Evergreen

A Guide to Writing with Readings

ELEVENTH EDITION

Annotated Instructor's Edition

Susan Fawcett

Australia • Brazil • Japan • Korea • Mexico • Singapore • Spain • United Kingdom • United States

Evergreen: A Guide to Writing with Readings
Eleventh Edition
Susan Fawcett

Product Director: Lauren Murphy
Content Developer: Rachel L. Kerns
Associate Content Developer: Julie Bizzotto
Senior Content Developers: Katherine Brundage and Brooke Foged
Digital Content Designer: Eric Newman
Executive Marketing Manager: Erica Messenger
Product Assistant: Katharine Werring
Senior Content Project Manager: Aimee Bear
Senior Designer: Diana Graham
Manufacturing Planner: Betsy Donaghey
IP Analyst: Ann Hoffman
Senior IP Project Manager: Kathryn Kucharek
Production Service/Compositor: Lachina Publishing Services
Text Designer: Lachina
Cover Designer: Diana Graham
Cover Image: Flas100/Shutterstock.com
Product Manager, Advanced and Elective Product Programs: Jeff Werle
Senior Content Developer, Advanced and Elective Product Programs: Ashley Jack
Product Assistant, Advanced and Elective Product Programs: Erica Pitcairn

Library of Congress Control Number: 2016952189

Student Edition:

ISBN: 978-1-337-09704-8

Loose-leaf Edition:

ISBN: 978-1-305-95100-6

Annotated Instructor's Edition:
ISBN: 978-1-337-10258-2

Cengage Learning
20 Channel Center Street
Boston, MA 02210
USA

Cengage Learning is a leading provider of customized learning solutions with employees residing in nearly 40 different countries and sales in more than 125 countries around the world. Find your local representative at **www.cengage.com**.

Cengage Learning products are represented in Canada by Nelson Education, Ltd.

To learn more about Cengage Learning Solutions, visit **www.cengage.com**.

Purchase any of our products at your local college store or at our preferred online store **www.cengagebrain.com**.

Printed in the United States of America
Print Number: 01 Print Year: 2016

Contents

Preface

Millions of students have become stronger, more confident writers with *Evergreen*. Its unsurpassed coverage of writing, grammar, and critical thinking have made the book a leader in the market and beloved by instructors and students alike. Based on author Susan Fawcett's experience teaching and directing the writing lab at Bronx Community College, City University of New York, *Evergreen* is designed for students who need to improve the writing skills necessary for success in college and in most careers. The goal of this eleventh edition of *Evergreen* is to build upon the proven success of the previous editions and continue to meet the changing needs of instructors and students.

To that end, revisions to this eleventh edition include a new chapter devoted to reading strategies, an increased focus on the reading and writing connection, and an expanded chapter on research and documentation. A robust technology package, featuring a brand-new MindTap for *Evergreen*, and rich instructor development resources support the text.

New Features of *Evergreen with Readings*, Eleventh Edition

Expanded Focus on Integrated Reading and Writing

A new Chapter 42, "Reading Strategies for Writers," focuses on the importance of active reading and describes specific strategies students can use to read print and digital texts more effectively.

Expanded Thesis Statement Coverage

In Chapter 14, students receive more guidance and practice with writing focused, powerful thesis statements.

Conducting Research and Documenting Sources

Chapter 19 better reflects the ways in which today's students conduct research in the library and online. In addition, this edition offers instruction in the updated, 8th edition MLA style and in APA style; it also compares the two.

Nine New Reading Selections

Nine new high-interest selections have been added to Unit 8: Melissa M. Ezarik on the benefits of volunteerism, Ryan Rigney on adapting and creating smartphone apps, Laurence Benhamou on the characteristics of Generation Z, Roberto A. Ferdman on the trend of owning dogs instead of having babies, Cade Metz on a robot workforce, Ali S. Khan on preparing for a zombie apocalypse, Christine Harrington on the nature of motivation, Evette Collins on accepting her natural hair and Hisham Almiraat on the challenges faced by bloggers in the Arab world. The selections were chosen as good examples of their representative modes and to encourage discussion and critical thinking; each selection is followed by questions addressing vocabulary development and comprehension and analysis, as well as by engaging writing assignments.

New and Updated High-Interest Models and Practices

Numerous exercises in the book have been updated for currency and interest; new subjects include African American filmmaker Oscar Micheaux, the economies of North and South Korea, the decline of student credit-card debt, errors in famous films, the first reality show, Doctors Without Borders, résumé tips, the impact of smartphones, and the careers of Jackson Pollock, Martin Scorsese, and Jennifer Lopez.

New Visual Images

Evergreen's critical-viewing program features over forty new photos, paintings, graphics, ads, and cartoons—many accompanied by critical-thinking questions. These images help visual learners and others grasp key writing concepts, evaluate visual material, and connect more deeply with the course. The flow of instruction and images is supported by *Evergreen*'s clear and purposeful design.

Existing Features of *Evergreen with Readings*, Eleventh Edition

Critical-Thinking Coverage

Evergreen has been the leader in integrating critical thinking with writing instruction. Coverage in this edition includes a feature for critical thinking or critical viewing in each rhetorical pattern chapter (see Chapters 5–13 and 16–17); if desired, these activities can easily be adapted into group work. Numerous thinking practices and Teaching Tips with critical-thinking suggestions challenge students to analyze, evaluate, infer, and apply writing concepts to real-life problems or visual images.

Academic Models and Assignments

Each of nine essay patterns in Chapters 16 and 17 is illustrated by one student essay in the first person and another in the third person. Enriched instruction on subject, audience, and purpose stresses the choice between writing about oneself or about impersonal material, and some textbook excerpts now serve as models.

Coverage of Every Common Core Standard for Developmental Writing

Colleges using the national K-12 Common Core standards as a guide to what students need to know will see that *Evergreen* thoroughly covers all bases, with its rich emphasis on critical thinking, academic and third-person writing, and deep commitment to preparing students for college and workplace challenges. These features continue to contribute to *Evergreen*'s success:

- Clear, step-by-step coverage of paragraph and essay writing, with many engaging practices, writing assignments, and critical-thinking activities
- Superior essay coverage, with two inspiring student models and a graphic organizer for each essay pattern

- Varied, thought-provoking writing assignments
- Collaborative Writers' Workshops that feature revision of student writing
- ESL coverage integrated throughout

Flexible Organization

Evergreen's full range of materials and flexible modular organization adapt easily to almost any course design and to a wide range of student needs. Because each chapter and unit is self-contained, chapters can be taught in any order, and the text works well for laboratory work, self-teaching, and tutorials.

Unit 1 provides an overview of the writing process and introduces five prewriting techniques. Unit 2 guides students step by step through the paragraph-writing process, while Unit 3 teaches students the rhetorical modes most often required in college writing (illustration, narration, description, process, definition, comparison/contrast, classification, cause/effect, and persuasion). Unit 4 devotes six chapters to essay writing: writing essays; applying the modes taught in Unit 3 to essays; crafting an introduction, conclusion, and title that stress the main idea; summarizing and quoting from sources (including coverage of APA and 8th edition MLA styles); strengthening an essay with research; and answering essay examination questions. Unit 5 teaches students to revise for consistency, sentence variety, and language awareness. Unit 6 thoroughly covers grammar and students' major problem areas, while Unit 7 reviews spelling and homonyms. Unit 8 includes a new chapter on reading strategies as well as twenty thought-provoking and richly varied reading selections by top authors. Headnotes, vocabulary glosses, vocabulary and language awareness questions, comprehension and analysis questions, and writing assignments accompany each piece. An ESL appendix gives additional support to ESL and ELL students.

Available Digital Resources

- ***MindTap for Evergreen*** is a personalized teaching experience with relevant assignments that guide students to analyze, apply, and improve thinking, allowing instructors to measure skills and outcomes with ease. MindTap lets you compose your course, your way.
  - *Personalized Teaching*: Adopt a learning path that is built with key student objectives. Control what students see and when they see it. Use it as-is or match to your syllabus exactly. Hide, rearrange, add, and create your own content.
  - *Guide Students*: Provide a unique learning path of relevant readings, activities, Aplia practice assignments, and engaging grammar videos designed specifically for *Evergreen*.
  - *Promote Better Outcomes*: Empower instructors and motivate students with visual analytics and reports that provide a snapshot of class progress, time in course, engagement, and completion rates. MindTap also provides seamless integration into your campus learning management system so you can keep all your course materials in one place.
  - *Time-saving tools: Write Experience* helps students improve written and critical-thinking skills with real-time guidance and instant automated feedback, allowing instructors to assess these skills without adding to their workloads.

- ***Aplia for Evergreen*** provides clear, succinct, and engaging writing instruction and practice to help students master basic writing and grammar skills. It features ongoing individualized practice, immediate feedback, and grades that can be automatically uploaded, so instructors can see where students are having difficulty. Add, drop, mix and match chapters and lessons, or opt for the **Individualized Study Path (ISP)**, which assesses students' skills through a comprehensive diagnostic and generates a list of assignments tailored to each student's needs.
- ***Cognero*** is Cengage Learning's flexible, online system that gives instructors the freedom to author, edit, and manage test-bank content from multiple Cengage Learning solutions.
- ***Evergreen Test Bank and Instructor's Manual***. The *Evergreen* Test Bank, available in print or online, provides assessment for every chapter in the book. The Instructor's Manual includes teaching suggestions, sample syllabi, a guide to teaching ESL students, and more.
- The password-protected ***Instructor Companion Site*** provides a downloadable version of the *Evergreen Test Bank and Instructor's Manual* as well as chapter-specific PowerPoint slides for classroom use.

Acknowledgments

Thanks to the following instructors who provided feedback for this edition:

Anna Carlson, San Joaquin Valley College
Carolyn Coward, Southwest Tennessee Community College
Mary Ellen Daniloff-Merrill, Southwest Minnesota State University
Margie Dernaika, Southwest Tennessee Community College
Mackenzie Escamilla, South Plains College
Susan Farmer, Dakota County Technical College
Robby Fowler, Meridian Community College
Judy Garner, Lake Land College
Geraldine Grunow, Henry Ford Community College
Maria Johnson, Georgia Piedmont Technical College
Liz Keefe, Gateway Community College
Rose McNeil, Southwest Tennessee Community College
Martha Perkins, Kellogg Community College
James Sodon, St. Louis Community College

Special thanks to the instructors who provided feedback for this edition's MindTap; to the team here at Cengage Learning; and to Chris Black and the team at Lachina Publishing Services. Grateful appreciation to Mark Connolly; Tanya Stanley of San Jacinto College; Theresa Suico of Saint Mary's College; and Anna Sarneso, Assistant Library Director at Mt. Ida College, who provided invaluable research and writing assistance.

Cengage Learning
2016

UNIT 1

Getting Started

CHAPTER 1

Exploring the Writing Process

A: The Writing Process

B: Subject, Audience, and Purpose

TEACHING TIP

You might engage students in a discussion about the kinds of writing they already have done for college or work, as well as the kinds of writing they expect to do in their future professions.

Did you know that the ability to write well characterizes the most successful college students and employees—in fields from education to medicine to computer science? Skim the job postings in career fields that interest you and notice how many stress "excellent writing and communication skills." Furthermore, reading and writing enrich our daily lives; in surveys, adults always rate reading, writing, and speaking well as the most important life skills a person can possess.

The goal of this book is to help you become a more skilled, powerful, and confident writer. You will see that writing is not a magic ability only a few are born with, but a life skill that can be learned. The first chapter presents a brief overview of the writing process, explored in greater depth throughout the book. Now I invite you to decide to excel in this course. Let *Evergreen* be your guide, and enjoy the journey.

A. The Writing Process

ESL TIP

Nonnative students may fail to understand the importance of *speaking English whenever possible*. Urge them to practice speaking and writing English with a friend or study partner. Stress that this discipline is key to success in this course and in their careers.

Many people have the mistaken idea that good writers simply sit down and write out a perfect letter, paragraph, or essay from start to finish. In fact, writing is a **process** consisting of a number of steps:

The Writing Process

1 Prewriting
- Thinking about possible subjects
- Freely jotting down ideas on paper or computer
- Narrowing the subject and writing your main idea in one sentence
- Deciding which ideas to include
- Arranging ideas in a plan or outline

2 Writing	Writing the first draft
3 Revising	Rethinking, rearranging, and revising as necessary Writing one or more new drafts Proofreading for grammar and spelling errors

Not all writers perform all the steps in this order, but most **prewrite**, **write**, and **revise**. Actually, writing can be a messy process of thinking, writing, reading what has been written, and rewriting. Sometimes steps overlap or need to be repeated. The important thing is that writing the first draft is just one stage in the process. "I love being a writer," jokes Peter De Vries. "What I can't stand is the paperwork."

LEARNING STYLES TIP
Visual representation of verbal processes helps *visual* and other learners. To underscore the recursive nature of the writing process, this graphic shows how a writer can move forward or back, from step to step.

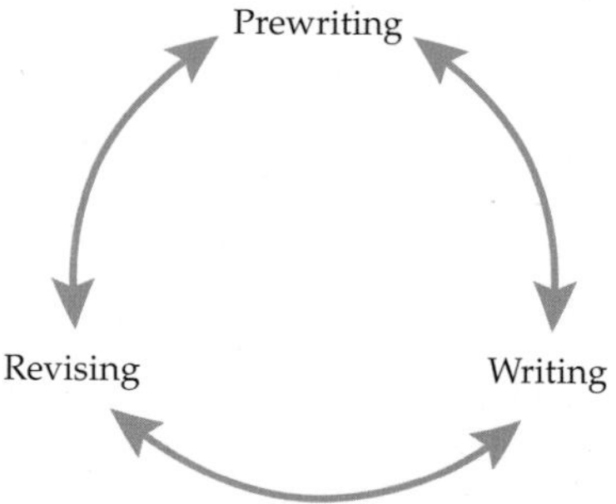

Good writers take time at the beginning to **prewrite**—to think, jot down ideas, and plan the paper—because they know it will save time and prevent frustration later. Once they write the first draft, they let it "cool off." Then they read it again with a fresh, critical eye and **revise**—crossing out, adding, and rewriting for more clarity and power. Good writers are like sculptors, shaping and reworking their material into something more meaningful. Finally, they **proofread** for grammar and spelling errors so that their writing seems to say, "I am proud to put my name on this work." As you practice writing, you will discover your own most effective writing process.

PRACTICE 1

TEACHING TIP
Encourage students to perform self-assessments when they receive feedback on their writing and to use them to set personal goals in this course.

Think of something that you wrote recently—and of which you felt proud—for college, work, or your personal life. Consider the *process* you followed in writing it. Did you do any *planning* or *prewriting*—or did you just sit down and start writing? How much time did you spend *rewriting* and *revising* your work? What one change in your writing process do you think would most improve your writing? Taking more time to prewrite? Taking more time to revise? Improving your grammar and spelling?

PRACTICE 2

Bring in several newspaper help-wanted sections. In a group with four or five classmates, study the ads in career fields that interest you. How many fields require writing and communication skills? Which job ad requiring these skills most surprised you or your group? Be prepared to present your findings to the class. If your class has Internet access, visit *Indeed.com* or other job-search websites and perform the same exercise.

EXPLORING ONLINE

www.google.com

Search "Writing: A Ticket to Work . . . or a Ticket Out" and read the summary. This survey of business leaders finds that good writing is the key to career success. What two facts or comments do you find most striking?

ESL TIP

Studies show that it is harder to remember information exchanged orally in a second language; thus, for ESL students (and visual learners), writing on the board, working directly from pages in the text, and using charts are useful memory aids.

B. Subject, Audience, and Purpose

Early in the prewriting phase, writers should give some thought to their **subject**, **audience**, and **purpose**.

In college courses, you may be assigned a broad **subject** by your instructor. First, make sure you understand the assignment. Then focus on one aspect of the subject that intrigues you. Whenever possible, choose something that you know and care about: life in Cleveland, working with learning-disabled children, repairing motorcycles, overcoming shyness, watching a friend struggle with drug addiction, playing soccer. You may not realize how many subjects you do know about.

To find or focus your subject, ask yourself:

- What special experience or expertise do I have?
- What inspires, angers, or motivates me? What do I love to do?
- What story in the news affected me recently?
- What campus, job, or community problem do I have ideas about solving?

Your answers will suggest good subjects to write about. Keep a list of all your best ideas.

TEACHING TIP

Some instructors distinguish between personal writing and more formal, third-person writing early in the term. Others start with first-person writing to establish fluency.

How you approach your subject will depend on your **audience**—your readers. Are you writing for your professor, classmates, boss, closest friend, young people in the community, or the editor of a newspaper?

To focus on your audience, ask yourself:

- For whom am I writing? Who will read this?
- How much do they know about the subject? Are they beginners or experts?
- Will they likely agree or disagree with my ideas?
- Will my readers expect a composition about my *personal experience* or about more *formal, factual material*?

Keeping your audience in mind helps you know what information to include and what to leave out. For example, if you are writing about a U.S. presidential election for a history class, you can assume your readers will understand how the

TEACHING TIP
You might bring in examples of different types of writing—an editorial, a magazine article, a humorous essay, or the text of a website. Have students determine audience and purpose in each.

Electoral College works. However, if you are writing for a general audience, you may have to explain why a candidate can win more popular votes than a rival and still fail to be elected president. Often in college courses like history as well as in the workplace, you will be expected to write about factual subjects—not yourself, your feelings, or your experiences. Consider how much your readers know about your subject and what kind of information they will need to understand your ideas.

Finally, keeping your **purpose** in mind will help you write more effectively. Do you want to explain something to your readers, persuade them that a certain view is correct, entertain them, tell a good story, or some combination of these?

PRACTICE 3

TEACHING TIP
Developmental students may think they have nothing to write about. To help counter this myth, ask volunteers to share their answers to some of the boxed questions at the beginning of Part B. Have them apply the questions to Practice 3.

List five subjects that you might like to write about. Consider your audience and purpose: For whom are you writing? What do you want them to know about your subject? Notice how the audience and purpose will help shape your paper.

	Subject	Audience	Purpose
EXAMPLE 1.	*my recipe for seafood gumbo*	*inexperienced cooks*	*to show how easy it is to make seafood gumbo*
2.	___	___	___
3.	___	___	___
4.	___	___	___
5.	___	___	___

PRACTICE 4

LEARNING STYLES TIP
To help students think about their learning styles, you might administer a questionnaire like the ones at **vark-learn.com**. Lead a class discussion about specific study and practice strategies for each style.

Jot down ideas for the following two assignments. Notice how your ideas and details differ depending on the audience and purpose.

1. Write a description of the home you grew up in. Your purpose is to share childhood memories and feelings. What rooms were your favorites? What did they look like? Did you have favorite places where you liked to play? What do you want your audience to know about your home and what it meant to you? What details should you include? Which details should you leave out?
2. Write a description of your childhood home for a real estate website. Your purpose is to describe the house or apartment in objective detail. What information would a buyer or renter need? What facts should you include? What personal impressions should you leave out?

PRACTICE 5

Read these sentences from real job-application letters and résumés, published in *Fortune* magazine. Each writer's *subject* was his or her job qualifications; the *audience* was an employer; and the *purpose* was to get a job. How did each person undercut his or her own purpose? What writing advice would you give each of these job seekers?

TEACHING TIP
Your students will enjoy doing Practice 5 in class. Remind them that the link between good writing and good jobs is strong.

1. I have lurnt Word and computer spreasheet programs.
2. Please don't misconstrue my 14 jobs as "job-hopping." I have never quit a job.
3. I procrastinate, especially when the task is unpleasant.
4. Let's meet, so you can "ooh" and "aah" over my experience.
5. It is best for employers that I not work with people.
6. Reason for leaving my last job: maturity leave.
7. As indicted, I have over five years of analyzing investments.
8. References: none. I have left a path of destruction behind me.

PRACTICE 6 CRITICAL THINKING AND WRITING

Analyze the following public service announcement and answer these questions: What *subject* is the ad addressing? Who is the target *audience*? What is the intended *purpose*? Can you summarize the ad's message in a sentence? Would this ad be more effective if it depicted a range of "role models" such as a teacher, a firefighter, a nurse, and a chef? Why or why not?

TEACHING TIP
Ads and cartoons are excellent tools to spark student interest and prompt critical thinking about subject, audience, and purpose.

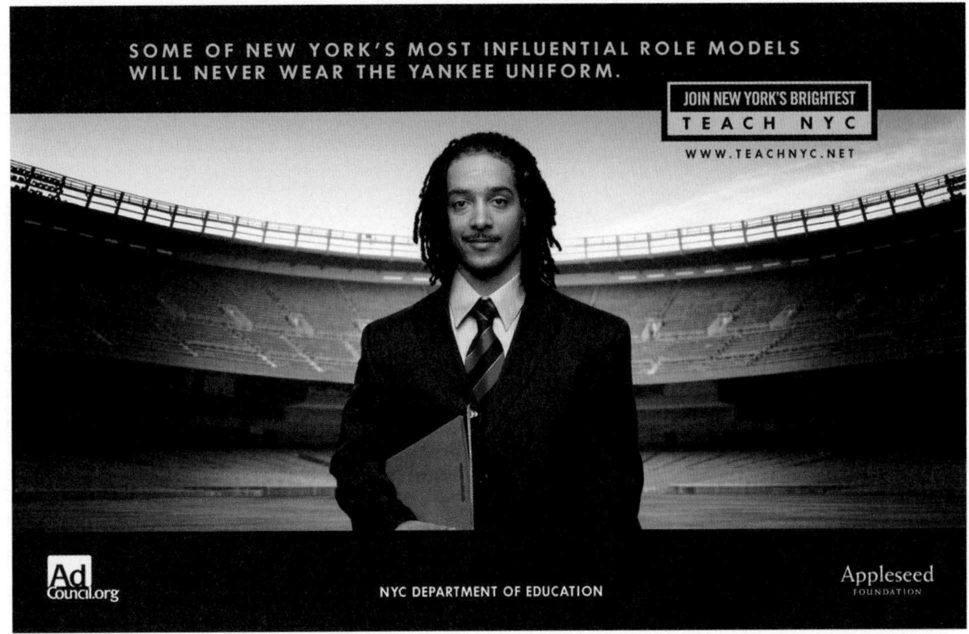

© Ad Council

EXPLORING ONLINE

Throughout this book, *Exploring Online* features will suggest ways to use the Internet to improve your writing and grammar. A number of online writing labs—called OWLs—based at colleges around the country offer excellent additional practice or review in areas where you might need extra help. Here are two good sites to explore:

owl.english.purdue.edu/owl
Purdue University's OWL

grammar.ccc.commnet.edu/grammar
Capital Community College Foundation's OWL

CHAPTER 2

Prewriting to Generate Ideas

A: Freewriting

B: Brainstorming

C: Clustering

D: Asking Questions

E: Keeping a Journal

TEACHING TIP

Emphasize to students that these prewriting techniques are tools for the *writer* and are not meant to be shared with others; therefore, the writer can feel free to explore.

This chapter presents five effective prewriting techniques that will help you get your ideas onto paper (or onto the computer). These techniques can help you overcome the "blank-page jitters" that many people face when they first sit down to write. You can also use them to generate new ideas at any point in the writing process. Try all five to see which ones work best for you.

In addition, if you write on a computer, try prewriting in different ways: on paper and on the computer. Some writers feel they produce better work if they prewrite by hand and only later transfer their best ideas onto the computer. Every writer has personal preferences, so don't be afraid to experiment.

A. Freewriting

Freewriting is an excellent method that many writers use to warm up and to generate ideas. These are the guidelines: for five, ten, or fifteen minutes, write rapidly, without stopping, about anything that comes into your head. If you feel stuck, just repeat or rhyme the last word you wrote, but *don't stop writing*. And don't worry about grammar, logic, complete sentences, or grades.

The point of freewriting is to write so quickly that ideas can flow without comments from your inner critic. The *inner critic* is the voice inside that says, every time you have an idea, "That's dumb; that's no good; cross that out." Freewriting

TEACHING TIP

Research indicates that freewriting can be confusing to some students with learning disabilities. Instead, they need to *verbalize* ideas before writing. Suggest that they talk with a partner for two minutes before they start to write.

helps you tell this voice, "Thank you for your opinion. Once I have lots of ideas and words on paper, I'll invite you back for comment."

After you freewrite, read what you have written, underlining or marking any parts you like.

Freewriting is a powerful tool for helping you turn thoughts and feelings into words, especially when you are unsure about what you want to say. Sometimes freewriting produces only nonsense; often, however, it can help you zoom in on possible topics, interests, and worthwhile writing you can use later. Focused freewriting can help you find subjects to write about.

Focused Freewriting

In **focused freewriting**, you simply try to focus your thoughts on one subject as you freewrite. The subject might be one assigned by your instructor, one you choose, or one you have discovered in unfocused freewriting. The goal of most writing is to produce a polished, organized piece of writing; focused freewriting can help you generate ideas or narrow a topic to one aspect that interests you.

Here is one student's focused freewriting on the topic of *someone who strongly influenced you*:

> Mr. Martin, the reason I'm interested in science. Wiry, five-foot-four-inch, hyperactive guy. A darting bird in the classroom, a circling teacher-bird, now jabbing at the knee bone of a skeleton, now banging on the jar with the brain in it. Like my brain used to feel, pickled, before I took his class. I always liked science but everything else was too hard. I almost dropped out of school, discouraged, but Martin was fun, crazy, made me think. Encouragement was his thing. Whacking his pencil against the plastic model of an eyeball in his office, he would bellow at me, "Taking too many courses! Working too many hours in that restaurant! Living everyone else's life but your own!" Gradually, I slowed down, got myself focused. Saw him last at graduation, where he thwacked my diploma with his pencil, shouting, "Keep up the good work! Live your own life! Follow your dreams!"

- This student later used this focused freewriting—its vivid details about Mr. Martin and his influence—as the basis for an effective paper. Underline any words or lines that you find especially striking or appealing. Be prepared to explain why you like what you underlined.

PRACTICE 1

ESL TIP

To encourage cross-cultural interaction, ask native English speakers to explain idioms or culturally specific ideas to your ESL students.

Do a three-minute focused freewriting on three of these topics:

jobs	celebrities	friendship
education	current events	traditions

Underline as usual. Did you surprise yourself by having so much to say about any one topic? Perhaps you would like to write more about that topic.

PRACTICE 2

TEACHING TIP

Before having students complete Practice 2, demonstrate the process by verbalizing your thoughts as you examine a freewriting for possible topics.

1. Read over your earlier freewritings and notice your underlinings. Would you like to write more about any underlined words or ideas? Write two or three such words or ideas here:

   Sample answers:

   people who are "Internet famous"

   My favorite family tradition is going ice skating on New Year's Eve.

2. Now choose one word or idea. Focus your thoughts on it and do a ten-minute focused freewriting. Try to stick to the topic as you write, but don't worry too much about keeping on track; just keep writing.

B. Brainstorming

ESL TIP

To draw out nonnative students who hesitate to share aloud, try the Anonymous Brainstorming Game, in which each student writes an idea related to the chosen topic (use precut scraps of paper if you wish). Ideas are then chosen randomly and discussed by the class.

Another prewriting technique that may work for you is **brainstorming**, or freely jotting down ideas about a topic. As in freewriting, the purpose is to generate lots of ideas so you have something to work with and choose from. Write everything that comes to you about a topic—words and phrases, ideas, details, examples.

After you have brainstormed, read over your list, underlining interesting or exciting ideas you might develop further. As with freewriting, many writers brainstorm on a general subject, underline, and then brainstorm again as they focus on one aspect of that subject.

Here is one student's brainstorm list on the topic of *managing your time*:

time, who has it?
classes, getting to campus
work 20 hours a week, plus time for Marina
always tired
hey Alicia, I don't feel like a Superwoman
help? I don't ask
studying falls to last place
why be in college if I don't study?
if only I had 10 hrs a week outside class to read, write
get help where?
library has study places, ask my counselor
trade child care time with Flo?
take 5 minutes every morning to read my spiritual books
start the day fresh
maybe I can plan my time to find time

With brainstorming, this writer generated many ideas and started to move toward a more focused topic: *By planning ahead, I am learning to find time for what matters*. With a narrowed topic, brainstorming once more can help the writer generate details and reasons to support the idea.

PRACTICE 3

Choose one of the following topics that interests you and write it at the top of your paper or computer screen. Then brainstorm. Write anything that comes into your head about the topic. Just let ideas pour out fast!

1. a place I want to go back to
2. my goals in this course
3. my best/worst job
4. qualities that will help me succeed
5. dealing with difficult people
6. an unforgettable person from work, school, or family life

Once you fill a page with your list, read it over, marking the most interesting ideas. Draw arrows or highlight and move text on your screen to connect related ideas. Is there one idea that might be the subject of a paper?

C. Clustering

LEARNING STYLES TIP
Encourage *visual learners* in particular to experiment with clustering as an idea-generation strategy.

Some writers use still another method—called **clustering** or **mapping**—to get their ideas on paper. To begin clustering, simply write an idea or a topic, usually one word, in the center of a piece of paper. Then let your mind make associations, and write these associations branching out from the center.

TEACHING TIP
Consider modeling the construction of a cluster, or have the class help you create one. Verbalize your mental process as you create it.

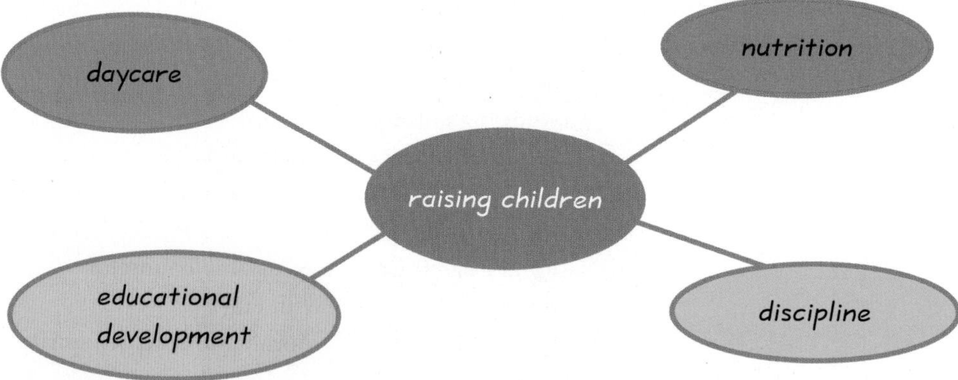

When one idea suggests other ideas, details, and examples, write these around it in a "cluster." After you finish, pick the cluster that most interests you. You may wish to freewrite for more ideas.

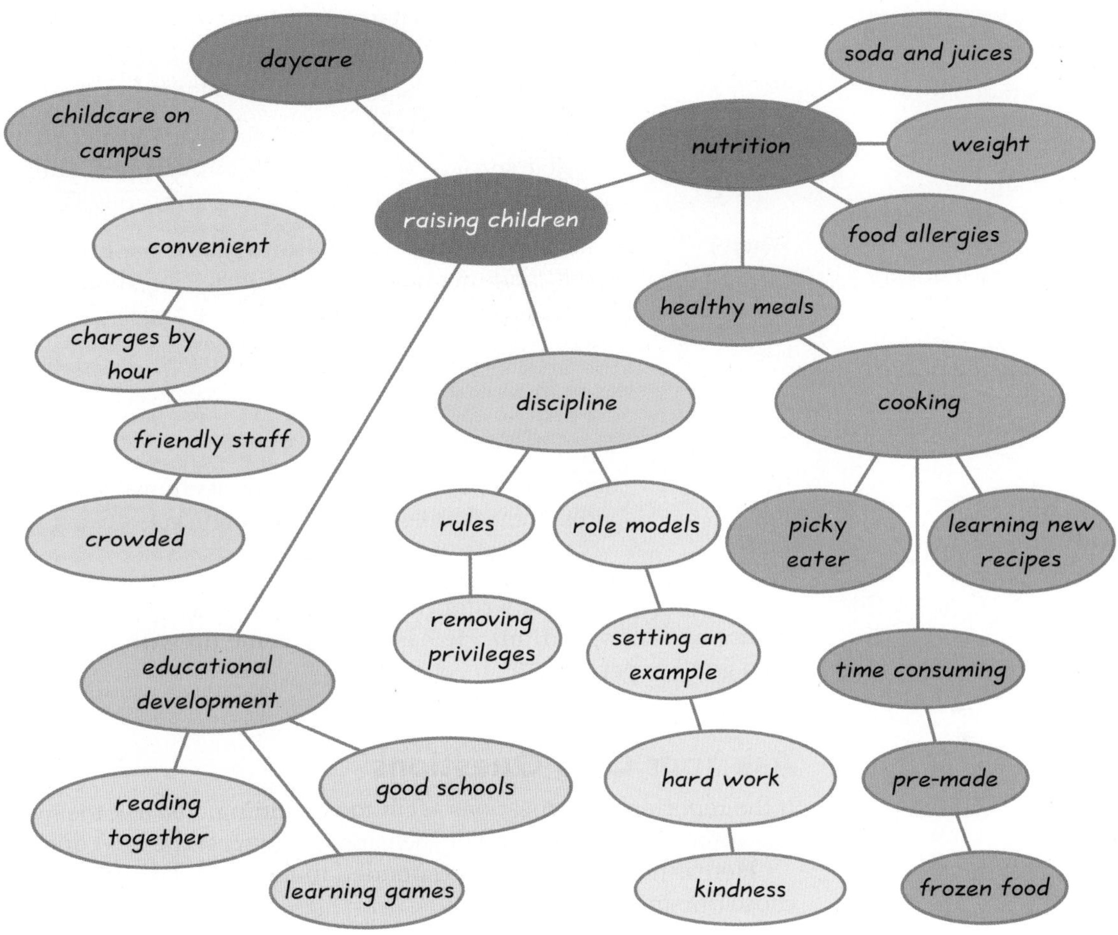

PRACTICE 4

TEACHING TIP

You might mention clustering, or mapping, as a *reading* technique, not just a writing technique. Some students use visual representation to help recall important material.

Choose one of these topics or another topic that interests you. Write it in the center of a piece of paper and then try clustering. Keep writing down associations until you have filled most of the page.

1. leadership
2. holidays
3. debt
4. online dating
5. a dream
6. reality TV shows

TEACHING TIP

Stress to students that practicing the two types of questioning taught here can enrich their learning, writing, and even self-knowledge.

D. Asking Questions

Many writers get ideas about a subject by asking questions and trying to answer them. This section describes two ways of doing this.

The Reporter's Six Questions

Newspaper reporters often answer six basic questions at the beginning of an article: **Who? What? Where? When? Why? How?** Here is the way one student used these questions to explore the general subject of *sports* assigned by his instructor:

LEARNING STYLES TIP

Students with a dominant *auditory learning style* might work with a partner, one asking the reporter's six questions aloud, the other answering and taking notes. Stress the value of talking about a topic with someone prior to writing.

Who?	Players, basketball and football players, coaches, fans. Violence—I'm tired of that subject. Loyal crazy screaming fans—Giants fans.
What?	Excitement. Stadium on the day of a game. Tailgate parties. Cookouts. Incredible spreads—Italian families with peppers, stuff to spread on sandwiches. All-day partying. Radios, TVs, grills, Giants caps.
Where?	Giants Stadium parking lot. People gather in certain areas—meet me in 10-B. Stadiums all over the country, same thing. People party on tailgates, in cars, on cars, plastic chairs, blankets.
When?	People arrive early morning—cook breakfast, lunch. After the game, many stay on in parking lot, talking, drinking beer. Year after year they come back.
Why?	Big social occasion, emotional outlet.
How?	They come early to get space. Some stadiums now rent parking spaces. Some families pass on season tickets in their wills!

Notice the way this writer uses the questions to focus his ideas about tailgate parties at Giants Stadium. He has already come up with many interesting details for a good paper.

Ask Your Own Questions

If the reporter's six questions seem too confining, just ask the questions *you* want answered about a subject. Let each answer suggest the next question.

Here is how one student responded to the subject *a career that interests you* (she chose nursing):

TEACHING TIP

Career planning intrigues most students. You might have them explore a field of interest on **stats.bls.gov/ooh/** and write about their findings.

What do I know about nursing? I know that hospitals never seem to have enough nurses, so many jobs must be available. Nurses work hard, but their work seems interesting, exciting. The pay is good. Nurses also help people, which is important to me.

What would I like to know? What kind of education and training do nurses need? Is it better to work in a hospital, clinic, doctor's office, school, nursing home? I think nurses specialize in certain areas, like ER medicine or pediatrics. I'd like to know how they pick and how they get specialized training.

Where can I get more information? A friend of my mom's is a nurse in the intensive care unit at Mt. Sinai. I could interview her. I could speak with the career counselor on campus. Kendra told me to check out a great U.S. government website on careers, **stats.bls.gov/ooh/**.

What would I like to focus on? Well, I'd like to know more about the real-life experience of being a nurse and the specific knowledge and skills nurses need. What are the rewards and drawbacks of a nursing career?

What is my angle or point? I want to give readers (and myself!) a sense of what it means to be a good nurse and how to prepare for a successful career. I think readers would be interested in practical tips about the education, choices, and requirements to become a nurse.

Who is my audience? I would like to write for people who might be considering nursing as a career.

PRACTICE 5

Answer the reporter's six questions on one of the following topics or on a topic of your own choice.

1. texting and driving
2. a sporting event
3. racial profiling
4. favorite music
5. heroes
6. a recent scandal or controversy

PRACTICE 6

Ask and answer at least five questions of your own about one of the topics in Practice 5. Use these questions if you wish: What do I know about this subject? What would I like to know? Where can I find answers to my questions? What would I like to focus on? What is my point of view about this subject? Who is my audience?

E. Keeping a Journal

TEACHING TIP

Ask students who are already in the habit of keeping a journal to share with the class the benefits of journaling.

Keeping a journal is an excellent way to practice your writing skills and discover ideas for further writing. Your journal is mostly for you—a private place where you record your experiences and your inner life; it is the place where, as one writer says, "I discover what I really think by writing it down."

You can keep a journal in a notebook or on a computer. If you prefer handwriting, write in a notebook. If you prefer to work on a computer, just open a "Journal" and keep your journal there. Then every morning or night, or several times a week, write for at least 15 minutes in this journal. Don't just record the day's events. ("I went to the store. It rained. I came home.") Instead, write in detail about what most angered, moved, or amused you that day.

Write about what you really care about—motorcycles, loneliness, building websites, working in a doughnut shop, family relationships, grades, ending or starting a relationship. You may be surprised by how much you know. Write, think, and write some more. Your journal is private, so don't worry about grammar or correctness. Instead, aim to capture your truth so exactly that someone reading your words might experience it too.

ESL TIP

ESL students may expect instructors to correct grammatical errors in their journals. Some instructors correct one or two chronic error types; others decline, explaining that a journal's purpose is idea generation and fluency.

You might also carry a little pad with you during the day for "fast sketches," jotting down things that catch your attention: a man playing drums in the street; a baby wearing a bib that reads *Spit Happens*; a compliment you receive at work; something your child just learned to do.

Every journal is unique—and usually private—but here is a sample journal entry to suggest possibilities. The student links a quotation he has just learned to a disturbing "lesson of love":

Apr. 11. Two weeks ago, our professor mentioned a famous quote: "It is better to have loved and lost than never to have loved at all." The words had no particular meaning for me. How wrong I was. Last Sunday I received some very distressing news that will change my life from now on.

My wife has asked me why I never notified any family members except my mother of the birth of our children. My reply has been an argument or an angry stare. Our daughter Angelica is now two months shy of her second birthday and we were also blessed with the birth of a son, who is five months old. I don't know whether it was maturity or my conscience, but last Sunday I decided it was time to let past grievances be forgotten. Nothing on this green earth would shelter me from what I was to hear that day.

I went to my father's address, knocked on his door, but got no response. Nervous but excited, I knocked again. Silence. On leaving the building, I bumped into his neighbor and asked for the possible whereabouts of my father. I couldn't brace myself for the cold shock of hearing from him that my father had died. I was angry as well as saddened, for my father was a quiet and gentle man whose love of women, liquor, and good times exceeded the love of his son.

Yes, it would have been better to have loved my father as he was than never to have gotten the opportunity to love such a man. A lesson of love truly woke me up to the need to hold dearly the ones you care for and overcome unnecessary grudges. "I love you, Pop, and may you rest in peace. Que Dios te guíe."

—Anthony Falu, Student

The uses of a journal are limited only by your imagination. Here are some ideas:

- Write down your goals and dreams; then brainstorm steps you can take to make them reality. (Notice negative thoughts—"I can't do that. That will never work." Focus on positive thoughts—"Of course I can! If X can do it, so can I.")
- Write about a problem you are having and creative ways in which you might solve it.
- Analyze yourself as a student. What are your strengths and weaknesses? What can you do to build on the strengths and overcome the weaknesses?
- What college course do you most enjoy? Why?
- Who believes in you? Who seems not to believe in you?
- If you could spend time with one famous person, living or dead, who would it be? Why?
- List five things you would love to do if they didn't seem so crazy.
- If you could change one thing about yourself, what would it be? What might you do to change it?
- Use your journal as a place to think about material that you have read in a textbook, newspaper, magazine, or online.
- What news story most upset you or made you laugh out loud in the past month? Why?
- Write down facts that impress you—the average American child watches 200,000 acts of violence before graduating from high school! Analyzing that one fact could produce a good paper.

TEACHING TIP

Explain to students that although they may prefer one prewriting technique, they should try using several techniques if they need to generate more ideas about a topic.

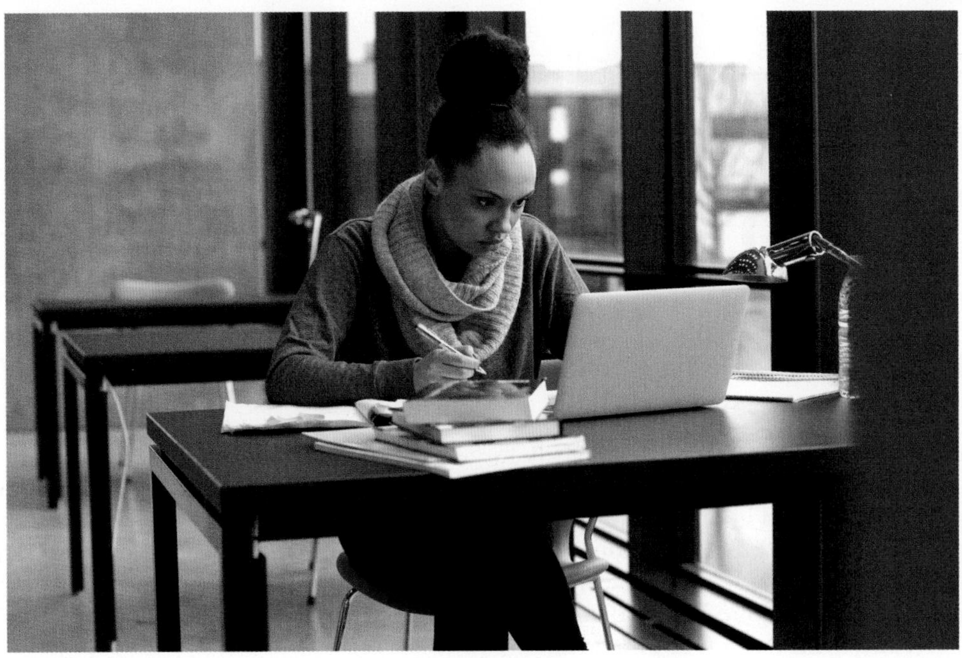
AmmentorpDK/Getty Images

This student likes to write using both a notebook and her laptop, particularly when she is working on assignments for school.

PRACTICE 7 CRITICAL VIEWING AND WRITING

Some people prefer to write on paper, while others prefer to write using a phone, tablet, or computer. Some writers, like the student pictured, use both methods, taking notes on paper and then typing on a computer, for example. Write a journal entry about the writing method(s) you prefer. How, if at all, do your preferences change depending on what you are writing?

PRACTICE 8

Get a notebook or set up your computer journal. Write for at least 15 minutes three times a week.

At the end of each week, reread what you have written or typed. Underline sections or ideas you like and highlight, or put a checkmark next to, subjects you might like to write more about.

PRACTICE 9

Choose one passage in your journal that you would like to rewrite and let others read. Mark the parts you like best. Now rewrite and polish the passage so you would be proud to show it to someone else.

EXPLORING ONLINE

www.powa.org/invent/choosing-your-subject

Practical advice about finding a subject *you* want to write about

grammar.ccc.commnet.edu/grammar/composition/brainstorm_freewrite.htm

Tips and timed practice on using freewriting to get started

writers' WORKSHOP

Using One or Two of Your Five Senses, Describe a Place

Readers of a finished paper can easily forget that they are reading the *end result* of someone else's writing process. The writer has already thought about audience and purpose, zoomed in on a subject, and prewritten to get ideas.

Here is one student's response to the following assignment: *Using one or two of the five senses—smell, hearing, taste, touch, or sight—describe a special place.* In your class or group, read the paper, aloud if possible. As you read, underline words or lines that strike you as especially well written or powerful.

Sounds and Smells of Home

At my grandmother's house in Puerto Rico, I woke to a hundred sounds and smells of happiness. As a child on vacation, I was called from my sleep by birds chirping in the trees. I kept my eyes closed and smiled to remember where I was. Then the distant lawnmowers started up, bringing ^the smell of cut grass. At the break of dawn, my grandma would sing, "Bésame mucho como si fuera la última vez," which means "kiss me a lot as though it is for the last time." She sang those words like a record that keeps repeating the same thing. The kitchen cabinets creaked open and closed, and I would hear the old, outdated radio tuning to her favorite talk show. A man's smooth radio voice spoke fast Spanish, like the rhythm of a different world. Clanking and pulling signaled that utensils were being laid out for breakfast. The cracking of the first egg, the sizzle of frying bacon, and the smell of fresh bread made me salivate. Time to get up. With heavy footsteps, my uncles came in, and their chair legs screeched against the tile floor. My grandmother's gardenia perfume embraced me as she kissed my forehead. This Christmas Eve, my dear grandma succumbed to cancer. I am grown, married, and have a son. But to this day, I can hear and smell those long-ago days when ^grandma gave me so much.

—Awilda Scarpetta, Student

1. How effective is Ms. Scarpetta's paper?

   _Y_ Good topic for a college audience?

   _Y_ Rich supporting details?

   _Y_ Clear main idea?

   _Y_ Logical organization?

2. Does the first sentence make you want to read on? Why or why not?
   Yes. "I woke to a hundred sounds and smells of happiness" is interesting.
3. Which of the five senses does the writer emphasize? What words show this?
   hearing: "chirping," "sang," "sizzle"; smell: "cut grass," "fresh bread," "perfume"
4. Discuss your underlinings with the group or class. Try to explain why a particular word or sentence is effective. For instance, the sentence "The cracking of the first egg, the sizzle of frying bacon, and the smell of fresh bread made me salivate" contains precise words and details of sound and scent.
5. Would you suggest that the writer make any changes or improvements? If so, what?
6. Last, proofread for grammar, spelling, and omitted words. Do you spot any error patterns (the same type of error made two or more times) that this student should watch out for? Yes, two omitted words

Of her prewriting process, Awilda Scarpetta writes: "I decided to write about my grandmother's house in Puerto Rico because I thought my classmates (my audience) would find that more interesting than the local neighborhood. This paper also taught me the importance of brainstorming. I filled two whole pages with my brainstorming list, and then it was easy to pick the best details."

GROUP WORK

Imagine that you have been given this assignment: *Using just one or two of the five senses, describe a special place.* Your audience will be your college writing class. Working as a group, plan a paper and prewrite. First, choose a place that your group will describe; if it is a place on campus, your instructor might even want you to go there. Second, decide whether you will emphasize sound, smell, taste, touch, or sight. Choose someone to write down the group's ideas, and then brainstorm. List as many sounds (or smells, etc.) as your group can think of. Fill at least one page. Now read back the list and put a check next to the best details; does your group agree or disagree about which ones are best?

You are well on your way to an excellent paper. Each group member can now complete the assignment, based on the list. If necessary, prewrite again for more details.

WRITING AND REVISING IDEAS

1. Using one or two of your five senses, describe a place. You might use a first sentence like this:

   At ________________ (place) I experienced a hundred ________________ (sounds, smells, etc.) of ________________ (an emotion).

2. List any interesting experiences or hobbies you know about that might interest your classmates and instructor (an intriguing job, time in another country, and so on). Choose one of these and prewrite; use the prewriting method of your choice and fill at least a page with ideas.

UNIT 2

Discovering the Paragraph

CHAPTER 3

The Process of Writing Paragraphs

This chapter will guide you step by step, from examining basic paragraphs to writing them. The paragraph makes a good learning model because it is short yet contains many of the elements found in longer compositions. Therefore, you can easily transfer the skills you gain by writing paragraphs to longer essays, reports, and letters.

In this chapter, you will first look at finished paragraphs and then move through the process of writing paragraphs of your own.

A. Defining and Looking at the Paragraph

A **paragraph** is a group of related sentences that develops one main idea. Although there is no definite length for a paragraph, it is often from 5 to 12 sentences long. A paragraph usually occurs with other paragraphs in a longer piece of writing—an essay, an article, or a letter, for example. Before studying longer compositions, however, we will look at single paragraphs.

ESL TIP
ESL students may require more explanation at the beginning of a new unit, task, or assignment. Clarifying instructions can sometimes improve their performance.

A paragraph looks like this on the page:

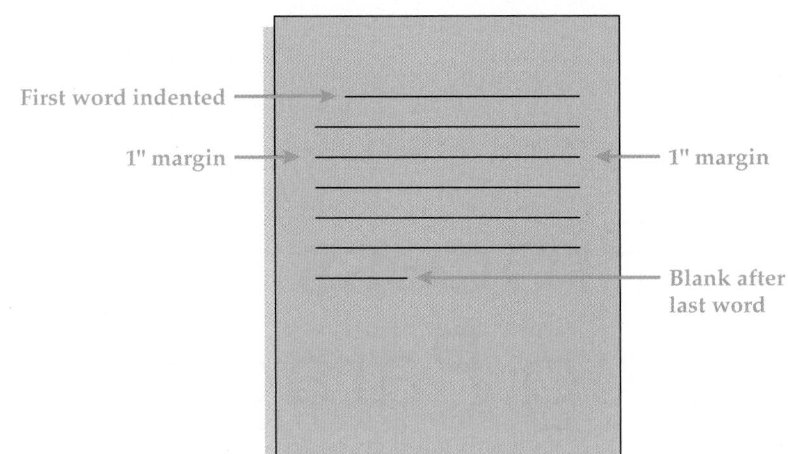

- Clearly **indent** the first word of every paragraph about 1 inch (five spaces on the computer).
- Extend every line of a paragraph as close to the right-hand margin as possible.
- However, if the last word of the paragraph comes before the end of the line, leave the rest of the line blank.

TEACHING TIP
Review with students the concepts of *general* and *specific* before covering the information about the main idea and topic sentence.

LEARNING STYLES TIP
Diagrams help *visual* and other learners grasp the concepts of *general* and *specific*. For example, draw a branching hierarchy of increasingly specific topics or an upside down triangle with a general topic in the widest part and ever more specific topics beneath.

Topic Sentence and Body

Most paragraphs contain one **main idea** to which all the sentences relate.

The **topic sentence** states this main idea.

The **body** of the paragraph develops and supports this main idea with particular facts, details, and examples:

> I allow the spiders the run of the house. I figure that any predator that hopes to make a living on whatever smaller creatures might blunder into a four-inch-square bit of space in the corner of the bathroom where the tub meets the floor needs every bit of my support. They catch flies and even field crickets in those webs. Large spiders in barns have been known to trap, wrap, and suck hummingbirds, but there's no danger of that here. I tolerate the webs, only occasionally sweeping away the very dirtiest of them after the spider itself has scrambled to safety. I'm always leaving a bath towel draped over the tub so that the big, haired spiders, who are constantly getting trapped by the tub's smooth sides, can use its rough surface as an exit ramp. Inside the house the spiders have only given me one mild surprise. I washed some dishes and set them to dry over a plastic drainer. Then I wanted a cup of coffee, so I picked from the drainer my mug, which was still warm from the hot rinse water, and across the rim of the mug, strand after strand, was a spider web.
>
> —Annie Dillard, *Pilgrim at Tinker Creek*

- The first sentence of Dillard's paragraph is the topic sentence. It states the main idea of the paragraph: that *the spiders are allowed the run of the house.*
- The rest of the paragraph, the body, fully explains and supports this statement. The writer first gives a reason for her attitude toward spiders and then gives particular examples of her tolerance of spiders.

TEACHING TIP
Ask students how paragraphs help the reader follow the writer's ideas. You might bring in a three- to five-paragraph passage reformatted as one long paragraph.

The topic sentence is more *general* than the other sentences in the paragraph. The other sentences in the paragraph provide specific information relating to the topic sentence. Because the topic sentence tells what the entire paragraph is about, *it is usually the first sentence*, as in the example. Sometimes the topic sentence occurs elsewhere in the paragraph, for instance, as the sentence after an introduction or as the last sentence. Some paragraphs contain only an implied topic sentence but no stated topic sentence at all.

As you develop your writing skills, however, it is a good idea to write paragraphs that *begin* with the topic sentence. Once you have mastered this pattern, you can try variations.

PRACTICE 1

Find and underline the **topic sentence** in each of the following paragraphs. Look for the sentence that states the **main idea** of the entire paragraph. Be careful: the topic sentence is not always the first sentence.

LEARNING STYLES TIP
Kinesthetic and *visual learners* may enjoy using different-colored highlighter markers to identify parts of a sentence or paragraph, as in Practices 1, 2, 3, and 12 in this chapter.

Paragraph 1

The United States Secret Service is one of the oldest federal law enforcement agencies in the country and ranks among the most elite in the world. With its origin dating back to the end of the American Civil War, the Secret Service was originally founded to combat the then-widespread counterfeiting of U.S. currency. In 1901, the agency was asked to begin its protective mission after the assassination of President William McKinley—the third sitting U.S. President to be assassinated. Today, the Secret Service continues to protect both national leaders and visiting foreign dignitaries while helping to secure the nation's financial infrastructure through financial and cybercrime investigations. The men and women who make up the Secret Service—both past and present—have embodied a tradition of excellence through integrity, commitment and honor. Their stories are the Secret Service's history—a proud history that continues to evolve and grow with every passing year.

—"USSS History," *United States Secret Service*

Courtesy of United States Secret Service

Secret Service agents providing protection services for papal visit to the United States, 2015

Paragraph 2

In the mid-1980s, 340,000 people in the United States owned cell phones. Today, that number is well over 380 million. Worldwide, five billion people have gone wireless, and most of them have no idea that inside the sleek, plastic exterior of every cell phone sits a package of electronics laden with hazardous substances called persistent, bioaccumulative and toxic chemicals (PBTs). When cell users toss their phones into the trash, PBTs like lead, arsenic, and cadmium leak into the land, air, and water, eventually entering the tissues of animals and humans. Every year, 150 million cell phones—complete with batteries and chargers—are pitched into the garbage instead of being recycled or safely disposed of. As the popularity of cellular phones soars, growing numbers of cell users are creating growing piles of toxic trash.

—Adapted from Rene Ebersole, "Recycle Cell Phones, Reduce Toxic Trash," *National Wildlife*

Paragraph 3

Bipolar disorder, also known as manic-depressive illness, is a brain disorder that causes unusual shifts in mood, energy, activity levels, and the ability to carry out day-to-day tasks. Symptoms of bipolar disorder are severe. They are different from the normal ups and downs that everyone goes through from time to time. Bipolar disorder symptoms can result in damaged relationships, poor job or school performance, and even suicide. But bipolar disorder can be treated, and people with this illness can lead full and productive lives.

—"What Is Bipolar Disorder?" *National Institute of Mental Health*

PRACTICE 2

ESL TIP

Because ways of organizing ideas and language vary from culture to culture, Practice 2 is very important. This practice works well in class.

Each group of sentences below could be unscrambled and written as a paragraph. Circle the letter of the **topic sentence** in each group of sentences. Remember: the topic sentence should state the main idea of the entire paragraph and should be general enough to include all the ideas in the body.

EXAMPLE

a. Next, a social phobia is an intense fear of a social or performance situation, like standing in a checkout line.

b. Agoraphobia, the third type, is a morbid terror of public places.

(c.) Phobias, the most common anxiety disorder, can be divided into three types.

d. A specific phobia, the first type, is an irrational fear of a specific thing, like spiders, dogs, elevators, or needles.

(Sentence c includes the ideas in all the other sentences.)

1. a. The United States military uses video games like *America's Army* to recruit and train soldiers for combat.

   b. Studies show that surgeons who improve their eye-hand coordination by playing video games perform difficult procedures faster and make 37 percent fewer mistakes.

c. More and more elementary schools employ the Wii gaming console to improve comprehension in math, geography, and science.

(d.) Video games are being used as creative learning tools in many settings.

2. a. Invited to join the space program, she trained as an astronaut and flew on the space shuttle *Endeavor* in 1992.

   b. The young Dr. Jemison headed to West Africa, where she worked in the Peace Corps for two years.

   c. Though a childhood teacher urged her to be a nurse, Mae Jemison knew she wanted to be a scientist and doctor.

   d. After eight years at NASA, she became a professor at Dartmouth College and started a company to help poor countries use solar energy.

   (e.) The life of Dr. Mae Jemison, the first African American female astronaut, is characterized by daring achievements and a strong desire to give back.

   f. A fine student, Jemison entered Stanford University at sixteen and later earned her M.D. degree from Cornell in 1981.

3. a. The left side of the human brain controls spoken and written language.

   b. The right side, on the other hand, seems to control artistic, musical, and spatial skills.

   c. Emotion is also thought to be controlled by the right hemisphere.

   (d.) The human brain has two distinct halves, or hemispheres, and in most people, each one controls different functions.

   e. Logical reasoning and mathematics are left-brain skills.

   f. Interestingly, the left brain controls the right hand, and vice versa.

4. a. Although David Ho was born in Taiwan to poor parents, they named him Da-I, or "great one," revealing their high expectations.

   b. When he arrived in the United States at age 12 and was teased about speaking no English, he focused on mathematics, developing a fierce work ethic.

   c. With a medical degree from Harvard, Ho worked in a large Los Angeles hospital, where he saw many of the world's first AIDS cases.

   (d.) A gift for math and science, plus luck and hard work, helped Dr. David Ho become one of the world's greatest AIDS researchers.

   e. As a young boy, Ho created a math and science laboratory in the family garage.

   f. In 1996, David Ho invented the cocktail of antiretroviral drugs that has since saved millions of lives around the world.

5. a. People who don't know basic algebra can be more easily fooled by dishonest manipulation of numbers.

   (b.) Because studying algebra has so many benefits, every college student should be required to pass an algebra course.

   c. Learning algebra helps build problem-solving skills and reasoning skills.

   d. According to the U.S. Secretary of Education, Americans must know algebra in order to compete with well-educated citizens from other nations in this global economy.

   e. An understanding of algebra is required in a surprising range of professions, from architect to banker to photographer.

6. a. Albert Einstein, whose scientific genius awed the world, did not speak until he was four and could not read until he was nine.

   b. Inventor Thomas Edison had such severe problems reading, writing, and spelling that he was called "defective from birth," taken out of school, and taught at home.

   (c.) Many famous people have suffered from learning disabilities.

   d. Film actress Keira Knightley suffers from dyslexia, yet she has mastered many complex roles and has been nominated for Golden Globe and Academy Awards.

7. (a.) Male and female insects are attracted to each other by visual, auditory, and chemical means.

   b. Through its chirping call, the male cricket attracts a mate and drives other males out of its territory.

   c. Butterflies attract by sight, and their brightly colored wings play an important role in courtship.

   d. Some female insects, flies among them, release chemicals called *pheromones* that attract males of the species.

8. a. Believe it or not, the first contact lens was drawn by Leonardo da Vinci in 1508.

   b. However, not until 1877 was the first thick glass contact actually made by a Swiss doctor.

   (c.) The journey of contact lenses from an idea to a comfortable, safe reality took nearly five hundred years.

   d. In 1948, smaller, more comfortable plastic lenses were introduced to enthusiastic American eyeglass wearers.

   e. These early glass lenses were enormous, covering the whites of the eyes.

   f. Today, contact lens wearers can choose ultra-thin, colored, or even disposable lenses.

B. Narrowing the Topic and Writing the Topic Sentence

TEACHING TIP
Students often need extra practice in recognizing topics that are too broad for a paragraph. List topics of varying levels of specificity on the board, or use students' own ideas from the prewriting exercises in Chapter 2, "Prewriting to Generate Ideas." Then lead a discussion about which topics should be narrowed.

A writer can arrive at the goal—a finished paragraph—in several ways. However, before writing a paragraph, most writers go through a process that includes these important steps:

1. Narrowing the topic
2. Writing the topic sentence
3. Generating ideas for the body
4. Selecting and dropping ideas
5. Arranging ideas in a plan or an outline

The rest of this chapter will explain these steps and guide you through the process of writing basic paragraphs.

Narrowing the Topic

As a student, you may be assigned broad writing topics by your instructor—success, cheating in schools, a description of a person. Your instructor is giving you the chance to cut the topic down to size and choose one aspect of the topic *that interests you*.

Suppose, for example, that your instructor gives this assignment: *Write a paragraph describing a social problem you have recently encountered.* The challenge is to pick a subject you would *like* to write about, something that interests you and also would probably interest your readers.

Thinking about your *audience* and *purpose* may help you narrow the topic. In this case, your audience probably will be your instructor and classmates; your purpose is to inform them about an issue you want to write about.

Many writers find it useful at this point—on paper or on the computer—to brainstorm, freewrite, or ask themselves questions: "What problem have I recently dealt with? Why did it bother me? Does it affect others? Why is this issue important to other people?"

Let's suppose that you choose to write about the problems single parents face attending college. But that subject is too broad a topic for one paragraph; you could write pages about the various problems single parents face. To narrow the topic further, you might focus on one issue: *daycare*. To give your paragraph greater focus and make it interesting to others, you might narrow it further to *the cost of daycare on campus*.

You might visualize the process like this:

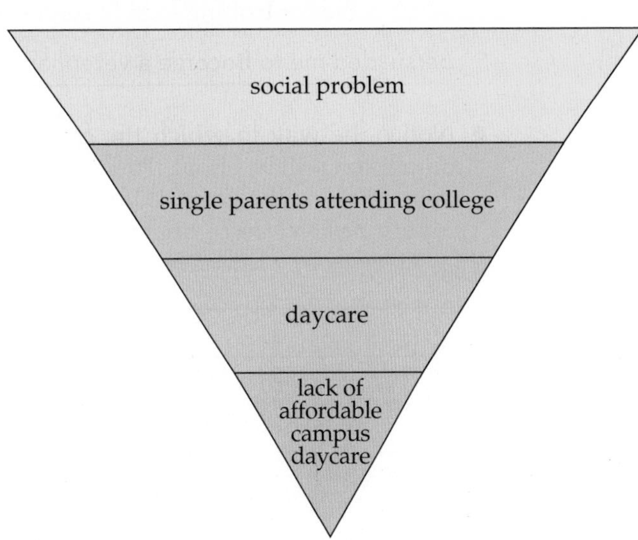

TEACHING TIP
Working on the board, help students narrow several broad topics and write viable topic sentences.

Writing the Topic Sentence

The next important step is to state your topic clearly *in sentence form*. Writing the topic sentence helps you further narrow your topic by forcing you to make a statement about it. The simplest topic sentence about campus daycare might read *Campus daycare is expensive,* but you might want to strengthen it by saying, for instance, *The lack of affordable daycare makes it difficult for single parents to attend college.*

Writing a good topic sentence is an important step toward an effective paragraph because the topic sentence controls the direction and scope of the body. A topic sentence should have a clear *controlling idea* and should be a *complete sentence.*

You can think of the topic sentence as having two parts, a **topic** and a **controlling idea**. The controlling idea states the writer's point of view or attitude about the topic.

topic — **controlling idea**

TOPIC SENTENCE: The lack of affordable daycare makes it difficult for single parents to attend college.

The controlling idea helps you focus on just one aspect or point. Here are three possible topic sentences about the topic *a memorable job*:

1. My job in the complaint department taught me how to calm down angry people.
2. Two years in the complaint department persuaded me to become an assistant manager.
3. Working in the complaint department persuaded me to become a veterinarian.

- These topic sentences all explore the same topic—working in a complaint department—but each controlling idea is different. The controlling idea in 1 is *taught me how to calm down angry people.*
- What is the controlling idea in sentence 2?

  persuaded me to become an assistant manager
  ____

  What is the controlling idea in sentence 3?

  persuaded me to become a veterinarian
  ____

- Notice the way in which the controlling idea lets the reader know what the paragraph will be about. There are many possible topic sentences for any topic, depending on the writer's interests and point of view. If you were assigned the topic *a memorable job*, what would your topic sentence be?

  ____
  ____
  ____
  ____

PRACTICE 3

Read each topic sentence below. Circle the topic and underline the controlling idea.

1. A low-fat diet provides many health benefits.
2. *Animal Planet* is both entertaining and educational.
3. Our football coach works to build players' self-esteem.
4. This campus offers many peaceful places where students can relax.
5. My cousin's truck looks like something out of *Star Wars*.

As a rule, the more specific and limited your topic and controlling idea, the better the paragraph; in other words, your topic sentence should not be so broad that it cannot be developed in one paragraph. Which of these topic sentences do you think will produce the best paragraphs?

4. Five wet, bug-filled days at Camp Nirvana made me a fan of the great indoors.
5. This town has problems.
6. Road rage is on the rise for three reasons.

- Topic sentences 4 and 6 are both specific enough to write a good paragraph about. In each, the topic sentence is carefully worded to suggest clearly what ideas will follow. From topic sentence 4, what do you expect the paragraph to include?

  The paragraph will probably discuss how weather and insects ruined the week.

- What do you expect paragraph 6 to include?

  The paragraph will probably discuss three reasons why road rage is on the rise.

- Topic sentence 5, on the other hand, is so broad that a paragraph could include almost anything. Just what problems does the town have? Strained relations between police and the community? Litter in public parks? Termites? The writer needs to rewrite the controlling idea, focusing on just one problem for an effective paragraph.

The topic sentence also must be a **complete sentence**. It must contain a subject and a verb, and express a complete thought.* Do not confuse a topic with a topic sentence. For instance, *a celebrity I would like to meet* cannot be a topic sentence because it is not a sentence; however, it could be a title† because topics and titles need not be complete sentences. One possible topic sentence might read, *A celebrity I would like to meet is writer Julia Alvarez.*

Do not write *This paragraph will be about . . .* or *In this paper I will write about . . . .* Instead, craft your topic sentence carefully to focus the topic and let your reader know what the paragraph will contain. Make every word count.

*For practice in correcting fragments, see Chapter 28, "Avoiding Sentence Errors," Part B.

†For practice in writing titles, see Chapter 15, "The Introduction, the Conclusion, and the Title," Part C.

PRACTICE 4

TEACHING TIP

Practice 4 works well as a small-group or full-class activity.

Put a check beside each topic sentence that is focused enough to allow you to write a good paragraph. If a topic sentence is too broad, narrow the topic according to your own interests and write a new topic sentence with a clear controlling idea.

EXAMPLES ✓ Keeping a journal can improve a student's writing.

Rewrite: ______________________________

_____ This paper will be about my family.

Rewrite: *My brother Mark has a unique sense of humor.*

1. ✓ Eugene's hot temper causes problems at work.

   Rewrite: ______________________________

2. _____ This paragraph will discuss my two closest friends.

   Rewrite: My two closest friends are alike in three ways.

3. ✓ Learning a foreign language has several benefits.

   Rewrite: ______________________________

4. _____ Child abuse is something to think about.

   Rewrite: Child abuse can be reduced through parenting classes.

5. ✓ Company officials should not read employees' e-mail.

   Rewrite: ______________________________

PRACTICE 5

Here is a list of broad topics. Choose three that interest you from this list. Narrow each topic, choose your controlling idea, and write a topic sentence focused enough to be the base of a good paragraph. Make sure that each topic sentence has a clear controlling idea and is a complete sentence.

overcoming fears

popular music

insider's tour of your community

balancing work and play

credit cards | a person you like or dislike
an act of cowardice or courage | a time when you were (or were not) in control

TEACHING AND ESL TIP
Practice 5 is difficult for some students and might be best done in small groups.

1. Narrowed topic: Overcoming fear of flying

   Controlling idea: Daryl boosted his career and calmed his nerves

   Topic sentence: Overcoming his fear of flying boosted Daryl's career and calmed his nerves.

2. Narrowed topic: I dislike Tom

   Controlling idea: his gossiping is destructive

   Topic sentence: I dislike Tom because his gossiping is a destructive habit.

3. Narrowed topic: Lack of balance when I worked several jobs

   Controlling idea: during this time I became less productive

   Topic sentence: The more hours a week I worked in part-time jobs, the less productive I was at school.

PRACTICE 6

Many writers adjust the topic sentence after they have finished drafting the paragraph. Study the body of each of these paragraphs to find the main, or controlling, idea. Then write the most exact and interesting topic sentence you can for each paragraph.

Paragraph 1

Animals occasionally rescue human beings.

A pet parrot recently saved his owner's life. Harry Becker was watching TV in his living room when he suddenly slumped over with a heart attack. The parrot screamed loudly until Mr. Becker's wife awoke and called 911. In another reported case of animal rescue, a family cat saved six-week-old Stacey Rogers. When the cat heard the baby gasping for breath in her crib, it ran howling to alert the baby's mother, who called paramedics. Even more surprising was an event reported in newspapers around the world. In 1996 in a Chicago zoo, a female gorilla rushed to save a three-year-old boy who fell accidentally into the gorilla enclosure. Still carrying her own baby on her back, the 150-pound gorilla gently picked up the unconscious child and carried him to the cage door to be rescued. Such stories reveal a mysterious and sometimes profound bond between animals and humans.

Paragraph 2

Smartphones offer four major advantages over regular cell phones.

The first advantage of smartphones is mobile Internet access. Gone are the days of having to return to the home or office computer in order to browse the Web. Instead, no matter where smartphone users are, they can quickly look up a weather forecast, the meaning of a word, or the best Thai restaurant within walking distance. Another major advantage is the ability to receive and send e-mails anywhere, anytime. The business benefits of this feature alone have prompted many companies to equip their employees with smartphones. Third, tools like a calendar, address book, international alarm clock, and GPS help smartphone users stay organized and efficient. Finally, thousands of downloadable apps can tailor a smartphone to each individual's needs. These apps range from music, video, and entertainment downloads to study tools and apps on parenting, car repair, diabetes, or stargazing.

C. Generating Ideas for the Body

ESL TIP
Many ESL and other students tend to overuse generalizations. Try the acronym FIRE (fact, incident, reason or result, explanation) to remind them to be specific.

TEACHING TIP
List on the board different kinds of supporting detail (facts, examples, anecdotes, expert opinions, testimonials, descriptive details, reasons, effects, etc.). Encourage students to consider all of these possibilities as they are brainstorming ideas for the body of their paragraph.

One good way to generate ideas for the body of a paragraph is **brainstorming**—freely jotting on paper or the computer anything that relates to your topic sentence: facts, details, examples, little stories. This step might take just a few minutes, but it is one of the most important elements of the writing process. Brainstorming can provide you with specific ideas to support your topic sentence. Later you can choose from these ideas as you compose your paragraph.

Here, for example, is a possible brainstorm list for the topic sentence *The lack of affordable daycare makes it difficult for single parents to attend college*:

1. Millions of college students are raising children.
2. Parents with small children need daycare in order to attend class.
3. In some colleges daycare costs more than tuition.
4. This campus has one daycare center located in the Student Center.
5. The daycare center is not open after 6 p.m.
6. The campus daycare center charges by the hour.
7. The high cost of daycare forces single parents to limit their time on campus.
8. The campus daycare workers are skilled and caring.
9. Daycare charges more per hour than I make at my job.
10. I can only attend college part-time because daycare is too expensive.
11. Expensive daycare makes it hard for single parents to go to college.
12. Paying for daycare is my biggest expense as a student.

Instead of brainstorming, some writers freewrite or ask themselves questions to generate ideas for their paragraphs. Some like to perform this step on paper, whereas others use a computer. Do what works best for you. The key is to write down lots of ideas during prewriting. If you need more practice in any of these methods, reread Chapter 2, "Prewriting to Generate Ideas."

PRACTICE 7

Now choose the topic from Practice 5 that most interests you. Write your narrowed topic, controlling idea, and topic sentence here.

Narrowed topic: ______________________________

Controlling idea: ______________________________

Topic sentence: ______________________________

____

Next, brainstorm. On paper or on the computer, write anything that comes to you about your topic sentence. Just let your ideas pour out. Try to fill at least one page.

D. Selecting and Dropping Ideas

TEACHING TIP
Create a paragraph with the class, honing a topic sentence, brainstorming, and selecting ideas for the body.

Next, simply read over what you have written, **selecting** those ideas that relate to and support the topic sentence and **dropping** those that do not. That is, keep the facts, examples, or little stories that provide specific information about your topic sentence. Drop ideas that just **repeat** the topic sentence but that add nothing new to the paragraph.

If you are not sure which ideas to select or drop, underline the **key word(s)** of the topic sentence, the ones that indicate the real point of your paragraph. Then make sure that the ideas you select are related to those key words.

Here again is the brainstorm list for the topic sentence *The lack of affordable daycare makes it difficult for single parents to attend college*. The key words in the topic sentence are *lack of affordable daycare*. Which ideas would you keep? Why? Which would you drop? Why?

LEARNING STYLES TIP
For the *kinesthetic learners* in your class, you might make sets of cards containing the ideas listed here. Have pairs or groups of students move the cards around to form logical groupings and then compare their groupings to the plan in Part E: "Arranging Ideas in a Plan or an Outline."

1. Millions of college students are raising children.
2. Parents with small children need daycare in order to attend class.
3. In some colleges daycare costs more than tuition.
4. This campus has one daycare center located in the Student Center.
5. The daycare center is not open after 6 p.m.
6. The campus daycare center charges by the hour.
7. The high cost of daycare forces single parents to limit their time on campus.
8. The campus daycare workers are skilled and caring.
9. Daycare charges more per hour than I make at my job.
10. I can only attend college part-time because daycare is too expensive.
11. Expensive daycare makes it hard for single parents to go to college.
12. Paying for daycare is my biggest expense as a student.

You probably dropped ideas 4, 5, and 8 because they do not relate to the topic—the lack of affordable daycare on campus. You should also have dropped idea 11 because it merely repeats the topic sentence.

PRACTICE 8

Read through your own brainstorm list from Practice 7. Select the ideas that relate to your topic sentence and drop those that do not. In addition, drop any ideas that just repeat your topic sentence. Be prepared to explain why you drop or keep each idea.

E. Arranging Ideas in a Plan or an Outline

TEACHING TIP
Organizing ideas is a key skill that many students lack. You might illustrate the process by "thinking aloud" as you reason out the best order of ideas for a paragraph. That is, model the mental process that writers go through when they plan.

TEACHING TIP
Students often resist outlining, and their papers suffer for it. Discuss with them the pitfalls of skipping outlining (e.g., underdevelopment, rambling). Outlining is covered in more depth in Chapter 14, "The Process of Writing an Essay."

After you have selected the ideas you wish to include in your paragraph, you can begin to make a **plan** or an **outline**. A plan briefly lists and arranges the ideas you wish to present in your paragraph. An outline does the same thing a bit more formally, but in an outline, letters or numbers indicate the main groupings of ideas.

First, group together ideas that have something in common, that are related or alike in some way. Then order your ideas by choosing which one you want to present first, which one second, and so on.

Below is a plan for a paragraph about the lack of affordable campus daycare:

TOPIC SENTENCE: The lack of affordable daycare makes it difficult for single parents to attend college.

Group 1
- Millions of college students are raising children.
- Parents with small children need daycare in order to attend class.

Group 2
- In some colleges daycare costs more than tuition.
- The high cost of daycare forces single parents to limit their time on campus.

Group 3
- The campus daycare center charges by the hour.
- Daycare charges more per hour than I make at my job.
- I can only attend college part-time because daycare is too expensive.
- Paying for daycare is my biggest expense as a student.

- Do you see the logic in this arrangement? How are the ideas in each group above related?

  Each group includes details about the lack of affordable daycare.

- Does it make sense to discuss the general facts about single parents needing campus daycare first, the high cost of daycare second, and how it affects the student personally third? Why?

  Yes. The order goes from the general to the specific, from background facts to how the issue affects one student personally.

- Once you have finished arranging ideas, you should have a clear **plan** from which to write your paragraph.*

*For more work on order, see Chapter 4, "Achieving Coherence," Part A.

PRACTICE 9

On paper or on the computer, arrange the ideas from your brainstorm list according to some plan or outline. First, group together related ideas; then decide which ideas will come first, which second, and so on.

Keep in mind that there is more than one way to group ideas. Think about what you want to say; then group ideas according to what your point is.

F. Writing and Revising the Paragraph

Writing the First Draft

The first draft should contain all the ideas you have decided to use in the order you have chosen in your plan. Be sure to start with your topic sentence. Try to write the best, most interesting, or most amusing paragraph you can, but avoid getting stuck on any one word, sentence, or idea. If you are unsure about something, put a check in the margin and come back to it later. Writing on every other line or double-spacing if you write on the computer will leave room for later corrections.

Once you have included all the ideas from your plan, think about adding a concluding sentence that summarizes your main point or adds a final idea. Not all paragraphs need concluding sentences. For example, if you are telling a story, the paragraph can end when the story does. Write a concluding sentence only if it will help to bring your thoughts to an end for your reader.

If possible, once you have finished the first draft, set the paper aside for several hours or several days.

PRACTICE 10

Write a first draft of the paragraph you have been working on.

Revising

TEACHING TIP

Explain the difference between *revising* and *proofreading*.

ESL TIP

Urge your ESL students to use English-only reference materials as they write and revise in English. Using bilingual dictionaries may result in incorrect word choice.

Revising means rethinking and rewriting your first draft and then making whatever changes, additions, or corrections are necessary to improve the paragraph. You may cross out and rewrite words or entire sentences. You may add, drop, or rearrange details.

As you revise, keep the *reader* in mind. Ask yourself these questions:

- Is my topic sentence clear?
- Can a reader understand and follow my ideas?
- Does the paragraph follow a logical order and guide the reader from point to point?
- Will the paragraph keep the reader interested?

In addition, check your paragraph for adequate support and unity, characteristics that we'll consider in the following pages.

Revising for Support

As you revise, make sure your paragraph contains excellent **support**—that is, specific facts, details, and examples that fully explain your topic sentence.

Be careful, too, that you have not simply repeated ideas—especially the topic sentence. Even if they are in different words, repeated ideas only make the reader suspect that your paragraph is padded and that you do not have enough facts and details to support your main idea properly.

Which of the following paragraphs contains the most convincing support?

Paragraph 1

(1) By making study time a priority every week, I raised my grade-point average from 2.4 to 3.3 in one year. (2) I have a really busy life, so I never studied enough. (3) When my average went down, I knew I had to do something. (4) I made myself study more often. (5) Because I made study time more important, my average went from C to B. (6) I also picked prime times to study, and this made a difference. (7) So sticking to my schedule definitely paid off.

Paragraph 2

(1) By making study time a priority every week, I raised my grade-point average from 2.4 to 3.3 in one year. (2) I work fifteen hours a week at the Gap while taking four courses a semester, so finding study time is hard. (3) I used to grab fifteen minutes here or twenty there, usually during breaks at work, on the subway to and from school, or right before bedtime. (4) When my average slipped to a C, I knew I had to take action and make my college education count. (5) I decided to make a real commitment to regular, high-quality study time. (6) I scheduled a two-hour study block at least four days a week, either at the library with a classmate from 12 to 2 p.m. or at home from 7 to 9 p.m. (7) It was really tough to resist the temptation to go out with friends, talk on the phone, or relax in front of the TV, but I scheduled my study times like appointments I had to keep. (8) As a result, I studied not only regularly but also for longer periods of time. (9) By increasing my study time this way, I began to understand the material much better. (10) In addition, I studied at times when I was more alert—not 10 or 11 p.m., when I was too tired to concentrate. (11) Soon I was earning more A's and B's, so sticking to my schedule definitely paid off.

TEACHING TIP
Emphasize to students the importance of including adequate supporting details in paragraphs. The number and quality of supporting details often make the difference between a mediocre and an excellent paragraph.

- *Paragraph 1* contains general statements but little specific information to support the topic sentence.
- *Paragraph 1* also contains needless repetition. What is the number of the sentence or sentences that just repeat the topic sentence? Sentence 5
- *Paragraph 2,* however, supports the topic sentence with specific details and examples: *fifteen hours at the Gap, four courses, two-hour study block at least four days a week, library with a classmate from 12 to 2 p.m.* What other specific support does it give?

Used to grab fifteen minutes here, twenty there, breaks at work, on the subway, temptation to go out with friends, talk on the phone, relax with TV, scheduled study times like appointments, times when more alert—not 10 or 11 p.m., soon earning more A's and B's.

PRACTICE 11

Check the following paragraphs for adequate support. As you read each one, decide which places need more or better support—specific facts, details, and examples. Then rewrite the paragraphs, inventing facts and details whenever necessary and dropping repetitious words and sentences.

Paragraph 1

(1) My uncle can always be counted on when the family faces hardship. (2) Last year, when my mother was very ill, he was there, ready to help in every way. (3) He never has to be called twice. (4) When my father became seriously depressed, my uncle's caring made a difference. (5) Everyone respects him for his willingness to be a real "family man." (6) He is always there for us.

Paragraph 2

(1) Lending money to a friend can have negative consequences. (2) For example, Ashley, a student at Tornado Community College, agreed to lend $200 to her best friend, Jan. (3) This was a bad decision even though Ashley meant well. (4) The results of this loan were surprising and negative for Ashley, for Jan, and for the friendship. (5) Both women felt bad about it but in different ways. (6) Yes, lending money to a friend can have very negative consequences, like anger and hurt.

Paragraph 3

(1) Many television talk shows don't really present a discussion of ideas. (2) Some people who appear on these shows don't know what they are talking about; they just like to sound off about something. (3) I don't like these shows at all. (4) Guests shout their opinions out loud but never give any proof for what they say. (5) Guests sometimes expose their most intimate personal and family problems before millions of viewers—I feel embarrassed. (6) I have even heard hosts insult their guests and guests insult them back. (7) Why do people watch this junk? (8) You never learn anything from these dumb shows.

TEACHING TIP

Stress to students that outlining first and then using the outline as a guide while writing will help prevent problems with unity.

Revising for Unity

It is sometimes easy, in the process of writing, to drift away from the topic under discussion. Guard against doing so by checking your paragraph for **unity**; that is, make sure the topic sentence, every sentence in the body, and the concluding sentence all relate to one main idea.*

This paragraph lacks unity:

> (1) A popular rival to the Barbie doll is provoking protests from angry parents. (2) Designed for four- to eight-year-olds and marketed with the slogan "a passion for fashion," the multi-ethnic Bratz dolls wear heavy makeup, sultry facial expressions, and skimpy outfits. (3) The "hooker chic" style of these dolls concerns many parents, who worry that such toys expose their daughters to adult sexuality too soon. (4) Boys are harmed too, they claim, because the dolls encourage them to see girls as sex objects in little tops and glittery mini-skirts.

*For more work on revising, see Chapter 24, "Putting Your Revision Skills to Work."

(5) Parents who buy Bratz dolls might think, "Hey, it's just a toy," but many child psychologists say that Bratz dolls send the wrong message and can negatively impact a developing girl's identity and values. (6) Many video games and music videos show damaging images of women. (7) Because Bratz accessories include items like a "party plane," drinks that look like cocktails, and jewelry with slivers of real diamond, critics maintain that these dolls glorify a lifestyle of partying and materialism while undermining the importance of education and achievement.

- What is the number of the topic sentence in this paragraph?

  Sentence 1

- Which sentence in the paragraph does not clearly relate to the topic sentence?

  Sentence 6

This paragraph also lacks unity:

(1) Quitting smoking was very difficult for me. (2) When I was 13, my friend Janice and I took up smoking because we thought it would make us look cool. (3) We practiced smoking in front of a mirror, striking poses with our cigarettes. (4) Even though we often were seized with violent fits of coughing, we thought we seemed grown up and sophisticated. (5) Gradually, I began to smoke not just to appear worldly but also to calm myself when I felt stressed. (6) I smoked to give myself confidence on dates and to feel less anxious before taking tests at school. (7) Reading, talking on the phone, and driving all became reasons to light up. (8) Soon, I was smoking all the time.

TEACHING TIP

To find sentences that disrupt unity, have students read backward, one sentence at a time, checking that each one relates directly to the idea in the topic sentence.

- Here the topic sentence itself, sentence 1, does not relate to the rest of the paragraph. The main idea in sentence 1, that quitting smoking was difficult, is not developed by the other sentences. Since the rest of the paragraph *is* unified, a more appropriate topic sentence might read, *As a teenager, I developed the bad habit of smoking.*

PRACTICE 12

TEACHING TIP

Practice 12 is fun to do in class. Once students find each sentence that does not belong, you might want to have them spot or highlight the topic sentence and supporting points.

Check the following paragraphs for unity. If a paragraph has unity, write *U* in the blank. If not, write the number of the sentence that does not belong in the paragraph.

Paragraph 1

_8_ (1) During the sweltering Miami summer of 1965, a worried football coach helped create the world's most popular sports drink. (2) The coach asked University of Florida scientist Tom Cade why so many players got sick in the heat, losing up to 18 pounds in one game. (3) Cade knew the athletes were losing vital water and minerals, so he mixed salt and potassium into a balancing drink.

(4) After players spit out the first, foul-tasting samples, Cade's wife suggested adding lemon juice and sweetener. (5) The rest is history. (6) Sipping the new beverage, the Florida Gators stopped wilting and roared into a winning streak. (7) The new drink was named in their honor. (8) Other Florida teams are the Hurricanes and the Seminoles. (9) Today eight million bottles of Gatorade are consumed daily.

Paragraph 2

_9_ (1) Technology enables people like the famous physicist Dr. Stephen Hawking to continue working despite serious physical disabilities. (2) For more than 45 years, Dr. Hawking has lived with Lou Gehrig's disease, which attacks the muscles, but his brilliant mind works perfectly. (3) He can no longer walk, speak, or feed himself. (4) Nevertheless, a high-tech wheelchair with computer attachments allows him to continue his research and stay in touch with friends and colleagues around the world. (5) His computer is hooked up full-time to the Internet. (6) To speak, he chooses words displayed on the computer screen, and then an electronic voice machine pronounces each word. (7) A pressure-sensitive joystick even lets Dr. Hawking make his way through traffic. (8) In his home, infrared remote controls operate doors, lights, and his personal entertainment center. (9) He has three children with his first wife, Jane, and one grandchild. (10) Dr. Hawking continues to search for new ways to overcome his problems through technology.

Paragraph 3

_5_ (1) Across the country, thousands of college students and others are attending or performing poetry at "poetry slams." (2) A poetry slam is a competitive event in which participants perform one original poem before an audience. (3) With words, rhymes, and dramatic skill as their only tools, these fast-talking bards have just three minutes to win over the audience. (4) After each performance, judges selected from the audience give a numerical score, usually from one to ten. (5) Gymnastics competitions are judged using a similar ten-point scoring system. (6) Although most slammers would love to win first prize, they say that poetry slams also allow them to express their deepest thoughts, boost self-esteem, hone their English skills, and connect with a community of people who "speak from the heart." (7) Poetry slams are gaining popularity as schools, arts organizations, and groups of young writers start poetry clubs or sponsor contests. (8) Now, as online videos of the winning performances reveal the power of poetry slams, the excitement has spread worldwide.

EXPLORING ONLINE

www.youtube.com

Search "national poetry slam winners" to watch winning poets. Would you like to attend or perform at a poetry slam? Why or why not? What do you think is the reason so many people attend slams?

Revising with Peer Feedback

Sometimes you may wish to show or read your first draft to a respected friend, who can give feedback using a template like this:

Peer Feedback Sheet

To ________________ From ________________ Date ________________

1. What I like about this piece of writing is ________________________________

____

2. Your main point seems to be ________________________________

____

3. These particular words or lines struck me as powerful:

Words or lines	I like them because
________________	________________
________________	________________
________________	________________

4. Some things aren't clear to me. These lines or parts could be improved (meaning not clear, supporting points missing, order seems mixed up, writing not lively):

Lines or parts	Need improving because
________________	________________
________________	________________
________________	________________

5. The one change you could make that would make the biggest improvement in this piece of writing is ________________________________

____

____

TEACHING TIP

For printable peer feedback sheets and rubrics for the paragraph, essay, and each rhetorical mode, see the *Instructor Companion Site.*

- Ask this person to give you an honest response, *not* to rewrite your work. You might want to ask your own specific questions or to modify the Peer Feedback Sheet.

Writing the Final Draft

ESL TIP
Alert nonnative writers to ESL Resources and to websites like **a4esl.org**.

When you are satisfied with your revisions, recopy your paper or print a fresh copy. If you are writing in class, the second draft will usually be the last one. Be sure to include all your corrections, writing neatly and legibly.

Compare the following first draft of the paragraph about campus daycare, showing the writer's changes, to the revised, final draft.

First Draft with Revisions

The lack of affordable daycare makes it difficult for single parents to attend college. Millions of parents attend colleges across the country. In some colleges daycare costs more than tuition. The high cost of daycare forces single parents to limit their time on campus. At our campus daycare charges more than I make at my job. Paying for daycare is my biggest expense as a student. I want to study nursing, but can only attend part-time.

add "single parents"
subsidies?
add details
awkward
how much?
better conclusion needed

Final Draft

TEACHING AND ESL TIP
Have students review their previous compositions to identify recurring language errors and focus on correcting these specific types of errors as they proofread. For ESL students, these errors may be caused by differences between their native language and English.

The lack of affordable daycare makes it difficult for single parents to attend college. Millions of parents attend community colleges across this country. Many of them are single mothers and fathers with small children who need campus daycare in order to attend class. College daycare can cost more than tuition, even in community colleges that offer subsidies. The high cost of daycare forces single parents to limit their time on campus, making it difficult for them to use the library or tutoring services. At our campus the daycare center charges 18 dollars an hour per child, which is more than I make at my job. Paying for daycare is my biggest expense as a student. I plan to study nursing, which requires many hours in the lab and all-day clinical courses. I wanted to graduate in two years, but because of the lack of affordable daycare, I can only attend college part-time.

- Note that the paragraph contains good support—specific facts, details, and examples that explain the topic sentence.
- Note that the paragraph has unity—every idea relates to the topic sentence.
- Note that the final sentence provides a brief conclusion, so that the paragraph *feels finished*.

TEACHING TIP

Using returned papers and suggestions from you, students should keep lists of their personal error patterns to make them better proofreaders.

Proofreading

Whether you write by hand or on the computer, be sure to **proofread** your final draft carefully for grammar and spelling errors. Pointing to each word as you read it will help you catch errors or words you might have left out, especially small words like *to, the,* or *a*. If you are unsure of the spelling of a word, consult a dictionary and run spell checker if you work on a computer.* Make neat corrections in pen or print a corrected copy of your paper. Chapter 39, "Putting Your Proofreading Skills to Work," and all of Units 6 and 7 in this book are devoted to improving your proofreading skills.

PRACTICE 13

Now read the first draft of your paragraph with a critical eye. Revise and rewrite it, checking especially for a clear topic sentence, strong support, and unity.

PRACTICE 14

Exchange revised paragraphs with a classmate. Ask specific questions or use the Peer Feedback Sheet.

When you give feedback, try to be as honest and specific as possible; saying a paper is "good," "nice," or "bad" doesn't really help the writer. When you receive feedback, think over your classmates' responses; do they ring true?

Now revise a second time, with the aim of writing a fine paragraph. Proofread carefully for grammar errors, spelling errors, and omitted words.

WRITING ASSIGNMENT

The assignments that follow will give you practice in writing basic paragraphs. Choose a paragraph and write (1) a topic sentence with a clear controlling idea and (2) a body that fully supports and develops the topic sentence.

Remember to narrow the topic, write the topic sentence, freewrite or brainstorm, and select and arrange ideas in a plan or an outline before you write. Rethink and revise as necessary before composing the final version of the paragraph. As you work, refer to the checklist at the end of this chapter.

TEACHING AND ESL TIP

Advise students to read writing assignments carefully and address all topics included in the prompt. Suggest that they underline all important words.

Paragraph 1

Discuss an important day in your life

Think back to a day when you learned something important. In the topic sentence, state what you learned. Freewrite or brainstorm to gather ideas. Then describe the lesson in detail, including only the most important steps or events in the learning process. Conclude with an insight.

---

*For tips and cautions on using a computer spell checker, see Chapter 39, "Putting Your Proofreading Skills to Work," Part B.

Paragraph 2

Describe your ideal job
Decide on the job for which you are best suited and, in your topic sentence, state what this job is. Then describe the qualities of this job that make it ideal. Include information about the pay, benefits, intangible rewards, working conditions, and duties this perfect job would offer you. Explain how each quality you describe matches your needs and desires. Revise your work, checking for support and unity.

Paragraph 3

TEACHING TIP
If you distinguish early in the term between personal and more formal or academic writing, you might point out that paragraph 3 lends itself to third-person writing; its focus is on the subject (a classmate), not the writer.

Interview a classmate about an achievement
Write about a time when your classmate achieved something important, like winning an award for a musical performance, getting an A in a difficult course, or helping a friend through a hard time. To gather interesting facts and details, ask your classmate questions like these and take notes: *Is there one accomplishment of which you are very proud? Why was this achievement so important?* Keep asking questions until you feel you can give the reader a vivid sense of your classmate's triumph. In your first sentence, state the person's achievement—for instance, *Being accepted into the honors program improved Gabe's self-esteem.* Then explain specifically why the achievement was so meaningful.

Paragraph 4

Tell a story of justice or injustice
Think about someone you know or heard about in a news report who did or did *not* get what he or she deserved. For example, you may have an athletic family member whose years of practice and hard work were rewarded with a college scholarship. On the other hand, you might have read about a person who spent time in prison for a crime he or she did not commit, thus losing precious years before being released. Make sure that you state your main idea and point of view clearly in a topic sentence. Then, use vivid supporting details to tell this person's story.

Paragraph 5

Discuss a quotation
Pick a quotation you strongly agree or disagree with. In your topic sentence, state how you feel about the quotation. Then explain why you feel the way you do, giving examples from your own experience to support or contradict the quotation. Make sure your reader knows exactly how you feel.

Paragraph 6

Give advice to busy students
Help busy students by giving them some advice that will make their lives easier. You might explain how to stay organized, establish a routine, balance coursework with other responsibilities, or keep a positive attitude. Use humor if you wish. State your controlling idea in the topic sentence and support this idea fully with details, explanations, and examples.

ESL TIP

Vary your editing responses on student papers. First, correct errors and have ESL students recopy the corrected text. Later, move to editing symbols and, eventually, underline or circle errors.

Checklist

The Process of Writing Basic Paragraphs

Refer to this checklist as you write a basic paragraph.

☐ 1. Narrow the topic to fit your audience and purpose.

☐ 2. Write a topic sentence that has a clear controlling idea and is a complete sentence. If you have trouble, freewrite or brainstorm first; then narrow the topic and write the topic sentence.

☐ 3. Freewrite or brainstorm, generating facts, details, and examples to develop your topic sentence.

☐ 4. Select and drop ideas for the body of the paragraph.

☐ 5. Arrange ideas in a plan or an outline, deciding which ideas will come first, which will come second, and so forth.

☐ 6. Write the best first draft you can.

☐ 7. Conclude. Don't just leave the paragraph hanging.

☐ 8. Revise as necessary, checking your paragraph for support and unity.

☐ 9. Proofread for grammar and spelling errors.

EXPLORING ONLINE

owl.english.purdue.edu/owl/resource/606/01

Quick review of paragraph writing

owl.english.purdue.edu/owl/resource/561/01

Good proofreading strategies to improve your writing and your grade

CHAPTER 4

Achieving Coherence

A: Coherence Through Order

B: Coherence Through Related Sentences

Every composition should have **coherence**. A paragraph *coheres*—holds together—when the sentences are arranged in a clear, logical *order* and are *related* like links in a chain.

A. Coherence Through Order

TEACHING TIP
Stress to students that coherence is necessary for the reader's comprehension of ideas.

An orderly presentation of ideas within the paragraph is easier to follow and more pleasant to read than a jumble. *After* jotting down ideas but *before* writing the paragraph, the writer should decide which ideas to discuss first, which second, which third, and so on, according to a logical order.

There are many possible orders, depending on the subject and the writer's purpose. This section will explain three basic ways of ordering ideas: **time order**, **space order**, and **order of importance**.

Time Order

One of the most common methods of ordering sentences in a paragraph is through **time**, or **chronological, order**, which moves from present to past or from past to present. Most stories, histories, and instructions follow the logical order of time.* The following paragraph employs time order:

(1) I love to talk, but I never thought twice about listening. (2) So when my College Skills instructor said that becoming an active listener improves

*For work on narrative paragraphs, see Chapter 6, "Narration," and for work on process paragraphs, see Chapter 8, "Process."

academic performance, I thought, "Whatever." (3) Now I believe that working on my listening skills has raised my GPA. (4) *First*, I arrive in the classroom early and pick a seat near the front of the room; that way, windows, latecomers, and jokers won't distract me. (5) *Then* I take out my paper, pen, and textbook. I like to converse with my classmates during these moments, but I have learned to politely end these conversations as soon as the instructor comes in. (6) *Next*, I stop slouching, sit up in my chair, and look straight at the instructor. (7) Doing this signals my brain that it's time to learn. (8) *As class proceeds*, I participate and keep my mind focused on the lesson. (9) If the instructor lectures, I take notes. (10) If the instructor leads a discussion, I think about what is being said, answer questions, and contribute my comments. (11) *Finally*, I resist the urge to have side conversations, text, make calls, or do homework during class. (12) Becoming an active listener takes some effort, especially if, like me, you have to break bad habits, but you'll be amazed at how much more you'll remember.

—Tony Aguera, Student

- The steps or actions in this paragraph are clearly arranged in the order of time. They are presented as they happen, *chronologically*.
- Throughout the paragraph, key words like *first, then, next, as class proceeds*, and *finally* emphasize time order and guide the reader from action to action.

Careful use of time order helps prevent confusing writing like this: *Oops, I forgot to mention that before the instructor comes in, I arrange my paper, pen, and book.*

Occasionally, when the sentences in a paragraph follow a very clear time order, the topic sentence is only implied, not stated directly, as in this example:

ESL TIP

You might use these two model paragraphs to contrast present and past tense. Ask students to identify the verb tense used in each and explain its use.

(1) In 1905, a poor washerwoman with a homemade hair product started a business—with $1.50! (2) In just five years, Madame C. J. Walker established offices and manufacturing centers in Denver, Pittsburgh, and Indianapolis. (3) The Madame C. J. Walker Manufacturing Company specialized in hair supplies, but Madame Walker specialized in independence for herself and for others. (4) Although she was not formally educated, she developed an international sales force, teaching her African American agents the most sophisticated business skills. (5) Eight years after starting her business, Madame Walker was the first African American woman to become a self-made millionaire. (6) In addition, she drew thousands of former farm and domestic workers into the business world. (7) One of her most original ideas was to establish "Walker Clubs," and she awarded cash prizes to the clubs with the most educational and philanthropic projects in their African American communities. (8) When she died in 1919, Madame Walker left two-thirds of her fortune to schools and charities. (9) Another of her contributions also lived on. (10) After her death, many of her former employees used their experience to start businesses throughout the United States and the Caribbean.

- Time order gives coherence to this paragraph. Sentence 1 tells us about the beginning of Madame Walker's career as a businessperson. However, it does not express the main idea of the entire paragraph.

- What is the implied topic sentence or main idea developed by the paragraph?

  With almost nothing but natural business ability, Madame Walker achieved success and helped others.

TEACHING TIP

Have students generate examples of academic, professional, and personal writing that might require time order.

- The implied topic sentence or main idea of the paragraph might read, *With nothing but natural business ability and vision, Madame C. J. Walker achieved history, making success for herself and others.*
- Because the writer arranges the paragraph in chronological order, the reader can easily follow the order of events in Madame Walker's life. What words and phrases indicate time order? Underline them and list them here:

  in 1905; in just five years; eight years after starting her business; when she died in 1919; after her death

PRACTICE 1

Arrange each set of sentences in logical time order, numbering the sentences *1, 2, 3,* and so on, as if you were preparing to write a paragraph. Underline any words and phrases, like *first, next,* and *in 1692,* that give time clues.

LEARNING STYLES TIP

For *kinesthetic learners,* consider adapting Practices 1 and 2, reproducing each sentence on a card or strip of paper; then let pairs of students put those strips or cards in order.

1. 5 Finally, network executives review the feedback from preview audiences to determine which pilots should be made into television series.

   1 The process of getting a television show into production is long and often difficult.

   4 Next, network executives decide which scripts will be turned into pilots, or test episodes.

   2 First, writers pitch ideas for television shows to network executives.

   3 Then the executives select a few ideas to be turned into scripts to be read and evaluated.

2. 3 Days later, the would-be saboteurs traveled across the United States, visiting old friends, shopping for new clothes, and dating former girlfriends.

   1 On June 12, 1942, a Nazi U-boat landed four secret agents on Long Island.

   2 The next morning the German spies, who had previously lived in the United States, took a train to New York City to destroy important military installations.

   4 A week after the landing, one of the saboteurs turned himself in to the FBI.

   5 Within days, the FBI rounded up all the spies before they committed a single act of sabotage.

3. 4 In 1957, *The Cat in the Hat* made famous both its hat-wearing tomcat with terrible manners and its author.

6 Before he died in 1991, Dr. Seuss inspired millions to love language with such creations as the Grinch, Nerds, Wockets, Bar-ba-loots, bunches of Hunches, and a fox in socks.

5 *Green Eggs and Ham* came out in 1960 and told a memorable story, using only fifty-five different words.

1 In his long career, Theodor Geisel, better known as Dr. Seuss, wrote forty-six wildly imaginative children's books, now read all over the world.

2 His first book was rejected by twenty-eight publishers, who found it "too strange for children."

3 In 1937, when it finally was published, readers loved the rhythmic march of tongue-twisting, invented words and the wacky characters.

WRITING ASSIGNMENT 1

Use **time order** to give coherence to a paragraph. Choose one of the following two topics. Compose a topic sentence, freewrite or brainstorm to generate ideas, and then arrange your ideas *chronologically*. You may wish to use transitional words and phrases like these to guide the reader from point to point:

first, second	before	soon	suddenly
then	during	when	moments later
next	after	while	finally

Paragraph 1

Narrate the first hour of your average day

Start with getting up in the morning and continue to describe what you do for that first hour. Record your activities, your conversations, if any, and possibly your moods as you go through this hour of the morning. As you revise, make sure that events clearly follow time order.

Paragraph 2

Record an unforgettable event

Choose a moment in sports or in some other activity that you vividly remember, either as a participant or as a spectator. In the topic sentence, tell in a general way what happened. *(It was the most exciting touchdown I have ever seen,* or *Ninety embarrassing seconds marked the end of my brief surfing career.)* Then record the experience, arranging details in time order.

Space Order

Another useful way to arrange ideas in writing is through **space order**—describing a person, a thing, or a place from top to bottom, from left to right, from foreground to background, and so on. Space order is often used in descriptive writing because it moves from detail to detail like a movie camera's eye:*

*For more work on space order, see Chapter 7, "Description."

(1) A rain forest actually consists of five different layers, each one teeming with life. (2) On the *forest's dark floor* live a wide variety of creatures, from the smallest insects and spiders to anteaters, wild boars, and even gorillas. (3) Rising a few feet above the ground is a layer of *shrubs and seedlings* struggling to grow in the deep shadows. (4) Still higher is the forest's *understory*, a cool, shady zone beneath the leaves of the taller trees where beetles, snakes, lizards, and frogs crawl over ferns and vines, and jaguars might lounge in tree branches, watching for prey. (5) The *canopy*—the leafy roof of the forest that is home to many mosses, orchids, birds, reptiles, and monkeys—chirps, squawks, hisses, and howls with life. (6) Bursting through the canopy into the sunlight are a few towering trees of the uppermost *emergent layer*, the habitat of birds like the brilliant red, blue, and yellow scarlet macaw.

- This paragraph uses space order.
- Sentence 1 clearly places the scene: the rain forest.
- Sentence 2 begins at the bottom, on the *forest's dark floor*.
- Sentences 3 and 4 move upward from the forest floor to describe the next two layers: *shrubs and seedlings* and the *understory*.
- Sentences 5 and 6 move further upward, describing the two highest areas of the rain forest: the *canopy* and the *emergent layer*.

Note how phrases like *rising a few feet above the ground, still higher, beneath the leaves of the taller trees, leafy roof,* and *bursting through the canopy into the sunlight* help the reader form a mental image of the rain forest as the paragraph moves from bottom to top.

PRACTICE 2

LEARNING STYLES TIP

Visual learners and others may find that sketching helps them comprehend space order. Practice 2 helps students apply verbal concepts to a visual image.

CRITICAL VIEWING AND WRITING

Some people draw a quick sketch to help them visualize space order as they read or write. Study this diagram of a rain forest, based on the boxed paragraph above. On the blank lines, name each forest layer from the ground up.

emergent layer

canopy

understory

shrubs and seedlings

forest floor

Some paragraphs that are clearly arranged according to space order have only an implied topic sentence:

TEACHING TIP

You might wish to have students sketch Costco's floor plan, showing the use of space order in this paragraph.

(1) At the entrance to Costco, inspectors check membership cards before letting customers enter the huge discount warehouse. (2) Just inside, flat-screen TVs flash larger and larger images of the same movie. (3) Behind them, wide aisles stretch toward the back of the store, each lined with tall metal shelves packed with merchandise. (4) Aisles on the left hold office supplies like bags with 50 ballpoint pens or cartons of paper. (5) In the center are games and toys, including life-sized plush bears at deep discounts. (6) To the right stretches a clothing section with every possible garment, even wedding dresses. (7) Farther back, shoppers cram their carts with groceries and cosmetics. (8) Who would want to walk miles on concrete floors for gallons of tomato sauce, 500 Huggies, and maybe even a casket at low, low prices? (9) Judging from the long lines snaking toward Costco's checkout, plenty of consumers do.

—Saron Huy, Student

TEACHING TIP

To give students more practice, list a person, a scene, and an object. Ask what kind of space order would be appropriate to describe each (front to back, top to bottom, and so on).

- The main idea of this paragraph is *implied,* not stated by a topic sentence. What is the main idea?

  Though huge and overwhelming, Costco is chock full of bargains.

- Because the paragraph is clearly arranged according to space order, the reader can easily follow it.
- Transitional phrases like *at the entrance, just inside,* and *behind them* guide the reader from sentence to sentence. What phrases in sentences 4 through 7 help guide the reader?

  on the left, in the center, to the right, farther back

PRACTICE 3

Below are topic sentences followed by supporting details. Arrange each group of details according to space order, numbering them *1, 2, 3,* and so on, as if you were preparing to write a descriptive paragraph. On the line after each topic sentence, tell what kind of space order you used: *left to right, back to front,* and so forth.

1. Describe the Empire State Building. top to bottom (or bottom to top)

   4 (2) street entrance and lobby

   3 (3) second-floor tourist center

   1 (5) rooftop antenna

   5 (1) basement

   2 (4) top observation deck

2. Describe the security measures protecting the original Declaration of Independence. inside to outside (or outside to inside)

 4 (2) room's perimeter ringed with security cameras and motion sensors

 3 (3) two armed guards standing next to the bronze and marble shrine

 5 (1) the National Archives building in Washington, D.C.

 1 (5) parchment of document touched only by decay-preventing helium gas

 2 (4) bulletproof glass case

3. Describe a firefighter's uniform. top to bottom (or bottom to top)

 4 (2) fire-retardant pants, called "turnouts"

 1 (5) black, hard plastic helmet with flashlight attached

 5 (1) steel-reinforced black rubber bunker boots

 3 (3) bright yellow, fireproof Kevlar jacket

 2 (4) compressed-air face mask

WRITING ASSIGNMENT 2

Use **space order** to give coherence to one of the following paragraphs. Compose a topic sentence, freewrite or brainstorm for more details, and then arrange them in space order. Use transitional words and phrases like these if you wish:

on the left	above	next to
on the right	below	behind
in the middle	beside	farther out

ESL TIP

Have your ESL students use objects in the classroom to generate additional words and phrases to denote spatial relationships and location.

Paragraph 1

Describe a memorable face

Describe the face of someone you know well, perhaps a friend, family member, or person you admire. Study the actual face of the person or visualize it vividly as you jot down the five or six most important or striking details. Then, before writing your paragraph, arrange these details according to space order—moving from left to right or from top to bottom.

Paragraph 2

Describe a possession

Choose one material object that you hold dear. As you examine or visualize it, brainstorm at least ten details that capture its essence. Now draft a topic sentence and choose your best details. Use space order to weave these details into sentences.

Order of Importance

Ideas in a paragraph can also be arranged in the **order of importance**. You may start with the most important idea and end with the least, or you may begin with the least important idea and build to a climax with the most important one.

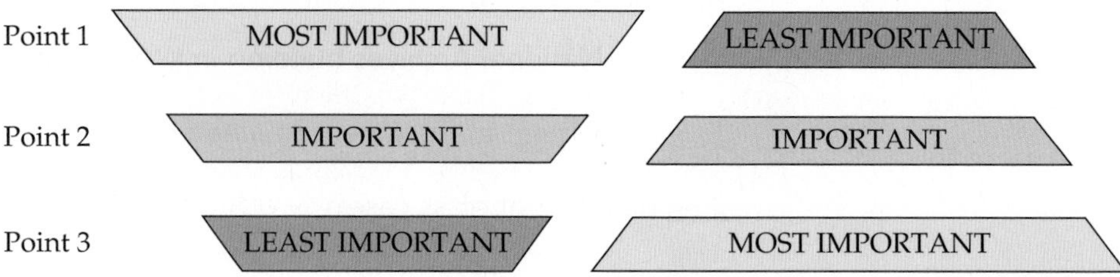

TEACHING TIP
Have students generate examples of academic, professional, and personal writing that might require order of importance.

If you wish to persuade your reader with arguments or examples, beginning with the most important points impresses the reader with the force of your ideas and persuades him or her to continue reading.* On essay examinations and in business correspondence, be especially careful to begin with the most important idea. In those situations, the reader definitely wants your important points first.

Read the following paragraph and note the order of ideas:

(1) Louis Pasteur is revered as a great scientist for his three major discoveries. (2) Most important, this Frenchman created vaccines that have saved millions of human and animal lives. (3) The vaccines grew out of his discovery that weakened forms of a disease could help the person or animal build up antibodies that would prevent the disease. (4) The vaccines used today to protect children from serious illnesses owe their existence to Pasteur's work. (5) Almost as important was Pasteur's brilliant idea that tiny living beings, not chemical reactions, spoiled beverages. (6) He developed a process, pasteurization, that keeps milk, wine, vinegar, and beer from spoiling. (7) Finally, Pasteur found ways to stop a silkworm disease that threatened to ruin France's profitable silk industry. (8) Many medical researchers regard him as "the father of modern medicine."

- The ideas in this paragraph are explained in the **order of importance**, from the *most important to the least important*:

  What was Pasteur's most important discovery? vaccines

  What was his next most important discovery? pasteurization

  What was his least important one? cure for silkworm disease

- Note how the words *most important, almost as important,* and *finally* guide the reader from one idea to another.

*See Chapter 5, "Illustration," and Chapter 13, "Persuasion."

TEACHING TIP
After students learn the three types of order, have each student choose one type of order and write a paragraph. Bring in the most successful examples of each type and ask authors to read them aloud.

Sometimes, if you wish to add drama and surprise to your paragraphs, you may want to begin with the least important idea and build toward a climax by saving the most important idea for last. This kind of order can help counter the tendency of some writers to state the most important idea first and then let the rest of the paragraph dwindle away.

Read the following paragraph and note the order of ideas:

> (1) Oscar Micheaux was the most successful and influential African American filmmaker in the first half of the twentieth century. (2) Born in Illinois in 1884, Micheaux moved to South Dakota, where he began writing about his experiences as a homesteader. (3) Micheaux published articles and wrote novels with some success. (4) More notably, he produced a film version of his novel *The Homesteader* in 1918, becoming the first African American to produce and direct a feature film. (5) In the following decades, Micheaux produced 44 motion pictures, many of which addressed racism and other issues facing African Americans. (6) Above all, Micheaux offered audiences positive and complex images of African Americans not otherwise seen in Hollywood films. (7) Since his death in 1951, Oscar Micheaux has been honored with a star on Hollywood Boulevard's Walk of Fame, numerous awards, and a commemorative postage stamp.

- The reasons for Micheaux's importance are discussed in the **order of importance**: *from the least to the most important*.
- Micheaux's film career is more important than his writing career. However, the fact that he offered audiences positive and complex images of African Americans in an era dominated by negative stereotypes is most important of all.
- Transitional words like *more notably* and *above all* help the reader follow clearly from one reason to the next.

Neftali/Shutterstock.com

Postage stamp honoring filmmaker Oscar Micheaux

EXPLORING ONLINE

www.oscarmicheaux.com

On this site, you can learn more about Oscar Micheaux and watch some of his films. Watch one of his movies; then write three things about it that command your attention, arrange them in order of importance, and write a paragraph.

PRACTICE 4

Arrange the ideas that develop each topic sentence in their **order of importance**, numbering them *1, 2, 3,* and so on. *Begin with the most important* (or largest, most severe, most surprising) and continue to the *least* important. Or reverse the order if you think that the paragraph would be more dramatic by beginning with the *least* important ideas and building toward a climax, with the most important last.

1. Cynthia Lopez's first year of college brought many unexpected expenses.

   3 (2) Her English professor wanted her to own a college dictionary.

   1 (4) All those papers to write made a $500 laptop computer a necessity.

   2 (3) She had to spend $235 for textbooks.

   4 (1) Her geometry class required various colored pencils and felt-tip pens.

2. Alcoholic beverages should not be sold at sporting events.

   1 (3) Injuries and even deaths caused by alcohol-induced crowd violence would be eliminated.

   3 (1) Fans could save money by buying soft drinks instead of beer.

   2 (2) Games and matches would be much more pleasant without the yelling, swearing, and rudeness often caused by alcohol.

3. The apartment needed work before the new tenants could move in.

   3 (2) The handles on the kitchen cabinets were loose.

   1 (4) Every room needed plastering and painting.

   4 (1) Grime marred the appearance of the bathroom sink.

   2 (3) Two closet doors hung off the hinges.

WRITING ASSIGNMENT 3

Use **order of importance** to give coherence to one of the paragraphs that follow. Use transitional words and phrases like these to guide the reader along:

TEACHING TIP
Stress the importance of outlining when arranging ideas in order of importance. Urge students to consider carefully the best order for their ideas before they write. Even a scratch outline will help them.

first	even more	another
next	last	least of all
above all	especially	most of all

Paragraph 1

Describe a day in which everything went right (or wrong)
Freewrite or brainstorm to generate ideas. Choose three or four of the day's best (or worst) events and write a paragraph in which you present them in order of importance—either from the most to the least important, or from the least to the most important.

Paragraph 2

Persuade someone to attend your college
Choose a person you know—a friend, relative, or co-worker—and write a paragraph to convince that person to enroll in classes at your college. Write your topic sentence and generate ideas; choose three to five reasons to use to convince your reader. Arrange these reasons according to their order of importance—either from the most to the least important or from the least to the most important.

B. Coherence Through Related Sentences

In addition to arranging ideas in a logical order, the writer can ensure paragraph coherence by linking one sentence to the next. This section will present four basic ways to link sentences: **repetition of important words, substitution of pronouns, substitution of synonyms**, and **transitional expressions**.

Repetition of Important Words and Pronouns

Link sentences within a paragraph by *repeating important words and ideas*:

LEARNING STYLES TIP
Using the examples here or paragraphs that you bring in, have students use highlighters to mark repeated words, pronouns, synonyms, and transitional expressions. Use a different color for each linking device.

(1) An Amber Alert is a notice to the general public that a child has been kidnapped. (2) This notification system was named after Amber Hagerman, a nine-year-old girl abducted from her neighborhood and found murdered a few days later. (3) The term *Amber Alert* is also an acronym for "America's Missing Broadcast Emergency Response." (4) The goal of an Amber Alert is to collect and spread information about the abduction with utmost speed, thus increasing the chances of finding the child alive. (5) First, police confirm that a child is missing and race to collect descriptive details about the child, the suspected abductor, and the suspect's vehicle. (6) Then broadcasts on television, radio, the Internet, and electronic highway signs spread these details and urge people to report any sightings or clues immediately. (7) To date, the program has saved 800 young lives.

- What important words are repeated in this paragraph?
- The words *Amber Alert* appear three times, in sentences 1, 3, and 4. The word *child* appears four times, in sentences 1, 4, and 5. The word *abducted* appears in sentence 2, *abduction* in sentence 4, and *abductor* in sentence 5.
- Repetition of these key words helps the reader follow from sentence to sentence as these terms are defined or the relationships between them are explained.

Although repetition of important words can be effective, it can also become boring if overused.* To avoid *unnecessary* repetition, substitute *pronouns* for words already mentioned in the paragraph, as this author does:

(1) Paul Revere's ride to warn of a British attack is the stuff of legend, yet few have heard of Sybil Ludington. (2) This courageous sixteen-year-old and *her* horse Star also rode through the night, saving thousands of lives. (3) Early one evening in April 1777, *her* father, Colonel Ludington, was warned by a messenger that Danbury, Connecticut, was burning and the British were pushing inland to attack. (4) When the messenger said *he* was too exhausted to ride on, the teenager volunteered, riding 40 miles at breakneck speed through Putnam County, New York, and rousing 400 militiamen from *their* beds.

- The use of pronouns in this paragraph avoids unnecessary repetition. The pronoun *her* in sentences 2 and 3 refers to the antecedent *this courageous sixteen-year-old.*†
- In sentence 4, the pronouns *he* and *their* give further coherence to the paragraph by referring to what antecedents?

the messenger ________ and the militiamen ________

Use pronoun substitution together with the repetition of important words for a smooth presentation of ideas.

PRACTICE 5

What important words are repeated in the following paragraph? Underline them. Circle any pronouns that replace them. Notice the varied pattern of repetitions and pronoun replacements.

I have always considered my father a very intelligent person. His intelligence is not the type usually tested in schools; perhaps he would have done well on such tests, but the fact is that he never finished high school. Rather, my father's intelligence is his ability to solve problems creatively as they arise. Once when I was very young, we were driving through the desert at night when the oil line broke. My father improvised a light, squeezed under the car, found the break,

*For practice in eliminating wordiness (repetition of unimportant words), see Chapter 23, "Revising for Language Awareness," Part B.

†For more work on pronouns and antecedents, see Chapter 33, "Pronouns," Parts A, B, and C.

and managed to whittle a connection to join the two severed pieces of tubing; then he added more oil and drove us over a hundred miles to the nearest town. Such intelligent solutions to unforeseen problems were typical of him. In fact, my father's brand of brains—accurate insight, followed by creative action—is the kind of intelligence that I admire and most aspire to.

WRITING ASSIGNMENT 4

Paragraph 1

Explain success

How do you measure *success*? By the money you make, the number or quality of friends you have? Freewrite or brainstorm for ideas. Then answer this question in a thoughtful paragraph. Give the paragraph coherence by repeating important words and using pronouns.

Paragraph 2

Discuss a public figure

Choose a public figure whom you admire—from the arts, politics, media, or sports—and write a paragraph discussing *one quality* that makes that person special. Name the person in your topic sentence. Vary repetition of the person's name with pronouns to give the paragraph coherence.

TEACHING TIP

Make sure your students can use a print or online thesaurus like the one at **www.thesaurus.com**.

ESL TIP

Remind ESL students to use English-only reference books to help them avoid word-choice errors.

Synonyms and Substitutions

When you do not wish to repeat a word or use a pronoun, give coherence to your paragraph with a **synonym** or **substitution**. **Synonyms** are two or more words that mean nearly the same thing. For instance, if you do not wish to repeat the word *car*, you might use the synonym *automobile* or *vehicle*. If you are describing a *sky* and have already used the word *bright*, try the synonym *radiant*.

Or instead of a synonym, **substitute** other words that describe the subject. If you are writing about Tom Brady, for example, refer to him as *this skilled quarterback* or *this versatile athlete*. Such substitutions provide a change from constant repetition of a person's name or a single pronoun.*

Use synonyms and substitutions together with repetition and pronouns to give coherence to your writing:

(1) *The main building of Ellis Island* in New York Harbor reopened as a museum in 1990. (2) Millions of people visit *the huge brick and limestone structure* every year. (3) From 1892 to 1954, *this famous immigrant station* was the first stop for millions of newcomers to American shores. (4) In fact, the ancestors of nearly 40 percent of American citizens passed through *this building*. (5) Abandoned in 1954, *it* deteriorated so badly that snow and rain fell on its floor. (6) Today visitors can follow the path of immigrants from a ferryboat, through the great arched doorway, into the room where the weary travelers left their baggage, up the

*For more work on exact language, see Chapter 23, "Revising for Language Awareness," Part A.

stairway where doctors kept watch, and into the registry room. (7) Here questions were asked that determined if each immigrant could stay in the United States. (8) *This magnificent monument to the American people* contains exhibits that help individuals search for their own relatives' names and that tell the whole immigration history of the United States.

- This paragraph effectively mixes repetition, pronouns, and substitutions. The important word *building* is stated in sentence 1 and repeated in sentence 4.
- Sentence 5 substitutes the pronoun *it*.
- In sentence 2, *the huge brick and limestone structure* is substituted for *building*, and a second substitution, *this famous immigrant station*, occurs in sentence 3. Sentence 8 refers to the building as *this magnificent monument to the American people* and concludes the paragraph.

EXPLORING ONLINE

www.libertyellisfoundation.org/genealogy/ellis_island.asp

This site has links to Ellis Island immigration stories and records; however, your name or a family story might be a fine writing topic, wherever you are from.

To find synonyms, check a **dictionary**. For instance, the entry for *smart* might list *clever, witty, intelligent*. An even better source of synonyms is the **thesaurus**, a book of synonyms. For example, if you are describing a city street and cannot think of other words meaning "noisy," look in the thesaurus. The number of choices will amaze you.

PRACTICE 6

Read each paragraph carefully. Then write on the lines any synonyms and substitutions that the writer has used to replace the word(s) in italics.

Paragraph 1

Quick thinking and creativity led fitness instructor Alberto Perez to invent *a popular workout routine* called Zumba. When Perez forgot the cassette tapes for his aerobics class in Cali, Colombia, he grabbed a few Latin music tapes from his car and taught the class some dance moves. This was the birth of Zumba, local slang for "fast moving." The rapid-fire exercise regimen combines steps from samba, salsa, and tango with aerobics and belly dance. Zumba quickly spread around the globe, offering an enjoyable way to lose weight or get in shape. The fitness craze, with its slogan "Ditch the workout, join the party," has even sparked a clothing line and video games.

A popular workout routine is also referred to as the rapid-fire exercise regimen

and the fitness craze.

Paragraph 2

Lori Arviso Alvord, M.D., spent her childhood playing on the red mesas of a New Mexico Indian reservation. Later, while training to become the first Navajo woman surgeon, she encountered a very different world, the sterilized steel-and-chrome environment of the modern hospital. There, as she broke her culture's taboos against touching the dead and removing parts of the body, she felt disconnected from her Native American heritage. Yet even as the skilled doctor used the latest medical technology to repair injuries and remove tumors, she felt that something important was missing. Returning to her roots to search for answers, she realized that scientific medicine alone cannot restore the harmony among body, mind, and spirit the Navajos call "walking in beauty." This pioneering healer resolved to integrate her culture's ancient healing traditions with high-tech procedures. Her skill with a scalpel begins a patient's healing process, but her blend of healing ceremonies and the involvement of families and neighbors restores the balance of good health.

Lori Arviso Alvord, M.D., is also referred to as the first Navajo woman surgeon, the skilled doctor, and this pioneering healer.

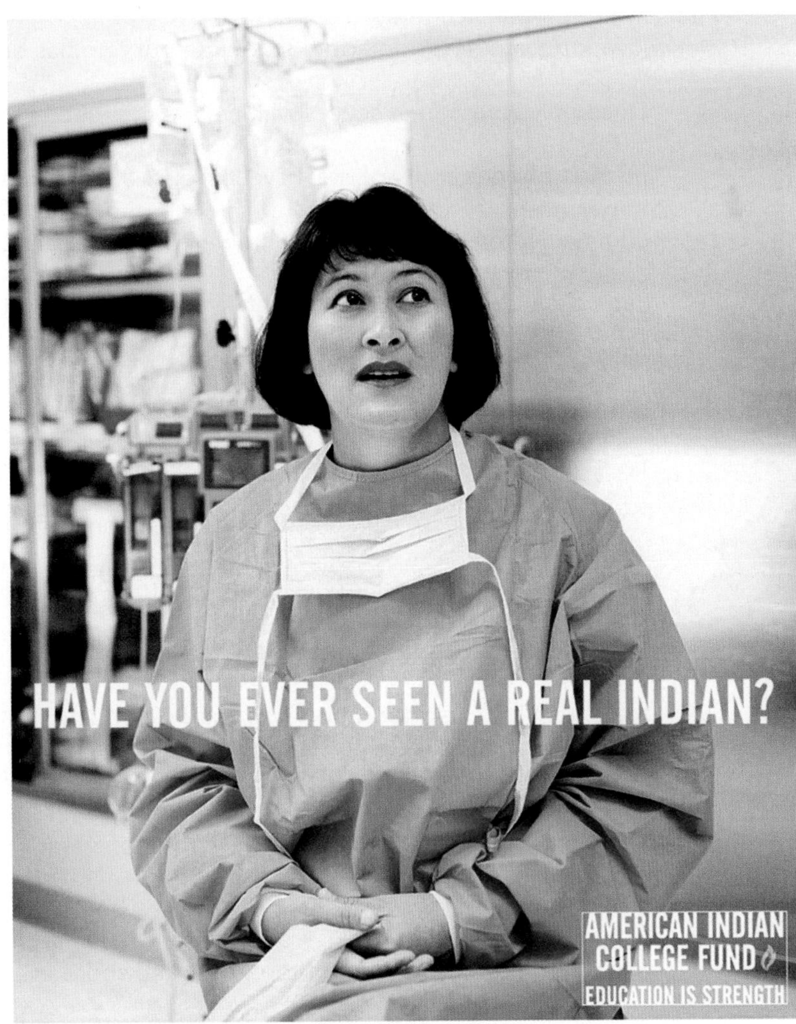

Courtesy of American Indian College Fund

Dr. Lori Alvord, surgeon, associate dean, and author, is featured in this ad for the American Indian College Fund. Why does the ad ask, "Have you ever seen a real Indian?"

PRACTICE 7

Give coherence to the following paragraphs by thinking of appropriate synonyms or substitutions for the words in italics. Then write them in the blanks. Answers will vary.

Paragraph 1

Social media is very popular with *teenagers*, who love to communicate with friends and express themselves online. Security experts, psychologists, and parents, however, are concerned that these ___young people___ are exposing themselves to a number of dangers. Too often ___adolescents___ thoughtlessly post information and images that reveal their identities and addresses to potential stalkers and sex offenders. Even an innocent photo might show a house number or a license plate in the background that could reveal their location to criminals. In addition, online bullying has become a serious problem. Once only harassed at school, victims are now subjected to threats and taunts on their phones and laptops. Psychologists also express a growing concern about what they call a "selfie culture" in which ___minors___ spend more time posting pictures of themselves to impress "contacts" rather than developing meaningful relationships with friends.

Paragraph 2

The hurricane devastated the seaside community. Many *houses* along the beach were flattened by the storm. A few blocks away a row of ___homes___ was flooded by seawater that collected in low-lying areas. A hilltop neighborhood was spared flooding, but the severe winds tore roofs from wooden ___structures___ facing the ocean. Hotels along the boardwalk sustained damage from flying debris that shattered windows, ripped down canopies, and battered signs. The amusement park's century-old Ferris wheel that drew thousands of tourists to the shore every summer was swept out to sea. The morning after the storm, the mayor toured the island, meeting with survivors and workers who cleared streets and restored power. People from the city drove to the island to salvage what they could from their beach ______cottages______.

WRITING ASSIGNMENT 5

As you do the following assignments, try to achieve paragraph coherence by using repetition, pronouns, synonyms, and substitutions.

Paragraph 1

Discuss your favorite form of relaxation

Write about what you like to do when you have free time. Do you like to get together with friends? Do you like to go to a movie or to some sporting event? Or do you prefer to spend your time alone, perhaps listening to music, reading, or going fishing? Whatever your favorite free-time activity, name it in your topic sentence. Be sure to tell what makes your activity *relaxing*. Then give your paragraph coherence by using pronouns and synonyms such as *take it easy, unwind,* and *feel free.*

Paragraph 2

Describe your ideal mate

Decide on three or four crucial qualities that your ideal husband, wife, or friend would possess, and write a paragraph describing this extraordinary person. Use repetition, pronouns, and word substitutions to give coherence to the paragraph. For example, *My ideal husband . . . he . . . my companion.*

Transitional Expressions

Skill in using transitional expressions is vital to coherent writing. **Transitional expressions** are words and phrases that point out the exact relation between one idea and another, one sentence and another. Words like *therefore, however, for example,* and *finally* are signals that guide the reader from sentence to sentence. Without them, even orderly and well-written paragraphs can be confusing and hard to follow.

The transitional expressions in this paragraph are italicized:

(1) Zoos in the past often contributed to the disappearance of animal populations. (2) Animals were cheap, and getting a new gorilla, tiger, or elephant was easier than providing the special diet and shelter needed to keep captive animals alive. (3) *Recently, however,* zoo directors have realized that if zoos themselves are to continue, they must help save many species now facing extinction. (4) *As a result,* some zoos have redefined themselves as places where endangered animals can be protected and even revived. (5) The San Diego Zoo and the National Zoo, in Washington, D.C., *for example,* have both successfully

bred giant pandas, a rapidly disappearing species. (6) The births of such endangered-species babies make international news, and the public can follow the babies' progress on zoo websites and "animal cams." (7) If zoos continue such work, perhaps they can, like Noah's ark, save some of Earth's wonderful creatures from extinction.

TEACHING TIP

Stress to students that transitional expressions point out specific *relationships* between ideas. Using them helps the reader follow the writer's thoughts.

- Each transitional expression in the previous paragraph links, in a precise way, the sentence in which it appears to the sentence before. The paragraph begins by explaining the destructive policies of zoos in the past.
- In sentence 3, two transitional expressions of contrast—*recently* (as opposed to the past) and *however*—introduce the idea that zoo policies have *changed*.
- The phrase *as a result* makes clear that sentence 4 is a *consequence* of events described in the previous sentence(s).
- In sentence 5, *for example* tells us that the National Zoo is *one particular illustration* of the previous general statement, and the San Diego Zoo is another.

AP Images/Eugene Hoshiko

Zoos in China and the United States are breeding pandas like this healthy six-month-old, thus helping to save this endangered species.

EXPLORING ONLINE

www.google.com

Search the words"endangered species, zoos." Take notes on writing ideas, and bookmark websites that intrigue you.

TEACHING AND ESL TIP
Transitional expressions to introduce details and points will be very helpful to both ESL and traditional students. Encourage them to keep personal lists with a variety of introductory expressions to use in their writing.

As you write, use various transitional expressions, together with the other linking devices, to connect one sentence to the next. Well-chosen transitional words also help stress the purpose and order of the paragraph.

Particular groups of transitional expressions are further explained and demonstrated in each chapter of Unit 3. However, here is a combined partial list for handy reference as you write:

Transitional Expressions at a Glance

Purpose	Transitional Expressions
to add	also, as well, besides, beyond that, first (second, third, last, and so on), for one thing, furthermore, in addition, moreover, next, then, what is more
to compare	also, as well, equally, in the same way, likewise, similarly
to contrast	be that as it may, however, in contrast, nevertheless, on the contrary, on the other hand
to concede (a point)	certainly, granted that, of course, no doubt, to be sure
to emphasize	above all, especially, indeed, in fact, in particular, most important, surely
to illustrate	as a case in point, as an illustration, for example, for instance, in particular, one such, yet another
to place	above, below, beside, beyond, farther, here, inside, nearby, next to, on the far side, opposite, outside, to the east (south, and so on)
to qualify	perhaps, maybe
to give a reason or cause	as, because, for, since
to show a result or effect	and so, as a consequence, as a result, because of this, consequently, for this reason, hence, so, therefore, thus
to summarize	all in all, finally, in brief, in other words, lastly, on the whole, to conclude, to sum up
to place in time	after a while, afterward, at last, at present, briefly, currently, eventually, finally, first (second, and so on), gradually, immediately, in the future, later, meanwhile, next, now, recently, soon, suddenly, then

PRACTICE 8

Carefully determine the exact relationship between the sentences in each pair below. Then choose a transitional expression from the list that clearly expresses this relationship and write it in the blank. Pay attention to punctuation and capitalize the first word of every sentence.* Answers will vary.

1. No one inquired about the money found in the lobby. __Consequently__, it was given to charity.

*For practice using conjunctions to join ideas, see Chapter 27, "Coordination and Subordination."

TEACHING TIP

As a class or in small groups, have students compare their answers to Practice 8 so that they can see different possibilities.

2. First, cut off the outer, fibrous husk of the coconut. __Then__, poke a hole through one of the dark "eyes" and sip the milk through a straw.

3. The English Department office is on the fifth floor. __Next__ to it is a small reading room.

4. Some mountains under the sea soar almost as high as those on land. One underwater mountain in the Pacific, __for example__, is only 500 feet shorter than Mount Everest.

5. All citizens should vote. Many do not, __however__.

6. Mrs. Dalworth enjoys shopping in out-of-the-way thrift shops. __Furthermore__, she loves bargaining with the vendors at outdoor flea markets.

7. In 1887, Native Americans owned nearly 138 million acres of land. By 1932, __in contrast__, 90 million of those acres were owned by whites.

8. Kansas corn towered over the fence. __Beside__ the fence, a red tractor stood baking in the sun.

9. Most street crime occurs between 2 and 5 a.m. __For this reason__, do not go out alone during those hours.

10. Dr. Leff took great pride in his work at the clinic. __Nevertheless__, his long hours often left him exhausted.

11. George Washington Carver developed hundreds of uses for a single agricultural product, the peanut. __For example__, he created peanut butter, peanut cooking oil, and printing ink from this legume.

12. We waited in our seats for over an hour. __Finally__ the lights dimmed, and the Fabulous String Band bounded on stage.

PRACTICE 9

Add **transitional expressions** to this essay to guide the reader smoothly from sentence to sentence. To do so, consider the relationship between sentences (shown in parentheses). Then write the transitional word or phrase that best expresses this relationship. Answers will vary.

TEACHING TIP

Students nearly always love discussing the provocative topic of birth order, which also affords an opportunity for critical thinking and writing. See Practice 10.

Oldest Child, Youngest Child—Does It Matter?

A number of studies show that birth order—whether a person is the first-born, middle, or last-born child in the family—can affect both personality and career choice. For example (illustration), first-borns carry the weight of their parents' expectations and frequently (time) are urged to be responsible and set a good example for their younger siblings. Consequently (result), they may develop leadership skills and a strong motivation to achieve. Many eldest children later (time) become leaders. High percentages of U.S. presidents and CEOs, for instance (illustration), are first-borns.

Middle children, in contrast (contrast), get less attention and applause in childhood. As a result (result), they tend to become flexible and good at resolving conflicts. In addition (addition), some middle children become rebellious or creative as they make their place in the world. Eventually (time), many choose careers as entrepreneurs, negotiators, or businesspeople. Finally (addition), later-born or last-born children, in order to compete with their older siblings, may become rule-breakers or family clowns. Professionally, babies of the family tend to become musicians, adventurers, and comedians. Of course (conceding a point), there are countless exceptions to these general rules; however (contrast) it is interesting to ponder the evidence that our birth order indeed (emphasis) helps shape who we are.

PRACTICE 10 CRITICAL THINKING AND WRITING

Consider what you learned about birth order and personality in Practice 9. What is your place in the family? Do the typical traits apply to you? Take notes for later writing while you describe the classic first-born, middle-born, or youngest child; then apply these traits to yourself or someone you know well who fills that birth spot. Is the portrait accurate? To learn more, visit **www.parents.com/baby/development/social/birth-order-and-personality**.

TEACHING TIP

Practice 10 can easily be adapted as a collaborative activity.

PRACTICE 11 REVIEW

Most paragraphs achieve coherence through a variety of linking devices: repetition, pronouns, substitutions, and transitional expressions. Read the following paragraphs with care, noting the kinds of linking devices used by each writer. Answer the questions after each paragraph.

Paragraph 1

(1) The film *Super Size Me* explores the effects of America's fast food diet. (2) Director Morgan Spurlock stars in this hilarious but shocking documentary, eating nothing but fast food from McDonald's for thirty days. (3) Doctors assess his physical condition before, during, and after the diet, which has such negative effects on his health that they urge him to quit early. (4) Woven into this plot is crucial information about the fast food industry, school lunch programs, and obesity. (5) This brilliant work is one to see.

—Jun Harada, *crazy4film.com*

1. What important words are repeated in sentences 1, 2, and 4? fast food

2. In sentences 2 and 5, "the film *Super Size Me*" is referred to as this hilarious but shocking documentary and this brilliant work.

Paragraph 2

(1) The Syrian refugee crisis has devastated that nation, destabilized much of the Middle East, and challenged European governments. (2) During the Arab Spring of 2011, Syrians demonstrated against their leader President Assad, whose forces responded by arresting demonstrators and firing upon crowds. (3) In the months that followed, opponents to Assad armed themselves, and Syrian soldiers deserted the army to join the insurgents. (4) That summer the first refugees crossed into neighboring Turkey to escape the violence. (5) A year later, some 80,000 refugees fled to Jordan. (6) In 2013, the Syrian economy collapsed, leaving millions without jobs, electricity, food, or water. (7) By that December two million Syrians had escaped to Jordan, Iraq, and Turkey. (8) As the crisis in their country intensified in 2015, Syrians began seeking refuge in Europe and the United States, raising humanitarian and security concerns.

1. Underline the transitional expressions in this paragraph.

2. What *order* of ideas does the paragraph employ? time order

PRACTICE 12 CRITICAL VIEWING AND WRITING

Study the photograph of Syrian and Iraqi refugees arriving in Greece. What do you think would drive them to risk their lives on such a flimsy raft? Are they running from or to something? Would anything make you take such a risk? What? What or whom would you bring with you?

Spencer Platt/Getty Images

Syrian and Iraqi refugees arrive on the island of Lesbos in Greece on October 13, 2015. What would you risk to escape terror and violence?

Paragraph 3

(1) *Phishing* is the term for tricking computer users into revealing sensitive information such as credit card or social security numbers. (2) A person who goes phishing first sets up a seemingly official website and e-mail address to pose as a legitimate individual or business. (3) Next, the phisher casts the bait. (4) He or she e-mails unsuspecting individuals, either threatening account suspension if a request for information is ignored or perhaps promising a funny or racy video. (5) When an unfortunate recipient takes the bait and sends back the information, the phisher can reel it in and use it to commit fraud or identity theft. (6) In recent years, social networking sites have become targets for phishing scams. (7) For example, a con artist might create a site that looks exactly like Facebook. (8) When victims log onto the dummy site, they unwittingly give their usernames, passwords, personal information, and entire address books to the waiting thief.

1. What important words are repeated in this paragraph? phishing, e-mail, site
2. What synonyms and pronouns are used for "a person who goes phishing"?

   the phisher, he or she, the con artist, the waiting thief
3. What transitional expressions are used in sentences 3 and 7? Next, for example

EXPLORING ONLINE

powa.org/arrange/arranging-and-ordering

Advice on ordering your ideas in the most powerful way

powa.org/arrange/showing-the-links

More help with transitional expressions

UNIT 2

writers' WORKSHOP

Discuss the Pressures of Living in Two Worlds

In this unit, you learned that most good paragraphs have a clear topic sentence, convincing support, and an order that makes sense. In your group or class, read this student's paragraph, aloud if possible. Underline any parts you find especially well written. Put a check next to anything that could be improved.

Young Immigrant Translators

~~This paper will discuss children as translators.~~ When immigrant children become translators for their parents, this can change the normal relationship between parent and child. Many immigrant parents do not have the time or opportunity to develop their English skills, even though they know that speaking English is the most important part of surviving in the United States. When they need to understand or speak English, they often ask their school-age children for help. The children must act like little adults, helping their parents with all kinds of problems. They end up taking time away from school and their friends because they are responsible for everything related to English. For example, they might have to answer the phone, fill out forms, pay bills, or shop for groceries. Even in more serious situations, like medical or financial problems, the children might have to translate for the doctor or accountant. Eventually, some children can start to resent their parents for relying on them so much. Instead of turning to their parents for help with homework or personal worries, they might turn instead to friends or teachers who understand the culture better. Although most immigrant children know their parents love them and want a better life for them, the role reversal of being child translators can make them become adults too soon.

—Mandy Li, Student

1. How effective is this paragraph?

   Y/N Clear topic sentence? Y Logical organization?

   Y Good supporting details? Y Effective conclusion?

2. Which sentence, if any, is the topic sentence? Is sentence 1 as good as the rest of the paragraph? If not, what revision advice would you give the writer? No. 2 is topic sentence. Drop No. 1.
3. Does this student provide adequate support for her main idea? Why or why not? Yes. She gives convincing examples.
4. Discuss your underlinings with the group or class. Which parts or ideas in this essay did you find most powerful? As specifically as you can, explain why. For example, the list of possible tasks a child translator must handle vividly supports the main idea of the paragraph.
5. Do you agree with Ms. Li that children being asked to translate for their parents makes children grow up too soon? Have you experienced or witnessed other situations in which children must become adults too soon? What are those situations?
6. Do you see any error patterns (one error made two or more times) that this student needs to watch out for? No.

GROUP WORK

In your group or class, make a plan or outline of Ms. Li's paragraph. How many points does she use to support her topic sentence? How can a writer know whether a paragraph has good support or needs better support? List three ways. Did this paragraph make you think? How would you rate the ideas in this paragraph? Extremely interesting? Interesting? Not very interesting? Be prepared to explain your rating to the full class.

WRITING AND REVISING IDEAS

1. Discuss the ways in which you or someone you know has had to live in two different cultures or "worlds."
2. What is the most important tool for surviving in the United States, in your view?

UNIT 3

Developing the Paragraph

CHAPTER 5

Illustration

TEACHING TIP
Point out that knowing how to choose excellent examples to develop a point will serve students well in college and on the job.

To **illustrate** is to explain a general statement by means of one or more specific examples.

Illustration makes what we say more vivid and more exact. Someone might say, "My math professor is always finding crazy ways to get our attention. Just yesterday, for example, he wore a high silk hat to class." The first sentence is a general statement about this professor's unusual ways of getting attention. The second sentence, however, gives a specific example of something he did that *clearly shows* what the writer means.

Writers often use illustration to develop a paragraph. They explain a general topic sentence with one, two, three, or more specific examples. Detailed and well-chosen examples add interest, liveliness, and power to your writing.

Topic Sentence

Here is the topic sentence of a paragraph that is later developed by examples:

> Great athletes do not reach the top by talent alone but by pushing themselves to the limit and beyond.

- The writer begins an illustration paragraph with a topic sentence that makes a general statement.
- This generalization may be obvious to the writer, but if he or she wishes to convince the reader, some specific examples would be helpful.

Paragraph and Plan

Here is the entire paragraph:

Great athletes do not reach the top by talent alone but by pushing themselves to the limit and beyond. For instance, basketball superstar LeBron James keeps striving to improve. Branded the next Michael Jordan in high school and drafted by the Cleveland Cavaliers, he propelled the Cavaliers to three NBA playoffs, led the Miami Heat to the NBA Championship in 2012, and later that year, won his second gold medal on a U.S. Olympic team. Even off-season, James perfects his agility, strength, and health routines, including adding squats on a vibrating platform to activate more muscles. In 2015, he was sidelined for two weeks with knee and back injuries but returned to become his team's all-time assists leader. Another example is record-breaking tennis player Serena Williams, who has been ranked number one in women's tennis six times. She has won 36 major titles and four Olympic gold medals. Williams overcame repeated knee and ankle injuries through hard work. She suffered a pulmonary embolism in 2011 but recovered and went on to win eight more titles. Few players in any sport, however, can match the work ethic of NFL quarterback Drew Brees, who suffered a nearly career-ending shoulder injury. During months of grueling rehabilitation, "Cool Brees" had to relearn how to throw a football. When the New Orleans Saints took a chance by signing him, Brees trained harder. Between seasons, he built strength, flexibility, and focus with three-hour workouts that ended when the coach threw playing cards in the air one at a time as Brees caught them one-handed. Four years after surgery, Brees led the Saints to a Super Bowl victory. Like many top athletes, he turned talent into greatness through sheer hard work.

- How many examples does the writer use to develop the topic sentence?

  three

- Who are they?

  LeBron James, Serena Williams, Drew Brees

AP Images/Kyodo

Serena Williams after her victory at the 2015 Wimbledon Championships in London

Before completing this illustration paragraph, the writer probably made an **outline** like this:

TOPIC SENTENCE: Great athletes do not reach the top by talent alone but by pushing themselves to the limit and beyond.

Example 1: LeBron James
—branded next Michael Jordan, drafted by Cavaliers
—brought Cavaliers to three NBA playoffs and Miami Heat to 2012 Championship
—won gold medals on two U.S. Olympic teams
—off-season, perfects agility, strength, and health routines
—does squats on a vibrating platform
—overcame injuries in 2015 to become his team's all-time assists leader

Example 2: Serena Williams
—ranked number one in women's tennis six times
—won 36 major titles
—won four Olympic gold medals
—overcame repeated knee and ankle injuries through hard work
—recovered from a pulmonary embolism to win eight more titles

Example 3: Drew Brees
—gifted NFL quarterback with severe shoulder injury
—months of rehab, relearned throwing a football
—between-season: strength, flexibility, focus, playing cards
—led Saints to Super Bowl win

CONCLUSION: Like many top athletes, he turned talent into greatness through sheer hard work.

- Note that each example clearly relates to and supports the topic sentence.

Instead of using three or four examples to support the topic sentence, the writer may prefer instead to discuss one single example:

ESL TIP
ESL students often fail to include specifics in their writing. Ask students to point out the details and facts that enhance the examples in this paragraph.

Dreams alone are not enough when it comes to creating the future. As professional life coach Diana Robinson says, "A dream is a goal without legs." And without legs, that goal is going nowhere. Making dreams come true requires planning and hard work. Gloria Gonzalez is an example. She chose the fashion design curriculum because she liked clothes, and people always admired her style. As she continues through college, however, she will need to master the nuts and bolts of the fashion business. Her abilities will be tested. Can she create under pressure, spot trends, meet tight deadlines, and work her way up? Perhaps she will learn that even brilliant fashion designer Yves Saint Laurent got his first big break, designing for Christian Dior, only after winning a major international design competition. Breaking into the fashion industry is challenging, but that doesn't mean Gloria should abandon her dream. Instead, she must find a reality-based path to help her turn that dream into goals.

—Adapted from Constance Staley, *Focus on College Success*

- What is the general statement?

  Dreams alone are not enough when it comes to creating the future.

- What specific example does the writer give to support the general statement?

  Gloria Gonzalez's dream of becoming a fashion designer

The single example may also be a **narrative,*** a *story* that illustrates the topic sentence:

> Aggressive drivers not only are stressed out and dangerous, but often they save no time getting where they want to go. Recently I was driving south from Oakland to San Jose. Traffic was heavy but moving. I noticed an extremely aggressive driver jumping lanes, speeding up, and slowing down. Clearly, he was in a hurry. For the most part, I remained in one lane for the entire 40-mile journey. I was listening to a new audiotape and daydreaming. I enjoyed the trip because driving gives me a chance to be alone. As I was exiting off the freeway, the aggressive driver crowded up behind me and raced on by. Without realizing it, I had arrived in San Jose ahead of him. All his weaving, rapid acceleration, and putting families at risk had earned him nothing except perhaps some high blood pressure and a great deal of wear and tear on his vehicle.
>
> —Adapted from Richard Carlson, *Don't Sweat the Small Stuff*

- What general statement does the aggressive driver story illustrate?

  Aggressive drivers not only are stressed out and dangerous, but often they save no time getting where they want to go.

- Note that this narrative follows time order.†

Transitional Expressions

The simplest way to tell your reader that an example is going to follow is to say so: "*For instance,* LeBron James . . ." or "Gloria Gonzalez *is an example*." This partial list should help you vary your use of **transitional expressions** that introduce an illustration:

Transitional Expressions for Illustration	
for instance	another instance of
for example	another example of
an illustration of this	another illustration of
a case in point is	here are a few examples (illustrations, instances)
to illustrate	

*For more on narrative, see Chapter 6, "Narration," and Chapter 16, "Types of Essays," Part B.

†For more work on time order, see Chapter 4, "Achieving Coherence," Part A.

- Be careful not to use more than two or three of these transitional expressions in a single paragraph.*

PRACTICE 1

Read each of the following paragraphs of illustration. Underline each topic sentence. Note in the margin how many examples are provided to illustrate each general statement.

TEACHING TIP
Students enjoy discussing the random kindness concept. Note the Critical Thinking and Writing activity later in this section.

ESL TIP
The word *random* may be unfamiliar to your ESL students. Have them work with a partner to discuss new words or retell a difficult text, which will deepen their comprehension.

Paragraph 1 (3 examples)

Random acts of kindness are those little sweet or grand lovely things we do for no reason except that, momentarily, the best of our humanity has sprung . . . into full bloom. When you spontaneously give an old woman the bouquet of red carnations you had meant to take home to your own dinner table, when you give your lunch to the guitar-playing beggar who makes music at the corner between your two subway stops, when you anonymously put coins in someone else's parking meter because you see the red "Expired" medallion signaling to a meter maid—you are doing not what life requires of you, but what the best of your human soul invites you to do.

—Daphne Rose Kingma, *Random Acts of Kindness*

Paragraph 2 (4 examples)

There are many quirky variations to lightning. A "bolt from the blue" occurs when a long horizontal flash suddenly turns toward the earth, many miles from the storm. "St. Elmo's Fire," often seen by sailors and mountain climbers, is a pale blue or green light caused by weak electrical discharges that cling to trees, airplanes, and ships' masts. "Pearl lightning" occurs when flashes are broken into segments. "Ball lightning" can be from an inch to several feet in diameter. Pearls and balls are often mistaken for flying saucers or UFOs, and many scientists believe they are only optical illusions.

—Reed McManus, *Sierra* magazine

PRACTICE 2

TEACHING TIP
Practice 2 makes a fine in-class activity. You might use it to review unity as well.

Each example in a paragraph of illustration must clearly relate to and support the general statement. Each general statement in this practice is followed by several examples. Circle the letter of any example that does *not* clearly illustrate the generalization. Be prepared to explain your choices.

EXAMPLE The museum contains many fascinating examples of African art.

a. It houses a fine collection of Ashanti fertility dolls.

b. Drums and shamans' costumes are displayed on the second floor.

(c.) The museum building was once the home of Frederick Douglass. (The fact that the building was once the home of Frederick Douglass is *not an example* of African art.)

---

*For complete essays developed by illustration, see Chapter 16, "Types of Essays, Part 1," Part A.

1. Antibiotic-resistant bacteria pose a threat to patients.
   a. Doctors are forced to prescribe larger doses of antibiotics to treat infections, subjecting patients to more serious side effects.
   b. According to a 2013 report by the CDC, at least 23,000 patients die every year from antibiotic-resistant infections.
   (c.) Simple hand-washing can reduce the transmission of germs.
   d. Patients with infections now require longer hospital stays, thereby exposing them to further risk of infection.
2. Today's global companies sometimes find that their product names and slogans can translate into embarrassing bloopers.
   a. Pepsi's slogan "Come alive with the Pepsi Generation" didn't work in Taiwan, where it meant "Pepsi will bring your ancestors back from the dead."
   b. When General Motors introduced its Chevy Nova in South America, company officials didn't realize that *no va* in Spanish means "it won't go."
   c. In Chinese, the Kentucky Fried Chicken slogan "finger-lickin' good" means "eat your fingers off."
   (d.) Nike runs the same ad campaign in several countries, changing the ad slightly to fit each culture.
3. Many life-enhancing products that we take for granted were invented by women.
   a. Josephine Cochran invented the dishwasher in 1893, declaring that if no one else would build a machine to perform this boring task, she would do it herself.
   b. In 1966, chemist Stephanie Louise Kwoleck patented Kevlar, a fabric five times stronger than steel, now used in bulletproof vests and other important products.
   (c.) Lonnie Johnson got the idea for the famous Super Soaker squirt gun after the homemade nozzle on his sink sprayed water across the room.
4. Reality television shows are becoming more numerous.
   (a.) Competition from cable and social media has led to a decline in viewership of network programming.
   b. Networks promote reality shows because they are cheap to produce.
   c. Reality shows often have unexpected events that build suspense and attract viewers.
   d. The public has an appetite for following the lives of "real people."
5. Single parents cope with a variety of stresses that couples do not.
   a. With just one paycheck instead of two, even single parents who receive child support can find themselves struggling to pay the monthly bills.
   b. Because single parents have no partner to share errands and household chores, they may have little time for stress-relieving recreation.
   (c.) Assigning household chores is a way to help children learn good habits.
   d. Stressful emotions like guilt can plague single parents, who wonder how their children will be affected by growing up without a full-time mom or dad.

Corbis RF/AGE Fotostock

The Great Sphinx of Giza

6. Historians have different ideas about the age of the Great Sphinx.
   a. Many believe that the Great Sphinx was built by the Pharaoh Khafre around 2500 BCE.
   b. Some scholars think that the Great Sphinx was constructed before Khafre's reign.
   c. The Great Sphinx has the head of a human and the body of a lion.
   d. Others argue that the Great Sphinx dates back as far as 7000 BCE.
7. A number of Native American musicians influenced popular music, although most are not well known.
   a. Shawnee guitarist Link Wray invented the reverberating power chord, the signature sound of Led Zeppelin and the Who.
   b. Buffy Sainte-Marie, a Cree Indian, wrote and introduced a new genre of songs protesting the plight of modern Native Americans.
   c. George Harrison, the famous Beatles guitarist, introduced the sitar, a stringed instrument from India, into pop music.
   d. Jesse Ed Davis, of Kiowa, Creek, and Seminole ancestry, was a fretboard innovator and guitarist for Jackson Browne, Willie Nelson, and Eric Clapton.
8. Colleges offer instruction in different formats to meet the needs of students.
   a. Courses are offered on weekends or in compressed three-week sessions to suit students' work schedules.
   b. Online courses allow students to earn credits without having to travel on campus.
   c. Independent study courses allow students to enroll year round and work at their own pace.
   d. Parking lots have been expanded to assist commuting students.

PRACTICE 3

TEACHING TIP
Practice 3 works well as a group exercise. Have each group develop its own example to support the same statement. Then share the examples and let the full class choose the most effective ones.

The secret of good illustration lies in well-chosen, well-written examples. Think of one example that illustrates each of the following general statements. Write out the example in sentence form (one to three sentences) as clearly and exactly as possible. Answers will vary.

1. A few contemporary singers work hard to send a positive message.

   Example Bono has made social values the center of his music and humanitarian work.

2. In a number of ways, this college helps students maintain a healthy lifestyle.

   Example Full-time students can use the student union's health club at no charge.

3. Believing in yourself is 90 percent of success.

   Example My friend Paco owns a successful restaurant because his enthusiasm and confidence attracted investors.

4. Many teenagers believe they must have expensive designer clothing.

   Example My nephew has a closet full of Ralph Lauren clothes that his mother cannot really afford.

5. Cell phones are a growing distraction in many families.

   Example Last night at dinner both my sisters texted friends and ignored my parents' attempts to talk about their schoolwork.

6. A number of my relatives have lived overseas.

   Example My aunt and uncle lived in France for six years.

7. Pets can teach children responsibility.

   Example My daughter walks her dog every day and saves her allowance to pay for his grooming.

8. Sadly, rudeness seems more and more common in America.

   Example My mother recently called to her neighbor to hold the elevator for her, and he shut the door in her face.

PRACTICE 4 CRITICAL THINKING AND WRITING

Illustrate Random Acts of Kindness

The phrase "random acts of kindness" refers to kind acts whose recipients are often perfect strangers. Read about random acts of kindness (Practice 1, paragraph 1). Now think of one good example of a real-life random act of kindness, performed by you or someone else—either at college or work, or in everyday life. Write up your example in one paragraph. Begin with a clear topic sentence and present the act of kindness as movingly as you can. Refer to the checklist, and ask yourself if you have included the most important details.

EXPLORING ONLINE

www.randomactsofkindness.org

On this site, you can find "kindness ideas" and look for writing topics in the "Inspiring Resources" section. Under "Kindness Stories," click "Write a Story" to submit your best writing for online publication.

TEACHING TIP

For downloadable rubrics corresponding to each rhetorical mode, go to the *Instructor Companion Site.*

Checklist

The Process of Writing an Illustration Paragraph

Refer to this checklist of steps as you write an illustration paragraph of your own.

☐ 1. Narrow the topic to fit your audience and purpose.

☐ 2. Compose a topic sentence that can honestly and easily be supported by examples.

☐ 3. Freewrite or brainstorm to find six to eight examples that support the topic sentence. If you wish to use only one example or a narrative, sketch out your idea. (You may want to freewrite or brainstorm before you narrow the topic.)

- ☐ 4. Select only the best two to four examples and drop any examples that do not relate to or support the topic sentence.
- ☐ 5. Make a plan or an outline for your paragraph, numbering the examples in the order in which you will present them.
- ☐ 6. Write a draft of your illustration paragraph, using transitional expressions to show that an example or examples will follow.
- ☐ 7. Revise as necessary, checking for support, unity, logic, and coherence.
- ☐ 8. Proofread for errors in grammar, punctuation, sentence structure, spelling, and mechanics.

Suggested Topic Sentences for Illustration Paragraphs

1. Even the busiest people can incorporate more exercise into their daily routines.
2. Most people have special places where they go to relax or find inspiration.
3. In my family, certain traditions (beliefs or activities) are very important.
4. In my chosen profession, I will have to write several kinds of documents.
5. Television shows and movies glamorize violence.
6. College students face a number of pressures.
7. Unfortunately, cheating at college (or stealing at work) is more common than most people realize.
8. The Internet makes it easy to spread gossip and conspiracy theories.
9. Sexual harassment is a fact of life for some employees.
10. Many popular fast food meals are high in calories.
11. Certain fellow students (or co-workers) inspire me to do my best.
12. Owning a home entails more work than people think.
13. Credit cards lead people to spend more than they should.
14. Part-time jobs teach students valuable lessons.
15. Writer's choice: ____

EXPLORING ONLINE

www.google.com

Search the words "une.edu, paragraph types illustration" for a visual review of illustration writing and sample illustration paragraphs from the University of New England.

writesite.cuny.edu/projects/keywords/example/hand2.html

Online practice: brainstorming examples for your paragraph

CHAPTER 6

Narration

TEACHING TIP
Ask students to brainstorm examples of narratives they might have to write on the job.

To **narrate** is to tell a story that explains what happened, when it happened, and who was involved.

A news report may be a narrative telling how a man was rescued from icy floodwaters or how a brave whistleblower risked her career and perhaps her life to expose an employer's harmful practices. When you read a bedtime story to a child, you are reading a narrative. In a college paper on campus drug use, telling the story of a friend who takes ecstasy would help bring that subject to life. In an e-mail to a friend, you might share an amusing story, narrating how you thought you locked yourself out of your car only to discover the keys in your bag.

We tell stories to teach a lesson, illustrate an idea, or make someone laugh, cry, or get involved. No matter what your narrative is about, every narrative should have a clear **point**: it should reveal what you want your reader to learn or take away from the story.

Topic Sentence

Here is the topic sentence of a **narrative** paragraph:

> The crash of a Brinks truck on a Miami overpass still raises disturbing questions.

- The writer begins a narrative paragraph with a topic sentence that tells or sets up the point of the narrative.
- What is the point of this narrative? to tell the story of a Brinks truck crash that raises disturbing questions

Paragraph and Plan

Here is the entire paragraph:

TEACHING TIP

Ethical issues and choices, like the subject of this paragraph, usually stimulate thinking and debate. Ask students to discuss the open-ended questions that conclude the paragraph.

The crash of a Brinks truck on a Miami overpass still raises disturbing questions. January 8, 1997, was just another crowded, rude, and crazy day in Miami traffic until an armored Brinks truck flipped and broke open, sending nearly a million dollars in cash swirling over the highway. Hundreds of motorists screeched to a stop, grabbing whatever money they could. People in nearby houses raced outside, shouting and scooping up bills. When it was over, a tiny handful of people returned some money. Firefighter Manny Rodriguez turned in a huge bale of bills worth $330,000, and one teenager returned some quarters. However, nearly half a million dollars was missing—stolen by everyday people like you and me. In the following days, some rationalized the mass theft as a kind of Robin Hood action because the truck had crashed in a poor area of town. Most people claimed to be shocked. Now we are all left with hard questions: *Why did a few people "do the right thing"? Why did the majority do the "wrong thing"? What causes people to act virtuously, even if no one is watching? What would you or I have done?*

- A narrative paragraph is developed according to time, or chronological, order.* That is, the writer explains the narrative—the entire incident—as a series of small events or actions in the order in which they occurred. By keeping to strict chronological order, the writer helps the reader follow the story more easily and avoids interrupting the narrative with, *But I forgot to mention that before this happened . . . .*

- What smaller events make up this paragraph? Brinks truck crashes; cash spills on highway; motorists and people in houses grab money; only a few return money, like Manny Rodriguez; half a million dollars gone; people react with excuses or shock

- What strong verbs or details help the writing come alive? crowded, rude, and crazy . . . flipped and broke open . . . cash swirling over the highway . . . motorists screeched . . . grabbing . . . shouting and scooping up bills . . . stolen by everyday people like you and me

TEACHING TIP

Narratives are enriched by lively verbs. Glean from your students' writing ten to twenty examples of sentences with weak verbs. As a class, revise the sentences so that their verbs sparkle.

- The writer ends the paragraph with some "hard questions." Do these questions express the point of the story? Yes, the topic sentence says this incident still raises disturbing questions, and the conclusion lists four of them.

*For more work on time, see Chapter 4, "Achieving Coherence," Part A.

Before writing this narrative paragraph, the writer may have brainstormed or freewritten to gather ideas, and then the writer may have made an **outline** like this:

TOPIC SENTENCE: The crash of a Brinks truck on a Miami overpass still raises disturbing questions.

Event 1: Brinks truck flips, spilling cash on the highway.
Event 2: Hundreds of motorists stop, grab money.
Event 3: People race out of houses, grabbing money.
Event 4: Later, firefighter Rodriguez returns $330,000.
Event 5: Just a few others give anything back; half million is gone.
Event 6: Days after, some call it "Robin Hood" action.
Event 7: Some say they are shocked.

CONCLUSION: Now we are all left with hard questions. (Some questions are listed.)

- Note that all of the events occur in chronological order.
- The conclusion provides a strong and thought-provoking ending.
- Finally, the specific details of certain events (like events 2 and 4) make the narrative more vivid.

Transitional Expressions

Because narrative paragraphs tell a story in **chronological** or **time order**, transitional expressions that indicate time can be useful.*

Transitional Expressions for Narratives		
afterward	finally	next
after that	first	now
currently	later	soon
eventually	meanwhile	then

PRACTICE 1

TEACHING TIP
After making sure students understand this tale, you might ask volunteers to share ways in which they feed the good wolf.

Read the following narrative paragraph carefully and answer the questions:

The Cherokee people tell the story of a young boy who has been badly wronged by someone he considered a friend. The boy, hurt and furious, tells his grandfather about the incident. His grandfather nods and replies, "At times, I too have felt hatred for those who do great harm and seem to feel no sorrow about it. But hate wears a person down and does not hurt the enemy. It is like taking poison and wishing the enemy would die. I have struggled with these feelings many times. It is as if two wolves live inside me; they live inside you, too. One wolf is good. He is peaceful, generous, compassionate, and wise. He lives in

*For complete essays developed by narration, see Chapter 16, "Types of Essays," Part B.

TEACHING TIP

Do any students come from a storytelling tradition? For a rich source of diverse stories, see **www.story-lovers.com/listsofstories.html**.

harmony with all those around him and does not easily take offense. He fights only when it is right to do so. But the other wolf lives in me as well—and in you. He is full of anger, envy, self-pity, and pain. The smallest thing infuriates him. He cannot think clearly because his anger is so great, yet that anger changes nothing. Sometimes, it is hard to live with two wolves inside me, for both of them struggle to dominate my spirit."

The boy looks intently into his grandfather's eyes and asks, "Which wolf wins, Grandfather?" The grandfather smiles and says quietly, "The one I feed."

1. What is the point of the narrative? This narrative warns that two wolves or selves exist in each person, and the one we "feed" is who we become.

2. What events make up this narrative? A boy has been hurt and speaks of it to his grandfather. The grandfather replies with a story about the two wolves inside him, one peaceful and wise, the other angry and self-centered. He explains that these wolves struggle to rule his soul as they do in everyone. The wolf who "wins" is the one we feed.

3. Do you relate to this story? In what way? Answers will vary.

PRACTICE 2

Here are three plans for narrative paragraphs. The events in the plans are not in correct chronological order. The plans also contain events that do not belong in each story. Number the events in the proper time sequence and cross out any irrelevant ones.

1. A combination of talent and hard work has propelled Jennifer Lopez to stardom.

   __1__ In 1991, Lopez first gained attention as a dancer on the television show *In Living Color*.

   __4__ In 2016, Lopez starred with Ray Liotta in the police drama *Shades of Blue*.

   __2__ Lopez had her first leading film role in *Selena* in 1997, and a year later she appeared in *Out of Sight*, becoming the first Latina actress to earn $1 million for a role.

Featureflash/Shutterstock.com

Jennifer Lopez receives a star on the Hollywood Walk of Fame in June 2013.

____ ~~More Hispanics are appearing in American films and television shows.~~

_3_ In 2001, she became the first entertainer to simultaneously have a number one film and record album.

2. After 80 years, Monopoly remains one of the most popular board games in the world.

   _2_ During World War II, the Allies hid real money and maps in Monopoly sets given to POWs to help them escape from German prison camps.

   _4_ Today Monopoly is produced in 26 languages.

   _1_ In 1935, Parker Brothers released Monopoly, a board game based on streets in Atlantic City.

   _3_ In 1997, computer game versions of Monopoly were released.

   ____ ~~Playing games gives friends and family a chance to interact and bond.~~

TEACHING TIP

You might teach students the uncommon but excellent adjective *Sisyphean* (Sis • y • phe • an). Have some fun using it in sentences. *Getting my degree (Housework, Improving my grammar, Parenting a teenager) feels like a Sisyphean task.* Can they think of synonyms? Futile, pointless, meaningless?

Artepics/Alamy Stock Photo

Sisyphus rolls a massive boulder up a hill

3. The ancient Greek story of Sisyphus depicts the terrible frustration of work that is never done.

 __4__ Every time Sisyphus neared the top of the hill, the massive boulder rolled back down, forcing him to start all over again.

 __1__ Sisyphus was a brutal king who murdered, stole, and fooled the gods by cheating death for years.

 __2__ When Sisyphus finally did die, the Greek god Zeus sought the worst possible punishment.

 __3__ Zeus condemned Sisyphus to roll a huge stone up a steep hill—forever.

 __5__ Thus, the story goes, for all eternity, Sisyphus has pointlessly pushed, sweated, and worked, forever deprived of the satisfaction of completing his task.

 ____ ~~According to Greek mythology, Zeus once turned himself into a swan.~~

PRACTICE 3 CRITICAL THINKING AND WRITING

Read the story of Sisyphus in Practice 2, item 3. Did you ever have a job, relationship, or situation that made *you* feel like Sisyphus? What was it about the experience that made you feel you kept doing the same thing without getting anywhere? Write a paragraph explaining what happened and how you felt.

PRACTICE 4

Here are topic sentences for three narrative paragraphs. Make a plan for each paragraph, placing the events of the narrative in the proper time sequence.

1. When I had trouble with ______________________, help came from an unexpected source.

   ____

   ____

   ____

   ____

   ____

2. Buying my first ______________________ took careful planning.

   ____

   ____

   ____

3. ______________________ was one of the memorable events that happened to me in high school.

   ____

   ____

   ____

   ____

   ____

PRACTICE 5 CRITICAL THINKING AND WRITING

Narrate an Experience of Stereotyping

TEACHING TIP
Dialogue or quotations can enliven narratives. If students want to include quotations, refer them to Chapter 38, "Mechanics," Part C, to review the rules.

Good narratives have a *point*; they bring to life a moral, lesson, or idea. Read this narrative passage about "The Latina Stereotype" by Judith Ortiz Cofer:

> My first public poetry reading took place at a restaurant where a luncheon was being held before the event. I was nervous and excited as I walked in with a notebook in hand. An older woman motioned me to her table, and thinking (foolish me) that she wanted me to autograph a copy of my newly published slender volume of verse, I went over. She ordered a cup of coffee from me, assuming that I was the waitress. (Easy enough to mistake my poems for menus, I suppose.) I know it wasn't an intentional act of cruelty. Yet of all the good things that happened later, I remember that scene most clearly, because it reminded me of what I had to overcome before anyone would take me seriously.

What is the point of this story? Exactly what *stereotype* did the writer encounter? What did the woman assume about her and why?

Have you ever been stereotyped? That is, has anyone ever treated you a certain way based only on your age, clothing, race, religion, gender, sexual orientation, major, accent, piercings or other decoration, or even things you are carrying, like books or a cell phone? What stereotype was imposed on you, and how did you react? Now narrate vividly in writing your experience of stereotyping. You might wish to place your topic sentence, stating the meaning or point, last. Refer to the checklist as you write, and determine if you selected the right details and organized them in a logical order.

EXPLORING ONLINE

www.tolerance.org

Explore this site about increasing tolerance. Take notes on any ideas for further writing.

Checklist

TEACHING TIP
For downloadable rubrics corresponding to each rhetorical mode, go to the *Instructor Companion Site.*

The Process of Writing a Narrative Paragraph

Refer to this checklist of steps as you write a narrative paragraph of your own.

- [ ] 1. Narrow the topic to fit your audience and purpose.
- [ ] 2. Compose a topic sentence that tells the point of the story.
- [ ] 3. Freewrite or brainstorm for all of the events and details that might be part of the story. (You may want to freewrite or brainstorm before you narrow the topic.)

- [ ] 4. Select the important events and details; drop any that do not clearly relate to the point in your topic sentence.
- [ ] 5. Make a plan or an outline for the paragraph, numbering the events in the correct time (chronological) sequence.
- [ ] 6. Write a draft of your narrative paragraph, using transitional expressions to indicate time sequence.
- [ ] 7. Revise as necessary, checking for support, unity, logic, and coherence.
- [ ] 8. Proofread for errors in grammar, punctuation, sentence structure, spelling, and mechanics.

Suggested Topics for Narrative Paragraphs

1. Your best (or worst) job interview
2. A telephone call that changed your life
3. An important family story or a story someone told you
4. Your first day on a job
5. An experience in a new town, city, or country
6. How you developed a career skill (in customer service, computers, attitude, and so on)
7. A breakthrough (emotional, physical, or spiritual)
8. A difficult decision
9. An incident that provoked an intense emotion (such as rage, grief, pride, or joy)
10. A triumphant (or embarrassing) moment
11. The first time you encountered a role model or important friend
12. A news story that affected you personally
13. An encounter with prejudice
14. A person you admire (interview the person and tell, in short form, his or her story)
15. Writer's choice: ______________________________

EXPLORING ONLINE

grammar.ccc.commnet.edu/grammar/composition/narrative.htm

Review the elements of a good narrative, and read some fine examples.

www.healingstory.org

Do you think that stories can heal? Explore this website and decide for yourself.

CHAPTER 7

Description

TEACHING TIP
Ask students to brainstorm examples of descriptions they might have to write on the job.

To **describe** something—a person, a place, or an object—is to capture it in words so others can imagine it or see it in their mind's eye.

The best way for a writer to help the reader get a clear impression is to use language that appeals to the senses: sight, sound, smell, taste, and touch. For it is through the senses that human beings experience the physical world around them, and it is through the senses that the world is most vividly described.

Imagine, for example, that you have just arrived home after being stuck in a traffic jam for an hour. You may not have taken a photograph, but your friends and family can receive an accurate picture of what you experienced if you *describe* the cars and trucks stuck bumper to bumper, the honking horns, the exasperated faces of drivers, the shouts of traffic cops, and the way you banged the steering wheel in frustration. Writing down what your senses experience will teach you to see, hear, smell, taste, and touch more accurately than ever before.

Description is useful in English class, the sciences, psychology—anywhere that keen observation is important.

Topic Sentence

Here is the topic sentence of a descriptive paragraph:

> On November 27, 1922, when archaeologist Howard Carter unsealed the door to the ancient Egyptian tomb of King Tut, he stared in amazement at the fantastic objects heaped all around him.

- The writer begins a descriptive paragraph by pointing out what will be described. What will be described in this paragraph?

  the fantastic objects in King Tut's tomb

- The writer can also give a general impression of this scene, object, or person. What overall impression of the tomb does the writer provide?

The writer gives the impression that the heaps of fantastic objects in King Tut's tomb were an amazing sight.

Paragraph and Plan

Here is the entire paragraph:

TEACHING TIP
Point out to students that this paragraph about King Tut's tomb is a good example of how exact, concise, fresh, and figurative language (all discussed in Chapter 23 "Revising for Language Awareness") work together to create vivid mental images in readers' minds.

On November 27, 1922, when archaeologist Howard Carter unsealed the door to the ancient Egyptian tomb of King Tut, he stared in amazement at the fantastic objects heaped all around him. On his left lay the wrecks of at least four golden chariots. Against the wall on his right sat a gorgeous chest brightly painted with hunting and battle scenes. Across from him was a gilded throne with cat-shaped legs, arms like winged serpents, and a back showing King Tut and his queen. Behind the throne rose a tall couch decorated with animal faces that were half hippopotamus and half crocodile. The couch was loaded with more treasures. To the right of the couch, two life-sized statues faced each other like guards. They were black, wore gold skirts and sandals, and had cobras carved on their foreheads. Between them was a second sealed doorway. Carter's heart beat loudly. Would the mummy of King Tut lie beyond it?

- The overall impression given by the topic sentence is that the tomb's many objects were amazing. List three specific details that support this impression.

Answers will vary.

wrecks of four golden chariots

chest painted with hunting and battle scenes

gilded throne with cat-shaped legs

ESL TIP
Encourage ESL students to broaden their vocabulary. Ask them to study any unfamiliar words from the sample paragraph with a partner.

- Note the importance of words that indicate richness and unusual decoration in helping the reader visualize the scene.* List as many of these words as you can:

fantastic, golden, gorgeous, brightly painted, gilded, cat-shaped legs, winged serpents, animal faces that were half hippopotamus and half crocodile, treasures, life-sized statues, gold skirts and sandals, cobras carved on their foreheads

- This paragraph, like many descriptive paragraphs, is organized according to space order.† The author uses transitional expressions that show where things are. Underline the transitional expressions that indicate place or position.

*For more work on vivid language, see Chapter 23, "Revising for Language Awareness."

†For more work on space order and other kinds of order, see Chapter 4, "Achieving Coherence," Part A.

Before composing this descriptive paragraph, the writer probably brainstormed and freewrote to gather ideas and then made an **outline** like this:

TOPIC SENTENCE: On November 27, 1922, when archaeologist Howard Carter unsealed the door to the ancient Egyptian tomb of King Tut, he stared in amazement at the fantastic objects heaped all around him.

1. **To the left**:	chariots —wrecked —golden
2. **To the right**:	a gorgeous chest —brightly painted with hunting and battle scenes
3. **Across the room**:	a throne —gilded —cat-shaped legs —arms like winged serpents
4. **Behind the throne**:	a couch —decorated with faces that were half hippopotamus and half crocodile
5. **To the right of the couch**:	two life-sized statues —black —gold skirts and sandals —cobras carved on foreheads
6. **Between the two statues**:	a second sealed doorway

CONCLUSION: King Tut's mummy was probably beyond the second door.

- Note how each detail supports the topic sentence.

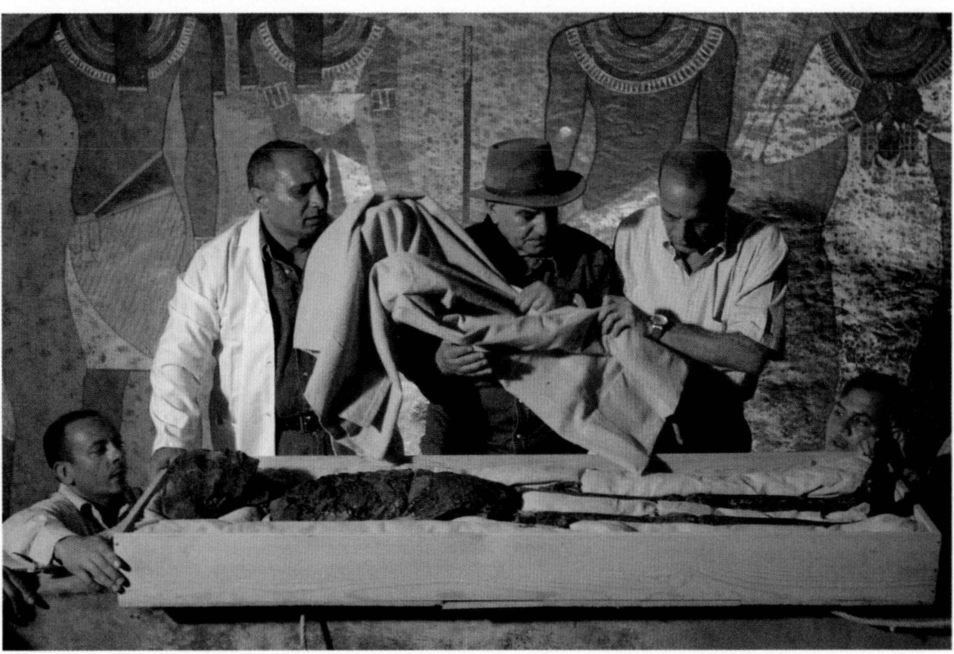

Corbis Wire/Corbis

Egyptian officials in King Tut's tomb prepare the boy king's mummy for placement in a climate-controlled glass box.

Transitional Expressions

Since space order is often used in description, **transitional expressions** indicating place or position can be useful:

Transitional Expressions Indicating Place	
next to, near	on top, beneath
close, far	toward, away
up, down, between	left, right, center
above, below	front, back, middle

Of course, other kinds of order are possible. For example, a description of a person might have two parts: details of physical appearance and details of behavior.*

PRACTICE 1

Read the following paragraph carefully and answer the questions.

> The woman who met us had an imposing beauty. She was tall and large-boned. Her face was strongly molded, with high cheekbones and skin the color of mahogany. She greeted us politely but did not smile and seemed to hold her head very high, an effect exaggerated by the abundant black hair slicked up and rolled on the top of her head. Her clothing was simple, a black sweater and skirt, and I remember thinking that dressed in showier garments, this woman would have seemed overwhelming.

1. What overall impression does the writer give of the woman?

   The impression is that the woman had a regal and imposing beauty.

2. What specific details support this general impression?

   tall; high cheekbones; mahogany skin; head held high; hair piled high on head; unsmiling expression

3. What kind of order does the writer use? space order

*For complete essays developed by description, see Chapter 16, "Types of Essays, Part 1," Part C.

PRACTICE 2

It is important that the details in a descriptive paragraph support the overall impression given in the topic sentence. In each of the following plans, one detail has nothing to do with the topic sentence; it is merely a bit of irrelevant information. Find the irrelevant detail and circle its letter.

1. Jane Perez announced her plan to run for mayor to an enthusiastic crowd.
   a. voters waving campaign posters
   b. volunteers passing out Perez for Mayor! T-shirts to eager supporters
   c. crowd chanting and clapping
   (d.) police officers providing security
   e. people reaching out to shake her hand
2. The new action movie *Terror at Midnight* failed with both fans and critics.
   a. bad reviews in major newspapers
   (b.) filmed at great expense on location in Paris
   c. empty theaters
   d. audiences walking out
   e. comedians renaming the film *Tedium at Midnight*
3. Wilson High School needs major renovations.
   a. leaking roofs
   b. crumbling plaster in classrooms
   (c.) located on Highland Avenue
   d. obsolete lab equipment
   e. rickety, unsafe elevators
4. Many people are taking steps to eat a more healthy diet.
   a. studying nutritional labels when shopping
   b. eating more fresh fruits and vegetables
   (c.) checking menu prices
   d. avoiding fried and processed foods
   e. lowering their intake of fat, sugar, and salt
5. National Savings and Loan is one of the most unusual banks in the city.
   a. mammoth dinosaur skeleton in the lobby
   (b.) offers free checking
   c. tellers wearing Halloween costumes year round
   d. safe deposit vault decorated as medieval dungeon
   e. Bonnie and Clyde mural

PRACTICE 3

TEACHING TIP
Practice 3 works well as a small-group activity.

Here are three topic sentences for descriptive paragraphs. Give five specific details that would support the overall impression given in each topic sentence. Appeal to as many of the senses as possible. Be careful not to list irrelevant bits of information. Answers will vary.

EXAMPLE Stopped in time by the photographer, my mother appears confident.

Details:

a. *her hair swept up in a sophisticated updo*

b. *a determined look in her young eyes*

c. *wide, self-assured smile*

d. *her chin held high*

e. *well-padded shoulders*

(These five details support *confident* in the topic sentence.)

LEARNING STYLES TIP
Some students draw a picture of the subject they plan to describe as part of their prewriting strategy. This exercise can stimulate creative thinking and ideas about which details to include.

1. The basement office is so cluttered we can't find anything.

   a. stacks of tattered newspapers and magazines

   b. piles of old bills and junk mail on the desk

   c. bookcases sagging with books and outdated manuals

   d. reels of tapes and home movies strewn on work bench

   e. file cabinets jammed with folders and dog-eared papers

2. Addressing the jury, the lawyer was obviously rattled.

   a. awkwardly repeated himself

   b. unable to look jurors in the eye

   c. forgot important facts

   d. mispronounced the defendant's name

   e. hands trembled while speaking

3. The stranded commuters remain in good spirits waiting for their bus.

   a. people trading jokes and stories

   b. a couple playing cards and laughing

   c. teenagers flirting

   d. students playing on their phones

   e. girl with headphones dancing

PRACTICE 4

Pick the description you like best from Practice 3. Prewrite for more details if you wish. Choose a logical order in which to present the best details, make a plan or an outline, and then write an excellent descriptive paragraph.

PRACTICE 5

CRITICAL VIEWING AND WRITING

Describe a Painting

LEARNING STYLES TIP
Brain research tells us that not only *visual learners* but all learners benefit from tasks like this one, requiring close observation, discussion, and conversion of visual cues into writing.

Study Edward Hopper's 1942 painting *Nighthawks*, below. Your task is to write one paragraph describing this painting so that someone who has never seen it can visualize it. Craft a good topic sentence that gives an overall impression of the scene. Your topic sentence might take this form:

"Edward Hopper's 1942 painting *Nighthawks* captures the isolation of city life late at night. ______________________________"

Brainstorm important details, using rich language to capture the scene.
Now decide the best order in which to present your details—right to left, center to sides, or some other. Use transitional expressions to guide the reader's eye from detail to detail. Revise the writing to make it as exact and fresh as possible. Read your paragraph aloud to locate missing details or awkward transitions.

Francis G. Mayer/Corbis

EXPLORING ONLINE

www.artic.edu

On this Art Institute of Chicago site, find a work of art that intrigues you and describe it.

www.moma.org

On this Museum of Modern Art site, find a work of art that captures you and write about it.

TEACHING TIP

For downloadable rubrics corresponding to each rhetorical mode, go to the *Instructor Companion Site*.

Checklist

The Process of Writing a Descriptive Paragraph

Refer to this checklist of steps as you write a descriptive paragraph of your own.

- [ ] 1. Narrow the topic to fit your audience and purpose.
- [ ] 2. Compose a topic sentence that clearly points to what you will describe or gives an overall impression of the person, object, or scene.
- [ ] 3. Freewrite or brainstorm to find as many specific details as you can to capture your subject in words. Remember to appeal to your readers' senses. (You may want to freewrite or brainstorm before you narrow the topic.)
- [ ] 4. Select the best details and drop any irrelevant ones.
- [ ] 5. Make a plan or an outline for the paragraph, numbering the details in the order in which you will present them.
- [ ] 6. Write a draft of your descriptive paragraph, using transitional expressions wherever they might be helpful.
- [ ] 7. Revise as necessary, checking for support, unity, logic, and coherence.
- [ ] 8. Proofread for errors in grammar, punctuation, sentence structure, spelling, and mechanics.

Suggested Topics for Descriptive Paragraphs

ESL TIP

Urge your ESL students to try out fresh vocabulary in their descriptions. They may require instructor feedback on word choice.

1. An unusual person you recently encountered
2. A food, object, or scene from another country
3. A workspace or place on campus that needs improvement (to be safer, more useful, more attractive)
4. A painting, sculpture, or other work of art
5. A scene of poverty or despair
6. Someone or something you found yourself staring at
7. Sounds heard at night in the city or country
8. A scene of peace (or of conflict)
9. A room that reveals something about its owner
10. A famous photograph of a historical event or person
11. A shop that sells only one type of item: cell phones, Western boots, flowers, car parts, cooking items
12. A lost object you wish you could replace
13. A crowded place: dance club, library, fast food restaurant, town square, or theater lobby
14. The clothing you would wear at a job interview
15. Writer's choice: ____________________

EXPLORING ONLINE

leo.stcloudstate.edu/acadwrite/descriptive.html

Good tips for improving your descriptive writing, with sample paragraphs

grammar.about.com/od/developingparagraphs/a/descparhub.htm

In-depth tutorial for writing a descriptive paragraph, with samples

CHAPTER 8

Process

TEACHING TIP
Ask students to think about their experiences with trying to follow directions and assemble something relatively complex (such as a piece of furniture). Can they see why clear directions are important?

Two kinds of **process paragraphs** will be explained in this chapter: the how-to paragraph and the explanation paragraph.

The **how-to paragraph** gives the reader directions on how he or she can do something: how to install a software program, how to get to the airport, or how to make tasty barbecued ribs. The goals of such directions are the installed software, the arrival at the airport, or the great barbecued ribs. In other words, the reader should be able to do something after reading the paragraph.

The **explanation paragraph**, on the other hand, tells the reader how a particular event occurred or how something works. For example, an explanation paragraph might explain how an internal combustion engine works or how palm trees reproduce. After reading an explanation paragraph, the reader is not expected to be able to do anything, just to understand how it happened or how it works.

Process writing is useful in history, business, the sciences, psychology, and many other areas.

Topic Sentence

Here is the topic sentence of a **how-to paragraph**:

> Careful preparation before an interview is the key to getting the job you want.

- The writer begins a how-to paragraph with a topic sentence that clearly states the goal of the process—what the reader should be able to do.
- What should the reader be able to do after he or she has read the paragraph following this topic sentence?

  The reader should be able to prepare for a job interview.
  ____

TEACHING TIP

Alert students to career and job-search resources, stressing the link between good writing and good jobs. Web searches will reveal much online help, including **career-advice.monster.com** and **www.indeed.com**.

Paragraph and Plan

Here is the entire paragraph:

"Luck is preparation meeting opportunity," it has been said, and this is true for a job interview. Careful preparation before an interview is the key to getting the job you want. The first step is to learn all you can about the employer. Read about the company on its websites. Use the names of its products, services, and key executives as search terms to examine local and national media sources for further information. Second, as you read, think about the ways your talents match the company's goals. Third, put yourself in the interviewer's place, and make a list of questions that he or she will probably ask. Employers want to know about your experience, training, and special skills, like your computer literacy. Remember, every employer looks for a capable and enthusiastic team player who will help the firm succeed. Fourth, rehearse your answers to the questions out loud. Practice with a friend or a voice recorder until your responses sound well prepared and confident. Finally, select and prepare a professional-looking interview outfit well in advance to avoid the last-minute panic of a torn hem or stained shirt. When a job candidate has made the effort to prepare, the interviewer is much more likely to be impressed.

- The topic sentence is the second sentence. In the first sentence, the writer has used a quotation to open the paragraph and spark the reader's interest.
- The body of the how-to paragraph is developed according to time, or chronological, order.* That is, the writer gives directions in the order in which the reader is to complete them. Keeping to a strict chronological order avoids the necessity of saying, *By the way, I forgot to tell you . . .*, or *Whoops, a previous step should have been to. . . .*
- How many steps are there in this how-to paragraph and what are they?

  There are five steps: (1) learn about the company, (2) match your talents to the company's goals, (3) list possible interviewer questions, (4) practice answering them, and (5) prepare your outfit.

LEARNING STYLES TIP

Visual learners may prefer using a flow chart to arrange their ideas. You might explain and illustrate by drawing a flow chart on the board.

Before writing this how-to paragraph, the writer probably brainstormed or freewrote to gather ideas and then made an **outline** like this:

TOPIC SENTENCE: Careful preparation before an interview is the key to getting the job you want.

Step 1: Learn about the employer
—study company website
—search local and national media sources

Step 2: Think how your talents match company goals

*For more work on order, see Chapter 4, "Achieving Coherence," Part A.

Step 3: List interviewer questions
—think about experience, training, special skills
—employers want capable team players

Step 4: Rehearse your answers out loud
—practice with friend or tape recorder

Step 5: Select your interview outfit
—avoid last-minute panic
—avoid torn hem, stained shirt

CONCLUSION: Interviewer more likely to be impressed

- Note that each step clearly relates to the goal stated in the topic sentence.

The second kind of process paragraph, the **explanation paragraph**, tells how something works, how it happens, or how it came to be:

TEACHING TIP
Some instructors object to the use of the *you* pronoun, even in some process writing. Advise the class of your standard.

Many experts believe that recovery from addiction, whether to alcohol or other drugs, has four main stages. The first stage begins when the user finally admits that he or she has a substance abuse problem and wants to quit. At this point, most people seek help from groups like Alcoholics Anonymous or treatment programs because few addicts can "get clean" by themselves. The next stage is withdrawal, when the addict stops using the substance. Withdrawal can be a painful physical and emotional experience, but luckily, it does not last long. After withdrawal comes the most challenging stage—making positive changes in one's life. Recovering addicts have to learn new ways of spending their time, finding pleasure and relaxation, caring for their bodies, and relating to spouses, lovers, family, and friends. The fourth and final stage is staying off drugs. This open-ended part of the process often calls for ongoing support or therapy. For people once defeated by addiction, the rewards of self-esteem and a new life are well worth the effort.

- What process does the writer explain in this paragraph? The writer explains how people recover from addiction.

- How many stages or steps are explained in this paragraph? four
  What are they? (1) deciding to quit, (2) withdrawing from substance, (3) changing one's life, (4) staying off drugs

- Make a plan of the paragraph in your notebook.

Daniel Dempster Photography/ Alamy Stock Photo

Just as these photos show each stage of a Monarch butterfly's life, so your paragraphs should clearly describe each step or stage for the reader. Before you write, try to visualize the process as if it were a series of photographs.

Transitional Expressions

Since process paragraphs rely on **chronological order**, or **time sequence**, words and expressions that locate the steps of the process in time are extremely helpful.

Transitional Expressions for Process

Beginning a Process	*Continuing a Process*		*Ending a Process*
first	afterward	then	finally
initially	after that	second	last
the first stage	later	third	the final step
the first step	meanwhile	the second stage	
	next	the next step	

PRACTICE 1

Read the following how-to paragraph carefully and answer the questions.

ESL TIP
ESL students may need help with command verbs in English. Have them point out command verbs in the sample paragraph.

If someone nearby collapses and does not respond to shouting or shaking, performing the three steps of cardiopulmonary resuscitation, or CPR, could determine whether that person lives or dies. The first step is to call for help by dialing 911. If you are not certified to deliver CPR, keep the emergency dispatcher on the line to talk you through the next two steps until paramedics arrive. The second step, performing chest compressions, should occur if the victim remains unresponsive and has stopped breathing or is breathing abnormally. With one hand over your other hand, push down two inches with the heel of your hand on the center of the victim's chest. Compress the chest hard and fast thirty times. Then perform the third step, blowing air into the victim's mouth. Tilt his or her head back and lift the chin. Pinch the victim's nose closed, cover his or her mouth with your mouth, and blow until you see the chest rise. Provide two breaths, each one second long. Continue alternating 30 pumps with two breaths until help arrives. Remember that time is the enemy of someone who is not breathing. By following these steps to keep precious oxygen and blood moving through the victim's body, you may save a life.

—Eleanor Steiger, Student

1. What should you be able to do after reading this paragraph? You should be able to perform the CPR procedure.

2. Are any "materials" necessary for this process? The only item is a telephone to call 911.

3. How many steps are there in this paragraph? List them. three: (1) call 911, (2) perform chest compressions, and (3) blow air into the victim's mouth. These steps are repeated until help arrives.

4. What order does the writer employ? time order

PRACTICE 2

Here are five plans for process paragraphs. The steps for the plans are not in the correct chronological order. The plans also contain irrelevant details that are not part of the process. Number the steps in the proper time sequence and cross out any irrelevant details.

1. The process of taking digital fingerprints, which requires specialized scanning equipment, consists of several simple steps.

   3 The computer converts these finger scans into digital data patterns, mapping points on the patterns.

   2 One by one, the subject places his or her fingers on the optical or silicon scanner surface for a few seconds while the computer scans.

   1 The technician begins by cleaning the subject's fingers with alcohol to remove any dirt or sweat.

   ____ ~~For years, the only fingerprints were made by rolling the fingers in wet ink and pressing the fingers onto a card.~~

   4 At the technician's command, the computer can compare this subject's fingerprint patterns to millions of patterns in the national database and identify possible matches.

2. Stress, which is your body's response to physical or mental pressures, occurs in three stages.

   __2__ In the resistance stage, your body works hard to resist or handle the threat, but you may become more vulnerable to other stressors, like flu or colds.

   __3__ If the stress continues for too long, your body uses up its defenses and enters the exhaustion stage.

   _____ ~~Trying to balance college courses, parenthood, and work is sure to cause stress.~~

   __1__ During the alarm stage (also called *fight or flight*), your body first reacts to a threat by releasing hormones that increase your heart rate and blood pressure, create muscle tension, and supply quick energy.

3. Chewing gum is made entirely by machine.

   __3__ Then the warm mass is pressed into thin ribbons by pairs of rollers.

   __1__ First, the gum base is melted and pumped through a high-speed spinner that throws out all impurities.

   _____ ~~The gum base makes the gum chewy.~~

   __2__ Huge machines mix the purified gum with sugar, corn syrup, and flavoring, such as spearmint, peppermint, or cinnamon.

   __5__ Finally, machines wrap the sticks individually and then package them.

   __4__ Knives attached to the last rollers cut the ribbons into sticks.

4. Sleep is a dynamic process consisting of five phases.

   __2__ In the next phase, eye movements cease and brain activity slows down.

   __1__ Light sleep is the first phase, when a person drifts in and out of sleep and can be woken up easily.

   __5__ The last phase is REM sleep, or rapid eye movement sleep.

   __3__ The third phase begins a period of deep sleep. If a person is woken up out of deep sleep, he or she will feel disoriented and groggy.

   _____ ~~Most doctors recommend getting eight hours of sleep per night.~~

   __4__ The next phase is also considered part of deep sleep.

5. Helping to save rare stranded sea turtles, our service learning project, was a rewarding series of steps.

   __3__ Inside, we rubbed Vaseline on each turtle's shell and put saline in its eyes; the sickest turtles needed IV fluids.

   __2__ We gently loaded each tired giant in the front seat of a pickup truck and hurried back to the sanctuary.

   __1__ In the fall, when temperatures dropped, we volunteers at the Wellfleet Wildlife Sanctuary raced to the beaches to find any giant sea turtles that had not swum south.

   _____ ~~Two volunteers so loved working with endangered turtles that they are now pursuing careers in marine biology.~~

   __4__ Within 12 hours, we drove our patients to the aquarium in Boston, to spend the winter and get well before their release in warm Florida seas.

PRACTICE 3

Here are topic sentences for three process paragraphs. Make a plan for each paragraph, listing in proper time sequence all the steps that would be necessary to complete the process. Then choose one plan and write an excellent process paragraph. Answers will vary.

TEACHING TIP

An enjoyable way to help students anticipate readers' questions about their process writing is to have them write and exchange how-to paragraphs with a classmate. Each reader should re-create the process, based *only* on what is written, and then report any unanswered questions to the writer.

1. I took steps to get my child ready for kindergarten.

   On his birthday I gave him several books. We began to read together every night. After we read the books, I encouraged him to draw pictures about what he had read. As the months passed, we spent more time reading and drawing than watching videos. Just before he turned five, I took him to school and introduced him to the teachers.

2. I have a plan to achieve my goal.

   First I will register for an online HTML and CSS course. After taking the online course, I will sign up for Web design classes at my school. Once I have learned the basics of Web design, I will ask my boss if I can help redesign our company's website. After I have enough experience to create a portfolio, I will try to get a job as a full-time Web designer.

3. Registering to vote in this state is a simple process.

First, obtain your driver's license or state ID. Log onto the "Register to Vote" site. Create a user name that contains the last four digits of your Social Security number and a password containing both letters and numbers. Fill in the required data; then press REGISTER ME.

PRACTICE 4 CRITICAL THINKING AND WRITING

Explain the Process of Intoxication

ESL TIP
For Practice 4, ESL students may need extra help choosing correct word forms.

Study these percentages that show rising blood alcohol content (BAC), a measure of intoxication. Now plan and write a paragraph that describes what happens as BAC rises. Your purpose is to inform your audience—nursing students—about this process. Write a topic sentence that gives an overview; in the body, include three or four percentages if you wish. In your concluding sentence or sentences, you might wish to emphasize the dangerous human meaning of these numbers.

BAC	Effect
0.03%	relaxation, mood change
0.05%	decrease in motor skills; legal driving limit in New York
0.07%	legal driving limit in 16 states
0.09%	delayed reaction time, decreased muscle control, slurred speech
0.15%	blurred vision, unsteadiness, impaired coordination
0.18%	difficulty staying awake
0.30%	semi-stupor
0.50%	coma and risk of death

Now assume your purpose is to write another paragraph convincing high school students not to binge drink. Would BAC percentages help persuade your audience, or would you take another approach? What might that approach be?

EXPLORING ONLINE

www.collegedrinkingprevention.gov

Under "Stats & Summaries," click "Snapshot of Drinking Consequences" for facts on alcohol's link to violence and other harmful behaviors. Under "NIAAA College Materials," click "A Call to Action" for facts on drinking as a "college culture."

TEACHING TIP

For downloadable rubrics corresponding to each rhetorical mode, go to the *Instructor Companion Site*.

Checklist

The Process of Writing a Process Paragraph

Refer to this checklist of steps as you write a process paragraph.

- ☐ 1. Narrow the topic to fit your audience and purpose.
- ☐ 2. Compose a topic sentence that clearly states the goal or end result of the process you wish to describe.
- ☐ 3. Freewrite or brainstorm to generate steps that might be part of the process. (You may want to freewrite or brainstorm before you narrow the topic.)
- ☐ 4. Drop any irrelevant information or steps that are not really necessary for your explanation of the process.
- ☐ 5. Make an outline or a plan for your paragraph, numbering the steps in the correct time (chronological) sequence.
- ☐ 6. Write a draft of your process paragraph, using transitional expressions to indicate time (chronological) sequence.
- ☐ 7. Revise as necessary, checking for support, unity, logic, and coherence.
- ☐ 8. Proofread for errors in grammar, punctuation, sentence structure, spelling, and mechanics.

Suggested Topics for Process Paragraphs

1. How to treat a first-degree burn or other minor injury
2. How to prepare your favorite dish
3. How to determine the best pet for your lifestyle
4. How to establish credit (or improve your credit score)
5. How to write a check
6. How an important discovery was made
7. How to find information in your library's online databases
8. How to sell something online
9. How to get the most out of a doctor visit
10. How to get fired, ruin a love affair, or alienate your in-laws (humorous)
11. How to break an unhealthy habit
12. A process you learned at work or school (how to handcuff a suspect, how to take blood pressure, how to make a customer feel welcome, how a lithograph is made, and so forth)
13. How to motivate someone to ______________________
14. How to shop on a budget for a computer, cell phone, or television
15. Writer's choice: ______________________

EXPLORING ONLINE

www.ehow.com/video_1323_make-peanut-butter.html

Do you think you can make a scrumptious peanut butter and jelly sandwich? Follow the clear instructions in this video.

www.ehow.com

Learn how to do all sorts of things; categories include careers, health, cars, legal, games, and more.

CHAPTER 9

Definition

A: Single-Sentence Definitions

B: The Definition Paragraph

To **define** is to explain clearly what a word or term means. As you write, you will sometimes find it necessary to explain words or terms that you suspect your reader may not know. For example, *net profit* is the profit remaining after all deductions have been taken; a *bonsai* is a dwarfed, ornamentally shaped tree. Such terms can often be defined in just a few carefully chosen words. However, other terms—like *courage, racism,* or *love*—are more difficult to define. They will test your ability to explain them clearly so that your reader knows exactly what you mean when you use them in your writing. They may require an entire paragraph for a complete and thorough definition.

In this chapter, you will learn to write one-sentence definitions and then whole paragraphs of definition. The skill of defining clearly will be useful in a wide variety of courses, such as as psychology, business, police science, nursing, engineering, history, and English.

A. Single-Sentence Definitions

TEACHING TIP

Students might wish to keep a thesaurus nearby while writing definitions. For an online thesaurus, go to **www.thesaurus.com**.

There are many ways to define a word or term. Three basic ways are **definition by synonym**, **definition by class**, and **definition by negation**.

Definition by Synonym

The simplest way to define a term is to supply a **synonym**, a word that means the same thing. A good synonym definition always uses an easier and more familiar word than the one being defined.

1. *Gregarious* means *sociable.*
2. *To procrastinate* means *to postpone needlessly.*
3. A *casement* is a *window.*
4. *Deftly* means *skillfully.*

Although you may not have known the words *gregarious, procrastination, casement,* and *deftly* before, the synonym definitions make it very clear what they mean.

A synonym should usually be the same part of speech as the word being defined, so it could be used as a substitute. *Gregarious* and *sociable* are both adjectives; *to procrastinate* and *to postpone* are verb forms; *casement* and *window* are nouns; *deftly* and *skillfully* are adverbs.

5. Quarterback Aaron Rodgers *deftly* moved his team up the field.
6. Quarterback Aaron Rodgers *skillfully* moved his team up the field.

- In this sentence *skillfully* can be substituted for *deftly*.

Unfortunately, it is not always possible to come up with a good synonym definition.

Definition by Class

The **class** definition is the one most often required in college and formal writing—in examinations, papers, and reports.

The class definition has two parts. First, the writer places the word to be defined into the larger **category**, or **class**, to which it belongs.

7. *Lemonade* is a *drink* . . .
8. An *orphan* is a *child* . . .
9. A *dictatorship* is a *form of government* . . .

ESL TIP

ESL students may require additional explanation of relative clauses. Refer them to Chapters 28, "Avoiding Sentence Errors," and 29, "Present Tense (Agreement)," for review.

Second, the writer provides the **distinguishing characteristics** or **details** that make this person, object, or idea *different* from all others in that category. What the reader wants to know is: What *kind* of drink is lemonade? What *specific* type of child is an orphan? What *particular* form of government is a dictatorship?

10. *Lemonade* is a drink *made of lemons, sugar, and water.*
11. An *orphan* is a child *without living parents.*
12. A *dictatorship* is a form of government *in which one person has absolute control over his or her subjects.*

Tatiana Grozetskaya/Getty Images

Here is a class definition of the structure pictured: *A pagoda is a sacred Hindu or Buddhist building characterized by upward-turning roofs.*

LEARNING STYLES TIP

Visual learners will understand and write class definitions more easily if they break them down in a chart like this.

Think of class definitions as if they were in chart form:

Word	Category or Class	Distinguishing Facts or Details
lemonade	drink	made of lemons, sugar, and water
orphan	child	without living parents
dictatorship	form of government	one person has absolute control over his or her subjects

When you write a class definition, be careful not to place the word or term in a category that is too broad or too vague. For instance, saying that lemonade is a *food* or that an orphan is a *person* will make your job of zeroing in on a distinguishing detail more difficult.

Besides making the category or class as limited as possible, be sure to make your distinguishing facts as specific and exact as you can. Saying that lemonade is a drink *made with water* or that an orphan is a child *who has lost family members* is not specific enough to give your reader an accurate definition.

Definition by Negation

A definition by **negation** means that the writer first says what something is not, and then says what it is.

13. A *good parent* does not just feed and clothe a child but loves, accepts, and supports that child for who he or she is.
14. *College* is not just a place to have a good time but a place to grow intellectually and emotionally.
15. *Liberty* does not mean having the right to do whatever you please but carries the obligation to respect the rights of others.

Definitions by negation are extremely helpful when you think that the reader has a preconceived idea about the word you wish to define. You say that *it is not* what the reader thought, but that *it is* something else entirely.

PRACTICE 1

TEACHING AND ESL TIP
To learn the meanings of words they don't know, students should refer to a dictionary while reading and writing.

Write a one-sentence definition by **synonym** for each of the following terms. Remember, the synonym should be more familiar than the term being defined.

1. *irate*: To be irate is to be angry.
2. *elude*: To elude someone is to keep away from him or her.
3. *pragmatic*: To be pragmatic is to be practical.
4. *fiasco*: A fiasco is a disaster.
5. *elated*: To be elated is to be overjoyed.

PRACTICE 2

TEACHING TIP
Practices 2 and 3 work well in class. Create sample class definitions on the board, perhaps in three columns: *Term*, *Class*, and *Differentiating Detail*.

Here are five **class** definitions. Circle the category and underline the distinguishing characteristics in each. You may find it helpful to make a chart.

1. An *airbag* is a rapidly inflated cushion designed to protect automobile passengers in a collision.
2. *Exculpatory evidence* is legal evidence that is favorable to the defendant in a criminal trial.
3. *Gluten* is a mixture of proteins found in grains that gives baked goods a chewy texture.
4. A *gaffer* is an electrician in charge of lighting a set for a film or TV production.
5. A *beanball* is a baseball pitch intentionally thrown to hit a batter.

PRACTICE 3

Define the following words by **class definition**. You may find it helpful to use this form:

"A ______________________ is a ______________________
(noun) (class or category)

that ____."
(distinguishing characteristic)

1. *hamburger*: A hamburger is a sandwich that consists of a split bun and a ground beef patty.

TEACHING TIP
Point out that effective definitions include exact language. For more on this topic, see Chapter 23, "Revising for Language Awareness."

2. *nightmare*: A nightmare is a bad dream that causes fear or distress.

3. *snob*: A snob is a person who thinks he or she is, and acts as if he or she were, socially superior to others.

4. *mentor*: A mentor is a counselor who guides, teaches, and assists another person.

5. *adolescence*: Adolescence is the period of life between puberty and maturity.

PRACTICE 4

Write a one-sentence definition by **negation** for each of the following terms. First say what each term is not; then say what it is.

1. *hero*: A hero is not someone with great athletic ability or wealth but a person admired for his or her acts of morality and fine character.

2. *final exam*: A final exam is not just a way to make students suffer but an enforced review of everything learned in the course.

3. *self-esteem*: Self-esteem does not mean conceit but rather a healthy respect for oneself.

4. *intelligence*: Intelligence is not knowledge in a specific area; it is the capacity to acquire and apply knowledge.

5. *freedom of speech*: Freedom of speech is not just a phrase we learn in history class; it is a right guaranteed to each American to express his or her beliefs in public.

B. The Definition Paragraph

Sometimes a single-sentence definition may not be enough to define a word or term adequately. In such cases, the writer may need an entire paragraph in which he or she develops the definition by means of examples, descriptions, comparisons, contrasts, and so forth.

Topic Sentence

The topic sentence of a definition paragraph is often one of the single-sentence definitions discussed in Part A: definition by synonym, definition by class, or definition by negation.

Here is the topic sentence of a definition paragraph:

> A *flashbulb memory* can be defined as a vivid and long-lasting memory formed at the moment a person experiences a highly emotional event.

- What kind of definition does the topic sentence use? class
- To what larger category or class does a *flashbulb memory* belong? a vivid and long-lasting memory
- What are the distinguishing details about a *flashbulb memory* that make it different from other kinds of memories? It is formed at the moment a person experiences a highly emotional event.

Paragraph and Plan

Here is the entire paragraph:

> A *flashbulb memory* can be defined as a vivid and long-lasting memory formed at the moment a person experiences a highly emotional event. It is as though a mental flashbulb pops, preserving the moment in great detail. Although flashbulb memories can be personal, they often are triggered by public events. For example, many older Americans recall exactly what they were doing when they heard that President John F. Kennedy had been assassinated in Dallas, Texas, on November 22, 1963. Time froze as people crowded around their radios and televisions to find out what had happened. Many more people recall in detail the shocking events of September 11, 2001, when hijacked airplanes crashed into the World Trade Center. Millions of people watched television as the horrifying scenes of the terror attack unfolded. The image of the towers collapsing is burned into the minds of people the world over, making it a flashbulb memory for an entire generation. As these examples show, flashbulb memories mark some of

our most permanent and haunting experiences, moments that were scored into our minds.

- One effective way for a writer to develop the body of a definition paragraph is to provide examples.*
- What two examples does this writer give to develop the definition in the topic sentence? the assassination of John F. Kennedy and the terrorist attack on the World Trade Center
- By repeating the word being defined—or a form of it—in the context of the definition paragraph, the writer helps the reader understand the definition better: "Although *flashbulb memories* can be personal" and "image of the towers collapsing is burned into the minds of people the world over, making it a flashbulb memory for an entire generation."

Before writing the paragraph, the writer probably brainstormed or freewrote to gather ideas and then made an **outline** like this:

TOPIC SENTENCE: A flashbulb memory is a vivid and long-lasting memory formed at the moment a person experiences a highly emotional event.

Example 1: John F. Kennedy's assassination
—older Americans recall what they were doing on November 22, 1963
—time froze as people heard what happened in Dallas

Example 2: World Trade Center attack
—many more recall the events of September 11, 2001
—millions watched television as horrifying events unfolded
—image of the towers collapsing is burned into the minds of an entire generation

CONCLUSION: Flashbulb memories mark our most permanent and haunting experiences.

- Note that the examples in the body of the paragraph clearly relate to the definition in the topic sentence.

Although examples are an excellent way to develop a definition paragraph, other methods of development are also possible. For instance, you might compare and contrast† *love* and *lust, assertiveness* and *aggressiveness,* or *the leader* and *the follower.* You could also combine definition and persuasion.‡ Such a paragraph might begin *College is a dating service* or *Alcoholism is not a moral weakness but a disease.* The rest of the paragraph would have to persuade readers that this definition is valid.

There are no transitional expressions used specifically for definition paragraphs. Sometimes phrases like *can be defined as* or *can be considered* or *means that* can help alert the reader that a definition paragraph will follow.§

*For more work on examples, see Chapter 5, "Illustration."

†For more work on contrast, see Chapter 10, "Comparison and Contrast."

‡For more work on persuasion, see Chapter 13, "Persuasion."

§For entire essays developed by definition, see Chapter 16, Part E.

PRACTICE 5

Read the following paragraph carefully and then answer the questions.

TEACHING TIP

Stereotyped labels or loaded terms for groups of people often make good topics for definition paragraphs (and definitions by negation). Ask the class for other terms (e.g., *immigrant*, *soccer mom*, or *rapper*).

A feminist is *not* a man-hater, a masculine woman, a demanding shrew, or someone who dislikes housewives. A feminist is simply a woman or man who believes that women should enjoy the same rights, privileges, opportunities, and pay as men. Because society has deprived women of many equal rights, feminists have fought for equality. For instance, Susan B. Anthony, a famous nineteenth-century feminist, worked to get women the right to vote. Today, feminists want women to receive equal pay for equal work. They support a woman's right to pursue her goals and dreams, whether she wants to be an astronaut, athlete, banker, or full-time homemaker. On the home front, feminists believe that two partners who work should equally share the housework and child care. Because the term is often misunderstood, some people don't call themselves feminists even though they share feminist values. But courageous feminists of both sexes continue to speak out for equality.

1. The definition here spans two sentences. What kind of definition does the writer use in sentence 1? definition by negation

2. What kind of definition appears in sentence 2? definition by class

3. The paragraph is developed by describing some key beliefs of feminists. What are these? equal rights, equal pay for equal work, freedom to pursue goals and dreams, working couples' sharing housework and child care

4. Which point is supported by an example? Feminists have fought for equality. Example: Susan B. Anthony

5. Make a plan or an outline of the paragraph. Topic sentence(s): A feminist is not a man-hater, a masculine woman, a demanding shrew, or someone who dislikes housewives. A feminist is simply a woman or man who believes that women should enjoy the same rights, privileges, opportunities, and pay as men.

    —fights for equal rights

—wants equal pay for equal work

—wants freedom for women to pursue goals and dreams

—believes working partners should share housework, child care

Conclusion: Courageous feminists of both sexes speak out for equality.

PRACTICE 6

Read the following paragraphs and answer the questions.

A *placebo* is a fake medical treatment. Prescribed as if it were the real thing, a placebo is used to test new drugs. One group of patients takes the real drug while the other takes a placebo, maybe a simple sugar pill. The results show how many people are truly helped by a new medication and how many feel better just because they *think* they've been treated.

Here it gets interesting. Many people who receive fake treatments do improve; they experience the mysterious *placebo effect.* The placebo effect is symptom relief that is caused by receiving a fake treatment. In one famous study, arthritis patients in Texas who thought they had knee surgeries reported the same improvement in pain and mobility as patients who had real surgeries! Apparently, if the patient believes in the treatment, the healing power of the mind might do the rest.

—Dan Robinson, *PsychologyWatch.com*

1. What two terms or concepts are defined? placebo and placebo effect

2. What kind of definition is used for *placebo*? synonym

3. What kind of definition is used for *placebo effect*? class

4. Into what larger category does the writer place *placebo effect*? symptom relief

5. What defining characteristic completes the definition? that is caused by receiving a fake treatment

6. What example does the author give to illustrate the *placebo effect*?

   patients who were told they had knee surgeries and then felt better

PRACTICE 7

Here are some topic sentences for definition paragraphs. Choose one that interests you and make a plan for a paragraph, using whatever method of development seems appropriate.

1. An egoist is a selfish, self-centered person who considers himself or herself superior to others.
2. Entitlements are government benefits granted to people who meet certain criteria, such as being elderly or disabled.
3. A healthy lifestyle consists of adequate exercise, a nutritious diet, and a rewarding social life.
4. Racial profiling is the unfair use of people's ethnic background to label them criminal suspects.
5. The "glass ceiling" refers to a barrier that prevents female employees from being promoted to higher levels of management.

PRACTICE 8

CRITICAL THINKING AND WRITING

Define a Team Player

TEACHING TIP
Job interviewers often ask, "Are you a team player?" An alternative writing assignment is a paragraph answering that question, with examples of support.

Whether or not we play sports, most of us know what it means to be a *team player* on a basketball or soccer team. But these days, many employers also want to hire "team players." What, exactly, are they looking for? What qualities does a team player bring to the job?

Consider the meaning of *team player*, listing all the qualities that you think a team player has. List at least eight qualities. Now craft a topic sentence of definition and write it down, using the form, "A team player is a(n) ____________ who ____________." Choose the three or four most important qualities and write a paragraph defining *team player*. Use examples or details to bring your paragraph to life.

EXPLORING ONLINE

www.studententerprise.ie/wp-content/uploads/are-you-a-team-player-quiz.pdf

Take this quiz and write about your results.

TEACHING TIP

For downloadable rubrics corresponding to each rhetorical mode, go to the *Instructor Companion Site.*

Checklist

The Process of Writing a Definition Paragraph

Refer to this checklist of steps as you write a definition paragraph.

- ☐ 1. Narrow the topic to fit your audience and purpose.
- ☐ 2. Compose a topic sentence that uses one of the three basic methods of definition discussed in this chapter: synonym, class, or negation.
- ☐ 3. Decide on the method of paragraph development that is best suited to what you want to say.
- ☐ 4. Freewrite or brainstorm to generate ideas that may be useful in your definition paragraph. (You may want to freewrite or brainstorm before you narrow the topic.)
- ☐ 5. Select the best ideas and drop any ideas that do not clearly relate to the definition in your topic sentence.
- ☐ 6. Make a plan or an outline for your paragraph.
- ☐ 7. Write a draft of your definition paragraph.
- ☐ 8. Revise as necessary, checking for support, unity, logic, and coherence.
- ☐ 9. Proofread for errors in grammar, punctuation, sentence structure, spelling, and mechanics.

TEACHING AND ESL TIP

Remind ESL students that they should *refer to* but not *plagiarize* dictionary definitions. Refer them to Chapter 18, "Summarizing, Quoting, and Avoiding Plagiarism," for review.

Suggested Topics for Definition Paragraphs

1. The gossip (or life of the party, Internet addict, co-worker from hell)
2. Professionalism
3. Identity theft
4. A term from your field of study (like *green building, concussion, Oedipus complex, Harlem Renaissance, Pacific garbage patch, Baroque*)
5. A term from popular culture (*Spanglish, sampling* in music, *whistleblower, Twitter, avatar*)
6. Underemployment
7. Terrorism
8. A disability, such as dyslexia, autism, or ADHD
9. A military term or symbol, such as the Purple Heart medal
10. A slang term you or your friends use
11. Urban legend (see **www.snopes.com**)
12. Plagiarism
13. Domestic violence
14. Disenfranchisement
15. Writer's choice: ______________________________

EXPLORING ONLINE

www.quintcareers.com/jobseeker-glossary

Check out this job seeker's glossary of career terms.

grammar.ccc.commnet.edu/grammar/composition/definition.htm

Read advice about writing longer definitions and one student's essay defining *Yankee*.

CHAPTER 10

Comparison and Contrast

A: The Contrast Paragraph and the Comparison Paragraph

B: The Comparison and Contrast Paragraph

TEACHING TIP
Point out to students that the ability to compare and contrast effectively improves decision-making ability, a useful skill in all areas of life.

To **contrast** two persons, places, or things is to examine the ways in which they are different. To **compare** them is to examine the ways in which they are similar.

Contrast and comparison are useful skills in daily life, work, and college. When you shop, you often compare and contrast. For instance, you might compare and contrast two dishwashers to get the better value. In fact, the magazine *Consumer Reports* was created to help consumers compare and contrast different product brands.

Your employer might ask you to compare and contrast two shipping options, two computers, or two Internet providers. Your job is to gather information about the similarities and differences to help your employer choose one over the other. In nearly every college course, you will be expected to compare and contrast—two novels, two methods of accounting, two historical events, or two ways of treating a psychological disorder.

A. The Contrast Paragraph and the Comparison Paragraph

Topic Sentence

Here is the topic sentence of a **contrast** paragraph:

> Although soul and hip hop both spring from African American roots, they are very different musical expressions.

- The writer begins a contrast paragraph with a topic sentence that clearly states what two persons, things, or ideas will be contrasted.
- What two things will be contrasted? soul and hip hop
- What word or words in the topic sentence make it clear that the writer will contrast soul and hip hop? very different

Paragraph and Plan

Here is the entire paragraph:

Although soul and hip hop both spring from African American roots, they are very different musical expressions. Soul music borrows from gospel and rhythm and blues. The singer's voice, backed up by live instruments, soars with emotion, with soul. This music captures the optimism of its time—the civil rights movement of the 1960s and hope for social change. There are two types of soul—the smooth Detroit style of the Supremes, Stevie Wonder, and The Temptations and the more gritty, gospel-driven Memphis style of Otis Redding and Booker T and the MGs. Soul music is upbeat and often joyful; its subjects are love and affirmation of the human condition. On the other hand, hip hop (or rap) draws on hard rock, funk, and techno. The rapper chants rhymes against a driving instrumental background that may be prerecorded. Rap grew out of the New York ghettos in the late 1970s and the 1980s, when crack and guns flooded "the hood" and many dreams seemed broken. Of the rival East and West Coast rappers, New Yorkers include Grandmaster Flash, LL Cool J, and the murdered Biggie Smalls, while Los Angeles rappers include Ice Cube and the murdered Tupac Shakur. The subjects of hip hop are racism, crime, and poverty. Both soul and hip hop claim to "tell it like it is." Hip hop's answer to the soulful Four Tops is the Furious Four. What's in a name? Perhaps the way the listener experiences reality.

—Maurice Bosco, Student

- The writer first provides information about (A) soul music and then gives contrasting parallel information about (B) hip hop.
- What information about (A) soul does the writer provide in the first half of the paragraph? The writer discusses musical influences, sound, time period, types, and subjects.
- What contrasting parallel information does the writer provide about (B) hip hop in the second half of the paragraph? The writer discusses the same five points: influences, sound, time period, types, and subjects.
- Why do you think the writer chose to present the points of contrast in this order? It makes sense to describe the sound and historical background of each kind of music first.

- Note that the last four sentences provide a thoughtful conclusion. What final point does the writer make? that the two kinds of music express two views of reality

Before composing the paragraph, the writer probably brainstormed or freewrote to gather ideas and then made an **outline** like this:

TEACHING TIP
Stress to students that outlining is particularly helpful in comparison and contrast writing because of its complexity.

TOPIC SENTENCE: Although soul and hip hop both spring from African American roots, they are very different musical expressions.

Points of Contrast	A. Soul	B. Hip Hop
1. influences	gospel, R&B	hard rock, funk, techno
2. sound	soaring voice, live instruments	chanted rhymes; instrumentals may be prerecorded
3. time period	1960s, civil rights, hope for change	1970s–1980s, crack, guns
4. types	Detroit, Memphis	New York, Los Angeles
5. subjects	love, affirmation	racism, crime, poverty

Organized in this manner, the plan for this contrast paragraph helps the writer make sure that the paragraph will be complete. That is, if the historical period of soul is discussed, that of hip hop must also be discussed, and so on, for every point of contrast.

Here is another way to write the same paragraph:

Although soul and hip hop both spring from African American roots, they are very different musical expressions. Soul music borrows from gospel and rhythm and blues, whereas hip hop (or rap) draws on hard rock, funk, and techno. The soul singer's voice, backed up by live instruments, soars with emotion, with soul; however, the rapper chants rhymes against a driving instrumental background that may be prerecorded. Soul music captures the optimism of its time—the civil rights movement of the 1960s and hope for social change. On the other hand, hip hop grew out of the New York ghettos in the late 1970s and the 1980s, when crack and guns flooded "the hood" and many dreams seemed broken. There are two types of soul—the smooth Detroit style of the Supremes, Stevie Wonder, and The Temptations and the more gritty, gospel-driven Memphis style of Otis Redding and Booker T and the MGs. Of the rival East and West Coast rappers, New Yorkers include Grandmaster Flash, LL Cool J, and the murdered Biggie Smalls, while Los Angeles rappers include Ice Cube and the murdered Tupac Shakur. Whereas soul music's subjects are love and affirmation of the human condition, the subjects of hip hop are racism, crime, and poverty. Both soul and hip hop claim to "tell it like it is." Hip hop's answer to the soulful Four Tops is the Furious Four. What's in a name? Perhaps the way the listener experiences reality.

- Instead of giving all the information about soul music and then going on to hip hop, this paragraph moves back and forth between soul and hip hop, dealing with *each point of contrast separately*.

Use either one of these two patterns when writing a contrast or a comparison paragraph:

1. Present all the information about A and then provide parallel information about B:

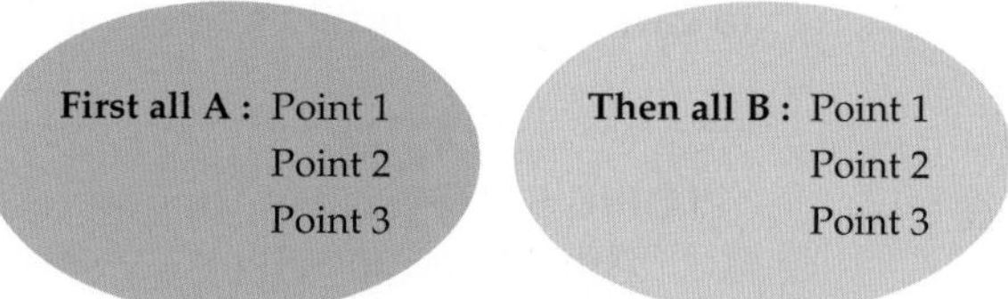

- This pattern is good for paragraphs and for short compositions. The reader can easily remember what was said about A by the time he or she gets to B.

2. Move back and forth between A and B. Present one point about A and then go to the parallel point about B. Then move to the next point and do the same:

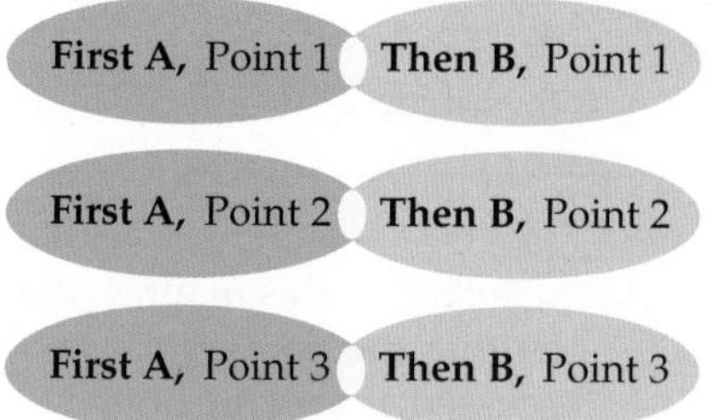

- The second pattern is better for longer papers, where it may be hard for the reader to remember what the writer said about A by the time he or she gets to B a few paragraphs later. By going back and forth, the writer makes it easier for the reader to keep the contrasts or comparisons in mind.

What you have learned so far about planning a contrast paragraph holds true for a comparison paragraph as well. Just remember that *contrast stresses differences* whereas *comparison stresses similarities.*

Here is a **comparison** paragraph:

In my family, personality traits are said to skip generations, so that might explain why my grandfather and I have so much in common. My grandfather arrived in the United States at sixteen, a penniless young man from Italy looking for a new life and ready to earn it. He quickly apprenticed himself to a shoe cobbler and never stopped working until he retired fifty-three years later. Similarly, when I was fourteen, I asked permission to apply for my first job as a bank teller. My parents smiled and said, "She's just like Grandpa." Though everyone else in my family spends money the minute it reaches their hands, my habit of saving every penny does not seem strange to them. My grandfather also was careful with money, building his own shoe repair business out of nothing. He loved to work in his large vegetable garden and brought bags of carrots and tomatoes to our house on Saturday mornings. Like him, I enjoy the feeling of dirt on my fingers and the surprise of seedlings sprouting overnight. Though I raise zinnias instead of zucchinis, I know where I inherited a passion to make things grow. Only in opportunities, we differed. Although my grandfather's education ended with third grade, I am fortunate to attend college—and hope that education will be my legacy to the generations that come after me.

—Angela De Renzi, Student

- What words in the topic sentence does the writer use to indicate that a comparison will follow?

  so much in common

- In what ways are the writer and her grandfather similar?

  They started working young and worked hard; both were careful with money; both were gardeners.

- What transitional words stress the similarities?

  Similarly, like Grandpa, also, like him

- What pattern of presentation does the writer use?

  The writer uses the A-B, A-B, A-B pattern.

TEACHING TIP
To give students more practice, have them work in small groups to brainstorm and organize ideas for comparison or contrast paragraphs.

- What one point of *contrast* serves as a strong punch line for the paragraph?

  Although the grandfather only attended third grade, the writer attended college.

- Make a plan or an outline of this comparison paragraph.

Transitional Expressions

Transitional expressions in contrast paragraphs stress *opposition* and *difference*:

TEACHING TIP
Transitional expressions are especially important in paragraphs organized with the A-B, A-B, A-B pattern. Readers will need transitions to help them follow the shifts from one topic to the other.

Transitional Expressions for Contrast	
conversely	nevertheless
however	on the contrary
in contrast	on the one hand
in opposition	on the other hand
although, even though, whereas, while*	but, yet†

*For more work on subordinating conjunctions like *although* and *while,* see Chapter 27, "Coordination and Subordination," Part B.

†For more work on coordinating conjunctions like *but* and *yet,* see Chapter 27, "Coordination and Subordination," Part A.

Transitional expressions in comparison paragraphs stress *similarities*:

Transitional Expressions for Comparison	
also	in a similar way
as well	in the same way
equally	likewise
in addition	similarly

ESL TIP
You might have ESL students write sentences using the transitional expressions in the charts.

As you write, avoid using just one or two of these transitional expressions. Learn new ones from the list and practice them in your paragraphs.*

PRACTICE 1

Read the following paragraph carefully and answer the questions.

Certain personality traits, like whether a person is more reactive or proactive, can predict success or its opposite. In his book *The Seven Habits of Highly Effective People,* Stephen Covey writes that reactive people tend to sit back and wait for life or circumstances to bring them opportunities. They react instead of act. When good things happen, they are happy, but when bad things happen, they feel like victims. Reactive people often say things like, "There's nothing I can do," "I can't because . . .," and "If only." In the short term, reactive people might feel comfortable playing it safe, holding back, and avoiding challenges; in the long term, though, they are often left dreaming. On the other hand, proactive people know that they have the power to choose their responses to whatever life brings. They act instead of react: if things aren't going their way, they take action to help create the outcome they desire. Proactive people can be recognized by their tendency to say things like "Let's consider the alternatives," "I prefer," "We can," and "I will." In the short term, proactive people might face the discomfort of failing because they take on challenges, set goals, and work toward them. But in the long term, Covey says, proactive people are the ones who achieve their dreams.

1. Can you tell from the topic sentence whether a contrast or comparison will follow?

   The words "more reactive or proactive" and "success or its opposite" suggest contrast.

2. What two personality types are being contrasted?

   reactive and proactive

3. What information does the writer provide about reactive people?

   They sit and wait; react, not act; say things like "There's nothing I can do"; avoid discomfort in the short term but are left dreaming.

4. What parallel information does the writer provide about proactive people?

   They know they have power; take positive action; say things like, "We can" and "I will"; face discomfort but often achieve their dreams.

*For entire essays developed by comparison or contrast, see Chapter 17, Part A.

5. What pattern does the writer of this paragraph use to present the contrasts?

 all A, then all B

6. What transitional expression does the writer use to stress the shift from A to B?

 On the other hand

PRACTICE 2

TEACHING TIP
North Korea is continually in the news as an isolated, hostile nation. Students, however, are familiar with South Korean products—Samsung smartphones and KIA automobiles. This fact can prompt discussions about foreign policy, media perceptions, imports, and cultural differences.

This paragraph is hard to follow because it lacks transitional words and expressions that emphasize contrast. Revise the paragraph, adding transitional words of contrast. Strive for variety. Answers may vary.

Since their creation in 1945, North and South Korea have developed very different economies. South Korea has twice the population of North Korea~~.~~ , but its ~~Its~~ economy is forty times larger. North Korea's exports total only $4 billion a year~~.~~ , whereas South Korea exports $572 billion worth of goods annually. The per capita GDP in North Korea is only $1,800 a year. In contrast, the ~~The~~ per capita GDP in South Korea is $35,000. South Korea has a prosperous middle class~~.~~ , while food ~~Food~~ and energy shortages remain widespread in North Korea. South Korea is the fifth largest car producer in the world, manufacturing over four million vehicles a year. North Korea , in contrast, produces fewer than 40,000 cars a year, mostly for military use. A final, striking difference between the two countries is their output of electricity. South Korea generates almost thirty times more electric power than North Korea. In North Korea the electricity is often turned off at night~~.~~ , but in ~~In~~ South Korea the cities blaze with light.

TEACHING TIP
Have students comment on what the satellite photograph reveals about North Korea and South Korea.

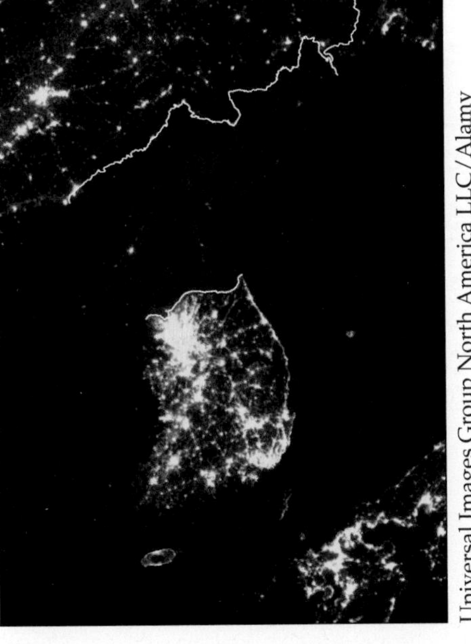

Universal Images Group North America LLC/Alamy Stock Photo

A satellite photograph of the Korean peninsula at night showing North Korea in near total darkness in contrast to the bright lights of South Korea

EXPLORING ONLINE

https://www.cia.gov/library/publications/resources/the-world-factbook

Select Korea, North and Korea, South from the dropdown list to learn about the differences between the two countries. Take notes on facts or ideas for further reading.

PRACTICE 3

Below are three plans for contrast paragraphs. The points of contrast in the second column do not follow the same order as the points in the first column. In addition, one detail is missing. First, number the points in the second column to match those in the first. Then fill in the missing detail.

LEARNING STYLES TIP

Activities like Practice 3 gain hands-on value for *kinesthetic learners* when the elements are reproduced as movable pieces (cards, paper strips). Students can rearrange the elements, using first the all-A-then-all-B pattern and then the A-B, A-B pattern.

1. Shopping at a Supermarket		Shopping at a Local Grocery
1. carries all brands	4	personal service
2. lower prices	3	closed on Sundays
3. open seven days a week	2	prices often higher
4. little personal service	1	doesn't carry all brands
5. no credit	5	credit available for steady customers

2. My Son		My Daughter
1. fifteen years old	4	good at making minor household repairs
2. likes to be alone	2	likes to be with friends
3. reads a lot	3	doesn't like to read
4. is an excellent cook	5	expects to attend a technical college
5. wants to go to culinary school	1	seventeen years old

3. Job A		Job B
1. good salary	3	three-week vacation
2. office within walking distance	4	work on a team with others
3. two-week vacation	2	one-hour bus ride to office
4. work alone	6	health insurance
5. lots of overtime	5	no overtime
6. no health insurance	1	low salary

PRACTICE 4

TEACHING TIP

Have diverse pairs of students identify and write collaboratively about one cultural difference of similarity (like "Italian Mama and Japanese Okasan"). This exercise builds writing and thinking skills—and it's fun.

Here are three topics for either contrast or comparison paragraphs. Compose two topic sentences for each topic, one for a possible contrast paragraph and one for a possible comparison paragraph. Answers will vary.

Topic	Topic Sentences
EXAMPLE Two members of my family	A. *My brother and sister have different attitudes toward exercise.*
	B. *My parents are alike in that they're easygoing.*
1. Two friends or co-workers	A. Tom Bogyo and Amanda Gill have very different attitudes toward success.
	B. Although Sylvia and Miako excel at different sports, both are talented athletes.
2. You as a child and you as an adult	A. I am less selfish than I was as a child.
	B. As an adult, I have some of the same dislikes I had as a child.
3. Two vacations	A. Some people like to relax on vacation, but others like to spend most of their time sightseeing.
	B. My vacations in both Barbados and Sun Valley included miles of walking.

PRACTICE 5

Here are four topic sentences for comparison or contrast paragraphs. For each topic sentence, think of one supporting point of comparison or contrast and explain that point in one or two sentences. Answers will vary.

1. When it comes to movies (TV shows, books, entertainment), Demetrios and Arlene have totally different tastes.

   Demetrios loves action and violence, whereas Arlene will leave the theater at the first sight of blood on the screen.

2. My mother and I have few personality traits in common.

   My mother is extremely temperamental, whereas I pride myself on keeping my cool.

3. Although there are obvious differences, the two neighborhoods (blocks, houses) have much in common.

   The large house has an extensive and beautiful garden. The smaller house also has a garden, less extensive but equally colorful.

4. Paying taxes is like having a tooth pulled.*

   Both are painful. It hurts to write that tax check and to have that tooth pulled. But by doing both, we avoid worse pain in the future.

*For more work on this kind of comparison, see Chapter 23, "Revising for Language Awareness," Part D.

PRACTICE 6 CRITICAL THINKING AND WRITING

Contrast Toys for Boys and Toys for Girls

Retail stores and websites frequently recommend toys for children, often dividing their gift ideas into two groups: "toys for boys" and "toys for girls." These were the top-selling toys in 2015, according to the National Retail Federation.

ESL TIP

ESL students may need an explanation of some toys here. Toys and games can be very culture-laden. Ask your ESL students to comment on how well the gender-based toy lists reflect non-U.S. cultures.

Top Toys for Boys	**Top Toys for Girls**
1. LEGO	1. Barbie
2. Star Wars	2. Disney's *Frozen*
3. Cars & Trucks	3. Dolls
4. Video Games	4. Monster High
5. Hot Wheels	5. American Girl
6. Teenage Mutant Ninja Turtles	6. My Little Pony
7. Xbox One	7. Shopkins
8. PlayStation 4	8. LEGO
9. Nerf	9. Disney Princess
10. Marvel Action Figures	10. Star Wars

Study these contrasting lists carefully and make notes about the similarities and differences. Do these lists indicate that boys and girls have different interests, or do they suggest that society sends children different messages based on their gender? Are "action figures" the same thing as dolls? Both boys and girls like LEGO and Star Wars, but could they play with them differently? Make notes and write a paragraph comparing or contrasting toys for boys and toys for girls.

EXPLORING ONLINE

www.google.com

Or visit your favorite search engine; search "toys, gender roles" and see what information you find.

TEACHING TIP

For downloadable rubrics corresponding to each rhetorical mode, go to the *Instructor Companion Site*.

Checklist

The Process of Writing a Comparison or Contrast Paragraph

Refer to this checklist of steps as you write a comparison or contrast paragraph.

- [ ] 1. Narrow the topic to fit your audience and purpose.
- [ ] 2. Compose a topic sentence that clearly states that a comparison or a contrast will follow.
- [ ] 3. Freewrite or brainstorm to generate as many points of comparison or contrast as you can think of. (You may want to freewrite or brainstorm before you narrow the topic.)
- [ ] 4. Choose the points you will use, and drop any details that are not really part of the comparison or the contrast.
- [ ] 5. List parallel points of comparison or of contrast for both A and B.
- [ ] 6. Make a plan or an outline, numbering all the points of comparison or contrast in the order in which you will present them in the paragraph.
- [ ] 7. Write a draft of your comparison or contrast paragraph, using transitional expressions that stress either differences or similarities.
- [ ] 8. Revise as necessary, checking for support, unity, logic, and coherence.
- [ ] 9. Proofread for errors in grammar, punctuation, sentence structure, spelling, and mechanics.

Suggested Topics for Comparison or Contrast Paragraphs

1. Compare or contrast two attitudes toward money (the spender and the saver) or partnership (the confirmed single and the committed partner).
2. Compare or contrast two ways of dealing with anger, loss, grief, or disappointment.
3. Compare or contrast two popular reality shows, TV series, or bands.
4. Compare or contrast being paid a salary and being paid by the hour.
5. Compare or contrast the way something is done in the United States and the way it is done in another country (or the ways something is done in two different states).
6. Compare or contrast two high schools or colleges you have attended (perhaps one in the United States and one in another country).
7. Compare or contrast two athletes in the same sport (or two entertainers, politicians, professors).
8. Compare or contrast your expectations of a person, place, or situation and the reality.
9. Compare or contrast living on campus and off campus.
10. Writer's choice: ______________________________

B. The Comparison and Contrast Paragraph

Sometimes you will be asked to write a paragraph that both compares and contrasts, one that stresses both similarities and differences.

Here is a comparison and contrast paragraph:

> Although contemporary fans would find the game played by the Knickerbockers—the first organized baseball club—similar to modern baseball, they would also note some startling differences. In 1845, as now, the four bases of the playing field were set in a diamond shape, ninety feet from one another. Nine players took the field. The object of the game was to score points by hitting a pitched ball and running around the bases. The teams changed sides after three outs. However, the earlier game was also different. The umpire sat at a table along the third-base line instead of standing behind home plate. Unlike the modern game, the players wore no gloves. Rather than firing the ball over the plate at ninety miles an hour, the pitcher gently tossed it underhand to the batter. Since there were no balls and strikes, the batter could wait for the pitch he wanted. The game ended not when nine innings were completed but when one team scored twenty-one runs, which were called "aces."

- How are the Knickerbockers' game and modern baseball similar?

  Both have four bases ninety feet apart in a diamond shape; nine players; both score points by runs; both have three outs.

- How are these two versions of the game different?

  In the Knickerbockers' game, umpire sat at a table on third-base line, players wore no gloves, pitcher gently tossed the ball, there were no balls and strikes, a team needed twenty-one "aces" to win, and there were no innings. In the modern game, umpire stands at home plate, pitcher fires the ball, there are balls and strikes, team with the most runs wins, and game is composed of nine innings.

- What transitional words and expressions in the paragraph emphasize similarities and differences?

  although, as now, however, unlike, rather than, not when, but when

Before composing this comparison and contrast paragraph, the writer probably brainstormed or freewrote to gather ideas and then made an **outline** like this:

TOPIC SENTENCE: Although contemporary fans would find the game played by the Knickerbockers—the first organized baseball club—similar to modern baseball, they would also note some startling differences.

Comparisons	**Knickerbockers**	**Modern Game**
Point 1	four bases, ninety feet apart, in diamond shape	
Point 2	nine players	
Point 3	scoring points	
Point 4	three outs	
Contrasts		
Point 1	umpire sat at third-base line	umpire at home plate
Point 2	no gloves	gloves
Point 3	pitcher gently tossed ball	pitcher fires ball at plate
Point 4	no balls and strikes	balls and strikes
Point 5	twenty-one "aces" to win, no innings	most runs to win, nine innings

- A plan or outline such as this makes it easier for the writer to organize a great deal of material.
- The writer begins by listing all the points of comparison—how the Knickerbockers' game and modern baseball are similar. Then the writer lists all the points of contrast—how they are different.

PRACTICE 7

Here is a somewhat longer comparison and contrast (two paragraphs). Read it carefully and answer the questions.

The New York and Los Angeles police departments are very different organizations. With 39,000 officers, the New York Police Department is larger than some European armies. In contrast, Los Angeles is served by only 9,000 officers. Because of the density of Manhattan, officers often walk beats, while in Los Angeles most officers work out of patrol cars to cover wider areas. The median pay for a police sergeant in New York is $91,000 a year, whereas in Los Angeles it is $84,000. The New York Police Department is more formal. Officers of higher rank wear different uniforms and badges. In addition, police officers are expected to salute superior officers and stand up when a superior enters the room. In contrast, Los Angeles officers wear the same uniform and only salute the flag or fallen officers at funerals.

Despite these differences, both departments share striking similarities. Both have inspired generations of hit television series and major motion pictures. Television shows have generally depicted the police in both cities as brave, honest, and caring professionals. Shows like *Kojak, Cagney and Lacey,* and *Law and Order* portrayed New

York police officers as dedicated crime fighters. Los Angeles officers were held up as moral crusaders in series like *Dragnet, Adam-12,* and *Police Story.* Motion pictures, however, often explore more complex themes. New York officers have been shown as corrupt and violent in films such as *Prince of the City, Serpico,* and *Bad Lieutenant.* Similarly, *LA Confidential, Training Day,* and *Internal Affairs* displayed Los Angeles officers as racist and crooked. Given their high profile in the media, both police departments will continue to inspire moviemakers and television writers.

1. What two persons or things does this writer compare and contrast?

   New York City and Los Angeles police departments

2. What words indicate that both contrast and comparison will follow?

   In contrast, Despite these differences...share similarities

3. How are the New York and Los Angeles police departments different?

   They differ in size, operation, pay, and formality.

4. How are the New York and Los Angeles police departments similar?

   Both have been widely depicted as honest and heroic in television shows and portrayed as violent and corrupt in motion pictures

5. Make a plan or outline for these paragraphs.

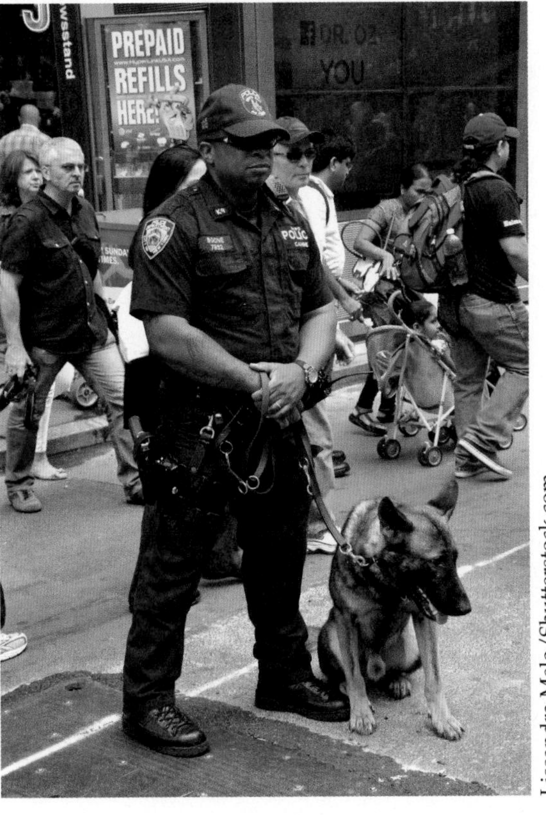

Lissandra Melo/Shutterstock.com

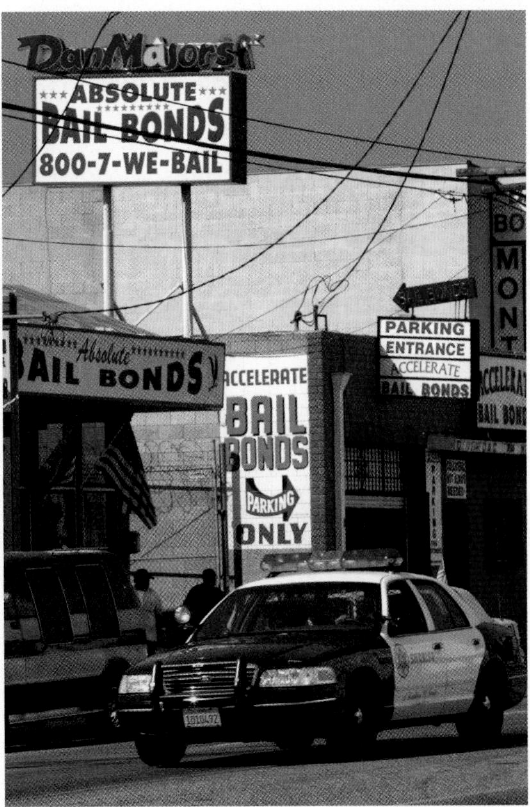

David McNew/Getty Images

A New York City police officer patrolling in Times Square and a Los Angeles police officer patrolling near Mission Junction

Working Through the Comparison and Contrast Paragraph

You can work through the comparison and contrast paragraph in the same way that you do a comparison paragraph or a contrast paragraph. Follow the steps in the earlier checklist, but make certain that your paragraph shows both similarities and differences.

Suggested Topics for Comparison and Contrast Paragraphs

1. Compare and contrast two different cars you have driven.
2. Compare and contrast the requirements of two jobs or careers.
3. Compare and contrast weddings, parties, or funerals in two different cultures.
4. Compare and contrast two smartphones, videos, or websites on similar subjects.
5. Compare and contrast your life now and your life five years ago.
6. Compare and contrast how two people you know coped with a similar problem such as the loss of a job, a divorce, or the death of a family member.
7. Compare and contrast shopping in person and shopping online.
8. Compare and contrast two popular television programs of the same type (newscasts, talk shows, situation comedies, and so on).
9. Compare and contrast two attitudes toward one subject (firearms, immigration, and so on).
10. Writer's choice: ______________________________

EXPLORING ONLINE

lrs.ed.uiuc.edu/students/fwalters/compcont.html

Review of the comparison/contrast paragraph, with examples

www.sbcc.edu/clrc/files/wl/downloads/WritingaCompareContrastEssay.pdf

Print these graphic outlines to help plan your paragraph.

CHAPTER 11

Classification

TEACHING TIP
To introduce the lesson, you might ask students to classify groups of everyday objects (shoes, cars, college courses, magazines, etc.) or even objects you bring in, from buttons to print advertisements.

To **classify** is to gather into types, kinds, or categories according to a single basis of division. Mailroom personnel, for example, might separate incoming mail into four piles: orders, bills, payments, and inquiries. Once the mail has been divided in this manner—according to which department should receive each pile—it can be efficiently delivered.

The same information can be classified in more than one way. The Census Bureau collects a variety of data about the people living in the United States. One way to classify the data is by age group—the number of people under eighteen, between eighteen and fifty-five, over fifty-five, and over seventy. Such information might be useful in developing programs for college-bound youth or for the elderly. Other ways of dividing the population are by geographic location, occupation, family size, level of education, and so on.

Whether you classify rocks by their origin for a geology course or children by their stages of growth for a psychology course, you will be organizing large groups into smaller, more manageable units that can be explained to your reader.

Topic Sentence

Here is the topic sentence for a classification paragraph:

> Gym-goers can be classified according to their priorities at the gym as sweaty fanatics, fashionistas, busybodies, or fit normals.

- The writer begins a classification paragraph with a topic sentence that clearly states what group of people or things will be classified.

- What group of people will be classified?

  gym-goers

- Into how many categories will they be divided? What are the categories?

  four: sweaty fanatics, fashionistas, busybodies, and fit normals

Paragraph and Plan

Here is the entire paragraph:

ESL TIP

ESL students may struggle to produce creative yet accurate names for groups in classification writing. Use the topic sentence about gym-goers to help students practice inventing terms.

Gym-goers can be classified according to their priorities at the gym as sweaty fanatics, fashionistas, busybodies, or fit normals. Sweaty fanatics take gym-going to the extreme. They hog the machines, drip sweat everywhere, and barely look up if someone falls off the treadmill beside them. Occasionally, they will stare at the mirror, admiring the muscle group they are working on. The fashionistas also admire their own reflections, but they barely break a sweat. For them, the gym is just another excuse to buy clothes. They wear perfectly matched workout clothes with color-coordinated sport watches and gym shoes. The third group, the busybodies, can't stop talking. Whether it's making idle chitchat or correcting another exerciser's form on a machine, they seem unable to shut up. Not even headphones and one-word answers can stop the busybodies from babbling. Luckily, the fit normals keep things from getting too far out of control. They come to the gym to work out, stay healthy, and go home, but they remember that basic good manners apply in every setting.

—Laurie Zamot, Student

- On what basis does the writer classify gym-goers?

  their priorities at the gym

- What information does the writer provide about the first type, sweaty fanatics?

  They hog machines, drip sweat, and don't notice anyone but themselves.

- What information does the writer provide about the second type, fashionistas?

  They admire themselves, barely sweat, and come to show off their outfits.

- What information does the writer provide about the third type, busybodies?

  They can't stop talking, even when others wear headphones and give short answers.

- What information does the writer provide about the fourth type, the fit normals?

  They balance things by working out but not forgetting good manners.

- Why do you think the writer discusses fit normals last?

  The writer starts with crazier and funnier types; the normals keep them all from going out of control.

Before composing the paragraph, the writer probably brainstormed or free-wrote to gather ideas and then made an **outline** like this:

TOPIC SENTENCE: Gym-goers can be classified according to their priorities at the gym as sweaty fanatics, fashionistas, busybodies, or fit normals.

Type 1: Sweaty fanatics
—hog machines; drip sweat
—barely look if someone falls
—stare in mirror, admiring muscles

Type 2: Fashionistas
—admire themselves but don't sweat
—excuse to buy clothes
—matched workout clothes
—coordinating sport watches and gym shoes

Type 3: Busybodies
—can't stop talking, advising
—headphones, short answers don't work

Type 4: Fit normals
—keep things from going out of control
—work out, go home
—remember good manners even in gym

- Note that the body of the paragraph discusses all four types of gym-goers mentioned in the topic sentence and does not add any new ones.

This classification paragraph sticks to a single method of classification: *the priorities of gym-goers at the gym*. If the paragraph had also discussed a fourth category—*left-handed gym-goers*—the initial basis of classification would fall apart because *left-handedness* has nothing to do with *the priorities of different gym-goers*.

The topic sentence of a classification paragraph usually has two parts: the *topic* and the *basis of classification*. The basis of classification is the controlling idea: it *controls* how the writer will approach the topic. Stating it in writing will help keep the paragraph on track.

There is no set rule about which category to present first, second, or last in a classification paragraph. However, the paragraph should follow some kind of **logical sequence** from the most to least outrageous, least to most expensive, from the largest to the smallest category, and so on.*

Transitional Expressions

Transitional expressions in classification paragraphs stress divisions and categories:

Transitional Expressions for Classification	
can be divided	the first type
can be classified	the second kind
can be categorized	the last category

PRACTICE 1

Read the following paragraph carefully and answer the questions.

TEACHING TIP

Stimulate critical thinking by asking students to give an example of each type of friend. Or ask, "Is anyone lucky enough to have a *friendship of the good*?"

In his classic discussion of friendship, the Greek philosopher Aristotle divided friends into three categories, based on the reason for the friendship. *Friendships of utility* are those in which two people are drawn together for mutual benefit. For example, two nurse's aides may develop a friendship through helping each other on the job, or two classmates may become friends because they study together. In this type of friendship, the connection frequently is broken when the situation changes, when one person takes another job, or the class ends. In the second type, *friendships of pleasure,* two people find it pleasurable to spend time together. Two passionate lovers fall into this category. Other examples are young people who hang out for fun, golf buddies, or hiking pals. When the pleasure fades, these friends may part ways. Either of these two types, however, can evolve into the more lasting third type, *friendships of the good*, or true friendships. These relationships are based on mutual admiration for the other's values and overall goodness, which creates a desire to interact and offer assistance. Lifelong friendships formed in childhood and friendships that endure despite separations, hardship, or changes in personal circumstances are true friendships. Aristotle's categories might explain why some people consider themselves lucky if they count just one true friend in a lifetime.

1. How many categories are there, and what are they?

three: friendships of utility, friendships of pleasure, and friendships of the good

2. On what basis does the writer classify friendships?

the reason for caring about each other

3. Make a plan or outline of the paragraph.

*For more work on order, see Chapter 4, "Achieving Coherence," Part A. For complete essays developed by classification, see Chapter 17, Part B.

PRACTICE 2

Each group of things or persons in this practice has been divided according to a single basis of classification. However, one item in each group does not belong—it does not fit that single basis of classification.

Read each group of items carefully; then circle the letter of the one item that does *not* belong. Next write the single basis of classification that includes the rest of the group.

EXAMPLE Television shows

a. game shows

b. reality shows

(c.) popular shows

d. talk shows

format ____________

1. Aircraft

a. single engine

b. twin engines

(c.) jet engine

d. four engines

number of engines ____________

2. Flooring

(a.) green

b. tile

c. hardwood

d. carpet

material ____________

3. Voters

(a.) donate to presidential campaigns

b. vote in every primary and general election

c. vote occasionally

d. never vote

frequency of voting ____________

4. Dresses

a. silk

b. cotton

(c.) formal

d. satin

material ____________

5. People

a. elderly

b. adolescent

c. infant

(d.) healthy

age ____________

6. Rock climbers

a. beginner

(b.) adventurous

c. professional

d. intermediate

level of experience ____________

PRACTICE 3

TEACHING TIP
Practice 3 works well as a small-group activity.

Any group of persons, things, or ideas can be classified in more than one way, depending on the basis of classification. For instance, students in your class can be classified on the basis of height (short, average, tall) or on the basis of class participation (often participate, sometimes participate, never participate). Both of these groupings are valid classifications of the same group of people.

Think of two ways in which each of the following groups could be classified. Answers will vary.

	Group	Basis of Classification
EXAMPLE	Houses	(A) *how large they are*
		(B) *how expensive they are*
	1. Politicians	(A) how they stand on an issue
		(B) how long they have served in office
	2. Infectious diseases	(A) how serious they are
		(B) how contagious they are
	3. Smartphones	(A) how much they cost
		(B) how durable they are
	4. Dieters	(A) how many calories they consume
		(B) how strictly they follow their diets
	5. Airline passengers	(A) how often they fly
		(B) how far they fly

ESL TIP
ESL students may prefer to narrow their classification topics by culture, for example, shopping in Cairo. Remind them that their cultural experiences offer many writing topics.

PRACTICE 4

TEACHING TIP
Have students share their answers to Practice 4 so that they can see others' ideas. This will reinforce the fact that, though different bases for classifying exist, the writer chooses one.

Listed below are three groups of people or things. Decide on a single basis of classification for each group and the categories that would develop from your basis of classification. Finally, write a topic sentence for each of your classifications. Answers will vary.

	Group	Basis of Classification	Categories
EXAMPLE	Professors at Pell College	*methods of instruction*	*lectures*
			class discussions
			both

TOPIC SENTENCE: *Professors at Pell College can be classified according to their methods of instruction: those who lecture, those who encourage class discussions, and those who do both.*

ESL TIP
ESL students may need to review word forms or parts of speech to express categories in parallel form. Use a model topic sentence from Practice 4 to illustrate.

Group	Basis of Classification	Categories
1. Car owners	how clean they keep their cars	very neat
		moderately neat
		not neat at all

TOPIC SENTENCE: Most car owners can be classified according to how clean they keep their vehicles: those whose cars are very neat, those whose cars are moderately neat, and those whose cars are not neat at all.

Group	Basis of Classification	Categories
2. Credit-card users	how much they use their cards	use only in emergencies
		use in moderation
		charge themselves into debt and into trouble

TOPIC SENTENCE: Credit-card users fall into three categories: those who use their cards only in emergencies, those who use their cards in moderation, and those who charge themselves into debt and into trouble.

Group	Basis of Classification	Categories
3. Ways of reacting to a crisis	how much emotion shown	people who cry or yell
		people who talk calmly
		people who don't talk at all

TOPIC SENTENCE: People react to crises in very different ways: by crying or yelling, by talking calmly, or by remaining completely silent.

PRACTICE 5

Now choose the classification in Practice 4 that most interests you and make a plan or outline for a paragraph. As you work, make sure that you have listed all possible categories for your basis of classification. Remember, every car owner, credit-card user, or person reacting to a crisis should fit into one of your categories. Finally, write your paragraph, describing each category briefly and perhaps giving an example of each.

PRACTICE 6 CRITICAL THINKING AND WRITING

Classify Students on Campus

Consider ways in which you might classify the students at your college. List at least five possible ways. You might focus on students in just one place—like the computer lab, swimming pool, coffee stand, library, or an exam room during finals week. Then come up with one basis of classification, either serious or humorous. For example, you could classify swimmers according to their level of expertise or splashing, students during finals week according to their fashion statements, or students standing in line for coffee according to their degree of impatience.

Now choose the most interesting basis of classification. Name three or four categories that cover the group, and write a paragraph classifying your fellow students. You might wish to enrich your categories with details and examples. Be prepared to read your paragraph to the class.

TEACHING TIP

For downloadable rubrics corresponding to each rhetorical mode, go to the *Instructor Companion Site.*

Checklist

The Process of Writing a Classification Paragraph

Refer to this checklist of steps as you write a classification paragraph.

- ☐ 1. Narrow the topic to suit your audience and purpose. Think in terms of a group of people or things that can be classified easily into types or categories.
- ☐ 2. Decide on a single basis of classification. This basis will depend on what information you wish to give your audience.
- ☐ 3. Compose a topic sentence that clearly shows what you are dividing into categories or types. If you wish, your topic sentence can state the basis on which you are making the classification and the types that will be discussed in the paragraph.
- ☐ 4. List the categories into which the group is being classified. Be sure that your categories cover all the possibilities. Do not add any new categories that are not logically part of your original basis of classification.
- ☐ 5. Freewrite, cluster, or brainstorm to generate information, details, and examples for each of the categories. (You may want to prewrite before you narrow the topic.)
- ☐ 6. Select the best details and examples, and drop those that are not relevant to your classification.
- ☐ 7. Make a plan or an outline for your paragraph, numbering the categories in the order in which you will present them.
- ☐ 8. Write a draft of your classification paragraph, using transitional expressions wherever they may be helpful.
- ☐ 9. Revise as necessary, checking for support, unity, logic, and coherence.
- ☐ 10. Proofread for errors in grammar, punctuation, sentence structure, spelling, and mechanics.

Suggested Topics for Classification Paragraphs

1. Ways that people manage their finances (organize or make decisions)
2. Co-workers at your job
3. Problems facing college freshmen or someone new to a job
4. Websites you have bookmarked
5. Types of viral videos on YouTube
6. Local restaurants
7. Dancers at a party or club
8. Ways that students prepare for exams
9. Online shoppers
10. Performers of one kind of music
11. Ways of commuting to work or school
12. Financial aid sources for college students
13. Styles of shoes
14. Hobbies
15. Writer's choice: ______________________________

EXPLORING ONLINE

www.filmratings.com
Click "How" for movie classifications.

blog.kaspersky.com/a-malware-classification/3037
A helpful breakdown of the types of computer malware

CHAPTER 12

Cause and Effect

TEACHING TIP

Ask students to brainstorm examples of cause and effect paragraphs they might have to write on the job.

The ability to think through **causes and effects** is a key to success in many college courses, jobs, and everyday situations. Daily we puzzle over the **causes** of, or reasons for, events: What caused one brother to drop out of school and another to succeed brilliantly? What causes Jenine's asthma attacks? Why did the stock market plunge 300 points?

Effects are the *results* of a cause or causes. Does playing violent computer games affect a child's behavior? What are the effects of being a twin, keeping a secret, or winning the lottery?

Most events worth examining have complex, not simple, causes and effects. That is, they may have several causes and several effects. Certainly, in many fields, questions of cause and effect challenge even the experts: *What is causing the rapid decline in the honeybee population? What will be the long-term effects of U.S. involvement in the war in Afghanistan?*

Topic Sentence

Here is the topic statement of a cause and effect paragraph; the writer has chosen to break the information into two sentences.

> What killed off the dinosaurs—and 70 percent of life on earth—65 million years ago? According to recent research, this massive destruction had three causes.

- The writer begins a cause and effect paragraph by clearly stating the subject and indicating whether causes or effects will be discussed. What is the subject of this paragraph? Will causes or effects be the focus?

  what killed the dinosaurs, causes

- The writer states the topic in two sentences rather than one. Is this effective? Why or why not? (A single sentence might read, "According to recent research, the massive destruction of dinosaurs and other creatures 65 million years ago had three causes.")

  Starting with a question sparks reader's interest.

- Words like *causes, reasons,* and *factors* are useful to show causes. Words like *effects, results,* and *consequences* are useful to show effects.

Paragraph and Plan

Here is the entire paragraph:

> What killed off the dinosaurs—and 70 percent of life on Earth—65 million years ago? According to recent research, this massive destruction had three causes. Dr. Peter Ward of the University of Washington reports that the first cause was simple "background extinction." This is the normal disappearance of some animals and plants that goes on all the time. Second, a drop in sea level during this period slowly destroyed about 25 percent more of the world's species. Last and most dramatic, a comet as big as Manhattan smashed into the earth near Mexico's Yucatan Peninsula, literally shaking the world. The huge buried crater left by this comet was found in 1991. Now Dr. Ward has proved that ash and a rare metal from that fiery crash fell around the globe. This means that the impact, fires, smoke, and ash quickly wiped out the dinosaurs and much of life on Earth. This great "die-off" cleared the way for mammals to dominate Earth.

- How many causes does this writer give for the destruction of the dinosaurs and other species? What are they?

  three: background extinction; drop in sea level; huge comet

- Did the writer make up these ideas? If not, who or what is the source of the information?

  no; Dr. Peter Ward, University of Washington

- What transitional words introduce each of the three causes?

  the first cause; second; last and most dramatic

- What kind of order is used in this paragraph?* ______

  order of importance

*For more work on order, see Chapter 4, "Achieving Coherence," Part A.

Before writing the paragraph, the writer probably brainstormed or freewrote to gather ideas and then made an **outline** like this:

TOPIC SENTENCE: According to recent research, this massive destruction had three causes.

—write a catchy introductory sentence?
—mention time, 65 million years ago

Cause 1: "background extinction"
—normal disappearance of animals and plants
—give credit to Dr. Ward

Cause 2: drop in sea level
—25 percent more species destroyed

Cause 3: giant comet hit earth
—big as Manhattan
—crater found in 1991 near Yucatan Peninsula
—now Ward proves ash and rare metal circled globe
—this comet destroyed dinosaurs and others

CONCLUSION: "Die-off" cleared way for mammals—OR tie to current news and films about comet danger

Other paragraphs examine *effects*, not causes. Either they try to predict future effects of something happening now, or they analyze past effects of something that happened earlier, as does this paragraph:

ESL TIP

Ask your ESL students to find synonyms for the word *effect* in this model paragraph. Have them brainstorm synonyms for *cause* and *effect* so they do not overuse these terms.

For Christy Haubegger, the lack of Latina role models had life-changing consequences. As a Mexican American girl adopted by Anglo parents, Christy found no reflection of herself in teen magazines or books. One result of seeing mostly blonde, blue-eyed models was an increase in her adolescent insecurities. A more damaging effect was Christy's confusion as she wondered what career to pursue; there were no Hispanic role models in schoolbooks to suggest possible futures for this excellent student. Even at Stanford Law School, Christy and her friends missed the inspiration and encouragement of professional Latina role models. At Stanford, Christy began to see this problem as an opportunity. She decided to start a national magazine that would showcase talented and successful Latinas. The 27-year-old made a detailed business plan and, incredibly, won the financial backing of the CEO of *Essence* magazine. In 1996, the first issue of *Latina* hit the newstands—the very positive consequence of an old loneliness.

- Underline the topic sentence in this paragraph.
- For Ms. Haubegger, the lack of Latina role models caused "life-changing consequences." What effects are discussed?

increased adolescent insecurities; no professional role models: her decision to start *Latina* magazine

ESL AND LEARNING STYLES TIP
ESL learners and others may prefer to brainstorm and organize causes or effects visually, in diagrams. To view many options, go to **faculty.bucks.edu/specpop/visual-org.htm.**

- What order does the writer follow? time order
- Notice that the paragraph first discusses negative effects and then a positive one.

Before you write about causes or effects, do some mental detective work. First, search out the three most important causes or effects. For example, if you are trying to understand the cause for the closing of a suburban shopping mall, you might consider changing consumer habits, the condition of the mall, and downtown redevelopment.

Causes	*Effect*	*Further Effects*
declining sales		*loss of jobs*
competition from online shopping	*closure of mall*	*loss of tax revenue to town*
aging, unappealing food court		*shoppers will head downtown*
popularity of downtown boutiques		*inconvenience to local residents*

In exploring the effects of something, consider both short-term and long-term effects and both negative and positive effects. (Although the mall closing will cause unemployment and revenue losses in the suburbs, it may increase business downtown as consumers shop elsewhere.)

What does this image illustrate? What is the cause and what is the effect? Can the last dominos be considered "further effects"? Can you think of technological, social, economic, or personal problems that follow a similar pattern?

Tetra Images/Alamy Stock Photo

TEACHING TIP
Ask students to think of news stories or personal opinions that illustrate these problems. These can be fun to share in class.

Problems to Avoid in Cause and Effect Writing

1. **Do not oversimplify.** Avoid the trap of naming one cause for a complex problem: Why did they divorce? Because he is moody. Or, The reason that reading scores have fallen in the school is television. Searching for the three most important causes or effects is a good way to avoid oversimplifying.
2. **Do not confuse time order with causation.** If your eye starts watering seconds after the doorbell rings, you cannot assume that the doorbell made your eye water. Were you peeling onions? Is it allergy season? Do you need to wet your contact lenses?

3. **Do not confuse causes and effects.** Separating causes and effects can be tricky. (Is Rita's positive attitude the cause of her success in sales or the result of it?)

Transitional Expressions

These transitional expressions are helpful in cause and effect paragraphs, which often imply order of importance or time order:*

Transitional Expressions for Cause and Effect	
To Show Causes	*To Show Effects*
the first cause (second, third)	one important effect
the first reason (second, third)	another result
yet another factor	a third outcome
because of	as a result
is caused by	consequently
results from	then, next, therefore, thus

PRACTICE 1

Read this paragraph and answer the questions.

> Type 2 diabetes is a damaging blood sugar disease that often can be prevented, but new cases in the United States have doubled in just ten years. To protect themselves and their families from type 2 diabetes, all Americans, especially parents, should understand its possible causes. The most important cause is obesity. The more fatty tissue a person has, the more his or her cells have trouble controlling blood sugar. Not surprisingly, as the numbers of overweight Americans increase, so do cases of type 2 diabetes. Second, inactivity feeds this disease. Inactive people gain more weight, but exercise doesn't just keep off pounds; it also turns blood sugar into energy and helps the cells control blood sugar. Third, a poor diet with lots of fried and fatty foods brings on type 2 diabetes, especially in people with a fourth cause, family history. Anyone with diabetes in the family or from certain racial backgrounds (for example, Hispanics, blacks, and Asians) has a higher risk. People can't change their genes, but they can fight type 2 diabetes by losing weight, exercising, and saying no to fatty foods.
>
> —Itan Harjo, Student

1. Underline the topic sentence. Does this paragraph discuss the causes or effects of type 2 diabetes?

   causes

*To read essays of cause and effect, see Chapter 17, Part C.

2. How many causes does this writer discuss? Which ones are controllable, and which are not?

   four: the first three are controllable

3. Make a plan or outline of this paragraph.

PRACTICE 2

To practice separating cause from effect, write the cause and the effect contained in each item below.

EXAMPLE Fewer people are attending concerts at the Boxcar Theater because ticket prices have nearly doubled.

Cause: *ticket prices nearly doubled*

Effect: *fewer people attending concerts*

TEACHING TIP
Many conjunctions and transitional expressions express cause and effect relationships. Reviewing these may help students more clearly present their ideas in cause and effect writing. (See Chapter 4, Part B; Chapter 22, Part D; and Chapter 26.)

1. A severe blizzard brought two feet of snow to the area, so school was canceled.

   Cause: a severe blizzard

   Effect: school cancelled

2. Seeing my father suffer because he could not read motivated me to excel in school.

   Cause: saw my father suffer because he could not read

   Effect: I excelled in school

3. One study showed that laughter extended the lives of cancer patients.

   Cause: laughter

   Effect: extended lives of cancer patients

4. Americans are having fewer children and doing so later in life. Some experts believe this is why they are spending more money every year on their pets.

   Cause: Americans having fewer children later

   Effect: spending more money on pets

5. Many doctors urged that trampolines be banned because of an "epidemic" of injuries to children playing on them.

   Cause: children playing on trampolines

   Effect: epidemic of injuries

6. I bought a bicycle for one reason only: cars are too expensive.

   Cause: cars are too expensive

   Effect: I bought a bicycle

7. As more people spend time surfing the Internet, television viewing is declining for the first time in fifty years.

   Cause: more people surfing the Internet

   Effect: first decline in TV viewing in fifty years

8. Due to improper management of the manufacturing plant, run-off from the plant polluted the surrounding groundwater. Consequently, the government declared the area a hazardous waste zone.

   Cause: improper management

   First Effect: polluted groundwater

   Second Effect: government declared the area a hazardous waste zone

PRACTICE 3

TEACHING TIP

Practice 3 works well as a small-group activity.

List three causes *or* three effects to support each topic sentence below. First, read the topic sentence to see whether causes or effects are called for. Then list your three best ideas.

1. The huge success of Barbie (or some other toy, game, or product) has a number of causes.

   ____

   ____

   ____

2. There are several reasons why teenagers start smoking despite widespread knowledge about the dangers of tobacco.

   ____

   ____

   ____

3. Using social media has many positive and negative effects on teenagers.

   ____

   ____

   ____

PRACTICE 4

Now choose one topic from Practice 3 that interests you and write a paragraph of cause or effect. Before you write a draft, make a plan. Have you chosen the three most important causes or effects and decided on an effective order in which to present them? As you write, use transitional expressions to help the reader follow your ideas.

PRACTICE 5 CRITICAL THINKING AND WRITING

Analyze Possible Reasons Why the High School Dropout Rate Has Declined

Read the following statistics. Then follow the directions.

1. The number of high school dropouts declined from over a million in 2008 to 750,000 in 2012, a 27 percent reduction.
2. The high school graduation rate increased from 74.7 percent in 2008 to 80.9 percent in 2012.
3. The number of "dropout factories," or schools where large numbers of students fail to graduate, dropped from 1,800 in 2008 to 1,000 in 2014.

—Lauren Camera, "Fewer Students Dropping Out of School," *U.S. News & World Report*, November 10, 2015

What do you think has caused the dropout rate to decrease since 2008? First, brainstorm a list of possible causes. Then list your strongest three causes in the order of importance. How would you try to persuade a teenage relative to stay in school?

TEACHING TIP
For downloadable rubrics corresponding to each rhetorical mode, go to the *Instructor Companion Site.*

Checklist

The Process of Writing a Cause and Effect Paragraph

Refer to this checklist of steps as you write a cause and effect paragraph.

☐ 1. Narrow the topic to fit your audience and purpose. Think of a subject that can be analyzed for clear causes or effects.

☐ 2. Decide whether you will emphasize causes or effects. What information would be most interesting to your audience?

☐ 3. Compose a topic sentence that states the subject and indicates whether causes or effects will be discussed.

☐ 4. Now freewrite, brainstorm, or cluster to find at least three possible causes or effects. Do your mental detective work. At this stage, think of all possible causes; think of short- and long-term effects, as well as positive and negative effects.

☐ 5. Select the best causes or effects with which to develop your paragraph. Drop those that are not relevant.

☐ 6. Make a plan or an outline for your paragraph, numbering the causes or effects in the order in which you will present them.

☐ 7. Write a first draft of your cause and effect paragraph, explaining each point fully so that your reader understands just how X caused Y. Use transitional expressions to emphasize these relationships.

- [ ] 8. Revise as necessary, checking for good support, unity, logic, and coherence. Does your paragraph have an interesting opening sentence?
- [ ] 9. Proofread for errors in grammar, punctuation, sentence structure, spelling, and mechanics. Especially watch for your personal error patterns.

Suggested Topics for Cause and Effect Paragraphs

1. Reasons why someone made an important decision
2. Causes of a politician's victory or defeat at the polls
3. Reasons why people want to start their own business
4. Causes of a marriage or divorce (friendship or end of friendship)
5. Reasons why a book, motion picture, video, commercial, or artistic performance created controversy
6. Causes of an act of courage or cowardice
7. Causes or effects of membership in a group (choir, band, sports team, church, or gang)
8. Effects of high blood pressure, alcoholism, diabetes, or some other illness
9. Effects of a certain event (like the death of a loved one, a medical diagnosis, or a move to a new place)
10. Effects of divorce on children
11. Effects of living in a particular place (such as a repressive country or home or a place that is rural, urban, poor, rich, ethnically diverse)
12. Effects (positive or negative) of working while going to college
13. Effects of conspiracy theories
14. Effects of social media, smartphones, or other technology on a person's life
15. Writer's choice: ______________________________

EXPLORING ONLINE

www2.elc.polyu.edu.hk/cill/exercises/cause&effect.htm

Review of vocabulary and grammar needed to describe causes and effects

web.calstatela.edu/faculty/lgarret/organiz1.htm

Helpful advice on organizing cause and effect papers

CHAPTER 13

Persuasion

TEACHING TIP
Let students know that this is one of the most important chapters in *Evergreen* because the ability to write logically and persuasively is central to success in college and most careers.

To **persuade** is to convince someone that a particular opinion or point of view is the correct one. Any time you argue with a friend, you are each trying to persuade or convince the other that your opinion is the right one. Commercials and advertisements are another form of persuasion. Advertisers attempt to convince the audience that the product they sell—whether jeans, a soft drink, or an automobile—is the best one to purchase.

You will often have to persuade in writing. For instance, if you want a raise, you will have to write a persuasive memo to convince your employer that you deserve one. You will have to back up, or support, your request with proof, listing important projects you have completed, noting new responsibilities you have taken upon yourself, or showing how you have increased sales.

Once you learn how to persuade logically and rationally, you will be less likely to accept the false, misleading, and emotional arguments that you hear and read every day. Persuasion is vital in daily life, in nearly all college courses, and in most careers.

Topic Sentence

Here is the topic sentence of a **persuasive** paragraph:

> Passengers should refuse to ride in any vehicle driven by someone who has been drinking.

- The writer begins a persuasive paragraph by stating clearly what he or she is arguing for or against. What will this persuasive paragraph argue against?

  This paragraph will argue against riding with a driver who has been drinking.

- Words like *should*, *ought*, and *must* (and the negatives *should not*, *ought not*, and *must not*) are especially effective in the topic sentence of a persuasive paragraph.

Paragraph and Plan

Here is the entire paragraph:

TEACHING TIP
Guide students to see how a fact or statistic improves credibility and helps persuade the reader. Point out the wealth of data available in print and online. (See also Chapter 19, "Strengthening an Essay with Research.")

Passengers should refuse to ride in any vehicle driven by someone who has been drinking. First and most important, such a refusal could save lives. The National Council on Alcoholism reports that drunk driving causes 25,000 deaths and 50 percent of all traffic accidents each year. Not only the drivers but the passengers who agree to travel with them are responsible. Second, riders might tell themselves that some people drive well even after a few drinks, but this is just not true. Dr. Burton Belloc of the local Alcoholism Treatment Center explains that even one drink can lengthen the reflex time and weaken the judgment needed for safe driving. Other riders might feel foolish to ruin a social occasion or inconvenience themselves or others by speaking up, but risking their lives is even more foolish. Finally, by refusing to ride with a drinker, one passenger could influence other passengers or the driver. Marie Furillo, a student at Central High School, is an example. When three friends who had obviously been drinking offered her a ride home from school, she refused, despite the driver's teasing. Hearing Marie's refusal, two of her friends got out of the car. Until the laws are changed and a vast re-education takes place, the bloodshed on American highways will probably continue. But there is one thing people can do: they can refuse to risk their lives for the sake of a party.

TEACHING TIP
Prompt critical thinking and writing by pairing alcohol advertising statistics (**www.madd.org**) and Adbusters' dark parody ads for vodka (**www.adbusters.org/spoofads/absolut-craze**). To grasp the latter, students should be familiar with the slick Absolut campaign.

- The first reason in the argument **predicts the consequence**. If passengers refuse to ride with drinkers, what will the consequence be?

  Lives could be saved.

- The writer also supports this reason with **facts**. What are the facts?

  Drunk driving causes 25,000 deaths and 50 percent of all traffic accidents each year.

- The second reason in the argument is really an **answer to the opposition**. That is, the writer anticipates the critics. What point is the writer answering?

  The writer is answering the point that some people believe they drive well even after having a few drinks.

- The writer supports this reason by **referring to an authority**. That is, the writer gives the opinion of someone who can provide unbiased and valuable information about the subject. Who is the authority, and what does this person say?

  Dr. Burton Belloc of the Alcoholism Treatment Center notes that even one drink affects a driver's reflexes.

- The third reason in the argument is that risking your life is foolish. This reason is really another **answer to the opposition**. What point is the writer answering?

  The writer is answering the point that people hesitate to be "party poopers."

- The final reason in the argument is that one passenger could influence others. What **example** does the writer supply to back up this reason?

  Marie Furillo refused a ride home from school because the driver had been drinking. Her refusal influenced the two passengers to get out of the car.

- Persuasive paragraphs either can begin with the most important reason and then continue with less important ones, or they can begin with the least important reasons, saving the most important for last.* This paragraph begins with what the author considers *most* important. How can you tell?

  The writer states that the first point is the most important.

Before composing this persuasive paragraph, the writer probably brainstormed or freewrote to gather ideas and then made an **outline** like this:

TEACHING TIP
Stress the importance of outlining before writing an argument. Urge students to consider carefully the order of their ideas before they write.

TOPIC SENTENCE: Passengers should refuse to ride in any vehicle driven by someone who has been drinking.

Reason 1: Refusal could save lives **(predicting a consequence)**.
—statistics on deaths and accidents **(facts)**
—passengers are equally responsible

Reason 2: Riders might say some drinkers drive well—not true **(answering the opposition)**.
—Dr. Belloc's explanation **(referring to authority)**

Reason 3: Others might feel foolish speaking up, but risking lives is more foolish **(answering the opposition)**.

Reason 4: One rider might influence other passengers.
—Marie Furillo **(example)**

CONCLUSION: Bloodshed will probably continue, but people can refuse to risk their lives.

- Note how each reason clearly supports the topic sentence.

*For work on order of importance, see Chapter 4, "Achieving Coherence," Part A.

Transitional Expressions

The following transitional expressions are helpful in persuasive paragraphs:

Transitional Expressions for Persuasion		
Give Reasons	*Answer the Opposition*	*Draw Conclusions*
another, next	granted that	consequently
first (second, third)	of course	hence
importantly	on the other hand	therefore
last, finally	some may say	thus

Methods of Persuasion

The drinking-and-driving example showed the basic kinds of support used in persuasive paragraphs: **facts**, **referring to an authority**, **examples**, **predicting the consequences**, and **answering the opposition**. Although you will rarely use all of them in one paragraph, you should be familiar with them all. Here are some more details:

TEACHING TIP
Students may benefit from reviewing the difference between facts and opinions. Facts are information that can be verified; opinions are personal value judgments that cannot be verified.

1. **Facts: Facts** are simply statements of what is. They should appeal to the reader's mind, not just to emotions. The source of your facts should be clear to the reader. If you wish to prove that children's eyesight should be checked every year by a doctor, you might look for supporting facts in appropriate books and magazines, or you might ask your eye doctor for information. Your paper might say, "Many people suffer serious visual impairment later in life because they received insufficient or inadequate eye care when they were children, according to an article in Better Vision."*

   Avoid the vague "everyone knows that" or "it is common knowledge that" or "they all say." Such statements will make your reader justifiably suspicious of your "facts."

TEACHING TIP
Engage students in a discussion about what kinds of education, training, or experience qualify someone as an authority on a subject.

2. **Referring to an authority:** An **authority** is an expert, someone who can be relied on to give unbiased facts and information. If you wish to convince your readers that asthma is a far more serious illness than most people realize, you might speak with an emergency-room physician about the numbers of patients treated for asthma attacks, or you might quote experts from the literature of national organizations like the Asthma and Allergy Foundation of America or the American Lung Association. These are all excellent and knowledgeable authorities whose opinions on medical matters would be considered valid and unbiased.

   Avoid appealing to "authorities" who are interesting, talented, or glamorous but who are not experts in the field in question. A football player certainly knows about sports, but he probably knows little about internal medicine.

3. **Examples:** An **example** should clearly relate to the argument and should be typical enough to support it.† If you wish to convince your reader that high schools should provide more funds than they do for women's sports, you might say, "Jefferson High School, for instance, has received inquiries from

*For more work on summarizing and quoting outside sources, see Chapter 19, "Strengthening an Essay with Research."

†For more work on examples, see Chapter 5, "Illustration."

sixty female students who would be willing to join a women's basketball or softball team if the school could provide the uniforms, the space, and a coach."

Avoid examples that are not typical enough to support your general statement. That your friend was once bitten by a dog does not adequately prove that all dogs are dangerous pets.

4. **Predicting the consequence: Predicting the consequence** helps the reader visualize what will occur if something does or does not happen. To convince your readers that a college education should be free to all qualified students, you might say, "If bright but economically deprived students cannot attend college because they cannot afford it, our society will be robbed of their talents."

   Avoid exaggerating the consequence. For instance, telling the reader, "If you don't eat fresh fruit every day, you will never be truly healthy," exaggerates the consequences of not eating fresh fruit and makes the reader understandably suspicious.

5. **Answering the opposition: Answering possible critics** shows that you are aware of the opposition's argument and are able to respond to it. If you wish to convince your readers that your candidate is the best on the ballot, you might say, "Some have criticized him for running a low-key campaign, but he feels that the issues and his stand on them should speak for themselves."

   Avoid calling the opposition "stupid," "lame," or "weak." Avoid hurling accusations without proof or trying to win over readers with comic or sarcastic remarks. Base your criticism on objective facts and evidence. Attack your opponents' ideas, not their personal characters.

TEACHING TIP

An effective answer to the opposition has two parts: a brief, fair statement of the opposition's view and a persuasive reply. Words like *although*, *but*, and *whereas* underscore the contrast.

Building Blocks of Effective Persuasive Writing

Topic: Every college student should complete an internship in his or her field of study.

Facts	• Many employers seek both academic and "real-world" experience. • 60% of new college hires today have held an internship.
Authority	• Dr. Bennet, Dean of Nursing, says her internship program helps students get and hold good jobs. • According to the National Association of Colleges and Employers, 30% of all workers started as interns.
Examples	• Majors like pharmacy and business already sucessfully require student internships. • Tisa's internship let her "test drive" work as a paralegal.
Consequences	• Required internships will help students find employment in bad economic times. • Those without internships will be disadvantaged.
Answering opposition	• Students will receive college help in balancing their intern duties, part-time jobs, schoolwork, and personal lives.

TEACHING TIP

To give students more practice matching the right evidence with the audience, have small groups create charts like this one for other persuasive topics.

TEACHING TIP

Ask each student to bring in an example of persuasive writing, such as a newspaper editorial or magazine piece. Then have each student identify the author's method(s) of persuasion.

TEACHING TIP

Critical-thinking experts like Richard Paul stress that students need to practice objectivity by putting themselves in their opponent's position. Debating, defending an opinion they *don't* believe in, and practicing self-rebuttal are useful, eye-opening activities.

Considering the Audience

In addition to providing adequate proof for your argument, pay special attention to the audience as you write persuasively. In general, we assume that our audience is much like us—reasonable people who wish to learn the truth. But because argument can evoke strong feelings, directing your persuasive paper toward a particular audience can be helpful. Consider just *what kind of evidence* this audience would respond to. For instance, if you were attempting to persuade parents to monitor their children's use of social media, you could present examples of cyberbullying to grab their attention and alert them to the dangers. You might introduce facts to demonstrate the scope of the problem, then include suggestions by authorities, such as psychologists and teachers, to provide solutions and offer advice. In addition, you might say that you realize that parents could view this as an invasion of their children's privacy. By doing so, you let them know that you understand their resistance to the argument and that you are sympathetic to their doubts. When you take your audience into consideration, you will make your persuasive paragraph more convincing.*

PRACTICE 1

TEACHING TIP

Students can practice answering the opposition by writing rebuttals to one or more of the persuasive paragraphs in this chapter.

Read the following persuasive paragraph carefully and answer the questions.

American women should stop buying so-called women's magazines because these publications lower their self-esteem. First of all, publications like *Glamour* and *Cosmo* appeal to women's insecurities and make millions doing it. Topics like "Ten Days to Sexier Cleavage" and "How to Attract Mr. Right" lure women to buy seven million copies a month, reports Claire Ito in *The Tulsa Chronicle*, May 4, 2009. The message: women need to be improved. Second, although many people—especially magazine publishers—claim these periodicals build self-esteem, they really do the opposite. One expert in readers' reactions, Deborah Then, says that almost all women, regardless of age or education, feel worse about themselves after reading one of these magazines. Alice, one of the women I spoke with, is a good example: "I flip through pictures of world-class beauties and six-foot-tall skinny women, comparing myself to them. In more ways than one, I come up short." Finally, if women spent the money and time these magazines take on more self-loving activities—studying new subjects, developing mental or physical fitness, setting goals and daring to achieve them—they would really build self-worth. Sisters, seek wisdom, create what you envision, and above all, know that you can.

—Rochelle Revard, Student

1. What is this paragraph arguing for or against?

   The paragraph argues that women should stop buying women's magazines.

   ____

2. What audience is the writer addressing? women

*For more work on audience, see Chapter 1, "Exploring the Writing Process," Part B. For complete essays developed by persuasion, see Chapter 17, Part D.

3. Which reason is supported by facts? the first reason

   What are the facts, and where did the writer get them? Women buy seven million copies a month, according to Claire Ito, *The Tulsa Chronicle*, May 4, 2009.

4. Which reason answers the opposition? the second reason

5. Which reason is supported by an example? the second reason

   What is the example? Alice, one of the women interviewed

6. Which reason appeals to an authority? the second reason

   Who is the authority? Deborah Then, expert in readers' reactions

PRACTICE 2

Read the following paragraph carefully and answer the questions.

This state should offer free parenting classes, taught by experts, to anyone who wishes to become a parent. First and most important, such parenting classes could save children's lives. Every year, over two million American children are hurt, maimed, or killed by their own parents, according to the National Physicians Association. Some of these tragedies could be prevented by showing parents how to recognize and deal with their frustration and anger. Next, good parenting skills do not come naturally, but must be learned. Dr. Phillip Graham, chairman of England's National Children's Bureau, says that most parents have "no good role models" and simply parent the way they were parented. The courses would not only improve parenting skills but might also identify people at high risk of abusing their children. Third, critics might argue that the state has no business getting involved in parenting, which is a private responsibility. However, the state already makes decisions about who is a fit parent—in the courts, child-protection services, and adoption agencies—but often this is too late for the well-being of the child. Finally, if we do nothing, the hidden epidemic of child abuse and neglect will continue. We train our children's teachers, doctors, daycare workers, and bus drivers. We must also educate parents.

TEACHING TIP
Explain that writers need not include *I think* or *I believe* to preface an argument.

1. What is this paragraph arguing for or against? It is arguing that the state should offer free parenting courses to all prospective parents.

2. Which reason appeals to an authority for support? reason two

   Who is the authority? Dr. Phillip Graham, chairman of England's National Children's Bureau

3. Which reason answers the opposition? reason three

4. Which reason includes facts? What is the source of these facts? reason one; the National Physicians Association

5. What consequence does the writer predict if parenting classes are not offered? Reason four predicts that the "hidden epidemic of child abuse and neglect" will continue.

6. Does this writer convince you that parenting classes might make a difference? If you were writing a persuasion paragraph to oppose or support this writer, what would your topic sentence be?

   Answers will vary.

PRACTICE 3

So far you have learned five basic methods of persuasion: **facts, referring to an authority, examples, predicting the consequence**, and **answering the opposition**. Ten topic sentences for persuasive paragraphs follow. Write one reason in support of each topic sentence, using the method of persuasion indicated. Answers will vary.

TEACHING TIP

Practice 3 encourages practical application of the persuasive methods students have learned and promotes critical thinking. Try it as a small-group exercise or full-class activity.

Facts

1. Consumers should read the fine print on their credit-card statements carefully.

   Reason: Many consumers do not realize how much interest rates and penalties are costing them.

2. People should not get married until they are at least twenty-five years old.

   Reason: Statistics show that 75 percent of couples who marry before that age eventually divorce.

Referring to an Authority

(If you cannot think of an authority offhand, name the kind of person who would be an authority on the subject.)

3. Business students should learn a second language.

   Reason: According to top business leaders, Americans need to speak languages other than English to compete in the global economy.

4. Most people should get at least one hour of vigorous exercise three times a week.

   Reason: Dr. Pamela Lu of the Fitness Research Corporation notes that regular exercise can help prevent heart attacks and other life-threatening afflictions.

Examples

5. Pets should be allowed in children's hospital rooms because they speed healing.

   Reason: Adam, a six-year-old cancer patient who was deeply depressed, began to recover once his doctor allowed his silky terrier, Cola, to visit him.

6. The health department should inspect local restaurants more rigorously.

   Reason: Last month people dining in three downtown restaurants developed food poisoning from improper food handling.

Predicting the Consequence

7. Companies should (should not) be allowed to conduct random drug testing on employees.

   Reason: If companies can perform such tests, innocent people will be embarrassed, inconvenienced, and insulted.

8. The federal government should (should not) prohibit the sale of drugs from overseas.

   Reason: Without such a prohibition, unwitting patients may buy counterfeit drugs that are ineffective or harmful.

Answering the Opposition

(State the opposition's point of view and then refute it.)

9. This college should (should not) drop its required-attendance policy.

   Reason: Although some might argue that students would quickly stop going to class, most students would make responsible decisions to attend classes and to get an education.

10. Teenagers should (should not) be required to get their parents' permission before being allowed to get a tattoo.

    Reason: Although some teenagers may make mature and informed decisions, not all teenagers realize the consequences of getting tattoos, which may be difficult or painful to remove.

PRACTICE 4

TEACHING TIP

Practice 4 is instructive and enjoyable as a class exercise. The humor of some statements helps students see the fallacies. Have them verbalize the rationale behind their choices.

Each of the following sentences tells what you are trying to persuade someone to do. Beneath each sentence are four reasons that attempt to convince the reader that he or she should take this particular course of action. Circle the letter of the reason that *seems irrelevant, illogical,* or *untrue.*

1. If you wanted to persuade someone to do holiday shopping earlier, you might say that

   a. shopping earlier saves time.

   b. more gifts will be in stock.

   c. stores will not be overly crowded.

   (d.) Beyoncé and Jay Z shop early.

2. If you wanted to persuade someone to buy a particular brand of cereal, you might say that it

   a. is inexpensive.

   b. contains vitamins and minerals.

   (c.) comes in an attractive box.

   d. makes a hearty breakfast.

3. If you wanted to persuade someone to move to your town, you might say that

   a. two new companies have made jobs available.

   (b.) by moving to this town, he or she will become the happiest person in the world.

   c. there is a wide selection of housing.

   d. the area is lovely and still unpolluted.

4. If you wanted to persuade someone to vote for a particular candidate, you might say that she

   a. has always kept her promises to the voters.

   b. has lived in the district for thirty years.

   c. has substantial knowledge of the issues.

   (d.) dresses very fashionably.

5. If you wanted to persuade someone to learn to read and speak a foreign language, you might say that

   a. knowledge of a foreign language can be helpful in the business world.

   b. he or she may want to travel in the country where the language is spoken.

   (c.) Shakira sings in two languages.

   d. being able to read great literature in the original is a rewarding experience.

6. If you wanted to persuade someone to quit smoking, you might say that

   a. smoking is a major cause of lung cancer.

   b. smoking stains teeth and softens gums.

   (c.) ashtrays are often hard to find.

   d. this bad habit has become increasingly expensive.

PRACTICE 5

TEACHING TIP
Practice 5 is an excellent and entertaining vehicle for honing students' critical-thinking skills.

As you write persuasive paragraphs, make sure that your reasons can withstand close examination. Here are some examples of *invalid* arguments. Read them carefully. Decide which method of persuasion is being used, and explain why you think the argument is invalid.

1. Men make terrible drivers. That one just cut right in front of me without looking.

   Method of persuasion: example

   Invalid because the example of one careless male driver isn't enough to support a general statement about all male drivers

2. Many people have become vegetarians during the past ten or fifteen years, but such people have lettuce for brains.

   Method of persuasion: answering the opposition

   Invalid because the writer attacks the opposition rather than countering the benefits of vegetarianism

3. Candy does not really harm children's teeth. Tests made by scientists at the Gooey Candy Company have proved that candy does not cause tooth decay.

   Method of persuasion: referring to an authority

   Invalid because the scientists are employed by a candy company and may therefore be biased

4. Stealing pens and pads from the office is perfectly all right. Everyone does it.

   Method of persuasion: example

   Invalid because saying "everyone does it" is vague and does not justify stealing

TEACHING TIP

Bring in advertisements for students to evaluate. Find some that are based on facts and logic and some that attempt to sell nonessential or harmful products (e.g., perfume, cigarettes, alcoholic beverages). Ask students to identify the method of persuasion used in each ad. Are the arguments valid or bogus?

5. We don't want ____________ in our neighborhood. We had a ____________ family once, and they made a lot of noise.

   Method of persuasion: example

   Invalid because generalizations about an entire group based on one family's behavior are stereotypes

6. If our city doesn't build more playgrounds, a crime wave will destroy our homes and businesses.

   Method of persuasion: predicting the consequence

   Invalid because this argument exaggerates the consequence

7. Studying has nothing to do with grades. My brother never studies and still gets A's all the time.

   Method of persuasion: example

   Invalid because one person's experience doesn't adequately support such a broad statement

8. Women bosses work their employees too hard. I had one once, and she never let me rest for a moment.

   Method of persuasion: example

   Invalid because a single example cannot justify this sweeping statement

9. The Big Deal Supermarket has the lowest prices in town. This must be true because the manager said on the radio last week, "We have the lowest prices in town."

   Method of persuasion: referring to an authority

   Invalid because the "authority" cited was advertising the store, not stating research findings

10. If little girls are allowed to play with cars and trucks, they will grow up wanting to be men.

    Method of persuasion: predicting the consequence

    Invalid because the writer cannot support such a sweeping prediction with facts

PRACTICE 6 CRITICAL THINKING AND WRITING

Persuade Through Words and Images

Advertisements bombard us every day—through TV, newspapers, magazines, billboards, store windows, and the labels on people's clothing and possessions. The billions of dollars that Americans spend on brand-name products tell us that ads are very persuasive, usually making their argument with a strong visual image and a few catchy words.

Advertising is not a new phenomenon, though. Study this 1930s ad for Lucky Strike cigarettes. What is the message of this ad? Write down the ad's "topic sentence" and argument. What methods of persuasion does Lucky Strike use? How accurate is its message?

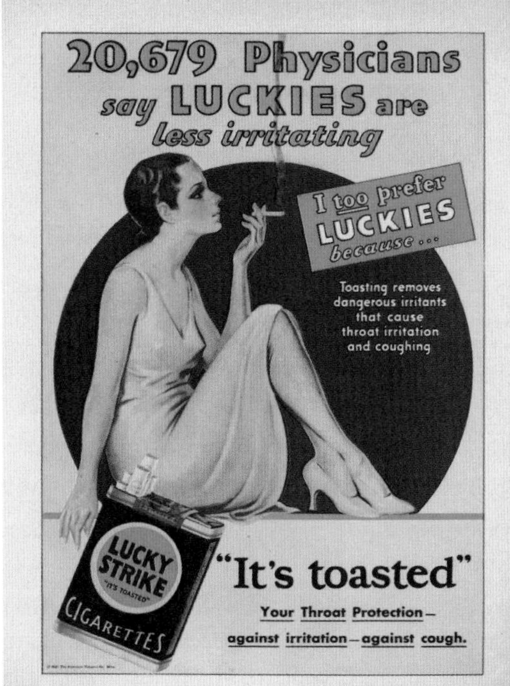

Image Courtesy of The Advertising Archives

EXPLORING ONLINE

www.adbusters.org/spoofads

To expose the power of advertising, a group called Adbusters creates stylish spoof ads for real products. Study the Adbuster spoof ads, especially those for fashion, alcohol, and tobacco. Pick one you like and write about its persuasive message.

WRITING ASSIGNMENT

To help you take a stand for a persuasive paragraph of your own, try the following exercises:

1. List five things you would like to see changed at your college.
2. List five things you would like to see changed in your home *or* at your job.
3. List five things that annoy you or make you angry. What can be done about them?
4. Imagine yourself giving a speech on national television. What message would you like to convey?

From your lists, pick one topic you would like to write a persuasive paragraph about and write the topic sentence here:

Sample answer: The college library should be open all day on Sundays.

Now make a plan or an outline for a paragraph. Use at least two of the five methods of persuasion. Arrange your reasons in a logical order, and write the most persuasive paragraph you can.

TEACHING TIP

For downloadable rubrics corresponding to each rhetorical mode, go to the *Instructor Companion Site.*

Checklist

The Process of Writing a Persuasive Paragraph

Refer to this checklist of steps as you write a persuasive paragraph of your own.

- ☐ 1. Narrow the topic to fit your audience and purpose. What do you wish to persuade your reader to believe or do?
- ☐ 2. Compose a topic sentence that clearly states your position for or against. Use *should, ought, must,* or their negatives.
- ☐ 3. Freewrite or brainstorm to generate all the reasons you can think of. (You may want to freewrite or brainstorm before you narrow the topic.)
- ☐ 4. Select the best three or four reasons and drop those that do not relate to your topic sentence.
- ☐ 5. If you use *facts*, be sure that they are accurate and that the sources of your facts are clear. If you use an *example*, be sure that it is a valid one and adequately supports your argument. If you *refer to an authority*, be sure that he or she is really an authority and *not biased.* If one of your reasons *predicts*

the consequence, be sure that the consequence flows logically from your statement. If one of your reasons *answers the opposition*, be sure to state the opposition's point of view fairly and refute it adequately.

☐ 6. Make a plan or an outline for the paragraph, numbering the reasons in the order in which you will present them.

☐ 7. Write a draft of your persuasive paragraph, using transitional expressions wherever they may be helpful.

☐ 8. Revise as necessary, checking for support, unity, logic, and coherence.

☐ 9. Proofread for errors in grammar, punctuation, sentence structure, spelling, and mechanics.

Suggested Topic Sentences for Persuasive Paragraphs

TEACHING TIP
Encourage your students to send their best writing to real-world audiences—the college president, the department of highways, an editor, or a webmaster.

A list of possible topic sentences for persuasive paragraphs follows. Pick one statement and decide whether you agree or disagree with it. Modify the topic sentence accordingly. Then write a persuasive paragraph that supports your view, explaining and illustrating from your own experience, your observations of others, or your reading.

1. The government should (or should not) be allowed to collect telephone records of American citizens.
2. Occasional arguments are good for friendship.
3. A required course at this college should be ______________ (Race Relations, Survey of World Art, How to Manage Money, or another).
4. The families of PTSD patients are the hidden victims of PTSD.
5. Sexual assault on college campuses is underestimated (or overestimated).
6. The death penalty should (or should not) be used to punish certain crimes.
7. Expensive weddings are an obscene waste of money.
8. Voters should be required to have picture IDs.
9. Smoking marijuana should be legal for adults over the age of twenty-one.
10. Drunk drivers who cause accidents with fatalities should be charged with murder.
11. ______________ is the most ______________ (hilarious, educational, mindless, racist) show on television.
12. To improve academic achievement, this town should create same-sex high schools (all boys, all girls).
13. The United States should insist that its allies play a greater role in "the war on terror."
14. ______________ (writer, singer, or actor) has a message that more people need to hear.
15. Writer's choice: ____

EXPLORING ONLINE

www.readwritethink.org/files/resources/interactives/persuasion_map

This online persuasion map helps you create your argument.

www.tesoltasks.com/ArgVocab.htm

Practice using the vocabulary of argument.

UNIT 3

writers' WORKSHOP

Give Advice to College Writers

When you are assigned a writing task, take a few minutes to think about the different types of paragraphs you have studied in this unit. Could a certain type of paragraph help you present your ideas more forcefully? You might ask yourself, "Would a paragraph developed by examples work well for this topic? How about a paragraph of cause and effect?"

When he received the assignment "Give advice to other college writers," this student not only made use of one paragraph pattern he had learned, but he also added something of his own—humor. In your class or group, read his work, aloud if possible, underlining any lines that you find especially funny or effective.

English Students, Listen Up!

You may think that years of school have taught you how to put off writing a paper; however, true procrastination is an art form, and certain steps must be followed to achieve the status of Master Procrastinator. The first step is to come up with a good reason to put off writing the paper. Reasons prevent others from hassling you about your procrastination. A reason should not be confused with an excuse. An excuse would be, "I am too tired." A reason would be, "It is important that I rest in order to do the best possible job." The second step is to come up with a worthwhile task to do before starting the paper. If you put off writing your paper by watching ~~*Gossip Girl*. You~~ *Gossip Girl*, you will feel guilty. On the other hand, if you put off writing your paper by helping your child do his or her homework or by doing three weeks' worth of laundry or by organizing your sock drawer, there will be no guilt. After completing your worthwhile ~~task. You~~ task, you will be hungry. In order to have the energy necessary to write the paper, you will need to eat something. The true artist can make this third step last even longer by either cooking a meal or going out for food. It is important not to risk your energy level by simply eating a bowl of cereal or a ketchup sandwich. After you eat, the fourth step is to prepare the space in which you will write the paper. This includes cleaning all the surfaces, sharpening ~~pencils. And~~ pencils, and making sure the lighting is exactly right. You may think that after this fourth step is completed, you will have no choice but to start your paper, but you do if you have done the other steps correctly. It is now too late in the day to start your paper. The fifth step is, of course, to go to bed and start over with step one in the morning.

—Thomas Capra, Student

1. How effective is this paragraph?

   Y Clear topic sentence? Y Good supporting details?

   Y Logical organization? Y Effective conclusion?

2. What type of paragraph development does Capra use here? How do you know? Does the topic sentence indicate what kind of paragraph will follow? process; topic

3. One step in the process of becoming a Master Procrastinator contains a *contrast*. Which step? What two things are contrasted? step one; reason and excuse

4. Discuss your underlinings with the group or class. Tell what parts of the paragraph you like best, explaining as specifically as possible why. For example, the mention of a ketchup sandwich in step three adds an extra dash of humor.

5. Although this writer is having fun, procrastination is a serious problem for some people. Do you think Capra is writing from experience? Why or why not?

6. This otherwise excellent writer makes the same grammar error three times. Can you spot and correct the error pattern that he needs to avoid? three sentence fragments

GROUP WORK

In your group or class, make a chart like the one below, listing all the types of paragraph development that you have studied. Now suppose that you have been assigned the topic *procrastination.* Discuss how different paragraphs could be developed on the subject of procrastination, each one using a different paragraph pattern. For instance, you could *illustrate* procrastination by discussing examples of procrastinators you have known. Fill in the chart with one idea per paragraph type. Then share your group's ideas with the class.

Topic: Procrastination

Method of Development	Paragraph Subject
Illustration	Give two to three examples of procrastinators.
Narration	Tell a story about someone who procrastinated.
Description	Describe what the desk of a procrastinator looks like.
Process	Give step-by-step advice about how to break the habit of procrastination.
Definition	Explain the meaning of the word *procrastination.*
Comparison and contrast	Explain the major differences between procrastinators and nonprocrastinators.
Classification	Describe different types of procrastinators.
Cause and effect	Explain the negative consequences of procrastination.
Persuasion	Give reasons why it's important to stop procrastinating.

WRITING AND REVISING IDEAS

1. Give humorous advice on how to get fired, how to fail a course, how to get robbed, or how to embarrass yourself for years to come by posting stupid pictures on the Internet.
2. Discuss procrastination, using one kind of paragraph development that you studied this term.

UNIT 4

Writing the Essay

CHAPTER 14

The Process of Writing an Essay

A: Looking at the Essay

B: Writing the Thesis Statement

C: Generating Ideas for the Body

D: Organizing Ideas into an Outline

E: Ordering and Linking Paragraphs in the Essay

F: Writing and Revising Essays

Although writing effective paragraphs will help you complete short-answer exams and brief writing assignments, much of the time—in college and in the business world—you will be required to write essays and reports several paragraphs long. Essays are longer and contain more ideas than the single paragraphs you have practiced so far, but they require many of the same skills that paragraphs do.

This chapter will help you apply the skills of paragraph writing to the writing of short essays. It will guide you from a look at the essay and its parts through planning and writing essays of your own.

A. Looking at the Essay

An **essay** is a group of paragraphs about one subject. In many ways, an essay is like a paragraph in longer, fuller form. Both have an introduction, a body, and a conclusion. Both explain one main, or controlling, idea with details, facts, and examples. An essay is not just a padded paragraph, however. An essay is longer because it contains more ideas.

The paragraphs in an essay are part of a larger whole, so each one has a special purpose.

- The **introductory paragraph*** opens the essay and tries to catch the reader's interest. It usually contains a **thesis statement**, one sentence that states the main idea of the entire essay.
- The **body** of an essay consists of one, two, three, or more paragraphs, each one making a different point about the main idea. Each paragraph within the body of an essay contains a topic sentence; details, facts, and examples that support the point of the paragraph (sometimes referred to as supporting ideas); and a concluding sentence.
- The **conclusion**† brings the essay to a close.

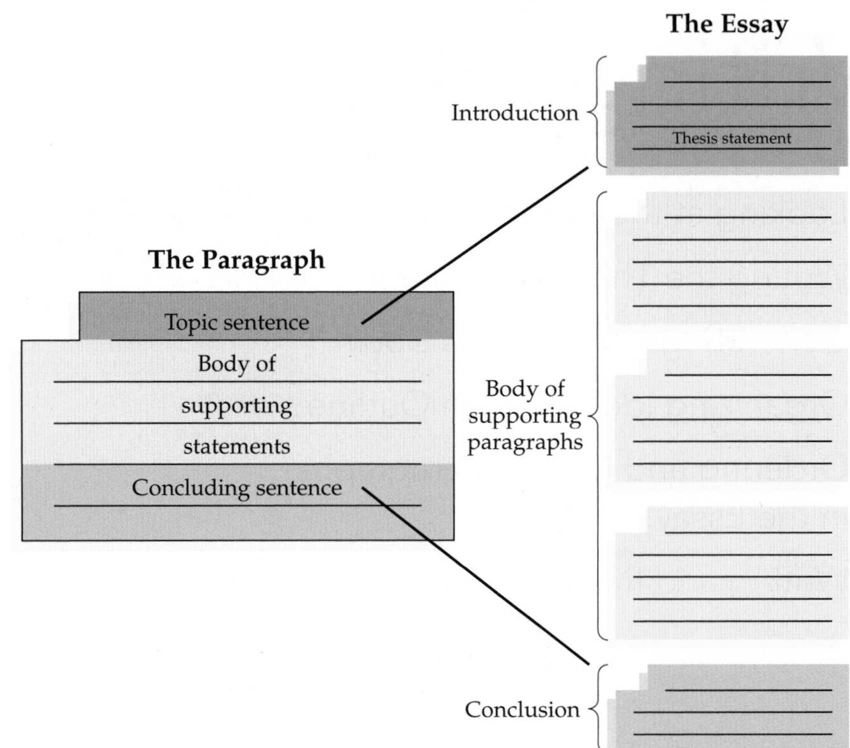

TEACHING AND ESL TIP
Using color coding to highlight parts of an essay or other written structures can help students—especially *visual learners*—understand.

Here is a student essay:

SUNLIGHT

Introduction

(1) An old proverb says, "He who brings sunlight into the lives of others cannot keep it from himself." Students who volunteer through the Center for Community Service often experience this wisdom firsthand. By giving their time and talents to the local community, these students not only enrich the lives of others, but they receive many surprising benefits for themselves.

Thesis statement

Topic sentence introducing point 1

(2) Most important, volunteering can bring a sense of empowerment, a knowledge that we can make a difference. This is significant because many students feel passive and hopeless about "the way things are." My first volunteer assignment was working with a group of troubled teenagers. Together we transformed a dismal vacant lot into a thriving business. The three-acre lot in the South Bronx, surrounded by abandoned buildings, was full of junk and heaps of wood. One teenager kicked a piece of wood and said, "Why don't we chop this up and sell it?" We surprised him by taking his idea seriously. We helped

Details, facts, examples supporting point 1

*For more work on introductions, see Chapter 15, "The Introduction, the Conclusion, and the Title."
†For more work on conclusions, see Chapter 15, "The Introduction, the Conclusion, and the Title."

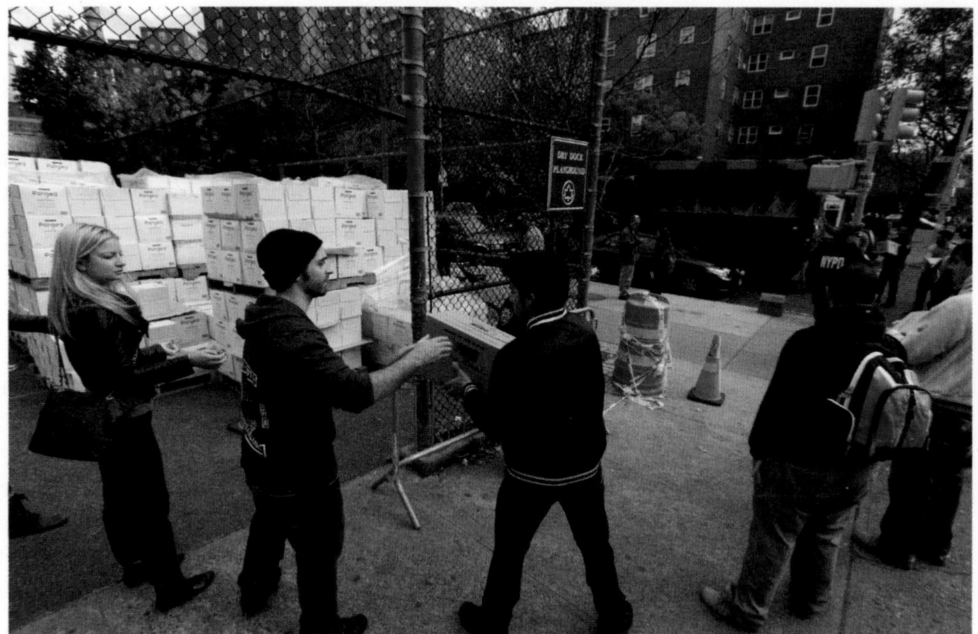

Volunteers unload supplies in New York City in the wake of Hurricane Sandy in November 2012.

Laurentiu Garofeanu/Barcroft Media/Getty Images

these young men, some of whom already had rap sheets, to chop up the wood, bundle it, contact restaurants with wood-burning ovens, and make deliveries. The restaurants, most of them very elegant, were happy to get cheap firewood, and the teenagers were thrilled to be treated like businesspeople. Most rewarding for me was seeing the changes in Raymond, "Mr. Apathy," as he took on a leading role in our project.

Topic sentence introducing point 2

Details, facts, examples supporting point 2

(3) Second, the volunteer often gains a deeper understanding of others. Another student, Shirley Miranda, worked with SHARE, a food cooperative that distributes bulk food once a month to its members. SHARE does not give food as charity; rather, each person does a job like unloading trucks at 5 A.M. on delivery day or packing boxes in exchange for healthy, inexpensive food. For Shirley, SHARE was a lesson in human relationships. Reflecting on her service, she wrote: "I learned that people may sometimes need guidance with dignity rather than total dependency on others. I saw that true teamwork is based on people's similarities, not their differences." SHARE so impressed Shirley that she worked in the program through her graduation.

Topic sentence introducing point 3

Details, facts, examples supporting point 3

(4) Finally, volunteering can be a way to "try on" a work environment. Sam Mukarji, an engineering student, volunteers on Saturdays as a docent, or guide, at the Museum of Science and Industry, which he describes as "my favorite place on the planet." Sam admires the creative uses of science in this museum, such as the virtual-reality experience of piloting an airplane. When many visitors asked Sam how the exhibit was put together, he suggested that the museum include signs explaining the technology. His idea was accepted, and he was asked to help implement it. Struggling to explain the exhibit in a clear way taught Sam how important writing skills are, even for an engineering major. Now he is paying closer attention to his English assignments and has discovered that working in a science museum would be his "dream job."

Conclusion

(5) Stories like these are not unusual at the Center for Community Service. Whenever the volunteers meet there, we always seem to end up talking about the positive ways in which volunteering has changed our lives. The Center is in a cinder-block basement without a single window, but it is filled with sunlight.

TEACHING TIP
Encourage students to read and study effective essays as models of good writing. The reading selections in Chapter 43, the Writers' Workshops concluding each unit, and even some practices in this text offer excellent examples.

- The last sentence in the introduction is the **thesis statement**. Just as a topic sentence sets forth the main idea of a paragraph, so the thesis statement sets forth the main idea of the whole essay. It must be *general enough to include the topic sentence of every paragraph in the body.*
- Note the underlined topic sentence of each supporting paragraph. Each topic sentence introduces one *benefit* that volunteers receive.
- Note that the thesis and topic sentences of paragraphs 2, 3, and 4 make a rough **outline** of the entire essay:

1. INTRODUCTION **and thesis statement:**	By giving their time and talents to the local community, these students not only enrich the lives of others, but they receive many surprising benefits for themselves.
2. **Topic sentence:**	Most important, volunteering can bring a sense of empowerment, a knowledge that we can make a difference.
3. **Topic sentence:**	Second, the volunteer often gains a deeper understanding of others.
4. **Topic sentence:**	Finally, volunteering can be a way to "try on" a work environment.
5. CONCLUSION	

TEACHING TIP
If your students seem interested in this topic, alert them to service learning opportunities on campus or share this site, which matches volunteers and local groups: **www.volunteermatch.org**.

- Note that every topic sentence supports the thesis statement. Every paragraph in the body discusses in detail one *benefit* that students receive from volunteering. Each paragraph also provides an *example* to explain that benefit.
- The last paragraph **concludes** the essay by mentioning sunlight, a reference to the proverb in paragraph 1.

PRACTICE 1

Read this student essay carefully and then answer the questions.

BOTTLE WATCHING

TEACHING TIP
Discussing Mr. Barnum's essay will likely engage your students. Ask whether a terrible job or other experience ever motivated them to dream bigger and take action.

(1) Every time I see a beer bottle, I feel grateful. This reaction has nothing to do with beer. The sight reminds me of the year I spent inspecting bottles at a brewery. That was the most boring and painful job I've ever had, but it motivated me to change my life.

(2) My job consisted of sitting on a stool and watching empty bottles pass by. A glaring light behind the conveyor belt helped me to spot cracked bottles or bottles with something extra—a dead grasshopper, for example, or a mouse foot. I was supposed to grab such bottles with my hooked cane and break them

ESL TIP
ESL students benefit greatly from textual analysis, which aids their understanding of organization, coherence markers, and vocabulary.

LEARNING STYLES TIP
Some instructors cut a paragraph or essay into sentence strips for groups of students to reconstruct, a technique especially helpful to *visual* and *kinesthetic learners*.

before they went into the washer. For eight or nine hours a day that was all I did. I got dizzy and sore in the eyes. I longed to fall asleep. I prayed that the conveyor would break down so the bottles would stop.

(3) After a while, to put some excitement into the job, I began inventing little games. I would count the number of minutes that passed before a broken bottle would come by, and I would compete against my own past record. Or I would see how many broken bottles I could spot in one minute. Once, I organized a contest for all the bottle watchers with a prize for the best dead insect or animal found in a bottle—anything to break the monotony of the job.

(4) After six months at the brewery, I began to think hard about my goals for the future. Did I want to spend the rest of my life looking in beer bottles? I realized that I wanted a job I could believe in. I wanted to use my mind for better things than planning contests for bleary-eyed bottle watchers. I knew I had to hand in my hook and go back to school.

(5) Today I feel grateful to that terrible job because it motivated me to attend college.

—Pat Barnum, Student

TEACHING TIP
Questions like these hone students' revising and writing skills. You might ask whether the one-sentence conclusion works or is just too short.

1. Which sentence in the introductory paragraph is the thesis statement?

   That was the most boring and painful job I've ever had, but it motivated me to change my life.

2. Did Mr. Barnum's introduction catch and hold your interest? Why or why not?

   Yes; the first sentence is surprising and makes you want to read on.

3. Underline the topic sentences in paragraphs 2, 3, and 4.

4. What is the controlling idea of paragraph 2?

   description of his duties on the job

5. What is the controlling idea of paragraph 3? What examples support this idea?

   games Barnum invented to add excitement; examples are competing against his record, counting broken bottles, prize for best dead critter

6. What do you like best about this essay? What, if anything, would you change?

   Answers will vary.

B. Writing the Thesis Statement

TEACHING AND ESL TIP
Point out to students that the first step in writing an effective academic essay is understanding the details of the assignment. Before proceeding, they should make sure that the instructor's requirements about the topic, length, and format are clear.

The steps in the essay-writing process are the same as those in the paragraph-writing process: **narrow the topic, write the thesis statement, generate ideas for the body, organize ideas in an outline, draft,** and **revise**. However, in essay writing, planning on paper, prewriting, and outlining are especially important because an essay is longer than a paragraph and more difficult to organize.

Narrowing the Topic

The essay writer usually starts with a broad subject and then narrows it to a manageable size. An essay is longer than a paragraph and gives the writer more room to develop ideas; nevertheless, the best essays, like the best paragraphs, are often quite specific. For example, if you are assigned a 400-word essay titled "An Experience I Won't Forget," a description of getting and moving into your first apartment might be too broad. You would need to *narrow* the topic to just one aspect of the experience. Many writers list possible narrowed subjects on paper or on a computer:

1. looking for an apartment through word-of-mouth and online ads
2. touring the apartment and making plans
3. meeting with the landlord and filling out the application
4. the excitement and fatigue of move-in day
5. realizing the expense of living on my own

Any one of these topics is narrow enough and specific enough to be the subject of a short essay. If you had written this list, you would now consider each narrowed topic and perhaps freewrite or brainstorm possible ways to support it. Keeping your audience and purpose in mind may also help you narrow your topic. Your audience here might be your instructor and classmates; your purpose might be to inform (by giving tips about searching for an apartment online) or to entertain (by narrating a funny or a dramatic incident). Having considered your topic, audience, and purpose, you would then choose the topic that you could best develop into a good essay.

If you have difficulty with this step, reread Chapter 2, "Prewriting to Generate Ideas."

Writing the Thesis Statement

The **thesis statement**—like the topic sentence in a paragraph—further focuses the narrowed subject because it must clearly state, in sentence form, the writer's **controlling idea**—the main point, opinion, or angle that the rest of the essay will support and discuss.

TEACHING TIP
Students will likely need extra practice with narrowing topics and writing thesis statements. You might demonstrate this process with several different topics, verbalizing your thoughts as you proceed.

Broad topic:	My most memorable job
Narrowed subject:	My job at the brewery
Controlling idea:	So bad it changed my life
Thesis statement:	That was the most boring and painful job I've ever had, but it motivated me to change my life.

- The controlling idea helps answer the question, "Why is this topic worth writing and reading about?" In this case, it lets us know that the job was so awful that it was life-changing.
- This thesis statement has a clear controlling idea. From it, we expect the essay to discuss specific ways in which this job was boring and painful and how it motivated a change.

LEARNING STYLES TIP

Remind *visual learners* to consider using graphic tools as they narrow the topic (e.g., the graphic triangle in Chapter 3, section titled "Narrowing the Topic").

The thesis statement and its controlling idea should be as **specific** as possible. By writing a specific thesis statement, you focus the subject and give yourself and your readers a clear idea of what will follow. Here are three ways to strengthen a vague thesis statement:

1. Replace vague words with more exact words* and replace vague ideas with more exact information:

Vague thesis statement:	Going deep-sea fishing when I was in Florida was really fun.
Revised thesis statement:	Going deep-sea fishing was the highlight of my trip to Florida because it let me spend time with my family in a relaxing setting.

- The first thesis statement lacks a clear controlling idea. The inexact words *really fun* do not say specifically enough *why* the activity was fun or *what* the rest of the essay might discuss.
- The second thesis statement is more specific. The words *really fun* are replaced by the more exact word *highlight.* In addition, the writer has added more complete information about why the activity was the highlight of the trip. From this thesis statement, it is clear that the essay will discuss how deep-sea fishing allowed the writer to spend time with family in a laid-back setting.

TEACHING TIP

Explain that specifying different aspects of the subject in the thesis statement is a great way to help the writer organize the essay and to help the reader follow it.

2. Ask yourself questions to narrow your thesis. These questions will help you make your thesis more specific. What aspects of your subject are noteworthy? Why are these aspects of your subject important? The most successful thesis statements go beyond observation and description (the *what*) and offer insight into the *why*.

Vague thesis statement:	The movie *Southern Smoke* seems fake.
Revised thesis statement:	The costumes, the dialogue, and the plot of the movie *Southern Smoke* all seem inauthentic.
Polished thesis statement:	The costumes, the dialogue, and the plot of the movie *Southern Smoke* all seem inauthentic and so make it an ineffective depiction of the South after the Civil War.

- The first thesis statement gives little specific direction to the writer or the reader.

*For more practice in choosing exact language, see Chapter 23, "Revising for Language Awareness," Part A.

- The second thesis statement, however, answers the question "What aspects of the movie seem inauthentic?" The thesis sets up a plan for the whole essay. The writer has divided the subject into three parts—the costumes, the dialogue, and the plot—and he or she will probably devote one paragraph to discuss how each one does not seem authentic, following the order in the thesis statement.
- The third statement takes the thesis a step further, answering the question "Why is that important?" This helps the thesis and the essay go beyond describing *what* the movie does and explain *why* this topic is worth exploring.

3. Avoid a heavy-handed thesis statement that announces, "Now I will write about . . ." or "This essay will discuss . . . ." Don't state the obvious. Instead, craft a specific thesis statement that will capture the reader's interest and control what the rest of your essay will be about. Make every word count.

Heavy-handed, vague thesis statement:	This essay will discuss an important benefit of taking online classes.
Revised thesis statement:	Online classes require students to work in virtual teams, giving them experience that is highly valued by most employers.

PRACTICE 2

Read each pair of thesis statements carefully. Then circle the letter of the stronger thesis statement. Explain your reasoning.

EXAMPLE a. This essay will discuss the main reason why Northern State Manufacturing should revise its attendance policy.

(b.) Northern State Manufacturing should revise its attendance policy because it encourages employees to commute in unsafe driving conditions.

Thesis statement b. is stronger because it isn't heavy-handed. It also states why the attendance policy should be revised.

1. (a.) Homeowners should install solar panels to reduce their consumption of fossil fuels.

   b. Homeowners should use solar panels because they are good for the environment.

   Thesis statement a. is stronger because it uses more exact words and more exact information.

2. a. *Dracula* is an example of a gothic novel.

   (b.) *Dracula* is considered a gothic novel because it includes a foreign location, supernatural elements, and a distressed heroine, all of which are features of the gothic genre.

Thesis statement b. is stronger because it states what aspects of *Dracula* make it a gothic novel.

3. a. This essay will discuss the Intolerable Acts, a series of laws put into place by the British Government that contributed to the American Revolutionary War.
   (b.) The Intolerable Acts imposed by the British Government in response to the Boston Tea Party sparked further rebellion by the American colonists, contributing to the outbreak of the American Revolutionary War.

   Thesis statement b. is stronger because it isn't heavy-handed. It also uses more exact words and more exact information.

PRACTICE 3

Revise each vague thesis statement, making it more specific. Remember, a good thesis statement should have a clear controlling idea and indicate what the rest of the essay will be about. Answers will vary.

EXAMPLE Watching TV news programs has its good points.

Watching news programs on TV can make one a more informed and responsible citizen.

TEACHING TIP
Ask students to share their rewritten thesis statements in small groups or with the class. Discuss different ways to narrow the topic or the point about that topic.

1. I will write about my job, which is very cool.

   Working as an administrative assistant at JamVision has given me a front-row seat to the triumphs and struggles of young musicians in the Chicago area.

2. My mother is a really good person.

   My mother, who raised my siblings and me by herself while working and going to school, is the strongest and most determined person I know.

3. School uniforms are a good idea.

   To reduce competition, school crime, and unnecessary distractions, students at Highland Middle School should be required to wear uniforms.

PRACTICE 4

TEACHING TIP
Practice 4 works well as a group activity or as the basis for a class discussion.

Eight possible essay topics follow. Pick three that interest you. For each one, *narrow* the topic, choose your *controlling idea,* and then compose a specific *thesis statement.* Answers will vary.

a volunteer experience	handling anger (or other emotion)
when parents work	a story or issue in the news now
an addictive habit	a problem on campus or at work
the value of a college degree	advantages or disadvantages of Internet research

EXAMPLE Subject: *handling anger*

Narrowed subject: *my angry adolescence*

Controlling idea: *channeling adolescent anger into art*

Thesis statement: *In a photography workshop for "at-risk" teenagers, I learned that anger can be channeled positively into art.*

1. Subject: ____________________

   Narrowed subject: ____________________

   Controlling idea: ____________________

   Thesis statement: ____________________

2. Subject: ____________________

   Narrowed subject: ____________________

   Controlling idea: ____________________

   Thesis statement: ____________________

3. Subject: ____________________

   Narrowed subject: ____________________

   Controlling idea: ____________________

   Thesis statement: ____________________

C. Generating Ideas for the Body

LEARNING STYLES TIP

For *kinesthetic* and *visual learners*, consider reproducing the ideas in this list on strips of paper or cards and letting pairs of students arrange those strips or cards into logical groups.

The thesis statement sets forth the main idea of the entire essay, but it is the **body** of the essay that must fully support and discuss that thesis statement. In composing the thesis statement, the writer should already have given some thought to what the body will contain. Now he or she uses one or more prewriting methods—*brainstorming, freewriting, clustering*, or *asking questions*—to generate ideas for the body.

To get enough material to flesh out an essay, many writers brainstorm or freewrite on paper or on the computer—jotting down any ideas that develop the thesis statement, including main ideas, specific details, and examples, all jumbled together. Only after creating a long list do they go back over it, drop any ideas that do not support the thesis statement, and then group ideas that might go together in body paragraphs.

Suppose, for instance, that you have written this thesis statement: *Although people often react to stress in harmful ways, there are many positive ways to handle stress.* By brainstorming and then dropping ideas that do not relate, you might eventually produce a list like this:

exercise
dig weeds or rake leaves

call a friend
talking out problems relieves stress
jogging
many sports ease tension
go to the beach
take a walk
taking breaks, long or short, relieves stress
talk to a therapist if the problem is really bad
escape into a hobby—photography, bird watching
go to a movie
talk to a counselor at the college
talk to a minister, priest, rabbi, etc.
many people harm themselves trying to relieve stress
they overeat or smoke
drinking too much, other addictions
do vigorous household chores—scrub a floor, wash dishes, do laundry
doing something physical relieves stress
some diseases are caused by stress
take a nap
some people get angry, but this hurts their relationships

Now read over the list, looking for groups of ideas that could become paragraphs. You might want to highlight related ideas. Some ideas might become topic sentences; others might be used to support a topic sentence. How many possible paragraphs can you find in this list?

four

PRACTICE 5

Choose one of the thesis statements you wrote for Practice 4 and generate ideas to develop an essay. Using your favorite prewriting method, try to fill at least a page. If you get stuck, reread the thesis statement to focus your thoughts or switch to another prewriting method.

D. Organizing Ideas into an Outline

Many writers make an **outline** before they write an essay. Because an essay is longer, more complex, and harder to control than a paragraph, an outline, even a rough one, helps the writer stay on track and saves time later. The outline should include the following:

1. Two to four main ideas to support the thesis statement
2. Two to four topic sentences stating these ideas
3. A plan for each paragraph in the body (developed in any of the ways explained earlier in this book)
4. A logical order in which to present paragraphs

Different writers create outlines in different ways. Some writers examine their brainstorming or other prewriting, looking for paragraph groups. Others write their topic sentences first and then generate ideas to support these topic sentences.

TEACHING TIP

Many students need additional guidance as they attempt to group ideas together. An instructor can often help students prevent major organizational problems by conferencing with them one-on-one about their outlines before they begin to write.

Reread prewriting and find paragraph groups. In Part C, you read one student's brainstorm list developing the thesis statement, *Although people often react to stress in harmful ways, there are many positive ways to handle stress*. Here is one possible way to group those ideas:

1. <u>many people harm themselves trying to relieve stress</u>
   they overeat or smoke
   drinking too much, other addictions
   some diseases are caused by stress
   some people get angry, but this hurts their relationships

2. exercise
   dig weeds or rake leaves
   jogging
   many sports ease tension
   take a walk
   do vigorous household chores—scrub a floor, wash dishes, do laundry
   <u>doing something physical relieves stress</u>

3. call a friend
   <u>talking out problems relieves stress</u>
   talk to a therapist if the problem is really bad
   talk to a counselor at the college
   talk to a minister, priest, rabbi, etc.

4. go to the beach
   <u>taking breaks, long or short, relieves stress</u>
   escape into a hobby—photography, bird watching
   go to a movie
   take a nap

- The main idea of each group is underlined. This idea could be a possible topic sentence for each paragraph.

Here is the completed outline from which the student wrote her essay:

TEACHING TIP

Explain to students that outlines can range from scratch jottings to formal outlines—whatever will help the writer organize ideas and plan the paper. Make clear which outline form you prefer.

---

1. INTRODUCTION and thesis statement:	Although people often react to stress in harmful ways, there are many positive ways to handle stress.
2. Topic sentence:	Many people actually harm themselves trying to relieve stress. —overeat, smoke, or drink too much —get stress-induced diseases —get angry

3. Topic sentence: For some people, doing something physical is a positive way to relieve stress.
—walk or jog
—exercise
—vigorous household chores
—dig weeds or rake leaves

4. Topic sentence: Taking breaks, long or short, is another positive way to relieve stress.
—take a nap
—escape into a hobby
—go to a movie, to the beach

5. Topic sentence: Discussing one's problems can relieve stress and sometimes resolve the cause of it.
—call a friend
—talk to a minister, etc.
—talk to a counselor at the college
—talk to a therapist if necessary

CONCLUSION: Stress is a fact of life, but we can learn positive responses to be happier and more productive.

TEACHING AND ESL TIP
Many ESL students find it helpful to use outlines. Explain that informal outlines are also useful in timed writing and examinations.

- Note that this writer now has a well-organized outline from which to write her paper.
- She has chosen a new order for the four supporting paragraphs. Does this order make sense? Explain.

harmful ways first, then physical work and breaks, getting help last

Write topic sentences and then plan paragraphs. Sometimes a writer can compose topic sentences directly from the thesis statement without taking extensive notes first. This is especially true if the thesis statement itself shows how the body will be divided or organized. Such a thesis statement makes the work of planning paragraphs easy because the writer has already broken down the subject into supporting ideas or parts:

Thesis statement: Because the student cafeteria has many problems, the college should hire a new administrator to see that it is properly managed in the future.

- This thesis statement contains two main ideas: (1) that the cafeteria has many problems and (2) that a new administrator should be hired. The first idea states the problem and the second offers a solution.

From this thesis statement, a writer could logically plan a two-paragraph body, with one paragraph explaining each idea in detail. He or she might compose two topic sentences as follows:

Thesis statement:	Because the student cafeteria has many problems, the college should hire a new administrator to see that it is properly managed in the future.
Topic sentence:	Foremost among the cafeteria's problems are unappetizing food, slow service, and high prices.
Topic sentence:	A new administrator could do much to improve these terrible conditions.

These topic sentences might need to be revised later, but they will serve as guides while the writer further develops each paragraph.

The writer might develop the first paragraph in the body by giving **examples*** of the unappetizing foods, slow service, and high prices.

He or she could develop the second paragraph through **process**,† by describing the **steps** that the new administrator could take to solve the cafeteria's problems. This planning will create a clear **outline** from which to write the essay.

PRACTICE 6

TEACHING TIP
This practice works well as a small-group activity.

Complete this outline as if you were planning the essay. First, state in sentence form each problem that will develop the topic sentence: unappetizing food, slow service, and high prices. Then develop each with details and examples.

1. **INTRODUCTION and thesis statement:** Because the student cafeteria has many problems, the college should hire a new administrator to see that it is properly managed in the future.

2. **Topic sentence:** Foremost among the cafeteria's problems are unappetizing food, slow service, and high prices.

   Problem 1: ______________________________

   ____

   ____

   ____

   Problem 2: ______________________________

   ____

   ____

   ____

   Problem 3: ______________________________

   ____

*For more work on developing paragraphs with examples, see Chapter 5, "Illustration."

†For more work on developing paragraphs by process, see Chapter 8, "Process."

____

____

3. Topic sentence: A new administrator could do much to improve these terrible conditions.

Step 1. Set minimum quality standards

—personally oversee purchase of healthful food

—set and enforce rules about how long food can be left out

—set cooking times for hot meals

Step 2. Reorganize service lines

—study which lines are busiest at different times of the day

—shift cooks and cashiers to those lines

—create a separate beverage line

Step 3. Lower prices

—better food and faster service would attract more student customers

—cafeteria could then lower prices

4. CONCLUSION

PRACTICE 7

TEACHING TIP

This practice can be done constructively in small groups. Urge groups to brainstorm and choose rich, interesting supporting details.

Write two to four topic sentences to support each of the thesis statements that follow. (You may wish to brainstorm or freewrite first.) Make sure that every topic sentence supports the thesis statement and that every one could be developed into a good paragraph. Then arrange your topic sentences in a rough outline in the space provided. Answers will vary.

EXAMPLE I vividly recall the sights, sounds, and smells of Times Square.

Topic sentence: *The streets were jammed with vehicles.*

Topic sentence: *My ears rang from the intensity of the noise around me.*

Topic sentence: *The air was filled with delicious aromas.*

1. Before you buy a phone, do these three things.

   Topic sentence: Decide how much you can spend, and determine your price range.

Topic sentence: Examine the models that are within your price range.

Topic sentence: Shop around; all phone dealers are not created equal.

2. Living alone has both advantages and disadvantages.

   Topic sentence: When you live alone, you can make spur-of-the-moment decisions about what you want to do.

   Topic sentence: Living by yourself, you can keep your apartment as neat or as sloppy as you like.

   Topic sentence: Living alone allows you to eat whatever and whenever you want.

   Topic sentence: Living alone, however, makes you especially vulnerable to loneliness.

3. Doing well at a job interview requires careful planning.

   Topic sentence: First, learn as much as possible about the company at which you are interviewing.

   Topic sentence: Try to anticipate the kinds of questions the interviewer might ask.

   Topic sentence: Choose appropriate clothing to wear at the interview.

   Topic sentence: Get a good night's sleep and practice relaxation techniques.

PRACTICE 8

Now choose *one* thesis statement you have written in the previous exercises, or write one now. Generate ideas for the body and organize them in an outline for an essay of your own. (For ideas, reread the thesis statements you wrote for Practice 4.) Your outline should include your thesis statement; two to three topic sentences; and supporting details, facts, and examples. Prewrite every time you need ideas; revise the thesis statement and the topic sentences until they are sharp and clear.

E. Ordering and Linking Paragraphs in the Essay

TEACHING TIP
Review the concept of coherence by referring students back to Chapter 4, "Achieving Coherence."

An essay, like a paragraph, should have **coherence**. That is, the paragraphs in an essay should be arranged in a clear, logical order and should follow one another like links in a chain.

Ordering Paragraphs

It is important that the paragraphs in your outline, and later in your essay, follow a **logical order**. The rule for writers is this: Use your common sense and plan ahead. Do *not* leave the order of your paragraphs to chance.

The types of order often used in single paragraphs—**time order, space order**, and **order of importance***—can sometimes be used to arrange paragraphs within an essay. Essays about subjects that can be broken into stages or steps, with each step discussed in one paragraph, should be arranged according to *time. Space order* is used occasionally in descriptive essays. A writer who wishes to save the most important or convincing paragraph for last would use *order of importance*. Or he or she might wish to reverse this order and put the most important paragraph first.

Very often, however, the writer simply arranges paragraphs in whatever order makes sense in the particular essay. Suppose, for example, that you have written the thesis statement, *Electric cars, which are now being developed by many vehicle manufacturers, have strong advantages and disadvantages*, and you plan four paragraphs with these topic sentences:

1. The high price tag and cost of parts for electric cars make them unaffordable for many Americans.
2. Electric cars will generate less pollution per mile than cars with gasoline engines even though they get their power from fossil fuel–burning electric plants.
3. Because electric cars must be plugged in and charged about six hours for every 50–100 miles driven, they will be impractical for those who drive long distances.
4. Electric cars will help to reduce America's dependence on foreign oil sources and thus improve our national security.

The writer lists four points about electric cars. Points two and four both state advantages of electric cars; therefore, it makes sense to order the paragraphs so that those two advantages are grouped together. Points one and three state two disadvantages—high cost and limits of operation—so these two points should be grouped together. The thesis statement refers to *advantages and disadvantages*, so it would make sense to discuss the advantages first. A logical order of paragraphs, then, might be the following:

---

1. INTRODUCTION and thesis statement:	Electric cars, which are now being developed by many vehicle manufacturers, have strong advantages and disadvantages.

*For more work on time order, space order, and order of importance, see Chapter 4, "Achieving Coherence," Part A.

2. **Topic sentence:** Electric cars will generate less pollution per mile than cars with gasoline engines even though they get their power from fossil fuel–burning electric plants.

3. **Topic sentence:** Electric cars will help to reduce America's dependence on foreign oil sources and thus improve our national security.

4. **Topic sentence:** The high price tag and cost of parts for electric cars make them unaffordable for many Americans.

5. **Topic sentence:** Because electric cars must be plugged in and charged about six hours for every 50–100 miles driven, they will be impractical for those who drive long distances.

6. CONCLUSION

LEARNING STYLES TIP

To give students more practice ordering and linking paragraphs, cut essays into paragraphs and then scramble those paragraphs. Ask students to use what they know about order, transitions, and other issues to put the paragraphs in the correct order.

Finally, if your thesis statement is divided into two, three, or four parts, the paragraphs in the body should follow the order in the thesis; otherwise, the reader will be confused. Assume, for instance, that you are planning three paragraphs to develop the thesis statement, *Visiting a foreign country for the first time can be overwhelming, exciting, and educational.*

Paragraph 2 should discuss its overwhelming aspects

Paragraph 3 should discuss its exciting aspects

Paragraph 4 should discuss its educational aspects

PRACTICE 9

Plans for three essays follow, each containing a thesis statement and several topic sentences in scrambled order. Number the topic sentences in each group according to *an order that makes sense.* Be prepared to explain your choices.

---

1. **Thesis statement:** An immigrant who wishes to become a U.S. citizen must complete a three-stage naturalization process.

Topic sentences:

2 After submitting an application, the would-be citizen interviews with an immigration officer and takes tests on the English language and American civics.

1 An immigrant who meets general requirements for minimum length of residency and good moral character begins by filling out Form N-400, the Application for Naturalization.

3 Applicants who perform well in the interview and on the tests take the Oath of Allegiance to the United States in a moving group ceremony, thus becoming American citizens.

TEACHING TIP

A sample Naturalization Self Test is available online: Google "Naturalization Self Test" and answer the questions.

TEACHING TIP

Have students complete Practice 9 on their own and then discuss their answers in small groups or with the class and explain the rationale behind the order they chose.

2. Thesis statement: To meet the demands of a growing computer industry and aging population, the fastest growing job markets through 2018 will be in the information technology and medical fields.

Topic sentences:

__3__ A second group of medical jobs will exist in private homes, where health-care aides will be needed to care for the elderly.

__1__ Skilled computer software engineers, systems designers, and database administrators will find many job opportunities from which to choose.

__2__ In hospitals and doctors' offices, the need for medical assistants, pharmacy technicians, and dental hygienists will grow rapidly.

3. Thesis statement: The practice of tai chi can improve one's concentration, health, and peace of mind.

Topic sentences:

__2__ In several ways, tai chi boosts physical health.

__3__ Peace of mind increases gradually as one becomes less reactive.

__1__ Concentrating on the movements of tai chi in practice promotes better concentration in other areas of life.

PRACTICE 10

Now, go over the essay outline that you developed in Practice 8 and reconsider which paragraphs should come first, which second, and so forth. Does time order, space order, or order of importance seem appropriate to your subject? Number your paragraphs accordingly.

Linking Paragraphs

Just as the sentences within a paragraph should flow smoothly, so the paragraphs within an essay should be clearly **linked** one to the next. As you write your essay, do not make illogical jumps from one paragraph to another. Instead, guide your reader. Link the first sentence of each new paragraph to the thesis statement or to the paragraph before. Here are four ways to link paragraphs:

1. Repeat key words or ideas from the thesis statement.
2. Refer to words or ideas from the preceding paragraph.
3. Use transitional expressions.
4. Use transitional sentences.

1. Repeat key words or ideas from the thesis statement.* The topic sentences in the following essay plan repeat key words and ideas from the thesis statement.

---

*For more work on repetition of key words, see Chapter 4, "Achieving Coherence," Part B. See also "Synonyms and Substitutions" in the same section.

TEACHING TIP

Mention to students that reading experts sometimes suggest highlighting key or repeated words to help follow the writer's ideas.

Thesis statement:	Spending time in nature can promote inner peace and a new point of view.
Topic sentence:	A stroll in the woods or a picnic by the sea often brings feelings of inner peace and well-being.
Topic sentence:	Natural places can even give us a new point of view by putting our problems in perspective.

- In the first topic sentence, the words *feelings of inner peace* repeat, in slightly altered form, words from the thesis statement. The words *a stroll in the woods or a picnic by the sea* refer to the idea of *spending time in nature*.
- Which words in the second topic sentence repeat key words or ideas from the thesis statement?

natural places, new point of view

2. Refer to words or ideas from the preceding paragraph. Link the first sentence of a new paragraph to the paragraph before, especially by referring to words or ideas near the end of the paragraph. Note how the two paragraphs are linked in the following passage:

(1) The Great Depression was the worst economic collapse of modern times, lasting ten years. It began with the stock market crash of 1929. By 1932, one-quarter of all Americans were unemployed. Manufacturing areas fared even worse. In Chicago, for instance, 40 percent of those seeking jobs could not find them. During one year, 80 percent of workers in Toledo, Ohio, were unemployed.

(2) Workers who did hold on to their jobs gladly took pay cuts. From 1929 to 1933, pay for manufacturing work fell from $25 to $17 a week. Farmers slashed prices, selling five bushels of wheat to buy one pair of shoes. By the winter of 1932–1933, farmers who couldn't sell their corn were burning it to heat their homes.

—adapted from Joseph R. Conlin,
The American Past: A Survey of American History, 9th Edition

- What words and groups of words in paragraph 2 clearly refer to paragraph 1?

Workers, jobs, 1929–1933, manufacturing

3. Use transitional expressions.* Transitional expressions—words like *for example, therefore,* and *later on*—are used within a paragraph to show the relationship between sentences. Transitional expressions can also be used within an essay to show the relationships between paragraphs:

*For a complete list of transitional expressions, see Chapter 4, "Achieving Coherence," Part B. See also the chapters in Unit 3 for ways to use transitional expressions in each paragraph and essay pattern.

(1) The house where I grew up was worn out and run-down. The yard was mostly mud, rock hard for nine months of the year but wet and swampy for the other three. Our nearest neighbors were forty miles away so it got pretty lonely. Inside, the house was shabby. The living room furniture was covered in stiff, nubby material that had lost its color over the years and become a dirty brown. Upstairs in my bedroom, the wooden floor sagged a little farther west every year.

(2) *Nevertheless,* I love the place for what it taught me. There I learned to thrive in solitude. During the hours I spent alone, when school was over and the chores were done, I learned to play the guitar and sing. Wandering in the fields around the house or poking under stones in the creek bed, I grew to love the natural world. Most of all, I learned to see and to appreciate small wonders.

- The first paragraph describes some of the negative details about the writer's early home. The second paragraph *contrasts* the writer's attitude, which is positive. The transitional expression *nevertheless* eases the reader from one paragraph to the next by pointing out the exact relationship between the paragraphs.
- Transitional expressions can also highlight the *order* in which paragraphs are arranged.* Three paragraphs arranged in time order might begin: *First . . .*, *Next . . .*, *Finally. . . .* Three paragraphs arranged in order of importance might begin: *First . . .*, *More important . . .*, *Most important. . . .* Use transitional expressions alone or together with other linking devices.

4. Use transitional sentences. From time to time, you may need to write an entire sentence of transition to link one paragraph to the next, as shown in this passage:

(1) Zainab Salbi lived through the ravages of war in her native Iraq. She experienced the violence committed against women under Saddam Hussein. After escaping to the United States, she worried about other women. In the 1990s, upset by stories of women in concentration camps in the former Yugoslavia, she and her husband Amjad Atallah decided to make a difference by volunteering. Unfortunately, they could find no organization dedicated to helping women affected by war.

(2) *This setback did not stop the couple, however.* Salbi and Atallah resolved to start their own group dedicated to helping women hurt physically and psychologically by war. The young couple spent their honeymoon connecting American female sponsors with female victims of the war in Bosnia and Herzegovina. They returned from the trip and started Women to Women International, which has since helped over 150,000 women in countries like Nigeria, Colombia, and Afghanistan, distributing over $40 million in aid. Salbi has become a champion of women's rights and published books about women's war experiences. "Women who survive war are strong and courageous," she says. "They just need some support to deal with the aftermath of conflict."

*For more work on transitional expressions of time, space, and importance, see Chapter 4, "Achieving Coherence," Part A.

- In paragraph 1, Salbi and Atallah focus on a goal but lack the tools to achieve it. In paragraph 2, they achieve their goal. The topic sentence of paragraph 2 is the second sentence: *Salbi and Atallah resolved to start their own group dedicated to helping women hurt physically and psychologically by war*.
- The first sentence of paragraph 2 is actually a **sentence of transition** that eases the reader from a challenge to success. (Note that it includes a transitional expression of contrast, *however*.)

Use all four methods of linking paragraphs as you write your essays.

PRACTICE 11

Read the essay that follows, noting the paragraph-to-paragraph *links*. Then answer the questions.

SKIN DEEP

(1) What do Winston Churchill, Rihanna, Bradley Cooper, and Miley Cyrus all have in common? Perhaps you guessed tattoos: body decorations made by piercing the skin and inserting colored pigments. In fact, tattoos have a long and nearly worldwide history, ranging from full-body art to a single heart, from tribal custom to pop-culture fad.

(2) The earliest known tattoo was found on the mummy of an Egyptian priestess dating back to 2200 BC. Tattoos were also used in the ancient world to decorate Japanese noblemen, mark Greek spies, and hide expressions of fear on Maori tribesmen in New Zealand. Full-body tattooing was practiced for centuries in the South Seas; in fact, the word *tattoo* comes from the Tahitian word *tattaw*. In medieval times, small tattoos were common in Europe. For instance, in 1066, after the famous Battle of Hastings, the only way that the body of the Anglo-Saxon King Harold could be identified was by the word *Edith* tattooed over his heart.

(3) For the next 600 years, however, Europeans lost interest in tattoos. Then, in the 1700s, explorers and sailors rekindled public excitement. Captain Cook, returning from a trip to Tahiti in 1761, described the wonders of tattoos.

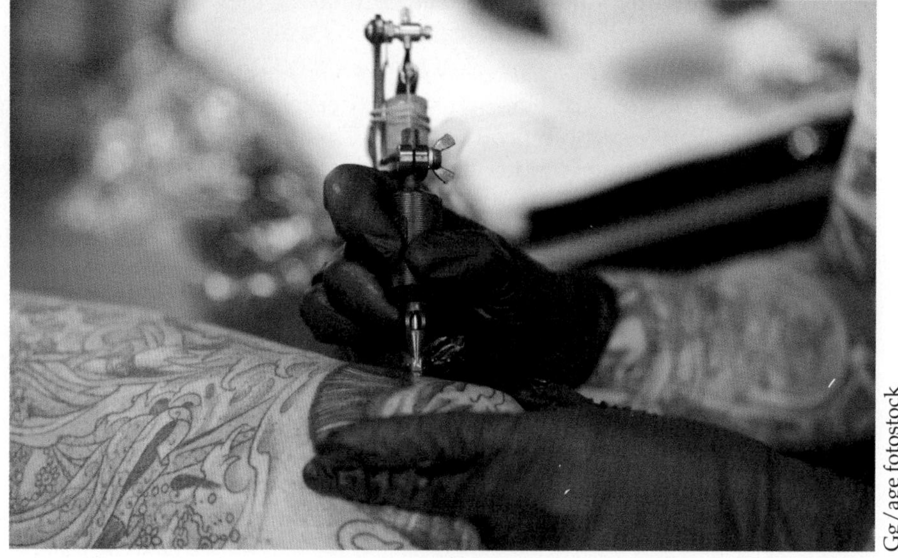
Gg/age fotostock

A tattoo artist at work

Cook enthusiastically paraded a heavily tattooed Tahitian prince named Omai through England's finest drawing rooms. People were intrigued by the colorful flowers, snakes, and geographical maps covering Omai's body. Although large tattoos were too much for the British, the idea of a pretty little bee or royal crest on the shoulder was very appealing. Tattooing remained popular with Europe's royalty and upper classes through the nineteenth century. The Prince of Wales, the Duke of York, Tsar Nicholas of Russia, and Winston Churchill all had tattoos.

(4) When tattooing first reached America, on the other hand, its image was definitely not refined. American soldiers and sailors, feeling lonely and patriotic during World War II, visited tattoo parlors in South Pacific ports and came home with *Mother* or *Death Before Dishonor* inked into their arms. Soon motorcyclists started getting tattoos as part of their rebellious, macho image. The process was painful, with a high risk of infection, so the more elaborate a cyclist's bloody dagger or skull and crossbones, the better.

(5) Tattooing did not remain an outlaw rite of passage for long. Safer and less painful methods developed in the 1970s and 1980s brought tattooing into the American mainstream, especially among the young. Designs ranged from one butterfly to black-and-white patterns like Native American textiles to flowing, multicolored, stained-glass designs. With the media documenting the tattoos of the rich and famous, tattooing became a full-blown fad by the 1990s. Now the one-time symbols of daring have become so common that many rebels are having their tattoos removed. About one-third of all the work performed by tattoo artists in the United States is "erasing" unwanted tattoos.

1. Find at least two transitional expressions the writer uses to link paragraphs.

   For the next 600 years, however; on the other hand

2. How does the writer link paragraphs 1 and 2? The key word *tattoo* from paragraph 1 is repeated in 2; "earliest known" refers to "long . . . history"

3. How does the writer link paragraphs 4 and 5? Transitional sentence in 5: "outlaw rite of passage" refers to motorcyclists in 4

F. Writing and Revising Essays

Writing the First Draft

Now you should have a clear plan or outline from which to write your first draft. This plan should include your thesis statement, two to four topic sentences that support it, details and facts to develop each paragraph, and a logical order. Explain your ideas fully, but avoid getting stuck on a particular word or sentence. When you have finished the draft, set it aside, if possible, for several hours or several days.

PRACTICE 12

Write a first draft of the essay you have been working on in Practices 8 and 10.

TEACHING TIP

Make sure that students understand the difference between revising and proofreading. Encourage them to avoid using the two terms interchangeably.

Revising and Proofreading

Revising is perhaps the most important step in the essay-writing process. Revising an essay involves the same principles as revising a paragraph.* Read your first draft slowly and carefully—aloud if possible. Imagine you are a reader who has never seen the paper before. As you read, underline trouble spots, draw arrows, and write in the margins, if necessary, to straighten out problems. Here are some questions to keep in mind as you revise:

1. Is the thesis statement clear?
2. Does the body of the essay fully support the thesis statement?
3. Does the essay have unity? Does every paragraph relate to the thesis statement?
4. Does the essay have coherence? Do the paragraphs follow a logical order?
5. Are the topic sentences clear?
6. Does each paragraph provide specific details and well-chosen examples?
7. Is the language exact, concise, and fresh?
8. Are the sentences varied in length and type?
9. Does the essay conclude, not just leave off?

If possible, ask a **peer reviewer**—a trusted classmate, friend, or tutor—to read your paper and give you feedback. Of course, this person should not rewrite or correct the essay but should simply tell you which parts are clear and which parts are confusing.

To guide your peer reviewer, you might ask him or her to use the Peer Feedback Sheet (see Chapter 3) or to answer these questions in writing:

1. What do you like about this piece of writing?
2. What seems to be the main point?
3. Which parts could be improved (unclear sentences, supporting points missing, order mixed up, writing not lively, and so forth)? Be specific.
4. What one change would most improve this essay?

*For more work on revising, see Chapter 3, "The Process of Writing Paragraphs," Part F, and Chapter 24, "Putting Your Revision Skills to Work."

TEACHING AND ESL TIP

Reinforce the notion that each student must learn his or her *error patterns*. These are the errors each should especially look for while proofreading.

Proofreading and Writing the Final Draft

Next, carefully **proofread** the draft for grammar and spelling. Check especially for those errors you often make: verb errors, comma splices, and so forth.* If you are unsure about the spelling of a word, check a dictionary or use the spell checker on your computer.

Finally, neatly recopy your essay or print out a final copy. Then, proofread the final copy.

The following sample essay by a student shows his first draft, the revisions he made, and the revised draft. Each revision has been numbered and explained to give you a clear idea of the thinking process involved.

First Draft

PORTRAIT OF A BIKE FANATIC

ESL TIP

Alert ESL students to the ESL Guidelines at the end of this text and to the excellent resources—quizzes and links—available online. Have them search the Web for help—for instance, **a4esl.org.**

(1) I first realized how serious Diane was when I joined her on a long trip one Sunday afternoon. Her bike looked new, so I asked her if it was. When she told me she had bought it three years ago, I asked her how she kept it looking so good. She showed me how she took good care of it.

(2) Diane had just about every kind of equipment I've ever seen. She put on her white helmet and attached a tiny rearview mirror on it—the kind the dentist uses to check out the backs of your teeth. She put a warning light on her left leg. She carried a whole bag full of tools. When I looked into it, I couldn't believe how much stuff was in there (wrenches, inner tubes, etc.)—tools to meet every emergency. I was tempted to see if it had a false bottom.

(3) I had no idea she was such a bike nut. We rode thirty miles and I was exhausted. Her equipment was something else, but useful because she had a flat and was able to fix it, saving our trip.

(4) She doesn't look like a bike fanatic, just a normal person. You'd never guess that her bike has more than 10,000 miles on it.

(5) As we rode, Diane told me about her travels throughout the Northeast (Cape Cod, Vermont, Penn., New York). Riding to work saved her money, kept her in shape. Her goal for the next summer was a cross-country tour over the Rockies!

(6) Our trip was no big deal to her but to me it was something. I might consider biking to work because it keeps you in shape. But basically I'm lazy. I drive a car or take the bus. I do like to walk though.

*For practice proofreading for individual errors, see chapters in Unit 6; for mixed-error proofreading, see Chapter 39, "Putting Your Proofreading Skills to Work."

Revisions

PORTRAIT OF A BIKE FANATIC

① *Add intro and thesis* I first realized how serious Diane was [② *about bicycling*] when I joined her on a ~~long~~ [③ *thirty-mile*] trip one Sunday afternoon. Her bike looked new, so I asked her if it was. When she told me she had bought it three years ago, I asked her how she kept it looking so good. ~~She showed me how she took good care of it.~~ ④ *Describe in detail*

Diane had just about every kind of equipment I've ever seen. [⑤ *For example,*] She put on her white helmet and attached a tiny rearview mirror on it—the kind the dentist uses to [⑥ *examine*] ~~check out~~ the backs of your teeth. She ~~put~~ [⑦ *strapped*] a warning light ~~on~~ [*to*] her leg [*just below the knee*]. ⑧ *Mention trip location*

She carried a whole bag full of tools. When I looked into it, I couldn't believe how much stuff was in there (wrenches, inner tubes, etc.)—tools to meet every emergency. I was tempted to see if it had a false bottom. ⑨ *New ¶ on tools, flat tire*

⑩ ~~I had no idea she was such a bike nut. We rode thirty miles and I was exhausted.~~ Her equipment was something else, but useful because she had a flat and was able to fix it, saving our trip. ⑪ *Combine into one ¶ on tools*

⑫ *Move to intro?* She doesn't look like a bike fanatic, just a normal person. You'd never guess that her bike has more than 10,000 miles on it.

⑬ *Describe in detail. Make interesting!* As we rode, Diane told me about her travels throughout the Northeast (Cape Cod, Vermont, Penn., New York). Riding to work saved her money, kept her in shape. [⑭ *Help Mother Earth!*] Her goal for the next summer was a cross-country tour over the Rockies!

⑮ *Better conclusion needed* Our trip was no big deal to her, but to me it was something. ~~I might consider biking to work because it keeps you in shape. But basically I'm lazy. I drive a car or take the bus. I do like to walk though.~~ ⑯ *Drop. Irrelevant*

TEACHING AND ESL TIP

The Writers' Workshops that conclude every unit model an effective way to teach revising skills through guided peer critique of student work.

Reasons for Revisions

1. No thesis statement. Add catchy introduction. (introduction and thesis statement)
2. Add *bicycling*. What she is serious *about* is not clear. (exact language)
3. Tell *how* long! (exact language)
4. Expand this; more details needed. (support, exact language)

TEACHING TIP

Go over the revisions and reasons with students so that they will better understand the changes that were made.

5. Add transition. (transitional expression)
6. Wrong tone for college essay. (exact language)
7. Find more active verb; be more specific. (exact language)
8. Conclude paragraph; add details to show time order. (order)
9. This section is weak. Add one paragraph on tools. Tell story of flat tire? (paragraphs, support)
10. Drop! Repeats thesis. Not really a paragraph. (unity, paragraphs)
11. Put this in tools paragraph. Order is mixed up. (order)
12. Put this in introduction? (order)
13. Add details; make this interesting! (support, exact language)
14. Add the point that biking helps the environment.
15. Write a better conclusion. (conclusion)
16. Drop! Essay is about Diane and biking, not my bad exercise habits. (unity)

Final Draft

PORTRAIT OF A BIKE FANATIC

(1) You'd never guess that the powder-blue ten-speed Raleigh had more than 10,000 miles on it. And you'd never guess that the tiny woman with the swept-back hair and the suntanned forearms had ridden those miles over the last two years, making trips through eleven states. But Diane is a bicycle fanatic.

(2) I first realized how serious Diane was about bicycling when I joined her on a thirty-mile trip one Sunday afternoon. Her bike looked new, so I asked her if it was. When she told me she had bought it three years ago, I asked her how she kept it looking so good. From her saddlebag she took the soft cloth that she wiped the bike down with after every long ride and the plastic drop cloth that she put over it every time she parked it outdoors overnight.

(3) Diane had just about every kind of bike equipment I've ever seen. For example, she put on her white helmet and attached a tiny rearview mirror to it—the kind the dentist uses to examine the backs of your teeth. She strapped a warning light to her left leg, just below the knee. Then we set off on our trip, starting at Walden Pond in Concord and planning to go to the Wayside Inn in Sudbury and back again before the sun set.

(4) We were still in Concord when Diane signaled me to stop. "I think I have a flat," she said. I cursed under my breath. I was sure that would mean the end of our trip; we'd have to walk her bike back to the car and she'd have to take it to the shop the next day. But she reached into her saddlebag again, and out came a wrench and a new tube. Before I knew it, she took the rear wheel off the bike, installed the new tube, and put the wheel back on. I began to wonder what else was in that saddlebag. When I asked, she showed me two sets of wrenches, another spare inner tube, two brake pads, a can of lubricating oil, two screwdrivers, a roll of reflective tape, extra bulbs for her headlight and taillight, and an extra chain. She had so much in the bag, I was tempted to see if it had a false bottom. Diane is one of those bicyclists who has tools to meet any emergency and knows how to use them.

(5) As we rode along, Diane told me about her travels throughout the Northeast. She had taken her bike on summer vacations on Cape Cod and fall foliage tours in Vermont. She had ridden all over Pennsylvania and upstate New York, covering as much as seventy miles in a single day. She also rode to and from work every day, which she said saved money, kept her in shape, and made a small contribution to the environment. Her goal for the next summer, she said, was a cross-country tour. "All the way?" I asked. "What about the Rockies?" "I know," she said. "What a challenge!"

(6) Our trip took a little less than three hours, but I'm sure Diane was slowing down to let me keep up with her. When we got back to the parked car, I was breathing hard and had worked up quite a sweat. Diane was already there waiting for me, looking as if she did this every day—which she does. For Diane, riding a bike is as easy and natural as walking is for most people. Look out, Rockies.

PRACTICE 13

Now, carefully read over the first draft of your essay from Practice 12 and revise it, referring to the list of nine questions that appear earlier in this section. You might wish to ask a peer reviewer for feedback before you revise. Ask specific questions or use the Peer Feedback Sheet. Take your time and write the best essay you can. Once you are satisfied, proofread your essay for grammar and spelling errors. Neatly write the final draft or print a final copy.

WRITING ASSIGNMENTS

The assignments that follow will give you practice in writing essays. In each, concentrate on writing a clear thesis statement and a full, well-organized body. Because introductions and conclusions are not discussed until Chapter 15, you may wish to begin your essay with the thesis statement and conclude as simply as possible.

Before you write, make sure you have the specific *audience* to whom you are writing and your *purpose* clearly in mind. Then make an outline that includes:

- a clear thesis statement
- two to four topic sentences that support the thesis statement
- details, facts, and examples to develop each paragraph
- a logical order of paragraphs

1. Do you socialize mostly with people from work or school? Why? Should you broaden your circle of friends to include more diverse people? Write an essay that explores in detail either the advantages or disadvantages of a diverse social life or the ways you could make this change happen. Begin by developing a clear thesis statement, and then write an outline to organize your essay.

2. Interview a classmate (or, if you do this assignment at home, someone with an unusual skill). As you talk to the person, look for a thesis: ask questions, take notes. What stands out about the person? Is there an overall impression

TEACHING TIP

If you want your students to practice less personal and more formal writing, note that the rhetorical tasks or audience requirements of assignments 2 through 6 lend themselves to third-person and/or more formal compositions.

or idea that can structure your essay? Do you notice an overall quality, skill, or goal that seems to characterize this person? Formulate a thesis statement that points out this quality or trait, organize your ideas, and write.

3. Write to a judge or probation officer explaining why a friend or family member deserves a second chance. Your friend or relative has gotten in trouble with the law (anything from a speeding ticket to armed robbery), and your goal is to convince the judge or officer to act with leniency. In your letter, briefly explain the crime or offense. Then set forth two to three solid reasons why you believe this person deserves a break. You could discuss stresses that contributed to the offense, as well as positive traits, a desire to change, or circumstances that predict a brighter future.

4. What are the most important qualities of a committed relationship? What factors help keep such a relationship positive and alive? Would it be shared interests, trust, humor, or nurturing each other's growth? Your audience is anyone who wants a devoted relationship. Jot your ideas, and perhaps ask happy couples for advice. Then write an essay that explains three key qualities of committed partnership. Support your points with details, examples, and perhaps a quote.

5. Some college students cheat on their papers and exams; some people cheat on the job. Why do people cheat? What are the advantages and disadvantages of cheating? Does cheating pay off? Does it achieve the end that the cheater desires? Focus on cheating at college or at work, and choose one main idea to write about. You might wish to use examples to support your thesis. Plan your essay carefully on paper before you write it.

6. Write a letter to an elected official, newspaper editor, school principal, college president, or other authority figure about an issue or incident that concerns you. Begin by crafting a thesis statement that mentions both the problem and at least one possible solution. Support your thesis first by clearly describing the problem, using specific details from your observations or experience. Then, carefully explain each of your proposed solutions, anticipating and answering all of the reader's potential questions.

Checklist

The Process of Writing an Essay

- ☐ 1. Narrow the topic to fit your audience and purpose. Be sure you can discuss this topic fully in a short essay.
- ☐ 2. Write a clear thesis statement. If you have trouble, freewrite or brainstorm first; then narrow the topic and write the thesis statement.
- ☐ 3. Freewrite or brainstorm, generating facts, details, and examples to support your thesis statement.

- [ ] 4. Plan or outline your essay, choosing from two to four main ideas to support the thesis statement.
- [ ] 5. Write a topic sentence that expresses each main idea.
- [ ] 6. Decide on a logical order in which to present the paragraphs.
- [ ] 7. Plan the body of each paragraph, using all you learned about paragraph development in Unit 2 of this book.
- [ ] 8. Write the first draft of your essay.
- [ ] 9. Revise as necessary, checking your essay for support, unity, and coherence. Refer to the list of revision questions in the "Revising and Proofreading" section of this chapter.
- [ ] 10. Proofread carefully for grammar, punctuation, sentence structure, spelling, and mechanics.

Suggested Topics for Essays

1. The career for which I am best suited
2. Tips for balancing work, school, and home
3. How to do something that will improve your life (get organized, learn a new language)
4. Why many Americans don't ________________ (save money for the future, stay motivated at work, value education, read poetry)
5. A valuable discipline or practice (lifting weights, rock climbing, bicycling, or other)
6. The advantages and disadvantages of online shopping
7. A story of courage
8. A lesson in diversity, race, or difference
9. The joys of homework (or housework or some other supposedly unpleasant task)
10. How to resolve a disagreement peacefully
11. A film, book, or magazine
12. The best (or worst) party I ever attended
13. Three ways that certain types of ads (for cereal or toys, for example) "hook" children
14. Whether courts should require a one-year "cooling-off" period before a divorce
15. Writer's choice: ____

EXPLORING ONLINE

www.powa.org

Click "Explain" for a good review of the college essay-writing process. Topics include "Subject to Thesis," "Stating Your Thesis," "Supporting Your Thesis," "Developing Your Paragraphs," and more.

www.gallaudet.edu/tip/english-center/writing/pre-writing-writing-and-revising.html

Review the steps of the writing process. If organizing is a problem for you, review the "Outlining" section.

owl.english.purdue.edu/owl/resource/561/01

On this page, find good revising and proofreading techniques to sharpen your awareness and raise your grade.

CHAPTER 15

The Introduction, the Conclusion, and the Title

A: The Introduction

B: The Conclusion

C: The Title

A catchy title and introduction are important parts of an essay. Both attract the reader's attention and make him or her want to read on. The conclusion of an essay performs a different job, leaving the reader with something to think about or with a sense of why the topic matters. Most writers polish these three elements *after* they have planned and written the essay, though sometimes a great title or the idea for a good introduction might occur to them earlier. This chapter will teach you how to write memorable introductions, conclusions, and titles.

A. The Introduction

An **introduction** has two functions in an essay. First, it contains the **thesis statement** and, therefore, tells the reader what central idea will be developed in the rest of the paper. Since the reader should be able to spot the thesis statement easily, it should be given a prominent place—for example, the first or the last sentence in the introduction. Second, the introduction has to interest the reader enough that he or she will want to continue reading the paper.

Sometimes the process of writing the essay will help clarify your ideas about how best to introduce it. So once you have completed your essay, you may wish to revise and rewrite the introduction, making sure that it clearly introduces the essay's main idea.

There is no best way to introduce an essay, but you should certainly avoid beginning your work with "I'm going to discuss" or "This paper is about." You needn't tell the reader you are about to begin; just begin!

Here are six basic methods for beginning your composition effectively. In each example, the thesis statement is italicized.

1. **Begin with a single-sentence thesis statement.** A single-sentence thesis statement can be effective because it quickly and forcefully states the main idea of the essay:

Time management should be a required course at this college.

- Note how quickly and clearly a one-sentence thesis statement can inform the reader about what will follow in the rest of the essay.

2. **Begin with a general idea and then narrow to a specific thesis statement.** The general idea gives the reader background information or sets the scene. Then the topic narrows to one specific idea—the thesis statement. The effect is like a funnel, from broad to narrow.

I spent most of my adolescent years surrounded by policemen, social workers, and counselors. I have been arrested, detained, and interrogated more times than I can remember. I wasn't a drug or criminal offender. *I was a teenage runaway.*

—Emelyn Cruz Lat, "Emancipated," *Mother Jones*

- What general idea precedes the thesis statement and then leads the reader to focus on the specific main point of the essay?

author's troubled adolescence

- The rest of the essay will focus on the experiences of a teenage runaway.

3. **Begin with an illustration or anecdote (a brief narrative).** A brief illustration or anecdote in the introduction of an essay makes the thesis statement more concrete and vivid, a good technique for catching the reader's interest.

The other day I was watching a Reebok commercial. It was about a young male who, after purchasing a pair of sneakers, was walking down the street to a smooth jazz tune. As this "pretty boy" walked in his new pair of sneakers, he drew the attention of all in his path, especially the females. For a second I was envious of this "dude." I've been purchasing sneakers for over eighteen years, and I haven't had one girl look at me the way they did him during his thirty-second stroll down some dark and filthy sidewalk. As I watched this ad and others like it, I started to analyze the ads' underlying message. *I wondered why the majority of sneaker ads are geared to inner-city youth, especially ads for brand-name sneakers.*

—Saladin Brown, Student, "The Illusion of Ads"

- Mr. Brown's thesis poses a question that his essay will try to answer.

- What example does the writer provide to make the thesis statement more concrete?

  the example of a young male who had just bought new sneakers

- The rest of the essay will discuss the reasons why athletic shoe advertisers seem to target inner-city males.

4. Begin with a surprising fact or idea. A surprising fact or idea arouses the reader's curiosity about how you will support this initial startling statement.

> *Millions of law-abiding Americans are physically addicted to caffeine—and most of them don't even know it.* Caffeine is a powerful central nervous system stimulant with substantial addiction potential. When deprived of their caffeine, addicts often experience severe withdrawal symptoms, which may include a throbbing headache, disorientation, constipation, nausea, sluggishness, depression, and irritability. As with other addictive drugs, heavy users develop a tolerance and require higher doses to obtain the expected effect.
>
> —Tom Ferguson and Joe Graedon, "Caffeine," *Medical Self-Care*

- Why are the facts in this introduction likely to startle or surprise the reader?

  So many people drink caffeine-containing beverages that they think caffeine is harmless.

- The rest of the essay will discuss caffeine addiction in depth.

TEACHING TIP
Present students with a list of different thesis statements. As a class or in small groups, have students discuss the introduction method(s) that would be most appropriate for each one.

5. Begin with a contradiction. In this type of introduction, your thesis statement contradicts what many or most people believe. In other words, your essay will contrast your opinion with the widely held view.

> When I became an Emergency Medical Technician (EMT), I was excited by the opportunity to assist others and save lives. Like most people, I didn't think of an EMT job as dangerous. After all, EMTs arrive *after* the accident or crime has occurred, so the riskiest part of our work would seem to be the high-speed ambulance ride to or from the scene. I never expected to encounter a situation that put my life and my partner's life in danger when we answered someone's call for help. *But one night a year ago, responding to a 911 call to aid a gunshot victim, we found ourselves in a situation that soon turned deadly dangerous.*
>
> —Marlena Torres Ballard, Student

- The writer first describes her excitement at becoming an EMT. What widely held view of this job does she set forth?

  the view that being an EMT is not dangerous

- How does she then contradict this idea?

  She writes that she and her partner found themselves in a "deadly dangerous" situation.

- The rest of the essay will tell the story of her frightening experience.

TEACHING TIP

Bring in magazines and newspapers and have students examine the introductions. Can they identify the methods used? (Illustration is the most frequently used.) Let them vote for the most effective one or two and explain their choices.

6. **Begin with a direct quotation.** A direct quotation is likely to catch your reader's attention and to show that you have explored what others have to say about the subject. You can then proceed to agree or to disagree with the direct quotation.

> "All glory comes from daring to begin," according to an old saying. The last two-and-a-half-year chapter of my life shows just how true this saying is. It started when I got laid off from my job at the furniture manufacturing plant in Morganton, North Carolina. I had worked there for 10 years after high school and assumed I always would. The chapter ended with me wearing a light blue cap and gown, walking across the stage to receive my college degree in dental assisting as my family and friends cheered me on. *By daring to find a new path and stay on it through the hardships, I have changed my life for the better.*
>
> —Sam Chaich, Student

- Does the writer agree or disagree with the quotation?

  The author agrees.

- Based on this introduction, what will the rest of the essay discuss?

  It will discuss the steps this student took to move from "laid off" to "graduated."

TEACHING TIP

Have students review their recently written essays and revise the introductions.

Of course, definitions, comparisons, or any of the other kinds of devices you have already studied can also make good introductions. Just make sure that the reader knows exactly which sentence is your thesis statement.

WRITING ASSIGNMENT 1

Here are five statements. Pick three that you would like to write about and compose an introduction for each one. Use any of the methods for beginning compositions discussed in this chapter thus far.

1. (Entrepreneurs, ex-offenders, student athletes, celebrities, or recovering addicts) should be considered role models for troubled youth.
2. Voter ID laws are necessary (unnecessary) and do not discriminate (discriminate) against low-income, minority, and elderly voters.
3. To avoid getting into debt, consumers have to use credit cards wisely.
4. The federal government should (not) be allowed to monitor phone calls, e-mails, and Internet activity.
5. Men today are more (less) responsible in parenting than their fathers were.

B. The Conclusion

A conclusion signals the end of the essay and leaves the reader with a final thought. As with the introduction, you may wish to revise and rewrite the conclusion once you have completed your essay. Be certain your conclusion flows logically from the body of the essay.

TEACHING TIP

Conclusions are often difficult for students because they feel that they've already said everything that they wanted to say. These three methods for concluding an essay will give them ideas for writing satisfying endings.

Like introductions, conclusions can take many forms, and the right one for your essay depends on how you wish to complete your paper—with what thought you wish to leave the reader. However, never conclude your paper with "As I said in the beginning," and try to avoid the overused "In conclusion" or "In summary." Don't end by saying you are going to end; just end!

Here are three ways to conclude an essay.

1. **End with a call to action.** The call to action says that in view of the facts and ideas presented in this essay, the reader should *do something*.

Single-gender schools work. As we have seen, boys-only and girls-only middle and high schools help steer young people toward academic achievement and higher self-esteem. Showing off for the opposite sex, dating too early, and, especially in the case of girls, failing to raise their hands for fear of outshining the boys, are problems avoided altogether in single-gender environments. Parents and concerned citizens must contact their representatives and school boards to demand the option of single-gender schools. We owe it to our children to fight for the schools that truly serve them.

- What does the writer want the reader to do?

The writer wants the reader to contact representatives and school boards to demand the option of single-gender schools.

2. **End with a final point.** Make a point that discusses one or more consequences of the ideas or experiences in your essay. Some writers also summarize their main ideas, but if you do this, be sure to add a new point or thought; don't just repeat what you have already said.

My struggles as a single mom made me grow up and change my values. Caring for a baby on a limited budget forced me to be responsible. Money once spent on shoes, makeup, pizza, and partying had to go towards food, doctor bills, baby clothes, and babysitters. I became less obsessed with myself and focused instead on my child, who was totally dependent on me. In order to provide for my son, I realized I would need a better job. That's what inspired me to enroll in college. Now I know I am the best mom I can be.

- With what final point does this student end her essay?

She states that becoming a single mom made her grow up and enroll in college.

TEACHING TIP

Bring in an essay with the conclusion removed. Have students, either individually or in groups, write two concluding paragraphs, each one using a different technique.

3. **End with a question.** By ending with a question, you leave the reader with a final problem that you wish him or her to think about.

Yes, it is embarrassing to speak with our children about sex. We will feel awkward not knowing what to say, stymied as they resist the discussion. However, knowing the pressures that kids today face, the terrible examples bombarding them from popular culture, and the real threat of diseases, can we afford not to?

—Amelia Garcia, Student, "Talking to Kids About Sex"

- What problem does the writer's final question point to?

  the problem of parents' difficulty in talking to kids about sex

WRITING ASSIGNMENT 2

Review two or three essays that you have written recently. Do the conclusions bring the essays clearly to an end? Are those conclusions interesting? How could they be improved? Using one of the three strategies taught in this section, write a new conclusion for one of the essays.

C. The Title

TEACHING TIP

Discuss with students the conventions for formatting a college paper.

If you are writing just one paragraph, chances are that you will not need to give it a title, but if you are writing a multiparagraph essay, a title is definitely in order.

The title is centered on the page above the body of the composition and separated from it by several blank lines (about 1 inch of space), as shown here.

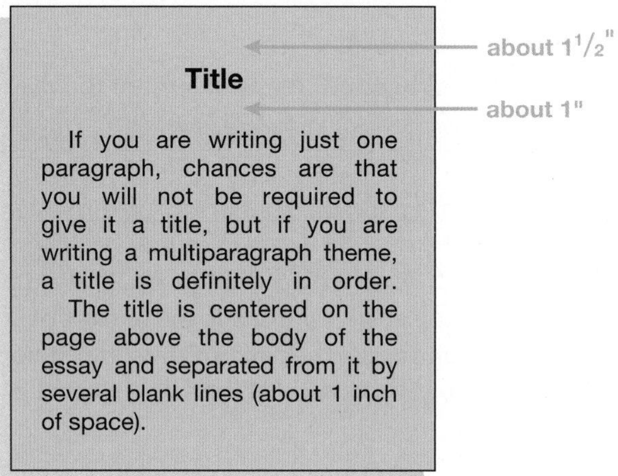
about $1^1/_2$"
Title
about 1"
If you are writing just one paragraph, chances are that you will not be required to give it a title, but if you are writing a multiparagraph theme, a title is definitely in order.
The title is centered on the page above the body of the essay and separated from it by several blank lines (about 1 inch of space).

- Do *not* put quotation marks around the title of your own paper.
- Do *not* underline or italicize the title of your own paper.
- Remember, unlike the topic sentence, the title is not part of the first paragraph; in fact, it is usually only four to five words long and is rarely an entire sentence.

A good title has two functions: to suggest the subject of the essay and to spark the reader's interest. Although the title is the first part of your essay the reader sees, the most effective titles are usually written *after* the essay has been completed.

To create a title, reread your essay, paying special attention to the **thesis statement** and the **conclusion**. Try to come up with a few words that express the main point of your paper.

Here are some basic kinds of titles.

1. The most common title used in college writing is the no-nonsense descriptive title. In this title, stress key words and ideas developed in the essay:

Anger in the Work of Jamaica Kincaid
Advantages and Disadvantages of Buying on Credit

2. Two-part titles are also effective. Write one or two words stating the general subject, and then add several words that narrow the topic:

Rumi: Poet and Mystic
Legal Gambling: Pro and Con

TEACHING TIP
Have fun by asking students to think of weak or bad titles they have given to past papers. Have volunteers share their worst title and suggest a new, better title—or they can ask the class to help them come up with a "grabber" title.

3. Write the title as a rhetorical question. Then answer the question in your essay:

What Can Be Done About the High Price of Higher Education?
Are Athletes Setting Bad Examples?

4. Relate the title to the method of development used in the essay (see Unit 3 and Chapters 16 and 17):

Illustration:	Democracy in Action Three Roles I Play
Narration:	The Development of Jazz Edwidge Danticat: The Making of a Storyteller
Description:	Portrait of a Scientist A Waterfront Scene
Process:	How to Start a Book Group How to Get in Shape Fast
Definition:	What It Means to Be Unemployed A Definition of Respect
Comparison:	Two Country Stars Who Crossed Over Unconventional Dads: Homer Simpson and Tony Soprano
Contrast:	Pleasures and Problems of Owning a Home Montreal: City of Contrasts
Classification:	Three Types of Soap Operas What Kind of E-Mail User Are You?
Cause and Effect:	What Causes Whales to Beach Themselves? The Effects of Divorce on Children
Persuasion:	Internet Pornography Should Be Banned The Need for Metal Detectors in Our Schools

TEACHING TIP
Have students browse through the reading selections in Chapter 43. Ask them to identify the titles that pique their interest and make them want to read on.

Use this list the next time you title a paper.*

*For more on how to capitalize in titles, see Chapter 38, "Mechanics," Part B.

WRITING ASSIGNMENT 3

Review two or three essays that you have written recently. Are the titles clear and interesting? Applying what you've learned in this chapter, write a better title for at least one paper.

EXPLORING ONLINE

www.powa.org

Click "Explain" and scroll to "Introductions and Conclusions." Read more about beginning and ending your essays effectively.

grammar.ccc.commnet.edu/grammar

Under "Essay & Research Paper Level," scroll to "Structural Considerations" and click "Beginnings" for lively sample introductions, plus tips for the writer.

CHAPTER 16

Types of Essays, Part 1

A: The Illustration Essay

B: The Narrative Essay

C: The Descriptive Essay

D: The Process Essay

E: The Definition Essay

TEACHING TIP

Go over the diagram at the beginning of Chapter 14 to review the similarities and differences between paragraphs and essays. The parts of Chapters 16 and 17 dovetail perfectly with the chapters in Unit 3.

Because an essay is like an expanded paragraph, the methods for developing and organizing a paragraph that you learned in Unit 3—illustration, process, and so forth—can also be used to develop an entire essay. Chapters 16 and 17 will show you how.

A. The Illustration Essay

The **illustration** essay is one of the most frequently used in college writing and in business. For papers and exams in history, health, psychology, English, and other subjects, you often will be asked to develop a main point with examples. In careers as varied as engineering, nursing, and advertising, you will author reports that include examples of advantages of one computer system, patients' symptoms and behavior, or successful product launches. In a job application, you might wish to give examples of achievements that demonstrate your special skills.

Here is an illustration essay:

GIRL HEROES IN THE HOUSE

Introduction

Thesis statement

(1) Although a visitor might not notice, the small apartment I share with my daughters is very crowded. We live with a group of fantastic characters who fill my young daughters' imaginations and therefore our daily lives. Mostly female, they reveal a world beyond Cinderella and Barbie. These role models

are teaching my girls to take pride in their heritage, their intelligence, and their unique talents.

Topic sentence introducing example 1

(2) A good example is *Dora the Explorer,* a spunky preschool adventurer with an international fan club. My third grader, who once knew every Dora song by heart, has since moved on, but her little sister now calls Dora her best friend. As a mother, I have good reasons to admire Dora. She is bilingual like our family, and while she is Mexican and we are Guatemalan, Dora gives my lovely brown daughters a reason to like themselves even if they don't look like Barbie. Dora plunges into the unknown day after day, armed with little more than a talking backpack and a belief that she can overcome any obstacle. The world outside can be an unsavory place for a four-year-old, so I am thankful for the pleasures Dora uncovers on her journeys and the dignity she brings to our heritage.

Facts & details developing example 1

Topic sentence introducing example 2

(3) A new role model in our home is Hermione, the brainy heroine in J. K. Rowling's *Harry Potter* books. She is my older daughter's current obsession, and I confess that I am hooked on her too. Like most parents, I was thrilled when my cartoon-addicted third grader wanted to read a chapter book, so every night we sit together absorbing the adventures of Harry and his best friends Ron and Hermione. We take turns reading pages, getting lost in the Hogwarts School of Witchcraft and Wizardry. I love that Hermione is neither graceful nor gorgeous and often comes across as a know-it-all. But experience reveals her as a brilliant young woman and a deeply loyal friend. Just two books into the series and Hermione has saved Harry more than once. I hope that my daughter internalizes the message that really cool girls value intelligence and loyalty more than superficial traits.

Facts & details developing example 2

Topic sentence introducing example 3

(4) With the "tween" years fast approaching, I suppose Hannah Montana will soon arrive in our home. While part of me dreads my girls' transition into rock music, boys, and fashion, there are worse role models than a perky high schooler who lives an average teenager's life by day and performs as a famous pop artist at night. The wild success of the *Hannah Montana* television show and merchandise shows the power this secret rock star has over little girls. Hannah solves everyday problems with a silly humor that girls love. She also offers a fantasy that preteens can escape into when their bodies begin to change and their social lives get complicated. Hannah's message is positive: pursue your talents, whatever they are.

Facts & details developing example 3

Conclusion

(5) The girl heroes in our home will keep changing as fast as my daughters do. I wonder if someday they will see me—raising them, working, going to college, pursuing my dreams—as a hero too. But for now, I am happy to share my home with a Latina adventurer, a smart witch-in-training, and a lively singer in lip gloss. They are helping me teach my daughters to embrace their lucky lives as modern girls.

—Irma Batres, Student

TEACHING AND ESL TIP

Discuss the three examples that develop this writer's thesis. Make sure students see how much specific detail and description help the reader understand each example.

- The **thesis statement** in an illustration essay states the writer's central point—a general statement that the rest of the essay will develop with examples.
- How many **examples** does the writer use to develop the thesis statement? What are they?

Three: Dora the Explorer, Hermione, Hannah Montana

TEACHING TIP

You might ask the class what role models they would name—for girls or for boys.

- What words connect each topic sentence to the introduction and thesis statement?

  "A good example is . . . ," "A new role model in our home is . . . ,"

  ". . . will soon arrive in our home."

- Notice that the thesis statement and topic sentences setting forth the three main examples create an **outline** for this essay. The writer no doubt made an outline well developed with specifics before she wrote the first draft.

PRACTICE 1

Read this student's illustration essay and answer the questions.

OTC: ONLY TAKE CARE!

IN

(1) Many people take over-the-counter (OTC) medications for headaches, colds, and such. Over 100,000 OTC medications are for sale in stores, a number that surprised me even though I am pursuing my Pharmacy Technician certification. Most consumers think that OTC drugs are harmless because no prescription is needed, but, in fact, they can be hazardous to your health.

E1

LEARNING STYLES TIP

Having students label the parts of essays in this chapter and the next will reinforce the structure of a well-organized essay for *visual learners* and others as well.

(2) Aspirin, for instance, is so common that people think it cannot hurt them. Every day, 43 million people take aspirin for pain, swelling, or fever; some take it on their doctors' orders to prevent a heart attack or stroke. An excellent drug if used correctly, aspirin can cause bleeding in the organs or even a brain bleed. Coated aspirin helps protect from stomach bleeding, but only your doctor can say whether the dangers are worth the risks. Many people don't know that those on blood thinners like warfarin should never take aspirin or that aspirin can cause serious brain, liver, and other damage in children and teens who have fevers; this condition is called Reyes Syndrome. A widespread myth among teenagers that mixing Coca-Cola with aspirin "gets you high" is not true; however, it can cause bleeding.

E2

(3) A second illustration is cold medications. The decongestants in many of these can dangerously raise blood pressure in people who take blood pressure medications and in those on certain antidepressants. People with irregular heartbeats can be "set off" by the stimulants in these drugs. A serious new problem with cold medications is addiction to a chemical found in over 100 of them, called Dextromethorphan (DXM). More and more young people are abusing cold medications for the DXM high. Overdoses and deaths have been reported.

E3

(4) Sleep aids are yet another example of problematic OTCs. Not being able to fall or stay asleep is a nerve-wracking problem for many people, but instead of studying their own habits to try and solve the problem naturally, often they just pop a pill. Most sleep aids contain antihistamines, which can cause not only drowsiness but also side effects during the day like sleepiness or headaches. Sleeping pills can become addictive, and people who use them should never drink alcohol. Studies differ as to whether these medications even work.

C (5) These are just three examples of OTC medications and their possible side effects. Easy access to these drugs means that mistakes and abuse are common. As a consumer, it's up to you to protect your body and your health. Always read the Drug Facts label on everything you take. Ask your doctor or pharmacist about both your OTC and prescription medications to make sure there are no interactions among them.

—Bradley K. Knight, Student

1. Underline or highlight the **thesis statement**. What main examples does this student use to support the thesis and develop the essay?

   aspirin, cold medications, sleep aids

2. Now, underline or highlight the **topic sentences**. Label the parts of this essay by writing these labels in the left margin opposite the correct part:

   IN Introduction
   C Conclusion
   E1 Example 1 and details
   E2 Example 2 and details
   E3 Example 3 and details

3. What transitional expressions of illustration help introduce each example?

   for instance, a second illustration, yet another example

4. The writer mentions in the introduction that he is pursuing a certain certification. Is this sentence relevant to the paper, or should it be dropped?

   It's relevant; pharmacy tech courses give him authority on the subject.

5. Mr. Knight drew on his curriculum to find a topic for his illustration essay. Have you learned material in your own courses that might interest your classmates? Can this material be presented through examples?

   Answers will vary.

PRACTICE 2 CRITICAL VIEWING AND WRITING

Often a writer will notice specific examples first, see a pattern, and then come up with a generalization—a thesis statement or topic sentence. Examine these three examples of graffiti attributed to Banksy, a British street artist. Can you make any *general* statements about Banksy's art, based just on these *examples*? Write down your generalizations.

David Silverman/Getty Images

Michaud Gael/Corbis

Murrissey72/Shutterstock.com

Planning and Writing the Illustration Essay

Before writing an illustration essay, you may wish to reread Chapter 5, "Illustration." As you pick a topic and plan the essay, make sure your thesis statement can be richly developed by examples. Prewrite to generate as many examples as possible, so you can choose the best two, three, or four. As you revise, make sure you have fully discussed each example, including all necessary details and facts.

The rest of the section will guide you as you write an illustration essay.

PRACTICE 3

TEACHING TIP
You may want to have students work together in small groups to practice writing a thesis statement and brainstorming to get strong examples.

1. Choose a topic from the list below or one your instructor has assigned. Make sure you can develop it well with examples. Determine your audience and purpose. Then brainstorm, cluster, or freewrite to get as many examples as possible. Choose the best ones.
   1. Role models (positive or negative)
   2. Learning from mistakes
   3. Qualities (or skills) that many employers look for
   4. TV shows that send a violent (hopeful, or other) message
   5. Everyday action steps to protect the environment
   6. Three people in the news who exemplify honesty or commitment to principles

ESL TIP
Ask students which suggested topics lend themselves to personal examples and which do not.

7. The skills, values, or traits that would make your friend a good store manager (police officer, cartoonist, and so forth)
8. Musicians or artists of a particular type (R&B, tropical Latin, surrealist, French impressionist, hip hop, and so on) or three works by the same artist
9. Experiences that shaped your attitudes toward education (or family or work)
10. Important advances in science or technology
11. Writer's choice: ______________________________

LEARNING STYLES TIP
Visual and other learners often find an organizer helpful as they generate ideas, plan, and compose.

2. Many students find using a graphic organizer helpful as they plan an essay. In your notebook or on a computer, create an outline for your illustration essay using an organizer like the one that follows. The information you write in each box will become a paragraph.

ILLUSTRATION ESSAY ORGANIZER

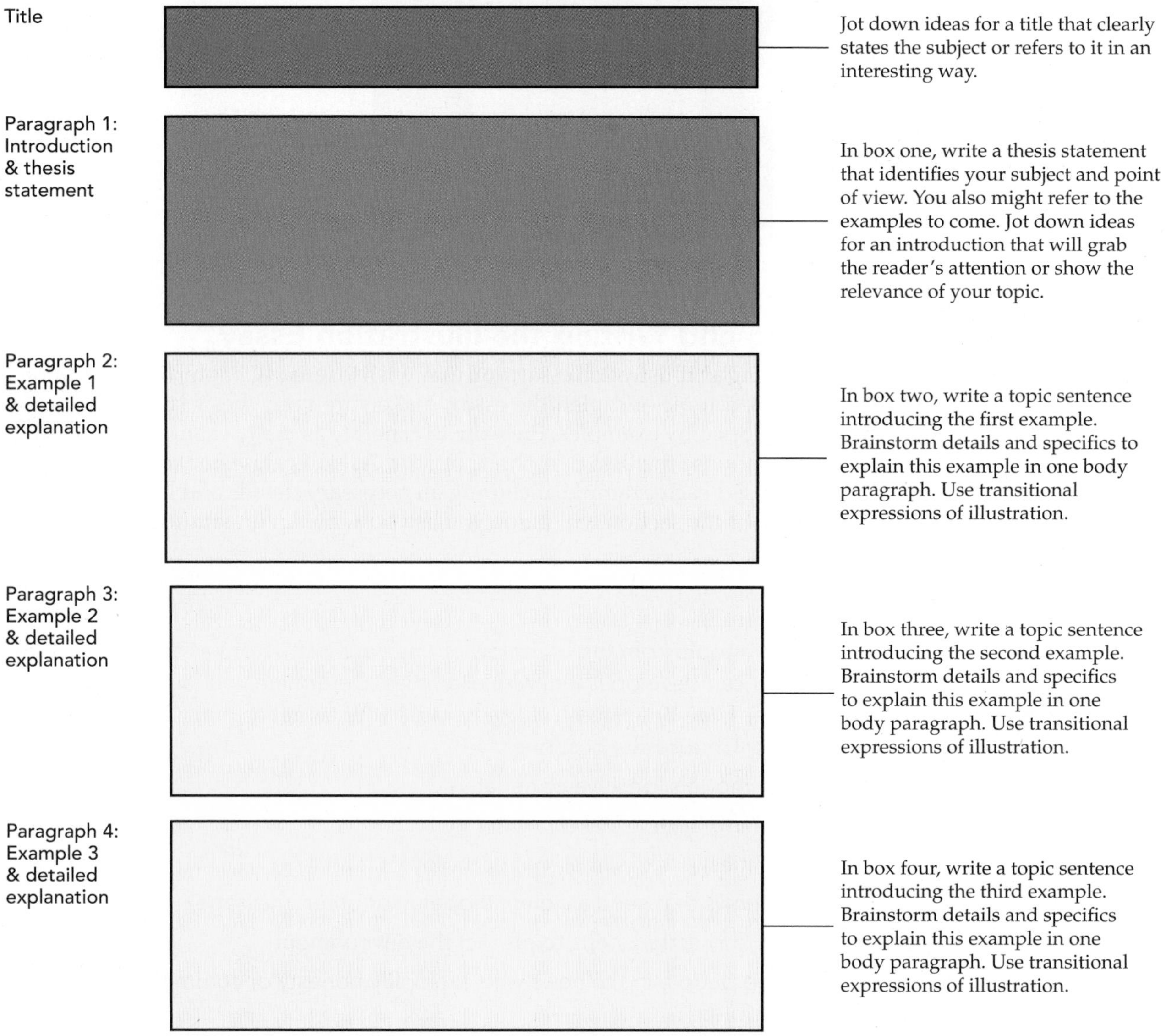

Title		Jot down ideas for a title that clearly states the subject or refers to it in an interesting way.
Paragraph 1: Introduction & thesis statement		In box one, write a thesis statement that identifies your subject and point of view. You also might refer to the examples to come. Jot down ideas for an introduction that will grab the reader's attention or show the relevance of your topic.
Paragraph 2: Example 1 & detailed explanation		In box two, write a topic sentence introducing the first example. Brainstorm details and specifics to explain this example in one body paragraph. Use transitional expressions of illustration.
Paragraph 3: Example 2 & detailed explanation		In box three, write a topic sentence introducing the second example. Brainstorm details and specifics to explain this example in one body paragraph. Use transitional expressions of illustration.
Paragraph 4: Example 3 & detailed explanation		In box four, write a topic sentence introducing the third example. Brainstorm details and specifics to explain this example in one body paragraph. Use transitional expressions of illustration.

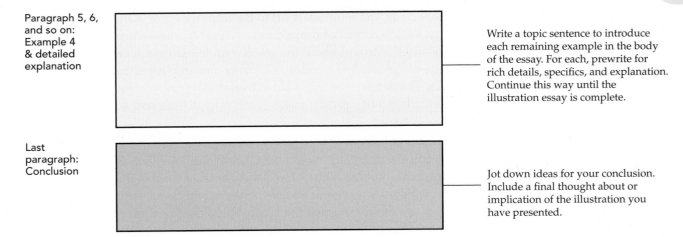

PRACTICE 4

Now, referring to your plan, write the best first draft you can. Aim for clarity as you help the reader develop an understanding of each category in your illustration. Check your paragraphing, and use *transitional expressions** to guide the reader from example to example.

Let your draft cool for an hour or a day; then reread it as if you were a helpful, eagle-eyed stranger. Now revise and rewrite, emphasizing clarity and completeness, and keeping your reader in mind. Is each paragraph developed fully? Do transitions make the flow of ideas clear? Proofread for spelling, grammar, and sentence errors.

B. The Narrative Essay

The urge to tell stories and listen to them is as old as human beings, so it's not surprising that the **narrative** essay is used frequently in college writing. For instance, in a history course, you might be assigned a paper on the major battles in World War I or be given an essay examination question about the struggle of women to gain the right to vote. An English teacher might ask you to write a composition retelling a meaningful incident or personal experience. In police work, nursing, and social work, your ability to organize facts and details in clear chronological, or time, order—to tell a story well—will be a crucial factor in the effectiveness of your writing.

Here is a narrative essay:

MAYA LIN'S VIETNAM VETERANS MEMORIAL

TEACHING TIP
Ask whether any students have visited the Vietnam Veterans Memorial. Why did they go, and what were their experiences like?

(1) The Vietnam War was the longest war in United States history, lasting from 1965 until 1975. Also our most controversial war, it left a deep wound in the nation's conscience. The creation of the Vietnam Veterans Memorial helped heal this wound and put an unknown architecture student into the history books.

(2) In 1980, when the call went out for designs for a Vietnam War memorial, no one could have predicted that as many as 14,000 entries would be submitted.

---

*For a list of transitional expressions of illustration, see Chapter 5.

The rules were clear. The memorial had to be contemplative, harmonize with its surroundings, list the names of those dead or missing, and—most important—make no political statement about the war. When the judges, all well-known architects and sculptors, met in April 1981, they unanimously chose entry number 1026. The winner was Maya Lin, a twenty-one-year-old Asian American architecture student who, ironically, was too young to have had any direct experience of the war.

TEACHING TIP
Point out to students that narration and description are commonly combined in essays.

(3) Lin envisioned shining black granite slabs embedded in a long V-shaped trench, with one end pointing toward the Lincoln Memorial and the other toward the Washington Monument. She defined the trench as a cut in the earth, "an initial violence that in time would heal." Names would be carved into the granite in the order of the dates on which the soldiers had died or disappeared. Lin felt that finding a name on the memorial with the help of a directory would be like finding a body on a battlefield.

(4) Although her design satisfied all the contest criteria and was the judges' clear favorite, it aroused much controversy. Some critics called it a "black gash of shame and sorrow," labeling it unpatriotic, unheroic, and morbid. They were upset that the memorial contained no flags, no statues of soldiers, and no inscription other than the names. Privately, some complained that Lin was too young to win the contest—and that she was female besides. She fought back. She claimed that a flag would make the green area around the memorial look like a golf course and that a traditional statue on her modern structure would be like a mustache drawn on someone else's portrait. At last, a compromise was reached: a flag and a statue were added to the memorial, and the critics withdrew their complaints. On Veterans Day, November 11, 1982, the Vietnam Veterans Memorial was finally dedicated.

(5) Since then, the memorial has become the most popular site in Washington, D.C. Some visit to see the monument and pay tribute to those who died in the war. Others come to locate and touch the names of loved ones. As they stand before the wall, they also learn the names of those who served and died with their relatives and friends. When the rain falls, all the names seem to disappear. Visitors often leave memorials of their own—flowers, notes to the departed, bits of old uniforms. A place of national mourning and of love, Maya Lin's monument has helped heal the wounds of the Vietnam War.

TEACHING TIP
"Facing It" is a moving, richly detailed poem on one man's visit to the Vietnam Memorial. You might wish to analyze its descriptive language with the class. For a printout or a video of the poet reading, search Google for "Facing It, Komunyakaa."

- The thesis statement of a narrative essay usually gives the point of the essay. Underline or highlight the thesis statement of this essay.
- Paragraphs 2, 4, and 5 of this essay tell in chronological order the incidents of the narrative.
- What are the incidents?

  the call for designs, the judges' decision, the controversy, the dedication, the healing result

- What is the main idea of paragraph 3?

  a description of Maya Lin's design

- Paragraph 1 provides background information that helps the reader understand the narrative. What background material is given in this paragraph?

The Vietnam War was the longest and most controversial war in U.S. history.

PRACTICE 5 CRITICAL THINKING AND WRITING

Study this photograph of a visitor to the Vietnam Veterans Memorial. Look closely at the man saluting the wall. Do you guess he is saluting to show respect to all those who died in the conflict or to honor a single person, such as a fallen friend or relative? What does this gesture symbolize? Write a paragraph in which you discuss the story this photograph tells.

Tom Williams/CQ Roll Call/Getty Images

A visitor to the Vietnam Veterans Memorial, 2012. What story does this picture tell?

PRACTICE 6

Read this student's narrative essay and answer the questions.

MY BLACK DOG

(1) I arrived at this college excited about changing my life. I was no longer the immature young man who thought education was boring. Through a neighbor in the field, I had become interested in studying to be a nuclear medicine technologist. My neighbor works in a cardiologist's office, interacts with patients, and does all the stress testing. He helped me pick a program, and I enrolled. But soon after starting school, I began to feel overwhelmed, upset, and irritated much of the time; I had no idea that this was the Black Dog.

(2) The fact is I could barely keep up with all the assignments, tests, and papers in five challenging classes. Further, this was an unfamiliar environment where math skills and brains ruled, not smart (make that stupid) remarks. I worried about failing but was embarrassed to talk to anyone—not my neighbor, not even my wife. One day she told me I was turning into a mean guy.

(3) In the student lounge, I happened to see a pamphlet published by the health service. It was mostly a list of questions, such as "Are you irritable, anxious, withdrawn?" "Do you often feel fatigued or low in energy?" "Do you experience extreme sadness or angry outbursts?" I was surprised to find myself answering "yes" to most of the questions. The pamphlet was on male depression. Like many guys, the last thing I wanted to do was face this and talk about it. In my mind, depression was not manly. Reading that 10 percent of college students are depressed and a third of freshmen feel overwhelmed helped a little.

(4) That night, I told my wife what was going on and decided to see a counselor. Amazingly, counseling at the college is free to students. I never loved talking about my insecurities, but it did help, especially problem solving with someone impartial. The counselor, Ron, encouraged me to use other campus resources, get a tutor, and improve the way I manage time. Ron, who knew that I like history, told me that the great leader Winston Churchill fought depression, which he called "the Black Dog." Before long, I felt more like the master of my Black Dog instead of the victim. I am still always rushing, but I don't feel so overwhelmed. My anger is gone, and my grades have climbed from Cs and Ds to As and Bs.

TEACHING TIP
You might ask students how the conclusion ties in with paragraph 4 and with the title.

(5) It's impressive that the college has these programs, and I urge anyone who's feeling depressed to reach out, discuss it, and get help. No one should suffer alone because depression grows more vicious in isolation.

—Paul Frey, Student

1. Instead of a thesis statement that tells the point of the story, Mr. Frey writes, "But soon after starting school, I began to feel overwhelmed, upset, and irritated much of the time; I had no idea that this was the Black Dog." Why do you think he does not define "Black Dog" in the first paragraph?

   He is creating suspense, making the reader wonder what the Black Dog is. Sometimes a good story keeps the reader guessing.

2. Underline the topic sentences of paragraphs 2, 3, and 4. What main incidents make up the story?

   Unable to keep up with college work, wife calls him mean, sees pamphlet on depression, talks to wife, sees a counselor, now copes better with stress

3. What is the point of this narrative? Is it effective that the writer does not reveal the point until paragraphs 3 and 4?

   The point is to discuss male depression. Yes, he creates suspense about the Black Dog and keeps readers interested.

4. The introduction, the incidents of the story, and the conclusion together form an outline for the narrative essay. Before sitting down to write, this student made such an outline to guide him as he wrote.

Planning and Writing the Narrative Essay

Before writing a narrative essay, you may wish to reread Chapter 6, "Narration." Pick a story idea that interests *you*—one with a point—and plan before you write. Your thesis statement will probably state the story's point. Supply any necessary background information. If your story consists of just a few major events, you may wish to devote one body paragraph to each one; if it has many small events, consider describing several events per paragraph. Follow chronological, or time, order. As you prewrite, search for exciting, precise details and words, just as you would if you were entertaining friends with a good story over lunch.

The rest of this section will guide you as you write a narrative essay.

PRACTICE 7

1. Choose a topic from the list below or one your instructor has assigned. Take your time deciding. Think of a story you want to tell—one with a point. Who is your audience? To whom will you tell your story?
   1. A favorite family story
   2. An immigrant's journey
   3. The story behind a key scientific discovery or invention
   4. How you chose your major or career path
   5. Your best or worst day at work or school
   6. A recent event you believe has been ignored or underreported
   7. The plot line of a movie or TV show you would like to produce
   8. The story of someone who inspires you (based on an interview you conduct)
   9. Learning a new language (or other subject or skill)
   10. An unforgettable incident you witnessed
   11. Writer's choice: ______________________

2. Many students find using a graphic organizer helpful as they plan an essay. In your notebook or on a computer, create an outline for your narrative essay using an organizer like the one that follows. The information you write in each box will become a paragraph.

LEARNING STYLES TIP

Visual and other learners often find an organizer helpful as they generate ideas, plan, and compose.

NARRATIVE ESSAY ORGANIZER

Title		In the title box, jot down ideas for a clear title if the subject is work-related or a "grabber" title if more personal.
Paragraph 1: Introduction & thesis statement		In box one, write your thesis statement and jot down any ideas for a catchy or engaging introductory paragraph.
Paragraph 2: Event 1 & detailed explanation		In box two, write a topic sentence introducing the first event (or series of events) in the narrative. Brainstorm details that will explain the incident.
Paragraph 3: Event 2 & detailed explanation		In box three, write the topic sentence for the second event or series of events. Prewrite for details.
Paragraph 4: Event 3 & detailed explanation		And so on to the end of the narrative . . .
Paragraph 5: Event 4 & detailed explanation		If your story has just three to six main events, write a topic sentence for each body paragraph, choosing the best details and supporting points from your prewriting. If the events are short or numerous, combine two or three in each paragraph.
Last paragraph: Conclusion		Prewrite ideas for a conclusion: a final thought or statement of the point, so the story will feel finished.

PRACTICE 8

Follow your plan and write the best first draft you can. Make sure to include all the key events, and aim for a smooth flow that will keep the reader interested. Conveying the meaning or point of the story and keeping it moving are the keys to good narration. As you write, inspire yourself by thinking of great storytellers you know or have heard. Use transitional expressions of time to help the reader follow.* Conclude with a final point or idea that follows from the story you have just narrated. Does your title capture the essence of the tale and make people want to read on?

Let your draft cool for an hour or a day; then reread it as if you were a helpful stranger. Now revise and rewrite, avoiding wordiness and keeping your reader in mind. Proofread for spelling, grammar, and sentence errors.

C. The Descriptive Essay

Although paragraphs of **description** are more common than whole essays, you will sometimes need to write a descriptive essay. In science labs, you may need to accurately describe cells under a microscope or a certain kind of rock. In business, you may need to describe a product, a piece of equipment, or the behavior of consumers in a test group. In social work, medicine, and psychology, case notes require precise description. No doubt you already use your descriptive powers in personal e-mails and letters. As this chapter will show, descriptive and narrative writing often overlap.

Here is one student's descriptive essay:

THE DAY OF THE DEAD

(1) One of the most important holidays in Mexico is the Day of the Dead, *El Día de los Muertos*. Surprisingly, this holiday is anything but depressing. In the weeks before, Mexicans excitedly prepare to welcome the souls of the dead, who come back each year to visit the living. From October 31 through November 2 this year, I attended this fiesta with my roommate Manuel. By sharing Day of the Dead activities in his family's home, in the marketplace, and in a cemetery, I have observed that Mexicans, unlike other North Americans, accept and celebrate death as a part of life.

ESL TIP

ESL students may not be aware that writers can use more than one verb tense in the same paragraph. Illustrate with examples from the essay.

(2) For this holiday, the home altar, or *ofrenda*, lovingly celebrates the dead. In the Lopez home, a trail of marigold petals and the rich smell of incense led us from the front door to the altar. The bright orange marigold blooms, the flowers of the dead, also trimmed a card table overflowing with everything the dead would need to take up their lives again. For Manuel's Uncle Angel there was a fragrant bowl of *mole*,† a glass of tequila, cigars, playing cards, and two Miles Davis jazz CDs. For Manuel's cousin Lucia, who died at 18 months, there was a worn stuffed puppy, a coral blanket, and a bowl of the rice pudding she loved. Heavy black and yellow beeswax candles threw a soft glow on photos of Angel and Lucia. It was as if the dead had never left and would always have a place of honor.

(3) While death is given an honored place in the home, it is celebrated with humor and mockery in the marketplace. Here the skeleton, or *calavera*, rules.

*For a list of transitional expressions of time, see Chapter 6.

†*mole*: A spicy Mexican sauce made of onions, chiles, and chocolate.

Judy Bellah/Alamy Stock Photo

Day of the Dead parade in Oaxaca, Mexico. Like a photograph, a good description creates a vivid picture.

ESL TIP
Students from Latin and South American countries might wish to share details about Day of the Dead celebrations in their countries. Do these differ from the experience of the student writer?

Shops sell sugar skulls, humorous bone figures, and even skeletons made of flowers. At the candy store, Manuel's niece picked out a white chocolate skull decorated with blue icing and magenta sequins in the eye sockets. In many bakeries, skull-and-crossbones designs decorated the delicious "bread of the dead." Most impressive were the stalls filled with *calacas*, handmade wooden skeletons, some no bigger than my thumb. The shelves showed a lively afterlife where skeleton musicians played in a band, skeleton writers tapped bony fingers on tiny typewriters, and teenage skeletons hoisted boom boxes on their matchstick-sized shoulder bones.

(4) On the evening of November first, reverence and fun combined in an all-night vigil at the cemetery. On a path outside the cemetery gate, rows of vendors sold soft drinks and cotton candy as if it were a sporting event. Men drank a strong fermented cactus beverage called *pulque* and played cards at picnic tables. The loud music of a mariachi band serenaded the dead, who would come back to eat the food laid out for them on the graves. Old grandmothers wearing hand-woven shawls mourned and wept while children chased each other around the pink- and blue-painted graves. Nobody scolded the children. Life and death did not seem so separate.

(5) While I have always felt fearful in cemeteries at home, there I felt excited and hopeful. When a soft breeze made the rows of candles flicker, I wondered if the souls of the children, the *angelitos*, had come back, laughing and giggling. Or was it the real children I heard laughing? I really didn't know. But I felt more alive than ever, waiting for the dead to arrive in a dusty cemetery in Mexico.

—Jason Eady, Student

- The **thesis statement** of a descriptive essay says what will be described and often gives an overall impression of it or tells how the writer will approach the subject. Underline or highlight the thesis statement in the introductory paragraph.

- Each paragraph in the body of this essay describes one scene or aspect of the topic. How many scenes or aspects are described, and what are they?

  three scenes: the home altar, the marketplace and shops, and the village cemetery

- What kind of order does the writer follow in organizing paragraph 2?

  space order: petals leading door to altar, marigolds trim the altar, offerings for Angel and Lucia, photos

- Paragraph 5 completes and **concludes** the essay. How effective is this student's conclusion?

  Very effective. He movingly describes the laughter of children—or *angelitos*. He has so well described the fiesta that we can see why he felt "more alive" in that cemetery.

PRACTICE 9

Read this student's descriptive essay and answer the questions.

TORNADO

(1) Tornados are one of the most terrifying natural events that occur, destroying homes and ending lives every year. On April 29th, 1995, a calm, muggy night, I learned this firsthand. Joey, a buddy I grew up with, agreed to travel across state with me so we could visit a friend in Lubbock, Texas. Joey and I were admiring the blue bonnets, which went on for miles like little blue birds flying close to the ground. The warm breeze brushed the tips of the blue bonnets and allowed them to dance under the clear blue sky. In the distance, however, we could see darkness.

(2) As we drove, thunderclouds continued to rumble in, like an ocean tide rolling closer and closer to the beach front, and within minutes the entire landscape was calm and dark. It looked like a total eclipse of the sun, and the blue bonnets were now completely still and somber. The rain began to trickle down out of the sky. The sound of the rain as it hit our car was like that of pins dropping on a metal surface. The intensity of the rain increased as we ventured farther into the eye of the storm.

(3) As we approached an overpass, we noticed a parking lot of cars underneath. By now, the rain had created a wall of water, which surrounded our car. We decided to pull over and sprint to the underpass to join the other frightened observers. What Joey and I were unaware of was that a tornado was already on the ground frantically spinning towards our position. The whirling "finger of God" was approaching us.

(4) The sound surrounding us was outrageous, like a steam locomotive roaring, whining, and whistling with an awful high-pitched roar. The rain had almost stopped, but the wind was nearly blowing us off the ground as we huddled together under the overpass. We could hear the screeching of car tires as they started sliding across the rain-soaked pavement. Electrical explosions lit up the darkened sky as the tornado ripped over power lines, snapping them as if they were toothpicks. Screams erupted

from the crowd as the tornado crossed directly over us, smashing large objects into the overpass pavement but leaving us untouched.

(5) Shortly thereafter the sky was bright again, revealing only shattered pieces of fence posts and telephone poles. Everyone unraveled from the huddle that had protected them moments earlier. The sun started poking holes in the dark rumbling sky; the wind and rain had ceased, leaving it morbidly calm. The sun burned away every trace of darkness. It was amazing to look back and see a mile-long trail of destruction surrounded by homes and fences that were totally untouched. I remember thinking how amazing this moment was, and how grateful I was to be alive.

—Wesley Duke, Student

1. This writer's thesis statement is actually two sentences. Underline or highlight them.
2. Every paragraph in this essay describes one scene or aspect of the topic. How many scenes or aspects are described, and what are they?

   five scenes or aspects: 1. blue day with distant darkness; 2. clouds, thunder, rain; 3. wall of water, race for the underpass; 4. tornado hits; 5. aftermath

3. This essay combines excellent, specific description with narration. What order does the writer use?

   time order

4. Which of the five senses does Mr. Duke emphasize in paragraph 4? Give some examples.

   hearing: sound of roaring locomotive, screeching tires, explosions, screams

5. The thesis statement, the scenes or phases in the description, and the conclusion together form an **outline** for the descriptive essay. Before sitting down to write, Mr. Duke made a detailed outline to guide his writing process.

PRACTICE 10 CRITICAL VIEWING AND WRITING

Study this diagram showing how lead exposure affects children and adults. The health risks are organized by the type of organ damage caused by lead. The diagram indicates that children suffer more significant damage. Convert the information shown here into the outline for an e-mail, a memo, or a short essay. Your audience is general readers and residents of a neighborhood with elevated lead levels.

First, list details that describe each important part of the diagram. Select the most important points to include and arrange them according to space order in an outline. If you have time, draft a clear essay or memo. Be prepared to share your work with the class.

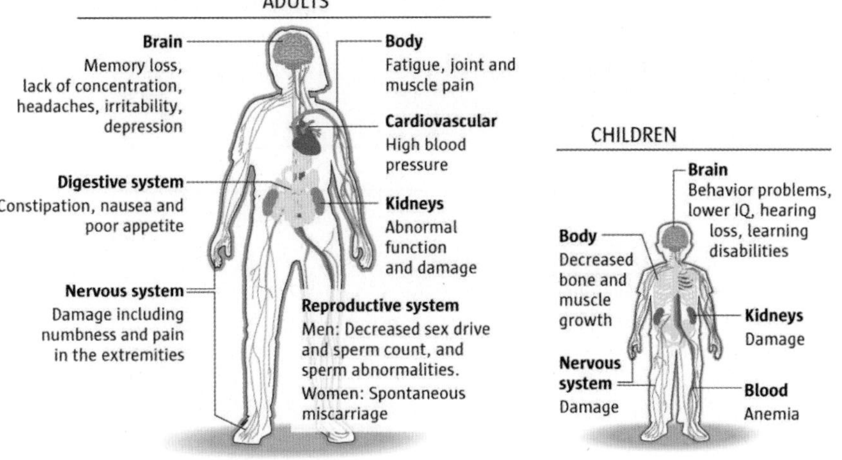

Source: Public Health – Seattle and King County; Centers for Disease Control and Prevention; National Institutes of Health. http://projects.seattletimes.com/2014/loaded-with-lead/3/.

Planning and Writing the Descriptive Essay

Before writing a descriptive essay, you may wish to reread Chapter 7, "Description." Use your senses—sight, smell, hearing, taste, and touch—as you plan and prewrite ideas. Pay special attention to organizing your details and observations; space order is often the best choice, but time order might work for your subject. As you revise, aim for rich details and exact language; these are what make good descriptions come alive.

The rest of the section will guide you as you write a descriptive essay.

PRACTICE 11

1. Choose a topic from the list below or one your instructor has assigned. Take your time deciding. Think of a subject that will make a good description, perhaps an important scene or experience that you can still see in your mind's eye. Who is your audience?
   1. A place you go to relax
   2. Your favorite neighborhood in your hometown or a city you have visited
   3. Your ideal house or apartment
   4. A lively public place, such as a campus hangout, a fitness center, or a dance club
   5. A tourist attraction or a place of natural beauty
   6. Your present or future workplace, including setting, people, and action
   7. A computer, vehicle, or piece of equipment from your job
   8. A group of students, customers, tourists, or neighbors you have observed
   9. The settings and costumes of a movie you admire
   10. A scene you will never forget
   11. Writer's choice: ______________________________

LEARNING STYLES TIP

Visual and other learners often find an organizer helpful as they generate ideas, plan, and compose.

2. Many students find using a graphic organizer helpful as they plan an essay. In your notebook or on a computer, create an outline for your descriptive essay using an organizer like the one that follows. The information you write in each box will become a paragraph.

DESCRIPTIVE ESSAY ORGANIZER

Title		In the title box, write a clear, engaging title.
Paragraph 1: Introduction & thesis statement		In box one, write a thesis statement that tells what will be described and conveys an overall impression. Jot down ideas for an engaging introductory paragraph.
Paragraph 2: Scene 1 in the description		In box two, write a topic sentence introducing the first scene or aspect of the description. Brainstorm details and specifics that "paint" the scene clearly in words.
Paragraph 3: Scene 2 in the description		In box three, write the topic sentence for the second scene or aspect of your description. Prewrite for rich details and specifics.
Paragraph 4: Scene 3 in the description		In box four, write a topic sentence for the third scene or aspect of your description. Prewrite for rich details and specifics.
Paragraph 5, 6, and so on: Scene 4 in the description		Write a topic sentence to introduce each remaining scene or aspect of the subject. For each, prewrite for rich details and specifics. Continue until the description is complete.
Last paragraph: Conclusion		Jot down ideas for your conclusion. Include a final thought or feeling that the description evokes.

PRACTICE 12

Now, referring to your plan, write the best first draft you can. Mentally see, hear, and smell the subject. Your *words* are your camera, paints, or graphic design program, so don't settle for the first words that occur to you. Follow the order of space or time, whichever you have selected, and be sure to use transitional expressions of space* or time† to guide the reader along. For inspiration, you might reread the conclusion of "Day of the Dead" before you conclude your paper.

Let your draft cool for an hour or a day; then reread it as if you were a helpful stranger. Now revise and rewrite, emphasizing exact language, avoiding wordiness, and keeping your reader in mind. Is each paragraph developed fully? Do transitions make the flow of ideas clear? Proofread for spelling, grammar, and sentence errors.

D. The Process Essay

The **process** essay is frequently used in college and business. Process essays either explain *how to do something* or describe *how something works* (or *how something happened*). In psychology, you might describe the stages of a child's moral development. In history, you might explain how a battle was won or lost, while in business, you might set forth the steps of an advertising campaign. In medicine, science, and technology, you must understand and perform numerous biological and technical processes.

Here is one student's process essay:

HOW TO PREPARE FOR A FINAL EXAM

(1) At the end of my first semester at college, I postponed thinking about final examinations, desperately crammed the night before, drank enough coffee to keep the city of Cincinnati awake, and then got Cs and Ds. I have since realized that the students who got As on their finals weren't just lucky; they knew how to *prepare*. There are many different ways to prepare for a final examination, and each individual must perfect his or her own style, but over the years, I have developed a method that works for me.

(2) First, when your professor announces the date, time, and place of the final—usually at least two weeks before—ask questions and take careful notes on the answers. What chapters will be covered? What kinds of questions will the test contain? What materials and topics are most important? The information you gather will help you study more effectively.

(3) Next, survey all the textbook chapters the test will cover, using a highlighter or colored pen to mark important ideas and sections to be studied later. Many textbooks emphasize key ideas with boldface titles or headlines; others are written so that key ideas appear in the topic sentences at the beginning of each paragraph. Pay attention to these guides as you read.

(4) Third, survey your class notes in the same fashion, marking important ideas. If your notes are messy or disorganized, you might want to rewrite them for easy reference later.

*For a list of transitional expressions of space order, see Chapter 7.

†For a list of transitional expressions of time, see Chapter 6.

(5) Fourth, decide approximately how many hours you will need to study. Get a calendar and clearly mark off the hours each week that you will devote to in-depth studying. If possible, set aside specific times: Thursday from 1 to 2 P.M., Friday from 6 to 8 P.M., and so on. If you have trouble committing yourself, schedule study time with a friend, but pick someone as serious as you are about getting good grades.

(6) Fifth, begin studying systematically, choosing a quiet place free from distractions in which to work—the library, a dorm room, whatever helps you concentrate. One of my friends can study only in his attic; another, in her car. As you review the textbook and your notes, ask yourself questions based on your reading. From class discussions, try to spot the professor's priorities and to guess what questions might appear on the exam. Be creative; one friend of mine puts important study material on cassette tapes, which he plays walking to and from school.

TEACHING TIP

Use this essay to illustrate that essays need not be confined to just five paragraphs.

(7) Finally, at least three days before the exam, start reviewing. At the least opportunity, refer to your notes, even if you are not prepared to digest all the material. Use the moments when you are drinking your orange juice or riding the bus; just looking at the material can promote learning. By the night before the exam, you should know everything you want to know—and allow for a good night's sleep!

(8) By following these simple procedures, you may find, as I do, that you are the most prepared person in the exam room, confident that you studied thoroughly enough to do well on the exam.

—Mark Reyes, Student

- The **thesis statement** in a process essay tells the reader what process the rest of the essay will describe. Underline or highlight the thesis statement.
- What **process** does this essay discuss?

  preparing for a test

- How many **steps or stages** make up this process? What are they?

  six: ask questions about the test, survey the chapters to be tested, survey class notes, plan studying time, begin studying systematically, review material

- What kind of **order** does the writer use to organize his essay?

  chronological order

- Before writing his first draft, Mr. Reyes made a clear **outline**. An outline is even more important in essay writing than paragraph writing because it keeps the writer organized and on track.
- Underline or highlight the topic sentences of Mr. Reyes' body paragraphs. Make an outline of Mr. Reyes' essay.

PRACTICE 13

Read this student's process essay and answer the questions.

THE MIRACLE OF BIRTH

TEACHING TIP
Ask students what words in the introduction indicate the level of seriousness in the essay.

(1) A woman is pregnant for approximately nine months. Within that time are three stages or trimesters, "tri" meaning three. Many women have said they loved being pregnant, but I like to refer to the trimesters as the puking stage, the fat stage, and the always-have-to-pee stage.

(2) In the first trimester, the baby is developing its nervous system and other important little body parts; while all of this is happening inside, the mom-to-be is usually puking her guts up. The fun doesn't stop there, however. Hormone levels skyrocket, and all of a sudden, mom-to-be is crying over the slightest thing, such as a McDonald's commercial that she finds unbearably sweet.

(3) The second trimester is often slightly gentler on one's stomach, perhaps because that stomach has doubled in size, along with mom's butt and thighs. The baby is growing fast now, and the vital organs are developing. The baby is beginning to do somersaults, and suddenly there is a new stabbing sensation, almost as if baby is using mom's ribs for gymnastic rings. Comfort is now a thing of the past.

TEACHING TIP
You might ask students to label the parts of this essay, which is very clearly structured.

(4) In the third trimester, baby is happily gaining about half a pound a week, but for the mother, the last stage of pregnancy never goes by fast enough. As all the intricate fine-tunings of development are happening on baby's major organs, hair, and skin, for some odd reason, sleep for mom is completely out of the question. Perhaps the lack of sleep is due to the up-and-coming gymnast in her stomach or the five hundred trips to the bathroom that mom must make in one night. The many sleepless nights may also be attributed to her anticipation of bladder control or actually having a waist again.

(5) Pregnancy is a wonderful experience as long as puking, gaining 40 to 60 pounds, and stumbling in and out of bed do not bother the mom-to-be. To me, pregnancy was a bummer, but like the old saying goes, "no pain, no gain." The end definitely justifies the means, and now that I am almost back to normal functioning with a beautiful, crying baby, the fun really starts.

—Heather Artley, Student

1. Underline or highlight this writer's thesis statement. What process does her essay discuss?

   pregnancy

2. How many stages or steps make up this process? What are they?

   three; first trimester, second trimester, and third trimester

3. Underline or highlight the topic sentences in paragraphs 2, 3, and 4. What order does the writer employ?

   time order

4. Is her tone serious or light? What words or phrases tell you this?

light; "the always-have-to-pee stage," "puking her guts up," "using mom's ribs for gymnastic rings," "five hundred trips to the bathroom," "bummer"

PRACTICE 14 CRITICAL VIEWING AND WRITING

Study this diagram showing that heart disease is actually a *process*. Read about the four stages.

Do you know anyone who is likely in the process of developing heart disease? How would you go about learning more about this process and how to stop or reverse it? Come up with least two trustworthy sources of information on heart disease. Be prepared to share your thoughts.

Heart disease is a process affecting 27.6 million Americans.

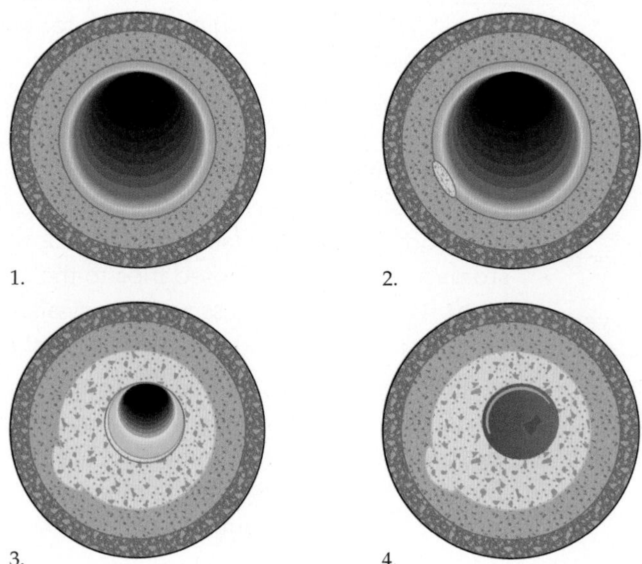

Stage 1. Normal arteries are healthy and open. **Stage 2.** Cholesterol begins to be deposited in a damaged or inflamed artery wall. **Stage 3.** Cholesterol continues to build up, narrowing the artery. **Stage 4.** The artery becomes so clogged that a blood clot can block it, causing heart attack or stroke.

Planning and Writing the Process Essay

Before writing a process essay, you may wish to reread Chapter 8, "Process." Choose a process topic that you know something about. What expertise, experience, or humorous attempt might you wish to share? If your process requires any equipment or ingredients (a recipe, for instance), list them in the first paragraph. As you plan the essay, list all the necessary steps or stages and arrange them logically, probably in time order. Then prewrite to gather details and examples about each step or stage.

The rest of this section will guide you as you write a process essay.

PRACTICE 15

1. Choose a topic from the list below or one your instructor has assigned. Take your time as you pick a process to describe that interests *you*. Who is your audience? That is, for whom are you explaining this process?
    1. A process that will help new students at your college learn how to register (how to drop or add courses, how to meet people on campus, how to apply for financial aid, and so on)
    2. How to get action on a community problem
    3. How to begin tracing your family's genealogy
    4. How to teach a child a skill or value
    5. How to perform a procedure at your workplace (help an elderly person dress, make Hollandaise sauce, handle a crime scene, and so on)
    6. How to set up a program or piece of technology (such as a cell phone, e-mail, a website, or a blog)
    7. The yearly cycle of a crop (corn, wheat, oranges, cocoa, and so on)
    8. How to impress the boss (in-laws, professor, person you are dating)
    9. An important process you learned in another course (stages of human moral development, how a lake becomes a meadow, and so on)
    10. How to get an A in ______________________________
    11. Writer's choice: ______________________________

LEARNING STYLES TIP

Visual and other learners often find an organizer helpful as they generate ideas, plan their essays, and compose.

2. Many students find using a graphic organizer helpful as they plan an essay. In your notebook or on a computer, create an outline for your process essay using an organizer like the one that follows. The information you write in each box will become a paragraph.

PROCESS ESSAY ORGANIZER

Title		Write a title that clearly states the process or refers to it in an interesting way.
Paragraph 1: Introduction & thesis statement		In box one, write a thesis statement that tells what process will be explained. Jot down ideas for a catchy and engaging introduction.
Paragraph 2: Step 1 or Stage 1 in the process		In box two, write a topic sentence stating the first step or stage in the process. Prewrite details that will explain this stage clearly.

Paragraph 3:
Step 2 or
Stage 2
in the process

In box three, write the topic sentence stating the second step or stage in the process. Prewrite details to explain this step.

Paragraph 4:
Step 3 or
Stage 3
in the process

In box four, write the topic sentence stating the third step or stage in the process. Prewrite details to explain this step.

Paragraph 5, 6,
and so on:
Step 4 or
Stage 4
in the process

Write a topic sentence to introduce each remaining step or stage in the process. For each, prewrite for rich details and specifics. Continue until the process is complete.

Last paragraph:
Conclusion

Jot down ideas for your conclusion. Include a final thought about or some implications of the process you have just analyzed.

PRACTICE 16

Now, referring to your plan, write the best first draft you can. Clear language and logical organization are keys to good process writing. Pay special attention to paragraphing; if the process is three to six steps, make each step a paragraph; if more, combine several steps per paragraph. Remember to use transitional expressions of time to help the reader follow.*

Let your draft cool for an hour or a day; then reread it as if you were a helpful, eagle-eyed stranger. Now revise and rewrite, avoiding wordiness and keeping your reader in mind. Proofread for spelling, grammar, and sentence errors.

E. The Definition Essay

Although paragraphs of **definition** are more common in college and the workplace than essays are, you may at some time have to write a definition essay. In a computer course, for example, you might be called on to define a *network* or *database*. In psychology, you might need to define the *Oedipus complex*, or in biology, the terms *DNA* or *stem cells*. Sometimes defining at length a term people think they know—like *work ethic* or *acquaintance rape*—can be illuminating.

Here is a definition essay:

*For a list of transitional expressions for process, see Chapter 8.

ESL AND TEACHING TIP

Point out that description, narration, and examples may be used in definition essays. In addition, this one is organized as process, the evolution of the showboat.

SHOWBOATS

(1) Years ago, the most appreciated quality in an athlete, aside from success, was dignity. Athletes like Joe DiMaggio and Joe Louis were admired not only because they were the best, but also because they carried themselves with quiet dignity. As sports got linked to television, however, athletes became entertainers as well as competitors. A player should not only succeed but also be a showboat. In the past, a showboat was a riverboat with a floating theater that entertained people at every stop. Now, a showboat is an athlete, usually male, who brags, struts, and calls attention to his own achievements.

(2) The first showboat in modern sports was Muhammad Ali. In 1964, he burst onto the boxing stage as Cassius Clay. Before his title fight against the "unbeatable" Sonny Liston, Clay bragged, "I'm young, I'm handsome, I'm fast, I'm pretty, and can't possibly be beat." After he shocked the experts by knocking out Liston, Ali mugged for the cameras, shouting, "I shook up the world! I must be the greatest!" Such loud self-confidence was unheard-of before Ali. As he won more fights, Ali rhymed about his skills, danced in the ring, and trash-talked to opponents. But he backed up his big words with big successes, beating Liston, Foreman, and Frazier.

(3) In 1991, showboating caught on after the University of Michigan recruited the talented "Fab Five" freshman basketball team. Chris Webber, Jalen Rose, Juwan Howard, Jimmy King, and Ray Jackson brought showboat style to college ball. They wore baggy shorts and dominated the court with in-your-face attitude. Meanwhile, in the NFL, two Dallas Cowboys Super Bowl (as in paragraph 4) champions perfected the touchdown celebration. High-stepping into the end zone or dancing after a touchdown, "Neon Deion" Sanders and Michael "The Playmaker" Irvin made sure that people noticed when they scored.

(4) Today, two NFL wide receivers define the new showboat. Terrell Owens and Chad Johnson have taken touchdown celebrations to an extreme level. A few of their on-field actions include removing a cell phone from the goalpost padding and then calling a sports agent, doing the Riverdance, proposing to a cheerleader, and using popcorn and pompoms as props. Off the field, Johnson changed his name to Ochocinco, his jersey number, and both men starred in reality TV shows. They are champion showboats, but neither has won a Super Bowl.

(5) With their bragging, bold style, and creative celebrations, showboats bring some welcome fun to serious sports. However, if an athlete focuses too much on getting his video clip on *Sports Highlights* or Twitter, it could interfere with winning the game. Maybe the trend has gone too far.

—Mitch Borsano, Student

- The **thesis statement** of a definition essay tells the reader what term will be defined and usually defines it briefly as well. Underline or highlight the thesis statement in this essay.
- Underline or highlight the **topic sentences** in paragraphs 2, 3, and 4. How do these three paragraphs develop the thesis statement?

  They give examples of showboats: Ali in 2; Fab 5, Sanders, and Irvin in 3; Owens and Johnson in 4.
- What order does the writer follow in paragraphs 2, 3, and 4?

  time order

- Is Mr. Borsano's conclusion effective or not? Has showboating gone too far?

  Answers will vary.

- Review the parts of this well-organized essay. You can see that the introduction and thesis statement; three body paragraphs, each explaining examples of "showboats"; and the conclusion form a clear **outline** of the essay. This student made just such an outline before he sat down to write.

PRACTICE 17

Now read another student's definition essay and answer the questions.

MORE THAN JUST GOOD

(1) I lean against our mango tree, waiting. The taxi is twenty minutes late, something only Americans like me would notice here in Costa Rica. I hear the roar of an engine that needs maintenance. A small gray Toyota speeds past and returns a few moments later, horn blasting. The driver sticks his head out the window and says, "Hello my friend, we go?" While I squeeze into the passenger seat, he says, "I no see you, *lo siento*. But *pura vida* man, where you going?" We seem to hit every pothole, and my body is jostled like a child playing with an old doll. Yet despite being late to meet my parents, despite the car having no air conditioning, and despite the driver's choice to blast salsa music loud enough for the entire neighborhood to throw a party, everything is indeed *pura vida*.

(2) The Spanish phrase *pura vida* is not just a Costa Rican slogan printed on T-shirts, and it does not merely mean "pure life." No other Latin American could tell you what it means beyond "something that *Ticos* (Costa Ricans) say." American culture lacks a similar idea. Often foreigners try to add *pura vida* to their pocket-dictionary vocabularies, but *pura vida* isn't planned. To experience *pura vida*, one must squeeze the best out of every experience—even bad lemons are used to make sweet *limonada*.

(3) *Pura vida* exists in the little things that make Costa Rica precious to the locals who have given so much to their country. *Pura vida* is the flavor of chilero sauce that spices up the rice and bean dish of *gallo pinto* that sits on their plates three meals a day. It is the plantain slices fried up to sweeten their palates when the rice and beans are finished. *Pura vida* is children and adults playing soccer together in the abandoned dirt field next door. They yell, "Oooooopaaa!" in unison when their only soccer ball is accidentally kicked into traffic. *Pura vida* is the sweet ocean air that blows in from the Pacific coast, rolls up the western mountains, and seeps throughout the central valley.

(4) While traveling the coast, I stop at a roadside spot that advertises rice, beans, and meat. I am greeted warmly by a waiter who wants to practice his English. "Hey man, you American?" he asks loudly, "You come to Costa Rica?" making sure that everyone can hear him. I nod, and when I tell him that I actually live here, he smiles and replies, "*pura vida*."

(5) This is the simple life, the pure life where you work hard to feed the family you love. Costa Rica is built on communities, friendship, and a willingness to help each other. When Ticos say *pura vida*, it's not just that life is good now. Life has always been good, and, if it's up to them, always will be.

—Anders Nelson, Student

1. In this essay, paragraph 1 introduces the term to be defined, but the thesis statement occurs in paragraph 2. Underline or highlight it.

2. How does the writer develop the definition of *pura vida* in paragraphs 3 and 4?

   He gives examples, like the chilero sauce, plantain slices, the soccer game, the ocean air, and the waiter greeting him as a Costa Rican.

3. Mr. Nelson uses careful description to help readers see and experience his subject. What descriptive details did you find especially powerful and effective?

   roar of an engine needing maintenance; salsa music loud enough for neighborhood to party; soccer game and "ooopah"; sweet ocean air flowing inland

4. Let this student's work inspire you. Can you think of a term from your home town, neighborhood, or native country that might lend itself to an essay of definition? Write ideas here. Ask some classmates if they would like to read more about the term.

   Answers will vary.

PRACTICE 18 CRITICAL VIEWING AND WRITING

Look closely at this poster called *The Illiterate.* The picture compares someone who cannot read and write with a blindfolded man walking off a cliff. What does the picture say about being illiterate? Does it accurately *define* illiteracy? Do you know anyone who is illiterate? If you were writing an essay called *The Illiterate*, how would you explain the term?

Hoover Institution Archives, Stanford University

The Illiterate by Aleksei Radakov

Planning and Writing the Definition Essay

Before writing a definition essay, you should reread Chapter 9, "Definition." Review the three types of definitions: by *synonym*, *class*, or *negation*. Take your time choosing a word or term that truly interests you—a word from your job, a college course, or your own experience. Prewrite for ideas to explain your definition. Consider using two or three examples to develop the term, one paragraph per example, the way the first student writer does. If you use some short examples like the second student, you might group them in one paragraph.

The rest of the section will guide you as you write a definition essay.

PRACTICE 19

1. Choose a topic from the list below or one your instructor has assigned. You might wish to define a term from an important college course, your job, or your culture. Decide who your audience is and what type of definition you will use.
    1. A special term from sports, technology, business, art, or psychology
    2. An environmental term (*global warming, endangered species, recycling, deforestation*, and so on)
    3. A best friend
    4. Hypocrisy
    5. Homelessness
    6. Maturity
    7. A disease or medical condition, such as diabetes, autism, depression, or alcoholism
    8. A slang term in current use
    9. A term from another language or culture (*salsa, joie de vivre, manga, machismo*, and so on)
    10. Twitter (use humor if you like)
    11. Writer's choice: ______________________________
2. Many students find using a graphic organizer helpful as they plan an essay. In your notebook or on a computer, create an outline for your definition essay using an organizer like the one that follows. The information you write in each box will become a paragraph.

LEARNING STYLES TIP

Visual and other students often find an organizer helpful as they generate ideas, plan, and compose.

DEFINITION ESSAY ORGANIZER

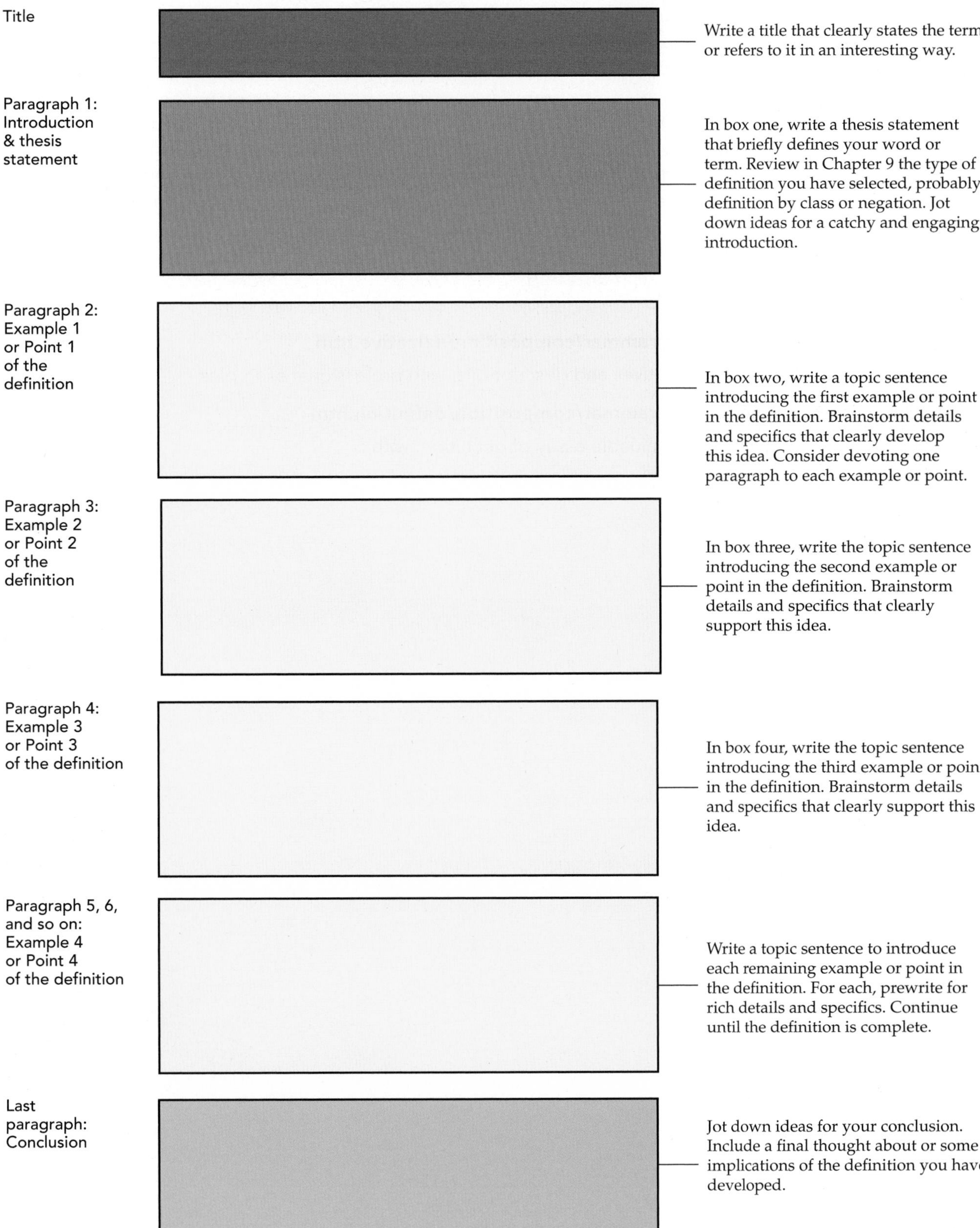
Title
Write a title that clearly states the term or refers to it in an interesting way.
Paragraph 1: Introduction & thesis statement
In box one, write a thesis statement that briefly defines your word or term. Review in Chapter 9 the type of definition you have selected, probably definition by class or negation. Jot down ideas for a catchy and engaging introduction.
Paragraph 2: Example 1 or Point 1 of the definition
In box two, write a topic sentence introducing the first example or point in the definition. Brainstorm details and specifics that clearly develop this idea. Consider devoting one paragraph to each example or point.
Paragraph 3: Example 2 or Point 2 of the definition
In box three, write the topic sentence introducing the second example or point in the definition. Brainstorm details and specifics that clearly support this idea.
Paragraph 4: Example 3 or Point 3 of the definition
In box four, write the topic sentence introducing the third example or point in the definition. Brainstorm details and specifics that clearly support this idea.
Paragraph 5, 6, and so on: Example 4 or Point 4 of the definition
Write a topic sentence to introduce each remaining example or point in the definition. For each, prewrite for rich details and specifics. Continue until the definition is complete.
Last paragraph: Conclusion
Jot down ideas for your conclusion. Include a final thought about or some implications of the definition you have developed.

PRACTICE 20

Now, referring to your plan, write the best first draft you can. Aim for clarity as you help the reader develop an understanding of this word or term. Check your paragraphing, and use *transitional expressions** to guide the reader from point to point.

Let your draft cool for an hour or a day; then reread it as if you were a helpful, eagle-eyed stranger. Now revise and rewrite, emphasizing exact language, avoiding wordiness, and keeping your reader in mind. Is each paragraph developed fully? Do transitions make the flow of ideas clear? Proofread for spelling, grammar, and sentence errors.

EXPLORING ONLINE

grammar.ccc.commnet.edu/grammar/composition/narrative.htm

Interesting tips on writing narratives and descriptions, with professional examples

grammar.ccc.commnet.edu/grammar/composition/definition.htm

Excellent advice on crafting a valuable essay of definition, with professional examples

*For a list of transitional expressions, see Chapter 4.

CHAPTER 17

Types of Essays, Part 2

A: The Comparison and the Contrast Essay

B: The Classification Essay

C: The Cause and Effect Essay

D: The Persuasive Essay

This chapter will show you how to apply four more methods of paragraph development that you learned in Unit 3 to the essay. Because an essay is like an expanded paragraph, the same methods you would use to prewrite, organize, and write a paragraph of comparison and contrast, for instance, can also be used to develop an entire essay. The rest of the chapter will show you how.

A. The Comparison and the Contrast Essay

Essays of **comparison** or **contrast** are frequently called for in college courses. In an English or a drama class, you might be asked to contrast two of Shakespeare's villains—perhaps Iago and Claudius. In psychology, you might have to contrast the training of the clinical psychologist and that of the psychiatrist, or in history, to compare ancient Greek and Roman religions.

Does the following essay compare or contrast?

E-NOTES FROM AN ONLINE LEARNER

Introduction

(1) This year I attended my first U.S. history class at midnight, clad in my dancing cow pajamas and fluffy slippers. No, I was not taking part in some bizarre campus ritual. I am enrolled in two courses in the University of Houston's Distance Education Program. Although I took classes on campus at the same college last year, my experiences in the traditional classroom and in the virtual classroom have been vastly different.

Thesis statement

Topic sentence introducing point 1

(2) Attending online courses has proved more convenient for me than traveling to regular classes each day. Because I live over an hour away from campus, I was often stalled in traffic when my 8 A.M. psychology lecture was beginning. Then I spent the last half hour of my afternoon English class praying that the discussion—however lively and interesting—would not go past 4 P.M. and make me late to pick up my son at daycare. In contrast, my online classes are always convenient to attend because I set my own schedule. Lectures for my history survey course are posted to the class website, so I can log on whenever I want to read new material or review. My writing seminar is "asynchronous." This means that students and instructors communicate at their convenience on an electronic bulletin board. I can e-mail my questions, file homework, and respond to other students' work at night or on weekends without leaving home.

Topic sentence introducing point 2

(3) Though some students miss the human energy of a real classroom, the online format actually encourages me to participate more in discussions. As a shy woman who is older than many of my peers, I used to hide in the back row to avoid having to speak. I only answered questions when called upon. On the other hand, writing online, I am more confident. I have time to think about what I want to say, and I know people are not judging me by anything except my ideas. Even though bulletin board discussions can be painfully slow and disjointed compared to the back-and-forth of a great classroom discussion, I like the equality in a virtual classroom. Surprisingly, there I feel freer to be the real me.

Topic sentence introducing point 3

(4) The biggest difference in moving from a regular classroom to a virtual one, in my view, is learning to be self-motivated. Attending classes on campus, I was motivated by the personal involvement of my instructors. I also caught that group adrenaline rush, seeing other students hunched over their notebooks in a lecture hall or coffee shop. While my online courses still require written papers each week and tests turned in on time, now no instructor is prodding me to get busy. Instead, only the soft bubbling noise of my aquarium screen saver reminds me to tap the keyboard and dive into my coursework. Fortunately, I am self-motivated and focused. As a returning student with a job and a child, I have to be. Honestly, however, I have already seen some classmates post homework assignments later and later until they drop off the screen entirely.

Conclusion

(5) Overall, my experience with online classes has been more positive than my experience on campus, but online learning is not for everyone. So far I find online classes convenient, welcoming for self-expression, and well-suited to my particular personality, which is organized, shy, and prone to bouts of midnight energy. In fact, it's 12:14 A.M. now as I input the final draft of this essay assignment. My son is asleep in the next room and my cat, Miss Fleason, is nuzzling my hot pink fluffy slippers.

—Brenda Wilson, Student

- The **thesis statement** of a comparison or contrast essay tells what two persons or things will be compared or contrasted.
- Will this essay **compare** or **contrast** the two kinds of classrooms? What word or words in the thesis indicate this?

contrast; vastly different

- Does the writer discuss all points about A and then all points about B, or skip back and forth between A and B?

  skips back and forth between A and B

- The pattern of supporting points in this essay might be shown like this:

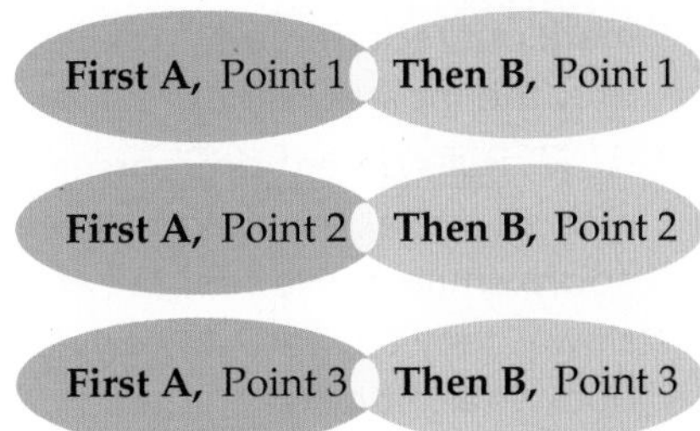

- Notice how the thesis statement, topic sentences, and supporting details form a clear **outline** of the essay.

PRACTICE 1

Now read this student's essay and answer the questions.

BAREBACK BRONC RIDING VERSUS BULL RIDING

IN

(1) There are many different events in the sport of rodeo. Two of the best-known, bareback bronc riding and bull riding, might seem quite similar to the casual onlooker. Although they are both rough stock (bucking) events, they differ in the equipment required, riding technique, animal size, and bucking style.

A, point 1

(2) Bareback bronc riding requires a lot of equipment for a safe and successful ride. The bareback rigging is probably most important. It is a combination of wood and leather, molded into a suitcase-type handle for the rider to wedge his hand in while wearing a thick leather glove. Another important piece of equipment is the neck roll, a thick pad attached to the back of the neck with long straps to prevent whiplash or fractures during the ride and dismount. Bareback riders are also required to wear straight-shanked, free-spinning spurs with rounded rowels (or wheels) to keep from cutting the horse. A vest and chaps are optional safety features for the legs and torso.

A, point 2

(3) Bareback bronc riding also entails a very unnatural technique. In this event, the rider positions himself almost completely reclined on the horse, with his head near the flanks and his feet at the shoulders. Once the gate is opened, the rider is required to "mark out" the horse. This means that the rider must reach up with his legs and mash his spurs into the horse's neck before the first buck is made. The rider is then judged on his spurring ability, which is done by pulling his feet in an upward motion and into an almost spread-eagle position.

A, points 3 and 4

(4) Size and bucking style of a bronc differ as well. An average bucking horse weighs between 1,200 and 1,500 pounds and is approximately five and one-half feet tall at the top of the shoulder. These horses are extremely quick and generally buck straight down the arena.

B, point 1

(5) In contrast to bareback bronc riding, bull riding does not require a rigging. Instead, a woven grass rope and a thin leather glove are used. The protective vest is a requirement in this event due to the rather aggressive nature of the

bulls. No neck roll is needed in this event because there is little strain on the neck. The spurs in bull riding have fixed rowels with sharp ends, and the shanks are angled inward at a 45-degree angle to make gripping easy. Helmets and face masks are optional safety features for this event.

B, point 2

(6) Unlike bronc riding, bull riding technique is fairly natural. The rider sits in the upright position, straddling the bull just behind the shoulders. There is no mark out requirement in bull riding, and spurring is just a scoring bonus. Usually only the most experienced riders practice spurring.

B, points 3 and 4

(7) Bulls differ from horses in both weight and bucking style. Bulls are heavier, with an average weight between 1,500 and 2,100 pounds, and they stand approximately five feet tall at the top of the shoulders. Although they buck fairly slowly, they are very powerful and very aggressive. Unlike broncs, bulls seldom buck straight down the arena; instead they often fade from side to side, spin, and twist.

C

(8) In short, there are many differences between bareback bronc riding and bull riding. The primary elements that set these events apart are the variations in equipment, riding technique, size, and bucking style. Both events, however, thrill rodeo fans and riders.

—Matt Bodson, Student

1. Underline or highlight the thesis statement and topic sentences in this essay. Does this writer compare or contrast bronc and bull riding? What words and phrases tell you this?

   contrast; the words *differ, in contrast,* and *unlike*

2. Does this writer follow the *all A, then all B* pattern or the *AB, AB, AB* pattern? If you aren't sure, label each part of the essay in the left margin. Use the terms below listed in scrambled order. A is bronc riding; B is bull riding.

B, point 2	B, points 3 and 4	C = Conclusion	A, point 1
A, point 2	IN = Introduction	A, points 3 and 4	B, point 1

   all A, then all B

3. Do you think Mr. Bodson picked a subject that he knows a lot about? What aspects of the essay give you this impression?

   Yes. All the detail seems to say he is a rodeo fan or even a rider.

4. If this writer asked you for peer feedback, what would you say? What do you like most about this essay? Do you have any suggestions for improvement?

   Answers will vary.

PRACTICE 2

TEACHING TIP

To compare and contrast well, a writer must *pay attention*, often to both visual and verbal cues. Practice 2 underscores the importance of close observation in the medical and environmental fields. Have groups compete to see who can write the most complete "field notes" contrasting the two images.

CRITICAL VIEWING AND WRITING

Comparing and contrasting two things requires concentration and focus. A few moments of thought are not enough to perceive all the similarities or differences. In fields like science, nursing, and medicine, close observation is key—for instance, spotting changes in a patient's appearance from day to day. Imagine you are a scientist describing the changes in the Aral Sea between 2000 and 2015. Take notes and describe at least three similarities and differences. What are the implications of this change?

THE ARAL SEA

Located in Central Asia, the Aral Sea was once the fourth largest lake in the world. Covering some 26,000 square miles, the lake was the size of West Virginia. Irrigation projects started by the Soviets in the 1960s diverted water from the rivers feeding the lake, causing it to shrink by 90 percent. Much of the Aral Sea is now called the Aral Desert.

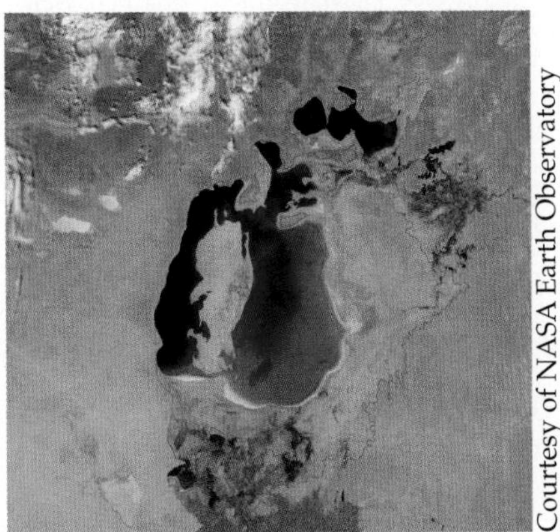

Courtesy of NASA Earth Observatory

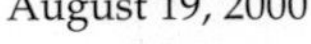

August 19, 2000

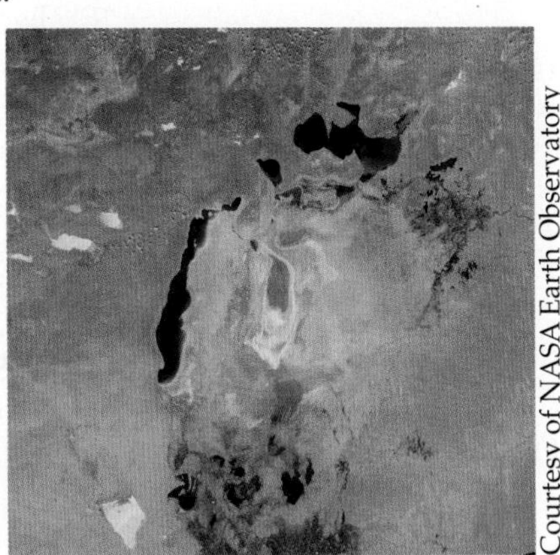

Courtesy of NASA Earth Observatory

August 13, 2015

Planning and Writing the Comparison and Contrast Essay

Before writing your essay, you may wish to reread Chapter 10, "Comparison and Contrast." Outlining is especially important in comparison and contrast. As you plan, make a chart of all your points of comparison or contrast to make sure you give balanced coverage. Decide which pattern will better present your ideas: *AB, AB, AB,* or *all A, then all B*. Be sure to use transitional expressions* to help the reader follow.

The rest of the section will guide you as you write a comparison and contrast essay.

PRACTICE 3

1. Choose a topic from the list below or one your instructor has assigned. Bear in mind that the most interesting essays usually compare two things that are

*For a list of transitional expressions of comparison and contrast, see Chapter 10.

TEACHING TIP
To give students more practice with comparison and/or contrast, have them work together in small groups to practice writing a thesis statement and outline for one of these topics.

different or contrast two things that are similar. Otherwise, you run the risk of saying the obvious ("Cats and dogs are two different animals"). Visualize the audience for whom you are writing.

1. Your mother's or father's childhood and your own
2. Two cultural attitudes about one subject such as education, marriage, money, or clothing
3. A neighborhood store and a chain store (bookstore, restaurant, music store, and so on)
4. Two politicians, entertainers, athletes, public figures, artists, or historical figures
5. Your expectations about parenthood (a job, or college) versus the realities
6. Two different social networking websites (like Facebook and Twitter)
7. Two ways of learning
8. Two views on a controversial issue
9. A book and a movie based on that book
10. Two job or career options you are considering
11. Writer's choice: ____________________

LEARNING STYLES TIP
Visual and other learners often find an organizer helpful as they generate ideas, plan, and compose.

2. Many students find using a graphic organizer helpful as they plan an essay. In your notebook or on a computer, create an outline for your comparison and contrast essay using an organizer like the one that follows. The information you write in each box will become a paragraph.

COMPARISON AND CONTRAST ESSAY ORGANIZER

Title		Write a title that states the two persons or things you will compare or contrast.
Paragraph 1: Introduction & thesis statement		In box one, write a thesis statement that clearly states the two persons or things and whether your essay will compare or contrast them. Jot down ideas for an engaging or informative introduction.
Paragraph 2: Point 1 of comparison or contrast		In box two, write a topic sentence introducing your first point of comparison or contrast. You should have decided by now whether to arrange your points in *AB, AB, AB* order or *all A, then all B*. Brainstorm details and specifics that clearly develop the topic sentence.
Paragraph 3: Point 2 of comparison or contrast		In box three, following your plan, write a topic sentence introducing the second point of comparison or contrast. Brainstorm details and specifics that clearly support this idea.

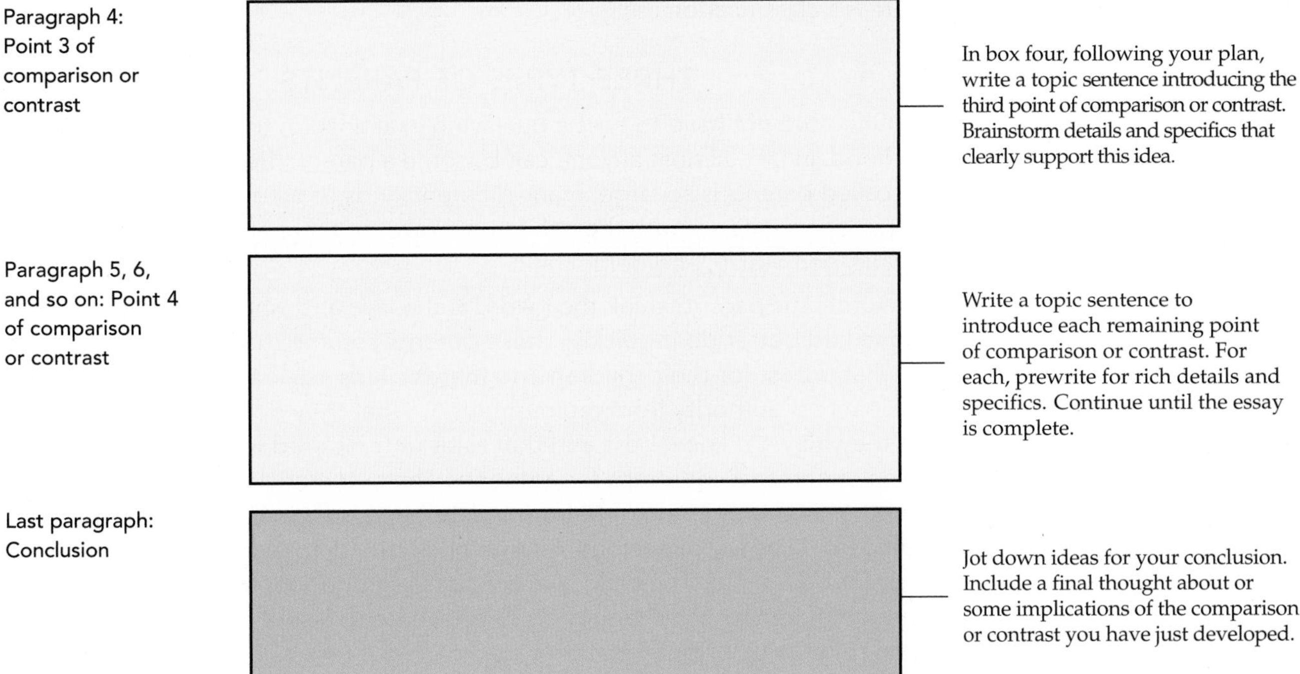
Paragraph 4: Point 3 of comparison or contrast
In box four, following your plan, write a topic sentence introducing the third point of comparison or contrast. Brainstorm details and specifics that clearly support this idea.
Paragraph 5, 6, and so on: Point 4 of comparison or contrast
Write a topic sentence to introduce each remaining point of comparison or contrast. For each, prewrite for rich details and specifics. Continue until the essay is complete.
Last paragraph: Conclusion
Jot down ideas for your conclusion. Include a final thought about or some implications of the comparison or contrast you have just developed.

PRACTICE 4

Once your plan is finalized, write the best first draft you can. Refer to your plan to make sure you have included every point of comparison or contrast. If any section seems weak, prewrite for more details and revise. Organization is very important in a comparison or contrast essay, so use *transitional expressions** to highlight the order and guide the reader from point to point.

Let your draft cool for an hour or a day; then reread it as if you were a helpful, eagle-eyed stranger. Now revise and rewrite, emphasizing completeness, clear organization, and exact language. Is each point developed fully? Do transitions make the flow of ideas clear? Proofread for spelling, grammar, and sentence errors.

B. The Classification Essay

The **classification** essay is useful in college and business. In music, for example, you might have to classify Mozart's compositions according to the musical periods of his life. A retail business might classify items in stock according to popularity—how frequently they must be restocked. All plants, animals, rocks, and stars are classified by scientists. Libraries classify and display books according to the Dewey Decimal Classification System. It seems that one way the human mind makes sense of the world is by grouping similar things and then dividing them into subcategories; a good classification does just that.

*For a list of transitional expressions of comparison and contrast, see Chapter 10.

Here is a classification essay:

THREE TYPES OF PARENTS

(1) One does not have to pass a qualifying examination to enter the state of parenthood. In fact, almost anyone can become a parent. Precisely because the group called *parents* is so large, many different kinds of parenting exist. In terms of how strict parents are with their children, however, there are three basic types: autocratic, permissive, and democratic.

TEACHING TIP
You might ask how many students knew the word *autocratic* before reading the essay. From the context of paragraph 2, can they now define the word?

(2) Autocratic parents think their word is the law, and when they say jump, everyone had better do it quickly. These parents assume that they alone know what is best for their children and that the kids will learn discipline and respect for authority from regimentation. What they do not even consider is that they may not know best and that rules untempered with mercy can breed rebellion and contempt for authority. The autocratic parent whose child comes home one hour late from a date because a major accident tied up traffic for miles will allow that child no opportunity to explain his or her reasons for being late. The child is immediately grounded, his or her allowance suspended. Parents of this type probably have good intentions, wanting their children to grow up "right," but they approach the task as if the family were in boot camp.

(3) At the other extreme, permissive parents set few or no rules for their children and offer little guidance. Frequently, these parents are too busy to take time with the children and tend to leave the child-rearing to TV, the computer, school, and chance. Since parents of this type set few rules for their children, it would be nearly impossible for their child to come home late. They allow their children to come and go as they please, either because they don't care what their youngsters do or because they think children need to learn to make their own rules. Permissive parents may not understand that all young people need guidance because when they mature, they will have to abide by society's rules. Not being taught to respect order early in life causes some children of permissive parents to resent the regulations everyone must obey.

(4) Democratic parents, the third type, are not as strict as autocrats and not as lenient as permissives. They are willing to discuss rules and punishments with their children and to listen to the other side of an argument. A democratic parent whose child comes in an hour late from a date will listen to the explanation about the major wreck that tied up traffic for miles. Since this is such an easily verifiable story, the democratic parent would suspend any punishment in this case when he or she hears the news or sees the morning paper. In general, democratic parents lay down fewer rules than their autocratic counterparts because they realize that children must learn some life lessons on their own. Democratic parents prefer to work in the role of advisors, always available when their children need help.

(5) Too few people with children are democratic parents, the most effective of the three types. Both too much authority and too little can breed disrespect and resentment. A good parent should offer boundaries and advice, trying neither to rule nor disregard his or her children completely.

—Sallie Duhling

- The **thesis statement** in a classification essay tells the reader what group will be classified and on what basis. Underline or highlight the thesis.
- Into how many categories are parents divided? What are they?

  Three: autocratic parents, permissive parents, democratic parents

- On what **basis** are these categories examined?

  strictness

- Can you see the logic of this writer's **order** of paragraphs? That is, why are autocratics discussed first, permissives second, and democratic parents last?

  The first type is very strict, the second not strict enough, and the last is a more balanced parenting style.

LEARNING STYLES TIP
To help students see the clear structure of this essay, ask them to make an outline of the essay.

- Note that the thesis statement, topic sentences setting forth the three categories, and the conclusion create an **outline** for this essay. The writer made such an outline before she wrote the first draft.

PRACTICE 5

Although the classification essay is usually serious, the pattern can make a good humorous essay, as this student's paper shows. Read it and answer the questions.

THE POTATO SCALE

(1) For years, television has been the great American pastime. Nearly every household has at least one TV, which means that people are spending time watching it, unless, of course, they bought it to serve as a plant stand. Television viewers can be grouped in many ways—by the type of shows they watch (but there is no accounting for taste) or by hours per week of watching (but that seems unfair since a working, twelve-hour-a-week viewer could conceivably become a fifty-hour-a-week viewer if he or she were out of a job). So I have developed the Potato Scale. The four major categories of the Potato Scale rank TV viewers on a combination of leisure time spent watching, intensity of watching, and the desire to watch versus the desire to engage in other activities.

(2) First, we have the True Couch Potatoes. They are diehard viewers who, when home, will be found in front of their televisions. They no longer eat in the dining room, and if you visit them, the television stays on. *TV Guide* is their Bible. They will plan other activities and chores around their viewing time, always hoping to accomplish these tasks in front of the tube. If a presidential address is on every channel but one, and they dislike the president, they will tune into that one channel, be it *Bugs Bunny* reruns or Polynesian barge cooking. These potatoes would never consider turning off the box.

(3) The second group consists of the Pseudo Couch Potatoes. These are scheduled potatoes. They have outside interests and actually eat at the table, but for a certain period of time (let's say from 7 to 11 in the evening), they will take on

the characteristics of True Couch Potatoes. Another difference between True and Pseudo Potatoes deserves note. The True Potato must be forced by someone else to shut off the television and do something different; however, if the Pseudo Potato has flipped through all the channels and found only garbage, he or she still has the capacity to think of other things to do.

(4) Third, we have the Selective Potatoes. These more discriminating potatoes enjoy many activities, and TV is just one of them. They might have a few shows they enjoy watching regularly, but missing one episode is not a world-class crisis. After all, the show will be on next week. They don't live by *TV Guide*, but use it to check for interesting specials. If they find themselves staring at an awful movie or show, they will gladly, and without a second thought, turn it off.

(5) The fourth group consists of Last Resort Potatoes. These people actually prefer reading, going to the theater, playing pickup basketball, walking in the woods, and many other activities to watching television. Only after they have exhausted all other possibilities or are dog tired or shivering with the flu, will they click on the tube. These potatoes are either excessively choosy or almost indifferent to what's on, hoping it will bore them to sleep.

(6) These are the principal categories of the Potato Scale, from the truly vegetable to the usually human. What type of potato are you?

—Helen Petruzzelli, Student

1. Underline or highlight the thesis statement and the topic sentences. Note that they form a clear outline of this well-organized classification essay.
2. The entire essay classifies people on the basis of their television viewing habits. Into how many categories are the TV viewers divided? What are they?

   Four: True Couch Potatoes, Pseudo Couch Potatoes, Selective Couch Potatoes, and Last Resort Couch Potatoes

3. Does the writer's order make sense? What is the logic in presenting True Couch Potatoes first, Pseudo Couch Potatoes second, Selective Couch Potatoes third, and Last Resort Couch Potatoes fourth?

   She moves from people who watch TV the most to those who watch it the least.

4. How successful is Ms. Petruzzelli's essay? Does it inspire you with any ideas for a humorous essay of your own?

   Answers will vary.

PRACTICE 6 CRITICAL VIEWING AND WRITING

Examine the plate below. It shows what experts believe to be the building blocks for a healthy diet. How is *classification* used in this illustration? How many food *classes* or *groups* are shown here? Label each food group; use nouns to keep your labels parallel. How do your personal eating habits compare to the ideal?

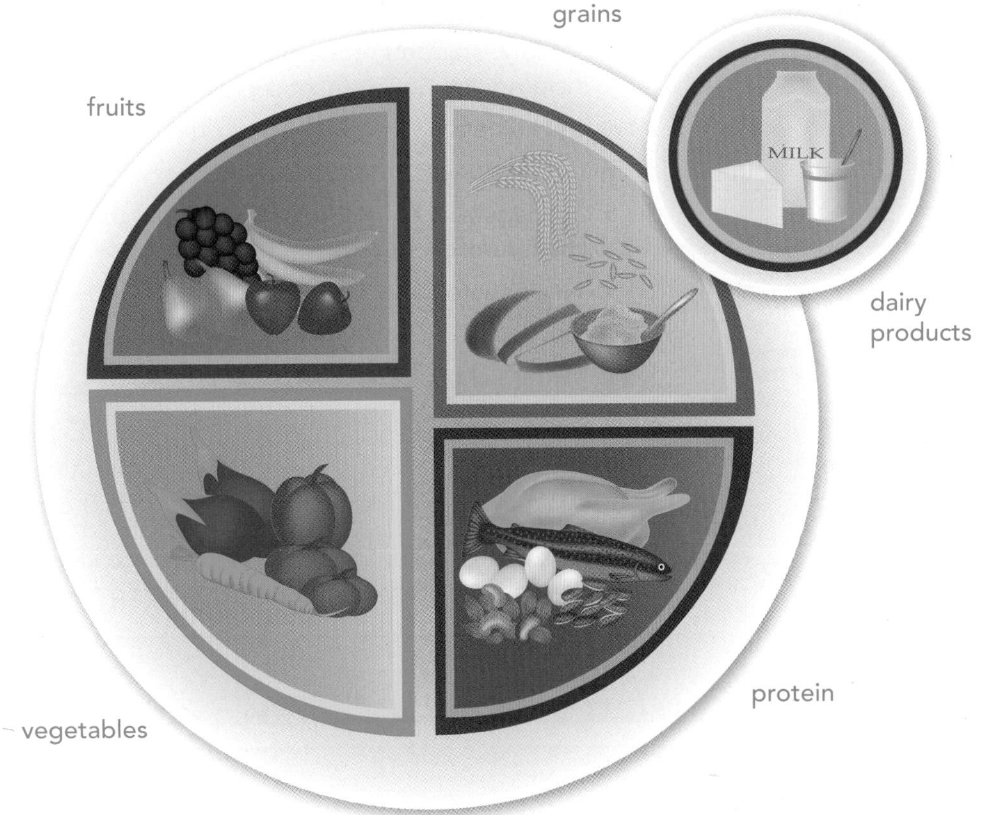

Planning and Writing the Classification Essay

Before writing a classification essay, you might reread Chapter 11, "Classification." Choose a topic that lends itself to this pattern, and then make sure your *basis of classification* includes every member of the group. For instance, *all* TV viewers fall somewhere on the Potato Scale (from those who watch TV nearly all the time to those who almost never watch). As you plan your essay, make sure your categories follow a logical order. As you write, use transitional phrases like "The first type . . ." and "The second category . . ." to help the reader follow.*

The rest of the section will guide you as you write a classification essay.

PRACTICE 7

1. Choose a topic from the list below or one your instructor has assigned, and then "try on" different bases of classification until you find one that inspires you. (For instance, you could discuss members of your family on the basis

*For a list of transitional expressions of classification, see Chapter 11.

of how they spend their leisure time . . . or how good they are at home repairs . . . or how they handle stress.) Be clear on your audience and purpose for this paper.

1. Places where you shop
2. Depictions of minorities or women in the media
3. Your monthly expenses
4. Your favorite restaurants
5. College students' attitudes toward plagiarism, racial profiling, sexual harassment, government surveillance, or any other issue
6. Pet owners
7. Job options in your career field
8. Teenagers whom you interview (about the value of education, hope about the future, or other subject)
9. News sources
10. Drivers
11. Writer's choice: ______________________________

LEARNING STYLES TIP

Visual and other learners often find an organizer helpful as they generate ideas, plan, and compose.

2. Many students find using a graphic organizer helpful as they plan an essay. In your notebook or on a computer, create an outline for your classification essay using an organizer like the one that follows. The information you write in each box will become a paragraph.

CLASSIFICATION ESSAY ORGANIZER

Title

Write a title that clearly states the classification subject or refers to it in an interesting way.

Paragraph 1: Introduction & thesis statement

In box one, write a thesis statement that sets forth the group you will classify and the basis of the classification; you also might name your categories (three or four is a good number). Jot down ideas for an introductory paragraph that will convey to the reader the value or point of your classification.

Paragraph 2: Category 1 of the classification

In box two, write a topic sentence introducing the first category. Brainstorm details, specifics, and perhaps an example or two to explain the category in one body paragraph. Use transitional expressions to guide the reader along.

Paragraph 3: Category 2 of the classification

In box three, write a topic sentence introducing the second category. Brainstorm details, specifics, and an example or two to explain the category.

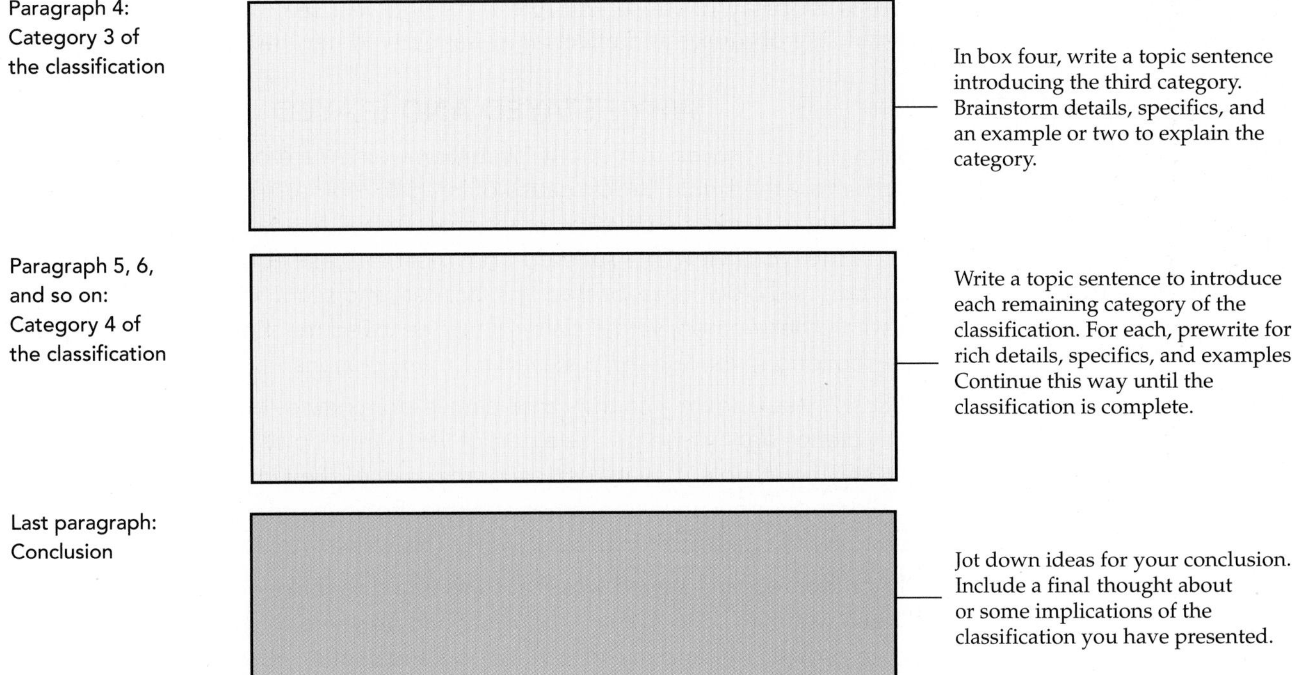
Paragraph 4:
Category 3 of
the classification
In box four, write a topic sentence introducing the third category. Brainstorm details, specifics, and an example or two to explain the category.
Paragraph 5, 6,
and so on:
Category 4 of
the classification
Write a topic sentence to introduce each remaining category of the classification. For each, prewrite for rich details, specifics, and examples. Continue this way until the classification is complete.
Last paragraph:
Conclusion
Jot down ideas for your conclusion. Include a final thought about or some implications of the classification you have presented.

PRACTICE 8

Now, referring to your plan, write the best first draft you can. Aim for clarity as you help the reader develop an understanding of each category in your classification. Check your paragraphing, and use *transitional expressions** to guide the reader from category to category.

Let your draft cool for an hour or a day; then reread it as if you were a helpful, eagle-eyed stranger. Now revise and rewrite, emphasizing clarity, completeness, and keeping your reader in mind. Is each paragraph developed fully? Do transitions make the flow of ideas clear? Proofread for spelling, grammar, and sentence errors.

C. The Cause and Effect Essay

Essays of **cause and effect** are among the most important kinds of essays to master because knowing how to analyze the causes and consequences of events will help you succeed in college, at work, and in your personal life. What *caused* a historic battle, an increase of homelessness, or a friendship to break apart? How will a certain child be *affected* by owning a computer, spending time at Sunshine Day Care, or being teased because he loves to dance? In business, the success of every company and product relies on a grasp of cause and effect in the marketplace. Why does this brand of smartphone outsell all others? What causes employees to want to work hard? How will the Internet affect business in 2030?

---

*For a list of transitional expressions of classification, see Chapter 11.

TEACHING TIP

Students are likely to want to discuss this powerful essay in class. The writer seeks reasons for her self-destructive behavior—a model of self-reflective critical thinking. You might ask why people engage in self-destructive actions—smoking, having unprotected sex, and so forth.

Here is an essay of cause and effect. As you will see, this writer's eventual understanding of causes and effects may have saved her life.

WHY I STAYED AND STAYED

(1) It has been proven that about 1.8 million women are battered each year, making battery the single largest cause of injury to women in the United States. Domestic violence can be physical, emotional, verbal, financial, or sexual abuse from a partner you live with. I suffered from most of these abuses for almost ten years. I have had black eyes, busted lips, bruises, and scars on my face. He had affairs with other women, yet he claimed that he loved me. People ask, "Why did you wait so long to leave him?" I stayed for many reasons.

(2) First, I was born in a country that is male-dominated. Many of my people accept violence against women as a part of life. I grew up seeing hundreds of women staying in violent relationships for the sake of their children. They wanted their children to grow up with a father at home. Relatives convinced these women to try to make their marriages work. This was all I knew.

(3) Another reason I stayed was that I was afraid to make changes in my life. I had been with him so long that I thought I had nowhere to go. I depended on him to provide me and my child with food and shelter. How could I manage on my own? Of course, the longer I believed these things, the more my self-confidence withered.

(4) Finally, I stayed because I was isolated. I felt ashamed to talk about the problem, believing it was somehow my fault. Fear was isolating, too. Living in a violent home is very frightening. Like many women, I was afraid to say anything to anyone, thinking he would get upset. If I just kept quiet, maybe he wouldn't hurt me. But nothing I did made any difference.

(5) When I finally realized that the abuse was not going to stop, I decided to do something about it. I was finally ready to end my pain. I began to talk to people and learn about ways to get help.

(6) On April 24th of this year, I fought back. When he punched me in the eye, I called 911. Thank God for changes in the way domestic violence cases are now being handled. The police responded quickly. He was arrested and taken to jail, where he waited for two days to go to court. The next day, I went to the courthouse to press charges. I spoke to the district attorney in charge, asking for an order of protection. This order forbids him from having any verbal or physical contact with me.

(7) It is very hard to see someone you love being taken away in handcuffs, but I had to put my safety and my child's well-being first. Although he is now out of jail, I feel safe with my order of protection; however, I understand that court orders sometimes do not stop abusers. These are very difficult days for me, but I pray that time will heal my wounds. I cry often, which helps my pain. But an innocent life depends on me for guidance, and I cannot let her down.

(8) Every case is different, and you know your partner better than anyone, but help is out there if you reach for it. Most cities have a 24-hour hotline. There is help at this college at the PASS Center and the Department of Student Development. You can go to a shelter, to a friend, to your family. These people will not fail you. You too can break the chain.

—Student, name withheld by request

- The **thesis statement** of a cause and effect essay identifies the subject and tells whether causes or effects will be emphasized. Underline or highlight the thesis statement in this essay. Does it emphasize causes or effects?

  causes

- How many **causes** does the writer discuss, and what are they?

  three: upbringing, fear of change, isolation

- Although some essays discuss either causes or effects, this one does both. Paragraph 5 marks a turning point, her decision to take action. What positive effects of this new decision does she discuss? Are there any negative effects?

  reached out for help and information, fought back by calling 911 and getting order of protection, acted for her daughter's welfare; negative feelings, sadness and guilt

- Before she wrote this essay, the writer probably made a **plan** or **outline** like this:

  Introduction and thesis statement
  Reasons for staying with abusive partner — upbringing; fear of change; isolation
  Decision to leave
  Effects of decision to leave abuser — reached out for help; fought back (911, order of protection); acted for daughter; sadness, guilt
  Advice for women in the same situation

- What order does this essay follow?

  time

- Do you think paragraph 8 makes an effective **conclusion**?

  good information, but might seem anticlimactic after dramatic personal story

PRACTICE 9

Now read another student's cause and effect essay and answer the questions.

UNFRIENDING FACEBOOK

(1) Facebook is the most popular social networking site in the world. Over half its 800 million users log in every day, uploading millions of photos, chatting with friends, and playing games. College students today have been "Facebooking" since high school. It is fun, but Facebook can have negative effects on a person's life like wasting time, hurting relationships, and even keeping a person from getting a good job.

(2) One of the most obvious effects of Facebook is that it wastes time. My college friends say that just reading and responding to posts takes an hour or more daily, but many jump on Facebook every chance they get. That's time they don't have to study history, write papers, or exercise. Then there are Facebook games. Farmville players manage pretend farms and harvest a friend's pretend crops while he takes a real exam. Gardens of Time, where friends team up to find hidden objects, logged more than five billion sessions in 2011. It's nice to relax, but that's a LOT of time spent on Facebook.

(3) A less obvious negative effect of Facebooking is the cost to friendships. Facebook encourages social networking, so it seems like it would strengthen relationships, but the opposite is true. People talk about "friending" each other, but that doesn't mean they have become actual friends. Having the most Facebook friends is a sort of contest among college students. One of my classmates brags about his 370 online friends, but he has met only about 30 of them in person. In addition, Facebook has been blamed for many romantic breakups. It is humiliating for lovers to broadcast their fights online or to read that one's significant other has changed his relationship status to "single." Facebook may be an easy way to update a list of people, but it will never replace personal sharing over coffee, the warmth of a phone call, or a loving, intimate relationship.

(4) A serious consequence of Facebook is revealing too much information, which can hurt a person professionally. Many students don't understand that some things should be kept private. When my friend Joi applied for an accounting internship, she never thought the interviewer would look her up online. On her Facebook page, Joi had photos of herself drinking at a party (she was underage) and complaints on her wall about "boring" classes and her supervisor at work, an "annoying ass." She hadn't set the privacy settings on her account, so these pictures and comments were the image she was broadcasting to the world. Yes, she lost the internship.

TEACHING TIP

You might ask whether Facebook overuse is a problem for any of your students. If so, have they invented solutions or limits, the way the writer's friends do in the last paragraph?

(5) Most people are not going to unfriend Facebook any time soon, but they can avoid its harmful effects. My roommate sets a timer when she gets on Facebook in the evening; when the timer goes off, so does her page. Another friend uses Facebook to keep up with her relatives in China, but for her friends and classmates here, she calls and texts instead. After losing a great internship, Joi opened a second Facebook account. The first one is now private, seen only by a few friends. Her second page is public and squeaky clean; Joi calls it her online résumé. These strategies can keep Facebook fun, not a time-wasting habit that might cause harm.

—Celia Menezes, Student

1. Underline or highlight the thesis statement and the topic sentences in paragraphs 2, 3, and 4.
2. Does the writer discuss causes or effects? What are they?

   effects: effect on time, on friendships, and on professional opportunities

3. What technique for the conclusion is used for this essay?

   end with a call to action

PRACTICE 10 CRITICAL VIEWING AND WRITING

Study this famous painting by Francisco Goya called *The Third of May.* The painting shows the execution of Spaniards in Madrid by French troops, and it is widely viewed as a moving depiction of wartime atrocities and political oppression. What are the effects of war and oppression? Why do you think Goya illuminated and highlighted the faces of the victims, but depicted the soldiers as faceless? How do their rifles contrast with the raised hands of the man in the white shirt? What is the significance of his clothing and his pose?

Hulton Fine Art Collection/Getty Images

Planning and Writing the Cause and Effect Essay

Before writing an essay of cause and effect, reread Chapter 12, "Cause and Effect," especially the section called "Problems to Avoid in Cause and Effect Writing." Choose a subject that lends itself to an analysis of causes or effects. Create a list of possible causes and effects; then choose the best three or four. Don't forget to consider short- and long-term effects, as well as positive and negative effects. Decide on a logical order—probably time order or order of importance—and use transitional expressions to introduce your points.*

The rest of the section will guide you as you write a cause and effect essay.

PRACTICE 11

1. Choose a topic from the list below or one your instructor has assigned. Make sure your topic lends itself to cause and effect analysis. This list and the one in Chapter 12 will give you ideas. Write a clear thesis statement that identifies

*For a list of transitional expressions for cause and effect, see Chapter 12.

your subject and indicates whether causes or effects will be emphasized. Then prewrite a number of possible causes or effects, so you can choose the most important ones to develop your essay. Decide on a logical order in which to present them.

1. What are the reasons why people do not vote?
2. What are the causes for the rising or falling popularity of a certain product, musical group, TV show, or game?
3. What caused you to do something you are (or are not) proud of?
4. Analyze the main causes of a problem in society (like child abuse, homelessness among military veterans, or teen pregnancy).
5. What causes people to end relationships?
6. What causes people to start smoking?
7. What are the effects of shyness on someone's life (or pride, rage, curiosity or the lack of it)?
8. Write a letter urging a young person not to make a bad choice with serious negative consequences (such as joining a gang or dropping out of school).
9. What are the effects of a new experience (a trip, military service, living in another country, dorm life)?
10. What are the effects of a divorce, death, or other loss?
11. Writer's choice: ______________________________

LEARNING STYLES TIP

Visual and other learners often find an organizer helpful as they generate ideas, plan, and compose.

2. Many students find using a graphic organizer helpful as they plan an essay. In your notebook or on a computer, create an outline for your cause and effect essay using an organizer like the one that follows. The information you write in each box will become a paragraph.

CAUSE AND EFFECT ESSAY ORGANIZER

Title		Write a title that clearly states the subject or refers to it in an interesting way.
Paragraph 1: Introduction & thesis statement		In box one, write a thesis statement that briefly states your subject and whether causes or effects will be emphasized. Jot down ideas for an engaging or informative introduction.
Paragraph 2: Cause or effect 1		In box two, write a topic sentence introducing the first cause or effect you will explain. Brainstorm details and specifics that clearly explain the importance of this cause or effect. Consider devoting one paragraph to each main cause or effect.

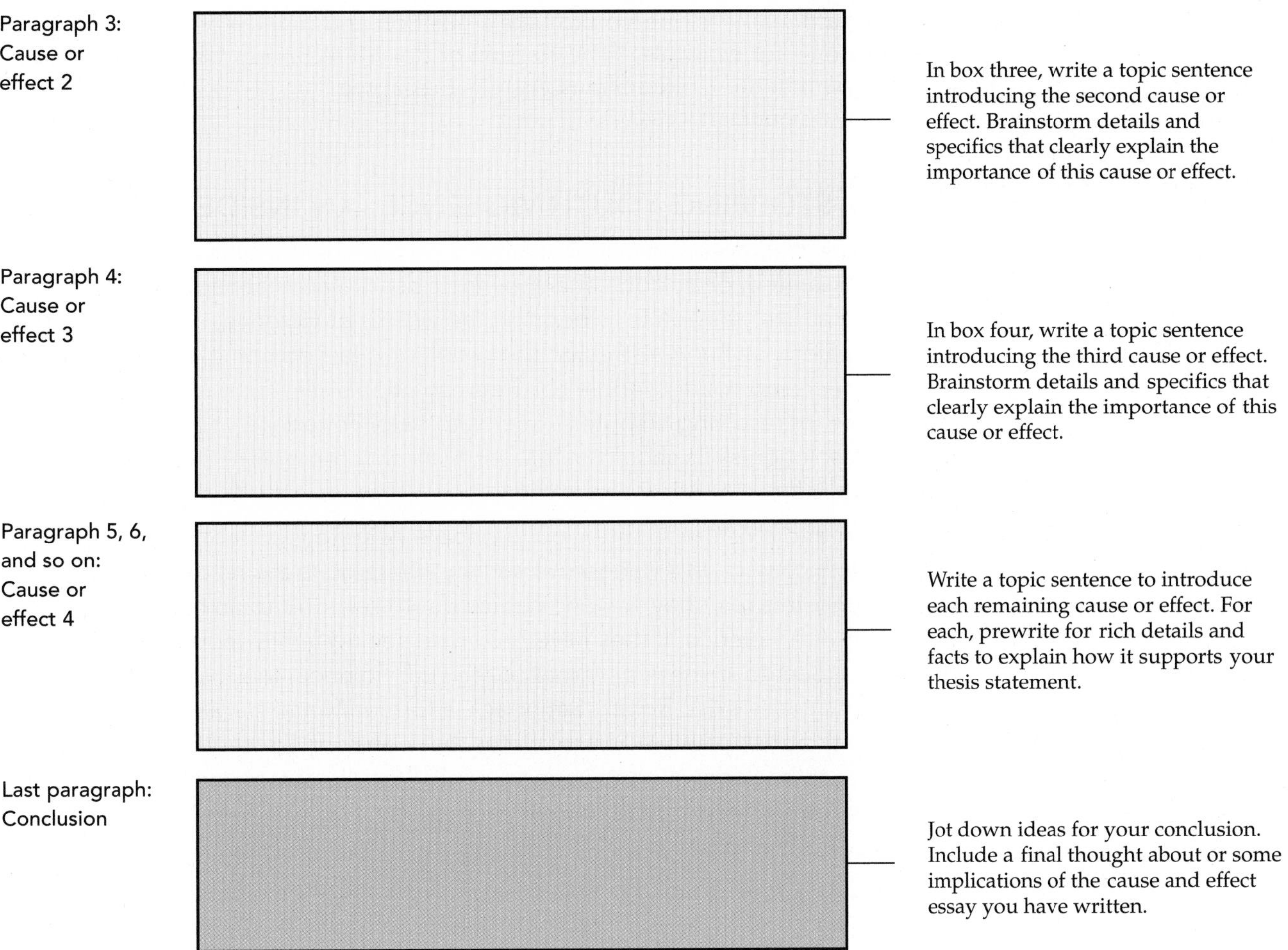

Paragraph 3: Cause or effect 2
In box three, write a topic sentence introducing the second cause or effect. Brainstorm details and specifics that clearly explain the importance of this cause or effect.
Paragraph 4: Cause or effect 3
In box four, write a topic sentence introducing the third cause or effect. Brainstorm details and specifics that clearly explain the importance of this cause or effect.
Paragraph 5, 6, and so on: Cause or effect 4
Write a topic sentence to introduce each remaining cause or effect. For each, prewrite for rich details and facts to explain how it supports your thesis statement.
Last paragraph: Conclusion
Jot down ideas for your conclusion. Include a final thought about or some implications of the cause and effect essay you have written.

PRACTICE 12

Now, referring to your plan, write the best first draft you can. Make sure that each cause and/or effect you discuss is clear to you and the reader. Is the order logical? Tie each cause or effect into your thesis statement and main idea. Use *transitional expressions** to help the reader follow what happened.

Let your draft cool for an hour or a day; then reread it as if you were a helpful, eagle-eyed stranger. Now revise and rewrite, emphasizing clarity and a thoughtful explanation of causes or effects. Is each paragraph developed fully? Do transitions make the flow of ideas clear? Proofread for spelling, grammar, and sentence errors.

D. The Persuasive Essay

Persuasive essays are the essay type most frequently called for in college, business, and daily life. That is, you will often be asked to take a stand on an issue—censorship on the Internet, whether a company should invest in on-site childcare, or whether a new superstore will help or hurt your community—and then try to persuade others to agree with you. Examination questions asking you to "agree or

*For a list of transitional expressions of cause and effect, see Chapter 12.

TEACHING TIP

Stress to students the importance of persuasive writing skills to career advancement. Ask for examples of career-related persuasive writing. Point out that documents like job-application letters, which are persuasive in nature, will help them get a job and then advance within an organization.

disagree" are really asking you to take a position and make a persuasive case for that position—for example, "The election of President Barack Obama signaled an end to racism in the United States. Agree or disagree."

Here is a persuasive essay:

STOPPING YOUTH VIOLENCE: AN INSIDE JOB

(1) Every year, over one million twelve- to nineteen-year-olds are murdered, robbed, assaulted, or bullied—many by their peers—and teenagers are more than twice as likely as adults to become the victims of violence, according to the Children's Defense Fund. Although the problem is far too complex for any one solution, teaching young people conflict-resolution skills—that is, nonviolent techniques for resolving disputes—seems to help. To reduce youth violence, conflict-resolution skills should be taught to all children before they reach middle school.

(2) First and most important, young people need to learn nonviolent ways of dealing with conflict. In a dangerous society where guns are readily available, many youngsters feel they have no choice but to respond to an insult or an argument with violence. If they have grown up seeing family members and neighbors react to stress with verbal or physical violence, they may not know that other choices exist. Robert Steinback, a former *Miami Herald* columnist who worked with at-risk youth in Miami, writes that behavior like carrying a weapon or refusing to back down gives young people "the illusion of control," but what they desperately need is to learn real control—for example, when provoked, to walk away from a fight.

(3) Next, conflict-resolution programs have been shown to reduce violent incidents and empower young people in a healthy way. Many programs and courses around the country are teaching teens and preteens to work through disagreements without violence. Tools include calmly telling one's own side of the story and listening to the other person without interrupting or blaming—skills that many adults don't have! Conflict Busters, a Los Angeles public school program, starts in the third grade; it trains students to be mediators, helping peers find their own solutions to conflicts ranging from "sandbox fights to interracial gang disputes," according to *Youthwatch: Statistics on Violence*, May 2012. Schools in Claremont, Connecticut, run a conflict-resolution course written by Dr. Luz Rivera, who said in a phone interview that fewer violent school incidents have been reported since the course began. Although conflict resolution is useful at any age, experts agree that students should first be exposed before they are hit by the double jolts of hormones and middle school.

(4) Finally, although opponents claim that this is a "Band-Aid" solution that does not address the root causes of teen violence—poverty, troubled families, bad schools, and drugs, to name a few—in fact, conflict-resolution training saves lives now. The larger social issues must be addressed, but they will take years to solve, whereas teaching students new attitudes and "people skills" will empower them immediately and serve them for a lifetime. For instance, fourteen-year-old Verna, who once called herself Vee Sinister, says that Ms. Rivera's course has changed her life: "I learned to stop and think before my big mouth gets me in trouble. I use the tools with my mother, and guess what? No more fights at school and screaming at home."

(5) The violence devastating Verna's generation threatens everyone's future. One proven way to help youngsters protect themselves from violence is conflict-resolution training that begins early. Although it is just one solution among many, this solution taps into great power: the hearts, minds, and characters of young people.

- The **thesis statement** in a persuasive essay clearly states the issue to be discussed and the writer's position on it. Underline or highlight the thesis statement.
- This introduction includes *facts*. What is the source of these facts, and why does the writer include them here?

  The Children's Defense Fund is the source. These facts show how serious a problem youth crime is.

- Sometimes a writer needs to define terms he or she is using. What term does the writer define?

  conflict-resolution skills

- How many reasons does this writer give to back up the thesis statement?

  three

- Notice that the writer presents one reason per paragraph. Which reasons refer to an *authority*?

  reason 1 and reason 2

- Who are these authorities?

  Robert Steinback, *Miami Herald* columnist who works with youth, and Dr. Luz Rivera, who wrote a conflict-resolution course

- How is the second reason supported?

  by examples

- What is the source of information on Conflict Busters?

  Youthwatch: Statistics on Violence, May 2012

- Which reason is really an *answer to the opposition?*

  reason 3

- This reason also uses an *example.* What or who is the example?

  Verna, a student whose life has changed

- Underline or highlight the topic sentence of each body paragraph. Note that the thesis statement, topic sentences, and conclusion make up an **outline** or **plan** for the whole essay.

PRACTICE 13

This student's persuasive essay won a national essay contest sponsored by CCBA (Community College Baccalaureate). Read it and answer the questions.

IMAGINE A FOUR-YEAR COMMUNITY COLLEGE

(1) Imagine four-year institutions that allow for a pace and schedule that meet the needs of nontraditional students with non-academic obligations. Imagine institutions with an affordability that allows students to pay their own tuition as it comes due, in the absence of family wealth or large scholarships. Imagine colleges that take pride in their program and the philosophy of open admissions, rather than their ability to selectively admit few while turning down many. Imagine institutions like these all over the country, allowing continuity of family, work, and community between students and their hometowns. You have just imagined community colleges with four-year degree programs. Schedule, affordability, and open admissions policies make community colleges ideal to offer four-year degrees.

(2) A key concept of community colleges is to tailor offerings to students with small, sporadic amounts of time available for classes. I work, help run a non-profit honor society on campus, attend full-time classes, and am a cadet in the Corona de Tucson Firefighter Academy. Without the flexible schedule that Pima Community College affords me, I would be unable to complete all of these tasks simultaneously. Community colleges generally have very accommodating schedules, with courses available nights and weekends, self-paced on campus, and even online. Students who deserve and desire to complete a bachelor's degree may simply not have the availability to schedule classes between seven A.M. and five P.M., but the community college would meet their needs.

(3) It is no coincidence that many students attending community colleges fall in the category of working poor. During freshman year, I struggled to pay tuition and book expenses; it was a year before I began receiving scholarships. Working in the food service industry, I had limited funds; luckily, I was able to utilize the library's books on reserve when I could not pay for my own. I saved thousands of dollars attending Pima Community College compared to what the University of Arizona would have charged me for the same number of credits. Yet my situation is not unique; millions of students would love to attend lavish universities, but incurring debts or failing to receive competitive scholarships deter worthy students from acquiring higher education. This is not to mention the fact that some full-capacity universities turn down valedictorians simply because they receive more perfect applications than they have seats available.

(4) Sometimes students need more than flexible hours or tuition to attend college; they need something nearby. Community colleges are exactly what the name entails, institutions of the community. Pima Community College has six campuses around town and online courses available. This has given me the ability to live with my sister and help her with mortgage payments while attending school. The community emphasis of these colleges allows students to stay in and help their community, family, and friends while pursuing higher education and personal enrichment. To imagine a solution to a problem and make it a reality is a staple of college education. Many have imagined a four-year community college—it must become a reality.

—John Windham, Student

1. What is this writer arguing *for*? Underline the thesis statement.

   He is arguing for the establishment of four-year community colleges.

2. In the introduction, instead of a thesis statement, the writer asks readers three times to "Imagine . . . ." The last sentence of the introduction says, "You have just imagined community colleges with four-year degree programs." How effective is this introduction?

   It is effective because the three "imagine" sentences tie to the main ideas developed in the thesis statement and body of the essay.

3. What three features of community colleges does the writer discuss in his argument?

   flexible scheduling, reasonable costs, and proximity to family and home

4. This writer uses himself as an example throughout the essay. Is this persuasive? Would you say that his experience makes him an authority?

   Yes, it is persuasive. His experience does make him an authority on the need for such a college.

PRACTICE 14 CRITICAL VIEWING AND WRITING

Look closely at the public service advertisement below, which appeared on buses and billboards. Like many advertisements, this one tries to *persuade* the viewer to adopt or agree with a certain view. Write down the ad's "thesis statement" and argument. How persuasive is this ad? Would you substitute other images or phrases?

YOU LOOK JUST AS STUPID WEARING THEIRS.

Friends of Animals
www.friendsofanimals.org

Courtesy Friends of Animals

Planning and Writing the Persuasive Essay

Before writing a persuasive essay, you should reread Chapter 13, "Persuasion." In particular, review the five methods of persuasion:

1. Use facts
2. Cite authority
3. Give examples
4. Predict consequences
5. Answer the opposition

Keeping your readers in mind is key to persuading them, so craft your thesis statement carefully. Plan to devote one paragraph to each of your reasons, developing each paragraph with facts and discussion. Ample factual support is vital to successful persuasion. A good way to find interesting factual support is to do some basic **research**—for example, to find books or articles by or about experts on your subject or even to conduct your own interviews, as does the author of "Stopping Youth Violence."*

The rest of the section will guide you as you write a persuasive essay.

PRACTICE 15

1. Choose a topic from the list below or one your instructor has assigned. If possible, choose a subject you feel strongly about. Argue for or against, as you wish.
   1. I deserve a better grade on my assignment (or in this course).
   2. America needs (does not need) to take drastic measures to curb climate change.
   3. Entitlements such as Medicare, Social Security, and Medicaid must (not) be cut to balance the federal budget.
   4. Every college student should be required to give three credit hours' worth of community service a year.
   5. The United States government should (not) require businesses to pay a living wage, provide health care, offer daycare, or give retirement benefits.
   6. A college education is (not) worth the time and money.
   7. Gay couples should be allowed to adopt children in all states.
   8. I am a good fit for the position of ____________________.
   9. To better prepare students for the world of work, this college should do three things.
   10. College student athletes should (not) be paid.
   11. Writer's choice: ____________________

LEARNING STYLES TIP

Visual and other learners often find an organizer helpful as they generate ideas, plan, and compose.

2. Many students find using a graphic organizer helpful as they plan an essay. In your notebook or on a computer, create an outline for your persuasive essay using an organizer like the one that follows. The information you write in each box will become a paragraph.

*For information on summarizing and quoting outside sources and on using research in an essay, see Chapter 18, "Summarizing, Quoting, and Avoiding Plagiarism" and Chapter 19, "Strengthening an Essay with Research."

PERSUASIVE ESSAY ORGANIZER

Title		Write a title that forcefully or provocatively sets forth the issue.
Paragraph 1: Introduction & thesis statement		In box one, write a thesis statement that clearly states the issue and your position about it. Jot down ideas for a strong and engaging introduction. Visualize your typical reader, and write with him or her in mind.
Paragraph 2: Reason 1 in the argument		In box two, write a topic sentence introducing the first reason (refer to the five methods of persuasion and try to use at least two in your essay). Prewrite ideas that clearly explain the first reason.
Paragraph 3: Reason 2 in the argument		In box three, write a topic sentence introducing the second reason. Especially if your topic is controversial, try to include an answer to the opposition. Brainstorm details and specifics that clearly and convincingly explain it.
Paragraph 4: Reason 3 in the argument		In box four, write a topic sentence introducing the third reason. Especially if your topic is controversial, try to include an answer to the opposition. Brainstorm details and specificsthat clearly and convincingly explain it.
Paragraph 5, 6, and so on: Reason 4 in the argument		Write a topic sentence to introduce each remaining reason that will support and explain your thesis statement. For each, prewrite for facts and specifics to explain it fully. Continue until your last reason is presented. Double-check the order in which you present the reasons; does it make logical sense?
Last paragraph: Conclusion		Jot down ideas for your conclusion that bring home to the reader why he or she should agree with your position. Include a brief review of your argument and/or a final thought about the issue and its importance.

PRACTICE 16

Now, referring to your plan, write the best first draft you can. Aim for clarity and persuasive power as you explain why your stand is the right one. Make sure your reasons follow the most effective order, and carefully choose *transitional expressions** to introduce each reason. Remember, factual support is key to a winning essay.

Let your draft cool for an hour or a day; then reread it as if you were a helpful, eagle-eyed stranger. Now revise and rewrite for clarity and ample support. Is each paragraph and reason developed fully? Do transitions make the flow of ideas clear? Does your conclusion bring the point home? Proofread for spelling, grammar, and sentence errors.

EXPLORING ONLINE

leo.stcloudstate.edu/acadwrite/comparcontrast.html

Helpful advice on writing a comparison or a contrast essay

grammar.ccc.commnet.edu/grammar/composition/argument.htm

Excellent tips on developing and supporting an argument

*For a list of transitional expressions for persuasion, see Chapter 13.

CHAPTER 18

Summarizing, Quoting, and Avoiding Plagiarism

A: Avoiding Plagiarism

B: Writing a Summary

C: Using Direct and Indirect Quotation (Paraphrase)

Now more than ever before, it is important for you to know how to find, evaluate, and use information from **outside sources**—that is, sources outside yourself (for example, books, articles, Internet sites, or other people). In some college courses, you will write papers with no outside sources. However, many courses and jobs will require you to refer to outside sources as you write reports, essays, and research papers. Besides, information from outside sources can vastly enrich your writing with facts, statistics, experts' ideas, and more.

In this chapter, you will learn what **plagiarism** is and how to avoid it. You will also learn and practice three ways to use outside sources in your writing: **summarizing**, **quoting directly**, and **quoting indirectly**.

A. Avoiding Plagiarism

ESL TIP
Ask students whether their cultures have a more lax attitude toward rigorous documenting of sources, and stress that in American colleges and businesses, plagiarism is considered a crime.

Before we discuss how to summarize or quote from an outside source, it is all-important that you understand—so you can avoid—**plagiarism**. Plagiarism is failing to give proper credit to an author whose words or ideas you have used. That is, plagiarism means passing off someone else's words or ideas as your own. Whether intentional or careless, plagiarism is stealing. A college student who plagiarizes a paper may be expelled from the course or from college. In the business world, publishing material copied from someone else is a crime.

To avoid plagiarism, you must give proper credit to the original author, as this chapter and the next will explain. Meanwhile, keep this simple rule in mind: **Always tell your reader the source of any words and ideas not your own. Give enough information so that a reader who wants to find your original source can do so.**

PRACTICE 1

TEACHING TIP
Discuss with students your college's policy on academic dishonesty and the consequences of cheating or plagiarizing.

What is your college's policy on plagiarism? That is, what consequences or penalties follow if a student is found to have plagiarized a paper or other work? Your writing instructor or the reference librarian can help you find this information. In addition, most colleges post plagiarism policies on their websites.

B. Writing a Summary

A **summary** presents the main idea and supporting points of a longer work *in much shorter form.* A summary might be one sentence, one paragraph, or several paragraphs long, depending on the length of the original and the nature of your assignment.

Summarizing is important both in college and at work. In a persuasive essay, you might summarize the ideas of an expert whose views support one of your points. A professor might ask you to summarize a book, a market survey, or even the plot of a film—that is, to condense it in your own words, presenting only the highlights. Of course, many essay exams also call for written summaries.

Compare this short newspaper article—the *source*—with the *summary* that follows:

Source

Fido may be cute, cuddly, and harmless. But in his genes, he's a wolf.

Researchers tracing the genetic family tree of man's best friend have confirmed that domestic dogs, from petite poodles to huge elkhounds, descended from wolves that were tamed 100,000 years ago.

"Our data show that the origin of dogs seems to be much more ancient than indicated in the archaeological record," said Robert K. Wayne of UCLA, the leader of a team that tested the genes from 67 dog breeds and 62 wolves on four continents.

Wayne said the study showed so many DNA changes that dogs had to have diverged genetically from wolves 60,000 to more than 100,000 years ago.

The study suggests that primitive humans living in a hunting and gathering culture tamed wolves and then bred the animals to create the many different types of dogs that now exist.

—Recer, Paul. "Dogs Tamed 100,000 Years Ago." *The Herald,* 13 June 1997, p. 9A.

TEACHING TIP
Point out to students that summarizing is an important academic and career skill. The ability to summarize improves comprehension as well as one's ability to communicate ideas to others.

Summary

Dogs began evolving from wolves between 60,000 and 100,000 years ago, reports Paul Recer in *The Herald*. Apparently, humans tamed wolves far earlier than was previously thought. Researchers at UCLA, led by Robert K. Wayne, came to these conclusions after studying the genes of 67 breeds of dogs and 62 wolves on four continents (9A).

- Notice that sentence 1 states the author and source of the original article. Sentence 1 also states the main idea of the article. What is its main idea?

  Dogs began evolving from wolves 60,000 to 100,000 years ago.

- What evidence supports this idea?

  a UCLA study

- The original is short, so the summary is very short—just three sentences long.
- The summary writer does not add his own opinions about dogs or evolution but simply states the main ideas of the source. Unlike many kinds of writing, a summary should not contain your personal opinions and feelings.
- Note that the page number of the original source appears in parentheses at the end of the summary.*

Preparing to Write a Summary

The secret of writing a good summary is clearly understanding the original. If you doubt this, try to summarize out loud a chapter of a biology book. To summarize well, you have to know the subject matter.

Before you summarize a piece of writing, notice the title and subtitle (if there is one); these often state the main idea. Read quickly for meaning; then carefully read the work again, underlining or jotting down notes for yourself. What is the author's thesis or main point? What points does he or she offer in support? Be careful to distinguish between the most and least important points; your summary should include only the most important ones.

To help you understand *what the author thinks is important,* notice which ideas get the most coverage. Read with special care the topic sentence of each paragraph and the first and last paragraphs of the work. If you are summarizing a magazine article or a textbook chapter, the subheads (often in boldface type) point out important ideas.

Your written summary should include the following:

1. The author, title, and source of the original
2. The main idea or thesis of the original, in your own words
3. The most important supporting ideas or points of the original, in your own words

ESL TIP

Stress to ESL students that plagiarizing does not help them improve their English writing skills.

Try to present the ideas in your summary in proportion to those in the original. For instance, if the author devotes one paragraph to each of four ideas, you might give one sentence to each idea. To avoid plagiarism, when you finish, compare your summary with the original; that is, make sure you have not just copied the phrasing and sentences of the original.

A summary differs from much other writing in that it should *not* contain your feelings or opinions—just the facts. Your job is to capture the essence of the original, with nothing added.

*For more precise information on how to cite sources, see Chapter 19, "Strengthening an Essay with Research," Part C.

Following are two summaries of a student essay in Chapter 17, Part A, of this book. Which do you think is the better summary, A or B? Be prepared to say specifically why.

Summary A

(1) In the essay "E-Notes from an Online Learner," printed in Fawcett, *Evergreen*, Eleventh Edition, student and mother Brenda Wilson contrasts her learning experiences in traditional and online classrooms. (2) Whereas Wilson's long commute to campus once made her late to class or anxious, she finds online classes more convenient because she can read lectures or submit coursework any time, from home. (3) Next, Ms. Wilson says that other students might prefer the energy of live class discussion, but she feels freer online, writing her thoughts with less self-consciousness. (4) Finally, she stresses that online students must be self-motivated, unlike regular students, who can rely on professors to prod them or on the "group adrenaline rush [of] seeing other students hunched over their notebooks." (5) Less focused students might procrastinate and drop out. (6) Overall, Wilson prefers distance learning (253–254).

Summary B

(1) This excellent essay is by Brenda Wilson, student. (2) I enjoyed reading about online learning because I have never taken a course online. (3) This year Ms. Wilson attended her history class dressed in dancing cow pajamas and fluffy slippers. (4) This was not a bizarre college ritual but part of the University of Houston's Distance Education Program. (5) Virtual courses are very different. (6) She has a job and a son, so she is very busy, like many students today. (7) Online classes are great for this type of student, more convenient. (8) Students have to motivate themselves, and Ms. Wilson has only the soft bubbling noise of her aquarium screen saver to remind her to work. (9) She ends by saying it is 12:14 A.M. and her cat is nuzzling her fluffy pink slippers. (10) I also liked her cat's name.

TEACHING TIP

Engage students in a discussion about their answers. They should be able to explain their rationale for choosing Summary A as better. Stress the *objectivity* of a good summary—no opinions added.

- The test of a good summary is how well it captures the original. Which better summarizes Ms. Wilson's essay, A or B?

  A is better because it summarizes the original and does not insert the opinions of the summarizer.

- If you picked A, you are right. Sentence 1 states the author and title of the essay, as well as the name and edition of the book in which it appears. Sentence 1 also states the main idea of the original, which *contrasts* the author's experience of traditional classes and virtual classes. Does any sentence in B state the main idea of the original essay?

  no

ESL TIP

If your ESL students struggle with finding main ideas in a reading, refer them to Chapters 3 and 14 to review paragraph and essay organization.

- Compare the original with the two summaries. How many points of contrast does A include? B?

  A includes three points of contrast; B includes one point, confusingly stated.

- Does each writer summarize the essay *in his or her own words*? If not, which sentences seem plagiarized?

  A does; B plagiarizes sentences 3, 4, 8, and 9.

- Writer A once quotes Ms. Wilson directly. How is this shown? Why do you think the summary writer chose this sentence to quote?

  Quotation marks set off Ms. Wilson's words in sentence 4; these words are richly descriptive and somewhat humorous.

- Do both summaries succeed in keeping personal opinion out? If not, which sentences contain the summary writer's opinion?

  A succeeds, but B inserts personal opinion in sentences 1, 2, and 10.

- Note that summary writer A includes the source page number in parentheses at the end of the summarized material. On the other hand, writer B refers to Brenda Wilson but does not name her essay or the source in which it appears.

PRACTICE 2

TEACHING TIP
Part C of this chapter discusses paraphrasing. Students may find it helpful to preview that information before they complete Practice 2.

In a group with three or four other classmates, choose one of the following essays to summarize: "Girl Heroes in the House" (Chapter 16, Part A); "The Day of the Dead" (Chapter 16, Part C); "Stopping Youth Violence: An Inside Job" (Chapter 17, Part D); or "Skin Deep" (Chapter 14, Part E). Read your chosen essay in the group, aloud if possible. Then each person should write a one-paragraph summary of it, referring to the checklist below (15–20 minutes).

Now read your finished summaries aloud to your group. How well does each writer briefly capture the meaning of the original? Has he or she kept out personal opinion? What suggestions for improvement can you offer? Your instructor may wish to have the best summary in each group read aloud to the whole class.

PRACTICE 3

Flip through a copy of a current magazine: *Time*, *People*, *Essence*, *Wired*, or another. Pick one article that interests you, read it carefully, and write a one- to three-paragraph summary of the article, depending on the length of the article. The points you include in your summary should reflect the emphasis of the original writer. Try to capture the essence of the article. Remember to give your source at the beginning, to keep out personal opinion, and to check your summary for plagiarism. Refer to the checklist.

TEACHING TIP

For a downloadable grading rubric for summaries, go to the *Instructor Companion Site.*

Checklist

The Process of Writing a Summary

- ☐ 1. Notice the title and subtitle of the original; do these state its main idea?
- ☐ 2. Read the original quickly for meaning; then carefully read it again, underlining important ideas and jotting down notes for yourself.
- ☐ 3. Determine the author's thesis or main idea.
- ☐ 4. Now find the main supporting points. Subheads (if any), topic sentences, and the first and last paragraphs of the original may help you find key points.
- ☐ 5. Write your topic sentence or thesis statement, stating the author's name and the thesis, title, source, and date of the original.
- ☐ 6. In your own words, give the author's most important supporting points, in the same order in which the author gives them. Keep the same proportion of coverage as the original.
- ☐ 7. Write your summary.
- ☐ 8. Now revise, asking yourself, "Will my summary convey to someone who has never read the original the author's main idea and key supporting points?"
- ☐ 9. Proofread carefully for grammar, punctuation, sentence structure, spelling, and mechanics.
- ☐ 10. Compare your final draft with the original to avoid plagiarism.

C. Using Direct and Indirect Quotation (Paraphrase)

TEACHING TIP

Discuss with students the dangers of copying and pasting information from websites directly into the papers they are composing on their computers. Warn students to be extra careful about citing sources and adequately paraphrasing source material.

Sometimes you will want to quote an outside source directly. A quotation might be part of a summary or part of a longer paper or report. Quoting the words of others can add richness and authority to your writing. Use short quotations in these ways:

- Use a quotation to stress a key idea.
- Use a quotation to lend expert opinion to your argument.
- Use a quotation to provide a catchy introduction or conclusion.
- Use a quotation about your topic that is wonderfully written and interesting.

However, avoid using very long quotations or too many quotations. Both send the message that you are filling up space because you don't have enough to say. Of course, to avoid plagiarism, you always must credit the original author or speaker.

Here are some methods for introducing quotations:

Ways to Introduce Quotations	
Mr. Taibi says, . . .	Ms. Luboff writes, . . .
One expert stated:	. . . , one authority reported.
In a recent *Times* column, Maureen Dowd observes . . .	According to Dr. Haynes, . . .

Here is another source:

Source

> Television, by its very nature, distorts the reality it claims to reflect and report on. Events are compressed, highlighted, sped up. Thus a person who occasionally watches sports highlights on TV will likely see more home runs and touchdowns than a person who attends local games regularly; television viewers are likely to see more murders than a police detective, more serious car crashes than a tow truck driver, and more plane crashes than a crash investigator.
>
> —Radford, Benjamin. *Media Mythmakers*. Prometheus, 2003, p. 69.

Two students who wrote about television correctly quoted Benjamin Radford.

Direct Quotation

> "Television, by its very nature, distorts the reality it claims to reflect and report on," Benjamin Radford observes in his book *Media Mythmakers* (69).

Indirect Quotation (Paraphrase)

> In *Media Mythmakers*, Benjamin Radford points out that television fundamentally mispresents the people and events it tries to capture (69).

TEACHING TIP
Consider demonstrating for students how to include a partial quotation, such as a phrase or part of a longer sentence.

- The first sentence gives Benjamin Radford's exact words inside quotation marks. This is **direct quotation**. Note the punctuation.
- The second sentence uses the word *that* and gives the *meaning* of Benjamin Radford's words without quotation marks. This is **indirect quotation**, or **paraphrase**. Note the punctuation.
- Both students correctly quote the writer and credit the source. Both include the page number in parentheses after the quoted material and before the period. (See Chapter 19, Part C, for more information on this style of citing sources.)

Now read this passage from a third student's paper:

Plagiarism

> Television basically mispresents what it claims to reflect and report on. Things are "compressed, highlighted, sped up." You see more home runs and touchdowns watching sports channels than you would at real games. Watching TV, you see more crimes than a policeman, more car accidents than a tow truck operator, and more plane accidents than a government investigator.

- Can you see why this passage is plagiarized?
- The ideas and many of the words are clearly Benjamin Radford's, yet the student never mentions him. Four words are placed in quotation marks, but the reader has no idea why. Instead, the student implies that all the ideas and words are his or her own. Changing words like "crash" to "accident" does not alter the fact that the student is copying someone else. What ideas and exact words are plagiarized from the source?

The idea that television distorts the events it covers; "it claims to reflect and report on", "compressed, highlighted, sped up."

- Revise this passage as if it were your own, giving credit to the original author and avoiding plagiarism.

PRACTICE 4

Following are passages from two sources. Read each one, and then, as if you were writing a paper, quote two sentences from each, one directly quoting the author's words and one indirectly quoting the author's ideas. Review the boxed ways to introduce quotations and try several methods. Finally, write a brief summary of each passage. Check your work to avoid plagiarism. Answers will vary.

LEARNING STYLES AND ESL TIP

Making a concept map or other type of graphic organizer of the main ideas may help some students to see the main ideas in a reading.

Source 1

In most cultures throughout history, music, dance, rhythmic drumming, and chanting have been essential parts of healing rituals. Modern research bears out the connection between music and healing. In one study, the heart rate and blood pressure of patients went down when quiet music was piped into their hospital coronary care units. At the same time, the patients showed greater tolerance for pain and less anxiety and depression. Similarly, listening to music before, during, or after surgery has been shown to promote various beneficial effects—from alleviating anxiety to reducing the need for sedation by half. When researchers played Brahms' "Lullaby" to premature infants, these babies gained weight faster and went home from the hospital sooner than babies who did not hear the music. Music may also affect immunity by altering the level of stress chemicals in the blood. An experiment at Rainbow Babies and Children's Hospital found that a single 30-minute music therapy session could increase the level of salivary IgA, an immunoglobulin that protects against respiratory infections.

—Institute of Noetic Sciences with William Poole.
The Heart of Healing. Turner Publishing, 1993, p. 134.

TEACHING AND ESL TIP

Have students work in pairs to paraphrase complex sentences. Model how they can simplify grammar and use synonyms in paraphrases.

Direct quotation: ______________________________

____

____

Indirect quotation: ______________________________

____

____

Summary: ______________________________

____

____

____

____

____

____

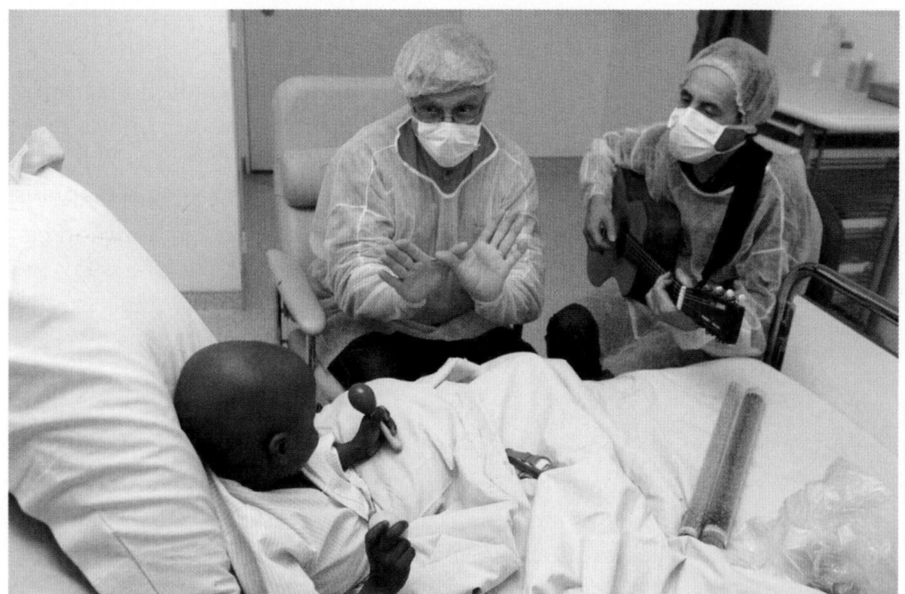

Encyclopedia/Corbis

In the children's cancer ward in Villejuif, France, musicians play for a patient during music therapy.

TEACHING TIP

Refer students to Chapter 38, "Mechanics," for information about punctuating direct quotations.

Source 2

The impact of Facebook on the college classroom goes far beyond technological innovations and the ability to build relationships. It has led young people to publicly announce intimate personal details without thought of the consequences. And that style of communication has led to some very uncomfortable encounters between students and their professors.

—Winzenburg, Stephen. "In the Facebook Era, Students Tell You Everything." *The Chronicle of Higher Education*, 29 July 2012, chronicle.com/article/In-the-Facebook-Era-Students/133169/.

Direct quotation: ______________________________

____

____

Indirect quotation: ______________________________

____

____

TEACHING TIP

If students need more practice with paraphrasing, bring in short passages from books and magazines and ask them to put the information in their own words. Point out any wording that is too close to that of the original source.

Summary: ______________________________

____

____

____

____

____

PRACTICE 5

Following are four sources and four quotations from student papers. If the student has summarized, directly quoted, or indirectly quoted the source correctly, write C. If you believe the source is plagiarized, write P; then revise the student's work as if it were your own to avoid plagiarism.

- Does each student clearly distinguish between his or her ideas and the source's?
- Does each student give enough information so that a reader could locate the original source?

Source 1

Binge drinking, according to criteria used in periodic surveys by the Harvard researchers, is defined as five or more drinks on one occasion for a man or four or more drinks on one occasion for a woman. Students who reported one or two such episodes in the two weeks preceding the survey were classified as occasional binge drinkers; those reporting three or more were considered frequent binge drinkers.

—Okie, Susan. "Survey: 44% of College Students Are Binge Drinkers." *The Washington Post*, 25 Mar. 2002, p. A6.

Student's Version

__P__ Binge drinking is a dangerous problem on campuses, but college
According to Susan Okie in *The Washington Post*, an
administrators are not doing enough to stop it. ~~An~~ amazing 44 percent of college
Using Harvard's definition, she defines
students are binge drinkers. ~~Let us define~~ binge drinking as five or more drinks
(A6)
on one occasion for a man or four or more drinks on one occasion for a woman.
College officials need to ask why so many students are drinking dangerously.

Source 2

Researchers measuring brain and heart activity found that volunteers were as stimulated by imagining someone they loved smiling at them as they were by being told they'd won a cash prize. David Lewis, a psychologist and director of research at Mindlab International in Brighton, England, which conducted the study, says a warm smile can create a "halo" effect, helping us "feel more optimistic, more positive, and more motivated."

—Rubin, Courtney. "Smile to Lift Your Mood." *U.S. News & World Report*, Dec. 2010, p. 63.

Student's Version

__P__ Research is revealing that a smile can improve your mood.
Psychologists in England have found that people who just think about being smiled at by a loved one feel as good as they do when they are told they have
(Rubin 63)
won money.

Source 3

The risk of stroke increases with the number of fast-food restaurants in a neighborhood. . . . Researchers found [that] residents of neighborhoods with the highest number of fast-food restaurants had a 13 percent higher relative risk of suffering ischemic strokes than those living in areas with the lowest numbers of restaurants.

—American Heart Association. "Number of Fast-Food Restaurants in Neighborhood Associated with Stroke Risk." *ScienceDaily*, 20 Feb. 2009, www.sciencedaily.com/releases/2009/02/090219202714.htm.

Student's Version

__C__ According to a news release by the American Heart Association, people who live near fast-food restaurants like McDonald's or Wendy's are at a higher risk for strokes than those who do not. As the number of restaurants rises, so does the risk.

Source 4

The United States has less than 5 percent of the world's population. But it has almost a quarter of the world's prisoners. Indeed, the United States leads the world in producing prisoners, a reflection of a relatively recent and now entirely distinctive American approach to crime and punishment. Americans are locked up for crimes—from writing bad checks to using drugs—that would rarely produce prison sentences in other countries. And in particular they are kept incarcerated far longer than prisoners in other nations.

—Liptak, Adam. "U.S. Prison Population Dwarfs That of Other Nations." *The New York Times*, 23 Apr. 2008, www.nytimes.com/2008/04/23/world/americas/23iht-23prison.12253738.html.

Student's Version

__P__ It is time to rethink the way that America punishes people for crimes. ~~We~~ *The New York Times* reports that we lock up people for crimes that don't carry prison sentences in other countries, and our prison sentences are longer. As a result, the United States has only 5% of the world population but 25% of the world's prisoners (Liptak).

EXPLORING ONLINE

owl.english.purdue.edu/owl/resource/589/2

Purdue OWL's site "Is It Plagiarism Yet?" gives helpful advice on what constitutes plagiarism.

owl.english.purdue.edu/owl/resource/563/01

Review of direct and indirect quotation and summary

CHAPTER 19

Strengthening an Essay with Research

A: Improving an Essay with Research

B: Finding and Evaluating Outside Sources: Using the Library and Searching the Internet

C: Adding Sources to Your Essay and Documenting Them Correctly Using MLA Style

D: Adding Sources to Your Essay and Documenting Them Correctly Using APA Style

E: MLA versus APA: A Quick Reference

You will have opportunities in college to prepare formal research papers with many outside sources. However, you should not limit your definition of "research" to just such assignments. Whenever you have a question and seek an answer from a source outside yourself, you are doing **research**. Most of us research every day, whether or not we call it that—when we gather facts and opinions about the cheapest local restaurant, the college with the best science program, the safest new cars, or various medical conditions. In this chapter, you will learn skills valuable both in college and at work: how to improve your writing with interesting information from outside sources.

A. Improving an Essay with Research

Almost any essay, particularly one designed to *persuade* your reader, can benefit from the addition of outside material. In fact, even one outside source—a startling statistic or a memorable quote—can enrich your essay. Supporting your main points with outside sources can be an excellent way to establish your credibility, strengthen your argument, and add power to your words.

Compare two versions of this student's paragraph:

TEACHING TIP
Stress to students that outside source material does not substitute for their own ideas; instead, it provides additional support for their ideas. Use the "Credit Cards Get Expelled" essay at the end of this chapter, for example, to point out that thesis statements and topic sentences do not refer to outside sources. They state the writer's ideas, and then the source material helps prove or support those ideas.

> Inexperienced hikers often get in trouble because they worry about rare dangers like snakebites, but they minimize the very serious dangers of dehydration and exposure to cold. For example, my brother-in-law once hiked into the Grand Canyon with only a granola bar and a small bottle of water. He became severely dehydrated and was too weak to climb back up without help.

- This paragraph makes an important point about the dangers that inexperienced hikers can face. The example of the brother-in-law supports the main point, but the paragraph needs more complete support.

Now read the revised paragraph, which the writer has strengthened with some relevant facts from an outside source:

> Inexperienced hikers often get in trouble because they worry about rare dangers like snakebites, but they minimize the very serious dangers of dehydration and exposure to cold. For example, my brother-in-law once hiked into the Grand Canyon with only a granola bar and a small bottle of water. He became severely dehydrated and was too weak to climb back up without help. He was lucky. According to the National Park Service website, over a hundred hikers die every year because they are not properly prepared for the environment. In addition, the NPS reports that nearly $5.2 million was spent in 2012 to perform 2,876 search-and-rescue operations, almost a third of them to save poorly prepared hikers like my brother-in-law ("Search and Rescue Report").

TEACHING TIP
Have your students work in pairs to brainstorm ways to introduce quotations, including reporting verbs. Have them start with the list in Chapter 18, Part C.

- What facts from the National Park Service website support the main point and add to the persuasive power of this paragraph?

Over 100 hikers die every year; nearly $5.2 million spent for 2,876 rescue operations

- What sentence of transition does the writer use to connect his example of the brother-in-law with facts from the outside source? What transitional words connect the fact about hikers' deaths each year?

He was lucky. According to the National Park Service. . .

- Remember that including just one well-chosen outside source can improve and enliven a paper.

Now, review this chart from the U.S. Census:

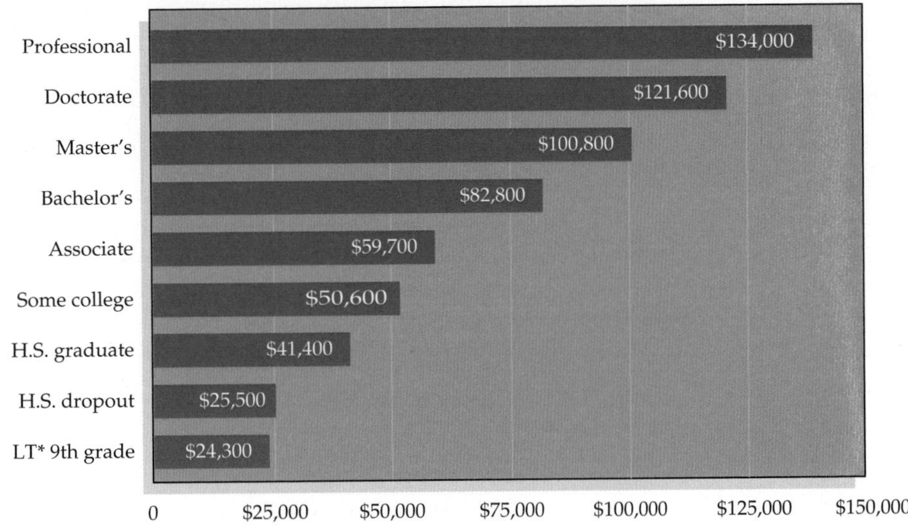

* LT: Less than

- What patterns do you see in this chart?
- How might you use this information in an essay?

You may also consider quoting an expert on the subject you are writing about. For example, if your subject is the lack of recycling receptacles on your campus, an opinion from an Environmental Protection Agency official would give authority to your essay. And don't forget experts closer to home; details about a student you know who has begun a recycling campaign on campus would add life and emotion to your work. If your essay is about your family history or the school's registration system, you could interview a relative or a school administrator and use that material to add authority to your paper.

A good way to begin using research is to pick an essay you have recently written. Reread it, marking any places where outside sources might make it even better. Write down any questions you want answers to or information that you would like to find:

LEARNING STYLES TIP

To engage *kinesthetic*, *visual*, and other learners, ask students to form pairs, exchange papers, and highlight the statements they feel could use additional support.

- What would I like to know more about?
- What outside source might make my essay more interesting?
- What information—fact, statistic, detail, or quotation—would make my essay more convincing?
- What people are experts on this topic? Where can I find them or their opinions?

Cristina's Research Process

Student Cristina Martin is learning to use outside sources. She plans to add research support to an essay she is writing for her English class. The paper examines the reasons why college students now have a lot less credit-card debt than they did when her older sister went to college ten years ago. In her paper, Cristina named two causes: the 2009 Credit CARD Act and the recession that started in the late 2000s. Now Cristina wants to add two or three sources to support her own ideas. She wonders if she can find evidence to confirm her observation that credit-card debt among students has decreased. She also wants to find information on how much credit-card debt students used to have versus how much debt they have now. Finally, she hopes to include some material from experts on what students know about credit-card debt to see if college students now are better informed about finances.

Here is one way to visualize the research process presented in this chapter:*

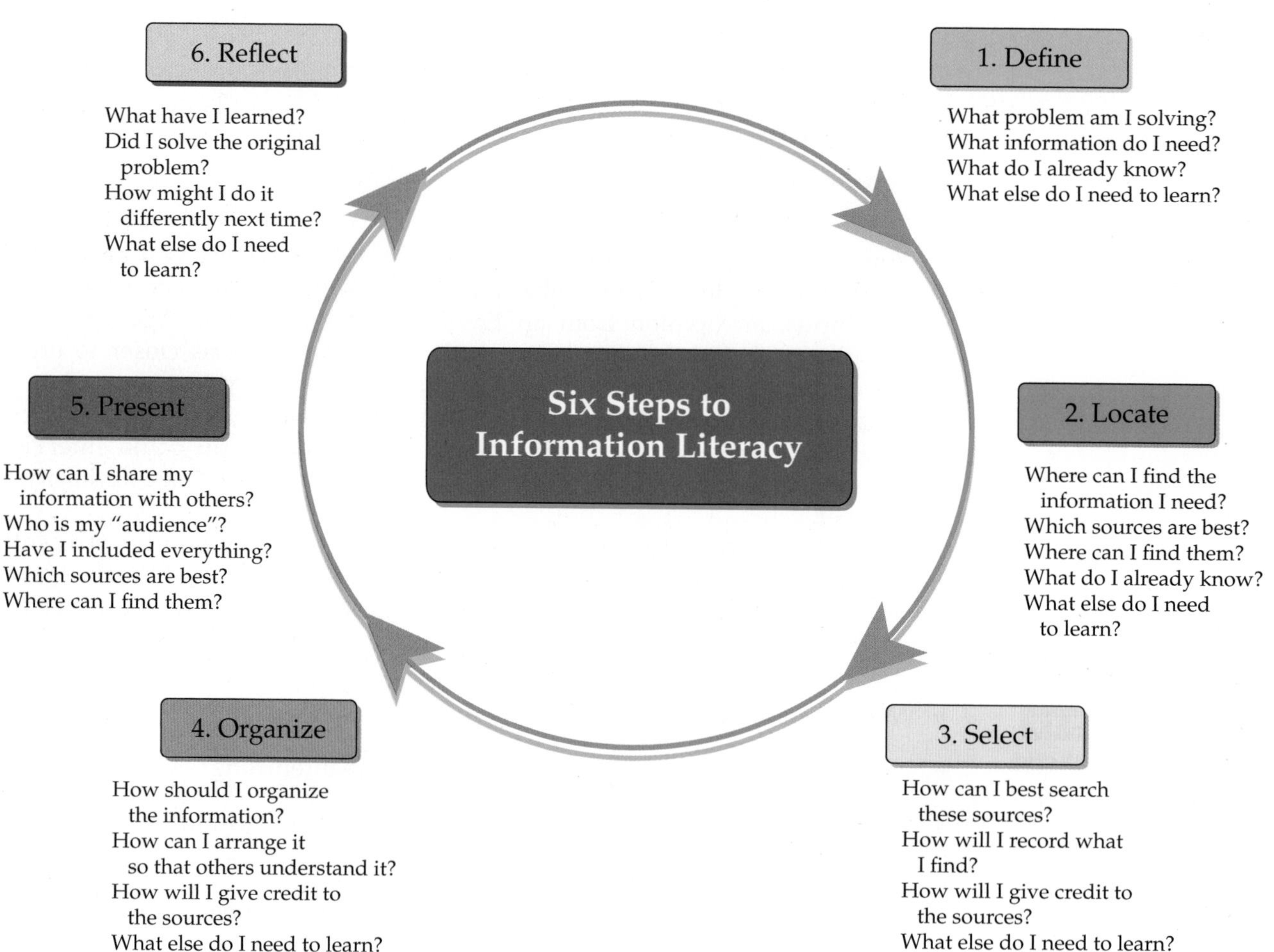

6. Reflect
What have I learned?
Did I solve the original problem?
How might I do it differently next time?
What else do I need to learn?
1. Define
What problem am I solving?
What information do I need?
What do I already know?
What else do I need to learn?
Six Steps to Information Literacy
5. Present
How can I share my information with others?
Who is my "audience"?
Have I included everything?
Which sources are best?
Where can I find them?
2. Locate
Where can I find the information I need?
Which sources are best?
Where can I find them?
What do I already know?
What else do I need to learn?
4. Organize
How should I organize the information?
How can I arrange it so that others understand it?
How will I give credit to the sources?
What else do I need to learn?
3. Select
How can I best search these sources?
How will I record what I find?
How will I give credit to the sources?
What else do I need to learn?

*From Wood, G. (2004). Academic original sin: Plagiarism, the Internet, and librarians. *The Journal of Academic Librarianship*, *30*(3), 237–242. Used by permission.

PRACTICE 1

Choose one of the following: either your favorite paper written this term or a paper on a topic assigned by your instructor. Then read through your paper, marking any spots where an outside source—fact, statistic, expert opinion, or quotation—might strengthen your essay. Write down any questions that you want to answer.

B. Finding and Evaluating Outside Sources: Using the Library and Searching the Internet

The next step is figuring out what information you need and where to find it. This section will show you how to find and evaluate sources in the library and on the Internet.

TEACHING TIP
Urge students to bookmark the library's homepage in addition to visiting the library in person.

Doing Research at the Library

Visit your college library, with your notes from Practice 1, to learn how to use the library's resources. Introduce yourself to the reference librarian, tell him or her what subject you are exploring, and ask for help finding and using any of these resources in your search:

1. **Catalog**. This will show you what books are available on your topic. For every book that looks like it might be interesting, jot down or export its title, author, and call number (the number that lets you find the book in the library). When you find a book that looks interesting, look at those near it as well. Books are arranged by subject, and most of the ones about your topic will probably be near each other.
2. **Databases**. The more current your topic, the more likely you are to find interesting information in electronic databases, which you can search for articles from magazines, journals, and newspapers. The library will have access to many general and subject-specific databases. Ask the librarian to help you explore these resources.
3. **Statistical Sources**. If you are looking for statistics and facts, the library has volumes such as *The Statistical Abstract of the United States* with information on population, education, immigration, crime, economic issues, and so on. The librarian can also help you find up-to-date information online.
4. **Reference Sources**. General books and articles on subjects like geology or psychology can be helpful. Special reference sources and encyclopedias exist for almost every area—for example, world soccer statistics, terrorism, or the birds of South America. These sources exist both in print and online.

TEACHING TIP
Engage students in a discussion about the effects of citing noncredible sources. They should understand that referring to questionable sources undermines their credibility as writers.

As you explore, you might see why experienced researchers often love what they do. They never know what they will find, and they learn the most interesting things. However, they must **evaluate** each source. If you are writing about the space shuttle, a current article in the *Chicago Tribune* would more likely impress readers as a reliable source than, say, a story in the *National Enquirer* called "Space Aliens Ate My Laundry." Look at the date of a book or article; if your subject is current, your sources should be too. Is the author a respected expert on this subject? Is the information balanced and objective? The librarian can help you find strong sources.

Once you discover good information that will strengthen your essay, take clear and careful notes. Use the techniques you learned in Chapter 18 to summarize and quote directly and indirectly; these will help you avoid accidental plagiarism. Write down everything you might need later. Save articles or chapters that are important. Don't leave the library without this information:

Book:	Author name(s), title and subtitle, year of publication, publisher, location of publisher (if you will be citing the source in APA format), exact pages of material quoted or summarized
Magazine or Journal:	Author name(s), title of article, title of magazine or journal, year, month, day of publication, volume and number, page numbers, title of database

Cristina's Research Process

Cristina visits her college library and gets help from the librarian using the database *Academic Search Premier.* Because Cristina's topic—changes to student credit-card debt—is current, she assumes that newspapers and magazines will give her the most up-to-date information. Searching "credit cards" and "college students," she finds a recent *USA Today* article called "College Prep Starts with Finance 101." She is excited to learn more about college students' thoughts and misunderstandings when it comes to credit card usage. She e-mails herself the article and adds it to her source folder.

PRACTICE 2

In your college or local library, find the answers to the following questions. Write down the answers and the complete source for each piece of information. Your instructor might wish to have you work in competing teams.

TEACHING TIP
Scavenger hunts like the one in Practice 2 are both fun and useful for familiarizing students with the library's different resources. For more ideas, ask the librarian or search "library scavenger hunt" online.

1. List the full titles of five novels by Toni Morrison. What major prize did she win and in what year?
2. How many acres of rain forest are destroyed every day in Brazil?
3. What is the average hourly wage of men in the United States? Of women?
4. How many murders were committed in your town or city last year? Is the number up or down from ten years ago?
5. What was the *New York Times* headline on the day and year of your birth? What stories dominated page 1?

PRACTICE 3

In your college or local library, find at least two excellent additions from outside sources that will improve the essay you worked on in Practice 1: a fact, statistic, example, quotation, or expert opinion. Record the information from each source precisely, using quotation marks as you learned in Chapter 18, Part C, or print or download the information. Write down everything you will need later to cite the source: the book or magazine, article name, author name(s), page numbers, and so on.

Doing Research on the Internet

The Internet is a wonderful source of information on just about everything—a great place to brainstorm, get ideas as you research, and find certain facts. However, once you leave the library website and its databases, it is harder to evaluate information, as this section will explain, so be careful.

If you have Internet access at the library or at home, use a search engine such as **www.google.com**. Type in search words that narrow your subject the same way you narrow a topic in writing—for example, *credit-card debt, college students.* Spell correctly, and try different words if necessary. If you do not see useful results on the first page, revise your search terms. Chances are your search terms are not specific enough.

Evaluate each website carefully. Who sponsors the site? How balanced and unbiased is the information? Is there an author given? Are any citations listed? Does the site have a recent updated or copyright date? With practice, Web researchers get better at spotting good and not-so-good sources of information. One tip is the Web address, or Uniform Resource Locator (URL) of each site. The last part of a URL indicates the type of organization that owns the site:

.com = company (aims to sell something and make a profit)

.org = nonprofit organization (aims to promote a cause)

.gov = government (provides many public information sites)

.edu = college or educational institution (aims to inform the public and promote itself)

TEACHING TIP

Many magazines' websites end in .com (e.g., the *U.S. News & World Report* site is **www.usnews.com**). Yet the information on such sites is generally thought to be credible.

For instance, if you are researching *asthma in children, treatments,* a government-sponsored health site might give more unbiased information than a company that sells asthma medications or a personal website called *Troy's Asthma Story.* For more help evaluating websites, ask the reference librarians.

As in the library—to avoid plagiarism later—take good notes, clearly marking words and ideas taken from your sources. Before you leave a website you wish to quote, bookmark or print the material you want to refer to, and make sure you have full information to cite the source later in your paper:

TEACHING TIP

You may need to explain to students how to bookmark sites using an online tool or in their browsers so that they can save and organize Web resources.

Website: URL, owner of site/publisher, author name(s), title of article, and date written.

TEACHING TIP

Students who conduct research online will no doubt copy and paste information from websites and electronic documents into their papers. Warn students who use this procedure to be extra careful about citing sources and adequately paraphrasing source material.

Cristina's Research Process

Cristina searches Google for "college students" and "credit-card debt, statistics." The search engine returns several thousand sources! Cristina scrolls quickly through many different hits until she finds one that looks promising. It's an article entitled "Credit Card Debt Statistics" on the website for NASDAQ, a major American stock exchange platform. While the article only has a small section devoted to college student credit-card debt, Cristina is happy to see that the information supports her observations on the downward trend. She also notes that figures in this section are from a report issued by Sallie Mae, a loan provider for college students. Before following the link to the Sallie Mae report, Cristina takes notes on a number of useful statistics and makes sure she has the URL and other pertinent information.

PRACTICE 4

TEACHING TIP
Have your students write sentences to answer the questions in Practice 4 to give them practice paraphrasing and trying out ways to introduce sources.

Answer these questions by doing research at the library or on the Internet. Be sure to use reliable sources.

1. How many people live in the United States?
2. What is the leading cause of death in American men? Women?
3. What is the leading export from your state?
4. How many different ethnic groups live in your state?
5. How many new AIDS cases were reported in your state last year? What groups were hardest hit?

PRACTICE 5

Using a search engine, find at least two good pieces of information to strengthen the essay you have worked on in Practices 1 and 3—facts, statistics, expert opinions, and so on. Hone your search words and evaluate what you find. Take careful notes, and save the information you need. Did you find any good material that you were not expecting? (Did you find exciting information on another subject that you might use in another paper? Be sure to take down any information you might use in the future.)

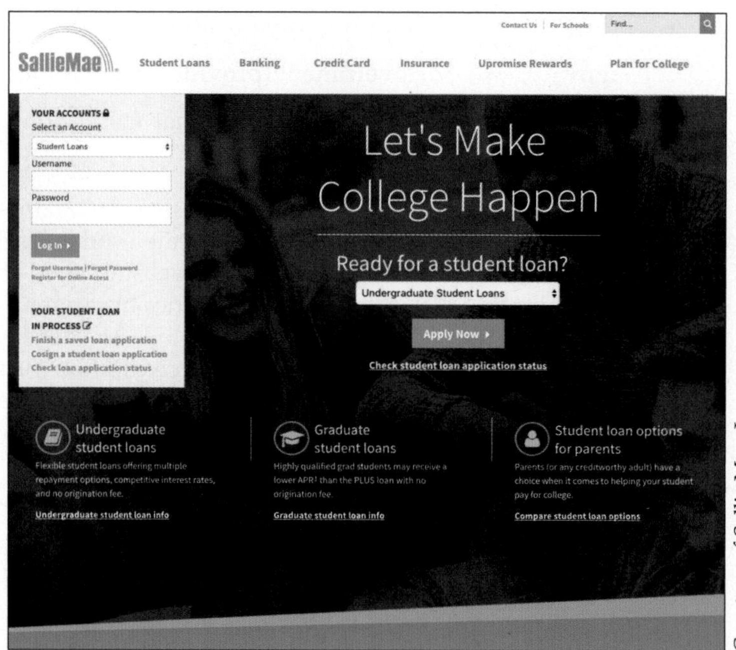

Courtesy of Sallie Mae, Inc.

This website, sponsored by the nation's largest company that helps people save, plan, and pay for college, is one of the sites Cristina visited.

C. Adding Sources to Your Essay and Documenting Them Correctly Using MLA Style

Now reread your original essay and the new material you found in your research process. Did you find other or better material than you looked for? Where in the paper will your outside sources be most effective? The next step is to use any of the three methods you learned in Chapter 18, Parts B and C—summary direct quotation, or indirect quotation (paraphrase)—as you revise your essay and add your outside sources. This section will show you how.

The **MLA style** (named after the Modern Language Association) is a common method used in the humanities, such as English and foreign language, for documenting sources quickly and clearly. MLA style is also called *parenthetical* documentation because it puts source information in the body of the essay, in parentheses, rather than in footnotes or endnotes.

A correct citation does two things:

- It tells your reader that the material is from an outside source.
- It gives your reader enough information to find the original source.

TEACHING TIP

Survey your students on their majors. Explain that those majoring in social science disciplines should eventually learn American Psychological Association (APA) documentation style. Information on APA style is in section D.

A correct citation appears in *two places* in your essay:

- **inside** the essay in parentheses
- at **the end** in a Works Cited list

Inside Your Essay: Summarize or Quote and Give Credit

TEACHING TIP

Encourage students to include a chapter number (if applicable) instead of a page number when they cite e-books: ([Author] ch. [#]).

When you quote an outside source in an essay, indicate that the material is not yours by introducing the quote with one of the phrases that you practiced in Part C of Chapter 18. In MLA style, if you use the author's name in this phrase, you will put only the page number in parentheses. If you leave the author unnamed, be sure to include both the author's last name and the page number in parentheses. If your source does not include page numbers, include the author's last name.

As a general rule, make sure to include enough information in parentheses so that the reader can locate the full documentation for the source in your Works Cited list—a complete list of the sources you summarized, directly quoted, or indirectly quoted in your essay. You will learn how to assemble a Works Cited list, which appears at the very end of an essay, later in this section.

Here is the introductory paragraph from Cristina's first draft of her essay on student credit-card debt.

> Even as the United States pulls its way out of the recession, credit-card debt continues to plague consumers. However, one segment of the population has seen a decrease in credit-card debt: college students. This was not always the case. Just a few years ago, credit-card debt among students posed a serious problem. This change stems from at least two major factors: the 2009 Credit CARD Act and the recession that started in the late 2000s. Still, students face challenges when it comes to graduating from college with a *summa cum laude* in financial knowledge.

- This is a clear introduction on a relevant subject. You can probably see why Cristina chose to research this topic.
- After reading her draft of the paragraph, Cristina decided to go beyond general observations by including some facts and figures to make it even more intriguing and to give it and the essay a stronger sense of purpose.

Now read the same paragraph, strengthened and expanded by facts Cristina found in her research:

TEACHING TIP

Make sure students know that MLA documentation not only indicates the sources of material but also shows where that material begins and ends so that readers can distinguish outside information from the writer's ideas.

Even as the United States pulls its way out of the recession, credit-card debt continues to plague consumers. According to Holly Johnson on *The Simple Dollar* website, the average American household owes over $7,000 in credit-card debt. However, one segment of the population has seen a decrease in credit-card debt: college students. This was not always the case. Just a few years ago, credit-card debt among students posed a serious problem; in 2009, education loan servicer Sallie Mae reported that the average college student had over $3,000 in credit card debt. Today the average balance is just under $500 (Sallie Mae, "How America Pays"). This change stems from at least two major factors: the 2009 Credit CARD Act and the recession that started in the late 2000s. Still, students face challenges when it comes to graduating from college with a *summa cum laude* in financial knowledge.

- Through her research online, Cristina learned that credit-card debt among students has decreased in the past few years. This information adds substance to her general observations.
- What transitional expression introduces the information from *The Simple Dollar* website?

  According to Holly Johnson on *The Simple Dollar* website. . .
- For the Sallie Mae references, the "author" of the article is a corporation. The full citations are found on the Works Cited pages at the end of the paper.

TEACHING TIP

The eighth edition of the MLA handbook represents a departure from the previous edition (e.g., students no longer have to identify the source's medium). If students are familiar with the old method of citations, be sure to explain how this new citation style differs.

At the End of Your Essay: List Works Cited

The last page of your essay will be a list of all the sources you summarized, directly quoted, or indirectly quoted in your essay, in alphabetical order by the author's last name. If there is no named author, list the entry alphabetically by its title. Title the page Works Cited, and center the title. If a citation goes beyond one line, indent any following lines half an inch to make it clear that the information belongs together.

MLA describes nine core elements of a Works Cited entry. Depending on the source, not all nine need to be included; only include the elements that apply to the source that you are citing. Remember, the goal of your citation is to be helpful to your reader.

Each element should be followed by a period or a comma as directed. A period should always follow the last element. Format your citation this way:

Author. Title of source. Title of container, Other contributors, Version, Number,
Publisher, Publication date, Location.

For more information on how to cite your sources, consult the *MLA Handbook*, Eighth Edition.

Element 1: Author

The author is the person or organization responsible for creating the source. For works with two authors, include the first author with last name first, followed by a comma and the second author in normal order. For works with three or more authors, use *et al.* (meaning "and others").

One author:

Eugenides, Jeffrey. *The Marriage Plot*. Farrar, Straus and Giroux, 2011.

Two authors:

Kessler, Lauren, and Duncan McDonald. *When Worlds Collide: A Media Writer's Guide to Grammar and Style.* 8th ed., Cengage Learning, 2012.

Three or more authors:

Berlin, Ira, et al. "The Destruction of Slavery, 1861–1865." *Slaves No More: Three Essays on Emancipation and the Civil War,* Cambridge UP*, 1992, pp. 1-76.

Element 2: Title of Source

If the title is a stand-alone work (such as a book, collection, periodical, TV series, or website), italicize it (or underline it if you are writing your essay by hand and cannot italicize it). If it is a work within a "container" or larger work, put quotation marks around it. Examples are an article in a newspaper, essay within a journal, story within an anthology, poem within an edited collection, song on an album, or episode of a TV series.

Title of a stand-alone work:

Eugenides, Jeffrey. *The Marriage Plot*. Farrar, Straus and Giroux, 2011.

Title of a work within a container:

Berlin, Ira, et al. "The Destruction of Slavery, 1861–1865." *Slaves No More: Three Essays on Emancipation and the Civil War,* Cambridge UP, 1992, pp. 1-76.

"Mandatory Minimums." *The West Wing*, season 1, episode 22, NBC, 3 May 2000.

Element 3: Title of Container

This is the title of the larger work (for example, a periodical, book, or website) that contains the source being cited. There can be more than one container (for example, for a periodical in a database). The name of the container is italicized.

One container:

Berlin, Ira, et al. "The Destruction of Slavery, 1861–1865." *Slaves No More: Three Essays on Emancipation and the Civil War,* Cambridge UP, 1992, pp. 1-76.

@deray. "We can disagree without attacking each other. Our ideas can be in conflict without us being in conflict. Everything isn't war." *Twitter,* 27 Apr. 2016, 9:08 a.m., twitter.com/deray/status/725355965911044096.

Two containers:

Tugend, Alina. "After a Tragedy, Calculating the Best Ways That People Can Help." *The New York Times,* 1 Jun. 2013, p. B5(L). *Global Issues in Context,* find.galegroup.com/gic/infomark.do?&source=gale&idigest=e5384996872d23352d960a942aa7c330&prodId=GIC&userGroupName=mlin_c_worstate&tabID=T006&docId=A331961786&type=retrieve&contentSet=IAC-Documents&version=1.0.

---

*UP: an abbreviation for "University Press"

Element 4: Other Contributors

This element refers to contributors other than the author, such as editors, translators, narrators, and directors. Use full words rather than abbreviations.

"New England." *The Concise Heath Anthology of American Literature,* edited by Paul Lauter et al., 2nd ed., vol. 1, Cengage Learning, 2013, pp. 173-77.

Element 5: Version

Only include this element if the work has different versions or editions. This may be identified by words or numbers.

Kessler, Lauren, and Duncan McDonald. *When Worlds Collide: A Media Writer's Guide to Grammar and Style.* 8th ed., Cengage Learning, 2012.

Zusak, Markus. *The Book Thief.* 10th anniversary ed., Knopf, 2016.

Element 6: Number

This element identifies the number, or volume, of the work. It is usually used for journal issues and comic books. It is also used for season and episode numbers for television series.

Drollette, Dan, Jr. "Elizabeth Kolbert: Covering the Hot Topic of Climate Change by Going to the Ends of the Earth." *Bulletin of the Atomic Scientists,* vol. 70, no. 4, July 2014, doi:10.1177/0096340214538957.

"Mandatory Minimums." *The West Wing,* season 1, episode 22, NBC, 3 May 2000.

Element 7: Publisher

The publisher is the organization responsible for making the source available to the public. This information is usually found on the title page, for a book, or on the home page, for a website. Do not list the city of publication.

Berlin, Ira, et al. "The Destruction of Slavery, 1861–1865." *Slaves No More: Three Essays on Emancipation and the Civil War,* Cambridge UP, 1992, pp. 1-76.

Schulten, Katherine. "Honoring Memorial Day." *The Learning Network,* The New York Times Company, 30 May 2016, learning.blogs.nytimes.com/2016/05/30/honoring-memorial-day.

Element 8: Publication Date

This element identifies the year, or the exact date, the work was published. List dates in this order: day month year. Abbreviate months with more than four letters.

@deray. "We can disagree without attacking each other. Our ideas can be in conflict without us being in conflict. Everything isn't war." *Twitter,* 27 Apr. 2016, 9:08 a.m., twitter.com/deray/status/725355965911044096.

Drollette, Dan., Jr. "Elizabeth Kolbert: Covering the Hot Topic of Climate Change by Going to the Ends of the Earth." *Bulletin of the Atomic Scientists,* vol. 70, no. 4, July 2014, doi:10.1177/0096340214538957.

"New England." *The Concise Heath Anthology of American Literature,* edited by Paul Lauter et al., 2nd ed., vol. 1, Cengage Learning, 2013, pp. 173-77.

TEACHING TIP

Discuss your preference for citing digital locations with your students. URLs are useful, but they are not always stable and can be lengthy. Some publishers assign DOIs (digital object identifiers) to their online publications. DOIs are preferred because they are stable, but they are not always available. While the *MLA Handbook* recommends including URLs or DOIs in citations, it directs students to consult with their instructors.

Element 9: Location

This element identifies the page number, or page numbers, within a container, or the URL of a website on which the source was found (exclude http://).

Page range:

Berlin, Ira, et al. "The Destruction of Slavery, 1861–1865." *Slaves No More: Three Essays on Emancipation and the Civil War,* Cambridge UP, 1992, pp. 1-76.

URL:

Orlin, Ben. "How to Fix the SAT." *Slate*, 21 May 2014, www.slate.com/articles/health_and_science/science/2014/05/revise_the_sat_the_college_board_should_give_out_fewer_standardized_test.html.

Cristina's Research Process

During her research, Cristina had carefully saved the quotes and facts that she wanted to use in her essay. Now, as she revises her essay to add these sources, she makes sure that she quotes her sources accurately and avoids unintentional plagiarism. As she rewrites her essay, she refers to Chapters 18 and 19. She uses transitional expressions to weave the outside sources smoothly into her essay. Then she prepares a Works Cited list, referring to the models in this chapter, as the last page of her paper.

Read Cristina's completed essay with research using MLA style citations, "Credit Cards Get Expelled: The Fall of Credit Cards on Campus," at the end of this section.

PRACTICE 6

TEACHING TIP

Have students form small groups to check their answers to Practice 6.

Below are five sources a student has compiled for a research essay on the history of the Boston Marathon. Using the models in this chapter to guide you, prepare a Works Cited list for the paper that includes all five sources, properly formatted and in alphabetical order.

- A book by Michael Connelly called *26.2 Miles to Boston: A Journey into the Heart of the Boston Marathon* that was published by Lyons Press in 2014
- An article in the April 21, 2014, issue of *Sports Illustrated* magazine (volume 120, number 16) called "Boston," which was written by S. L. Price and appeared on pages 52–69
- A webpage called "Boston Marathon History" from the Boston Athletic Association website (www.baa.org/races/boston-marathon/boston-marathon-history.aspx)
- A book by Paul C. Clerici titled *Boston Marathon: History by the Mile* published by The History Press in 2014, 144 pages long
- An article from *The Atlantic*'s web magazine called "Why Does Boston Hold a Marathon on Patriots' Day?" that was written by Yoni Appelbaum and was published on April 17, 2013 (the student viewed the article at www.theatlantic.com/national/archive/2013/04/the-history-of-the-boston-marathon-a-perfect-way-to-celebrate-patriots-day/275023/)

TEACHING TIP

For answers to this exercise in APA format, visit the *Instructor Companion Site*.

Works Cited

Appelbaum, Yoni. "Why Does Boston Hold a Marathon on Patriots' Day?" *The Atlantic,* 17 Apr. 2013, www.theatlantic.com/nationalarchive/2013/04/the-history-of-the-boston-marathon-a-perfect-way-to-celebrate/-patriots-day/275023/.

"Boston Marathon History." *Boston Athletic Association*, www.baa.org/races/boston-marathon/boston-marathon-history.aspx.

Clerici, Paul C. *Boston Marathon: History by the Mile.* The History Press, 2014.

Connelly, Michael. *26.2 Miles to Boston: A Journey into the Heart of the Boston Marathon.* Lyons Press, 2014.

Price, S. L. "Boston." *Sports Illustrated,* vol. 120, no. 16, 21 Apr. 2014, pp. 52-69.

PRACTICE 7

TEACHING TIP

Students might work in pairs to check their essays for plagiarism and correct citation style. Have them bring their original source material to class.

Now, using two of the three methods—summary, direct quotation, or indirect quotation—add your research findings to your essay. Review Chapters 18 and 19 if you need to. Aim to achieve two things: First, try to add the new material seamlessly, using introductory phrases so that it relates clearly to your ideas in the essay. Second, be careful to avoid plagiarism by documenting your sources correctly, both inside the essay and in your Works Cited list.

Following is the final draft of Cristina's essay, which she has strengthened with research.

Martin 1

Every research paper should begin on a new page.

Cristina Martin
Professor Tate
English 100
4 March 2016

Credit Cards Get Expelled: The Fall of Credit Cards on Campus

Introduction

Indirectly quoted facts from The Simple Dollar and Sallie Mae expand the topic.

The website citation gives a shortened title and no page number.

Thesis statement

Even as the United States pulls its way out of the recession, credit-card debt continues to plague consumers. According to Holly Johnson on *The Simple Dollar* website, the average American household owes over $7,000 in credit-card debt. However, one segment of the population has seen a decrease in credit-card debt: college students. This was not always the case. Just a few years ago, credit-card debt among students posed a serious problem; in 2009, education loan servicer Sallie Mae reported that the average college student had over $3,000 in credit-card debt. Today the average balance is just under $500 (Sallie Mae, "How America Pays"). This change stems from at least two major factors: the 2009 Credit CARD Act and the recession that started in the late 2000s. Still, students face challenges when it comes to graduating from college with a *summa cum laude* in financial knowledge.

Topic sentence: cause #1

One of the main contributors to a decrease in credit-card usage with college students is the 2009 Credit Card Accountability Responsibility and Disclosure (CARD) Act, which has protection for college students. The most widely known protections involve credit-card marketing and student access to cards. Prior to this act, credit-card companies were allowed to market on college campuses. Walking across campus, students would encounter energetic salespeople tempting students to fill out applications in exchange for T-shirts, pizzas, Frisbees, and other freebies. Easy applications for credit cards littered the campus mailroom and filled students' mailboxes. The Credit CARD Act put a stop to these practices. It also requires young applicants under the age of twenty-one to prove they can make the payments on their own or have an adult co-signer (McClure). These safeguards have cut college students' credit-card access and use, which helps prevent them from getting credit-card debt.

Topic sentence: cause #2

Direct quotes support the student's ideas

Experts also point to another factor that has helped reduce student credit-card debt: the financial crisis of the late 2000s. At first, this seems to go against a 2009 Sallie Mae report, which stated that "in this time of. . . economic downturn, college students are relying on credit cards more than ever before" (2). However, Sallie Mae's "How America Pays for College 2013" states that the combination of the 2009 Credit CARD Act and the recession has led to the decline of student credit-card use. This is due, in part, to the recession's impact on young adults' economic prospects. In *The Nation*, Lizzy Ratner reports that the recession affected people under thirty more than it did any other demographic because of a combination of college loan debt and high unemployment rates. The implication is that the combination of student loan debt and dismal job hopes, in addition to the lack of access to credit cards, resulted in students turning to debit rather than credit cards.

Martin 2

Topic sentence: college students' ongoing financial hardships

The ideas are developed by a newspaper article summarizing a study on college students' financial knowledge. A direct quote and an indirect quote are clearly cited.

At first glance, the drop in student credit-card debt seems like good news. After all, this appears to show that students will graduate with less credit-card debt, which should put them on firmer financial footing. However, reality is less clear-cut. As previously mentioned, student loan debt is growing, with students graduating with tens of thousands of dollars in student loans. Additionally, lack of student credit-card debt might be more indicative of lack of access rather than financial savviness. A 2015 article by Michael Schramm describes a recent U.S. Bank study on college students that found that "many students are misinformed about essential financial facts" (B5). The article also remarks that a majority of students had misconceptions on how credit history is established and how credit-card debt works.

Topic sentences: The effects of the Credit CARD Act and the recession on student credit-card debt and the remaining challenges students face when it comes to finances.

Advice to students forms conclusion

Clearly, the 2009 Credit CARD Act and the recession have had positive impacts on college students' credit-card debt. However, it remains to be seen if limiting students' access to credit cards will actually help them establish strong financial practices in the future or if it is merely delaying the inevitable, especially given high student loans and students' widespread misunderstandings about credit. To truly become adept at managing their finances, students should take it upon themselves to make wise decisions. From scrutinizing college costs and having frank discussions with parents, guardians, or other trusted adults regarding what is reasonable when it comes to student loans to learning about how to establish a good credit history to taking a financial literacy class, students have opportunities to ace real-life finances 101.

Martin 3

Works Cited

Works Cited should start a new page

Johnson, Holly. "The State of American Credit Card Debt in 2015." *The Simple Dollar*, 3 June 2015, www.thesimpledollar.com/the-state-of-american-credit-card-debt-in-2015.

McClure, Ann. "Curtailing Credit Cards." *University Business*, Feb. 2010, p. 7.

Ratner, Lizzy. "Generation Recession." *The Nation*, 23 Nov. 2009, pp. 23-26.

Sallie Mae. "How America Pays for College 2013." *Salliemae.com*, 2013, www.salliemae.com/assets/Core/how-America-pays/howamericapays2013.pdf.

Sallie Mae. "How Undergraduate Students Use Credit Cards: Sallie Mae's National Study of Usage Rates and Trends." *Salliemae.com*, Apr. 2009, static.mgnetwork.com/rtd/pdfs/20090830_iris.pdf.

Schramm, Michael. "College Prep Starts with Finance 101." *USA Today*, 1 Sept. 2015, p. B5.

D. Adding Sources to Your Essay and Documenting Them Correctly Using APA Style

After you've finished writing your first draft, reread it and the new material you found in your research process. You might have found other or better material than you were originally looking for. You also need to determine the places in your paper where your research makes the most sense and has the most impact. The three methods you learned in Chapter 18, Parts B and C—summary, direct quotation, or indirect quotation (paraphrase)—can help you as you revise your essay and incorporate your additional resources. This section will guide you on how to do this using the American Psychological Association (APA) style.

APA style is typically used in writing assignments for courses in the social sciences, such as psychology, political science, and education, and in nursing and business. APA style lets you document your sources in a quick and clear way that allows readers to locate information on your sources, particularly the authors' names and the dates of publication. APA style is also called *parenthetical* documentation because it puts source information in the body of the essay, in parentheses, rather than in footnotes or endnotes.

In APA style, a correct citation accomplishes three things:

- It tells your reader that the material is from an outside source.
- It establishes the relevance of the material to your reader by identifying the authors and the dates of publication.
- It gives your reader enough information to find the original source.

A correct citation appears in *two places* in your essay:

- **inside** the essay in parentheses
- at **the end** in a References list

Inside Your Essay: Summarize or Quote and Give Credit

Quotations from outside sources in APA style should be introduced with an appropriate phrase, like the ones you practiced in Part C of Chapter 18. If you use the author's name in this phrase, it should be followed by the date of publication in parentheses (in most instances, just the year is needed). The quotation will then be followed by the page number in parentheses (the page number should be introduced by a "p."). If you leave the author unnamed in your introductory phrase, the quote should be followed by the author's last name, the year of publication, and the page number in parentheses. If you are using a source where no date is given, you should note this using the abbreviation "n.d." (for "no date") in the place that the date would usually go. For websites, indicate the section heading (if the source has section headings) or the paragraph number (if the site has paragraphs that are numbered) where the passage is located.

Here is the introductory paragraph from Cristina's first draft of her essay on student credit-card debt.

> Even as the United States pulls its way out of the recession, credit-card debt continues to plague consumers. However, one segment of the population has seen a decrease in credit-card debt: college students. This was not always the case. Just a few years ago, credit-card debt among students posed a serious problem. This change stems from at least two major factors: the 2009 Credit CARD Act and the recession that started in the late 2000s. Still, students face challenges when it comes to graduating from college with a *summa cum laude* in financial knowledge.

- This is a clear introduction on a relevant subject. You can probably see why Cristina chose to research this topic.
- After reading her draft of the paragraph, Cristina decided to go beyond general observations by including some facts and figures to make it even more intriguing and to give it and the essay a stronger sense of purpose.

Now read the same paragraph, strengthened and expanded by facts Cristina found in her research, which are cited using APA style:

> Even as the United States pulls its way out of the recession, credit-card debt continues to plague consumers. According to Holly Johnson (2015) on *The Simple Dollar* website, the average American household owes over $7,000 in credit-card debt. However, one segment of the population has seen a decrease in credit-card debt: college students. This was not always the case. Just a few years ago, credit-card debt among students posed a serious problem; in 2009, education loan servicer Sallie Mae reported that the average college student had over $3,000 in credit card debt. Today the average balance is just under $500 (Sallie Mae, 2013). This change stems from at least two major factors: the 2009 Credit CARD Act and the recession that started in the late 2000s. Still, students face challenges when it comes to graduating from college with a *summa cum laude* in financial knowledge.

- Through her research online, Cristina learned that credit-card debt among students has decreased in the past few years. This information adds substance to her general observations.
- What transitional expression introduces the information from *The Simple Dollar* website?

  According to Holly Johnson (2015) on *The Simple Dollar* website. . .

- For the Sallie Mae references, the "author" of the article is a corporation. The full citation is found on the References page at the end of the paper.

At the End of Your Essay: List References

In APA style, the last page of your essay will be a list of all the sources you summarized, directly quoted, or indirectly quoted in your essay, in alphabetical order by the author's last name. If there is no named author, list the entry alphabetically by its title (in quotation marks). Title the page References, and center it. Use these models to format the most commonly used sources properly. (Don't worry about memorizing the forms; even experienced writers often have to check an APA manual for the correct form.) If a citation goes beyond one line, indent any following lines half an inch to make it clear that the information belongs together.

Books

One author:

Berman, A. (2015). *Give us the ballot: The modern struggle for voting rights in America*. New York, NY: Farrar, Straus, and Giroux.

More than one author:

Finn, P., & Couvée, P. (2014). *The Zhivago affair: The Kremlin, the CIA, and the battle over a forbidden book*. New York, NY: Pantheon.

Encyclopedia:

Tirro, F. (2016). Jazz. In *The World Book Encyclopedia* (Vol. 11, pp. 68–74). Chicago, IL: World Book.

Periodicals

Article in a newspaper:

Smith, M. (2016, January 13). Troops to help Flint address water crisis. *New York Times*, p. A16.

Article in a magazine:

Park, A. (2015, December 28). Road to the Olympics. *Time, 186*(27/28), 86–93.

Article in a journal:

Williams, R. M., Welch, C. E., Parsons, J. T., & McLeod, T. C. (2015). Athletic trainers' familiarity with and perceptions of academic accommodations in secondary school athletes after sports-related concussion. *Journal of Athletic Training, 50*(3), 262–269.

Electronic Sources

When citing sources found on the World Wide Web, APA style recommends that you include the URL for websites and the Digital Object Identifier (DOI) for online scholarly articles when one is available. Unlike URLs, which can change, DOIs provide a longer-lasting way for readers to locate a source. In cases where no DOI is assigned to an online article or source, you should include the URL of the journal home page, which can help readers find the article.

A page on a website (no named author for the page):

Ending child poverty. (2016). Retrieved from http://www.childrensdefense.org/policy/endingchildpoverty/

Article in an online periodical (no DOI):

Orlin, B. (2014, May 21). How to fix the SAT. *Slate*. Retrieved from http://www.slate.com/articles/health_and_science/science/2014/05/revise_the_sat_the_college_board_should_give_out_fewer_standardized_test.html

Work from a subscription service (with a DOI):

Drollette, D., Jr.. (2014). Elizabeth Kolbert: Covering the hot topic of climate change by going to the ends of the Earth. *Bulletin of the Atomic Scientists, 70*(4), 1–9. doi:10.1177/0096340214538957

Multimedia

Film or video:

Guggenheim, D., MacDonald, L., & Parkes, W. F. (Producers), & Guggenheim, D. (Director). (2015). *He named me Malala* [Motion picture]. United States: 20th Century Fox.

Radio or television program:

Iserson, D., & Weiner, M. (Writers), & Manley, C. (Director). (2014). The runaways [Television series episode]. In S. Hornbacher & M. Weiner (Executive producers), *Mad men*. Los Angeles, CA: Lionsgate Television.

Personal Communications

Personal interviews and other forms of personal communication should not be included in your References list. You can note these types of sources parenthetically in the body of your paper by including the participant's name, the phrase "personal communication," and the date of the communication. For instance, a personal interview with Mariela Santos would appear in the body of your paper as (M. Santos, personal communication, January 3, 2013).

These models cover the most common outside sources you will encounter in your research. For more information, or if you need assistance with a different type of source, you can reference the APA style guide or other websites that have APA style guidelines, such as Purdue's Online Writing Lab at **owl.english.purdue.edu/owl/resource/560/1/**.

PRACTICE 8

Below are five sources a student has compiled for a research essay on cyberbullying. Using the models above to guide you, prepare a References list for the paper that includes all five sources, properly formatted and in alphabetical order.

- A book by Justin W. Patchin and Sameer Hinduja called *Words Wound: Delete Cyberbullying and Make Kindness Go Viral* that was published in Minneapolis, MN, by Free Spirit Publishing in 2013
- An article in the July 7, 2014, issue of *Time* magazine, volume 184, issue 1, called "The Antisocial Network," which was written by Jack Dickey and appeared on pages 40–45
- A webpage called "Cyberbullying and Social Media" from the Megan Meier Foundation website (MeganMeierFoundation.org) without a date of publication (the student viewed it at http://www.meganmeierfoundation.org/cyberbullying-social-media.html). No additional publication information is provided on the page.
- A book by Emily Bazelon titled *Sticks and Stones: Defeating the Culture of Bullying and Rediscovering the Power of Character and Empathy* published by Random House in New York, New York, in 2013
- An article from *CNN.com* called "The Health Risks of Cyberbullying in College" that was written by Sandee LaMotte and was published on March 3, 2015 (the student viewed the article at http://www.cnn.com/2015/03/02/health/cyberbullying-in-college/index.html)

TEACHING TIP

For answers to this exercise in MLA format, visit the *Instructor Companion Site*.

References

Bazelon, E. (2013). *Sticks and stones: Defeating the culture of bullying and rediscovering the power of character and empathy.* New York, NY: Random House.

Cyberbullying and social media. (n.d.). Retrieved from http://www.meganmeierfoundation.org/cyberbullying-social-media.html

Dickey, J. (2014, July 7). The antisocial network. *Time, 184*(1), pp. 40–45.

LaMotte, S. (2015, Mar. 3). The health risks of cyberbullying in college. Retrieved from http://www.cnn.com/2015/03/02/health/cyberbullying-in-college/index.html

Patchin, J. W., & Hinduja, S. (2013). *Words wound: Delete cyberbullying and make kindness go viral.* Minneapolis, MN: Free Spirit Publishing.

PRACTICE 9

Now, using two of the three methods—summary, direct quotation, or indirect quotation—add your research findings to your essay using APA style. Review Chapters 18 and 19 if you need to. Aim to achieve two things: first, try to add the new material gracefully, using introductory phrases so that it relates clearly to your ideas in the essay. Second, be careful to avoid plagiarism by documenting your sources correctly, both inside the essay and in your References list.

Following is the final draft of Cristina's essay, which she has strengthened with research that is cited using APA style.

Every research paper should begin on a new page. Also, note that true APA style asks students to have a cover page with slightly different information. For this paper, Cristina's professor had the students forgo the cover page and the traditional running head.

Cristina Martin
Professor Tate
English 100
4 March 2016

Credit Cards Get Expelled: The Fall of Credit Cards on Campus

Introduction

Indirectly quoted facts from The Simple Dollar and Sallie Mae expand the topic.

The website citation gives a shortened title and no page number.

Thesis statement

Even as the United States pulls its way out of the recession, credit-card debt continues to plague consumers. According to Holly Johnson (2015) on *The Simple Dollar* website, the average American household owes over $7,000 in credit-card debt. However, one segment of the population has seen a decrease in credit-card debt: college students. This was not always the case. Just a few years ago, credit-card debt among students posed a serious problem; in 2009, education loan servicer Sallie Mae reported that the average college student had over $3,000 in credit-card debt. Today the average balance is just under $500 (Sallie Mae, 2013). This change stems from at least two major factors: the 2009 Credit CARD Act and the recession that started in the late 2000s. Still, students face challenges when it comes to graduating from college with a *summa cum laude* in financial knowledge.

Topic sentence: cause #1

One of the main contributors to a decrease in credit-card usage with college students is the 2009 Credit Card Accountability Responsibility and Disclosure (CARD) Act, which has protection for college students. The most widely known protections involve credit-card marketing and student access to cards. Prior to this act, credit-card companies were allowed to market on college campuses. Walking across campus, students would encounter energetic salespeople tempting students to fill out applications in exchange for T-shirts, pizzas, Frisbees, and other freebies. Easy applications for credit cards littered the campus mailroom and filled students' mailboxes. The Credit CARD Act put a stop to these practices. It also requires young applicants under the age of twenty-one to prove they can make the payments on their own or have an adult co-signer (McClure, 2010). These safeguards have cut college students' credit-card access and use, which helps prevent them from getting credit-card debt.

Topic sentence: cause #2

Direct quotes support the student's ideas.

Experts also point to another factor that has helped reduce student credit-card debt: the financial crisis of the late 2000s. At first, this seems to go against a 2009 Sallie Mae report, which stated that "in this time of. . . economic downturn, college students are relying on credit cards more than ever before." However, Sallie Mae's "How America Pays for College 2013" states that the combination of the 2009 Credit CARD Act and the recession has led to the decline in student credit-card use. This is due, in part, to the recession's impact on young adults' economic prospects. In *The Nation*, Lizzy Ratner (2009) reports that the recession affected people under thirty more than it did any other demographic because of a combination of college loan debt and high unemployment rates. The implication is that the combination of student loan debt and dismal job hopes, in addition to the lack of access to credit cards, resulted in students turning to debit rather than credit cards.

Martin 2

Topic sentence: college students' ongoing financial hardships

The ideas are developed by a newspaper article summarizing a study on college students' financial knowledge. A direct quote and an indirect quote are clearly cited.

Topic sentences: The effects of the Credit CARD Act and the recession on student credit-card debt and the remaining challenges students face when it comes to finances

Advice to students forms conclusion.

At first glance, the drop in student credit-card debt seems like good news. After all, this appears to show that students will graduate with less credit-card debt, which should put them on firmer financial footing. However, reality is less clear cut. As previously mentioned, student loan debt is growing, with students graduating with tens of thousands of dollars in student loans. Additionally, lack of student credit-card debt might be more indicative of lack of access rather than financial savviness. A 2015 article by Michael Schramm describes a recent U.S. Bank study on college students that found that "many students are misinformed about essential financial facts" (p. B5). The article also remarks that a majority of students had misconceptions on how credit history is established and how credit-card debt works.

Clearly, the 2009 Credit CARD Act and the recession have had positive impacts on college students' credit-card debt. However, it remains to be seen if limiting students' access to credit cards will actually help them establish strong financial practices in the future or if it is merely delaying the inevitable, especially given high student loans and students' widespread misunderstandings about credit. To truly become adept at managing their finances, students should take it upon themselves to make wise decisions. From scrutinizing college costs and having frank discussions with parents, guardians, or other trusted adults regarding what is reasonable when it comes to student loans to learning about how to establish a good credit history to taking a financial literacy class, students have opportunities to ace real-life finances 101.

Martin 3

References should start a new page.

References

Johnson, H. (2015, June 3). The state of American credit card debt in 2015. Retrieved from http://www.thesimpledollar.com/the-state-of-american-credit-card-debt-in-2015/

McClure, A. (2010, February). Curtailing credit cards. *University Business, 13*(2), 7.

Ratner, L. (2009, November 23). Generation recession. *The Nation, 289*(17), 23–26.

Sallie Mae. (2009, April). *How undergraduate students use credit cards: Sallie Mae's national study of usage rates and trends*. Retrieved from http://static.mgnetwork.com/rtd/pdfs/20090830_iris.pdf.

Sallie Mae. (2013). *How America pays for college 2013*. Retrieved from https://www.salliemae.com/assets/Core/how-america-pays/howamericapays2013.pdf

Schramm, M. (2015, September 1). College prep starts with Finance 101. *USA Today,* p. B5.

E. MLA versus APA: A Quick Reference

As you might have noticed, MLA style and APA style seem alike at first glance. Both share the goal of informing the reader of the sources that were used when writing the paper and giving the reader the information needed to locate these original sources. They both use parenthetical documentation, where source information is found in the essay's body and in a separate listing at the end. The styles also require much of the same information, and the in-text and works cited or reference citations look somewhat similar. However, there are some key differences between MLA and APA styles. The chart below will give you a quick overview of the similarities and differences between MLA and APA styles so that you can tell which one is being used in a given paper or reading.

MLA Versus APA

	MLA Style	**APA Style**
General Style		
Subjects That Use This Style	MLA style is typically used in the humanities, including English and foreign language.	APA style is typically used in nursing, business, and the social sciences, such as psychology and education.
Citations	Citations appear: • Inside the essay in parentheses • At the end in a "Works Cited" list	Citations appear: • Inside the essay in parentheses • At the end in a "References" list
In-Text Citations	In-text citations should include: • The author's (or authors') last name • The page number No commas are used to separate the information. Example: (Corrigan 151)	In-text citations should include: • The author's (or authors') last name • The date of publication (appearing directly after the author's name) • The page number proceeded by a "p." Commas are used to separate the information. Example: (Corrigan, 2014, p. 151)
End-of-the-Paper Citations		
Title of the Page	The page is titled "Works Cited"	The page is titled "References"
Information Included	Each citation should include (when available): • Author(s) • Title of source • Title of container • Other contributors • Version • Number • Publisher • Publication date • Location	Each citation should include (when available): • Author(s) • Publication date • Title(s) • City and state (two-letter abbreviation) of publication (for books) • Volume and issue number (for periodicals and journals) • Publisher (for books)

Author Information	The author's full name is listed starting with the author's last name.	The author's last name as well as the first initial of the first and middle name (if given) is listed.
Title Formatting	Capitalize all of the principal words. Italicize full-length works (books, journals, magazines) and use quotation marks for works that are part of larger works (poems, articles, essays).	For books, articles, and other nonperiodical works, capitalize only the first word of the title and of the subtitle (if one is used) as well as any proper nouns. For titles of periodicals (journals, magazines), capitalize all principal words. Italicize full-length works (books, journals, magazines), but do not italicize, underline, or put quotation marks around the titles of works that are part of larger works (poems, articles, essays).
Date of Publication	The date follows the publisher information.	The date follows the author's name.
Sample End Text Citation for a Book	Goldstein, Dana. *The Teacher Wars: A History of America's Most Embattled Profession.* Anchor, 2014.	Goldstein, D. (2014). *The teacher wars: A history of America's most embattled profession.* New York, NY: Anchor Books.
Sample End Text Citation for a Magazine Article	Schneider, Nathan. "The Joy of Slow Computing." *The New Republic,* 1 June 2015, pp. 10-11.	Schneider, N. (2015, June 1). The joy of slow computing. *The New Republic, 246*(5), 10–11.
Sample End Text Citation for a Journal Article	Gavaler, Chris. "The Well-Born Superhero." *The Journal of American Culture*, vol. 37, no. 2, June 2014, pp. 182–197.	Gavaler, C. (2014, June). The well-born superhero. *The Journal of American Culture, 37*(2), 182–197.

Suggested Topics for Research Papers

1. Types of fat in foods
2. The effects of (or solutions for) illegal immigration
3. Zoos
4. Environmental topics, such as coral reef destruction or green burial (in ecopods)
5. Arguments for or against stem cell research
6. Prisons in America
7. Methods of persuasion in advertisements
8. Media violence
9. An idea to reform public schools
10. Gun control
11. Writer's choice: ______________________________

EXPLORING ONLINE

owl.english.purdue.edu/owl/resource/658/1

A review of the research-paper process

style.mla.org/works-cited-a-quick-guide

More help with MLA citations, from the Modern Language Association

www.csuohio.edu/writing-center/apa-resources

For writers using APA style, this site gives clear, practical examples of how to insert material from outside sources in your papers.

CHAPTER 20

Writing Under Pressure: The Essay Examination

A: Budgeting Your Time

B: Reading and Understanding the Essay Question

C: Choosing the Correct Paragraph or Essay Pattern

D: Writing the Topic Sentence or the Thesis Statement

Being able to write under pressure is a key skill both in college and in the workplace. Throughout your college career, you will be asked to write **timed papers** in class and to take **essay examinations**. In fact, many English programs base placement and passing on timed essay exams. Clearly, the ability to write under pressure is crucial.

An **essay question** requires the same writing skills that a student uses in composing a paragraph or an essay. Even in history and biology, how well you do on an essay test depends partly on how well you write; yet many students, under the pressure of a test, forget or fail to apply what they know about good writing. This chapter will improve your ability to write under pressure. Many of the sample exam questions on the following pages were taken from real college examinations.

A. Budgeting Your Time

To do well on a timed essay or an essay test, it is not enough to know the material. You must also be able to call forth what you know, organize it, and present it in writing—all under pressure in a limited time.

Since most essay examinations are timed, it is important that you learn how to **budget** your time effectively so that you can devote adequate time to each question *and* finish the test. The following six tips will help you use your time well.

1. **Make sure you know exactly how long the examination lasts.** A one-hour examination may really be only fifty minutes; a two-hour examination may last only one hour and forty-five minutes.
2. **Note the point value of all questions and allot time accordingly to each question.** That is, allot the most time to questions that are worth the most points and less time to ones that are worth fewer.
3. **Decide on an order in which to answer the questions.** You do not have to begin with the first question on the examination and work, in order, to the last. Instead, you may start with the questions worth the most points. Some students prefer to begin with the questions they feel they can answer most easily, thereby guaranteeing points toward the final grade on the examination. Others combine the two methods. No matter which system you use, be sure to allot enough time to the questions that are worth the most points—whether you do them first or last.
4. **Make sure you understand exactly what each question asks you to do; then quickly prewrite and plan your answer.** It is important to take a breath, study the question, and make a quick scratch outline or plan of your answer *before you start to write*. Parts B through D of this chapter will guide you through these critical steps.
5. **Time yourself.** As you begin a particular question, calculate when you must be finished with that question in order to complete the examination, and note that time in the margin. As you write, check the clock every five minutes so that you remain on schedule.
6. **Finally, do not count on having enough time to recopy your work.** Skip lines and write carefully so that the instructor can easily read your writing as well as any neat corrections you might make.

ESL TIP
Ask students whether sharing or copying answers on exams is acceptable in their cultures. Stress that in the United States such behaviors are not acceptable unless the exam is collaborative.

PRACTICE 1

ESL TIP
Have students underline the important words in each question in Practice 1. Ask what they should include in each answer. Refer them to the instruction words in Part C.

Imagine that you are about to take the two-hour history test shown below. Read the test carefully, noting the point value of each question, and then answer the questions that follow the examination. Answers may vary.

Part I Answer both questions. 15 points each.

1. Do you think that the Versailles Peace Treaty was a "harsh" one? Be specific.
2. List the basic principles of Karl Marx. Analyze them in terms of Marx's claim that they are scientific.

Part II Answer two of the following questions. 25 points each.

3. Describe the origins of, the philosophies behind, and the chief policies of either Communist Russia or Fascist Italy. Be specific.

4. What were the causes of Nelson Mandela's presidential victory in South Africa in 1994?
5. European history of the nineteenth and twentieth centuries has been increasingly related to that of the rest of the world. Why? How? With what consequences for Europe?

Part III Briefly identify ten of the following. Two points each.

a. John Locke
b. Franco-Prussian War
c. Stalingrad
d. Cavour
e. Manchuria, 1931
f. Entente Cordiale
g. Existentialism
h. Jacobins
i. The Opium Wars
j. Social Darwinism
k. The Reform Bill of 1832
l. The most interesting reading you have done this term (from the course list)

TEACHING TIP

Lead a class discussion about students' answers to the questions in Practice 1. They should be able to explain why they answered as they did.

1. Which part would you do first and why?

 I would do Part II first because it is worth the most points (50).

 How much time would you allot to the questions in this part and why?

 I would allot approximately half of my time because it is half of the exam.

2. Which part would you do second and why?

 I would do Part I second because it is worth 30 points.

 How much time would you allot to the questions in this part and why?

 I would allot about half my remaining time because this part is about one-fourth of the exam.

3. Which part would you do last and why?

 I would do Part III last because it is worth the least number of points (20).

 How much time would you allot to the questions in this part and why?

 I would allot most of my remaining time, answering all of the questions I could. I'd save some time to review my other answers.

B. Reading and Understanding the Essay Question

Before you begin writing, carefully examine each question to decide exactly what your purpose is: that is, what the instructor expects you to do.

- This question contains three sets of instructions.

Question: Using either Communist China or Nazi Germany as a model, (a) describe the characteristics of a totalitarian state, and (b) explain how such a state was created.

- First, you must use "either Communist China or Nazi Germany as a model." That is, you must **choose** *one or the other* as a model.
- Second, you must **describe**, and third, you must **explain**.
- Your answer should consist of two written parts, a **description** and an **explanation**.

It is often helpful to underline the important words, as shown in the previous box, to make sure you understand the entire question and have noted all its parts.

The student must (1) choose to write about either Communist China or Nazi Germany, not both; (2) describe the totalitarian state; (3) explain how such a state was created.

PRACTICE 2

TEACHING TIP
Consider having students complete Practice 2 in small groups so that they can talk through their answers.

Read each essay question and underline key words. Then, on the lines beneath the question, describe in your own words exactly what the question requires: (1) What directions does the student have to follow? (2) How many parts will the answer contain?

EXAMPLE What were the causes of the Cold War? What were its chief episodes? Why has there not been a "hot" war?

Student must *(1) tell what caused the Cold War (two or more causes), (2) mention main events of Cold War, (3) give reasons why we haven't had a full-scale war. The essay will have three parts: causes, main events, and reasons.*

1. State Newton's First Law and give examples from your own experience.

   Student must (1) write out Newton's First Law and (2) give examples of the law from his or her own experience. The essay will have two parts: the law and examples.

2. Choose one of the following terms. Define it, give an example of it, and then show how it affects patients: (a) postpartum depression, (b) bipolar disorder, (c) borderline personality disorder.

   Student must (1 and 2) define and give an example of one term: postpartum depression, bipolar disorder, or borderline personality disorder; and (3) explain how it affects patients. The essay will have three parts: a definition, an example, and effects.

3. Shiism and Sunnism are the two great branches of Islam. Discuss the religious beliefs and the politics of each branch.

   Student must (1) discuss the religious beliefs and the politics of Shiism and (2) discuss the religious beliefs and the politics of Sunnism. The essay will have two parts: Shiism and Sunnism.

4. Name and explain three types of educational institutions. What are three factors that influence one's choice of an educational institution?

   Student must (1) identify and describe three types of educational institutions and (2) name three factors influencing one's choice of an educational institution. The essay will have two parts: types and factors.

5. Explain the causes and effects of brain concussions. Discuss how concerns about concussions may affect the sport of football in the United States.

   Student must (1) define what brain concussions are and (2) explain how concerns about concussions may affect the future of football. The essay will have two parts: a definition stating causes and effects and a discussion of anticipated results.

6. Discuss the causes and consequences of the Cuban Missile Crisis in 1962. What was the role of President John Kennedy?

   Student must (1) discuss the causes of the Cuban Missile Crisis, (2) discuss its consequences, and (3) explain President Kennedy's role. The essay will have three parts: causes, effects, and role of Kennedy.

7. Erik Erikson has theorized that adult actions toward children may produce either (a) trust or mistrust, (b) autonomy or self-doubt, (c) initiative or guilt. Choose one of these pairs and give examples of the kinds of adult behavior that might create these responses in a child.

   Student must (1) choose one pair of terms, (2) give examples of adult behavior that might create trust (autonomy, initiative) in a child, and (3) give examples of adult behavior that might create mistrust (self-doubt, guilt) in a child. The essay will have two parts: behavior creating positive traits and behavior creating negative traits.

8. The sixteenth century is known for the Renaissance, the Reformation, and the Commercial Revolution. Discuss each event, showing why it was important to the history of Western civilization.

   Student must discuss the historical importance of (1) the Renaissance, (2) the Reformation, and (3) the Commercial Revolution. The essay will have three parts: the Renaissance, the Reformation, and the Commercial Revolution.

9. Define the Monroe Doctrine of the early nineteenth century and weigh the arguments for and against it.

   Student must (1) define the Monroe Doctrine, (2) evaluate the arguments for it, and (3) evaluate the arguments against it. The essay will have three parts: definition, arguments for, and arguments against.

10. The 2008 recession fundamentally changed the economy and the way Americans view homeownership. Agree or disagree.

    Student must give reasons to support or oppose the statement that the 2008 recession (1) fundamentally changed the economy and (2) the way Americans view homeownership. The essay will have two parts: a description of the 2008 recession and views of homeownership and the supporting or opposing evidence.

C. Choosing the Correct Paragraph or Essay Pattern

Throughout this book, you have learned how to write various types of paragraphs and compositions. Many examinations will require you to **illustrate**, **define**, **compare**, and so forth. How well you answer questions may depend partly on how well you understand these terms.

1. *Illustrate* "behavior modification."
2. *Define* "greenhouse effect."
3. *Compare* the themes in two Charles Dickens novels.

- The key words in these questions are *illustrate, define,* and *compare*—**instruction words** that tell you what you are supposed to do and what form your answer should take.

Review this list of common instruction words used in college examinations:

TEACHING TIP

You can reduce students' test anxiety by reviewing these terms, most of which they now know.

1. **Classify**:	Gather into categories, types, or kinds according to a single basis of division (see Chapter 11).
2. **Compare**:	Point out similarities (see Chapter 10). Instructors often use *compare* to mean point out both *similarities* and *differences*.
3. **Contrast**:	Point out differences (see Chapter 10).
4. **Describe**:	Give an account of or capture pictorially (see Chapter 7).
5. **Define**:	State clearly and exactly the meaning of a word or term (see Chapter 9). You may be required to write a single-sentence definition or a full paragraph. Instructors may use *identify* as a synonym for *define* when they want a short definition.
6. **Discuss**: (analyze, describe, or explain)	Often an instructor uses these terms to mean "thoughtfully examine a subject, approaching it from different angles." These terms allow the writer more freedom of approach than many of the others.
7. **Discuss causes**:	Analyze the reasons or causes for something; answer the question, Why? (see Chapter 12).
8. **Discuss effects**:	Analyze the effects, consequences, or results of something (see Chapter 12).
9. **Evaluate**:	Weigh the pros and cons, advantages and disadvantages (see Chapters 10 and 13).
10. **Identify**:	Give a capsule who-what-when-where-why answer. Sometimes *identify* is a synonym for *define*.
11. **Illustrate**:	Give one or more examples (see Chapter 5).

12. **Narrate**: (trace)	Follow the development of something through time, event by event (see Chapters 6 and 8).
13. **Summarize**:	Write the substance of a longer work in condensed form (see Chapter 18, Part B).
14. **Take a stand**:	Persuade; argue for a particular position (see Chapter 13).

PRACTICE 3

You should have no trouble deciding what kind of paragraph or composition to use if the question uses one of the terms just defined—*contrast, trace, classify,* and so on. However, questions are often worded in such a way that you have to discover what kind of paragraph or essay is required. What kind of paragraph or essay is required by each of the following questions?

EXAMPLE What is *autism*? (*Write a paragraph to. . . .*) *define*

1. In one concise paragraph, give the main ideas of Simone de Beauvoir's famous book *The Second Sex*. summarize
2. What is the difference between veins and arteries? contrast
3. Follow the development of social media. narrate
4. How do bacterial and viral infections differ? contrast
5. Who or what is each of the following: Putin, NATO, ISIS? identify or define
6. Explain the causes of the American Civil War. discuss causes
7. Explain what is meant by "magical thinking." define
8. Take a stand for or against background checks for gun purchasers in this country. Give reasons to support your stand. persuade, give reasons
9. Give two recent instances of racial profiling you consider "out of control." illustrate
10. Categorize the different websites giving out medical information. classify

D. Writing the Topic Sentence or the Thesis Statement

A good way to ensure that your answer truly addresses itself to the question is to compose a topic sentence or a thesis statement that contains the key words of the question.

Question: How do fixed-rate and adjustable-rate mortgages differ?

- The key words in this question are *fixed-rate* and *adjustable-rate mortgages,* and *differ.*
- What kind of paragraph or essay would be appropriate for this question?

a paragraph or essay of contrast

Topic sentence or *thesis statement* of answer: Fixed-rate and adjustable-rate mortgages differ in three basic ways.

- The answer repeats the key words of the question: *fixed-rate, adjustable-rate, mortgages,* and *differ.*

PRACTICE 4

Here are five examination questions. Write a topic sentence or thesis statement for each question by using the question as part of the answer. Pretend that you know all the material. Even though you may not know anything about the subjects, you should be able to formulate a topic sentence or thesis statement based on the question. Answers may vary.

1. Contrast high school requirements in Jamaica with those in the United States.

   Topic sentence or thesis statement: High school requirements in Jamaica are more demanding than those in the United States.

2. What steps can a busy person take to reduce the destructive impact of stress in his or her life?

   Topic sentence or thesis statement: A busy person can take three steps to help reduce the destructive impact of stress in his or her life.

TEACHING TIP

These questions come from real college exams. Bring in other essay exams from classes across disciplines. Have students work in groups to discuss the exam questions.

3. Assume that you manage a small shop that sells men's apparel. What activities would you undertake to promote the sale of sportswear?

   Topic sentence or thesis statement: As manager of a small shop that sells men's apparel, I would do three things to promote the sale of sportswear.

4. The state should subsidize students in medical school because the country needs more doctors. Agree or disagree with this statement.

   Topic sentence or thesis statement: The state should not subsidize students in medical school.

5. Does religion play a more vital role in people's lives today than it did in your parents' generation?

   Topic sentence or thesis statement: Religion plays a more vital role in people's lives today than it did in my parents' generation.

TEACHING TIP

Have students practice these steps by writing a timed essay. Ask them to choose from three writing prompts that you provide.

Checklist

The Process of Answering an Essay Question

- ☐ 1. Survey the test and note the point value for each question.
- ☐ 2. Calculate how much time you need for each question. Then check the clock as you write so that you complete all the questions.
- ☐ 3. Read each question carefully, underlining important words.
- ☐ 4. Determine how many parts the answer should contain.
- ☐ 5. Considering your audience (usually the teacher) and purpose, choose the paragraph or essay pattern that would best answer the question.
- ☐ 6. Write a topic sentence or a thesis statement that repeats the key words of the question.
- ☐ 7. Quickly freewrite or brainstorm ideas and arrange them in a logical order, making an outline or plan.
- ☐ 8. Write your paragraph or essay.

EXPLORING ONLINE

www.google.com

Don't get nervous; get an A. Search "taking essay exams" and find advice that truly helps you.

www.studygs.net/tsttak4.htm

This site offers valuable strategies for reading and writing essay examinations.

counselingcenter.illinois.edu/brochures/test-anxiety

Do you get so anxious taking tests that you don't do your best? Explore this excellent site from the University of Illinois for tips and a deeper understanding of the problem.

writers' WORKSHOP

Analyze a Social Problem

Because essays are longer and more complex than paragraphs, organizing an essay can be a challenge, even for experienced writers. Techniques like having a clear *controlling idea*, a good *thesis statement*, and a *plan or an outline* all help an essay writer manage the task. Another useful approach is dividing the subject into three parts, as one student does here. In your group or class, read the essay, aloud if possible, underlining the parts you find most powerful and paying special attention to organization.

It's Great to Get Old

(1) I knock at the door and patiently await an answer. I listen and hear the thump of a cane on the hard wood floor, edging slowly toward the door. "It's great to get old," my grandmother says facetiously[1] as she opens the door, apologizing for making me wait. Through her I learn firsthand the problems of the aged. Loneliness, lack of money, and ailing health are just some of the problems old people must deal with.

(2) For one thing, loneliness seems endemic[2] among old people in America. With difficulty getting around, many spend most of their time confined to their apartments, awaiting visits from family or friends. Through my grandmother, I realize that as much as old people's families may care about them, the family members obviously have lives of their own and cannot visit as much as old persons would like. And when people are very old, most of their friends have already died, so they spend most of their time alone.

(3) Poor health is also a major problem. Any number of physical ailments create a problem. Cataracts, for example, are a common eye problem among old people. Health problems can make life very difficult for an old person.

(4) Last but not least is the financial burden old people must cope with. The rising costs of basic necessities such as food, housing, and health care are especially difficult for old people to meet. Sadly, most are forced to compromise what they need for what they can afford. Take, for example, an old person who must choose between food and medications. This person might buy inexpensive pasta for dinner every night or sometimes not eat at all in order to pay for medications. Good nutrition must be forfeited for what he or she can afford. Financial problems also make life very difficult for an old person.

---

[1]facetiously: humorously

[2]endemic: typical in a certain place or population

(5) There is no easy way to ease the problems of the aged. Simply being aware of them is an important step in the right direction. If we turn our attention and compassion toward the elderly, we can begin to help them find solutions.

—Denise Nelley, Student

1. How effective is Ms. Nelley's essay?

   ___Y___ Strong thesis statement? ___Y/N___ Good supporting details? (see 5 below)

   ___Y/N___ Logical organization? (see 4 below) ___Y___ Effective conclusion?

2. Did the introductory paragraph catch your interest? Explain why or why not.
3. What is the controlling idea of the essay? What is the thesis statement? That the elderly face difficult problems, last sentence in first paragraph
4. This writer has skillfully organized her ideas. Her thesis names three problems facing the elderly. What are they? Does the body of the essay discuss these three problems in the same order that the thesis names them? If not, what changes would you suggest? No. Discuss money second, health third.
5. Are the three problems fully explained in paragraphs 2, 3, and 4? That is, does Ms. Nelley provide enough support for each problem? If not, what revision suggestions would you give the writer, especially for paragraph 3?*
6. This student movingly presents some problems of the elderly. Do you think she should have included solutions? Why or why not?
7. Can you spot any error patterns (the same error two or more times) that this student should watch out for? No

GROUP WORK

In your group or class, evaluate (or grade) Ms. Nelley's essay. Then, based on your evaluation, decide what changes or revisions would most improve the essay and revise it accordingly, as if it were your own. If your group wishes to add any new ideas or support, brainstorm together and choose the strongest ideas. Rewrite as needed.

When you are done, evaluate the essay again, with your changes.

WRITING AND REVISING IDEAS

1. Discuss the ways in which a loved one's experience has taught you about a problem (addiction, AIDS, disability, and so on).
2. Analyze a social problem (racial profiling or shoplifting, for example).

*Prewrite again for more support on health problems. Develop paragraph 3 more fully. Avoid using "problem" four times.

UNIT

5

Improving Your Writing

CHAPTER 21

Revising for Consistency and Parallelism

A: Consistent Tense

B: Consistent Number and Person

C: Parallelism

ESL TIP
Ask students to define and offer synonyms for the word *consistent*. The most helpful meanings are *uniform* or *unchanging*.

All good writing is **consistent**. That is, each sentence and paragraph in the final draft moves along smoothly without confusing shifts in **tense**, **number**, or **person**. In addition, good writing uses **parallel structure** to balance two or more similar words, phrases, or clauses.

Although you should be aware of consistency and parallelism as you write the first draft of your paragraph or essay, you might find it easier to **revise** for them—that is, to write your first draft and then, as you read it again later, check and rewrite for consistency and parallelism.

A. Consistent Tense

ESL TIP
Nonnative writers may need extra work on avoiding tense shifts and on verb tenses in general.

Consistency of tense means using the same verb tense whenever possible throughout a sentence or an entire paragraph. Do not shift from one verb tense to another—for example, from present to past or from past to present—unless you really mean to indicate different times.

1. Inconsistent tense: We *stroll* down Bourbon Street as the jazz bands *began* to play.
2. Consistent tense: We *strolled* down Bourbon Street as the jazz bands *began* to play.
3. Consistent tense: We *stroll* down Bourbon Street as the jazz bands *begin* to play.

TEACHING TIP

Ask the class to discuss cases where present or past tense might be more effective or appropriate.

- Sentence 1 begins in the present tense with the verb *stroll* but then slips into the past tense with the verb *began*. Both actions (strolling and beginning) occur at the same time, but the verb tenses are inconsistent. Both verbs should be in the same tense.
- Sentence 2 is consistent. Both verbs, *strolled* and *began*, are now in the past tense.
- Sentence 3 is also consistent, using the present tense forms of both verbs, *stroll* and *begin*. The present tense here gives a feeling of immediacy, as if the action is happening now.*

Of course, you should use different verb tenses in a sentence or paragraph if they convey the meaning that you wish to convey:

4. Last fall I *took* English 02; now I *am taking* English 13.

- The verbs in this sentence accurately show the time relationship between the two classroom experiences.†

PRACTICE 1

Read the following sentences carefully for meaning. Then correct any inconsistencies of tense by changing the verbs that do not accurately show the time of events.

EXAMPLE I took a deep breath and opened the door; there stands a well-dressed man with a large box.

Consistent: I took a deep breath and opened the door; there ~~stands~~ *stood* a well-dressed man with a large box.

or

Consistent: I ~~took~~ *take* a deep breath and ~~opened~~ *open* the door; there stands a well-dressed man with a large box.

1. Two seconds before the buzzer sounded, LeBron James sank a basket from midcourt, and the crowd ~~goes~~ went wild.
2. Nestlé introduced instant coffee in 1938; it ~~takes~~ took eight years to develop this product.
3. We ~~expand~~ expanded our sales budget, doubled our research, and soon saw positive results.

---

*For more work on spotting verbs, see Chapter 26, "The Simple Sentence," Part C.

†For more work on particular verb tenses and forms, see Chapters 29, 30, and 31.

4. For twenty years, Dr. Dulfano observed animal behavior and ~~seeks~~ sought clues to explain the increasing violence among human beings.

5. I knew how the system ~~works~~ worked.

6. I was driving south on Interstate 90 when a truck ~~approaches~~ approached with its high beams on.

7. Two brown horses ~~graze~~ grazed quietly in the field as the sun rose and the mist disappeared.

8. Lollie had a big grin on her face as she ~~begs~~ begged the lead singer for an autograph.

9. Kelly ~~races~~ raced into the lobby, grabbed my arm, and shouted "Call 911!"

10. The nurses quietly paced the halls, making sure their patients ~~rest~~ rested comfortably.

PRACTICE 2

Inconsistencies of tense are most likely to occur within paragraphs and longer pieces of writing. Therefore, it is important to revise your writing for tense consistency. Read this paragraph for meaning. Then revise, correcting inconsistencies of tense by changing incorrect verbs.

TEACHING TIP

Tell the class to beware of tense shifts in writing. As writers relive past events in their minds, they may shift from past to present verbs.

In 1869, workers digging a well on a farm in Cardiff, New York, ~~unearth~~ unearthed a stone statue. The ten-foot-high figure attracted crowds, and the farmer, William Newell, ~~begins~~ began charging visitors to see the strange figure some believed ~~is~~ was the petrified body of an ancient giant. Seeing thousands flocking to Newell's farm, businessmen ~~buys~~ bought the statue, now called the Cardiff Giant. An expert noticed fresh chisel marks on the statue and ~~declares~~ declared the discovery a fake. Newell admitted he ~~pay~~ paid stonecutters to carve the statue then ~~plant~~ planted it on his farm the year before. Although ~~label~~ labeled a scam, the Cardiff Giant still drew onlookers. P. T. Barnum ~~offer~~ offered to buy the statue for his museum. The owners ~~refuse~~ refused to sell, so Barnum ~~exhibit~~ exhibited a plaster replica. People were so fascinated with the Cardiff Giant, they ~~line~~ lined up to see a copy of a fake they ~~nickname~~ nicknamed Old Hoaxy.

AP Images/Jean-Marc Bouju

U.S. soldiers trying to rest in "Ranger graves" like those the student describes in Practice 3.

PRACTICE 3

TEACHING TIP

Transforming activities like Practice 3 promote verbal agility.

The following paragraph is written in the past tense. Rewrite it in consistent present tense. Cross out each past tense verb and write the present tense form above it. Make sure all verbs agree with their subjects.*

The desert heat ~~was~~ is vicious under the burlap that ~~camouflaged~~ camouflages me. I ~~lay~~ lie in my "Ranger grave," Army slang for the shallow holes soldiers ~~dug~~ dig into the sand, just big enough to conceal their bodies. A few thoughts ~~worked~~ work their way through the haze of my brain, but mostly I ~~dreamed~~ dream about water—icy, sparkling water. I almost ~~heard~~ hear the clink of ice cubes in a Mason jar, dripping with condensation. I barely ~~noticed~~ notice the fine sand in my eyes. I ~~didn't~~ don't have enough fluid in my body to make tears. "Water truck!" The call ~~floated~~ floats down the nearly invisible line of graves that ~~stretched~~ stretch across the sand. I ~~peeked~~ peek out as the water truck ~~drove~~ drives away through shimmering waves of heat. It ~~left~~ leaves behind a water buffalo, a huge tank of water for the ground troops in our area. As the new guy in the squad, I ~~had~~ have to fill our canteens. With my monkey suit for chemical attack, my machine gun, and extra ammo, I ~~trudged~~ trudge out. The desert ~~coated~~ coats me with sand. My helmet ~~felt~~ feels huge on my head. Finally, I ~~reached~~ reach the tank and mentally ~~pumped~~ pump myself up. I ~~was~~ am a paratrooper, a member of the 82nd Airborne, elite fighting force of the U.S. Army! My sense of duty and my mental ice ~~pushed~~ push me onward. I ~~sipped~~ sip a little hot water, ~~filled~~ fill the canteens, and ~~dragged~~ drag them back to the men.

—Ray Christian, Student

*For more work on agreement, see Chapter 29, "Present Tense (Agreement)."

PRACTICE 4

TEACHING TIP
Ask students to color-code the verb tenses in their compositions with highlighters. This graphic presentation may enhance their awareness of a tense-shifting problem.

The following paragraph is written in the present tense. Rewrite it in consistent past tense,* crossing out each present tense verb and writing the past tense form above it.

In the summer of 1816, four friends ~~share~~ shared a house in Switzerland. Days of rain ~~force~~ forced them to stay indoors. They ~~begin~~ began telling ghost stories to ease the boredom. For a while, they ~~recite~~ recited aloud from *Tales of the Dead*, a collection of horror stories full of eerie graveyards, swirling fog, and restless spirits. Then one night, they ~~decide~~ decided to hold a contest to see who ~~can~~ could write the most frightening ghost story. All four ~~feel~~ felt eager to compete. Two of the friends—Percy Bysshe Shelley and Lord Byron—~~are~~ were already famous poets. The other two—Dr. John Polidori and Mary Wollstonecraft Godwin, Shelley's wife-to-be—~~are~~ were also writers. Midnight ~~passes~~ passed, and they ~~retire~~ retired to their bedrooms. Mary ~~closes~~ closed her eyes, and imagination ~~takes~~ took over. In her mind's eye, she ~~sees~~ saw a science student kneeling beside a creature he constructed. It ~~is~~ was a hideous corpse of a man, but suddenly, it ~~twitches~~ twitched with life. Horror-stricken, the young man ~~runs~~ ran away from his creation, hoping that the spark of life ~~will~~ would sputter and die. Later, though, he ~~wakes~~ woke to find the monster standing over his bed. Following this nightmare, Mary ~~writes~~ wrote her novel *Frankenstein* in a two-month rush. Published in 1818, *Frankenstein* ~~becomes~~ became a classic, read by people around the world.

PRACTICE 5

Longer pieces of writing often use both the past tense and the present tense. However, switching correctly from one tense to the other requires care. Read the following essay carefully and note when a switch from one tense to another is logically necessary. Then revise verbs as needed.

A QUICK HISTORY OF CHOCOLATE

TEACHING TIP
Suggest that students read Practice 5 aloud, listening and marking switches in tense. Then they can go back and make the necessary corrections to the verbs they marked.

Most of us now take solid chocolate—especially candy bars—so much for granted that we find it hard to imagine a time when chocolate didn't exist. However, this delicious food ~~becomes~~ became an eating favorite only about 150 years ago.

*For more work on the past tense, see Chapter 30, "Past Tense."

The ancient peoples of Central America began cultivating cacao beans almost 3,000 years ago. A cold drink made from the beans ~~is~~ was served to Hernando Cortés, the Spanish conqueror, when he ~~arrives~~ arrived at the Aztec court of Montezuma in 1519. The Spaniards took the beverage home to their king. He ~~likes~~ liked it so much that he kept the formula a secret. For the next 100 years, hot chocolate was the private drink of the Spanish nobility. Slowly, it ~~makes~~ made its way into the fashionable courts of France, England, and Austria. In 1657, a Frenchman living in London opened a shop where devices for making the beverage ~~are~~ were sold at a high price. Soon chocolate houses appeared in cities throughout Europe. Wealthy clients met in them, sipped chocolate, conducted business, and ~~gossip~~ gossiped.

During the 1800s, chocolate became a chewable food. The breakthrough ~~comes~~ came in 1828 when cocoa butter was extracted from the bean. Twenty years later, an English firm mixed the butter with chocolate liquor, which ~~results~~ resulted in the first solid chocolate. Milton Hershey's first candy bar ~~come~~ came on the scene in 1894, and Tootsie Rolls hit the market two years later. The popularity of chocolate bars ~~soar~~ soared during World War I when they ~~are~~ were given to soldiers for fast energy. M&Ms gave the industry another boost during World War II; soldiers needed candy that wouldn't melt in their hands.

On average, Americans today eat ten pounds of hard chocolate a year. Their number-one choice is Snickers, which ~~sold~~ sells more than a billion bars every year. However, Americans consume far less chocolate than many Western Europeans. The average Dutch person ~~gobbled~~ gobbles up more than fifteen pounds a year, while a Swiss ~~packed~~ packs away almost twenty pounds. Chocolate is obviously an international favorite.

B. Consistent Number and Person

Just as important as verb tense consistency is consistency of **number** and **person**.

Consistency of Number

Consistency of number means avoiding confusing shifts from singular to plural or from plural to singular within a sentence or paragraph. Choose *either* singular *or* plural; then be *consistent*.

1. Inconsistent number: *The wise jogger* chooses *their* running shoes with care.
2. Consistent number: *The wise jogger* chooses *his or her* running shoes with care.
3. Consistent number: *Wise joggers* choose *their* running shoes with care.

- Because the subject of sentence 1, *the wise jogger*, is singular, use of the plural pronoun *their* is *inconsistent*.
- Sentence 2 is *consistent*. The singular pronoun *his* (or *her*) now clearly refers to the singular *jogger*.
- In sentence 3, the plural number is used *consistently*. *Their* clearly refers to the plural *joggers*.

If you begin a paragraph by referring to a website designer as *she*, continue to refer to *her* in the **third person singular** throughout the paragraph:

> The new *website designer* created this streamlined website for our company. *She* explained that our old site was hard for customers to navigate. A slight increase in orders despite the difficult economy is probably the result of *her* work. Needless to say, we plan to hire *her* again.

Do not confuse the reader by shifting unnecessarily to *they* or *you*.

PRACTICE 6

Correct any inconsistencies of **number** in the following sentences.* Also make necessary changes in verb agreement.

EXAMPLE A singer must protect ~~their~~ *his or her* voice.

ESL TIP

Have your ESL students correct pronoun errors in sentences (e.g., *himself* versus *hisself*) to check their knowledge.

1. An individual's self-esteem can affect ~~their~~ his or her performance.
2. The new restaurant offers a range of dishes, but I find most of ~~it~~ them too spicy.
3. The auto show displayed a new hybrid vehicle, and ~~they~~ it drew a lot of attention.

*For more practice in agreement of pronouns and antecedents, see Chapter 33, "Pronouns," Part B.

4. The defendant has decided that he will represent ~~oneself~~ himself.
5. Dreams fascinate me; ~~it is~~ they are like another world.
6. If ~~a person doesn't~~ people don't know how to write well, they will face limited job opportunities.
7. Oxford University boasts of the great number of ancient manuscripts ~~they own~~ it owns.
8. Always buy corn and tomatoes when ~~it is~~ they are in season.
9. The average American takes ~~their~~ his or her freedom for granted.
10. ~~Women have~~ A woman has more opportunities than ever before. She is freer to go to school, get a job, and choose the kind of life she wants.

TEACHING TIP
You might want to explain how the three "persons," or points of view, differ. First person is informal and is not welcomed in some courses and most workplaces. Second person usually should be avoided except in "how-to" writing. Third person is often the best choice for academic writing.

Consistency of Person

Consistency of person—closely related to consistency of number—means using the same *person,* or indefinite pronoun form, throughout a sentence or paragraph whenever possible.

First person is the most personal and informal in written work: (singular) *I,* (plural) *we*
Second person speaks directly to the reader: (singular and plural) *you*
Third person is the most formal and most frequently used in college writing: (singular) *he, she, it, one, a person, an individual, a student,* and so on; (plural) *they, people, individuals, students,* and so on

Avoid confusing shifts from one person to another. Choose one, and then be *consistent*. When using a noun in a general way—*a person, the individual, the parent*—be careful not to slip into the second person, *you*, but continue to use the third person, *he or she*.

ESL TIP
Some ESL instructors advise students to avoid verb and article errors by sticking to third person plural.

4. Inconsistent person	A *customer* gets a discount when *you* present a coupon.
5. Consistent person:	A *customer* gets a discount when *he or she* presents a coupon.
6. Consistent person:	*You* get a discount when *you* present a coupon.

- In sentence 4, the person shifts unnecessarily from the third person, *a customer*, to the second person, *you*. The result is confusing.
- Sentence 5 maintains consistent third person. *He or she* now clearly refers to the third person subject, *a customer*.
- Sentence 6 is also consistent, using the second person, *you*, throughout.

Of course, inconsistencies of person and number often occur together, as shown in the next box.

TEACHING TIP

Students might ask you about the use of "one," as in "One should practice the piano every day." Share your policy on person with the class—whether you prefer "one," the most formal, or some other, and whether you discourage second person, except in instructions.

7. Inconsistent person and number:	Whether *one* enjoys or resents commercials, *we* are bombarded with them every hour of the day.
8. Consistent person and number:	Whether *we* enjoy or resent commercials, *we* are bombarded with them every hour of the day.
9. Consistent person and number:	Whether *one* enjoys or resents commercials, *he or she* (or *one*) is bombarded with them every hour of the day.

- Sentence 7 shifts from the third person singular, *one,* to the first person plural, *we.*
- Sentence 8 uses the first person plural consistently.
- Sentence 9 uses the third person singular consistently.

PRACTICE 7

Correct the shifts in **person** in these sentences. If necessary, change the verbs to make them agree with any new subjects.

EXAMPLE One should eliminate saturated fats from ~~your~~ *one's* diet.

TEACHING TIP

If your students need to review pronoun agreement, refer them to Chapter 33 for more help and practice.

1. Sooner or later, most addicts realize that ~~you~~ they can't just quit when ~~you~~ they want to.
2. One problem facing students on this campus is that ~~a person doesn't~~ they don't know when the library will be open and when it will be closed.
3. One should rely on reason, not emotion, when ~~they are~~ he or she is forming opinions about such controversial issues as abortion, immigration, or gun control.
4. I have reached a time in my life when what others expect is less important than what ~~one~~ I really ~~wants~~ want to do.
5. Members of the orchestra should meet after the concert and bring ~~your~~ their instruments and music.
6. The wise mother knows that she is asking for trouble if ~~you let~~ she lets a small child watch violent television shows.
7. The contestant whose design is chosen will receive a scholarship to the Fashion Institute of Technology. ~~You~~ He or she will also be invited to attend Fashion Week in New York.

8. You shouldn't judge a person by the way ~~they dress~~ he or she dresses.
9. Don't let peer pressure lead you to make decisions ~~one later regrets~~ you later regret.
10. People who visit the Caribbean for the first time are struck by the lushness of the landscape. The sheer size of the flowers and fruit amazes ~~you~~ them.

PRACTICE 8

The following paragraph consistently uses third person singular—*the job applicant, the job seeker, he or she.* For practice in revising for consistency, rewrite the paragraph in **consistent third person plural.** Begin by changing *the job applicant* to *job applicants.* Then change verbs, nouns, and pronouns as necessary.

TEACHING TIP

To give students practice writing in third person, preferred in much college and professional writing, you might distribute paragraphs written in first or second person and have students rewrite them in third person.

In a job interview these days, the job applicant should stress his or her personal skills, rather than only technical skills. This strategy could increase his or her chances of getting hired. The job seeker should point out such skills as speaking and writing confidently, working well on a team, solving problems quickly, or managing people. These days, many employers assume that if an applicant has excellent "soft skills" like these, he or she can be trained in the technical fine points of the job.

In a job interview these days, job applicants should stress their personal skills, rather than only technical skills. This strategy could increase their chances of getting hired. Job seekers should point out such skills as speaking and writing confidently, working well on a team, solving problems quickly, or managing people. These days, many employers assume that if applicants have excellent "soft skills" like these, they can be trained in the technical fine points of the job.

PRACTICE 9

Revise the following essay for inconsistencies of person and number. Correct any confusing shifts (changing words if necessary) to make the writing clear and *consistent* throughout.

IS OUR IDEA OF RACE CHANGING?

What is race, anyway? Is it skin color, country of origin, cultural traditions, biology? The students in Samuel Richards' sociology class at Pennsylvania State University are pondering these questions. Professor Richards encourages ~~him or her~~ them to move beyond the black and white labels most people apply to ~~themself~~ themselves and others.

To make his point that race and ethnicity are complex aspects of identity, Richards began offering a DNA test to any student who wanted to learn more about ~~their~~ his or her racial heritage. Most students, naturally curious about ~~his or her~~ their ancestors, rushed to sign up. The DNA tests were performed through a simple mouth swab by a professor of genetics, Mark Shriver. He tested for four DNA groups: Western European, West African, East Asian, and Native American.

The results received national attention. Many students discovered that ~~he or she was~~ they were mixed race, including some who believed they were 100 percent Caucasian or Asian. One white student, for example, learned that 14 percent of his DNA was African and 6 percent East Asian. "I was like, oh my God, that's me," he recalls. A.J. Dobbins knew he was black and perhaps had a white ancestor, but he was amazed to learn that ~~one's~~ his DNA is 28 percent Caucasian, 70 percent sub-Saharan African, and 2 percent Native American.

Many hope that this experiment will chip away at prejudice, shaking people out of ~~his~~ their rigid thinking. Critics, however, say the genetic tests are incomplete. They call DNA testing a fad and scoff at some of Richards' students who hoped to test multiracial in order to upset ~~his or her~~ their parents. Yet more and more everyday people and celebrities are getting their DNA tested. Columnist Leonard Pitts, Jr., Oprah, and Brazilian soccer star Obina, to name just three, have used DNA results and historic records to trace ~~one's~~ their heritage.

C. Parallelism

TEACHING TIP

You might begin Part C by discussing the pairs or series of elements in the six boxed sentences. Make sure students can recognize the revised *parallel structures* before moving on.

Parallelism, or **parallel structure**, is an effective way to add smoothness and power to your writing. **Parallelism** is a balance of two or more similar words, phrases, or clauses.

Compare the two versions of each of these sentences:

1. She likes dancing, swimming, and to box.
2. She likes *dancing*, *swimming*, and *boxing*.
3. The cable runs across the roof; the north wall is where it runs down.
4. The cable runs *across the roof* and *down the north wall*.
5. He admires people with strong convictions and who think for themselves.
6. He admires people *who have strong convictions* and *who think for themselves*.

TEACHING TIP

Most students are completely unaware of the concept of parallelism. Explain that, once grasped and put to use, parallel structures add sophistication and structure to one's writing.

- Sentences 2, 4, and 6 use **parallelism** to express parallel ideas.
- In sentence 2, *dancing*, *swimming*, and *boxing* are parallel; all three are the *-ing* forms of verbs, used here as nouns.
- In sentence 4, *across the roof* and *down the north wall* are parallel prepositional phrases, each consisting of a preposition and its object.
- In sentence 6, *who have strong convictions* and *who think for themselves* are parallel clauses beginning with the word *who*.

Sometimes two entire sentences can be parallel:

> In a democracy we are all equal before the law. In a dictatorship we are all equal before the police.
>
> —Millor Fernandes

- In what way are these two sentences parallel?

  Both use the same format: "In a ——— we are all equal before the ———."

Certain special constructions require parallel structure:

7. The fruit is *both* tasty *and* fresh.
8. He *either* loves you *or* hates you.
9. Yvette *not only* plays golf *but also* swims like a pro.
10. I would *rather* sing in the chorus *than* perform a solo.

- Each of these constructions has two parts:
  both . . . and
  (n)either . . . (n)or
  not only . . . but also
  rather . . . than
- The words, phrases, or clauses following each part must be parallel:
  tasty . . . fresh
  loves you . . . hates you
  plays golf . . . swims like a pro
  sing in the chorus . . . perform a solo

PRACTICE 10

Rewrite each of the following sentences, using parallel structure to accent parallel ideas.

EXAMPLE The summer in Louisiana is very hot and has high humidity.

The summer in Louisiana is very hot and humid.

TEACHING TIP

Suggest that students read this chapter's examples and exercise items aloud so that they can better "hear" the parallel and nonparallel structures.

1. Teresa is a gifted woman—a chemist, does the carpentry, and she can cook.

   Teresa is a gifted woman—a chemist, a carpenter, and a cook.

2. The shape of the rock, how big it was, and its color reminded me of a small turtle.

   The rock's shape, size, and color reminded me of a small turtle.

3. He is an affectionate husband, a thoughtful son, and kind to his kids.

   He is an affectionate husband, a thoughtful son, and a kind father.

4. Marvin was happy to win the chess tournament and he also felt surprised.

   Marvin was happy and surprised to win the chess tournament.

TEACHING TIP

Point out to students that correcting parallelism errors often eradicates wordiness. Ask which version of sentence 5 is more concise—the original or the revised.

5. Dr. Tien is the kindest physician I know; she has the most concern of any physician I know.

   Dr. Tien is the kindest and most concerned physician I know.

6. Joe would rather work on a farm than spending time in an office.

   Joe would rather work on a farm than spend time in an office.

7. Every afternoon in the mountains, it either rains or there is hail.

   Every afternoon in the mountains, it either rains or hails.

8. *Sesame Street* teaches children nursery rhymes, songs, how to be courteous, and being kind.

   Sesame Street teaches children nursery rhymes, songs, courtesy, and kindness.

9. Alexis would rather give orders than taking them.

   Alexis would rather give orders than take them.

10. His writing reveals not only intelligence but also it is humorous.

   His writing reveals not only intelligence but also humor.

PRACTICE 11

Write one sentence that is parallel to each sentence that follows, creating pairs of parallel sentences. Answers will vary.

TEACHING TIP
Have students compare their answers to Practice 11 and help each other identify any inconsistent structures.

EXAMPLE On Friday night, she dressed in silk and sipped champagne.

On Monday morning, she put on her jeans and crammed for a history test.

1. When he was twenty, he worked seven days a week in a fruit store.

   When he was forty, he worked four days a week as the owner of a chain of fruit stores.

2. The child in me wants to run away from problems.

   The adult in me knows I must face them.

3. The home team charged enthusiastically onto the field.

   The visiting team sat dejectedly in the dugout.

4. "Work hard and keep your mouth shut" is my mother's formula for success.

   "Nothing ventured, nothing gained" is mine.

5. The men thought the movie was amusing.

   The women thought it was insulting.

PRACTICE 12

The following paragraph contains both correct and faulty parallel structures. Revise the faulty parallelism.

TEACHING TIP
Students are often intrigued to learn that good orators—and good writers—use parallelism to help the audience follow their ideas. Bring in Martin Luther King Jr.'s "I Have a Dream" speech or Abraham Lincoln's "Gettysburg Address." Let students find and analyze uses of parallelism.

During World War II, United States Marines who fought in the Pacific possessed a powerful and unbeatable weapon ~~that was also unbeatable~~: Navajo Code Talkers. Creating a secret code, Code Talkers sent and translated ~~were translating~~ vital military information. Four hundred twenty Navajos memorized and used the code ~~and it was used by them~~. It consisted of both common Navajo words and ~~there were also~~ about 400 invented words. For example, Code Talkers used the Navajo words for *owl*, *chicken hawk*, and *swallow* to describe different kinds of aircraft. Because Navajo is a complex and uncommon language ~~that is also uncommon~~, the Japanese military could not break the code. Although Code Talkers helped the Allied Forces win the war, their efforts were not publicly recognized until the code was declassified in 1968. On August 14, 1982, the first Navajo Code Talkers Day honored these heroes, who not only had risked their lives but also had developed ~~been developing~~ one of the few unbroken codes in history.

PRACTICE 13

The following essay contains both correct and faulty parallel structures. Revise the faulty parallelism.

TEACHING TIP
Ask students to use a highlighter to mark parallel elements (words, phrases, and clauses) in a piece of their own writing.

VINCENT VAN GOGH

Vincent Van Gogh sold only one painting in his lifetime, but his oil paintings later influenced modern art and established ~~establishing~~ him as one of the greatest artists of all time. Born in Holland in 1853, Van Gogh struggled to find an inspiring career. After failing as a tutor and ~~being~~ a clergyman, he began to paint. Van Gogh's younger brother Theo supported him with money and ~~also sending~~ art supplies. Eventually, Van Gogh went to live with Theo in Paris, where the young artist was introduced to Impressionism, a style of painting that emphasizes light at different times of day. Using vivid colors and ~~also with~~ broad brush strokes, Van Gogh made powerful pictures full of feeling. His favorite subjects were landscapes, still

TEACHING TIP

Remind students to be alert for parallelism errors in sentences that contain coordinating conjunctions, particularly *and*, *or*, *but*, and *nor*.

TEACHING TIP

To prompt critical thinking, ask students whether there is an activity or art form they would pursue even if they knew they would never receive money or recognition in their lifetime.

lifes, sunflowers, and ~~drawing~~ everyday people. Perhaps his most famous picture, *Starry Night*, shows a wild night sky over a French village, with the moon and stars swirling in fiery circles.

Starry Night was painted in southern France, a place of great beauty and ~~the light was wonderful~~ wonderful light. There, in the last three years of his life, Van Gogh created 186 of his greatest works. Always shy and sometimes ~~feeling~~ depressed, he began to suffer from episodes of mental illness. Theo ~~gentle~~ gently but firmly urged him to keep painting. For years, Van Gogh's death in 1890 was considered a suicide by gunshot, but one book claims that the artist was bullied ^and shot^ by local teenagers ~~and they shot him~~. When Theo died soon after, his widow Joanna took the paintings back to Holland and ~~was working~~ worked hard to get recognition for her brother-in-law's genius. Today, the dynamic paintings of Vincent Van Gogh are admired, studied, and ~~receive love~~ loved all over the world.

Starry Night by Vincent Van Gogh

EXPLORING ONLINE

TEACHING TIP
Suggest that students visit one of the websites and describe the experience, using parallel structure at least three times.

www.vangoghmuseum.nl/en

Visit the Van Gogh Museum in the Netherlands and explore. Take notes on your experience.

www.vangoghgallery.com

Find *Wheatfield with Crows*. Do you see any details in the painting that would suggest it was made just before the artist committed suicide?

EXPLORING ONLINE

grammar.ccc.commnet.edu/grammar/consistency.htm

Review consistency with examples, "repairs," and self tests.

grammar.ccc.commnet.edu/grammar/parallelism.htm

Give your writing more style by using parallel words and phrases.

CHAPTER 22

Revising for Sentence Variety

A: Mix Long and Short Sentences

B: Use a Question, a Command, or an Exclamation

C: Vary the Beginnings of Sentences

D: Vary Methods of Joining Ideas

E: Avoid Misplaced and Confusing Modifiers

F: Review and Practice

TEACHING TIP

Tell students that mixing different sentence types and lengths has two important effects:

1. Sentence variety adds sophistication to one's writing.

2. Sentence variety makes writing more interesting to read, thus engaging readers and improving their comprehension.

Good writers pay attention to **sentence variety**. They notice how sentences work together within a paragraph, and they seek a mix of different sentence lengths and types. Experienced writers have a variety of sentence patterns from which to choose. They try not to overuse one pattern.

This chapter will present several techniques for varying your sentences and paragraphs. Some of them you may already know and use, perhaps unconsciously. The purpose of this chapter is to make you more conscious of the **choices** available to you as a writer.

Remember, you achieve sentence variety by practicing, by systematically **revising** your papers, and by trying out new types of sentences or combinations of sentences.

A. Mix Long and Short Sentences

One of the basic ways to achieve sentence variety is to use both long and short sentences. Beginning writers tend to overuse short, simple sentences, which quickly become monotonous. Notice the length of the sentences in the following paragraph:

TEACHING TIP
Caution your students not to avoid errors by writing short, childish sentences. This chapter will give them longer, correct options.

(1) There is one positive result of the rising crime rate. (2) This has been the growth of neighborhood crime prevention programs. (3) These programs really work. (4) They teach citizens to patrol their neighborhoods. (5) They teach citizens to work with the police. (6) They have dramatically reduced crime in cities and towns across the country. (7) The idea is catching on.

The sentences in the paragraph above are all nearly the same length, and the effect is choppy and almost childish. Now read this revised version, which contains a variety of sentence lengths:

(1) One cause of the falling crime rate in some cities is the growth of neighborhood crime prevention programs. (2) These programs really work. (3) By patrolling their neighborhoods and working with the police, citizens have shown that they can dramatically reduce crime. (4) The idea is catching on.

LEARNING STYLES TIP
Consider having students use highlighters to color-code sentences in something they've written. Have them use yellow for short sentences and other colors for medium-length and long sentences, so they can *visually* analyze their sentence variety.

This paragraph is more effective because it mixes two short sentences, 2 and 4, and two longer sentences, 1 and 3. Although short sentences can be used effectively anywhere in a paragraph or an essay, they can be especially useful as introductions or conclusions, as in sentence 4. Note the powerful effect of short sentences used between longer ones in the paragraph that follows. Underline the short sentences:

(1) Biting into a tabasco pepper is like aiming a flame-thrower at your parted lips. (2) There might be little reaction at first, but then the burn starts to grow. (3) A few seconds later the chili mush in your mouth reaches critical mass and your palate prepares for liftoff. (4) The message spreads. (5) The sweat glands open, your eyes stream, your nose runs, your stomach warms up, your heart accelerates, and your lungs breathe faster. (6) All this is normal. (7) But bite off more than your body can take, and you will be left coughing, sneezing, and spitting. (8) Tears stripe your cheeks, and your mouth belches like a dragon celebrating its return to life. (9) Eater beware!

—Jeremy MacClancy, *Consuming Culture: Why You Eat What You Eat*

PRACTICE 1

TEACHING AND ESL TIP
Have students analyze a partner's essay for overused connectors—another way to vary writing.

Revise and rewrite the following paragraph in a variety of sentence lengths. Recombine sentences in any way you wish. You may add connecting words or drop words, but do not alter the meaning of the paragraph. Answers will vary.

The park is alive with motion today. Joggers pound up and down the boardwalk. Old folks watch them from the benches. Couples row boats across the lake. The boats are green and wooden. Two teenagers hurl a Frisbee back and forth. They yell and leap. A shaggy white dog dashes in from nowhere. He snatches the red disk in his mouth. He bounds away. The teenagers run after him.

TEACHING TIP
Have students apply what they have learned by looking for short, choppy sentences in a paragraph they have written.

The park is alive with motion today. Joggers pound up and down on the boardwalk, and old folks watch them from the benches. Couples row green wooden boats across the lake. On the nearby grass, two teenagers hurl a Frisbee back and forth, yelling and leaping. Suddenly, a shaggy white dog dashes in from nowhere, snatches the red disk in his mouth, and bounds away. The teenagers run after him.

B. Use a Question, a Command, or an Exclamation

The most commonly used sentence is the **declarative sentence**, which is a statement. However, an occasional carefully placed **question**, **command**, or **exclamation** is an effective way to achieve sentence variety.

The Question

Can exercise make us smarter? Amazingly, the answer is yes, but only if we do certain kinds of exercise. After a decade of study, sports scientists report that students who ran or walked briskly for thirty minutes scored better on memory tests. Other studies confirm these results. Aerobic exercises like running, swimming, and brisk walking cause a dramatic increase in blood flow that stimulates the growth of new brain cells. Thus, a heart-pounding "cardio" workout three to five times a week actually boosts intelligence.

This paragraph begins with a question. The writer does not really expect the reader to answer it. Rather, it is a **rhetorical question**, one that will be answered by the writer in the course of the paragraph. A rhetorical question used as a topic sentence can provide a colorful change from the usual declarative sentences: *How healthy is the American diet? What is courage? Is cheating worth the risks?*

The Command and the Exclamation

(1) Try to imagine using failure as a description of an animal's behavior. (2) Consider a dog barking for fifteen minutes, and someone saying, "He really isn't very good at barking, I'd give him a C." (3) How absurd! (4) It is impossible for an animal to fail because there is no provision for evaluating natural behavior. (5) Spiders construct webs, not successful or unsuccessful webs. (6) Cats hunt mice; if they aren't successful in one attempt, they simply go after another. (7) They don't lie there and whine, complaining about the one that got away, or have a nervous breakdown because they failed. (8) Natural behavior simply is! (9) So apply the same logic to your own behavior and rid yourself of the fear of failure.

—Dr. Wayne W. Dyer, *Your Erroneous Zones*

TEACHING TIP
Stress to students that exclamation points are rarely used in academic and professional writing.

The previous paragraph begins and ends with **commands**, or **imperative sentences**. Sentences 1, 2, and 9 address the reader directly and have as their implied subject *you*. They tell the reader to do something: *(You) try to imagine . . . , (you) consider . . . , (you) apply. . . .* Commands are most frequently used in giving directions,* but they can be used occasionally, as in the previous paragraph, for sentence variety.

Sentences 3 and 8 in the Dyer paragraph are **exclamations**, sentences that express strong emotion and end with an exclamation point. These should be used very sparingly. In fact, some writers avoid them altogether, striving for words that convey strong emotion instead.

Be careful with the question, the command, and the exclamation in your writing. Try them out, but use them—especially the exclamation—sparingly.

WRITING ASSIGNMENT

Write a paragraph that begins with a rhetorical question. Choose one of the questions below or compose your own. Be sure that the body of the paragraph really does answer the question.

1. How has college (or anything else) changed me?
2. Do children see too much violence on television?
3. Is marriage worth the risks?

C. Vary the Beginnings of Sentences

TEACHING TIP
Remind students that varying the beginnings of sentences, like varying types of sentences, is key. They should avoid overusing one type or technique.

Begin with an Adverb

Since the first word of many sentences is the subject, one way to achieve sentence variety is by occasionally starting a sentence with a word or words other than the subject.

For instance, you can begin with an **adverb**:†

1. He *laboriously* dragged the large crate up the stairs.
2. *Laboriously*, he dragged the large crate up the stairs.
3. The contents of the beaker *suddenly* began to foam.
4. *Suddenly*, the contents of the beaker began to foam.

- In sentences 2 and 4, the adverbs *laboriously* and *suddenly* are shifted to the first position. Notice the difference in rhythm that this creates, as well as the slight change in meaning: Sentence 2 emphasizes *how* he dragged the crate—*laboriously*; sentence 4 emphasizes the *suddenness* of what happened.
- A comma usually follows an adverb that introduces a sentence; however, adverbs of time—*often, now, always*—do not always require a comma. As a general rule, use a comma if you want the reader to pause briefly.

*For more work on giving directions, see Chapter 8, "Process."

†For more work on adverbs, see Chapter 35, "Adjectives and Adverbs."

PRACTICE 2

Rewrite the following sentences by shifting the adverbs to the beginning. Punctuate correctly.

EXAMPLE He skillfully prepared the engine for the race.

Skillfully, he prepared the engine for the race.

1. We carefully applied varnish on the antique desk.

   Carefully, we applied varnish on the antique desk.

2. Drivers frequently ignore the warning signs.

   Frequently, drivers ignore the warning signs.

3. Jane eagerly accepted the job offer.

   Eagerly, Jane accepted the job offer.

4. We immediately reported the accident to the manager.

   Immediately, we reported the accident to the manager.

5. The mayor swiftly demanded their resignations.

   Swiftly, the mayor demanded their resignations.

PRACTICE 3

Begin each of the following sentences with an appropriate adverb. Punctuate correctly. Answers may vary.

1. Cautiously, the detective approached the ticking suitcase.
2. Enthusiastically, Roger Federer powered a forehand past his opponent.
3. Gleefully, she received her check for $25,000 from the state lottery.
4. Reluctantly, he left the beach.
5. Slowly, the submarine sank out of sight.

PRACTICE 4

Write three sentences of your own that begin with adverbs. Use different adverbs from those in Practices 2 and 3; if you wish, use *graciously, furiously, sometimes.* Punctuate correctly. Sample answers:

1. Graciously, Rosa offered us use of her vacation home.
2. Furiously, she slammed the door.
3. Sometimes I go for long walks on the beach.

ESL TIP

English prepositions are particularly confusing for ESL students. If they need additional help and exercises, refer them to the appendix at the end of the book, "Additional Help and Practice for ESL/ELL Students."

Begin with a Prepositional Phrase

A **prepositional phrase** is a group of words containing a **preposition** and its **object** (a noun or pronoun). *To you*, *in the evening*, and *under the old bridge* are prepositional phrases.*

Preposition	Object
to	you
in	the evening
under	the old bridge

Here is a partial list of prepositions:

Common Prepositions			
about	beneath	into	throughout
above	beside	near	to
across	between	of	toward
against	by	on	under
among	except	onto	up
at	for	out	upon
behind	from	over	with
below	in	through	without

For variety in your writing, begin an occasional sentence with a prepositional phrase:

5. Charles left the room *without a word.*
6. *Without a word*, Charles left the room.
7. A fat yellow cat lay sleeping *on the narrow sill.*
8. *On the narrow sill,* a fat yellow cat lay sleeping.

TEACHING TIP

Does word order affect meaning? Ask students whether placing an adverb or prepositional phrase first instead of last in a sentence changes the emphasis. (Words in first position often receive the greatest emphasis.)

- In sentences 6 and 8, the prepositional phrases have been shifted to the beginning. Note the slight shift in emphasis that results. Sentence 6 stresses that Charles left the room *without a word*, and 8 stresses the location of the cat, *on the narrow sill.*
- Prepositional phrases that begin sentences are usually followed by commas. However, short prepositional phrases need not be.

Prepositional phrases are not always movable; rely on the meaning of the sentence to determine whether they are movable:

9. The dress *in the picture* is the one I want.
10. Joelle bought a bottle *of white wine for dinner*.

*For work on spotting prepositional phrases, see Chapter 34, "Prepositions."

- *In the picture* in sentence 9 is a part of the subject and cannot be moved. *In the picture the dress is the one I want* makes no sense.
- Sentence 10 has two prepositional phrases. Which one *cannot* be moved to the beginning of the sentence? Why?

  "Of white wine" cannot be moved because it describes the word *bottle* and should therefore follow it.

PRACTICE 5

Underline the prepositional phrases in each sentence. Some sentences contain more than one prepositional phrase. Rewrite each sentence by shifting a prepositional phrase to the beginning. Punctuate correctly.

EXAMPLE A large owl with gray feathers watched us from the oak tree.

From the oak tree, a large owl with gray feathers watched us.

1. The coffee maker turned itself on at seven o'clock sharp.

   At seven o'clock sharp, the coffee maker turned itself on.

2. A growling Doberman paced behind the chain-link fence.

   Behind the chain-link fence, a growling Doberman paced.

3. A man and a woman held hands under the street lamp.

   Under the street lamp, a man and a woman held hands.

4. They have sold nothing except athletic shoes for years.

   For years, they have sold nothing except athletic shoes.

5. A group of men played checkers and drank iced tea beside the small shop.

   Beside the small shop, a group of men played checkers and drank iced tea.

PRACTICE 6

TEACHING TIP
Have students examine a piece of their own writing for adverbs or prepositional phrases that could be shifted to the beginnings of sentences.

Begin each of the following sentences with a different prepositional phrase. Refer to the list and be creative. Punctuate correctly. Answers will vary.

1. During the night, the blizzard dumped sixteen inches of snow on the city.
2. At the top of the hill, stranded skiers signaled for help.
3. Before the exam, the teachers reminded everyone to relax.
4. Below sea level, the houses were vulnerable to flooding.
5. Under the freeway, bikers took shelter during the rainstorm.

PRACTICE 7

Write three sentences of your own that begin with prepositional phrases. Use these phrases if you wish: *in the dentist's office, under that old dock, behind his friendly smile.* Punctuate correctly. Answers will vary.

1. In the dentist's office, the patients waited nervously.
2. Under that old dock, a large snapping turtle makes its home.
3. Behind his friendly smile, he is a dishonest salesman.

D. Vary Methods of Joining Ideas*

TEACHING TIP
Sentence-combining exercises like these expose students to variant structures and underscore the choices that good writers make as they write. Tell your students that the combining techniques in this section will add style and conciseness to their writing.

Join Ideas with a Compound Predicate

A sentence with a **compound predicate** contains more than one verb, but the subject is *not* repeated before the second verb. Such a sentence is really composed of two simple sentences with the same subject:

1. The nurse entered.
2. The nurse quickly closed the door.
3. The nurse *entered* and quickly *closed* the door.

- *The nurse* is the subject of sentence 1, and *entered* is the verb; *the nurse* is also the subject of sentence 2, and *closed* is the verb.
- When these sentences are combined with a compound predicate in sentence 3, *the nurse* is the subject of both *entered* and *closed* but is not repeated before the second verb.
- Because the subject is not repeated before the second verb, the sentence does not contain two independent clauses. Therefore, no comma is necessary when the conjunctions *and, but, or,* and *yet* join the verbs in a compound predicate.

A compound predicate is useful in combining short, choppy sentences:

4. He serves elaborate meals.
5. He never uses a recipe.
6. He *serves elaborate meals* yet *never uses a recipe.*

7. Aviators rarely get nosebleeds.
8. They often suffer from backaches.
9. *Aviators rarely get nosebleeds* but *often suffer from backaches.*

- Sentences 4 and 5 are joined by *yet*; no comma precedes *yet*.
- Sentences 7 and 8 are joined by *but*; no comma precedes *but*.

---

*For work on joining ideas with coordination and subordination, see Chapter 27, "Coordination and Subordination."

PRACTICE 8

Combine each pair of short sentences into one sentence with a compound predicate. Use *and*, *but*, *or*, and *yet*. Punctuate correctly.

Answers will vary.

ESL TIP

ESL students may overuse *and*. Illustrate the appropriate use of this connector.

EXAMPLE Toby smeared peanut butter on a thick slice of white bread. He devoured the treat in thirty seconds.

Toby smeared peanut butter on a thick slice of white bread and devoured the treat in thirty seconds.

1. Americans eat more than 800 million pounds of peanut butter. They spend more than $1 billion on the product each year.

   Americans eat more than 800 million pounds of peanut butter and spend more than $1 billion on the product each year.

2. Peanut butter was first concocted in the 1890s. It did not become the food we know for thirty years.

   Peanut butter was first concocted in the 1890s but did not become the food we know for thirty years.

3. George Washington Carver did not discover peanut butter. He published many recipes for pastes much like it.

   George Washington Carver did not discover peanut butter yet published many recipes for pastes much like it.

4. The average American becomes a peanut butter lover in childhood. He or she loses enthusiasm for it later on.

   The average American becomes a peanut butter lover in childhood but loses enthusiasm for it later on.

5. Older adults regain their passion for peanut butter. They consume great quantities of the delicious stuff.

   Older adults regain their passion for peanut butter and consume great quantities of the delicious stuff.

PRACTICE 9

Complete the following compound predicates. Do *not* repeat the subjects.

Answers will vary.

1. Sharon offered to produce the film and agreed to hire Taylor to direct.

2. The children rushed to the buffet table but refused to take any of the vegetables.

3. Jack will drive us to the airport or call us a cab.

4. The quarterback stumbled yet managed to throw a winning pass.

5. The governor toured the accident site and promised to provide help for the victims.

PRACTICE 10

Write three sentences with compound predicates. Be careful to punctuate correctly. Sample answers:

1. Many people like to cook but do not like to clean up.
2. We could see a movie or go out to dinner.
3. Renée can drive a car but has never parallel parked.

Join Ideas with an *-ing* Modifier

An excellent way to achieve sentence variety is by occasionally combining two sentences with an ***-ing* modifier**.

10. He peered through the microscope.
11. He discovered a squiggly creature.
12. *Peering through the microscope,* he discovered a squiggly creature.

- Sentence 10 has been converted to an *-ing* modifier by changing the verb *peered* to *peering* and dropping the subject *he*. *Peering through the microscope* now introduces the main clause, *he discovered a squiggly creature*.
- A comma sets off the *-ing* modifier from the word it refers to, *he*. To avoid confusion, the word referred to must appear in the immediately following clause.

TEACHING TIP
Misplaced and dangling modifiers are discussed more thoroughly in Part E of this chapter.

An *-ing* modifier indicates that two actions are occurring at the same time. The main idea of the sentence should be contained in the main clause, not in the *-ing* modifier. In the preceding example, the discovery of the creature is the main idea, not the fact that someone peered through a microscope.

Be careful; misplaced *-ing* modifiers can result in confusing sentences: *He discovered a squiggly creature peering through the microscope.* (Was the creature looking through the microscope?)*

Convert sentence 13 into an *-ing* modifier and write it in the blank:

*For more work on avoiding confusing modifiers, see Part E of this chapter.

13. We drove down Tompkins Road.
14. We were surprised by the number of "for sale" signs.
15. Driving down Tompkins Road, we were surprised by the number of "for sale" signs.

- The new *-ing* modifier is followed directly by the word to which it refers, *we*.

PRACTICE 11

Combine the following pairs of sentences by converting the first sentence into an *-ing* modifier. Make sure the subject of the main clause directly follows the *-ing* modifier. Punctuate correctly.

EXAMPLE Jim searched for his needle-nose pliers.
He completely emptied the tool chest.

Searching for his needle-nose pliers, Jim completely emptied the tool chest.

1. She installed the air conditioner.
She saved herself $50 in labor.

Installing the air conditioner, she saved herself $50 in labor.

2. The surgeons raced against time.
The surgeons performed a liver transplant on the child.

Racing against time, the surgeons performed a liver transplant on the child.

3. They conducted a survey of Jackson Heights residents.
They found that most opposed construction of the airport.

Conducting a survey of Jackson Heights residents, they found that most opposed construction of the airport.

4. Three flares spiraled upward from the little boat.
They exploded against the night sky.

Spiraling upward from the little boat, three flares exploded against the night sky.

5. Virgil danced in the Pennsylvania Ballet.
Virgil learned discipline and self-control.

Dancing in the Pennsylvania Ballet, Virgil learned discipline and self-control.

6. The hen squawked loudly.
The hen fluttered out of our path.

Squawking loudly, the hen fluttered out of our path.

7. The engineer made a routine check of the blueprints.
He discovered a flaw in the design.

Making a routine check of the blueprints, the engineer discovered a flaw in the design.

8. Dr. Salazar opened commencement exercises with a humorous story.
He put everyone at ease.

Opening commencement exercises with a humorous story, Dr. Salazar put everyone at ease.

PRACTICE 12

Add either an introductory *-ing* modifier *or* a main clause to each sentence. Make sure that each *-ing* modifier refers clearly to the subject of the main clause. Answers will vary.

EXAMPLE *Reading a book a week*, Jeff increased his vocabulary.

Exercising every day, *I became stronger*.

1. Finally finishing her report, she felt a sense of accomplishment.
2. Growing up in Hollywood, he was not dazzled by movie stars.
3. Talking over their differences at last, the father and son were reconciled.
4. Interviewing his relatives, Jason collected many family stories.
5. Moving slowly on its long chain, the wrecking ball swung through the air and smashed into the brick wall.

PRACTICE 13

Write three sentences of your own that begin with *-ing* modifiers. Make sure that the subject of the sentence follows the modifier, and be careful of the punctuation. Answers will vary.

1. Giving myself a pep talk, I sat down to study Japanese.
2. Practicing with her roommate's manual, Ellen finally learned to use PowerPoint.
3. Rummaging through his drawers, Joe found a stack of unpaid bills.

Join Ideas with a Past Participial Modifier

Some sentences can be joined with a **past participial modifier**. A sentence that contains a *to be* verb and a **past participle*** can be changed into a past participial modifier:

*For more work on past participles, see Chapter 31.

ESL TIP
The use of participles as adjectives is often troublesome for ESL students. This concept might have to be reviewed throughout the term.

16. Judith *is trapped* in a dead-end job.
17. Judith decided to enroll at the local community college.
18. *Trapped in a dead-end job,* Judith decided to enroll at the local community college.

- In sentence 18, sentence 16 has been made into a past participial modifier by dropping the helping verb *is* and the subject *Judith.* The past participle *trapped* now introduces the new sentence.
- A comma sets off the past participial modifier from the word it modifies, *Judith.* To avoid confusion, the word referred to must directly follow the modifier.

Be careful; misplaced past participial modifiers can result in confusing sentences: *Packed in dry ice, Steve brought us some ice cream.* (Was Steve packed in dry ice?)*

Sometimes two or more past participles can be used to introduce a sentence:

19. The term paper *was revised* and *rewritten.*
20. It received an A.
21. *Revised and rewritten,* the term paper received an A.

- The past participles *revised* and *rewritten* become a modifier that introduces sentence 21. What word(s) do they refer to?

the term paper

PRACTICE 14

Combine each pair of sentences into one sentence that begins with a past participial modifier. Convert the sentence containing a form of *to be* plus a past participle into a past participial modifier that introduces the new sentence.

EXAMPLE Duffy was surprised by the interruption.
He lost his train of thought.

Surprised by the interruption, Duffy lost his train of thought.

TEACHING TIP
For a review of past participle formation, see Chapter 31.

1. My mother was married at the age of sixteen.
My mother never finished high school.

Married at the age of sixteen, my mother never finished high school.

2. The 2:30 flight was delayed by an electrical storm.
It arrived in Lexington three hours late.

Delayed by an electrical storm, the 2:30 flight arrived in Lexington three hours late.

*For more work on avoiding confusing modifiers, see Part E of this chapter.

3. The old car was waxed and polished.
   It shone in the sun.

   Waxed and polished, the old car shone in the sun.

4. The museum was built by Frank Gehry.
   It has become famous.

   Built by Frank Gehry, the museum has become famous.

5. The Nineteenth Amendment was ratified in 1920.
   It gave women the right to vote.

   Ratified in 1920, the Nineteenth Amendment gave women the right to vote.

6. The manuscript seems impossible to decipher.
   It is written in code.

   Written in code, the manuscript seems impossible to decipher.

7. Dr. Bentley will address the pre-med students.
   He has been recognized for his contributions in the field of immunology.

   Recognized for his contributions in the field of immunology, Dr. Bentley will address the pre-med students.

8. Ms. Witherspoon was exhausted by night classes.
   She declined the chance to work overtime.

   Exhausted by night classes, Ms. Witherspoon declined the chance to work overtime.

PRACTICE 15

Complete each sentence by filling in *either* the past participial modifier *or* the main clause. Remember, the past participial modifier must clearly refer to the subject of the main clause. Answers will vary.

ESL TIP
It is beneficial for ESL students to recognize sentences in which two ideas are joined by participles even if they cannot yet produce them.

EXAMPLE Wrapped in blue paper and tied with string, *the gift arrived* _____.

Chosen to represent the team ___, Phil proudly accepted the trophy.

1. Constructed entirely of lightweight plastic, the lifeboat weighed less than 30 pounds _____.

2. Stuck in traffic outside the airport, we missed our flight ______.

3. Released last summer ______, the movie broke box office records.

4. Decorated with red, white, and blue frosting, the cake was served at our annual Fourth of July party ______.

5. Buried in snow ______, the abandoned cars were hard to locate.

PRACTICE 16

Write three sentences of your own that begin with past participial modifiers. If you wish, use participles from this list:

shocked	dressed	interested	bent
awakened	lost	stuffed	pleased

Make sure that the subject of the sentence clearly follows the modifier.
Sample answers:

1. Awakened by the fire alarm, the hotel guests rushed outside.
2. Interested in a career in tech, Cecilia enrolled in engineering courses.
3. Lost for several hours, the hikers were cold and tired when they were rescued.

Join Ideas with an Appositive

A fine way to add variety to your writing is to combine two choppy sentences with an appositive. An **appositive** is a word or group of words that renames or describes a noun or pronoun:

22. Carlos is the new wrestling champion.
23. He is a native of Argentina.
24. Carlos, *a native of Argentina,* is the new wrestling champion.

- *A native of Argentina* in sentence 24 is an appositive. It renames the noun *Carlos*.
- An appositive must be placed either directly *after* the word it refers to, as in sentence 24, or directly *before* it, as follows:

25. *A native of Argentina,* Carlos is the new wrestling champion.

- Note that an appositive is set off by commas.

Appositives can add versatility to your writing because they can be placed at the beginning, in the middle, or at the end of a sentence. When you join two ideas with an appositive, place the idea you wish to stress in the main clause and make the less important idea the appositive:

26. Naomi wants to become a fashion model.
27. She is the daughter of an actress.
28. *The daughter of an actress,* Naomi wants to become a fashion model.

29. FACT made headlines for the first time only a few years ago.
30. FACT is now a powerful consumer group.
31. FACT, *now a powerful consumer group*, made headlines for the first time only a few years ago.

32. Watch out for Smithers.
33. He is a dangerous man.
34. Watch out for Smithers, *a dangerous man*.

Using an appositive to combine sentences eliminates unimportant words and creates longer, more fact-filled sentences.

PRACTICE 17

TEACHING TIP

As students work on Practice 17, they may try to turn one of the sentences in each pair into a relative clause. If so, review the difference between relative clauses and appositives. A discussion of relative clauses begins later in this section.

Combine the following pairs of sentences by making the *second sentence* an appositive. Punctuate correctly.

These appositives should occur at the *beginning* of the sentences.

EXAMPLE My uncle taught me to use watercolors.
He is a well-known artist.

A well-known artist, my uncle taught me to use watercolors.

1. Dan has saved many lives.
   He is a dedicated firefighter.

   A dedicated firefighter, Dan has saved many lives.

2. Acupuncture is becoming popular in the United States.
   It is an ancient Chinese healing system.

   An ancient Chinese healing system, acupuncture is becoming popular in the United States.

3. The Cromwell Hotel was built in 1806.
   It is an elegant example of Mexican architecture.

   An elegant example of Mexican architecture, the Cromwell Hotel was built in 1806.

These appositives should occur in the *middle* of the sentences. Punctuate correctly.

EXAMPLE His American history course is always popular with students.
It is an introductory survey.

His American history course, an introductory survey, is always popular with students.

4. The Korean ping-pong champion won ten games in a row.
   She is a small and wiry athlete.

   The Korean ping-pong champion, a small and wiry athlete, won ten games in a row.

5. The pituitary is located below the brain.
   It is the body's master gland.

   The pituitary, the body's master gland, is located below the brain.

6. The accused thief demanded to represent herself at trial.
   She is a law school graduate.

   The accused thief, a law school graduate, demanded to represent herself at trial.

These appositives should occur at the *end* of the sentences. Punctuate correctly.

EXAMPLE I hate fried asparagus.
It is a vile dish.

I hate fried asparagus, a vile dish.

7. Jennifer flaunted her new camera.
   It was a Nikon with a telephoto lens.

   Jennifer flaunted her new camera, a Nikon with a telephoto lens.

8. The police located a single witness.
   She was a six-year-old neighbor.

   The police located a single witness, a six-year-old neighbor.

9. We met for pancakes at the Cosmic Cafe.
   It was a greasy diner on the corner of 10th and Vine.

   We met for pancakes at the Cosmic Cafe, a greasy diner at the corner of 10th and Vine.

PRACTICE 18

Write three sentences using appositives. In one sentence, place the appositive at the *beginning*; in one sentence, place the appositive in the *middle*; and in one sentence, place it at the *end*. Sample answers:

1. An avid sailor, my brother-in-law dreams of owning a 30-foot sailboat.
2. We serve gazpacho, a cold soup made of raw vegetables, on hot summer days.
3. The tall woman standing on the dock is Isabel, my mother's neighbor.

ESL TIP

ESL students face formidable challenges with relative clauses. In English and most European languages, the relative clause *follows* the noun being modified, but in several languages (e.g., Japanese, Chinese, and Korean), the relative clause *precedes* the noun being modified.

Join Ideas with a Relative Clause

Relative clauses can add sophistication to your writing. A **relative clause** begins with *who*, *which*, or *that* and describes a noun or pronoun. It can join two simple sentences in a longer, more complex sentence:

35. Jack just won a scholarship from the Arts Council.
36. He makes wire sculpture.
37. Jack, *who makes wire sculpture*, just won a scholarship from the Arts Council.

- In sentence 37, *who makes wire sculpture* is a relative clause, created by replacing the subject *he* of sentence 36 with the relative pronoun *who*.
- *Who* now introduces the subordinate relative clause and connects it to the rest of the sentence. Note that *who* directly follows the word it refers to, *Jack*.

The idea that the writer wishes to stress is placed in the main clause, and the subordinate idea is placed in the relative clause. Study the combinations in sentences 38 through 40 and 41 through 43.

TEACHING TIP

Students will need to memorize that the pronoun *that* is not used with a comma and the pronoun *which* is.

38. Carrots grow in cool climates.
39. They are high in vitamin A.
40. Carrots, *which* are high in vitamin A, grow in cool climates.

41. He finally submitted the term paper.
42. It was due six months ago.
43. He finally submitted the term paper *that* was due six months ago.

LEARNING STYLES TIP

For ESL students and *visual learners*, color coding can help show how relative clauses can be embedded in the main sentence or independent clause.

- In sentence 40, *which are high in vitamin A* is a relative clause, created by replacing *they* with *which*. Which word in sentence 40 does *which* refer to?

  carrots

- What is the relative clause in sentence 43?

  that was due six months ago

- Which word does *that* refer to?

  term paper

TEACHING TIP

A caution for students: improper punctuation of relative pronoun clauses can create fragments, and wrong placement can create dangling or misplaced modifiers.

ESL TIP

Spanish does not always distinguish between personal (*who*) and impersonal (*which, that*) pronouns. Furthermore, a relative pronoun cannot be omitted in Spanish, as it has been in the sentence *The girls we saw looked so happy.*

Punctuating relative clauses can be tricky; therefore, you will have to be careful:*

44. Claude, *who grew up in Haiti*, speaks Creole.

- *Who grew up in Haiti* is set off by commas because it adds information about Claude that is not essential to the meaning of the sentence. In other words, the sentence would make sense without it: *Claude speaks Creole.*
- *Who grew up in Haiti* is called a **nonrestrictive clause**. It does not restrict or provide vital information about the word it modifies.

45. People *who crackle paper in theaters* annoy me.

- *Who crackle paper in theaters* is not set off by commas because it is vital to the meaning of the sentence. Without it, the sentence would read, *People annoy me*; yet the point of the sentence is that people *who crackle paper in theaters* annoy me, not all people.
- *Who crackle paper in theaters* is called a **restrictive clause** because it restricts the meaning of the word it refers to, *people.*

Note that *which* usually begins a nonrestrictive clause and *that* usually begins a restrictive clause.

PRACTICE 19

Combine each pair of sentences by changing the second sentence into a relative clause introduced by *who*, *which*, or *that*. Remember, *who* refers to persons, *that* refers to persons or things, and *which* refers to things.

These sentences require *nonrestrictive relative clauses*. Punctuate correctly.

EXAMPLE My cousin will spend the summer hiking in the Rockies.
She lives in Indiana.

My cousin, who lives in Indiana, will spend the summer hiking in the Rockies.

1. Scrabble has greatly increased my vocabulary.
It is my favorite game.

Scrabble, which is my favorite game, has greatly increased my vocabulary.

2. Contestants on game shows often make fools of themselves.
They may travel thousands of miles to play.

Contestants on game shows, who may travel thousands of miles to play, often make fools of themselves.

*For more practice in punctuating relative clauses, see Chapter 37, "The Comma," Part D.

3. Arabic is a difficult language to learn.
   It has a complicated verb system.

   Arabic, which has a complicated verb system, is a difficult language to learn.

The next sentences require *restrictive relative clauses*. Punctuate correctly.

EXAMPLE He described a state of mind.
I have experienced it.

He described a state of mind that I have experienced.

4. The house is for sale.
   I was born in it.

   The house that I was born in is for sale.

5. My boss likes reports.
   They are clear and to the point.

   My boss likes reports that are clear and to the point.

6. People know how intelligent birds are.
   They have owned a bird.

   People who have owned a bird know how intelligent birds are.

PRACTICE 20

Combine each pair of sentences by changing one into a relative clause introduced by *who*, *which*, or *that*. Remember, *who* refers to persons, *that* refers to persons or things, and *which* refers to things.

Be careful of the punctuation. (Hint: *Which* clauses are usually set off by commas and *that* clauses are usually not.)

1. The novel is now a best seller.
   It was first published in 1912.

   The novel, which was first published in 1912, is now a best seller.

2. Exercise boosts my energy, sharpens my concentration, and keeps my weight down. I used to hate it.

   Exercise, which I used to hate, boosts my energy, sharpens my concentration, and keeps my weight down.

3. We waited for the plane.
It was ninety minutes late.

We waited for the plane that was ninety minutes late.

4. The children were hiking when the thunderstorm hit.
They found shelter in a cave.

The children, who were hiking when the thunderstorm hit, found shelter in a cave.

5. Edgar Allan Poe became one of America's favorite writers.
He attended West Point for one year.

Edgar Allan Poe, who attended West Point for one year, became one of America's favorite writers.

E. Avoid Misplaced and Confusing Modifiers

ESL TIP
ESL learners may be more likely to misplace phrases and clauses when they think in their native language and then try to translate a thought into English. Urge them to think through their sentences in English to avoid errors of this kind.

As you practice varying your sentences, be sure that your modifiers say what you mean. Revise your work to avoid **misplaced**, **confusing**, or **dangling modifiers**.

1. Perching on a scarecrow in the cornfield, the farmer saw a large crow.

- Probably the writer did not mean that the farmer was perching on a scarecrow. Who or what, was *perching on a scarecrow in the cornfield*?
- *Perching* refers to the *crow,* but the order of the sentence does not show this. This misplaced modifier can be corrected by turning the ideas around:

The farmer saw a large crow perching on a scarecrow in the cornfield.

Do these sentences say what they mean? Are the modifiers misplaced or correct?

2. Covered with whipped cream, Tyrone carried a chocolate cake.
3. I sold the tin soldiers to an antique dealer that I found in the basement.
4. A homeless teenager, the nun helped the girl find a place to live.

- In sentence 2, does the past participial modifier *covered with whipped cream* refer to Tyrone or the cake? Rewrite the sentence so that the modifier is placed correctly:

Tyrone carried a chocolate cake covered with whipped cream.

- In sentence 3, who or what does the relative clause *that I found in the basement* refer to? Rewrite the sentence so that the modifier is placed correctly:

  I sold the tin soldiers that I found in the basement to an antique dealer.

- In sentence 4, the misplaced appositive totally changes the meaning of the sentence. What did this writer mean to say?

  The nun helped the girl, a homeless teenager, find a place to live.

TEACHING TIP
In addition to creating misplaced or dangling modifiers with *-ing* phrases, students are also likely to create fragments by punctuating these phrases as independent sentences.

Sometimes a modifier is confusing because it does not refer to anything in the sentence. This is called a **dangling modifier** and must be corrected by rewriting.

5. Drilling for oil in Alaska, acres of wilderness were destroyed.
6. Tired and proud, the website was completed at midnight.

- In sentence 5, who or what was *drilling for oil*? The sentence doesn't tell us.
- *Drilling for oil* is a dangling modifier. It can be corrected only by rewording the sentence:

7. Drilling for oil in Alaska, the company destroyed acres of wilderness.

- In sentence 6, *tired and proud* is a dangling modifier. Surely the website isn't tired and proud, so who is? Rewrite the sentence to say what the writer probably intended.

  Tired and proud, we completed the website at midnight.

PRACTICE 21

Correct any confusing, misplaced, or dangling modifiers. Rearrange words or rewrite as necessary.

TEACHING TIP
Misplaced and confusing modifiers may be a new notion for many students, and learning to fix them will add clarity to their writing. The unintentional humor in Practice 21 makes it an excellent one to do with the full class.

1. Plump sausages, the dinner guests looked forward to the main course.

   The dinner guests looked forward to the main course, plump sausages.

2. Soaring over the treetops in a hot air balloon, the view was spectacular.

   Soaring over the treetops in a hot air balloon, they enjoyed the spectacular view.

3. Powered by hydrogen, the engineers designed a new kind of car.

   The engineers designed a new kind of car, powered by hydrogen.

ESL TIP
Pairing an ESL student with a native-English student may help your nonnative students complete Practice 21.

4. The tourists asked for British attorneys, who did not know anything about English law.

   The tourists, who did not know anything about English law, asked for British attorneys.

5. Revised to highlight his computer expertise, Marcelo was proud of his new résumé.

   Marcelo was proud of his new résumé, revised to highlight his computer expertise.

6. Jim, who loved to lick car windows, drove his dog to the vet.

   Jim drove his dog, who loved to lick car windows, to the vet.

7. Clanking inside the dryer, Carla heard the lost keys.

   Carla heard the lost keys clanking inside the dryer.

8. The manager who was caught shoplifting wrestled the man to the floor until the police arrived.

   The manager wrestled the man who was caught shoplifting to the floor until the police arrived.

F. Review and Practice

TEACHING TIP
You might suggest that students bookmark or copy this chart and keep it handy as they write. This will remind them to try new techniques.

Before practicing some of the techniques of sentence variety discussed in this chapter, review them briefly:

1. Mix long and short sentences.
2. Add an occasional question, command, or exclamation.
3. Begin with an adverb: *Unfortunately*, the outfielder dropped the fly ball.
4. Begin with a prepositional phrase: *With great style*, the pitcher delivered a curve.
5. Join ideas with a compound predicate: The fans *roared and banged* their seats.
6. Join ideas with an *-ing* modifier: *Diving chin-first onto the grass*, Beltran caught the ball.
7. Join ideas with a past participial modifier: *Frustrated by the call*, the batter kicked dirt onto home plate.
8. Join ideas with an appositive: Beer, *the cause of much rowdiness*, should not be sold at games.
9. Join ideas with a relative clause: Box seats, *which are hard to get for important games*, are frequently bought up by corporations.

TEACHING TIP
Consider having students exchange papers with a partner and mark short sentences that could be combined. Like many revising issues, lack of sentence variety is often easier to spot in others' writing at first.

Of course, the secret of achieving sentence variety is practice. Choose one, two, or three of these techniques to focus on and try them out in your writing. Revise your paragraphs and essays with an eye to sentence variety.

PRACTICE 22

Revise and then rewrite this essay, aiming for sentence variety. Vary the length and pattern of the sentences. Vary the beginnings of some sentences. Join two sentences in any way you wish, adding appropriate connecting words or dropping unnecessary words. Punctuate correctly. Answers will vary.

TEACHING TIP

Practice 22 works well as a group exercise. Ask groups to work on one paragraph each. Then have someone read aloud the "before" and "after" versions so the class can hear how much smoother the revision sounds.

CLEAN AIR CRUSADER

At age seventeen, Erica Fernandez became an unlikely environmental hero. She had grown up in rural Mexico. In Mexico she took blue skies and clean water for granted. She was ten. The family emigrated to Oxnard, California. Erica was shocked by the terrible quality of her new environment. Thousands of cars, visible smog, and stifling air were daily realities. Worse, Erica's father suffered from respiratory problems. His respiratory problems grew dramatically worse. So did her own asthma.

Erica was a teenager. She heard about a proposed natural gas pipeline just off the coast. The pipeline would further pollute the air. It would release carbon dioxide. This was more carbon dioxide every year than 48,000 cars. Erica was angry. There was a large public hearing of the California State Lands Commission. Erica walked to the podium. She gave an electrifying speech. She expressed passionate concern for her father's lungs and the health of the community. The proposal failed. Erica Fernandez became a local hero. She was suddenly in demand as an environmental speaker.

The experience taught her that committed people can make a difference. She was accepted at Stanford University. At Stanford, she was named one of the ten outstanding college women in the U.S. She won a Jane Goodall Global Leadership Award. This allowed her to spend a summer in her native Mexico. There she fought the destruction of important forests. Erica Fernandez plans to become an environmental lawyer.

CLEAN AIR CRUSADER

At age seventeen, Erica Fernandez became an unlikely environmental hero. Growing up in rural Mexico, she took blue skies and clean water for granted. When she was ten, the family emigrated to Oxnard, California, and Erica was shocked by the terrible quality of her new environment. Thousands of cars, visible smog, and stifling air were daily realities. Worse, Erica's father suffered from respiratory problems that grew dramatically worse. So did her own asthma.

When Erica was a teenager, she heard about a proposed natural gas pipeline just off the coast. The pipeline would further pollute the air and release more

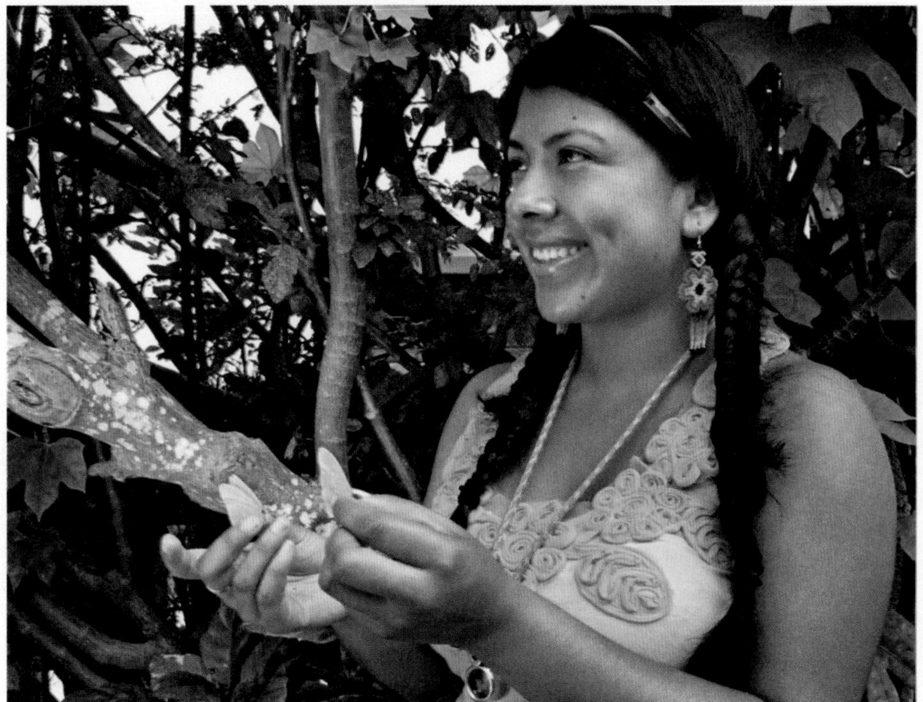

Erica Fernandez, who as a teenager became an environmental hero

carbon dioxide than 48,000 cars. Erica was angry. Attending a large public hearing of the California State Lands Commission, she walked to the podium and gave an electrifying speech. She expressed passionate concern for her father's lungs and the health of the community; as a result, the proposal failed. Erica Fernandez became a local hero, suddenly in demand as an environmental speaker.

The experience taught her that committed people can make a difference. Accepted at Stanford University, she was named one of the ten outstanding college women in the U.S. She also won a Jane Goodall Global Leadership Award, which allowed her to spend a summer in her native Mexico fighting the destruction of important forests. Erica Fernandez plans to become an environmental lawyer.

EXPLORING ONLINE

grammar.ccc.commnet.edu/grammar/combining_skills.htm

Add sophistication to your writing. Review and scroll down for interactive, sentence-combining quizzes.

owl.english.purdue.edu/owl/resource/597/01

Are your modifiers dangling? Don't blush; revise.

CHAPTER 23

Revising for Language Awareness

Although it is important to write grammatically correct English, good writing is more than just correct writing. Good writing has life, excitement, and power. It captures the attention of the reader and compels him or her to read further.

The purpose of this chapter is to increase your awareness of the power of words and your skill at making them work for you. The secret of effective writing is **revision**. Do *not* settle for the first words that come to you, but go back over what you have written, replacing dull or confusing language with exact, concise, fresh, and sometimes figurative language.

A. Exact Language: Avoiding Vagueness

Good writers express their ideas as *exactly* as possible, choosing *specific*, *concrete*, and *vivid* words and phrases. They do not settle for vague terms and confusing generalities.

Read the following sentences. Which sentence in each pair gives the more *exact* information? That is, which uses specific and precise language? Which words in these sentences make them sharper and more vivid?

1. A car went around the corner.
2. A battered blue Mustang careened around the corner.

3. Janet quickly ate the main course.
4. Janet devoured the plate of ribs in two and a half minutes.

5. The president did things that caused problems.
6. The president's military spending increased the budget deficit.

ESL TIP

Stress to ESL students that using bilingual dictionaries may result in vague and inexact word choice.

- Sentences 2, 4, and 6 contain language that is *exact*.
- Sentence 2 is more exact than sentence 1 because *battered blue Mustang* gives more specific information than the general term *car.* The verb *careened* describes precisely how the car went around the corner, fast and recklessly.
- What specific words does sentence 4 substitute for the more general words *ate, main course,* and *quickly* in sentence 3?

devoured; plate of ribs; in two and a half minutes

- Why are these terms more exact than those in sentence 3?

They tell exactly how Janet ate, what she ate, and how quickly she ate it.

- What words in sentence 6 make it clearer and more exact than sentence 5?

military spending; increased the budget deficit

Concrete and detailed writing is usually exciting and makes us want to read on, as does this passage by N. Scott Momaday. Here this Native American writer describes his grandmother at prayer. Read it aloud if possible:

TEACHING TIP

Ask students to bring in examples of writing they consider to be evocative and interesting. As a class, share the passages and discuss how specific, concrete, and vivid language makes readers want to read more.

The last time I saw [my grandmother], she prayed standing by the side of her bed at night, naked to the waist, the light of a kerosene lamp moving upon her dark skin. Her long, black hair, always drawn and braided in the day, lay upon her shoulders and against her breasts like a shawl. I do not speak Kiowa, and I never understood her prayers, but there was something inherently sad in the sound, some merest hesitation upon the syllables of sorrow. She began in a high and descending pitch, exhausting her breath to silence; then again and again—and always the same intensity of effort, of something that is, and is not, like urgency in the human voice. Transported so in the dancing light among the shadows of her room, she seemed beyond the reach of time. But that was illusion; I think I knew then that I should not see her again.

—N. Scott Momaday, *The Way to Rainy Mountain*

Now compare a similar account written in general and inexact language:

The last time I saw my grandmother, she was praying next to her bed. Her long hair was down, covering her. In the day, she always wore it up. I remember that her room had a kerosene lamp. I don't speak Kiowa, so I didn't understand what she was saying, but there was definitely something sad about it. I think I knew somehow that I was not going to see her again.

TEACHING TIP
For an online thesaurus, refer students to **www.thesaurus.com**.

You do not need a large vocabulary to write exactly and well, but you do need to work at finding the right words to fit each sentence. As you revise, cross out vague or dull words and phrases and replace them with more exact terms. When you are tempted to write *I feel good*, ask yourself exactly what *good* means in that sentence: *relaxed*? *proud*? *healthy*? *in love*? When people walk by, do they *flounce, stride, lurch, wiggle,* or *sneak*? When they speak to you, do people *stammer, announce, babble, murmur,* or *coo*? Question yourself as you revise; then choose the right words to fit that particular sentence.

PRACTICE 1

Lively verbs are a great asset to any writer. The following sentences contain four overused general verbs—*to walk, to see, to eat,* and *to be*. In each case, replace the general verb in parentheses with a more exact verb *chosen to fit the context of the sentence*. Use a different verb in every sentence. Consult a dictionary or thesaurus* if you wish. Answers will vary.

EXAMPLES In no particular hurry, we ___*strolled*___ (walked) through the botanical gardens.

ESL TIP
Have an ESL and non-ESL student work together to find synonyms in Practice 1.

1. With guns drawn, three police officers ___crept___ (walked) toward the door of the warehouse.
2. As we stared in fascination, an orange lizard ___crawled___ (walked) up the wall.
3. The four-year-old ___teetered___ (walked) onto the patio in her mother's high-heeled shoes.
4. A furious customer ___strode___ (walked) into the manager's office.
5. Two people who ___witnessed___ (saw) the accident must testify in court.
6. We crouched for hours in the underbrush just to ___spy___ (see) a rare white fox.
7. Three makeshift wooden rafts were ___spotted___ (seen) off the coast this morning.
8. For two years, the zoologist ___studied___ (saw) the behavior of bears in the wild.
9. There was the cat, delicately ___munching___ (eating) my fern!
10. Senator Gorman astounded the guests by loudly ___slurping___ (eating) his soup.
11. All through the movie, she ___crunched___ (ate) hard candies in the back row.
12. Within seconds, Dan had bought two tacos from a street vendor and ___devoured___ (eaten) them both.

TEACHING TIP
You might tie this practice to the value of accurate verbs in the business world. Many career sites now list precise action verbs to help résumé writers describe their skills. See **www.quintcareers.com/action-skills**.

TEACHING TIP
Using student examples, create a handout of sentences containing weak verbs. As a class or with students working in pairs, revise the sentences with more vivid verbs.

*A thesaurus is a book of *synonyms*—words that have the same or similar meanings.

PRACTICE 2

The following sentences contain dull, vague language. Revise them using vivid verbs, specific nouns, and colorful adjectives. As the examples show, you may add and delete words. Answers will vary.

ESL TIP
ESL writers often have trouble with adjective order. Shed light on this confusing subject with the Royal Order of Adjectives chart at **grammar.ccc.commnet.edu/grammar/adjectives.htm**.

EXAMPLES A dog lies down in the shade.

A mangy collie flops down in the shade of a parked car.

My head hurts.

My head throbs.

I have shooting pains in the left side of my head.

1. The shopper was mad.

   The shopper slammed his fist on the counter when he heard that his 50 percent off coupon was no longer valid.

2. I feel good today for several reasons.

   I feel giddy today because it's Saturday, it's springtime, and I'm in love.

TEACHING TIP
Have students share with the class or a small group their answers to Practice 2.

3. A woman in unusual clothes went down the street.

   A six-foot-tall woman in flowing African robes strode regally down the street.

4. The sunlight made the yard look pretty.

   The streaming sunlight painted every corner of the yard in brilliant colors.

5. What the company did bothered the townspeople.

   The company's dumping practices enraged the townspeople.

6. The doctor's waiting room was crowded.

   The pediatrician's waiting room overflowed with whining children and impatient parents.

7. As soon as he gets home from work, he hears the voice of his pet asking for dinner.

   The minute he walks in the door from work, his ears are assailed by Rover's piteous yelps begging for dinner.

8. The noises of construction filled the street.

   A cacophony of jackhammers, diesel engines, and rumbling dump trucks rose from the construction site.

9. When I was sick, you were helpful.

   When I had the flu for a week, you brought me chicken soup every day.

10. This college does things that make the students feel bad.

    The inadequate security in the college's dormitories worries and angers many students.

PRACTICE 3

A word that works effectively in one sentence might not work in another sentence. In searching for the right word, always consider the **context** of the sentence into which the word must fit. Read each of the following sentences for meaning. Then circle the word in parentheses that *most exactly fits* the context of the sentence.

TEACHING AND ESL TIP

Before asking students to complete Practice 3, you might want to review the concept of *context*. Show them examples of sentences that contain words with multiple meanings (e.g., *dressing* and *fast*) in different contexts. Ask students to determine from the context which meaning of the word is intended.

EXAMPLE Machu Picchu, which means "old peak" in the Quechua (words, language, lingo), is known as the "Lost City of the Incas."

1. Ever since the ruins of Machu Picchu were (buried, invented, discovered) in 1911 by Yale archaeologist Hiram Bingham, people all over the world have been fascinated by this mysterious site.
2. The ancient city (perches, hangs, wobbles) high atop a peak in the rugged Andes Mountains of Peru.
3. In the 1400s, using gray Andes granite, the Inca people (arranged, constructed, piled) the palace, temples, baths, and houses of Machu Picchu.
4. The carved stone blocks are so (strong, massive, long) that thousands of men would have been needed to move just one of them into place.
5. The (sophisticated, fluid, bubbly) plumbing and drainage system that brought running water to Machu Picchu still works today.

View of Machu Picchu, Peru

saraporn/Shutterstock.com

ESL TIP

ESL students may benefit from *collocation* study. Choose five to ten target words from Practice 3. Ask students to list words that commonly occur before and after the target words, such as *accidentally fell*.

6. The city served not only as a (hideout, getaway, retreat) and fortress for the nobility but also as an observatory.
7. Many ceremonies took place around the Intihuatana stone, a kind of sundial that (casts, manufactures, emits) no shadow at noon on the two equinoxes, in March and in September.
8. According to legend, when spiritually sensitive people touch their foreheads to the Intihuatana stone, it (magically, accidentally, weirdly) opens their vision to the spirit world.
9. In 1533, Spanish conquistadors (ruthlessly, destructively, properly) destroyed the Inca civilization, but the invaders never found Machu Picchu.
10. Nevertheless, the cloud-capped city was (abandoned, missed, set aside) for 400 years.
11. Its rediscovery (torched, entered, ignited) the imaginations of scientists and adventurers, who still labor to unlock Machu Picchu's secrets.
12. Today many tourists (enjoy, battle, are awed by) altitude sickness just to trek up the mountain and gaze upon this beautiful, well-preserved sanctuary.

PRACTICE 4

The following paragraph begins a description. Using specific and vivid language, revise the paragraph to make it as exciting as possible. Then finish the essay; be careful to avoid vague language. Answers will vary.

TEACHING TIP

Read aloud the best three or four revisions of the paragraph in Practice 4.

The hurricane was really bad for the town. The boardwalk was in disrepair. The street was filled with downed trees. Many businesses popular with tourists were affected by the storm. The windows of the hotels along the shore showed signs of damage. Many of the houses on Atlantic Avenue were destroyed. The beach was covered with broken things.

B. Concise Language: Avoiding Wordiness

TEACHING TIP
Explain to students that many people write a wordy and imprecise first draft. Revising later includes searching for the right words to express one's thoughts.

ESL TIP
Many world dialects of English, such as African and Indian English, value wordy, flowery language. You may need to stress that U.S. English writers prefer conciseness.

Concise writing comes quickly to the point. It avoids **wordiness**—unnecessary and repetitious words that add nothing to the meaning.

Which sentence in each of the following pairs is more *concise*? That is, which does *not* contain unnecessary words?

1. Because of the fact that the watch was inexpensive in price, he bought it.
2. Because the watch was inexpensive, he bought it.

3. In my opinion I think that the financial aid system at Ellensville Junior College is in need of reform.
4. The financial aid system at Ellensville Junior College needs reform.

5. On October 10, in the fall of 2003, we learned the true facts about the Peruvian mummies.
6. On October 10, 2003, we learned the facts about the Peruvian mummies.

- Sentences 2, 4, and 6 are *concise,* whereas sentences 1, 3, and 5 are *wordy.*
- In sentence 1, *because of the fact that* is really a *wordy* way of saying *because. In price* simply repeats information already given by the word *inexpensive.*
- The writer of sentence 3 undercuts the point with the wordy apology of *in my opinion I think.* As a general rule, leave out such qualifiers and simply state the opinion; but if you do use them, use either *in my opinion* or *I think,* not both. Sentence 4 replaces *is in need of* with one direct verb, *needs.*
- *In the fall of* in sentence 5 is *redundant*; it repeats information already given by which word?

  October

- Why is the word *true* also eliminated in sentence 6?

  Facts are always true.

Concise writing avoids wordiness, unnecessary repetition, and padding. Of course, conciseness does not mean writing short, bare sentences, but simply cutting out all deadwood and never using fifteen words when ten will do.

PRACTICE 5

The following sentences are *wordy.* Make them more *concise* by crossing out or replacing unnecessary words or by combining two sentences into one concise sentence. Rewrite each new sentence on the lines beneath, capitalizing and punctuating correctly.

EXAMPLES The U.S. Census uncovers many interesting facts that have a lot of truth to them.

The U.S. Census uncovers many interesting facts.

In the year 1810, Philadelphia was called the cigar capital of the United States. The reason why was because the census reported that the city produced 16 million cigars each year.

In 1810, Philadelphia was called the cigar capital of the United States because the census reported that the city produced 16 million each year.

TEACHING TIP

Students may pad their papers, thinking this satisfies minimum page requirements. Urge them to break the habit and write as concisely as possible. If padding "feels" necessary, either the topic is too narrow for the assignment or they have not yet generated enough ideas and should do more prewriting.

1. The Constitution requires and says that the federal government of the United States must take a national census every ten years.

   The Constitution requires the federal government to take a national census every ten years.

2. At first, the original function of the census was to ensure fair taxation and representation.

   The original function of the census was to ensure fair taxation and representation.

3. Since the first count in 1790, however, the census has been controversial. There are several reasons why the census has been controversial.

   Since the first count in 1790, however, the census has been controversial for several reasons.

4. One reason why is because there are always some people who aren't included.

   One reason is that some people aren't included.

5. The 1990 census, for example, missed almost 5 million people, many of whom were homeless with no place to live.

   The 1990 census, for example, missed almost 5 million people, many of whom were homeless.

6. For the 2000 census, the Census Bureau considered using statistical methods. The statistical methods would have been used instead of the traditional direct head count.

   For the 2000 census, the Census Bureau considered using statistical methods instead of the traditional direct head count.

7. The Bureau would have directly counted about 90 percent of U.S. residents who live in the United States and then estimated the number and characteristics of the remainder of the rest of the people.

   The Bureau would have directly counted about 90 percent of U.S. residents and then estimated the number and characteristics of the remainder.

8. Those who opposed the idea believed that in their opinion statistical methods would have introduced new errors that were mistaken into the count.

   Those who opposed the idea believed that statistical methods would have introduced new errors into the count.

TEACHING TIP
You may wish to review with the class a list of common wordy expressions. For several such lists, see **owl.english.purdue.edu/owl/owlprint/572.**

9. The distribution of $100 billion in money, as well as the balance of power in the House of Representatives, depended on how and in which manner the census was conducted.

   The distribution of $100 billion, as well as the balance of power in the House of Representatives, depended on how the census was conducted.

10. Despite controversy, the U.S. census still continues to serve a beneficial purpose that is for the good of the United States.

    Despite controversy, the census serves a beneficial purpose for the United States.

PRACTICE 6

Rewrite this essay *concisely,* cutting out all unnecessary words. Reword or combine sentences if you wish, but do not alter the meaning. Answers may vary.

DR. ALICE HAMILTON, MEDICAL PIONEER

At the age of forty ~~years old~~, Dr. Alice Hamilton became a pioneer in ~~the field of~~ industrial medicine. In 1910, the governor of Illinois appointed her to investigate rumors that ~~people who were doing the work~~ workers in Chicago's paint factories were dying from lead poisoning. The result of her investigation was the first state law ~~that was passed~~ to protect workers.

The following year, the U.S. Department of Labor hired ~~this woman,~~ Dr. Hamilton~~,~~ to study industrial illness throughout the country ~~of the United States~~. In the next decade, she researched ~~and studied~~ many occupational diseases, including tuberculosis among quarry workers and silicosis—clogged lungs—among sandblasters. To gather information, Dr. Hamilton went to the workplace—deep in mines, quarries, and underwater tunnels. She also spoke to the workers in their homes ~~where they lived~~.

With great zeal, Dr. Hamilton spread her message about poor health conditions on the job. ~~What happened with her reports is that they~~ Her reports led to new safety regulations, workers' compensation insurance, and improved working conditions in many industries. She wrote many popular articles and spoke to groups of interested citizens. In ~~the year of~~ 1919, she became the first woman to ~~hold courses and~~ teach at Harvard University. Her textbook ~~which she wrote~~, *Industrial Poisons in the U.S.*, became the standard book on the subject. By the time she died in 1970—she was 101—she had done much to improve the plight of many working people. ~~The reason why she~~ She is remembered today ~~is~~ because she cared at a time when many others seemed not to care at all.

C. Fresh Language: Avoiding Triteness

Fresh writing uses original and lively words. It avoids **clichés**, those tired and trite expressions that have lost their power from overuse.

Which sentence in each pair that follows contains fewer expressions that you have heard or read many times before?

1. Some people can relate to the hustle and bustle of city life.
2. Some people thrive on the energy and motion of city life.

3. This book is worth its weight in gold to the car owner.
4. This book can save the car owner hundreds of dollars a year in repairs.

- You probably found that sentences 2 and 4 contained fresher language. Which words and phrases in sentences 1 and 3 have you heard or seen before, in conversation, on TV, or in magazines and newspapers? List them:

  the hustle and bustle; worth its weight in gold

Clichés and trite expressions like the following have become so familiar that they have almost no impact on the reader. Avoid them. Say what you mean in your own words:

Cliché: She is pretty as a picture.
Fresh: Her amber eyes and wild red hair mesmerize me.

Or occasionally, play with a cliché and turn it into fresh language:

Cliché: . . . as American as apple pie.
Fresh: . . . as American as a Big Mac.

Cliché: The grass is always greener on the other side of the fence.
Fresh: "The grass is always greener over the septic tank."
—Erma Bombeck

The following is a partial list of trite expressions to avoid. Add to it any others that you overuse in your writing.

TEACHING TIP
Ask students for other examples of overused expressions. Write these on the board and have students think of fresher and more interesting ways to say the same thing.

Trite Expressions and Clichés	
at this point in time	hustle and bustle
awesome	in this day and age
better late than never	last but not least
break the ice	living hand to mouth
cold, cruel world	one in a million
cool, hot	out of this world
cry your eyes out	sad but true
easier said than done	tried and true
free as a bird	under the weather
green with envy	work like a dog

PRACTICE 7

Cross out clichés and trite expressions in the following sentences and replace them with fresh and exact language of your own. Answers may vary.

1. Getting a good job in this ~~cold, cruel~~ [harsh] economy can be ~~easier said than done~~ [challenging].
2. Many Americans are ~~living hand to mouth~~ [struggling financially], and even college graduates may be ~~hitting a brick wall in the job market~~ [having a hard time finding a job].
3. The keys are to ~~keep your chin up and think outside the box~~ [stay positive and be creative], says career coach Bob Martinez.

ESL TIP
Your ESL students may not recognize trite language. Have them partner with native English speakers to complete Practice 7.

4. He offers three useful tips for job seekers who ~~are between a rock and a hard place~~ don't know how to proceed.

TEACHING AND ESL TIP
Urge your students to learn and use new words systematically. Alert them to the challenging vocabulary site at the end of the chapter, or have them Google "free SAT vocabulary."

5. First, don't cling ~~like there's no tomorrow~~ to one limited career goal.
6. If your dream is to become assistant marketing director for the Portland Trail Blazers, consider starting at any sports organization ~~as low man on the totem pole~~ by getting coffee and helping out.
7. Don't ~~throw out the baby with the bathwater by ruling~~ rule out an internship.
8. Next, don't rely only on ~~tried and true~~ reputable job-searching websites.
9. ~~Reach out and touch someone by networking~~ Network in person because having a contact inside the company is often the best way to get hired.
10. ~~Last but not least~~ Finally, at job fairs or interviews, set yourself apart by bringing a writing sample or demonstrating your people skills.

D. Figurative Language: Similes and Metaphors

ESL TIP
Point out that using figurative language may be an accessible tool for improving writing because similes and metaphors exist in most languages.

One way to add sparkle and precision to your writing is to use an occasional simile or metaphor. A **simile** is a comparison of two things using the word *like* or *as*:

"He was *as ugly as* a wart." —Anne Sexton

"The water made a sound *like* kittens lapping." —Marjorie Kinnan Rawlings

A **metaphor** is a similar comparison *without* the word *like* or *as*:

"My soul is a dark forest." —D. H. Lawrence

Love is a virus.

- The power of similes and metaphors comes partly from the surprise of comparing two apparently unlike things. A well-chosen simile or metaphor can convey a lot of information in very few words.
- Comparing a person to a wart, as Sexton does, lets us know quickly just how ugly that person is. And to say that the water sounds *like kittens lapping* describes the sound so precisely that we can almost hear it.

- What do you think D. H. Lawrence means by his metaphor? In what ways is a person's soul like a *dark forest*?

  It is a tangle of emotions containing scary, unexplored areas.

- The statement *love is a virus* tells us something about the writer's attitude toward love. What is it? In what ways is love like a virus?

  The writer thinks that love is contagious; love is a kind of sickness with predictable symptoms.

Similes and metaphors should not be overused; however, once in a while, they can be a delightful addition to a paper that is also exact, concise, and fresh.

PRACTICE 8

The following paragraph describes airplanes. The author uses at least three similes and three metaphors. Underline the similes and circle the metaphors.

The Concordes no longer fly. These planes, the world's fastest airliners, are now displayed in museums like exotic dragonflies. As thin as darts, they once shot across the Atlantic in less than four hours. Their javelin fuselages, however, meant that seating was Volkswagen tight with little room for amenities. A rising tide of maintenance costs made the jets impractical, and they were grounded in 2003. Stressing style over speed, today's luxury planes advertise themselves like leisure resorts featuring bars, showers, and gourmet dining.

PRACTICE 9

Think of several similes to complete each sentence that follows. Be creative! Then circle your favorite simile, the one that you think best completes each sentence. Answers will vary.

EXAMPLE The cafeteria is like an assembly line.
a hurricane.
an action movie.
a courtroom.

TEACHING TIP
This practice is great fun to do in class.

1. Job hunting is like a game of chess.
   rock climbing.
   a plunge into cold water.
   ______.

2. My room looks like yesterday's scrambled eggs.
a shipwreck.
a supernova.
__________.

3. Writing well is like riding down the freeway.
sailing in a stiff wind.
reaching the top of a mountain.
__________.

4. Marriage is like a broken record.
a trip around the world.
completing a puzzle.
__________.

PRACTICE 10

Think of several metaphors to complete each sentence that follows. Then circle the metaphor that you think best completes the sentence. Answers will vary.

EXAMPLE Love is *a blood transfusion* (circled).
a sunrise.
a roller coaster ride.
a magic mirror.

1. The Internet is a bottle of sedatives.
a palace with many rooms.
an undiscovered continent.
__________.

2. Registration is a battlefield.
a snake pit.
a lesson in patience.
__________.

3. My car is a two-eyed monster.
a goldfish bowl.
another child.
__________.

4. Courage is a taut rope ____.
a doorway ____.
a searchlight ____.
____.

WRITING ASSIGNMENTS

1. Good writing can be done on almost any subject if the writer approaches the subject with openness and with "new eyes." Take a piece of fruit or a vegetable—a lemon, a green pepper, a cherry tomato. Examine it as if for the first time. Feel its texture and parts, smell it, weigh it in your palm.

   Now capture your experience of the fruit or vegetable in words. First jot down words and ideas, or freewrite, aiming for the most exact description possible. Don't settle for the first words you think of. Keep writing. Then go back over what you have written, underlining the most exact and powerful writing. Compose a topic sentence and draft a paragraph that conveys your unique experience of the fruit or vegetable.

2. In the paragraph that follows, Rick Bragg describes his home state in such rich, exact detail that it comes to life for the reader. Read his paragraph, underlining or highlighting language that strikes you as *exact* and *fresh*. Can you spot the two similes? Can you find any especially vivid adjectives or unusual verbs?

   My mother and father were born in the most beautiful place on earth, in the foothills of the Appalachians along the Alabama–Georgia line. It was a place where gray mists hid the tops of low, deep-green mountains, where redbone and bluetick hounds flashed through the pines as they chased possums into the sacks of old men in frayed overalls, where old women in bonnets dipped Bruton snuff and hummed "Faded Love and Winter Roses" as they shelled purple hulls, canned peaches and made biscuits too good for this world. It was a place where playing the church piano loud was near as important as playing it right, where fearless young men steered long, black Buicks loaded with yellow whiskey down roads the color of dried blood, where the first frost meant hog killin' time, and the mouthwatering smell of cracklin's would drift for acres from giant, bubbling pots. It was a place where the screams of panthers, like a woman's anguished cry, still haunted the most remote ridges and hollows in the dead of night, where children believed they could choke off the cries of night birds by circling one wrist with a thumb and forefinger and squeezing tight, and where the cotton blew off the wagons and hung like scraps of cloud in the branches of trees.

   —Rick Bragg, *All Over But the Shoutin'*

   Write a paragraph or essay in which you describe a place you know well and perhaps love. As you freewrite or brainstorm, try to capture the most precise and minute details of what you experienced or remember. Now revise your writing, making the language as *exact, concise,* and *fresh* as you can.

EXPLORING ONLINE

grammar.ccc.commnet.edu/grammar/composition/abstract.htm

Practice choosing exact language.

grammar.ccc.commnet.edu/grammar/concise.htm

Practice pruning excess words.

grammar.ccc.commnet.edu/grammar/vocabulary.htm

Build a powerful, college-level vocabulary with these tips, quizzes, and links.

CHAPTER 24

Putting Your Revision Skills to Work

In Units 2 and 3, you learned to **revise** basic paragraphs, and in Unit 4, you learned to revise essays. All revising requires that you rethink and rewrite with such questions as these in mind:

Can a reader understand and follow my ideas?
Is my topic sentence or thesis statement clear?
Does the body of my paragraph or essay fully support the topic or thesis statement?
Does my paragraph or essay have unity? That is, does every sentence relate to the main idea?
Does my paragraph or essay have coherence? That is, does it follow a logical order and guide the reader from point to point?
Does my writing have a logical conclusion, or does it just leave off?

Of course, the more writing techniques you learn, the more options you have as you revise. Unit 5 has moved beyond the basics to matters of style: consistency and parallelism, sentence variety, and exact language. This chapter will guide you again through the revision process, adding questions like the following to your list:

Are my verb tenses and pronouns consistent?
Have I used parallel structure?
Have I varied the length and type of my sentences?
Is my language exact, concise, and fresh?

Many writers first revise and rewrite with questions like these in mind. They do *not* worry about grammar and minor errors at this stage. Then in a separate, final process, they **proofread*** for spelling and grammatical errors.

Here are two sample paragraphs by students, showing the first draft, the revisions made by the student, and the revised draft of each. Each revision has been numbered and explained to give you a clear idea of the thinking process involved.

Writing Sample 1

First Draft

I like to give my best performance. I must relax completely before a show. I often know ahead of time what choreography I will use and what I'll sing, so I can concentrate on relaxing completely. I usually do this by reading, etc. I always know my parts perfectly. Occasionally I look through the curtain to watch the people come in. This can make you feel faint, but I reassure myself and say I know everything will be okay.

Revisions

(1) *In order*
~~I like~~ to give my best performance, I must relax completely before a show.

(2) *and vocals*
I often know ahead of time what choreography I will use, and ~~what I'll sing,~~

(3) *during that long, last hour before curtain,*
(4)
so I can concentrate on relaxing. ~~completely.~~ I usually do this by reading
(5) *an action-packed mystery, but sometimes I joke with the other performers or just walk around backstage.*
(6) (7) *peek*
~~etc.~~ I always know my parts perfectly. Occasionally I ~~look~~ through the curtain to

audience file (8) *me*
watch the ~~people come~~ in. This can make ~~you~~ feel faint, but I reassure myself

(9) *"Vickie," I say, "the minute you're out there singing to the people, everything will be okay."*
~~and say I know everything will be okay.~~

TEACHING TIP

Go over these reasons with students as they examine the changes to this paragraph and to Writing Sample 2. Use these examples as opportunities to review anything they don't fully understand.

Reasons for Revisions

1. Combine two short sentences. (sentence variety)
2. Make *choreography* and *vocals* parallel and omit unnecessary words. (parallelism)
3. Make time order clear: first discuss what I've done during the days before the performance, and then discuss the hour before performance. (time order)
4. Drop *completely*, which repeats the word used in the first sentence. (avoid wordiness)

---

*For practice in proofreading for particular errors, see individual chapters in Units 6 and 7. For practice in proofreading for mixed errors, see Chapter 39, "Putting Your Proofreading Skills to Work."

5. This is important! Drop *etc.*, add more details, and give examples. (add examples)
6. This idea belongs earlier in the paragraph—with what I've done during the days before the performance. (order)
7. Use more specific and interesting language in this sentence. (exact language)
8. Use the first person singular pronouns *I* and *me* consistently throughout the paragraph. (consistent person)
9. Dull—use a direct quotation, the actual words I say to myself. (exact language, sentence variety)

Revised Draft

In order to give my best performance, I must relax completely before a show. I often know ahead of time what choreography and vocals I will use, and I always know my parts perfectly, so during that long, last hour before curtain, I can concentrate on relaxing. I usually do this by reading an action-packed mystery, but sometimes I joke with the other performers or just walk around backstage. Occasionally I peek through the curtain to watch the audience file in. This can make me feel faint, but I reassure myself. "Vickie," I say, "the minute you're out there singing to the people, everything will be okay."

—Victoria DeWindt, Student

Writing Sample 2

First Draft

When I was little, I stuttered. I didn't even know it. Kids at school started teasing me, and I realized. Children can be very cruel. I became withdrawn and stopped talking at school. My grades were poor. My parents decided to put me in speech therapy, which really helped. I got faster and could often speak normally, without repeating any syllables. My speech therapists taught me lessons of compassion and patience. They totally put me on the path I am on today. They not only helped me in childhood, but in my career decision as well. I hope to help other young people.

Revisions

a child, — (2) until some children

(1) When I was ~~little~~ I stuttered. I didn't even know it. ~~Kids~~ at school started

(3) yelling "Suh-Suh-Sarah."

teasing me, ~~and I realized. Children can be very cruel.~~ I became withdrawn and

(4) When realized how poor my grades were, they

stopped talking at school. ~~My grades were poor.~~ My parents decided to put me in

(5) Add new section below*

speech therapy, ~~which really helped.~~ I got faster and could often speak normally,

at all — Early

without repeating any syllables. ~~My speech therapists taught me~~ lessons

from my speech therapists

of compassion and patience. ~~They totally~~ put me on the path I am on today.

* Miss Lindsey and Mister Bob, my speech therapists, taught me to slow down and relax to pronounce words correctly. They taught me exercises and breathing techniques. Even when I struggled to get something right, they would praise and encourage me. Over time,

(6) *My speech therapists* (7) *they inspired me to become a speech-language pathologist.* ~~They~~ not only helped me in childhood, but ~~in my career decision as well~~. I hope to help other young people. (8) *conquer their speaking obstacles because I know that speaking easily will give them the confidence to succeed.*

Reasons for Revisions

1. Add topic sentence that better fits the revised paragraph. (topic sentence)
2. Combine two short sentences. (sentence variety)
3. Add a good example of the children's cruelty. (exact language, avoid wordiness)
4. Combine two sentences and make order clear. (sentence variety, time order)
5. This is important! Tell in detail how these therapists helped me, and name them. (add examples, exact language)
6. *They* now seems to refer to *syllables;* change to *my speech therapists.* (pronoun substitution)
7. Tell what career I'm referring to. (exact language)
8. Be specific. Tell how I want to help young people, so the reader understands my passion. (add examples, exact language, sentence variety)

Revised Draft

Early lessons of compassion and patience from my speech therapists put me on the path I am on today. When I was a child, I stuttered. I didn't even know it until some children at school started teasing me, yelling, "Suh-Suh-Sarah." I became

British singer Ed Sheeran overcame his stutter by learning how to rap. In 2014, Sheeran was nominated for Best New Artist at the Grammy Awards.

JStone/Shutterstock.com

withdrawn and stopped talking at school. When my parents realized how poor my grades were, they decided to put me in speech therapy. Miss Lindsey and Mister Bob, my speech therapists, taught me to slow down and relax to pronounce words correctly. They taught me exercises and breathing techniques. Even when I struggled to get something right, they would praise and encourage me. Over time, I got faster and could often speak normally, without repeating any syllables at all. My speech therapists not only helped me in childhood, but they inspired me to become a speech-language pathologist. I hope to help other young people conquer their speaking obstacles because I know that speaking easily will give them the confidence to succeed.

—Sarah Washington, Student

PRACTICE 1

TEACHING TIP
Consider having students work together in groups on their revisions to this essay. Encourage them to talk through their ideas for improvement.

Because revising, like writing, is a personal process, the best practice is to revise your own paragraphs and essays. Nevertheless, here is a first draft that needs revising.

Revise it *as if you had written it.* Use and build on the good parts, removing unnecessary words, rewriting unclear or awkward sentences, adding details, and perhaps reordering parts. Then, write or type your final draft. Ask yourself these questions:

Are my verb tenses and pronouns consistent?

Have I used parallel structure to highlight parallel ideas?

Have I varied the length and type of my sentences?

Is my language exact, concise, and fresh?

First Draft

TEACHING TIP
Encourage students to double-space their first drafts, allowing space for revisions.

BREAKING THE YO-YO SYNDROME

For years, I was a yo-yo dieter. I bounced from fad diets to eating binges when I ate a lot. This leaves you tired and with depression. Along the way, though, I learned a few things. As a result, I personally will never go on a diet again for the rest of my life.

First of all, diets are unhealthy. Some of the low-carbohydrate diets are high in fat. Accumulating fat through meat, eggs, and the eating of cheese can raise blood levels of cholesterol and led to artery and heart disease. Other diets are too high in protein and can cause kidney ailments, and other things can go wrong with your body, too. Most diets also leave you deficient in essential vitamins and minerals that are necessary to health, such as calcium and iron.

In addition, diets are short-term. I lose about ten pounds. I wind up gaining more weight than I originally lost. I also get sick and tired of the restricted diet. On one diet, I ate cabbage soup for breakfast, lunch, and dinner. You are allowed to eat some fruit on day one, some vegetables on day two, and so on, but mostly you are supposed to eat cabbage soup. After a week, I never want to see a bowl of cabbage soup again. Because the diet was nutritionally unbalanced, I ended up craving bread, meat, and all the other foods I am not supposed to eat. Moreover, in the short term, all one loses is water. You cannot lose body fat unless you reduce regularly and at a steady rate over a long period of time.

The last diet I tried was a fat-free diet. On this diet I actually gained weight while dieting. I am surprised to discover that you can gain weight on a fat-free diet snacking on fat-free cookies, ice cream, and cheese and crackers. I also learn that the body needs fat—in particular, the unsaturated fat in foods like olive oil, nuts, avocados, and salad dressings. If a dieter takes in too little fat, you are constantly hungry. Furthermore, the body thinks it is starving, so it makes every effort to try to conserve fat, which makes it much harder for one to lose weight.

In place of fad diets, I now follow a long-range plan. It is sensible and improved my health. I eat three well-balanced meals, exercise daily, and am meeting regularly with my support group for weight control. I am much happier and don't weigh as much than I used to be.

Revised Draft

BREAKING THE YO-YO SYNDROME

For years, I was a yo-yo dieter, bouncing from fad diets to eating binges that left me tired and depressed. Along the way, though, I learned a few things. As a result, I will never go on a diet again.

First, diets are unhealthy. Some of the low carbohydrate diets are high in fat, and fat from meat, eggs, and cheese can raise blood levels of cholesterol and lead to artery and heart disease. Other diets are too high in protein and can cause kidney ailments and other disorders. Most diets also leave a person deficient in essential vitamins and minerals, such as calcium and iron.

In addition, diets are short-term. I lose about ten pounds; then I wind up gaining more weight than I originally lost. I also get bored on the restricted diet. On one diet, I ate cabbage soup for breakfast, lunch, and dinner. I was allowed to eat some fruit on day one, some vegetables on day two, and so on, but mostly I was supposed to eat cabbage soup. After a week, I never wanted to see a bowl of cabbage soup again. Because the diet was nutritionally unbalanced, I ended up craving bread, meat, and all the other foods I was not supposed to eat. Moreover, in the short term, all you lose is water. You cannot lose body fat unless you reduce steadily over a long period of time.

The last diet I tried was a fat-free diet. I was surprised to discover that you can actually gain weight snacking on fat-free cookies, ice cream, and cheese and crackers. I also learned that the body needs fat—in particular, the unsaturated fat in foods like olive oil, nuts, avocados, and salad dressings. If you take in too little fat, you are constantly hungry. Furthermore, the body thinks it is starving, so it tries to conserve fat, which makes losing weight much harder.

In place of fad diets, I now follow a long-range plan that is sensible and healthful. I eat three well-balanced meals, exercise daily, and meet regularly with my support group for weight control. I am much happier and thinner than I used to be.

EXPLORING ONLINE

owl.english.purdue.edu/owl/resource/561/05

Guidance for the writer who is about to revise

owl.english.purdue.edu/owl/resource/561/01

Guidance for the writer who is about to revise and proofread

writers' WORKSHOP

Examine Something That Isn't What It Appears to Be

Revising is the key to all good writing—taking the time to sit down, reread, and rethink what you have written. In this unit, you have practiced revising for consistent verb tense, consistent person, parallelism, sentence variety, and language awareness.

In your group or class, read this student's essay, aloud if possible. Underline the parts that strike you as especially effective, and put a checkmark by anything that might need revising. Answers will vary.

Behind the Face of Beauty

(1) Beauty is her name. She walks with her head up high, five foot three ~~in height~~, a hundred and ten pounds ~~in weight~~, small waist and round figure ~~figure round in shape~~. Her hair is long with light brown eyes and a "killer smile." She has a caramel complexion that turns bronze ~~in color~~ during the summer.

(2) She has style and wears ~~wore~~ flashy jewelry that will make you stare in amazement. She has a ton of clothing that would make a movie star jealous. She is ~~was~~ very sociable and does ~~did~~ not have any trouble getting people to like her, mainly because of her sense of humor. Everyone enjoys ~~enjoyed~~ being around her, just as she enjoys having everyone around her. Men want to marry her, and women would just about do anything to have her confidence and strength.

(3) Heavenly is what she seems, but she is only disguised as an angel. She does not pay attention to men on foot, meaning, men without cars. Everything and everybody has to be within her control. If she can't dictate to you, she will try to destroy you and do it in a way you won't at first recognize. She'll criticize your brand new shoes so that you will return them. Once you have returned the shoes, you will see her wearing the same pair. Blasphemy is what she will accuse you of if you ever call her envious.

(4) Well into her thirties, the oldest of five, and raised in a broken home with her careless teenaged mother, she ran away and chose a life of so-called freedom. Self-hate is inside her soul, but she covers it up with a smile and a bag full of tricks ~~and trades~~. Using manipulation and deceit is the only way she feels she can get her vengeance.

(5) When I was a girl, I used to watch different sweethearts shower her with gifts. The family adored her. She was my mother's firstborn. Her young friends catered to her. To them, she was

a goddess. I cherished the ground she walked on. I had every intention of being just like her someday. She said she loved her "baby sis," but the minute ~~you~~ I showed signs of confidence, she would make ~~you~~ me cry by saying ~~you were~~ I was not strong.

(6) Now, tears are what I shed for her because she is lost. Until she finds the right path, she will continue to cover up with lavishness and luxury. She will hypnotize both men and women into being under her control. With time, others will learn that she is shallow and, to those who open their hearts to her, even dangerous.

—Tyesha Wiggins, Student

1. How effective is Ms. Wiggins's essay?

   __Y__ Strong thesis statement? __Y__ Good supporting details?

   __Y__ Logical organization? __Y__ Effective conclusion?

2. What do you like best about this essay? What details or sections most command your attention or make you think?
3. Although this student writes about someone she knows, she is also trying to make sense for herself and the reader of her sister's outward beauty and inner ugliness. Do you think she succeeds?
4. How do you think the author of this essay would define beauty? Do you think ideas of beauty are changing?
5. Are all the verb tenses correct, or do you notice any inconsistent tense? Inconsistent tense in paragraph 2
6. Are there any places where short, choppy sentences detract from the excellent content? Yes, paragraph 5
7. Can you spot any error patterns (the same error two or more times) that this student should watch out for? Yes, wordiness in paragraph 1 and inconsistent person in paragraph 5. (See corrections in blue.)

GROUP WORK

In your group, revise Ms. Wiggins' essay as if it were your own. First, decide what problems need attention. Then rewrite those parts, sentence by sentence, aiming for a truly fine paper. Share your revision with the class, explaining why you made the changes you did.

WRITING AND REVISING IDEAS

1. Examine something that isn't what it appears to be or someone whose presentation contrasts with his or her character.
2. Write a definition of the word *beauty* or *ugliness*.

UNIT 6

Reviewing the Basics

CHAPTER 25

Proofreading to Correct Your Personal Error Patterns

A: Identifying and Tracking Your Personal Error Patterns

B: Proofreading Strategies

The important last step in the writing process is proofreading: slowly reading your revised paragraph or essay in order to find and correct any errors in grammar, punctuation, and spelling.

Proofreading your own work before turning it in is vitally important because grammatical and other mistakes not only distract readers, but also give a negative impression of your skills and even intelligence. Many employers won't interview a candidate whose cover letter or résumé contains errors. Yet many new writers avoid proofreading or rush through it so quickly that they set themselves up for failure.

In fact, the more mistakes you tend to make, the more important proofreading is for you. This chapter will give you tools to build your skills as an error detective and writer. Then the rest of this unit and Unit 7 will further develop your proofreading skills, teaching you how to spot and correct many specific errors. In each chapter ahead, you'll get to practice a proofreading strategy that targets a particular mistake.

A. Identifying and Tracking Your Personal Error Patterns

Knowing what errors you tend to make and then proofreading for these errors will boost your success in college and at work.

Learn Your Error Patterns

An **error pattern** is any error you make two, three, or more times. For example, if a teacher has noted that one of your papers has several comma splices or numerous verb errors, those are *error patterns* that you need to work on. The first step in getting rid of these errors is becoming aware of them.

Here are four ways to discover your error patterns:

Papers. Study recently returned papers, making sure you understand the errors that have been marked. Check the Revising and Proofreading Symbols Chart for proofreading symbols your instructor might use, like *frag* for sentence fragment. Count the number of times each mistake appears.

Instructor. Ask your instructor to identify your error patterns. List them. Ask which three are the most serious.

Textbook. As you work through this book, notice chapters or practices where you keep making mistakes or writing incorrect answers. These are your error patterns.

Writing lab. Go to the writing lab with a paper you recently wrote. Ask a tutor to help identify the kinds of errors you make. Ask which three are the most serious.

PRACTICE 1

Consult your instructor, or bring a recent paper to the college writing lab. Get help in identifying your error patterns and start a written list. Ask which three error patterns most harm your written communication and your grade.

Create a Personal Error Patterns Chart

Let's say your instructor marks twelve errors on your English paper, and eight of them are verb agreement mistakes. This means that eight of your errors are really one error repeated eight times! Mastering this one error pattern would certainly improve your grade.

An excellent tool for tracking and beginning to master your errors is an **error chart** or **log**. This tool will show you what to study and what mistakes to watch for in your writing. Here is an example of one student's chart:

Personal Error Patterns Chart

Error Type & Symbol	Specific Error	Correction	Rule or Reminder
Fragment *frag*	The house was saved. Because firefighters quickly doused the flames.	The house was saved because firefighters quickly doused the flames.	Don't punctuate a dependent clause as a complete sentence. (Ch. 28)
Sound-alikes *sp*	The scholarship committee has made it's decision.	The scholarship committee has made its decision.	*It's* = it is *Its* is possessive.
Pronoun agreement *agr*	Everyone brought their best dish to the feast.	Everyone brought his or her best dish to the feast.	*Everyone* is singular (indefinite pronoun) so pronoun must be singular. (Ch. 33, B)

- Each time you receive a marked paper, write every error name or type in column 1 (like *fragment* or *pronoun agreement*). Check the Revising and Proofreading Symbols Chart to understand your instructor's proofreading symbols: for instance, *frag* for fragment.
- In column 2, copy the error as you wrote it.
- In column 3, correct the error. If you have trouble understanding what you did wrong, ask your instructor or search the index of this book for the sections you need.
- In column 4, jot down the rule or ideas for fixing this type of mistake.

When you have filled a page or more, look for *error patterns* that keep coming up. Keep a count of these in the left margin. Any error that appears in paper after paper will need a special plan of attack.

Continue to add errors from future papers, instructor conferences, and tests. As you work in this textbook, add to your chart any grammatical concepts that still confuse you. Whenever you master the correction of an error, cross it off the chart and celebrate your achievement.

PRACTICE 2

Using a recent paper of yours that was graded by an instructor, begin your Personal Error Patterns Chart. You can use the blank chart in this book or create your own chart, adding rows as you need them. Some students design and draw their own charts. Follow this format:

LEARNING STYLES TIP

Visual and all learners benefit from converting their errors into graphic, chart form. Often just seeing that one or two error types dominate is illuminating. Encourage students to personalize and embellish their charts but to include the four categories.

Error Type & Symbol	Specific Error	Correction	Rule or Reminder

B. Proofreading Strategies

Whenever you write, honor your own writing process by setting aside enough time to perform each step, including proofreading. Just as it helps to take a break of hours or days between writing your first draft and revising, taking a break *before you proofread* is beneficial. Go for a walk. Call a friend. You cannot do a good job proofreading when you are tired. You will catch more errors with a rested mind and fresh outlook.

If possible, proofread in a quiet place where you won't be distracted—not at a dance club, not standing in the kitchen preparing dinner with the kids.

Many writers have found that the **proofreading strategies** described below help them see their own writing with a fresh eye. You will learn more strategies in subsequent chapters of this book. Try a number of methods and see which ones work best for you.

Proofreading Strategy 1: Allow enough time to proofread.

Many students don't proofread at all, or they skim their paper for grammatical errors two minutes before class. This just doesn't work. Set aside enough time to proofread slowly and carefully, searching for errors and especially hunting for your personal error patterns.

Proofreading Strategy 2: Work from a paper copy.

People who proofread on computers tend to miss more errors. If you write on a computer, do not proofread on the monitor. Instead, print a copy of your paper, perhaps enlarging the type to 14 point. Switching to a paper copy seems to help the brain see more clearly.

Proofreading Strategy 3: Read your words aloud.

Reading silently makes it easier to skip over errors or mentally fill in missing details. If you read your paper aloud, you will catch more mistakes. It is easier to *hear* than *see* errors like missing and misspelled words, fragments, wordy phrases, and awkward sentences. Listen and follow along on your printed copy, marking errors as you hear them.

TEACHING TIP

Students might wish to have the computer read their work aloud; various programs do this.

a. Read your paper aloud to *yourself.* Be sure to read *exactly* what's on the page, and read with enthusiasm.
b. Ask *a friend* or *writing tutor* to read your paper out loud to you. Tell the reader you just want to hear your words and that you don't want any other suggestions right now.

Proofreading Strategy 4: Read "bottoms up," from the end to the beginning.

One way to fool the brain into taking a fresh look at something you've written is to proofread the last sentence first. Read slowly, word by word. Then read the second-to-last sentence, and so on, all the way back to the first sentence.

Proofreading Strategy 5: Isolate your sentences.

If you write on a computer, spotting errors is often easier if you reformat so that each sentence appears isolated, on its own line. Double-space between sentences. This visual change can help the brain focus clearly on one sentence at a time.

Proofreading Strategy 6: Check for one error at a time.

If you make many mistakes, proofread separately all the way through your paper for each error pattern. Although this process takes time, you will catch many more errors this way and make real progress. You will begin to eliminate some errors altogether as you learn about fixing each error and as you get better at spotting and correcting it. You will learn more recommended proofreading strategies in upcoming chapters.

PRACTICE 3

Grammar CSI. Help solve crimes against English! Working in teams, proofread newspapers, signs, ads, and other printed materials (like campus flyers and publications). When you locate an error in grammar, punctuation, capitalization, or spelling, collect the evidence: write down, photocopy, or use your phone to snap a picture of the offending mistake. Collect five to ten errors and create a presentation—a report, collage, or PowerPoint presentation displaying evidence from your crime scenes.

PRACTICE 4

Print out or make two copies of something you wrote recently for school or work. Ask someone to read the original piece out loud as you listen. On your copy, underline or highlight sentences or places that sound wrong. Also mark any places where the reader stumbles verbally. Rewrite the marked sentences.

PRACTICE 5

Choose a paper you wrote recently. Select one of the proofreading strategies and try it out on this paper. Read with full attention, keenly watching for your personal error patterns. Put a check in the margin beside each error. Then correct your errors.

EXPLORING ONLINE

www.writing.wisc.edu/Handbook/Proofreading.html

Excellent proofreading advice from the University of Wisconsin OWL

owl.english.purdue.edu/owl/resource/561/01

Proofreading tips from the Purdue University OWL, plus advice on correcting common errors made by college students

CHAPTER 26

The Simple Sentence

A: Defining and Spotting Subjects

B: Spotting Prepositional Phrases

C: Defining and Spotting Verbs

A. Defining and Spotting Subjects

ESL TIP

If you have many nonnative students, you might discuss possible differences between their language and English, such as word order or singulars and plurals, that might confuse them as they write sentences in English.

To write well, you need to know how to write correct sentences. A sentence is a group of words that contains a **subject** and a **verb** and expresses a complete thought.

A subject is the *who* or *what* word that performs the action or the *who* or *what* word the sentence is about:

1. Three *hunters* tramped through the woods.
2. The blue *truck* belongs to Ralph.

- In sentence 1, *hunters,* the *who* word, performs the action—"tramped through the woods."
- In sentence 2, *truck* is the *what* word about which a statement is made—"belongs to Ralph."

Some sentences have more than one subject, joined by *and*:

3. Her *aunt and uncle* love country music.

- In sentence 3, *aunt and uncle,* the *who* words, perform the action—they "love country music."
- *Aunt and uncle* is called a **compound subject**.

Sometimes an *-ing* word can be the subject of a sentence:

4. *Reading* strains my eyes.

- *Reading* is the *what* word that performs the action—"strains my eyes."

PRACTICE 1

Circle the subjects in these sentences.

1. Kwanzaa is an African-American holiday celebrated from December 26 through January 1.
2. It was created in 1966 by Maulana Karenga.
3. The name in Swahili means "first fruits of the harvest."
4. During the week-long holiday, families serve foods that have special meanings.
5. For example, certain fruits and vegetables represent group effort.
6. Each evening a candle is lit that represents one of Kwanzaa's seven principles.
7. Unity, self-determination, collective work and responsibility, cooperative economics, purpose, creativity, and faith form the seven principles of Kwanzaa.
8. In addition to food and candles, traditional African clothing plays an important role in celebrating black culture.
9. In recent years, the holiday has spread to Canada.
10. In 2009, Maya Angelou narrated a documentary film about Kwanzaa called *The Black Candle.*

Rolf Bruderer/Corbis

Lighting the candles at Kwanzaa

B. Spotting Prepositional Phrases

TEACHING TIP
Part B anticipates and addresses a common problem: many basic writers confuse the object of a preposition with the subject of the sentence.

ESL TIP
Explain, perhaps with a simple drawing, that prepositions express relationships: *on the lake, in the lake, beside the lake.* Ask students for more examples.

One group of words that may confuse you as you look for subjects is the prepositional phrase. A **prepositional phrase** contains a **preposition** (a word like *at, in, of, from,* and so forth) and its **object**.

Preposition	Object
at	the beach
on	time
of	the students

The object of a preposition *cannot* be the subject of a sentence:

1. One of my friends is working tonight.

- The subject of the sentence is *One*, not *friends*.

Spotting and crossing out prepositional phrases will help you find the subject:

2. The sweaters in the window look handmade.
3. The sweaters ~~in the window~~ look handmade.
4. ~~On Tuesday~~, a carton ~~of oranges~~ was left ~~on the porch~~.

- In sentence 1, you might have trouble finding the subject. But once the prepositional phrase is crossed out in sentence 2, the subject, *sweaters*, is easier to spot.
- In sentence 3, once the prepositional phrases are crossed out, the subject, *carton*, is easier to spot.

Here are some common prepositions that you should know:

ESL TIP
If ESL students have trouble with English prepositions, refer them to Chapter 34, "Prepositions."

Common Prepositions			
about	beneath	in	round
above	beside	inside	since
across	between	into	through
after	beyond	like	to
against	by	near	toward
among	concerning	of	under
around	despite	off	unlike
as	down	on	until
at	during	outside	up
before	except	over	upon
behind	for	past	with
below	from	regarding	

PRACTICE 2

Cross out the prepositional phrases in each sentence. Then circle the subject of the sentence.

1. The bus leaves ~~from Highland Avenue~~ each morning ~~at six~~.
2. ~~During the storm,~~ we heard a tree crash ~~on the roof~~.
3. The car ~~in the driveway~~ belongs ~~to Ted~~.
4. One ~~of my sisters~~ plans to open a restaurant ~~after she graduates~~.
5. ~~Under the street,~~ a maze ~~of tunnels~~ carries rainwater ~~to the treatment plant~~.
6. ~~Before the exam,~~ a review will be held ~~in the library~~.
7. The man ~~behind the curtain~~ spoke ~~with a megaphone~~.
8. ~~Over spring break,~~ many students travel ~~to Florida~~.
9. The plan ~~regarding student loans~~ was approved ~~by the dean~~.
10. ~~Over the winter,~~ raccoons burrowed ~~under the garage~~.

PRACTICE 3

Cross out the prepositional phrases in each sentence. Then circle the subject of the sentence.

1. ~~After the hurricane~~, the governor faced several challenges.
2. ~~With communications disrupted~~, her staff had little information ~~about the damage~~.
3. ~~After touring the shoreline by helicopter~~, she appeared ~~on television~~.
4. She appealed ~~for calm,~~ then took questions ~~from reporters~~.
5. ~~During the next few hours,~~ dozens ~~of survivors~~ were found taking shelter ~~in cellars~~.
6. ~~By the end of the day~~, rescuers reported that no lives had been lost.
7. ~~Across the state,~~ grateful citizens credited the governor's evacuation order ~~for saving lives~~.
8. ~~In previous emergencies,~~ local officials determined when ~~to evacuate shore towns~~.
9. ~~During the summer,~~ this policy caused confusion ~~among visiting tourists~~.
10. ~~With a statewide evacuation order,~~ confusion was eliminated.

TEACHING TIP
After students have completed Parts A and B, they might highlight all subjects in a recent paragraph of their own, exchange work, and check each other's answers.

C. Defining and Spotting Verbs

Action Verbs

In order to be complete, every sentence must contain a **verb**. One kind of verb, called an **action verb**, expresses the action that the subject is performing:

1. The star quarterback *fumbled*.
2. The carpenters *worked* all day, but the bricklayers *went* home early.

- In sentence 1, the action verb is *fumbled*.
- In sentence 2, the action verbs are *worked* and *went*.*

Linking Verbs

Another kind of verb, called a **linking verb**, links the subject to words that describe or identify it:

3. Sophia *is* a fine mathematician.
4. This fabric *feels* rough and scratchy.

- In sentence 3, the verb *is* links the subject *Sophia* with the noun *mathematician*.
- In sentence 4, the verb *feels* links the subject *fabric* with the adjectives *rough* and *scratchy*.

Here are some common linking verbs:

Common Linking Verbs	
appear	feel
be (am, is, are, was, were, has been, have been, had been . . .)	look
become	seem

Verbs of More Than One Word—Helping Verbs

So far you have dealt with verbs of only one word—*fumbled, worked, is, feels,* and so on. But many verbs consist of more than one word:

5. He *should have taken* the train home.
6. *Are* Tanya and Joe *practicing* the piano?
7. The lounge *was painted* last week.

- In sentence 5, *taken* is the main verb; *should* and *have* are the **helping verbs**.
- In sentence 6, *practicing* is the main verb; *are* is the helping verb.
- In sentence 7, *painted* is the main verb; *was* is the helping verb.†

PRACTICE 4

TEACHING TIP
Practices 4 and 5 make enjoyable full-class exercises.

Underline the verbs in these sentences.

1. Students jog along the lake every morning.
2. The police investigated the robbery last night.

*For work on compound predicates, see Chapter 22, "Revising for Sentence Variety," Part D.
†For more work on verbs in the passive voice, see Chapter 31, "The Past Participle," Part E.

3. We are accepting applications until the end of the month.
4. Marion and Sid bought a new car last week.
6. He translated my poems into Spanish.
7. Reading these graphs requires special training.
8. Searching for oil in the desert, engineers discovered an ancient temple.
9. Pilots are using a new navigation system to fly through fog.
10. The judge must decide whether she can testify.

PRACTICE 5

ESL TIP
ESL students may be confused by the variety of verb forms and tenses in Practice 5. Be prepared to refer them to Chapters 29 and 30 for explanations.

Underline the verbs in these sentences.

1. Historians and librarians are racing against time to preserve images and documents.
2. Throughout the twentieth century, pictures and text were recorded on equipment that is now obsolete.
3. Few people or even libraries have access to machines that can play reel-to-reel tapes.
4. Rare films and videos are deteriorating faster than researchers can transfer them to digital formats.
5. Microfilm was designed to be more durable than paper.
6. Librarians report, however, that microfilm reels are becoming brittle and often break when read.
7. Ironically, the newspapers and magazines they were supposed to replace can last longer if carefully stored.
8. Preservationists believe that many films and videos will be lost before they can be restored or transferred.
9. Film historians estimate that 80 percent of silent films decayed before they could be saved.
10. Many families discover that important moments like vacations and weddings were photographed on slides and tapes they can no longer see.

PROOFREADING STRATEGY

TEACHING TIP
Point out to students that spotting complete ideas is the key building block in correcting many serious errors: comma splices, fragments, and verb errors.

Being able to identify subjects and verbs will help you check your sentences for completeness and correct many serious writing errors (like fragments and run-on sentences in Chapter 28). To find subjects and verbs, **cross out** and **color code**:

1. Read each sentence slowly, crossing out any prepositional phrases.
2. Then either circle the subject and underline the verb or *color code your subjects and verbs*, using two different highlighters, like this:

   ~~In the United States,~~ distances ~~in length~~ are measured ~~in feet and miles~~.

   Europeans calculate distances ~~in meters and kilometers~~.
3. Finally, read each sentence slowly to make sure it expresses a complete thought and ends with a period.

PRACTICE 6 REVIEW

LEARNING STYLES TIP

Interactive computer exercises often engage *visual* and *kinesthetic learners*, thereby increasing their comprehension and retention.

Cross out any prepositional phrases in each of the sentences below. Then either circle each subject and underline each verb or highlight the subject and verb in different colors.

1. ~~In 1908~~, a strange fireball streaked across the sky ~~over Siberia~~.
2. ~~Within minutes~~, a mammoth explosion devastated a remote area ~~near the Tunguska River~~.
3. ~~In an instant~~, a herd ~~of reindeer~~ was vaporized.
4. The blast flattened 80 million trees ~~in an area covering 800 square miles~~.
5. Political events ~~in Russia~~ delayed scientific expeditions ~~to the remote region~~.
6. ~~In 1927~~, the first researchers explored the site.
7. They were amazed ~~by the extent of the devastation~~.
8. Strangely, no crater was found.
9. Scientists later estimated the blast was hundreds of times more powerful than an atomic bomb.
10. After exploring many theories, most scientists now believe that an asteroid burst ~~about five or six miles above the Earth~~.

EXPLORING ONLINE

grammar.ccc.commnet.edu/grammar/quizzes/subjector.htm

Interactive subject quiz

dailygrammar.com/archive.html

Click "Lessons 6-10" (Verbs) and "Lessons 11-15" (Verbs) for a verb review.

a4esl.org/a/g3.html

Interactive preposition quizzes: scroll down to "Prepositions"

CHAPTER 27

Coordination and Subordination

A. Coordination

LEARNING STYLES TIP

It can be fun and effective, when teaching coordination, subordination, and sentence errors, to get *kinesthetic learners* up out of their seats. Reproduce sentence parts, punctuation marks, and conjunctions on cards, and pass out the cards. Ask students holding relevant parts to go to the front of the room, arranging themselves into correctly joined and punctuated clauses.

A **clause** is a group of words that includes a subject and a verb. If a clause can stand alone as a complete idea, it is an **independent clause** and can be written as a **simple sentence**.*

Here are two independent clauses written as simple sentences:

1. The dog barked all night.
2. The neighbors didn't complain.

You can join two clauses together by placing a comma and a **coordinating conjunction** between them:

3. The dog barked all night, *but* the neighbors didn't complain.
4. Let's go to the beach today, *for* it is too hot to do anything else.

- The coordinating conjunctions *but* and *for* join together two clauses.

*For more work on simple sentences, see Chapter 26, "The Simple Sentence."

- Note that the clause on each side of the coordinating conjunction can stand alone as a complete sentence.
- A comma precedes each coordinating conjunction.

TEACHING TIP
Students often overuse the conjunction *and.* Encourage them to think critically about the exact *relationship* between two independent ideas before they select a conjunction.

Here is a list of coordinating conjunctions. To help you remember them, just think FANBOYS (the first letter of *for, and, nor, but, or, yet,* and *so*).

Coordinating Conjunctions			
and	for	or	yet
but	nor	so	

Be sure to choose the coordinating conjunction that best expresses the *relationship* between the two clauses in a sentence:

TEACHING TIP
The conjunctions *for* and *yet* may be particularly difficult for students. Explain that *for* means *because* and *yet* is closely related to *but.*

5. It was late, *so* I decided to take a bus home.
6. It was late, *yet* I decided to take a bus home.

- The *so* in sentence 5 means that the lateness of the hour caused me to take the bus. (The trains don't run after midnight.)
- The *yet* in sentence 6 means that despite the late hour I still decided to take a bus home. (I knew I might have to wait two hours at the bus stop.)
- Note that a comma precedes the coordinating conjunction.

PRACTICE 1

TEACHING TIP
After students complete Practice 1, consider discussing their answers as a class so that they can see which conjunctions work in a sentence and which don't.

Read the following sentences for meaning. Then fill in the coordinating conjunction that *best* expresses the relationship between the two clauses. Don't forget to add the comma.

1. In 1853, a customer at Moon Lake Lodge in Saratoga, New York, thought his fried potatoes were too thick and soggy __, so__ he sent them back to the kitchen.
2. The Native American/African American chef, George Crum, took offense at this criticism of his cooking __, for__ he was a confident and cranky fellow.
3. Crum wanted to annoy his fussy customer__, so__ he angrily sliced some potatoes very thin, poured salt all over them, and fried them hard.
4. The chef expected the complaining patron to leave in a huff __, but__ he didn't.
5. Instead, the crispy potato thins pleased the customer immensely __, so/and__ he ordered more.

6. Crum, who soon opened his own restaurant, called his lucky invention "potato crunches" __, but__ he later renamed them "Saratoga Chips."

7. In the 1920s, traveling salesman Herman Lay began selling potato chips out of the trunk of his car __, and__ other companies began manufacturing them, too.

8. Now customers could order the tasty treat in restaurants __, or__ they could munch them at home.

9. However, chips at the bottom of the barrel or tin would not stay fresh __, nor__ would they stay crispy.

10. Entrepreneur Laura Scudder solved this problem by putting the chips between sheets of wax paper that she ironed together __, and__ the potato chip quickly became America's favorite snack.

PRACTICE 2

TEACHING TIP

Students may try to combine these sentences using subordinating conjunctions like *because* and *then*. Remind them to use only the conjunctions in the list earlier in this chapter.

Combine these simple sentences with a coordinating conjunction. Punctuate correctly.

1. My daughter wants to be a mechanic. She spends every spare minute at the garage.

   My daughter wants to be a mechanic, so she spends every spare minute at the garage.

2. Ron dared not look over the edge. Heights made him dizzy.

   Ron dared not look over the edge, for heights made him dizzy.

3. The movie got rave reviews. It failed at the box office.

   The movie got rave reviews, but it failed at the box office.

TEACHING TIP

Have students apply what they have learned by looking for short, choppy sentences in a paragraph they have written and then revising, using coordinating conjunctions.

4. Join the health club. Exercise at home if you can't afford the fees.

   Join the health club, or exercise at home if you can't afford the fees.

5. In 1969, the first astronauts landed on the moon. Most Americans felt proud.

   In 1969, the first astronauts landed on the moon, and most Americans felt proud.

B. Subordination

TEACHING TIP
To begin a lesson on subordinating conjunctions, you might review with students the meanings of the terms *coordinate* and *subordinate*.

Two clauses can also be joined with a **subordinating conjunction**. The clause following a subordinating conjunction is called a **subordinate** or **dependent clause** because it depends on an independent clause to complete its meaning:

1. We will light the candles *when Flora arrives.*

- *When Flora arrives* is a subordinate or dependent clause introduced by the subordinating conjunction *when.*
- By itself, *when Flora arrives* is incomplete; it depends on the independent clause to complete its meaning.*

ESL TIP
ESL students tend to write dependent clause fragments. In some languages, like Japanese, freestanding dependent clauses are accepted as correct. Further, ESL students often duplicate English oral patterns, in which freestanding dependent clauses are common.

Note that sentence 1 can also be written this way:

2. *When Flora arrives,* we will light the candles.

- The meaning of sentences 1 and 2 is the same, but the punctuation is different.
- In sentence 1, because the subordinate clause *follows* the independent clause, *no comma* is needed.
- In sentence 2, however, because the subordinate clause *begins* the sentence, it is followed by a *comma.*

TEACHING TIP
Remind students that conjunctions express precise *relationships* between ideas. Discuss the meanings of any conjunctions that confuse them.

Here is a partial list of subordinating conjunctions:

Subordinating Conjunctions		
after	if	unless
although	if only	until
as	in order that	when
as if	once	whenever
as though	provided that	where
because	rather than	whereas
before	since	wherever
even if	so that	whether
even though	though	while

Be sure to choose the subordinating conjunction that *best expresses the relationship* between the two clauses in a sentence:

3. This course was excellent *because* Professor Green taught it.
4. This course was excellent *even though* Professor Green taught it.

---

*For more work on incomplete sentences, or fragments, see Chapter 28, "Avoiding Sentence Errors," Part B.

- Sentence 3 says that the course was excellent *because* Professor Green, a great teacher, taught it.
- Sentence 4 says that the course was excellent *despite the fact that* Professor Green, apparently a bad teacher, taught it.

PRACTICE 3

TEACHING TIP

After students complete Practice 3, consider discussing the answers as a class so that students can see which conjunctions work in the sentence and which don't.

Read the following sentences for meaning. Then fill in the subordinating conjunction that *best* expresses the relationship between the two clauses.

1. We called a cab ____because____ my car wouldn't start.
2. ____After____ Jane graduates, she plans to move to Nevada.
3. Fans were stunned ____when____ the coach replaced the quarterback.
4. Classes were cancelled ____because____ there were severe ice storms.
5. You should review your notes ____before____ you retake the driver's test.

PRACTICE 4

TEACHING TIP

For Practice 4, encourage students to locate and circle the subordinating conjunction before deciding if the sentence needs a comma.

TEACHING TIP

The subject of this practice might prompt discussion or ideas for further writing. A good source of facts on the benefits of music education is **www.childrensmusicworkshop.com/twelve-benefits-of-music-education**.

Punctuate the following sentences by adding a comma where necessary. Put a *C* after any correct sentences.

1. Thousands of low-income children in Venezuela have been given a new life because José Antonio Abreu taught them to play classical music. C
2. While some people only talked about the poverty and drugs destroying many young Venezuelans, Abreu took action.
3. After he convinced government leaders that musical training builds self-worth, Abreu got funding to start children's orchestras. C
4. The results have been amazing as communities proudly support their young musicians. C
5. When the children practice their violins or oboes, they are also learning discipline, valuable skills, and the joys of musical teamwork.
6. The program ignores pop and tropical musicians like Christina Aguilera and Oscar D'León because Abreu wants his students to master classical artists like Mozart and Beethoven. C
7. Since the program was launched, a generation of talented Venezuelan musicians is already performing, composing, and teaching classical music.

Carlos Cazalis/Corbis News/Corbis

The National Network of Youth and Children's Orchestras of Venezuela performs in Caracas, Venezuela.

8. Because the program has been so successful, it is the model for new youth orchestras now being formed throughout the world.

PRACTICE 5

TEACHING TIP

Ask your students to describe the impression that short, choppy sentences give readers about the writer. (The effect can seem monotonous, unsophisticated, even childlike.)

ESL TIP

A common ESL error is to use both a subordinating and a coordinating conjunction in the same sentence (e.g., *Although it was raining, but she forgot her umbrella*). Remind students to check carefully for this overuse problem.

Combine each pair of the following ideas by using a subordinating conjunction. Write each combination twice, once with the subordinating conjunction at the beginning of the sentence and once with the subordinating conjunction in the middle of the sentence. Punctuate correctly.

EXAMPLE We stayed on the beach.
The sun went down.

We stayed on the beach until the sun went down.

Until the sun went down, we stayed on the beach.

1. This cactus has flourished.
2. I talk to it every day.

Because I talk to it every day, this cactus has flourished.

This cactus has flourished because I talk to it every day.

3. Ralph takes the train to Philadelphia.
4. He likes to sit by the window.

Whenever Ralph takes the train to Philadelphia, he likes to sit by the window.

Ralph likes to sit by the window whenever he takes the train to Philadelphia.

5. My dad offered to buy me a car.
6. I paid for the insurance.

My dad offered to buy me a car provided that I paid for the insurance.

Provided that I paid for the insurance, my dad offered to buy me a car.

7. He was the first person to eat a slice of meat between two pieces of bread.
8. The sandwich was named after the Earl of Sandwich.

The sandwich was named after the Earl of Sandwich because he was the first person to eat a slice of meat between two pieces of bread.

Because he was the first person to eat a slice of meat between two pieces of bread, the sandwich was named after the Earl of Sandwich.

9. Akila was about to answer the final question.
10. The buzzer sounded.

Akila was about to answer the final question when the buzzer sounded.

When the buzzer sounded, Akila was about to answer the final question.

11. Jason grew up on the Jersey shore.
12. He never learned to swim.

Although he grew up on the Jersey shore, Jason never learned to swim.

Jason never learned to swim although he grew up on the Jersey shore.

13. She connected the speakers.
14. The room filled with glorious sound.

When she connected the speakers, the room filled with glorious sound.

The room filled with glorious sound when she connected the speakers.

15. The chimney spewed black smoke and soot.
16. Nobody complained to the local environmental agency.

Nobody complained to the local environmental agency although the chimney spewed black smoke and soot.

Although the chimney spewed black smoke and soot, nobody complained to the local environmental agency.

C. Semicolons

TEACHING TIP
Students may have a tendency to use semicolons inappropriately. You might want to emphasize that there are only *two* uses for the semicolon: (1) to separate two sentences, and (2) to separate items in a series that contains internal commas.

You can join two independent clauses by placing a semicolon between them. The semicolon takes the place of a conjunction:

1. She hopes to receive good grades this semester; her scholarship depends on her maintaining a 3.5 average.
2. Tony is a careless driver; he has had three minor accidents this year alone.

- Each of the sentences above could also be made into two *separate sentences* by replacing the semicolon with a period.
- Note that the first word after a semicolon is *not* capitalized (unless, of course, it is a word that is normally capitalized, like someone's name).

PRACTICE 6

TEACHING TIP
Stress to students that semicolons connect only *related* ideas. If two ideas do not have a close relationship (such as a cause and an effect, a comparison of two like things, a time order relationship, etc.), they probably should be separated with a period.

Combine each pair of independent clauses by placing a semicolon between them.

1. The senator appeared ill at ease at the news conference; he seemed afraid of saying the wrong thing.
2. Madison is the capital of Wisconsin; Springfield is the capital of Illinois.
3. On Thursday evening, Hector decided to go camping; on Friday morning, he packed his bags and left.
4. The flight was cancelled; the airline provided passengers with hotel rooms.
5. Not a single store was open at that hour; not a soul walked the streets.

PRACTICE 7

Each independent clause that follows is the first half of a sentence. Add a semicolon and a second independent clause. Make sure your second thought is also independent and can stand alone. Answers will vary.

ESL TIP
Few languages use the semicolon as English does. Some ESL instructors explain semicolon use but advise students to stick to periods and commas to avoid errors.

TEACHING TIP
Ask students to share their answers to Practice 7. You might have each student write one of his or her sentences on the board and then have the class verify that the second thought is independent.

1. My car refused to start this morning ; I was late to work.

2. The play was sparsely attended ; it closed after a week.

3. Nancy grew up in southern France ; her husband is from Germany.

4. Two feet of snow fell last night ; the roads are icy this morning.

5. The mayor refused to speak with the press ; Ava thought he had something to hide.

D. Conjunctive Adverbs

TEACHING TIP
Point out to students that using conjunctive adverbs correctly will significantly increase the sophistication of their writing.

In earlier chapters on paragraph and essay writing, you practiced using **transitional expressions** like *however, for example*, and *therefore*. Most transitional expressions are **conjunctive adverbs**. A conjunctive adverb placed after a semicolon can help clarify the relationship between two clauses:

1. I like the sound of that speaker; *however,* the price is too high.
2. They have not seen that film; *moreover,* they have not been to a theater for three years.

- Note that a comma follows the conjunctive adverb.

Here is a partial list of conjunctive adverbs, or transitional expressions.*

Conjunctive Adverbs or Transitional Expressions	
Addition:	also, besides, furthermore, in addition, moreover
Comparison:	likewise, similarly
Contrast:	however, nevertheless, on the contrary, on the other hand
Emphasis:	indeed, in fact, of course
Example:	for example, for instance
Result:	consequently, therefore, thus

*For more transitional expressions, see Chapter 4, "Achieving Coherence," Part B.

PRACTICE 8

Punctuate each sentence correctly by adding a semicolon, a comma, or both where necessary. Put a *C* after any correct sentences.

1. I hate to wash my car windows; nevertheless, it's a job that must be done.
2. Sonia doesn't know how to play chess; however, she would like to learn.
3. I never met Jack Dawson; in fact, I never heard his name until now.
4. Deep water makes Maurice nervous; therefore, he does not want to join the scuba diving team.
5. I like this painting; the soft colors remind me of tropical sunsets. C
6. The faculty approved of the new trimester system; furthermore, the students liked it too. C
7. They only have one truck; consequently, I doubt they can ship all our goods on time.
8. Shoplifting has increased dramatically; therefore, the mall is hiring additional security guards.

TEACHING TIP

Use sets of closely related sentences to demonstrate how the lack of a conjunctive adverb forces readers to discern the relationship between the two ideas on their own. Thus, readers are more likely to miss the connection or to misunderstand it.

PRACTICE 9

Proofread this paragraph for coordination errors, missing punctuation, and one conjunctive adverb that does not express the right relationship between ideas. Add the correct punctuation or write your corrections above the lines, using a mix of semicolons and semicolons plus conjunctive adverbs.

(1) Successful college students learn how to take good notes in class. (2) One excellent note-taking method is the Cornell ~~method experts~~ method; experts say that it actually helps the brain learn. (3) A student using the Cornell method performs several steps. (4) Before class, he or she draws a line dividing notebook paper into two columns. (5) The narrower left-hand column will contain key words, and the wider right-hand column, notes. (6) During the lesson, the student records the professor's main ideas in the notes column, jotting important phrases, symbols, and abbreviations, but not complete sentences. (7) At the

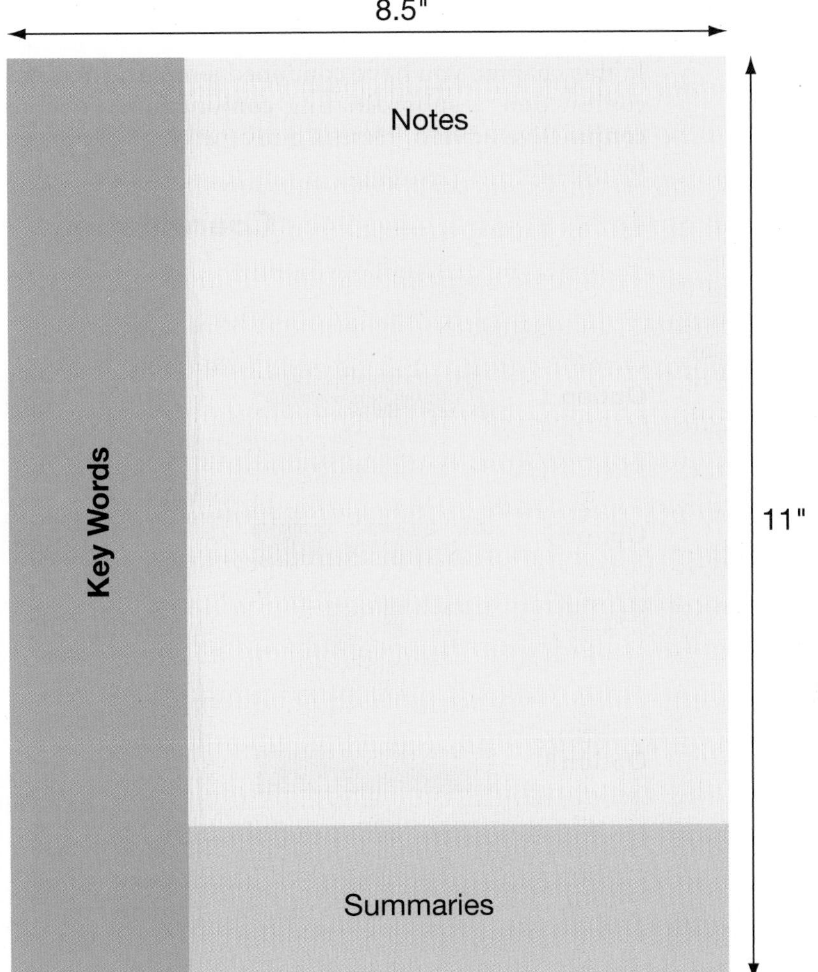

A sample page showing the Cornell note-taking method. Do you think this method would work better than the one you now use? Why or why not?

TEACHING TIP

You might go over the Cornell note-taking method in class. Ask students to try it for a week in all their classes (notes, key words, summaries) and then report on their results.

bottom of the page, the student leaves five or six lines blank. (8) As soon as possible after class, he or she rereads the notes and reduces them further by writing a few key words or questions in the left-hand ~~column furthermore~~ column; furthermore, at the bottom of the page, the student writes a brief summary of the notes. (9) These "reducing" steps help the brain understand and remember the ~~material, nevertheless,~~ material; consequently, studying later for a test is easier. (10) To study, the student simply covers up the notes and recites the information aloud from memory, glancing at the key words and questions for hints. (11) Periodically reviewing like this helps the brain move course concepts gradually into long-term memory and improves recall on exams. (12) Finally, students should reflect on what they are ~~learning, for example;~~ learning; for example, they might ask how the ideas in their notes apply to real-life situations. Some people call the Cornell system the Five R's, for *record, reduce, recite, review*, and *reflect*.

E. Review

In this chapter, you have combined simple sentences by means of a **coordinating conjunction**, a **subordinating conjunction**, a **semicolon**, and a **semicolon** and **conjunctive adverb**. Here is a review chart of the sentence patterns discussed in this chapter.*

TEACHING TIP

Most students find this chart extremely helpful as a summary of correct options for joining ideas. Suggest that they tab or copy it, referring to it as they write.

Coordination

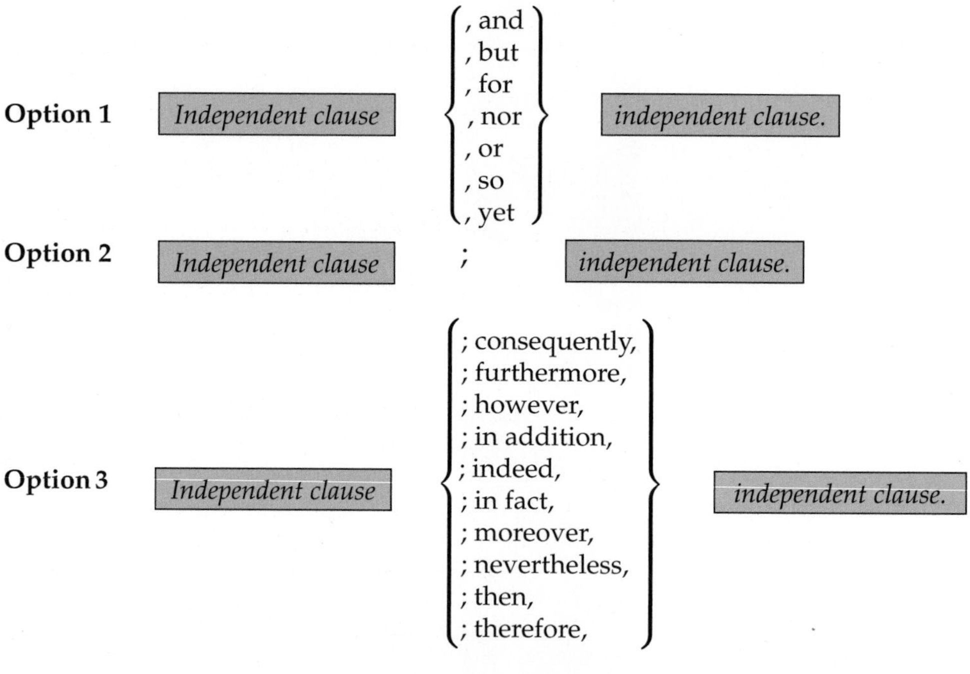

Subordination

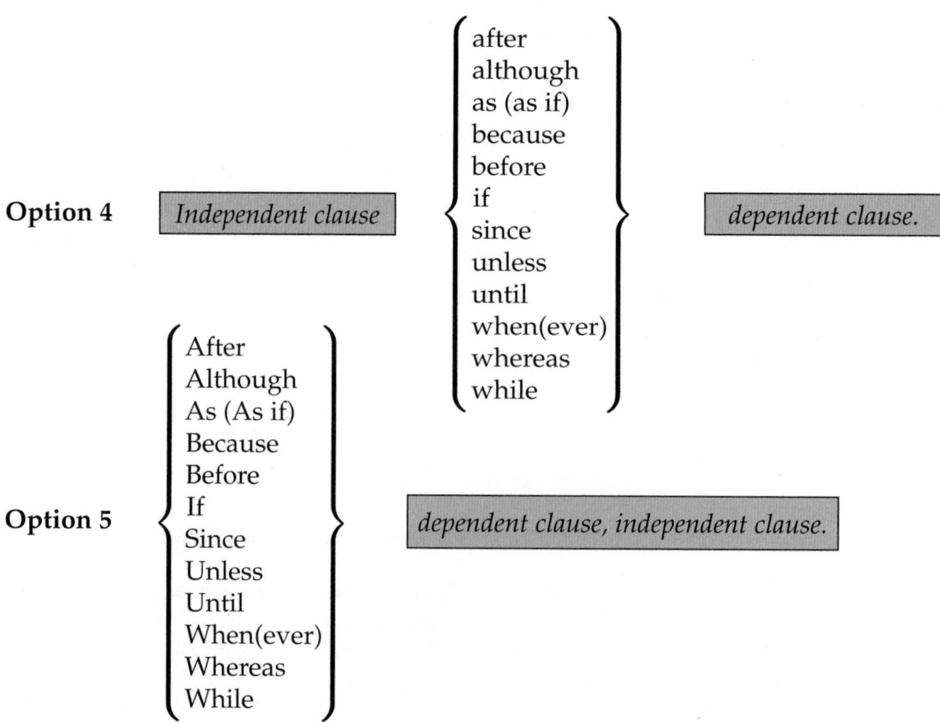

*For more ways to combine sentences, see Chapter 22, "Revising for Sentence Variety," Part D.

PRACTICE 10

Read each pair of simple sentences to determine the relationship between them. Then join each pair in three different ways, using the conjunctions or conjunctive adverbs in parentheses at the left. Punctuate correctly. Answers will vary.

EXAMPLE The company picnic was canceled.
Rain started to fall in torrents.

(for) *The company picnic was canceled, for the rain started to fall in torrents.*

(because) *Because the rain started to fall in torrents, the company picnic was canceled.*

(therefore) *The rain started to fall in torrents; therefore, the company picnic was canceled.*

1. My grandmother is in great shape.
   She eats right and exercises regularly.

   (for) My grandmother is in great shape, for she eats right and exercises regularly.

   (because) Because my grandmother eats right and exercises regularly, she is in great shape.

   (therefore) My grandmother eats right and exercises regularly; therefore, she is in great shape.

2. We just put in four hours paving the driveway.
   We need a long break and a cold drink.

   (since) Since we just put in four hours paving the driveway, we need a long break and a cold drink.

   (because) We need a long break and a cold drink because we just put in four hours paving the driveway.

   (consequently) We just put in four hours paving the driveway; consequently, we need a long break and a cold drink.

3. The bank robber was caught on videotape.
   He eluded the police for months.

   (but) The bank robber was caught on videotape, but he eluded the police for months.

(although) Although the bank robber was caught on videotape, he eluded the police for months.

(however) The bank robber was caught on videotape; however, he eluded the police for months.

4. Don is an expert mechanic.
   He intends to open a service center.

   (and) Don is an expert mechanic, and he intends to open a service center.

   (because) Because Don is an expert mechanic, he intends to open a service center.

   (furthermore) Don is an expert mechanic; furthermore, he intends to open a service center.

5. Our sales are declining.
   We plan to expand our store.

   (but) Our sales are declining, but we plan to expand our store.

   (although) Although our sales are declining, we plan to expand our store.

   (nevertheless) Our sales are declining; nevertheless, we plan to expand our store.

PROOFREADING STRATEGY

Using coordination and subordination will improve your writing, but you must proofread to make sure that you punctuate correctly.

1. First, **search for the seven coordinating conjunctions**, or FANBOYS, and highlight or underline each one. If the idea on each side of the comma can stand alone as a complete sentence, make sure that a comma comes before the coordinating conjunction.

   Correct — Correct

   Every day, she clocks out and leaves the pediatric ward tired but satisfied.

   Incorrect — Correct

   Baby Chandra has improved but the doctor and nurses continue to monitor her.

2. Next, **search your document for any subordinating conjunctions** (like *although, because, before, when,* etc.). Highlight or underline these words. If the dependent idea comes first in the sentence, make sure that a comma separates the dependent from the independent idea. Here are two examples:

Independent idea — Dependent idea

Schools are closed today because the city is buried under two feet of snow.

Dependent idea — Incorrect — Independent idea

Until the airport shuttle bus arrives [,] we can wait in the lounge.

PRACTICE 11 REVIEW

TEACHING TIP

After students try Practice 11 on their own, consider reading aloud "before" and "after" versions of a paragraph so that students can hear how much smoother the revision sounds. Also, ask them whether the newly combined sentences help them understand the information better.

In your writing, aim for variety by mixing coordination, subordination, and simple sentences.* Revise the following paragraphs to eliminate monotonous simple sentences. First, read the paragraph to determine the relationships between ideas; then choose the conjunctions that best express these relationships, making your corrections above the lines. Proofread your work, making sure you punctuate correctly.

Paragraph 1

Most people know about Howard Hughes' giant airplane *The Spruce Goose*~~. Most~~ [, but most] have never heard of his steam car. By the 1920s, steam cars were considered obsolete. Steam cars took several minutes to start~~. They~~ [; moreover, they] had to stop for water every sixty miles. ~~In~~ [Nevertheless, in] 1926, Hughes hired two engineers~~. He~~ [and] told them to build a revolutionary steam car. He wanted it to start in 20 seconds~~. He~~ [, and he] wanted it to have a range of 400 miles. The engineers worked in secret for three years~~. They~~ [, and they] spent a half million dollars. ~~They~~ [After they] completed the car~~. The~~ [, the] engineers invited Hughes to inspect their creation. ~~Hughes was impressed. He~~ [Impressed, he] asked how it worked. The builders explained that the entire body of the car contained a network of radiators. [When] Hughes realized that the radiators could burst in a crash and scald the driver~~. He~~ [, he] ordered his half-million-dollar car to be cut to pieces.

Paragraph 2

Businessman Robert Johnson has blazed new trails throughout his career. No existing television network targeted African ~~Americans. Johnson~~ [Americans, so Johnson] created the Black Entertainment Television network. ~~The~~ [Although the] company started with a tiny budget and just two hours of daily ~~programming. It~~ [programming, it] became a huge success.

*For more work on sentence variety, see Chapter 22, "Revising for Sentence Variety."

~~BET~~ As BET grew to be the largest black-owned and black-operated company in the ~~country. Johnson~~ country, Johnson created new jobs for hundreds of people. ~~He~~ After he became America's first African American billionaire~~. Johnson~~ , Johnson devoted more time to philanthropy. In 2007, he invested thirty million dollars to create a fund that loans money to Liberian entrepreneurs. In 2011, he raised money to help the Bahamas cope with hurricanes~~. In~~ ,and in 2012, he launched a business to raise money to fight malaria worldwide.

Paragraph 3

Cleopatra became Queen of Egypt at ~~seventeen. She~~ seventeen; nevertheless, she displayed a flair for ruling and was soon worshipped by her subjects. ~~Julius~~ When Julius Caesar, ruler of Rome, was sent to calm civil wars in Egypt in 51 ~~B.C. Cleopatra~~ B.C., Cleopatra was in hiding. She directed her servants to roll her up inside a large rug and smuggle her into the palace. Caesar was fifty-two and the most powerful man in the ~~world. He~~ world, but he was amazed to receive a gift-wrapped queen. Their relationship became one of history's greatest love ~~stories. It~~ stories, and it lasted until Caesar's enemies murdered him.

North Wind Picture Archives/ Alamy Stock Photo

Caesar Augustus (Julius Caesar's great-nephew) finds Cleopatra's body after she has committed suicide by snakebite.

Later, Marc Antony came to Egypt to add African lands to the Roman Empire. He, too, fell in love with the spirited ~~queen. He~~ queen, and he moved into her palace on the island of Antirhodos. This betrayal was too much for the ~~Romans. Their~~ Romans; their navy attacked Cleopatra's fleet. Both Antony and Cleopatra killed ~~themselves. They~~ themselves because they would not bow in defeat. The Romans smashed all statues of the ~~queen. An~~ queen, and an earthquake sank her palace into the Mediterranean Sea. Fifteen hundred years ~~passed.~~ passed before ~~Undersea~~ undersea explorer Franck Goddio discovered Cleopatra's lost palace in 1996. Neither the Roman Empire nor the forces of nature could erase one of the most powerful and intriguing women who ever lived.

EXPLORING ONLINE

grammar.ccc.commnet.edu/grammar/quizzes/nova/nova1.htm
Interactive coordination quiz

depts.dyc.edu/learningcenter/owl/exercises/conjunctions_ex2.htm
Exercises in subordination, with answers

CHAPTER 28

Avoiding Sentence Errors

A: Avoiding Run-Ons and Comma Splices

B: Avoiding Fragments

A. Avoiding Run-Ons and Comma Splices

TEACHING TIP

Stress to students that run-ons and comma splices are among the most common—and most serious—grammatical errors. By forcing readers to stop, back up, and try to figure out where one thought ends and another begins, these errors confuse and irritate the audience.

Be careful to avoid **run-ons** and **comma splices**.

A **run-on sentence** incorrectly runs together two independent clauses without a conjunction or punctuation. This error confuses the reader, who cannot tell where one thought stops and the next begins:

Run-on: 1. My neighbor Mr. Hoffman is seventy-five years old he plays tennis every Saturday afternoon.

A **comma splice** incorrectly joins two independent clauses with a comma but no conjunction:

Comma splice: 2. My neighbor Mr. Hoffman is seventy-five years old, he plays tennis every Saturday afternoon.

The run-on and the comma splice can be corrected in five ways:

ESL TIP

Modern Arabic now uses a full stop to separate sentences, but Arabic-speaking ESL students may still make comma splice errors.

Use two separate sentences.	My neighbor Mr. Hoffman is seventy-five years old. He plays tennis every Saturday afternoon.
Use a coordinating conjunction. (See Chapter 27, Part A.)	My neighbor Mr. Hoffman is seventy-five years old, but he plays tennis every Saturday afternoon.
Use a subordinating conjunction. (See Chapter 27, Part B.)	Although my neighbor Mr. Hoffman is seventy-five years old, he plays tennis every Saturday afternoon.
Use a semicolon. (See Chapter 27, Part C.)	My neighbor Mr. Hoffman is seventy-five years old; he plays tennis every Saturday afternoon.
Use a semicolon and a conjunctive adverb. (See Chapter 27, Part D.)	My neighbor Mr. Hoffman is seventy-five years old; however, he plays tennis every Saturday afternoon.

PRACTICE 1

ESL TIP

ESL students often benefit from group activities, especially with a mix of native and ESL speakers. Try using Practice 1 as a pair or group activity. Ask the groups to present and explain each of their answers.

TEACHING TIP

After students complete Practice 1, go over the answers in class so that you can demonstrate how to use all five revision methods for each sentence.

Some of these sentences contain run-ons or comma splices; others are correct. Put a *C* next to the correct sentences. Revise the run-ons and comma splices in any way you choose. Be careful of the punctuation. Answers may vary.

1. Identity theft is the fastest-growing crime in the United States it costs society $49 to $50 billion a year.

   Revised: Identity theft is the fastest-growing crime in the United States, and it costs society $49 to $50 billion a year.

2. The identity thief doesn't just steal someone's cash or jewelry, he or she poses as that person to open new accounts, take out loans, or even buy houses.

   Revised: The identity thief doesn't just steal someone's cash or jewelry; he or she poses as that person to open new accounts, take out loans, or even buy houses.

3. For the victim, identity theft can mean the shock of violation, large financial losses, and ruined credit.

   Revised: C

4. Individuals today must protect themselves against identity theft the U.S. Department of Justice recommends the SCAM approach.

   Revised: Because individuals today must protect themselves against identity theft, the U.S. Department of Justice recommends the SCAM approach.

5. *S* is for *stingy* people should be stingy about giving their valuable social security, bank account, and credit-card numbers to others.

   Revised: *S* is for *stingy*, for people should be stingy about giving their valuable social security, bank account, and credit-card numbers to others.

6. *C* stands for *check* all financial statements carefully for unauthorized withdrawals or purchases.

   Revised: C ____

   ____

7. The *A* in SCAM reminds everyone to *ask* periodically for a copy of his or her credit report fraudulent accounts and activity will show up there.

   Revised: The *A* in SCAM reminds everyone to *ask* periodically for a copy of his or her credit report because fraudulent accounts and activity will show up there.

8. The final step is *M, maintaining* careful records of bank and financial accounts, these records can help dispute any problems.

   Revised: The final step is *M, maintaining* careful records of bank and financial accounts; these records can help dispute any problems.

9. Trash cans and dumpsters still provide identity thieves with most of their valuable information, a final *S* might stand for *shred*.

   Revised: Trash cans and dumpsters still provide identity thieves with most of their valuable information, so a final *S* might stand for *shred*.

10. Old checks, bank records, and credit-card offers from today's mail should never be tossed out they should be shredded or burned.

    Revised: Old checks, bank records, and credit-card offers from today's mail should never be tossed out; instead, they should be shredded or burned.

PRACTICE 2

TEACHING TIP

Refer students to Chapter 27, Part E for a useful and graphic summary of five ways to join ideas. Many students refer to this chart often and keep it handy as they write.

TEACHING TIP

You can use this exercise to illustrate the role of coincidence in critical thinking. Did a novel really "predict" a disaster fourteen years later, or was it simply a coincidence?

Proofread the following paragraph for run-ons and comma splices. Correct them in any way you choose. Answers will vary.

(1) In 1898, Morgan Robertson published a novel that eerily paralleled the sinking of the *Titanic* fourteen years later. (2) His book was called *Futility* , and it ~~it~~ was about the sinking of a luxury liner. (3) Robertson named the ship *Titan* ; it resembled the *Titanic* in many ways. (4) Both ships could carry 3,000 passengers , and both ~~both~~ had three propellers. (5) Because both ~~Both~~ ships were considered "unsinkable," they did not have enough lifeboats for all the passengers. (6) In Robertson's novel, the *Titan* struck an iceberg on an April night 400 nautical miles from Newfoundland. (7) In 1912, the *Titanic* hit an iceberg in April 400 nautical miles

from Newfoundland. (8) The fictional *Titan* lost over half of its 2,500 passengers
; similarly,
the *Titanic* lost over half of its 2,200 passengers. (9) Robertson denied his
disaster; instead, he
book predicted the ~~disaster, he~~ claimed his story was based on his extensive knowledge of shipbuilding.

PROOFREADING STRATEGY

Proofread your work very carefully if comma splices are among your error patterns:

1. Go back through your draft and **circle every comma.**
2. For each comma, ask yourself, ***"Would substituting a period for this comma create complete sentences that could stand alone on <u>both</u> sides of the comma?"***

   No
   When a strong hurricane is approaching, officials may order a mandatory

   Yes
   evacuation, residents must leave the area.

3. If the answer is yes, you have written a comma splice and will need to **replace the comma with a period or keep the comma and add a coordinating conjunction after it**.

   When a strong hurricane is approaching, officials may order a mandatory evacuation, **and** residents must leave the area.

PRACTICE 3

TEACHING TIP
Because run-ons and comma splices, like fragments, are most likely to occur in longer pieces of writing, proofreading exercises like these are especially important.

Proofread the following essay for run-ons and comma splices. Correct them in any way you choose, writing your revised essay on a separate sheet of paper. Be careful of the punctuation. Answers will vary.

HOW TO READ AN AD

(1) Most people insist that advertising does not affect them and that they tune out ads and commercials. (2) If these claims are true, however, why do companies spend billions a year on advertising? (3) For the Super Bowl alone,
each; in
corporations rush to buy 30-second commercial spots at $4.5 million ~~each, in~~ fact,
Garey. They
ads work very well, declares former advertising executive Stephen ~~Garey, they~~
bombard people with attractive pictures and the hidden message, "buy, buy, buy." (4) The best defense against this ad blitz is learning to read ads critically.

TEACHING TIP

Ask students to study the list at the end of paragraph 2 and then apply it to this advertisement.

(5) Advertisers are master ~~persuaders, their~~ persuaders; however, their techniques are very different from those used in college and at work. (6) A student or worker often must take a stand, arguing for or against ~~something he~~ something, and he or she uses logical reasons and arguments to try to persuade others. (7) Advertisers, on the other hand, use illogical but powerful visual methods to persuade people to buy their products. (8) The Center for Media Literacy lists ten such "techniques of persuasion" in ads:

Humor	Friends	Fun	Sex appeal	Celebrity
Macho	Family	Nature	Cartoons	Wealth

(9) These techniques are emotional and ~~indirect, often~~ indirect, and often pictures are used to suggest pleasant associations with a product. (10) For instance, one ad might show happy people enjoying an energy drink; thus, it links "friends" and "fun" with an energy drink. (11) Another ad shows a well-dressed man helping a beautiful woman into a car, associating "wealth," "macho," and perhaps "sex appeal" with that brand of automobile. (12) Flip through any popular magazine

Image Courtesy of The Advertising Archives

Study this ad. Reread Practice 3, especially the list at the end of the second paragraph. How many advertisers' "techniques of persuasion" can you spot in the ad?

and see which techniques each ad ~~uses look~~ uses; look closely and ask yourself what *audience* is targeted by each ad. (13) What *methods* attract your attention and call to your dollars? (14) Are there *hidden messages*? (15) Looking critically at ads not only creates smarter ~~consumers, it~~ consumers. It also trains the critical thinking skills that many professors and employers value.

B. Avoiding Fragments

TEACHING TIP
Students should know that sentence fragments are considered a serious and distracting error in college and the workplace.

Another error to avoid is the **sentence fragment.** A **sentence** must contain a subject and a verb and must be able to stand alone as a complete idea. A **sentence fragment** is incomplete. It lacks a subject, a verb, or both—or it does not stand alone as a complete idea.

Here are six common fragments and ways to correct them. The first three are among the most frequently made errors in college and business writing.

Dependent Clause Fragments

A dependent clause fragment often starts with a subordinating conjunction like *although, because, if, when,* and so on.*

TEACHING TIP
Many dependent clause fragments could be called "afterthoughts." This idea helps some students. Often, attaching such a fragment to the preceding sentence is the best method of correction.

Complete sentence: 1. Kirk decided to major in business.
Fragment: 2. After his parents opened a restaurant.

- Example 1 is a complete sentence.
- Example 2 is a fragment because it is a dependent clause beginning with the subordinating conjunction *after.* Furthermore, it is not a complete idea.

This fragment can be corrected in two ways:

Corrected: 3. Kirk decided to major in business after his parents opened a restaurant.
Corrected: 4. Kirk decided to major in business. His parents opened a restaurant.

- In sentence 3, the fragment is combined with the sentence before.
- In sentence 4, the fragment is changed into a complete sentence.

Relative Clause Fragments

A dependent clause fragment can also start with *who, whose, which,* or *that.*†

*For a longer list of subordinating conjunctions and more work on dependent clauses, see Chapter 27, "Coordination and Subordination," Part B.

†For more work on relative clauses, see Chapter 22, "Revising for Sentence Variety," Part D, and Chapter 29, "Present Tense (Agreement)," Part G.

ESL TIP
Many ESL students begin sentences with subordinators like *because* and *although*, so this type of fragment is a common problem. Some are copying the oral speech patterns they hear. Others come from language backgrounds, like Japanese, in which this construction is accepted written practice.

Complete sentence:	5. Ms. Costa is a popular history professor.
Fragment:	6. Who never runs out of creative ideas.

- Example 5 is a complete sentence.
- Example 6 is a fragment because it is a relative clause beginning with *who.* It is not a complete idea.

This fragment can be corrected in two ways:

Corrected:	7. Ms. Costa is a popular history professor who never runs out of creative ideas.
Corrected:	8. Ms. Costa is a popular history professor. She never runs out of creative ideas.

- In sentence 7, the fragment is combined with the sentence before.
- In sentence 8, the fragment is changed into a complete sentence.

-ing Fragments

An *-ing* fragment starts with an *-ing* verb form.

Complete sentence:	9. Joaquin can be seen on the track every morning.
Fragment:	10. Running a mile or two before breakfast.

- Example 9 is a complete sentence.
- Example 10 is a fragment because it lacks a subject and because an *-ing* verb form cannot stand alone without a helping verb.*

This fragment can be corrected in two ways:

Corrected:	11. Joaquin can be seen on the track every morning, running a mile or two before breakfast.
Corrected:	12. Joaquin can be seen on the track every morning. He runs a mile or two before breakfast.

- In sentence 11, the fragment is combined with the sentence before.
- In sentence 12, the fragment is changed into a complete sentence.

Watch out for fragments beginning with a subordinating conjunction; *who, which,* or *that;* or an *-ing* verb form. These groups of words cannot stand alone, but must be combined with another sentence or changed into a complete sentence.

---

*For more work on joining ideas with an *-ing* modifier, see Chapter 22, "Revising for Sentence Variety," Part D.

PRACTICE 4

TEACHING TIP

You might wish to complete Practice 4 in class so that everyone can see the ways each fragment can be corrected and understand why some sentences are correct.

Some of these examples are fragments; others are complete sentences. Put a *C* next to the complete sentences. Revise the fragments any way you choose. Answers will vary.

1. When Sandra completes her commercial jet training.

   Revised: When Sandra completes her commercial jet training, she will interview with United Airlines and Southwest Air.

2. Loudly talking on his cell phone, Ivan strolled through the mall.

   Revised: C

3. A city that I have always wanted to visit.

   Revised: Moscow is a city that I have always wanted to visit.

4. If she speaks Portuguese fluently, she will probably get the job.

   Revised: C

5. The comic strip *Peanuts*, which was created by Charles Schulz.

   Revised: The comic strip *Peanuts*, which was created by Charles Schulz, has become the most widely printed comic strip in the world.

6. Speaking three languages fluently.

   Revised: Speaking three languages fluently, Sarah plans to become a translator.

7. After the building was demolished.

   Revised: After the building was demolished, tourists took home bricks as souvenirs.

8. Frantically scanning the beach for the lost child.

   Revised: Frantically, she scanned the beach for the lost child.

Prepositional Phrase Fragments

Complete sentence:	13. A huge telescope in Green Bank, West Virginia, scans for signs of life.
Fragment:	14. On stars 20 to 30 light years away.

- Sentence 13 is a complete sentence.
- Sentence 14 is a fragment because it is a prepositional phrase beginning with *on*. It lacks both a subject and a verb.

This fragment can be corrected in two ways:

Corrected:	15. A huge telescope in Green Bank, West Virginia, scans for signs of life on stars 20 to 30 light years away.
Corrected:	16. A huge telescope in Green Bank, West Virginia, scans for signs of life. Its target is stars 20 to 30 light years away.

- Sentence 15 shows the easiest way to correct this fragment—by connecting it to the sentence before.
- In sentence 16, the fragment is changed into a complete sentence by adding a subject, *its target,* and a verb, *is.*

Appositive Phrase Fragments

Fragment:	17. A fine pianist.
Complete sentence:	18. Cecilia won a scholarship to Juilliard.

- Sentence 17 is a fragment because it is an appositive—a noun phrase. It lacks a verb, and it is not a complete idea.*
- Sentence 18 is a complete sentence.

This fragment can be corrected in two ways:

Corrected:	19. A fine pianist, Cecilia won a scholarship to Juilliard.
Corrected:	20. Cecilia is a fine pianist. She won a scholarship to Juilliard.

- In sentence 19, the fragment is combined with the sentence after it.
- In sentence 20, the fragment is changed into a complete sentence by adding a verb, *is*, and a subject, *she* (to avoid repeating *Cecilia*).

---

*For more work on appositives, see Chapter 22, "Revising for Sentence Variety," Part D.

Infinitive Phrase Fragments

Complete sentence:	21. Maya has always wanted to become a biologist.
Fragment:	22. To protect the environment.

- Sentence 21 is a complete sentence.
- Sentence 22 is a fragment because it lacks a subject and contains only the infinitive form of the verb—*to* plus the simple form of *protect*.

  This fragment can be corrected in two ways:

Corrected:	23. Maya has always wanted to become a biologist and to protect the environment.
Corrected:	24. Maya has always wanted to become a biologist. Her goal is to protect the environment.

- In sentence 23, the fragment is combined with the sentence before it.
- In sentence 24, the fragment is changed into a complete sentence.

Watch out for phrase fragments. A prepositional phrase, appositive phrase, or infinitive cannot stand alone, but must be combined with another sentence or changed into a complete sentence.

PRACTICE 5

TEACHING TIP

Have students share their answers to Practice 5 so that everyone can see possibilities other than the ones they wrote.

Now, proofread for fragments. Some of these examples are fragments; others are complete sentences. Put a *C* next to the complete sentences. Revise the fragments any way you choose. Answers will vary.

1. Constructed entirely of recycled plastic.

   Revised: The park benches were constructed entirely of recycled plastic.

2. Jogging reduces stress.

   Revised: C

3. Ellen, an investigator for the FBI.

   Revised: Ellen, an investigator for the FBI, analyzes cases of identity theft.

4. Working past midnight.

   Revised: Working past midnight, Terry was exhausted.

5. Caring for a pet.

   Revised: Caring for a pet teaches children responsibility.

6. At the top of the hill.

   Revised: A radio tower is located at the top of the hill.

7. Filmed on location in the Andes.

   Revised: The movie was filmed on location in the Andes.

8. The Picasso sketch.

   Revised: The Picasso sketch was sold for half a million dollars.

ESL TIP
ESL and *visual learners* will find this review chart especially useful. Suggest that students keep it handy as they write and revise.

Review Chart: Correcting Sentence Fragments

Type of Fragment	F *Fragment* C *Corrected*
1. Dependent clause	**F** After Jake moved to Colorado. **C** After Jake moved to Colorado, he learned to ski.
2. Relative clause	**F** Who loves computer games. **C** My niece, who loves computer games, repairs my computer.
3. *-ing* modifier	**F** Surfing the Web. **C** Surfing the Web, we visited European art museum sites.
4. Prepositional phrase	**F** Inside the cave. **C** They found mastodon bones inside the cave.
5. Appositive	**F** A slow student. **C** Einstein, a slow student, proved to be a genius.
6. Infinitive	**F** To go dancing tonight. **C** She wants to go dancing tonight.

PROOFREADING STRATEGY

Sentence fragments are a serious error. To spot and correct them more easily in your writing, try the **bottom-up proofreading technique**. Start by reading the last sentence of your paper, carefully, word by word. Then read the second-to-last sentence, and so on, all the way from the "bottom to the top." For each sentence, ask:

1. Does this sentence have a *subject*, a *complete verb*, and express a *complete thought*?
2. Is this an incomplete thought that starts with a word like *because*, *although*, or *when*? If so, fragments like this often can be fixed by connecting them to the sentence before or after.
3. Is this an incomplete thought containing *who*, *which*, or *that*? If so, such fragments often can be fixed by connecting them to the sentence before or after.

If sentence fragments are one of your error patterns, log them in your Personal Error Patterns Chart and proofread every paper once through, looking specifically for fragments.

PRACTICE 6

Fragments are most likely to occur in paragraphs or longer pieces of writing. Proofread the paragraph below for fragments. Correct them in any way you choose, either adding the fragments to other sentences or making them into complete sentences. Answers will vary.

(1) F. Scott Fitzgerald's novel *The Great Gatsby* inspired a Broadway play and four motion pictures, (2) ~~All~~ all of them focusing on Gatsby's obsession with Daisy. (3) The first film starring Warner Baxter (4) ~~Was~~ was released in 1927. (5) Alan Ladd played the lead in the 1949 version directed by Elliot Nugent. (6) In 1974, Jack Clayton ~~directing~~ directed Robert Redford and Mia Farrow as the doomed couple. (7). Francis Ford Coppola, best known for directing *The Godfather* two years before, (8) ~~Wrote~~ wrote the script. (9) To be true to the novel, (10) Coppola used much of the book's dialogue. (11) The Australian director Baz Luhrmann used extensive computer graphics to recreate New York City in the early 1920s for his film, (12) ~~Shot~~ shot in New South Wales. (13) Released in 2013, (14) ~~This~~ this version of *The Great Gatsby* starred Leonardo DiCaprio and Carey Mulligan.

AF archive/Alamy Stock Photo

Leonardo DiCaprio (as Jay Gatsby) and Carey Mulligan (as Daisy Buchanan) in the 2013 film *The Great Gatsby*

PRACTICE 7

TEACHING TIP

Practice 7 challenges students to spot and correct fragments even as Ms. Ibanez's story makes them want to read on. Have them think critically about the qualities that made her successful. Can these qualities be learned?

Proofread this essay for fragments. Correct them in any way you choose, either adding the fragments to other sentences or making them into complete sentences. Be careful of the punctuation. Answers will vary.

HER FOCUS IS SUCCESS

(1) If the way we react to adversity reveals our true character~~.~~, (2) Maria Elena Ibanez is extraordinary. (3) This successful computer engineer and businesswoman is a master at refusing to let obstacles keep her from a goal.

(4) In 1973, nineteen-year-old Maria Elena left Colombia and arrived alone in Miami~~.~~, (5) ~~Speaking~~ speaking just a few words of English. (6) Her goal was to learn fifty new words a day~~.~~ (7) ~~By~~ by talking to people and reading children's books. (8) Soon she spoke well enough to enroll at Florida International University and earn a computer science degree; she so impressed college officials that they hired her as a programmer.

(9) In 1982, Maria Elena started her first company. (10) Because computers cost much more in South America than they did in the United States~~.~~, (11) ~~She~~ she decided to sell reasonably priced computers to South American dealers. (12) When some dealers hesitated to do business with such a young woman, she won their respect with her expertise and willingness to teach them about the new technology. (13) Soon she sold International Micro Systems~~.~~, (14) ~~The~~ the nation's 55th fastest growing private company, at a huge profit.

(15) In spite of this success, people laughed out loud when Maria Elena announced her new goal. (16) To sell computers throughout Africa. (17) She paid no attention and returned from her first selling trip with handfuls of orders. (18) Then in 1992, disaster struck.

(19) Hurricane Andrew plowed into Miami, exploding Maria Elena's house. (20) As she and her two small children hid in a closet. (21) In the morning, dazed, she walked to the offices and warehouse of her new company. (22) The building was a mangled mess of fallen walls, trees, wet paper, and smoking wires. (23) Sitting down on a curb, she cried, but as her employees began arriving. (24) She sprang into action.

(25) One worker said the company could set up in his home. (26) Which had electricity. (27) Working 24 hours a day and using cell phones, the employees called all their African customers. (28) To say everything was fine and their orders would be shipped on time. (29) International High Tech grew 700 percent that year. (30) Despite the most damaging hurricane in U.S. history.

(31) Maria Elena moved her company into its rebuilt offices. (32) Today she and the children live in an apartment. (33) Not a house. (34) Asked about losing every piece of clothing, every picture, every possession in her former home. (35) She laughs, says that most problems hide opportunities, and adds that now she has no lawn to mow.

PRACTICE 8 REVIEW

Proofread these paragraphs for run-ons, comma splices, and fragments. Correct the errors in any way you choose. Answers will vary.

Paragraph 1

(1) Scenes in movies often require multiple takes, some may be shot over days or even weeks. (2) Despite careful planning. (3) Mistakes can happen. (4) Hair and makeup may be hard to duplicate and props can be forgotten or misplaced. (5) Concentrating on the important aspects of a dramatic scene. (6) Directors and technicians sometimes miss details. (7) Some of Hollywood's most famous films contain errors in continuity, some of them are quite noticeable. (8) In *Casablanca*, for example, Rick, played by Humphrey Bogart, is shown waiting on a train platform in a driving rain. (9) His trench coat is soaking

TEACHING TIP
You might ask students if they have noticed obvious goofs in movies. You can use this topic as a critical viewing exercise. Samples of movie "goofs" are posted online and can motivate class discussion.

wet, ~~when~~ yet when he boards the train in the next shot, his coat is crisp and dry. (10) The holiday classic *It's a Wonderful Life* includes a scene showing Jimmy Stewart tossing a Christmas wreath on a table to pick up a telephone. (11) As he holds the phone in the next shot, the wreath magically reappears around his arm. (12) After a fight scene in *LA Confidential*~~.~~, (13) ~~Bruises~~ bruises appear and disappear on Guy Pearce's face. (14) Today, as soon as films are released, alert fans are bound to spot goofs and share them online.

Paragraph 2

(1) Some teenagers seem to start the day tired~~,~~. ~~they~~ They are worn out even before they leave for school. (2) Once in class, they might doze off, even in the middle of an exciting lesson. (3) Are these students lazy~~,~~? ~~have~~ Have they stayed out too late partying? (4) Medical research provides a different explanation for the exhaustion of these teens. (5) As children become adolescents, they develop an increased need for sleep, especially in the morning. (6) Unfortunately, most American high schools start around 7:30 A.M., and many students have to get up as early as 5:00 A.M. (7) Scientists suggest that if students could start school later in the day~~.~~, (8) ~~They~~ they might get the extra sleep they need. (9) To test this theory, many schools have begun to experiment with later hours. (10) Congress is even paying the extra operating costs for schools that start after 9:00 A.M. (11) The hope is that teens will be less tired~~,~~; furthermore, because schools that start later will end later, students will be off the streets and out of trouble during the late afternoon~~.~~, (12) ~~Which~~ which is prime mischief time.

TEACHING TIP
Students may enjoy debating or writing about keeping or changing early start times for school and/or work.

PRACTICE 9 REVIEW

Proofread this essay for run-ons, comma splices, and fragments. Correct the errors in any way you choose. Answers will vary.

FRIENDS AND ENEMIES

(1) Thomas Jefferson and John Adams were fellow patriots, political rivals, bitter presidential candidates, and friends. (2) As Founding Fathers~~.~~, (3) Adams and Jefferson worked in the Continental Congress to draft the Declaration of Independence~~.~~, (4) ~~Forming~~ forming a lasting friendship. (5) Both men were known for

their high principles. (6) Adams agreed to represent the British soldiers who fired on the crowd in the Boston Massacre Jefferson wanted to include a paragraph opposing slavery in the Declaration of Independence.

(7) In 1796 Adams and Jefferson both ran for president. (8) Representing different parties. (8) At this time presidential candidates did not have "running mates" they campaigned alone. (9) John Adams won the presidency, Jefferson became vice president. (10) Though once close friends. (11) Adams and Jefferson disagreed over governing policies. (12) Adams favored a strong central government in contrast, Jefferson believed in states' rights. (13) Four years later. (14) Adams ran for re-election. (15) Jefferson decided to run against him. (16) The only time a serving president and vice president ran against each other.

(17) The campaign of 1800 was especially negative. (18) Adams was denounced as a "hideous hermaphroditical character" who was neither male nor female Jefferson was called a low-life of mixed race. (18) Jefferson won the presidency, Adams retired to his farm in Massachusetts. (19) After serving two terms. (20) Jefferson left the White House and returned to Virginia.

(21) Urged by a mutual friend. (22) The rivals resumed their friendship. (23) Writing over a hundred and fifty letters over fourteen years. (24) Coincidentally, both men died on the same day, July 4, 1826. (25) The fiftieth anniversary of the Declaration of Independence.

TEACHING TIP

To prompt critical thinking, ask students if they think American political campaigns have always been negative. You might introduce examples of negative campaign ads, cartoons, and handbills from the past. Many classic campaign ads and cartoons are available online. Ask students if negative campaigning is effective.

PRACTICE 10 REVIEW

Proofread this essay for run-ons, comma splices, and fragments. Correct the errors in any way you choose. Answers will vary.

AN AMERICAN FAMILY

(1) Today television is dominated by reality TV shows that follow the lives of celebrities, contestants, and working people. (2) The first reality show aired in 1973 broadcast by PBS, the show was a documentary called *An American Family.* (3) Filmmaker Craig Gilbert convinced public broadcasting executives to fund a proposed documentary about the private lives of a real family. (4) After examining several potential subjects. (5) Gilbert chose the Loud family of Santa Barbara. (6) The Louds appeared as a typical American family Bill and Pat Loud lived in

an upscale neighborhood and had five children. (7) The Louds agreed to let Gilbert's crew have access to their home. (8) In the spring and summer of 1971, (9) ~~Cameras~~ cameras recorded the Louds having dinner, talking on the phone, and playing music. (10) Looking at the raw footage, (11) ~~Network~~ network executives were dismayed. (12) Nothing interesting seemed to be happening.

(13) But as the weeks passed, Gilbert's cameras began to record dramatic moments. (14) The Louds' eldest son Lance (15) ~~Announced~~ announced that he was gay. (16) Bill Loud returned home from a business trip, and his wife Pat greeted him by declaring she wanted a divorce and ordering him out of the house. (17) After shooting 300 hours of film, (18) Gilbert edited his work down to twelve one-hour episodes. (19) In the spring of 1973, *An American Family* premiered, and it quickly became the most popular show on public television. (20) Viewers were riveted by the documentary's uncensored look into an American home. (21) The Louds became controversial national figures. (22) ~~Displayed~~ They were displayed on magazine covers and interviewed on talk shows.

(23) Though divorced, (24) Bill and Pat Loud appeared on talk shows claiming that the series misrepresented their lives. (25) The 2011 film *Cinema Verite*, starring Tim Robbins and Diane Lane, (26) ~~Offered~~ offered a fictional account about the making of *An American Family*.

EXPLORING ONLINE

www.pbs.org/video/2045835722

You can watch a compilation of *An American Family* on PBS. What do you think of Craig Gilbert's project? Was it an accurate depiction of a family? What role does editing play in shaping how film shapes our perceptions of reality? How does this program contrast with current reality television shows?

EXPLORING ONLINE

grammar.ccc.commnet.edu/grammar/quizzes/runons_quiz.htm

Take this quiz to help you root out run-ons.

grammar.ccc.commnet.edu/grammar/fragments.htm

Tips and quizzes to help you find and fix sentence fragments

CHAPTER 29

Present Tense (Agreement)

A. Defining Subject-Verb Agreement

ESL TIP
Many ESL students have trouble with verbs and verb tenses in English. You can tailor this comprehensive unit to your needs by assigning some chapters and parts to the full class and other parts selectively.

ESL TIP
In many languages—such as Chinese, Japanese, and Korean—subject-verb number agreement does not exist. Thus, ESL students may need extra help with the concept.

Subjects and verbs in the present tense must **agree** in number; that is, singular subjects take verbs with singular endings, and plural subjects take verbs with plural endings.

Verbs in the Present Tense
Sample Verb: *To Leap*

	Singular		**Plural**	
	If the subject is	**the verb is**	**If the subject is**	**the verb is**
1st person:	I	leap	we	leap
2nd person:	you	leap	you	leap
3rd person:	he she it	leaps	they	leap

TEACHING TIP

Write two or three sentences containing subject-verb agreement errors on the board. Explain that, in general, an *-s* follows *either* the subject *or* the verb, not both, dispelling the common misconception that a subject with an *-s* requires a verb with an *-s*.

- Use an *-s* or *-es* ending on the verb only when the subject is *he*, *she*, or *it* or the equivalent of *he*, *she*, or *it*.

The subjects and verbs in the following sentences agree:

1. He *bicycles* to the steel mills every morning.
2. They *bicycle* to the steel mills every morning.
3. This student *hopes* to go to social work school.
4. The planets *revolve* around the sun.

- In sentence 1, the singular subject, *he*, takes the singular form of the verb, *bicycles*. *Bicycles* agrees with *he*.
- In sentence 2, the plural subject, *they*, takes the plural form of the verb, *bicycle*. *Bicycle* agrees with *they*.
- In sentence 3, the subject, *student*, is equivalent to *he* or *she* and takes the singular form of the verb, *hopes*.
- In sentence 4, the subject, *planets*, is equivalent to *they* and takes the plural form of the verb, *revolve*.

Subjects joined by the conjunction *and* usually take a plural verb:

5. Kirk and Quincy *attend* a pottery class at the Y.

- The subject, *Kirk and Quincy*, is plural, the equivalent of *they*.
- *Attend* agrees with the plural subject.*

PRACTICE 1

Underline the subject and circle the correct present tense verb.

1. Many people (confuses, confuse) the roles of the FBI and the CIA.
2. Both organizations (addresses, address) issues of national security.
3. The government, however, (establishes, establish) clear assignments for both.
4. The FBI (serves, serve) as a domestic intelligence service and a national law enforcement agency.
5. An FBI agent (operates, operate) much like a police officer, investigating and arresting American citizens for engaging in crime or terrorism.
6. The CIA, on the other hand, (gathers, gather) information on foreign governments and individuals.

---

*For work on consistent verb tense, see Chapter 21, "Revising for Consistency and Parallelism," Part A.

TEACHING TIP
Consider doing Practice 1 with the whole class, or let smaller groups complete it, competing for the best verb agreement score.

ESL TIP
Remind ESL students of the importance of *pronouncing* plurals in English. Native Spanish speakers often do not pronounce the final -*s*, so correcting pronunciation can improve their comprehension, verb agreement, and spelling.

7. CIA agents (does, do) not investigate or arrest American citizens.
8. The traditional lines between the agencies (blurs, blur) in an era of international terrorism and global crime.
9. Today FBI agents often (travels, travel) overseas to cooperate with foreign law enforcement agencies to track criminals.
10. In the digital age the online criminals victimizing American citizens and businesses often (operates, operate) out of foreign countries.
11. Increasingly, FBI investigations (unearths, unearth) links to foreign organizations.
12. Today CIA agents frequently (engages, engage) in overt actions, especially in fighting terrorists.
13. Instead of collecting and analyzing information, the CIA often (takes, take) direct action to eliminate terrorists.
14. According to some experts, the two agencies (needs, need) to work closer together to combat terrorism, money laundering, and cyberattacks.
15. Many other countries (has, have) a single intelligence service covering both domestic and international issues.

B. Three Troublesome Verbs in the Present Tense: *To Be, To Have, To Do*

ESL TIP
A common ESL error is omitting the "be" verb in sentences (e.g., *He a student*) because some other languages do not require a verb in this instance.

Choosing the correct verb form of *to be, to have,* and *to do* can be tricky. Study these charts:

Reference Chart—*To Be* Present Tense

	Singular		**Plural**	
	If the subject is	**the verb is**	**If the subject is**	**the verb is**
1st person:	I	am	we	are
2nd person:	you	are	you	are
3rd person:	he she it	is	they	are

Reference Chart—*To Have* Present Tense

	Singular		Plural	
	If the subject is	**the verb is**	**If the subject is**	**the verb is**
1st person:	I	have	we	have
2nd person:	you	have	you	have
3rd person:	he, she, it	has	they	have

Reference Chart—*To Do* Present Tense

	Singular		Plural	
	If the subject is	**the verb is**	**If the subject is**	**the verb is**
1st person:	I	do	we	do
2nd person:	you	do	you	do
3rd person:	he, she, it	does	they	do

PRACTICE 2

Write the correct present tense form of the verb in the space at the right of the pronoun.

To be	**To have**	**To do**
I ___am___	we ___have___	it ___does___
we ___are___	she ___has___	they ___do___
he ___is___	he ___has___	she ___does___
you ___are___	they ___have___	you ___do___
it ___is___	I ___have___	he ___does___
they ___are___	it ___has___	we ___do___
she ___is___	you ___have___	I ___do___

PRACTICE 3

ESL TIP
To help ESL students improve their error recognition, ask them to read a paper aloud, stopping every time they see or hear an error. If students read past an error, you will know which errors they cannot yet identify.

Fill in the correct present tense form of the verb in parentheses.

1. Surfing ___is___ (to be) an extreme sport, and it ___has___ (to have) many fans.
2. Most beginners ___do___ (to do) basic moves on dry land—lying on the board, kneeling, and then rising to a hunched standing position.
3. An ocean beach with gentle, regular waves ___is___ (to be) the ideal place to start surfing.
4. Expert surfers ___have___ (to have) exceptional skills and ___are___ (to be) at home in the monster waves off Hawaii or Australia.
5. An expert ___does___ (to do) a "roller coaster" by soaring from the bottom to the top of a giant wave and down again.
6. "Riding a tube" ___is___ (to be) a thrilling trip through the transparent green tunnel of a giant wave.
7. Hawaiian coastlines ___have___ (to have) some of the world's best surfing.
8. Banzai Pipeline in Oahu ___is___ (to be) a famous surfing break; it ___has___ (to have) excellent tubes and waves three stories high.
9. Oahu's Sunset Rip, a notorious break, ___has___ (to have) several international surfing competitions.
10. For the surfer, wipeouts, flying boards, and sharks ___are___ (to be) constant dangers.
11. Yet the sport ___has___ (to have) new converts every year.
12. Many say that it ___is___ (to be) a spiritual experience.

C. Special Singular Constructions

TEACHING TIP
The special problems in Parts C–G are tricky for many students and may need extra explanation and practice.

Each of these constructions takes a **singular** verb:

Special Singular Constructions	
each (of) . . .	neither (of) . . .
either (of) . . .	one (of) . . .
every one (of) . . .	which one (of) . . .

1. *Neither* of the birds *has* feathers yet.
2. *Each* of the solutions *presents* difficulties.

- In sentence 1, *neither* means *neither one*. *Neither* is a singular subject and requires the singular verb *has*.
- In sentence 2, *each* means *each one*. *Each* is a singular subject and requires the singular verb *presents*.

However, an exception to this general rule is the case in which two subjects are joined by (*n*)*either* . . . (*n*)*or*. . . . Here, the verb agrees with the subject closer to it:

3. Neither the teacher nor the *pupils want* the semester shortened.
4. Either the graphs or the *map has* to be changed.

- In sentence 3, *pupils* is the subject closer to the verb. The plural subject *pupils* takes the verb *want*.
- In sentence 4, *map* is the subject closer to the verb. The singular subject *map* takes the verb *has*.

PRACTICE 4

TEACHING TIP

Suggest that students cross out the intervening prepositional phrase and then say the sentence aloud without that phrase. They may be able to better "hear" the verb that's correct.

Underline the subject and circle the correct verb in each sentence.

1. Each of these ferns (needs, need) special care.
2. One of the customers always (forget, forgets) his or her umbrella.
3. Which one of the flights (goes, go) nonstop to Dallas?
4. Every one of those cameras (costs, cost) more than I can afford.
5. Either you or Emma (is, are) correct.
6. One of the players on the team (is, are) sick today.
7. Do you really believe that one of these oysters (holds, hold) a pearl?
8. Neither of the twins (resembles, resemble) his parents.
9. One of the scientists (believes, believe) he can cure baldness.
10. Each of these inventions (has, have) an effect on how we spend our leisure time.

D. Separation of Subject and Verb

Sometimes a phrase or a clause separates the subject from the verb. First, look for the subject; then make sure that the verb agrees with the subject.

1. The economist's *ideas* on this matter *seem* well thought out.
2. *Radios* that were made in the 1930s *are* now collectors' items.

- In sentence 1, the *ideas* are well thought out. The prepositional phrase *on this matter* separates the subject *ideas* from the verb *seem.**
- In sentence 2, *radios* are now collectors' items. The relative clause *that were made in the 1930s* separates the subject *radios* from the verb *are*.

PRACTICE 5

TEACHING TIP

If students erroneously make the verb agree with the object of the preposition in these constructions, remind them to cross out the intervening prepositional phrase and then verify agreement.

Read each sentence carefully for meaning. Cross out any phrase or clause that separates the subject from the verb. Underline the subject and circle the correct verb.

1. The plums ~~in that bowl~~ (tastes, taste) sweet.
2. The instructions ~~on the package~~ (is, are) in French and Japanese.
3. Our new community center, ~~which has a swimming pool and tennis courts~~, (keeps, keep) everyone happy.
4. The lampshades ~~that are made of stained glass~~ (looks, look) beautiful at night.
5. All the smartphones ~~on that shelf~~ (comes, come) with free apps.
6. A movie ~~that lasts more than three hours usually~~ (puts, put) me to sleep.
7. The man ~~with the dark sunglasses~~ (looks, look) like a typical movie villain.
8. The two nurses ~~who check blood pressure~~ (enjoys, enjoy) chatting with the patients.
9. The function ~~of these metal racks~~ (remains, remain) a mystery to me.
10. The van ~~on the street~~ (has, have) two flat tires.

---

*For more work on prepositional phrases, see Chapter 26, "The Simple Sentence," Part B.

ESL TIP
In some languages, *there is* sentences do not exist, so ESL students may need to practice using them. A typical sentence error where *there is* or *there are* should be used is the following: *On the bus had many people.*

E. Sentences Beginning with *There* and *Here*

In sentences that begin with *there* or *here*, the subject usually follows the verb:

1. There *seem* to be two *flies* in my soup.
2. Here *is* my *prediction* for the coming year.

- In sentence 1, the plural subject *flies* takes the plural verb *seem*.
- In sentence 2, the singular subject *prediction* takes the singular verb *is*.

You can often determine what the verb should be by reversing the word order: *two flies seem* . . . or *my prediction is*. . . .

PRACTICE 6

Underline the subject and circle the correct verb in each sentence.

1. There (goes, go) Jennifer Lawrence.
2. There (is, are) only a few seconds left in the game.
3. Here (is, are) a terrific way to save money—make a budget and stick to it!
4. There (has, have) been robberies in the neighborhood lately.
5. Here (is, are) the plantains you ordered.
6. Here (comes, come) Jimmy, the television talk-show host.
7. There (is, are) no direct route to Black Creek from here.
8. There (seems, seem) to be something wrong with the doorbell.
9. Here (is, are) the teapot and sugar bowl I've been looking for.
10. There (is, are) six reporters in the hall waiting for an interview.

F. Agreement in Questions

ESL TIP
ESL students might need to be reminded that normal English word order is inverted in questions.

In questions, the subject usually follows the verb:

1. What *is* the *secret* of your success?
2. Where *are* the *copies* of the review?

- In sentence 1, the subject *secret* takes the singular verb *is*.
- In sentence 2, the subject *copies* takes the plural verb *are*.

You can often determine what the verb should be by reversing the word order: *the secret of your success is . . .* or *the copies are. . . .*

PRACTICE 7

Underline the subject and circle the correct verb in each sentence.

1. How (does, do) the combustion engine actually work?
2. Why (is, are) Robert and Jade so suspicious?
3. Where (is, are) the new suitcases?
4. Which tour guide (have, has) a pair of binoculars?
5. (Are, Is) Dianne and Ramone still recording podcasts?
6. What (seems, seem) to be the problem here?
7. Why (is, are) those boxes stacked in the corner?
8. (Is, Are) the mattress factory really going to close in June?
9. How (does, do) you explain that strange footprint?
10. Who (is, are) those people on the fire escape?

G. Agreement in Relative Clauses

A **relative clause** is a subordinate clause that begins with *who, which,* or *that.* The verb in the relative clause must agree with the antecedent of the *who, which,* or *that.**

1. People *who have a good sense of humor* make good neighbors.
2. Be careful of a scheme *that promises you a lot of money fast.*

- In sentence 1, the antecedent of *who* is *people. People* should take the plural verb *have.*
- In sentence 2, the antecedent of *that* is *scheme. Scheme* takes the singular verb *promises.*

PRACTICE 8

Underline the antecedent of the *who, which,* or *that.* Then circle the correct verb.

1. Most patients prefer doctors who (spends, spend) time talking with them.

*For more work on relative clauses, see Chapter 22, "Revising for Sentence Variety," Part D.

LEARNING STYLES TIP
Occasionally turning grammar exercises or review sessions into competitive games is a great way to focus attention. Divide the class into teams and give each team a point for every correct answer. Reward the winning team with small prizes.

2. The gnarled oak that (shades, shade) the garden is my favorite tree.
3. Tablets, which (has, have) some advantages over laptop computers, are becoming more popular.
4. My neighbor, who (swims, swim) at least one hour a day, is seventy years old.
5. Planning ahead, which (saves, save) hours of wasted time, is a good way to manage time effectively.
6. Employers often appreciate employees who (asks, ask) intelligent questions.
7. Students enjoy the new student union, which (features, feature) a free coffee bar.
8. Everyone admires her because she is someone who always (sees, see) the bright side of a bad situation.
9. He is the man who (creates, create) furniture from scraps of walnut, cherry, and birch.
10. You should avoid foods that (contains, contain) added sugar.

PROOFREADING STRATEGY

If present tense verb agreement is one of your error patterns, you might **isolate** and **color code**. First, if you are writing on a computer, *isolate each sentence* on its own line. This will help your brain and eye focus on one sentence at a time. Next, find the subject and verb in each sentence; use highlighters to *color code* subjects yellow and verbs green. Cross out any confusing prepositional phrases.

Now check each color-coded pair for subject-verb agreement. 1. If you aren't sure, *change the subject to a pronoun*, and see if it agrees with the verb. 2. Do a final "audio check" and read the sentence aloud. Here are two examples:

they / are owned
The apartments ~~on State Street~~ is owned ~~by the college~~.

he / wants
My friend want to rent one of them this fall.

PRACTICE 9 REVIEW

TEACHING TIP
Students should be able to recognize that this essay is developed by illustration. Ask them to identify the examples that develop the topic sentences in the second and third paragraphs.

Proofread the following essay for agreement errors. You might try out the proofreading strategy to see if it works for you.

JOB HUNTING? THINK GREEN.

(1) These days, many job fairs and sites ~~features~~ feature green jobs, or green-collar jobs. (2) Just what is a green job? (3) A green job ~~provide~~ provides solid wages yet preserves rather than drains the earth's resources. (4) Workers who build hybrid cars have green jobs. (5) So do people who install "green roofs" on buildings—garden areas that ~~purifies~~ purify the air and prevent diseases like asthma.

(6) Green-collar employees often take pride in their work because they contribute to the health of the community. (7) Many colleges now offer courses that ~~prepares~~ prepare students for a greener workforce. (8) Robert, Cheree, and Han ~~illustrates~~ illustrate this trend.

(9) Robert Gomez of Oakland, California, remembers his shock at losing a good job in commercial construction two years ago. (10) Today, at 52, thanks to a poster in the unemployment office, Robert ~~have~~ has a certificate in solar panel installation from Merritt College and a new lease on life. (11) He installs solar energy panels on homes and buildings, a job he enjoys. (12) According to career counselors, people like Robert ~~does~~ do well even during hard times because they stay flexible and get new training.

(13) Cheree Williams wants a green career. (14) She attends Evergreen State College in Eugene, Oregon, a school that wins awards for its environmental efforts. (15) Cheree ~~study~~ studies in the Food, Health, and Sustainability program; she learns earth-friendly farming methods in the school's organic garden. (16) With her degree, she ~~hope~~ hopes to work in the public schools, building children's health and achievement through wise food choices.

(17) A third example is Han Bae, who loves chemistry and cars. (18) A career in the growing biofuels industry ~~make~~ makes sense for him, he believes. (19) At Central Carolina Community College, Han gets hands-on experience making and testing new fuels because a factory right on campus makes ethanol from different plant sources. (20) College vehicles actually ~~runs~~ run on these fuels.

(21) Nationwide, enrollment in green courses ~~increase~~ increases every year, touching fields as diverse as prison administration and small business entrepreneurship.

heshphoto/Getty Images

A construction crew installs solar panels on a roof.

EXPLORING ONLINE

grammar.ccc.commnet.edu/grammar/sv_agr.htm

Review the rules of subject-verb agreement; then scroll to the bottom for interactive quizzes.

a4esl.Org/q/h/vm/svagr.html

Take this verb quiz and get instant feedback on your answers.

CHAPTER 30

Past Tense

A: Regular Verbs in the Past Tense

B: Irregular Verbs in the Past Tense

C: A Troublesome Verb in the Past Tense: *To Be*

D: Troublesome Pairs in the Past Tense: *Can/Could, Will/Would*

A. Regular Verbs in the Past Tense

TEACHING TIP
For students who don't pronounce or hear the -*ed* on regular verbs, these forms can be more problematic than irregulars. Help such students see that this is their error pattern.

Regular verbs in the past tense take an -*ed* or -*d* ending:

1. The captain *hoisted* the flag.
2. They *purchased* a flat screen TV yesterday.
3. We *deposited* a quarter in the meter.

- *Hoisted, purchased,* and *deposited* are regular verbs in the past tense.
- Each verb ends in -*ed* or -*d*.

PRACTICE 1

ESL TIP
Verb tense can be a difficult concept for nonnative writers, requiring extra help and practice.

Fill in the past tense of the regular verbs in parentheses.*

1. On July 8, 1947, the headline of the Daily Record in Roswell, New Mexico, ___announced___ (announce) the U.S. military's capture of a "flying saucer."

*If you have questions about spelling, see Chapter 40, "Spelling," Parts D, E, and F.

TEACHING TIP
You may wish to review spelling rules for adding *-d* or *-ed*. 1. If the verb ends in *e*, add *-d* (*lived, skated*). 2. If the verb ends in *y*, change the *y* to *i* and add *-ed* (*cried, applied*). 3. If the last two letters of the verb are a vowel plus a consonant (except *w* and *y*), double the consonant and add *-ed* (*tapped, committed*). 4. For all other verbs, add *-ed* (*picked, stayed, followed*).

2. Events surrounding this incident __produced__ (produce) one of the most famous and controversial UFO stories of all time.

3. A local sheep rancher first __stumbled__ (stumble) upon a large field of wreckage that __resembled__ (resemble) sheets of tough, wafer-thin metal.

4. Several people who __stopped__ (stop) at the crash site __reported__ (report) seeing bodies of space aliens.

5. Army officials __gathered__ (gather) the fragments, __transported__ (transport) them to the Roswell Army Air Field, and __issued__ (issue) a press release about a mysterious disc.

6. Soon afterward, however, the military __changed__ (change) its story and __identified__ (identify) the object as a fallen weather balloon.

7. Reporters and the public __ignored__ (ignore) the incident for thirty years, but in 1978, an Army major who __searched__ (search) the wreckage __accused__ (accuse) the military of lying.

8. Other eyewitnesses to the crash __admitted__ (admit) seeing strange bodies, which they __portrayed__ (portray) as short, hairless beings with large heads.

9. Over sixty years later, scientists are debating whether the military actually __seized__ (seize) and __studied__ (study) the remains of beings from outer space.

10. For years, UFO skeptics __claimed__ (claim) that the strange debris found in 1947 __consisted__ (consist) of special membranes used in a top secret high altitude spy balloon.

B. Irregular Verbs in the Past Tense

ESL TIP
Irregular verbs can be a problem for ESL students and speakers of languages that do not include irregular verbs, such as Chinese.

Irregular verbs do not take an *-ed* or *-d* ending in the past but change internally:

1. I *wrote* that letter in ten minutes.
2. Although the orange cat *fell* from a high branch, she escaped unharmed.
3. The play *began* on time but ended fairly late.

TEACHING TIP
Tell students that many irregular verbs fall into one of three categories. 1. Do not change (*cut/cut, hit/hit*). 2. Change their vowel (*ride/rode, get/got, drink/drank*). 3. Change completely (*teach/taught, think/thought*).

- *Wrote* is the past tense of *write*.
- *Fell* is the past tense of *fall*.
- *Began* is the past tense of *begin*.

Here is a partial list of irregular verbs:

Reference Chart
Irregular Verbs in the Past Tense

Simple Form	Past Tense	Simple Form	Past Tense
be	was, were	leave	left
become	became	let	let
begin	began	lie	lay
blow	blew	lose	lost
break	broke	make	made
bring	brought	mean	meant
build	built	meet	met
buy	bought	pay	paid
catch	caught	put	put
choose	chose	quit	quit
come	came	read	read
cut	cut	ride	rode
deal	dealt	rise	rose
dig	dug	run	ran
dive	dove (dived)	say	said
do	did	see	saw
draw	drew	seek	sought
drink	drank	sell	sold
drive	drove	send	sent
eat	ate	shake	shook
fall	fell	shine	shone (shined)
feed	fed	sing	sang
feel	felt	sit	sat
fight	fought	sleep	slept
find	found	speak	spoke
fly	flew	spend	spent
forbid	forbade	split	split
forget	forgot	spring	sprang
forgive	forgave	stand	stood
freeze	froze	steal	stole
get	got	stink	stank
give	gave	swim	swam
go	went	take	took
grow	grew	teach	taught
have	had	tear	tore
hear	heard	tell	told
hide	hid	think	thought

TEACHING TIP

Pair students and ask them to take turns using verbs from this list in spoken sentences. Doing so will give them a chance to hear the correct forms.

hold	held	throw	threw
hurt	hurt	understand	understood
keep	kept	wake	woke (waked)
know	knew	wear	wore
lay	laid	win	won
lead	led	write	wrote

PRACTICE 2

Fill in the past tense of the regular and irregular verbs in parentheses. If you are not sure of the past tense, use the Reference Chart. Do not guess.

TEACHING AND ESL TIP

This practice works well in class. Students may wish to write in the past tense about someone who "broke through" in some way, as these individuals have done. In a diverse class, this can be an opportunity for cultural sharing.

LEARNING STYLES TIP

Reading passages like Practice 2 aloud in class is a great way to train *aural learners* and others to hear (and correct) verb errors. Speakers who drop *-ed* verb endings are helped by learning to hear and articulate those *-eds*.

HISPANIC HEROES: SHAKING UP HOLLYWOOD

(1) For much of the last century Hispanics in Hollywood __remained__ (remain) a small minority. (2) Many Latin actors either __accepted__ (accept) such stereotyped roles as the gardener or __changed__ (change) their names, hoping to snag better roles. (3) Jo Raquel Tejada __billed__ (bill) herself as Raquel Welch, and Ramon Estevez __became__ (become) Martin Sheen. (4) But a new century __brought__ (bring) deeper change—in the form of determined individuals who __dreamed__ (dream) of making or starring in movies and then __fought__ (fight) to open doors.

(5) Director Robert Rodriguez, for instance, __succeeded__ (succeed) after a rocky beginning. (6) As a young Texan, Rodriguez was rejected by the film school to which he __applied__ (apply). (7) Instead of getting discouraged, the twenty-three-year-old __took__ (take) off for Mexico with a movie camera, some friends, and $7,000. (8) The result was the film *El Mariachi*, a Spanish-language action comedy that Rodriguez later __sold__ (sell) to Columbia Pictures for worldwide distribution. (9) After that, he __kept__ (keep) entertaining moviegoers with low-budget, action-packed English-language films like *Desperado*, *Spy Kids*, and *From Dusk Till Dawn*. (10) He __raked__ (rake) in millions with his violent shoot-'em-up scenes and special effects.

(11) Perhaps more important, Rodriguez __put__ (put) Hispanics in top roles—for instance, casting Antonio Banderas as a dad, not a Hispanic dad, in *Spy Kids*. (12) "I find that the best way through a closed door," Rodriguez once __proclaimed__ (proclaim), "is to kick it open."

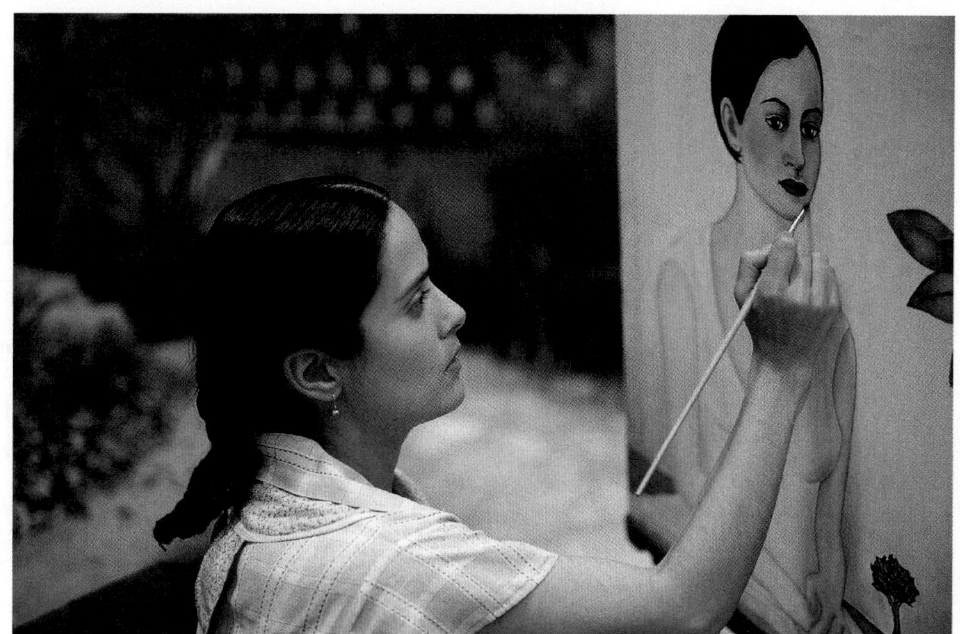

AF archive/Alamy Stock Photo

Salma Hayek as the Mexican painter Frida Kahlo, the dream role for which she fought.

(13) Another Hispanic who ___helped___ (help) make her own opportunities is Mexican-born actress and producer Salma Hayek. (14) Ironically, it was Rodriguez who ___battled___ (battle) Hollywood for approval to cast this unknown actress in one of *Desperado's* leading roles. (15) She ___did___ (do) not disappoint him, and her performance ___catapulted___ (catapult) her to fame. (16) From the time she was thirteen, Hayek ___admired___ (admire) Frida Kahlo and ___longed___ (long) to play the spirited Mexican painter in a film about her life. (17) Behind the scenes, Salma ___strategized___ (strategize) brilliantly to get the movie made, secure rights, and beat out Madonna for the part. (18) In the end, Hayek ___produced___ (produce) and ___starred___ (star) in *Frida*, which ___opened___ (open) in 2002. (19) Her performance in that lead role ___earned___ (earn) her an Academy Award nomination. (20) This movie and Salma's depiction of the brainy scientist in *Spy Kids* ___expanded___ (expand) Hollywood's ideas about "suitable" Hispanic roles.

(21) Rodriguez and Hayek are just two examples of the new infusion of talent in American movies. (22) In addition, Hispanics have achieved success on the small screen. (23) Comedian George Lopez ___appeared___ (appear) in several situation comedies and specials. (24) *Forbes* estimated that Sofia Vergara, star of *Modern Family*, ___earned___ (earn) $37 million in a year, making her the highest paid TV actress.

C. A Troublesome Verb in the Past Tense: *To Be*

To be is the only verb that in the past tense has different forms for different persons. Be careful of subject-verb agreement:

Reference Chart—*To Be* Past Tense

	Singular		Plural	
	If the subject is	the verb is	If the subject is	the verb is
1st person:	I	was	we	were
2nd person:	you	were	you	were
3rd person:	he she it	was	they	were

TEACHING TIP
In English, only *to be* changes in the past tense. Students might need extra help with *wasn't* and *weren't*—and the double whammy of agreement plus an apostrophe.

- Note that the first person singular form and the third person singular form are the same—*was*.

Be especially careful of agreement when adding *not* to *was* or *were* to make a contraction:

was + not = wasn't
were + not = weren't

PRACTICE 3

TEACHING TIP
A number of students use *was* with plural subjects (e.g., *we was* or *you was*) in informal conversation. Impress upon them that these errors are unacceptable in writing.

Circle the correct form of the verb *to be* in the past tense. Do not guess. If you are not sure of the correct form, use the Reference Chart in Part B of this chapter.

1. Oprah Winfrey (was, were) always an avid reader.
2. In fact, books (was, were) sometimes her only comfort during her difficult childhood and painful adolescence.
3. When her producers (was, were) considering a TV book club, the world's most popular talk-show host (was, were) sure she could get the whole country reading.
4. Her first book club selection (was, were) *The Deep End of the Ocean* by Jacquelyn Mitchard, the story of a kidnapped child; the public's rush to buy books (wasn't, weren't) anticipated.

5. Mitchard's publishers (was, were) astonished to have to reprint the book nearly twenty times; all in all, 900,000 hardcovers and over 2 million paperbacks (was, were) sold.
6. Every book club pick (was, were) a huge success, and even people who didn't read found they (was, were) eagerly awaiting Winfrey's next selection.
7. Toni Morrison's *Sula* (was, were) suddenly a best seller, as (was, were) older classics by William Faulkner, John Steinbeck, and Carson McCullers.
8. Controversy (was, were) no stranger to the show; Oprah publically chided James Frey after *A Million Little Pieces,* his "true life story," (was, were) shown to be lies.
9. When the final season of Oprah's show (was, were) announced in 2009, many readers (was, were) upset.
10. In 2012, however, Oprah (was, were) so enthusiastic about Cheryl Strayed's book *Wild* that she launched Oprah's Book Club 2.0 with digital and social media features.

D. Troublesome Pairs in the Past Tense: *Can/Could, Will/Would*

ESL TIP
Point out that *can* does not require an *-s* in third person singular.

Use *could* as the past tense of *can.*

1. Maria is extraordinary because she *can* remember what happened to her when she was three years old.
2. Before construction on the bridge started, I *could* drive home in 20 minutes.

- In sentence 1, *can* shows the action is in the present.
- In sentence 2, *could* shows the action occurred in the past.

PRACTICE 4

TEACHING AND ESL TIP
For in-class practice, ask volunteers to read these items aloud, correcting the verbs as they go. Have the class check their work by ear.

Fill in either the present tense *can* or the past tense *could.*

1. Tom is so talented that he ____can____ play most music on the piano by ear.
2. He ____can____ leave the hospital as soon as he feels stronger.
3. Last week we ____could____ not find fresh strawberries.

4. When we were in Spain last summer, we ___could___ see all of Madrid from our hotel balcony.

5. As a child, I ___could___ perform easily in public, but I ___can___ no longer do it.

6. Anything you ___can___ do, he ___can___ do better.

7. Nobody ___could___ find the guard after the robbery yesterday.

8. Today polls ___can___ usually predict who will win elections.

Use *would* as the past tense of *will*.

3. Roberta says that she *will* arrive with her camera in ten minutes.
4. Roberta said that she *would* arrive with her camera in ten minutes.

- In sentence 3, *will* points to the future from the present.
- In sentence 4, *would* points to the future from the past.

PRACTICE 5

Fill in either the present tense *will* or the past tense *would*.

1. Sean expected that he ___would___ arrive at midnight.

2. Sean expects that he ___will___ arrive at midnight.

3. I hope the sale at the used car lot ___will___ continue for another week.

4. I hoped the sale at the used car lot ___would___ continue for another week.

5. When Benny had time, he ___would___ organize his digital photos.

6. When Benny has time, he ___will___ organize his digital photos.

7. The chefs assure us that the wedding cake ___will___ be spectacular.

8. The chefs assured us that the wedding cake ___would___ be spectacular.

PROOFREADING STRATEGY

To proofread for past tense verb errors, especially if these are one of your error patterns, **highlight** and **read aloud**. First, read slowly through the text, underlining or highlighting the *main verb* or *verbs* in every sentence.

- Make sure that every *regular past tense verb* ends in *-d* or *-ed*.
- Carefully consider every *irregular past tense verb* to make sure it is in the correct form. If you aren't sure, check the past tense chart. Here are some examples:

discovered
After we got home from vacation, we discover water dripping from the ceiling.

were
Holes was punched in our roof when tree limbs fell on our house while we were gone.

PRACTICE 6 REVIEW

Proofread the following essay for past tense errors. Using highlighters, try the proofreading strategy to see if it works for you. Correct any errors by writing above the lines.

TEACHING TIP
Urge students to think critically about the pros and cons of video games. Perhaps suggest that they research the cognitive benefits of the games. Do any students want to work in this or another technology field?

VIDEO GAME NATION

(1) In 1972, when Nolan Bushnell introduced the first video game to the mass market, few people imagined what the future ~~hold~~ held. (2) Bushnell ~~call~~ called his new company Atari; the game was Pong. (3) To play, two people simply bounced a digital ball back and forth on a black-and-white console, turning knobs to control their paddles. (4) Primitive by today's standards, Pong ~~were~~ was a sensation in arcades and bars across the United States. (5) In 1975, Atari's home version of Pong ~~outsolded~~ outsold all other items in the Sears Christmas catalog. (6) But that was just the beginning. (7) Over the next thirty-five years, electronic games ~~becomed~~ became one of America's most popular pastimes, spawning a booming industry and new jobs.

(8) During the 1980s, the first generation of gamers ~~flock~~ flocked to arcades to play Pac-Man, Donkey Kong, and Centipede. (9) Far-sighted tech companies like Sony, Nintendo, and Microsoft ~~seen~~ saw this growing market and ~~gone~~ went to work. (10) They ~~create~~ created home consoles, handheld systems, and of course, more and better games. (11) With the evolution of eye-popping 3-D graphics, realistic sound and action, and imaginative characters, video games ~~begin~~ began to look more like television and movies than the electronic paddle-and-ball game that started it all. (12) The public ~~keeped~~ kept buying. (13) In 2014 alone, sales of computer and video games in the United States ~~total~~ totaled $5.5 billion.

(14) As the industry grew, so ~~do~~ did controversy. (15) Critics warned that gamers just ~~set~~ sat on the couch instead of playing outside. (16) Many ~~worryied~~ worried about the violent content of some games. (17) Others argued that the puzzle-based adventure games of the 1990s and early 2000s ~~teached~~ taught useful skills. (18) Gamers

~~has~~ had to reason, invent strategies, and foresee the consequences of their actions. (19) Despite the controversy, video games are now part of life for most American children, teens, and even adults. (20) In recent years, the average age of the video game player ~~rise~~ rose to thirty-five.

(21) Some gamers longed to work in the field, but they needed training. (22) They ~~knowed~~ knew that companies, hoping to create the latest, greatest game, formed development teams composed of graphic designers, artists, musicians, and computer technicians. (23) So it ~~were~~ was students themselves who ~~clamor~~ clamored for degree programs to teach them the necessary skills. (24) Some colleges—like New York's Rensselaer Polytechnic Institute and Pittsburgh's Carnegie Mellon University—responded quickly. (25) They ~~establish~~ established interdisciplinary programs to prepare students for the fast-moving video game industry of the future.

EXPLORING ONLINE

grammar.ccc.commnet.edu/grammar/quizzes/irregular_verbs.htm

Type in the irregular verbs; the computer checks you.

web2.uvcs.uvic.ca/elc/studyzone/330/grammar/pasted.htm

Review and quizzes: regular verbs

CHAPTER 31

The Past Participle

A. Past Participles of Regular Verbs

TEACHING TIP
Past participles are the source of problems for many students. Those who don't pronounce the *-ed* ending of regular verbs are more likely to make written mistakes. Explain that verb errors are a serious blot in college and work.

The **past participle** is the form of the verb that can be combined with helping verbs like *have* and *has* to make verbs of more than one word:

Present Tense	Past Tense	Helping Verb plus Past Participle
1. They *skate.*	1. They *skated.*	1. They *have skated.*
2. Beth *dances.*	2. Beth *danced.*	2. Beth *has danced.*
3. Frank *worries.*	3. Frank *worried.*	3. Frank *has worried.*

- *Skated, danced,* and *worried* are all past participles of regular verbs.
- Note that both the *past tense* and the *past participle* of regular verbs end in *-ed* or *-d*.

PRACTICE 1

ESL TIP
English verbs—tenses, endings, and forms—are a challenge for ESL students, who will benefit from exercises like Practice 1.

The first sentence of each pair that follows contains a regular verb in the past tense. Fill in *have* or *has* plus the past participle of the same verb to complete the second sentence.

1. Arlen Ness earned his title, King of the Choppers.

   Arlen Ness ___has___ ___earned___ his title, King of the Choppers.

2. Since 1967, Ness designed and manufactured one-of-a-kind motorcycles.

   Since 1967, Ness ___has___ ___designed___ and ___manufactured___ one-of-a-kind motorcycles.

3. The craftsmanship, performance, and eye-popping style of Ness bikes attracted worldwide attention.

   The craftsmanship, performance, and eye-popping style of Ness bikes ___have___ ___attracted___ worldwide attention.

4. Shaquille O'Neal and Aerosmith's Steven Tyler ordered custom Ness creations.

   Shaquille O'Neal and Aerosmith's Steven Tyler ___have___ ___ordered___ custom Ness creations.

LEARNING STYLES TIP
Have students read sentences in Practice 1 aloud. This helps *aural learners* and others hear (and correct) verb errors. Because many speakers drop *-ed* verb endings in speech, practice in hearing and pronouncing the *-eds* helps them reprogram.

5. A master builder and bike painter, Arlen Ness received many first-place trophies.

   A master builder and bike painter, Arlen Ness ___has___ ___received___ many first-place trophies.

6. Crowds lined up just to glimpse his elongated yellow chopper, "Top Banana."

   Crowds ___have___ ___lined___ up just to glimpse his elongated yellow chopper, "Top Banana."

Michael Macor/Corbis

Arlen Ness poses with a custom motorcycle he calls "Ness Stalgia," inspired by a 1957 Chevrolet.

TEACHING TIP

You may wish to review spelling rules for adding *-d* or *-ed*. 1. If the verb ends in *e*, add *-d* (*lived*, *skated*). 2. If the verb ends in *y*, change the *y* to *i* and add *-ed* (*cried*, *applied*). 3. If the last two letters of the verb are a vowel plus a consonant (except *w* and *y*), double the consonant and add *-ed* (*tapped*, *committed*). 4. For all other verbs, add *-ed* (*picked*, *stayed*, *followed*).

7. Ness picked witty names like "Jelly Belly" for many bikes.

   Ness ___has___ ___picked___ witty names like "Jelly Belly" for many bikes.

8. The curvy, green beauty, "Smooth-Ness," and the silver monster, "Mach Ness," both played on his famous name.

   The curvy, green beauty, "Smooth-Ness," and the silver monster, "Mach Ness," both ___have___ ___played___ on his famous name.

9. Corey Ness joined his father's multimillion-dollar company.

   Corey Ness ___has___ ___joined___ his father's multimillion-dollar company.

10. Custom motorcycles turned into big business.

    Custom motorcycles ___have___ ___turned___ into big business.

B. Past Participles of Irregular Verbs

LEARNING STYLES TIP

Kinesthetic learners may want to use flash cards to review the past participle forms of irregular verbs.

ESL TIP

Some ESL teachers rely on memorization to teach irregular verb forms, while others use only practice in context. A variety of approaches will address different learning and teaching styles.

Most verbs that are irregular in the past tense are also irregular in the past participle, as shown in the following chart.

Present Tense	Past Tense	Helping Verb plus Past Participle
1. We *sing*.	1. We *sang*.	1. We *have sung*.
2. Bill *writes*.	2. Bill *wrote*.	2. Bill *has written*.
3. I *think*.	3. I *thought*.	3. I *have thought*.

- Irregular verbs change from present to past to past participle in unusual ways.
- *Sung*, *written*, and *thought* are all past participles of irregular verbs.
- Note that the past tense and past participle of *think* are the same—*thought*.

Reference Chart
Irregular Verbs, Past and Past Participle

Simple Form	Past Tense	Past Participle
be	was, were	been
become	became	become
begin	began	begun
blow	blew	blown
break	broke	broken
bring	brought	brought
build	built	built
buy	bought	bought
catch	caught	caught

choose	chose	chosen
come	came	come
cut	cut	cut
deal	dealt	dealt
dig	dug	dug
dive	dove (dived)	dived
do	did	done
draw	drew	drawn
drink	drank	drunk
drive	drove	driven
eat	ate	eaten
fall	fell	fallen
feed	fed	fed
feel	felt	felt
fight	fought	fought
find	found	found
fly	flew	flown
forbid	forbade	forbidden
forget	forgot	forgotten
forgive	forgave	forgiven
freeze	froze	frozen
get	got	got (gotten)
give	gave	given
go	went	gone
grow	grew	grown
have	had	had
hear	heard	heard
hide	hid	hidden
hold	held	held
hurt	hurt	hurt
keep	kept	kept
know	knew	known
lay	laid	laid
lead	led	led
leave	left	left
let	let	let
lie	lay	lain
lose	lost	lost
make	made	made
mean	meant	meant
meet	met	met
pay	paid	paid
put	put	put
quit	quit	quit
read	read	read
ride	rode	ridden
rise	rose	risen

TEACHING TIP

You might have students write sentences using past participles from this list, then exchange papers and check each other's work.

ESL TIP

Remind students to keep track of their personal error patterns—including any irregular verbs that give them trouble. They should proofread their writing with these errors in mind.

run	ran	run
say	said	said
see	saw	seen
seek	sought	sought
sell	sold	sold
send	sent	sent
shake	shook	shaken
shine	shone (shined)	shone (shined)
sing	sang	sung
sit	sat	sat
sleep	slept	slept
speak	spoke	spoken
spend	spent	spent
split	split	split
spring	sprang	sprung
stand	stood	stood
steal	stole	stolen
stink	stank	stunk
swim	swam	swum
take	took	taken
teach	taught	taught
tear	tore	torn
tell	told	told
think	thought	thought
throw	threw	thrown
understand	understood	understood
wake	woke (waked)	woken (waked)
wear	wore	worn
win	won	won
write	wrote	written

PRACTICE 2

The first sentence of each pair that follows contains an irregular verb in the past tense. Fill in *have* or *has* plus the past participle of the same verb to complete the second sentence.

1. Sean took plenty of time buying the groceries.

   Sean ___has___ ___taken___ plenty of time buying the groceries.

2. We sent our latest budget to the mayor.

   We ___have___ ___sent___ our latest budget to the mayor.

3. My daughter hid her diary.

   My daughter ___has___ ___hidden___ her diary.

4. The jockey rode all day in the hot sun.

   The jockey ___has___ ___ridden___ all day in the hot sun.

5. Hershey, Pennsylvania, became a great tourist attraction.

   Hershey, Pennsylvania, ___has___ ___become___ a great tourist attraction.

6. The company's managers knew about these hazards for two years.

   The company's managers ___have___ ___known___ about these hazards for two years.

7. Carrie floated down the river on an inner tube.

   Carrie ___has___ ___floated___ down the river on an inner tube.

8. At last, our team won the bowling tournament.

   At last, our team ___has___ ___won___ the bowling tournament.

9. Larry and Marsha broke their long silence.

   Larry and Marsha ___have___ ___broken___ their long silence.

10. Science fiction films were very popular this past year.

    Science fiction films ___have___ ___been___ very popular this past year.

TEACHING TIP

For Practices 2 and 3, you might want to ask students to first circle the subject and ask whether it is singular or plural before choosing *has* or *have*.

PRACTICE 3

Complete each sentence by filling in *have* or *has* plus the past participle of the verb in parentheses. Some verbs are regular, some are irregular.

1. Soccer ___has___ ___gained___ (gain) popularity in the United States ever since the 1994 World Cup was held in Pasadena, California.

2. Sports fans ___have___ ___seen___ (see) the enthusiasm and passion that soccer arouses in such countries as Argentina, Brazil, Italy, and Portugal.

3. The United States also ___has___ ___demonstrated___ (demonstrate) that it can win games in the biggest soccer competition in the world.

4. The U.S. women's soccer team ___has___ ___won___ (win) worldwide respect, earning Olympic gold medals in 2004, 2008, and again in 2012.

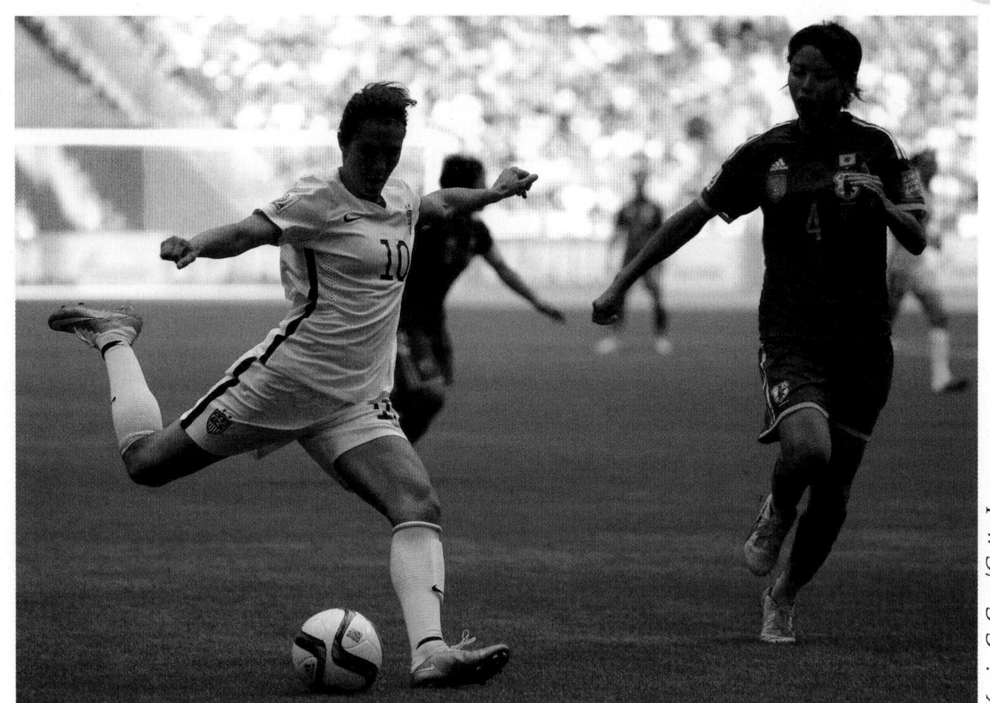
Kevin C. Cox/Getty Images

Carli Lloyd of the United States kicks the ball during the 2015 Women's World Cup final.

5. The names of female stars like Abby Wambach ____have____ ____become____ (become) household words, along with great male players like David Beckham.

6. Television coverage of matches ____has____ ____increased____ (increase); in fact, 23 million Americans watched the thrilling 2015 Women's World Cup final, in which the United States beat Japan 5 to 2.

7. Major League Soccer ____has____ ____added____ (add) new franchises and recently ____has____ ____begun____ (begin) to attract stars from other countries.

8. Significantly, the game ____has____ ____grown____ (grow) in popularity with suburban boys and girls.

9. The parents of these children ____have____ ____encouraged____ (encourage) them to play a relatively safe but exciting sport.

10. Experts say that this generation, which ____has____ ____fallen____ (fall) in love with soccer, is changing the future of American athletics.

C. Using the Present Perfect Tense

ESL TIP
The perfect tenses are not unique to English, but they are difficult for ESL students. Extra help and discussion of the differences between their native language and English may help.

The **present perfect tense** is composed of the present tense of *to have* plus the past participle. The present perfect tense shows that an action has begun in the past and is continuing into the present.

1. Past tense: Beatrice *taught* English for ten years.
2. Present perfect tense: Beatrice *has taught* English for ten years.

- In sentence 1, Beatrice *taught* English in the past, but she no longer teaches it. Note the use of the simple past tense, *taught*.
- In sentence 2, Beatrice *has taught* for ten years and is still teaching English *now*. *Has taught* implies that the action is continuing.

PRACTICE 4

ESL TIP
You might give ESL students a list of common time expressions often used with either simple past or with present perfect (for example, *so far*, *today*, *since May 1, I* have watched . . . or *yesterday*, *at 10 A.M.* today, *on May 1, I* watched . . .).

Read these sentences carefully for meaning. Then circle the correct verb—either the *past tense* or the *present perfect tense*.

1. He (directed, has directed) the theater group for many years now.
2. Emilio lifted the rug and (has swept, swept) the dust under it.
3. She (went, has gone) to a poetry slam last night.
4. For the past four years, I (took, have taken) art classes in the summer.
5. We (talked, have talked) about the problem of your lateness for three days; it's time for you to do something about it.
6. While he was in Japan, he (took, have taken) many photographs of shrines.
7. She (won, has won) that contest ten years ago.
8. The boxers (fought, have fought) for an hour, and they look very tired.
9. He (applied, has applied) to three colleges and attended the one with the best sociology department.
10. The auto mechanics (had, have had) a radio show together for five years and are now extremely popular.

D. Using the Past Perfect Tense

The **past perfect tense** is composed of the past tense of *to have* plus the past participle. The past perfect tense shows that an action occurred further back in the past than other past action.

TEACHING TIP

You might explain the past perfect tense as describing two actions in the past. The first action to occur will use a past perfect verb, and the second action to occur will use a simple past verb.

1. Past tense: Rhonda *left* for the movies.
2. Past perfect tense: Rhonda *had* already *left* for the movies by the time we *arrived*.

- In sentence 1, *left* is the simple past.
- In sentence 2, the past perfect *had left* shows that this action occurred even before another action in the past, *arrived*.

PRACTICE 5

ESL TIP

Tense sequence can be especially tricky for ESL learners. Using a tense sequence chart might help them. Try **grammar.ccc.commnet.edu/grammar/sequence.htm**.

Read these sentences carefully for meaning. Then circle the correct verb—either the *past tense* or the *past perfect tense*.

1. Tony came to the office with a cane last week because he (sprained, had sprained) his ankle a month ago.
2. As Janice (piled, had piled) the apples into a pyramid, she thought, "I should become an architect."
3. Juan (finished, had finished) his gardening by the time I (drove, had driven) up in my new convertible.
4. The man nervously (looked, had looked) at his watch and then walked a bit faster.
5. Roberto told us that he (decided, had decided) to enlist in the Marines.
6. The caller asked whether we (received, had received) our free toaster yet.
7. Last week he told me that he (forgot, had forgotten) to mail the rent check.
8. As the curtain came down, everyone (rose, had risen) and applauded the Brazilian dance troupe.
9. Scott (closed, had closed) his books and went to the movies.
10. The prosecutor proved that the defendant was lying; until then I (believed, had believed) he was innocent.

E. Using the Passive Voice (*To Be* and the Past Participle)

TEACHING TIP
To help students improve their writing style, use these and other examples to show that passive voice sentences are often wordier than active voice sentences. Passive voice also allows for omission of the subject—desirable only when the subject is unknown or diplomacy is required (e.g., *The situation was mishandled*).

The **passive voice** is composed of the past participle with some form of *to be* (*am, is, are, was, were, has been, have been,* or *had been*). In the passive voice, the subject does not act but is *acted upon*.

Compare the passive voice with the active voice in the following pairs of sentences.

1. Passive voice: This newspaper *is written* by journalism students.
2. Active voice: Journalism students *write* this newspaper.
3. Passive voice: My garden *was devoured* by rabbits.
4. Active voice: Rabbits *devoured* my garden.

- In sentence 1, the subject, *this newspaper*, is passive; it is acted upon. In sentence 2, the subject, *students*, is active; it performs the action.
- Note the difference between the passive verb *is written* and the active verb *write*.
- However, both verbs (*is written* and *write*) are in the *present tense*.
- The verbs in sentences 3 and 4 are both in the *past tense*: *was devoured* (passive) and *devoured* (active).

Use the passive voice sparingly. Write in the passive voice when you want to emphasize the receiver of the action rather than the doer.

PRACTICE 6

Fill in the correct *past participle* form of the verb in parentheses to form the passive voice. If you are not sure, check the chart in Part B of this chapter.

1. The barn was ___built___ (build) by friends of the family.
2. These ruby slippers were ___given___ (give) to me by my grandmother.
3. A faint inscription is ___etched___ (etch) on the back of the old gold watch.
4. At the garden party Sheila and Una were ___bitten___ (bite) by mosquitoes and gnats.
5. The getaway car is always ___driven___ (drive) by a man in a gray fedora.
6. Her articles have been ___published___ (publish) in *Texas Monthly*.

PRACTICE 7

Whenever possible, write in the *active*, not the *passive*, voice. Rewrite these sentences in the active voice, making all necessary verb and subject changes. Be sure to keep the sentence in the original tense.

EXAMPLE Too many personal questions were asked by the interviewer.

The interviewer asked too many personal questions.

1. The shot was blocked by the goalie.

   The goalie blocked the shot.

2. Her reputation was hurt by her rudeness.

   Her rudeness hurt her reputation.

3. The law boards were passed by Eduardo and Noah.

   Eduardo and Noah passed the law boards.

4. The noisy group was warned by the usher.

   The usher warned the noisy group.

5. We were shown how to create PowerPoint slides by the instructor.

   The instructor showed us how to create PowerPoint slides.

F. Using the Past Participle as an Adjective

ESL TIP

The use of participles as adjectives is often troublesome for ESL and some native-born students, as well.

The **past participle** form of the verb can be used as an **adjective** after a linking verb:

1. The window is *broken*.

- The adjective *broken* describes the subject *window*.

The **past participle** form of the verb can sometimes be used as an adjective before a noun or a pronoun.

2. This *fried* chicken tastes wonderful.

- The adjective *fried* describes the noun *chicken*.

PRACTICE 8

Use the past participle form of the verb in parentheses as an adjective in each sentence.

1. My __used__ (use) laptop was a great bargain at only $200.
2. Bob is highly __qualified__ (qualify) to install a water heater.

TEACHING TIP

Remind students that not pronouncing a final *-ed* can contribute to written errors. Urge them to practice saying *pleased to meet you*, *case closed*, *well-dressed*, and so on.

3. The ___air-conditioned___ (air-condition) room was making everyone shiver.
4. The newly ___risen___ (rise) cinnamon bread smelled wonderful.
5. Were you ___surprised___ (surprise) to hear about my raise?
6. He feels ___depressed___ (depress) on rainy days.
7. She knows the power of the ___written___ (write) word.
8. My gym teacher seems ___prejudiced___ (prejudice) against short people.
9. The ___embarrassed___ (embarrass) child pulled her jacket over her head.
10. We ordered ___tossed___ (toss) salad, ___broiled___ (broil) salmon, ___mashed___ (mash) potatoes, and ___baked___ (bake) apple rings.

PRACTICE 9

Proofread the following paragraph for errors in past participles used as adjectives. Correct the errors by writing above the lines.

(1) To experience the food of another culture is to appreciate that culture in new ways. (2) A fine example is the traditional Chinese wedding banquet, where each beautiful dish is chosen, ~~prepare~~ prepared, and presented to carry a promise for the couple's future. (3) Carefully ~~season~~ seasoned shark's fin soup opens the feast; this rare and expensive treat signifies health and long life to both family lines. (4) Each table receives its own glazed Peking Duck to indicate the couple's fidelity. (5) In Chinese tradition, chicken represents the phoenix, a magic bird that rises from the ashes, and lobster represents the dragon. (6) Often ~~combine~~ combined and ~~bake~~ baked in a single dish, these two foods mark the peaceful union of two families. (7) Because the Chinese word for fish sounds like "abundance," a whole steamed fish is offered to the newly ~~marry~~ married couple—a wish for prosperity. (8) At the end of the meal, ~~satisfy~~ satisfied guests enjoy dessert buns filled with lotus seeds, promising fertility and future children. (9) It should come as no surprise that an old-~~fashion~~ fashioned Chinese banquet can last an entire day.

PROOFREADING STRATEGY

If past participle problems are among your error patterns, read your draft one word at a time and **search for the helping verbs *has, have, had, is, am, are, was,* and *were*.** Every time you find a helping verb, highlight or underline it. If you are using a computer, use the *"Find"* feature to locate these words in your draft. Whenever these helping verbs are part of a past participle verb, **check the past participle form.** If it's a regular verb, it should end in *-d* or *-ed.* If it's an irregular verb and you aren't sure, check the verb chart. How should the writer correct the incorrect past participles in these examples?

The manager has interviewed [Correct] all the candidates, and she has chose [Incorrect] our new sales associate.

My steak was grill [Incorrect] and season [Incorrect] to perfection.

PRACTICE 10 REVIEW

Proofread the following essay for past participle errors. Try the proofreading strategy to see if it works for you. Correct the errors by writing above the lines.

LAUGHING AT THE NEWS

(1) In recent years, many people have ~~stop~~ stopped reading newspapers and watching the nightly news. (2) Meanwhile, comedy news shows like *The Daily Show with Trevor Noah* and *Full Frontal with Samantha Bee* have ~~growed~~ grown more popular. (3) ~~Watch~~ Watched by many people, they are a major news source for many Americans.

(4) Since the mid-1970s, generations of television viewers have seen NBC's *Saturday Night Live* mock the news with its "Weekend Update," where comic actors posing as news anchors offer a few sentences about a current issue, ~~follow~~ followed by a punch line. (5) SNL's writers have ~~took~~ taken aim at everything from global warming and the budget crisis to world leaders. (6) Actress and writer Tiny Fey outdid herself in 2008 with her impressions of vice presidential candidate Sarah Palin, complete with winks, "beauty pageant walkin'," and a phony moose ~~shoot~~ shot dead on stage. (7) ~~View~~ Viewed millions of times on YouTube, Fey's skits are classics.

(8) Mixing a little news with a lot of laughs has ~~rose~~ risen to new heights on *The Daily Show* and *Full Frontal.* (9) The topics are all ~~lift~~ lifted from current headlines, but

Brad Barket/Getty Images

Trevor Noah took over *The Daily Show*'s desk from Jon Stewart in 2015.

the wise-cracking hosts have ~~became~~ become masters at mining humor from serious topics. (10) Both Trevor Noah and Samantha Bee have ~~address~~ addressed sensitive political and social issues. (11) ~~Praise~~ Praised by critics, both hosts have wide audiences, especially among young people.

(12) As the line between news and comedy has ~~blur~~ blurred, questions are being ~~raise~~ raised about the effects of "infotainment." (13) ~~Worry~~ Worried about the trend, CNN reporter Christiane Amanpour fears viewers are becoming less ~~educate~~ educated. (15) Others insist that those who watch comedy news think more critically and that humor comes closer to the truth than wooden seriousness.

EXPLORING ONLINE

www.grammar-quizzes.com/participles1.html

Test your knowledge of past tense and past participles.

grammar.ccc.commnet.edu/grammar/quizzes/final-ed_option.htm

To add or not to add *-ed*? This one is tricky; test yourself.

CHAPTER 32

Nouns

A. Defining Singular and Plural

Nouns are words that refer to people, places, or things. They can be either singular or plural. **Singular** means one. **Plural** means more than one.

Singular	Plural
the glass	glasses
a lamp	lamps
a lesson	lessons

- As you can see, nouns usually add *-s* or *-es* to form the plural.

Some nouns form their plurals in other ways. Here are a few examples:

Singular	Plural	Singular	Plural
child	children	medium	media
crisis	crises	memorandum	memoranda (memorandums)
criterion	criteria	phenomenon	phenomena
foot	feet	syllabus	syllabi
goose	geese	tooth	teeth
man	men	woman	women

ESL TIP
ESL students in particular have trouble with spelling rules for adding *-s* to regular nouns. Refer them to www.eslcafe.com/grammar/nouns02.html.

TEACHING TIP
Many students will know some or all of the material in this chapter, so you may wish to assign topics selectively.

ESL TIP

Some ESL writers add -*s* to non-count words (e.g., *equipments*, *furnitures*). Refer them to the "Additional Help and Practice for ESL/ELL Students" appendix of this book.

These nouns ending in -*f* or -*fe* change endings to -*ves* in the plural:

Singular	Plural
half	halves
knife	knives
life	lives
scarf	scarves
shelf	shelves
wife	wives
wolf	wolves

LEARNING STYLES TIP

To supply useful *visual reinforcements* to ESL and other learners, use the board, charts, or flash cards—prepare cards with the singular form of a noun on one side, plural on the other.

Hyphenated nouns form plurals by adding -*s* or -*es* to the main word:

Singular	Plural
brother-in-law	brothers-in-law
maid-of-honor	maids-of-honor

Other nouns do not change at all to form the plural; here are a few examples:

Singular	Plural
deer	deer
equipment	equipment
fish	fish
merchandise	merchandise

If you are unsure about the plural of a noun, check a dictionary. For example, if you look up the noun *woman* in the dictionary, you may see an entry like this:

woman, women

The first word listed, *woman*, is the singular form of the noun; the second word, *women*, is the plural.

Some dictionaries list the plural form of a noun only if the plural is unusual. If no plural is listed, that noun probably adds -*s* or -*es*.* Remember: do not add an -*s* to words that form plurals by changing an internal letter. For example, the plural of *man* is *men*, not *mens*; the plural of *woman* is *women*, not *womens*; the plural of *foot* is *feet*, not *feets*.

*For more work on spelling plurals, see Chapter 40, "Spelling," Part H.

PRACTICE 1

Make these singular nouns plural.

1. man men
2. half halves
3. foot feet
4. son-in-law sons-in-law
5. moose moose
6. life lives
7. tooth teeth
8. medium media
9. woman women
10. crisis crises
11. maid-of-honor maids-of-honor
12. criterion criteria
13. shelf shelves
14. mouse mice
15. child children
16. father-in-law fathers-in-law
17. knife knives
18. deer deer
19. secretary secretaries
20. goose geese

B. Signal Words: Singular and Plural

ESL TIP

ESL students need to be careful about using words in English that resemble words in other languages but mean something different—for example, the French *librairie* means *bookstore* in English.

A **signal word** tells you whether a singular or a plural noun usually follows. These signal words tell you that a singular noun usually follows:

Signal Words	
a(n) a single another each every one	house

These signal words tell you that a plural noun usually follows:

Signal Words	
all both few many most several some two (or more) various	houses

PRACTICE 2

ESL TIP

For an interesting list of discussion questions about gender roles in different cultures, see **iteslj.org/questions/gender.html**.

Some of the following sentences contain incorrect singulars and plurals. Correct the errors. Put a *C* after correct sentences.

1. By three years old, most children have firm ideas about how men and ~~woman~~ women should behave.

2. Children develop their concepts about gender differences through *conditioning*, a process of learning that reinforces certain behaviors while discouraging ~~other~~ others.

3. Conditioning occurs through the messages delivered by parents, ~~peer~~ peers, and the media.

4. Research shows that parents begin to treat their ~~childrens~~ children differently as early as 24 ~~hour~~ hours after birth.

5. Fathers hold their infant girls gently and speak softly to them, but they bounce baby boys, playing "airplane" and tickling their ~~feets~~ feet.

6. Mothers, too, condition gender roles; they reward little girls who play quietly and help with chores, while excusing the loud play of boys as natural. C

7. Once in school, children quickly learn that certain kinds of make-believe—such as playing house or having tea parties—are girls' games; boys are encouraged by their ~~friend~~ friends to crash cars and shoot toy guns.

8. While the boundaries are less rigid for girls at this stage, most boys who show any interest in feminine clothes or ~~activity~~ activities will be mocked by their peers.

9. Many TV ~~ad~~ ads play a key conditioning role by showing boys involved in sports or jobs and girls playing indoors with toy ovens or dolls.

10. By limiting choices for most ~~child~~ children, perhaps we ignore many talents and ~~interest~~ interests that might greatly enhance their ~~lifes~~ lives and society as a whole.

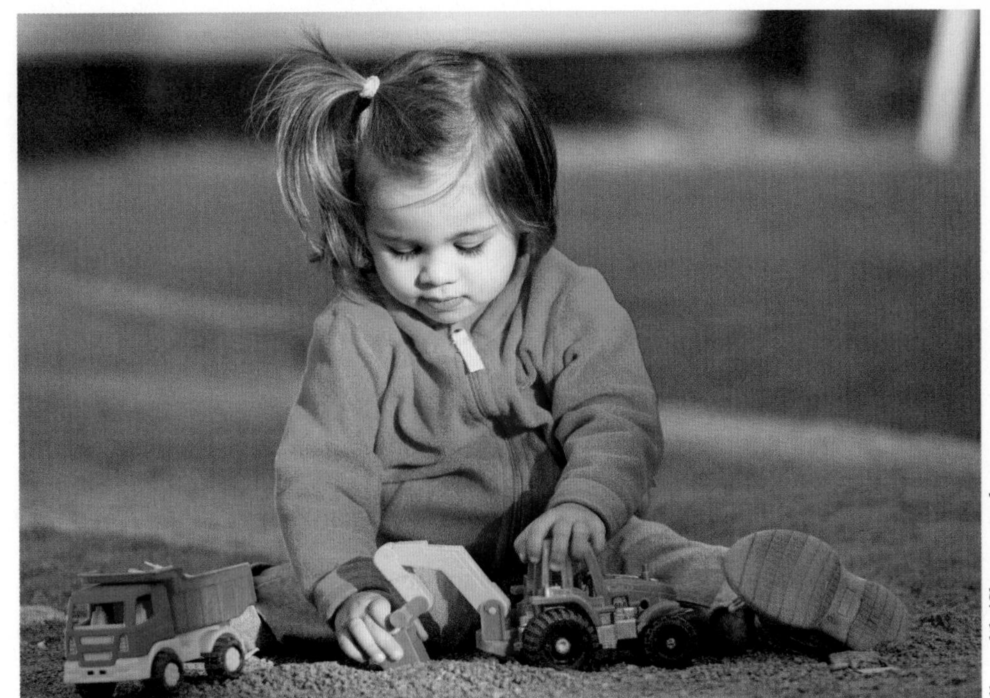

ilkercelik/Shutterstock.com

Gender conditioning starts early. How does this photograph support, or challenge, gender stereotypes?

C. Signal Words with *of*

TEACHING TIP
The constructions in Part C confuse many students and can lead to both noun and verb agreement errors. Remind students to cross out the prepositional phrase in order to find the subject and determine its number.

Many signal words are followed by *of* . . . or *of the*. . . . Usually, these signal words are followed by a **plural** noun (or a collective noun) because they really refer to one or more from a larger group.

one of the each of the	pictures is . . .
many of the a few of the both of the lots of the	pictures are . . .

ESL TIP
ESL students may need extra practice using singular and plural nouns appropriately. Have them write sentences using the signal word charts in Part B and here.

- **Be careful:** The signal words *one of the* and *each of the* are followed by a **plural** noun, but the verb is **singular** because only the signal word (*one* or *each*) is the real subject.*

One of the coats *is* on sale.
Each of the flowers *smells* sweet.

*For more work on this type of construction, see Chapter 29, "Present Tense (Agreement)," Part C.

PRACTICE 3

TEACHING TIP
You might wish to review relevant spelling rules; for example, for words that end in *-y*, drop the *-y* and add *-ies* (*victory, victories*).

Fill in your own nouns in the following sentences. Use a different noun in each sentence. Answers will vary.

1. Since Jacob wrote each of his ___exams___ with care, the A's came as no surprise.
2. You are one of the few ___people___ I know who can listen to the radio and play video games at the same time.
3. Naomi liked several of the new ___singers___ but remained faithful to her long-time favorites.
4. Many of the ___students___ carried laptops.
5. Determined to win the Salesperson of the Year award, Clyde called on all of his ___clients___ two or three times a month.
6. One of the ___categories___ makes no sense.

PROOFREADING STRATEGY

Incorrect singular and plural nouns are considered serious errors, so proofread with care if these are among your error patterns.

First, **search each sentence for signal words and phrases** (such as *an, each, one, many, several, a few*) that "announce" the need for either a singular or a plural noun. Underline or color code these signal words. Code in a different color all phrases like *one of the* . . . and *a few of the* . . . that are always followed by a plural. **Locate the noun** following each signal word and check for correctness.

Notice how the color-coded signal words in this example make it easier to see if the nouns are correct.

> C
> Many architects submitted designs for the new monument, but only one of the ~~drawing~~ [drawings] impressed both ~~judge~~ [judges].

PRACTICE 4

REVIEW

Proofread the following essay for errors in singular and plural nouns. Try out the proofreading strategy to see if it works for you. Correct the errors by writing above the lines.

HAPPINESS 101

(1) At Harvard University, up to 900 ~~student~~ [students] per semester pack a lecture hall for Professor Tal Ben-Shahar's course on happiness. (2) Called "Positive Psychology,"

the class explores current research on what makes people ~~peoples~~ truly happy. (3) It is one of the most popular courses ~~course~~ on campus. (4) Students learn that they are more likely to experience joy if they participate in activities ~~activitys~~ that they find meaningful as well as pleasurable. (5) For example, a person who enjoys playing the piano might perform once a month for the residents of a nursing home ~~homes~~, thus adding meaning to pleasure. (6) Students also discover that more happiness comes to people who accept every one of their feelings ~~feeling~~—even fear, sadness, and anger—without self-judgment.

(7) Professor Ben-Shahar's students learn a few more criteria ~~criterion~~ for a cheerful life. (8) They find out that rushing to do too much in a short time increases anxiety and depression, while simplifying life increases enjoyment. (9) Furthermore, several studies ~~study~~ prove that expressing gratitude ~~gratitudes~~ can lift a person's spirits, so it seems the many women ~~woman~~ and men ~~man~~ who keep a daily gratitude journal ~~journals~~ are on to something.

(10) One of the most important lessons ~~lesson~~, though, is that contentment depends on a person's state of mind, not his or her status or bank account. (11) Happy people see the glass ~~glasses~~ as half full rather than half empty. (12) They also view all of their failures ~~failure~~ not as disasters or crises ~~crisis~~ but as learning opportunities. (13) Fortunately, research indicates that this kind of optimism ~~optimisms~~ can be learned. (14) Those who are able to shift their thoughts to focus on the positive can change their lives ~~lifes~~ for the better.

PRACTICE 5 CRITICAL THINKING AND WRITING

Think about which one of Professor Ben-Shahar's principles for happiness in Practice 4 is the most important. Based on your own experience, what three reasons best explain why you came to this conclusion? Write a paragraph explaining your reasoning.

EXPLORING ONLINE

grammar.ccc.commnet.edu/grammar/quizzes/cross/plurals_gap.htm

Interactive noun plurals quiz: test yourself!

grammar.ccc.commnet.edu/grammar/quizzes/final-s_option.htm

Do you know when to add -s to nouns and verbs? Test yourself.

CHAPTER 33

Pronouns

A: Defining Pronouns and Antecedents

B: Making Pronouns and Antecedents Agree

C: Referring to Antecedents Clearly

D: Special Problems of Case

E: Using Pronouns with *-self* and *-selves*

A. Defining Pronouns and Antecedents

ESL TIP

Pronoun forms usually do not present a learning hardship to ESL students because the English pronoun system is far simpler than that of many other languages.

Pronouns take the place of or refer to nouns, other pronouns, or phrases. The word that the pronoun refers to is called the **antecedent** of the pronoun.

1. *Eric* ordered *baked chicken* because *it* is *his* favorite dish.
2. *Simone and Lee* painted *their* room.
3. *I* like *camping in the woods* because *it* gives *me* a chance to be alone with *my* thoughts.

- In sentence 1, *it* refers to the antecedent *baked chicken*, and *his* refers to the antecedent *Eric*.
- In sentence 2, *their* refers to the plural antecedent *Simone and Lee*.
- In sentence 3, *it* refers to the antecedent *camping in the woods*. This antecedent is a whole phrase. *Me* and *my* refer to the pronoun antecedent *I*.

PRACTICE 1

In each sentence, circle the pronoun and then write its antecedent, as shown in the example.

EXAMPLE Have you ever wondered why we exchange rings in (our) wedding ceremonies? we

TEACHING AND ESL TIP

Point out to students that animals and inanimate object antecedents are referred to with the pronouns *it* and *its* and, in the case of plurals, *they* and *their.*

1. Today when people buy wedding rings, they follow an age-old tradition. ______ people ______
2. Rich Egyptian grooms gave their brides gold rings 5,000 years ago. ______ grooms ______
3. To Egyptian couples, the ring represented eternal love; it was a circle without beginning or end. ______ ring ______
4. By Roman times, gold rings had become more affordable, so ordinary people could also buy them. ______ rings ______
5. Still, many a Roman youth had to scrimp to buy his beloved a ring. ______ youth ______
6. The first bride to slip a diamond ring on her finger lived in Venice about 500 years ago. ______ bride ______
7. The Venetians knew that setting a diamond in a ring was an excellent way of displaying its beauty. ______ diamond ______
8. Nowadays, two partners exchange rings to symbolize the equality of their relationship. ______ partners ______

B. Making Pronouns and Antecedents Agree

TEACHING TIP

Explain to students that although we might not make our subjects and pronouns agree in casual conversation, we must do so in writing. Students have particular trouble with the special cases covered in Part B and with Part C on vague or repeated pronouns.

A pronoun must *agree* with its antecedent in number and person.*

1. When *Tom* couldn't find *his* pen, *he* asked to borrow mine.
2. The three *sisters* wanted to start *their* own business.

- In sentence 1, *Tom* is the antecedent of *his* and *he.* Since *Tom* is singular and masculine, the pronouns referring to *Tom* are also singular and masculine.
- In sentence 2, *sisters* is the antecedent of *their.* Since *sisters* is plural, the pronoun referring to *sisters* must also be plural.

There are three special cases that can be particularly tricky when making pronouns and antecedents agree.

1. Indefinite Pronouns

Indefinite pronouns refer to undefined people or things. Indefinite pronouns can be singular or plural.

*For more work on pronoun agreement, see Chapter 21, "Revising for Consistency and Parallelism," Part B.

TEACHING TIP
Challenge students to memorize these lists of indefinite pronouns. In groups or as a class, invent a mnemonic device to help remember them.

TEACHING TIP
Discuss with the class the modern view that using only *he*, *his*, or *him* when referring to both genders is sexist. It is better to switch to plural rather than risk offending someone.

TEACHING TIP
Words like *all*, *any*, *more*, *most*, *none*, and *some* can take the singular or plural form depending on whether they refer to a single unit or several individuals or items: Some *of the guests are bringing* their *friends to the party* vs. Some *of the money is missing, and* it *will be hard to replace*. Discuss these special cases with students.

Singular Indefinite Pronouns

anybody anyone everybody everyone nobody no one one somebody someone	Each of these words is **singular**. Any pronoun that refers to one of them must also be singular: *he, him, his, she*, or *her*.

3. *Anyone* can quit smoking if *he* or *she* wants to.
4. *Everybody* should do *his* or *her* best to keep the reception area uncluttered.

- *Anyone* and *everybody* require the singular pronouns *he, she, his,* and *her.*

If *everyone* or *someone* is a woman, use *she* or *her*; if *everyone* or *someone* is a man, use *he* or *him*. For example:

5. *Someone* left *her* new dress in a bag on the sofa.

Plural Indefinite Pronouns

both few many	These words are **plural**. Any pronoun that refers to them must also be plural: *they, their,* or *them.*

6. *Both* of *them* forgot *their* keys.
7. *Many* are bringing *their* best friends to the party.

- *Both* and *many* require the plural pronouns *them* and *their.*

PRACTICE 2

Circle the antecedent and then fill in the correct pronoun. Make sure each pronoun agrees in number and person with its antecedent.

1. (Anyone) can become a good cook if ___he or she___ tries.
2. (One) of the men dropped ___his___ bow tie behind the bookcase.
3. (No one) in the mixed doubles let ___his or her___ guard down for a minute.

4. Everybody wants his or her career to be rewarding.

5. Everyone is entitled to his or her full pension.

6. Both of my friends will be joining us, so please have their tickets ready.

7. One should wear a necktie that doesn't clash with one's suit.

8. The movie theater was so cold that few took off their coats.

TEACHING TIP
In Chapter 29, "Present Tense (Agreement)," students learned to cross out prepositional phrases between the subject and verb. Suggest that they continue this practice here.

2. Special Singular Antecedents

each (of) . . . either (of) . . . every one (of) . . . neither (of) . . . one (of) . . .	Each of these constructions is **singular**. Any pronoun that refers to one of them must also be singular.*

8. *Neither* of the two men paid for *his* ticket to the wrestling match.
9. *Each* of the houses has *its* own special charm.

ESL TIP
To give ESL students extra practice, have them write original sentences using each of these singular antecedents.

- The subject of sentence 8 is the singular *neither*, not *men*; therefore, the singular masculine pronoun *his* is required.
- The subject of sentence 9 is the singular *each*, not the plural *houses*; therefore, the singular pronoun *its* is required.

PRACTICE 3

Circle the antecedent and then fill in the correct pronoun. Make sure each pronoun agrees in number and person with its antecedent.

TEACHING TIP
Encourage your students to practice making pronouns and antecedents agree, even in casual conversation. Mastering pronoun agreement in speech will help make it an automatic habit when writing.

1. Each of the men wanted to be his own boss.

2. One of the women forgot her keys at the gym.

3. Every one of the colts has a white star on its forehead.

4. Neither of the actors knew his or her lines by heart.

5. Each of the dentists had his or her offices remodeled.

6. Each of these arguments has its flaws and its strengths.

7. Every one of the jazz bands had its own distinctive style.

8. Either of these smartphones will work very well if it is properly cared for.

*For more work on prepositional phrases, see Chapter 26, "The Simple Sentence," Part B.

3. Collective Nouns

Collective nouns represent a group of people but are usually considered **singular**. They usually take singular pronouns.

10. The *jury* reached *its* decision in three hours.
11. The debating *team* is well known for *its* fighting spirit.

TEACHING TIP
A good list of collective nouns often amazes students (e.g., *a murder of crows*). See **www.enchantedlearning.com/grammar/partsofspeech/nouns/collective/**. Craft a lesson on agreement, using these or collective nouns that your students invent (*an absence of waiters, a wallet of doctors*).

- In sentence 10, *jury* is a collective noun. Although it has several members, the jury acts as a unit—as one. Therefore, the antecedent *jury* takes the singular pronoun *its*.
- In sentence 11, why does the collective noun *team* take the singular pronoun *its*?

Here is a partial list of collective nouns:

Common Collective Nouns

class	family	panel
college	flock	school
committee	government	society
company	group	team
faculty	jury	tribe

PRACTICE 4

Read each sentence carefully for meaning. Circle the antecedent and then fill in the correct pronoun.

ESL TIP
ESL students may need extra help in choosing appropriate collective nouns, but they will reap new vocabulary from the exercise.

1. My (family) gave me all ___its___ support when I went back to school.
2. The (government) should reexamine ___its___ domestic policy.
3. The (college) honored ___its___ oldest graduate with a reception.
4. (Eco-Wise) has just begun to market a new pollution-free detergent that ___it___ is proud of.
5. The (panel) will soon announce ___its___ recommendations to the hospital.
6. The two (teams) gave ___their___ fans a real show.
7. The (jury) deliberated for six days before ___it___ reached a verdict.
8. After touring the Great Pyramid, the (class) headed back to Cairo in ___its___ air-conditioned bus.

C. Referring to Antecedents Clearly

A pronoun must refer *clearly* to its antecedent. Avoid vague, repetitious, or ambiguous pronoun references.

1. Vague pronoun:		At the box office, they said that tickets were no longer available.
2. Revised:	{	The cashier at the box office said . . .
		or
3. Revised:		At the box office, I was told . . .

- In sentence 1, who is *they*? *They* does not clearly refer to an antecedent.
- In sentence 2, *the cashier* replaces *they*.
- In sentence 3, the problem is avoided by a change of language.*

4. Repetitious pronoun:		In the article, *it* says that Tyrone was a boxer.
5. Revised:	{	The article says that. . .
		or
6. Revised:		It says that . . .

- In sentence 4, *it* merely repeats *article,* the antecedent preceding it.
- Use either the pronoun or its antecedent, but not both.

7. Ambiguous pronoun:	Mr. Tedesco told his son that *his* car had a flat tire.
8. Revised:	Mr. Tedesco told his son that the younger man's car had a flat tire.
9. Revised:	Mr. Tedesco told his son Paul that Paul's car had a flat tire.

- In sentence 7, *his* could refer either to Mr. Tedesco or to his son.

PRACTICE 5

TEACHING TIP
Ask students to identify each pronoun error in Practice 5 as vague, repetitious, or ambiguous.

Revise the following sentences, removing vague, repetitious, or ambiguous pronoun references. Make the pronoun references clear and specific.
Answers will vary.

1. In this book it says that hundreds of boys are injured each year copying wrestling stunts they see on TV.

   Revised: This book says that hundreds of boys are injured each year copying wrestling stunts they see on TV.

*For more work on using exact language, see Chapter 23, "Revising for Language Awareness," Part A.

2. On the radio they warned drivers that the Interstate Bridge was closed.

   Revised: The radio announcer warned drivers that the Interstate Bridge was closed.

3. Sandra told her friend that she shouldn't have turned down the promotion.

   Revised: Sandra told her friend Janet that Janet shouldn't have turned down the promotion.

4. In North Carolina they grow tobacco.

   Revised: Tobacco is grown in North Carolina.

5. The moving van struck a tree; luckily, no one was injured, but it was badly damaged.

   Revised: The moving van struck a tree; luckily, no one was injured, but the van was badly damaged.

6. Professor Grazel told his parrot that he had to stop chewing phone chargers.

   Revised: Professor Grazel told his parrot to stop chewing phone chargers.

7. On the news, it said that more Americans than ever are turning to nontraditional medicine.

   Revised: The news broadcast reported that more Americans than ever are turning to nontraditional medicine.

8. Keiko is an excellent singer, yet she has never taken a lesson in it.

   Revised: Keiko is an excellent singer, yet she has never taken a voice lesson.

9. Vandalism was once so out of control at the local high school that they stole sinks and lighting fixtures.

   Revised: Vandalism was once so out of control at the local high school that sinks and lighting fixtures were stolen.

10. Rosalie's mother said she was glad she had decided to become a paralegal.

    Revised: Rosalie's mother said she was glad Rosalie had decided to become a paralegal.

D. Special Problems of Case

ESL TIP
Point out to your ESL students that in compound constructions with a noun and a pronoun, the noun goes first. They should not write: *I and my friend went shopping.*

Personal pronouns take different forms depending on how they are used in a sentence. Pronouns can be **subjects**, **objects**, or **possessives**.

Pronouns used as **subjects** are **in the subjective case**:

1. *He* and *I* go snowboarding together.
2. The peaches were so ripe that *they* fell from the trees.

- *He, I,* and *they* are in the subjective case.

Pronouns that are **objects of verbs** or **prepositions** are in the **objective case**. Pronouns that are **subjects of infinitives** are also in the **objective case**:

3. A sudden downpour soaked *her.* (object of verb)
4. Please give this card to *him.* (object of preposition)
5. We want *them* to leave right now. (subject of infinitive)*

- *Her, him,* and *them* are in the objective case.

ESL TIP
Although most languages have a way of signaling possession, they don't all regard the same nouns as "possessable." In Spanish, one refers to parts of the body using the definite article, whereas in English, we use a possessive form. One would say, in Spanish, *I have broken the leg.*

ESL TIP
Ask students to write sentences using each of the pronoun cases listed in the chart.

TEACHING TIP
Create a quiz on pronoun cases by removing the pronouns from this chart and having students fill them in.

Pronouns that **show ownership** are in the **possessive case**:

6. The carpenters left *their* tools on the windowsill.
7. This flower has lost *its* brilliant color.

- *Their* and *its* are in the possessive case.

Pronoun Case Chart

Singular	**Subjective**	**Objective**	**Possessive**
1st person	I	me	my (mine)
2nd person	you	you	your (yours)
3rd person	he	him	his (his)
	she	her	her (hers)
	it	it	its (its)
	who	whom	whose
	whoever	whomever	
Plural	**Subjective**	**Objective**	**Possessive**
1st person	we	us	our (ours)
2nd person	you	you	your (yours)
3rd person	they	them	their (theirs)

Three problems require special care when determining the correct case.

*An infinitive is *to + the simple form of a verb* (to purchase, to study).

TEACHING TIP
Crossing out the noun half of a compound construction is a good way to choose the correct case: e.g., ~~Luke and~~ I work out; join ~~Luke and~~ me.

1. Case in Compound Constructions

A **compound construction** consists of two nouns, two pronouns, or a noun and a pronoun joined by *and*. Make sure that the pronouns in a compound construction are in the correct case.

8. *Serge* and *I* went to the pool together.
9. Between *you* and *me*, this party is a bore.

- In sentence 8, *Serge* and *I* are subjects.
- In sentence 9, *you* and *me* are objects of the preposition *between*.

Never use *myself* as a substitute for either *I* or *me* in compound constructions.

PRACTICE 6

Determine the case required by each sentence, and circle the correct pronoun.

1. Harriet and (he, him) plan to enroll in the police academy.
2. A snowdrift stood between the subway entrance and (I, me).
3. Tony used the software and then returned it to Barbara and (I, me, myself).
4. The reporter's questions caught June and (we, us) off guard.
5. By noon, Julio and (he, him) had already cleaned the garage and mowed the lawn.
6. These charts helped (she, her) and (I, me) with our statistics homework.
7. Professor Woo gave Diane and (she, her) extra time to finish the geology final.
8. Between you and (I, me), I have always preferred country music.

2. Case in Comparisons

TEACHING TIP
Many people wrongly substitute *I* for *me* because they think it sounds more formal; thus, they assume that it must be correct.

Pronouns that complete **comparisons** may be in the **subjective**, **objective**, or **possessive** case:

10. His son is as stubborn as *he*. (subjective)
11. The cutbacks will affect you more than *me*. (objective)
12. This essay is better organized than *mine*. (possessive)

TEACHING TIP
Students will better "hear" the correct pronoun if they supply the missing words of a comparison and then determine the correct pronoun case.

To decide on the correct pronoun, simply complete the comparison mentally and then choose the pronoun that naturally follows:

13. She trusts him more than I . . . (trust him).
14. She trusts him more than . . . (she trusts) . . . me.
15. Orlo's dog is as energetic as theirs . . . (is).

- Note that in sentences 13 and 14, the case of the pronoun in the comparison can change the meaning of the entire sentence.

PRACTICE 7

Circle the correct pronoun.

1. Your hair is much shorter than (she, her, hers).
2. We tend to assume that others are more self-confident than (we, us).
3. She is just as funny as (he, him).
4. Is Hanna as trustworthy as (he, him)?
5. Although they were both research scientists, he received a higher salary than (she, her).
6. I am not as involved in this project as (they, them).
7. Sometimes we become impatient with people who are not as quick to learn as (we, us).
8. Michael's route involved more overnight stops than (us, our, ours).

3. Use of *Who* (or *Whoever*) and *Whom* (or *Whomever*)

Who and **whoever** are in the **subjective** case. **Whom** and **whomever** are in the **objective** case.

16. *Who* is at the door?
17. For *whom* is that gift?
18. *Whom* is that gift for?

- In sentence 16, *who* is the subject.
- The same question is written two ways in sentences 17 and 18. In both, *whom* is the object of the preposition *for*.

Sometimes, deciding on *who* or *whom* can be tricky:

19. I will give the raise to *whoever* deserves it.
20. Give it to *whomever* you like.

- In sentence 19, *whoever* is the subject in the clause *whoever deserves it*.
- In sentence 20, *whomever* is the object in the clause *whomever you like*.

If you have trouble deciding on *who* or *whom*, change the sentence to eliminate the problem.

21. I prefer working with people *whom* I don't know as friends.
    Or
    I prefer working with people I don't know as friends.

PRACTICE 8

Circle the correct pronoun.

1. (Who, Whom) will deliver the layouts to the ad agency?
2. To (who, whom) are you speaking?
3. (Who, Whom) prefers hiking to skiing?
4. For (who, whom) are those boxes piled in the corner?
5. The committee will award the scholarship to (whoever, whomever) it chooses.
6. (Who, Whom) do you wish to invite to the open house?
7. At (who, whom) did the governor fling the cream pie?
8. I will hire (whoever, whomever) can use a computer and speak Korean.

E. Using Pronouns with *-self* and *-selves*

ESL TIP

For an interactive quiz on those pesky pronouns with *-self* and *-selves*, send students to **a4esl .org/q/j/tm /fb-reflexive.html**.

Pronouns with *-self* or *-selves* can be used in two ways—as reflexives or as intensives.

A reflexive pronoun indicates that someone did something to himself or herself:

1. My daughter Miriam felt very grown up when she learned to dress *herself*.

- In sentence 1, Miriam did something to *herself*; she *dressed herself*. An intensive pronoun emphasizes the noun or pronoun it refers to:

2. Anthony *himself* was surprised at how relaxed he felt during the interview.

- In sentence 2, *himself* emphasizes that Anthony—much to his surprise—was not nervous at the interview.

The following chart will help you choose the correct reflexive or intensive pronoun:

TEACHING TIP
Students have no doubt heard the words *hisself* and *theirselves* in casual conversation. Point out that these are not real words.

Antecedent		**Reflexive or Intensive Pronoun**
Singular	I	myself
	you	yourself
	he	himself
	she	herself
	it	itself
Plural	we	ourselves
	you	yourselves
	they	themselves

Note that in the plural *-self* is changed to *-selves*.

Be careful: do not use reflexives or intensives as substitutes for the subject of a sentence:

Incorrect: Harry and *myself* will be there on time.
Correct: Harry and *I* will be there on time.

PRACTICE 9

Fill in the correct reflexive or intensive pronoun. Be careful to make pronouns and antecedents agree.

1. Though he hates to cook, André __himself__ sautéed the mushrooms.
2. Rhoda found __herself__ in a strange city with only the phone number of a cousin whom she had not seen for years.
3. Her coffee machine automatically turns __itself__ on in the morning and off in the evening.
4. The librarian and I rearranged the children's section __ourselves__.
5. When it comes to horror films, I know that you consider __yourself__ an expert.
6. They __themselves__ didn't care if they arrived on time or not.
7. After completing a term paper, I always buy __myself__ a little gift to celebrate.
8. Larry __himself__ was surprised at how quickly he grew to like ancient history.

PROOFREADING STRATEGY

One of the most common pronoun errors is using the plural pronouns *they, them,* or *their* incorrectly to refer to a singular antecedent. If this one of your error patterns, **search your draft for *they, them,* and *their*** and **highlight or underline them**. If you are using a computer, use the "Find" feature to locate these words.

Take a moment to **identify the antecedent** for each of these highlighted words by drawing an arrow from the highlighted word to its antecedent. Do the two words agree?

> Because **anyone** can create a website and post ~~their~~ his or her opinions, **researchers** must use their critical thinking skills to make sure that online information is correct.

PRACTICE 10 REVIEW

ESL TIP

Pronoun errors often persist even among advanced ESL students. Have your students use Practice 10 as a guide to finding and correcting pronoun errors in their own writing.

Proofread the following essay for pronoun errors. You might wish to try the proofreading strategy. Then correct each pronoun error in any way you choose.

THE MANY LIVES OF JACKIE CHAN

(1) Few movie stars can claim a career as unusual as ~~him~~ his. (2) For one thing, Jackie Chan performs his death-defying stunts ~~hisself~~ himself. (3) Although he was a huge star in Asia for more than twenty years, fame eluded him in the United States until recently.

(4) Chan was born in Hong Kong in 1954. (5) Because ~~him~~ he and his parents were so poor, he was sent to live and study at the Peking Opera School. (6) There, ~~they~~ experts trained him in acting, dancing, singing, sword fighting, and kung fu. (7) When the school closed in 1971, ~~their~~ its lessons paid off for Chan in an unexpected way.

(8) Chan worked as a stuntman and fight choreographer and landed acting roles in several films, including Bruce Lee's *Enter the Dragon.* (9) Lee~~, he~~ died in 1973, and Chan was the natural choice to fill Lee's shoes. (10) In several films, Chan tried to imitate Lee, but the films were unsuccessful. (11) In 1978, however, Chan came up with the idea of turning Lee's tough style into comedy. (12) *Snake in the Eagle's Shadow* and *Drunken Master* were hilarious hits; ~~it~~ they established "kung fu comedy." (13) Jackie Chan became one of Hong Kong's most popular stars.

AF archive/Alamy Stock Photo

Jackie Chan in the 2000 film *Shanghai Noon*

(14) However, Hollywood directors did not appreciate Chan as a stuntman, actor, comedian, director, and scriptwriter all in one, and ~~its~~ his early American films flopped. (15) Chan understood his own strengths better than ~~them~~ they. (16) He returned to Hong Kong, but ~~him~~ he and his fans always believed he could make a U.S. comeback. (17) This happened when *Rumble in the Bronx*, China's most popular film ever, was dubbed in English. (18) Finally, ~~they~~ Americans began to appreciate this manic, bruised, and battered action hero ~~who~~ whose films were refreshingly nonviolent. (19) After that, Chan's U.S. films, like *Rush Hour* (and its sequels) and *Shanghai Noon*, were received as well as ~~its~~ their Hong Kong counterparts.

EXPLORING ONLINE

grammar.ccc.commnet.edu/grammar/quizzes/cases_quiz1.htm

Interactive pronoun quiz

a4esl.Org/q/h/vm/pronouns.html

Pronoun quiz: especially helpful for ESL writers

CHAPTER 34

Prepositions

A: Working with Prepositional Phrases

B: Prepositions in Common Expressions

A. Working with Prepositional Phrases

TEACHING TIP
Illustrate the fact that prepositions show precise *relationships*: *in the boat, under the boat, against the boat*, and so on.

Prepositions are words like *about, at, behind, into, of, on,* and *with.** They are followed by a noun or a pronoun, which is called the **object** of the preposition. The preposition and its object are called a **prepositional phrase**.

1. Ms. Fairworth hurried *to the computer lab.*
2. Students *with a 3.5 grade point average* will receive a special award.
3. Traffic *at this corner* is dangerously heavy.

- In sentence 1, the prepositional phrase *to the computer lab* explains where Ms. Fairworth hurried.
- In sentence 2, the prepositional phrase *with a 3.5 grade point average* describes which students will receive a special award.
- Which is the prepositional phrase in sentence 3, and what word does it describe?

  at this corner; traffic

ESL TIP
English prepositions often confuse nonnative students, even those who are highly proficient in English. One reason is that some languages (such as German, Russian, and Latin) use inflections to perform the work of prepositions. Another reason is the variability of preposition use.

In/On for Time

Two prepositions often confused are *in* and *on.* Use *in* before months not followed by a specific date, before seasons, and before years that do not include specific dates.

1. *In March,* the skating rink will finally open for business.
2. Rona expects to pay off her car *in 2018.*

*For more work on prepositions, see Chapter 26, "The Simple Sentence," Part B.

ESL TIP
Suggest that students try practicing with flash cards, memorizing when necessary.

Use *on* before days of the week, before holidays, and before months if a date follows.

3. *On Sunday*, the Kingston family spent the day at the beach.
4. *On January 6*, Bernard left for a month of mountain climbing.

In/On for Place

In means *inside* a place.

1. Tonia put her TV *in the bedroom*.
2. Many country groups got their start *in Nashville*.

On means *on top of* or *at a particular place*.

3. That mess *on your desk* needs to be cleared off.
4. Pizza Palace will be opening a new parlor *on Highland Avenue*.

PRACTICE 1

Fill in the correct prepositions in the following sentences. Be especially careful of *in* and *on*.

1. __In__ a little town __on__ the coast of the Dominican Republic, baseball is a way of life.

2. Once known for cattle and sugar, San Pedro de Macoris has been exporting world-class baseball players __to__ the major leagues __for__ over fifty years.

3. Hall-of-Famer Juan Marichal and versatile shortstop José Reyes are just two Dominicans who have made names __for__ themselves __in__ the majors.

4. Other stars born in or __near__ San Pedro de Macoris are Pedro Martinez, Alfonso Soriano, and David Ortiz.

5. Baseball was first introduced __on__ the island __by__ American mill and plantation owners, who encouraged their workers to learn the game.

6. Because equipment was expensive, boys from poor families often batted __with__ a tree branch, using a rolled-up sock __in__ place __of__ a ball.

7. Each young man dreamed that he would be discovered __by__ the baseball scouts and sent to play __in__ *las ligas mayores.*

8. Amazing numbers __of__ these players succeeded, and many Dominican athletes later returned to invest __in__ the local economy.

9. For example, Robinson Cano bought 6,000 baseball uniforms __for__ children and donated four ambulances and four school buses __to__ his hometown.

10. Major league teams, including the Dodgers, Giants, and Expos, now operate year-round training camps __on__ the island, hoping to cultivate the athletes __of__ tomorrow.

B. Prepositions in Common Expressions

ESL TIP

Have students think of other verbs that change meaning when their accompanying prepositions change (e.g., *run over, run into, run out of; take on, take up, take in; turn out, turn in, turn over*). Ask them to write sentences to check their understanding.

Prepositions are often combined with other words to form fixed expressions. Determining the correct preposition in these expressions can sometimes be confusing. Following is a list of some troublesome expressions with prepositions. Consult a dictionary if you need help with others.

Expressions with Prepositions

Expression	Example
according to	*According to* the directions, this flap fits here.
acquainted with	Tom became *acquainted with* his classmates.
addicted to	He is *addicted to* soap operas.
afraid of	Tanya is *afraid of* flying.
agree on (a plan)	Can we *agree on* our next step?
agree to (something or another's proposal)	Roberta *agreed to* her secretary's request for a raise.
angry about or at (a thing)	Jake seemed *angry about* his meager bonus.
angry with (a person)	Sonia couldn't stay *angry with* Felipe.
apply for (a position)	By coincidence, the twins *applied for* the same job.

approve of	Do you *approve of* bilingual education?
argue about (an issue)	I hate *arguing about* money.
argue with (a person)	Edna *argues with* everyone about everything.
capable of	Mario is *capable of* accomplishing anything he attempts.
complain about (a situation)	Patients *complained about* the long wait to see the dentist.
complain to (a person)	Knee-deep in snow, Jed vowed to *complain to* a maintenance person.
comply with	Each contestant must *comply with* contest regulations.
consist of	This article *consists of* nothing but false accusations and half-truths.
contrast with	The light blue shirt *contrasts* sharply *with* the dark brown tie.
correspond with (write)	We *corresponded with* her for two months before we met.
deal with	Ron *deals* well *with* temporary setbacks.
depend on	Miriam can be *depended on* to say embarrassing things.
different from	Children are often *different from* their parents.
differ from (something)	An iPhone *differs from* an Android in many ways.
differ with (a person)	Kathleen *differs with* you on cutting taxes.
displeased with	Ms. Withers was *displeased with* her doctor's advice to eat less fat.
fond of	Ed is *fond of* his pet tarantula.
grateful for	Be *grateful for* having so many good friends.
grateful to (someone)	The team was *grateful to* the coach for his inspiration and confidence.
identical to	Scott's ideas are often *identical to* mine.
inferior to	Saturday's performance was *inferior to* the one I saw last week.
in search of	I hate to go *in search of* change at the last moment before the toll.
interested in	Willa is *interested in* results, not excuses.
interfere with	That dripping faucet *interferes with* my concentration.
object to	Martin *objected to* the judge's comment.
protect against	This heavy wool scarf will *protect* your throat *against* the cold.

ESL TIP
Refer students to these interactive quizzes on idioms and phrasal verbs: **a4esl org/q/h/idioms.html**.

ESL TIP
Explain to students that many frequently used idioms like *in order to, at all, by the way,* and *according to* include prepositions.

reason with	It's hard to *reason with* an angry person.
rely on	If Toni made that promise, you can *rely on* it.
reply to	He wrote twice, but the company did not *reply to* his e-mails.
responsible for	Kit is *responsible for* making two copies of each document.
sensitive to	Professor Godfried is *sensitive to* his students' concerns.
shocked at	We were *shocked at* the graphic violence in that film.
similar to	Some poisonous mushrooms appear quite *similar to* the harmless kind.
speak with (someone)	Geraldine will *speak with* her supervisor about a raise.
specialize in	The dance teacher *specializes in* ballet.
struck by	We were *struck by* the brilliant colors of fish and coral on the reef.
succeed in	Oscar *succeeded in* painting the roof in less than five hours.
superior to	It's clear that the remake is *superior to* the original.
take advantage of	Celia *took advantage of* the snow day to visit the science museum.
worry about	Never *worry about* more than one problem at a time.

PRACTICE 2

Fill in the preposition that correctly completes each of the following expressions.

1. Today's students feel more dedicated to social and political causes than past generations, according ___to___ the annual American Freshman Survey.

2. Every year since 1966, the Higher Education Research Institute has been responsible ___for___ this survey of hundreds of thousands of college students.

3. The results show what students each year hope ___for___, worry ___about___, complain ___about___, depend ___on___, and hold dear.

TEACHING TIP
You might ask students to design and conduct their own survey of college classmates. Have them work in groups, each with a different five-question focus, and later report their findings to the class.

4. According ___to___ the survey conducted in 2015, 8 percent ___of___ incoming freshmen anticipated participating in demonstrations while in college, the highest rate recorded since 1967.

5. Students also are more interested ___in___ serving their communities and working ___for___ social change.

6. Nearly 75 percent ___of___ students ranked "helping others ___with___ difficulties" as being "very important" or "essential" ___in___ their lives.

7. Nine out ___of___ ten students stated that they had performed some sort ___of___ volunteer work in the previous year.

8. Almost 60 percent were concerned ___about___ learning about other countries and cultures.

9. Forty percent of students reported having an interest ___in___ political news and events, and 22 percent maintained that "influencing the political structure" was important in their lives.

10. The survey also revealed that most students are concerned ___about___ the cost of higher education, with women being more troubled ___by___ their financial situation than men.

PROOFREADING STRATEGY

If preposition mistakes are one of your error patterns, try this strategy. Using the feedback you've received from instructors and tutors who know your writing, **record the five prepositions that give you the most trouble** on your Personal Error Patterns Chart.

Carefully scan your writing for each of these five prepositions. If you are using a computer, use the "Find" feature to locate these words in your draft or color code them as in the example below. Then **make sure that you have used each of the prepositions correctly**.

On / in
In May 5, many people on the United States celebrate the holiday Cinco de Mayo with Mexican food, music, and dancing.

PRACTICE 3 REVIEW

Proofread this essay for preposition errors. Try the proofreading strategy to see if it works for you. Cross out the errors and write your corrections above the lines.

DOCTORS WITHOUT BORDERS

(1) ~~In~~ On December 20, 1971, a small group ~~with~~ of French doctors and journalists formed an organization called Médecins Sans Frontières, or Doctors Without Borders. (2) Concerned ~~in~~ about a humanitarian crisis in Nigeria, they believed that all people deserved medical care, regardless ~~with~~ of their race, religion, or political beliefs. (3) They also believed that health services should not be limited ~~in~~ by national borders.

(4) The group's first mission took place ~~on~~ in December 1972 following a devastating earthquake in Managua, the capital ~~on~~ of Nicaragua. (5) The disaster killed 6,000 people and left a quarter-million homeless. (6) Doctors Without Borders provided medical aid ~~with~~ to the survivors. (7) Two years later, the organization established its first long-term health mission ~~about~~ in Honduras to help the victims ~~in~~ of Hurricane Fifi, which caused major flooding of the Central American country. (8) ~~On~~ In 1975, South Vietnam fell and millions ~~in~~ of refugees fled ~~in~~ to Thailand. (9) Doctors Without Borders established another long-term mission to provide medical care ~~with~~ for the displaced people housed ~~for~~ in makeshift refugee camps.

(10) In 1976, Doctors Without Borders provided medical assistance ~~about~~ during the civil war ~~of~~ in Lebanon, the first time the organization came under hostile fire. (11) The medical volunteers helped wounded soldiers from both sides. (12) Doctors Without Borders remained in Lebanon ~~before~~ until 1984, ~~that~~ when the conflict worsened and security could no longer be guaranteed to protect their volunteers.

(13) In the 1980s, the organization expanded its services and began raising money ~~for~~ to fund medical missions in Africa and Asia. (14) Volunteers established aid centers ~~on~~ in Afghanistan to treat Afghan warriors fighting against invading Soviet forces. (15) The organization provided famine relief ~~about~~ in Ethiopia but

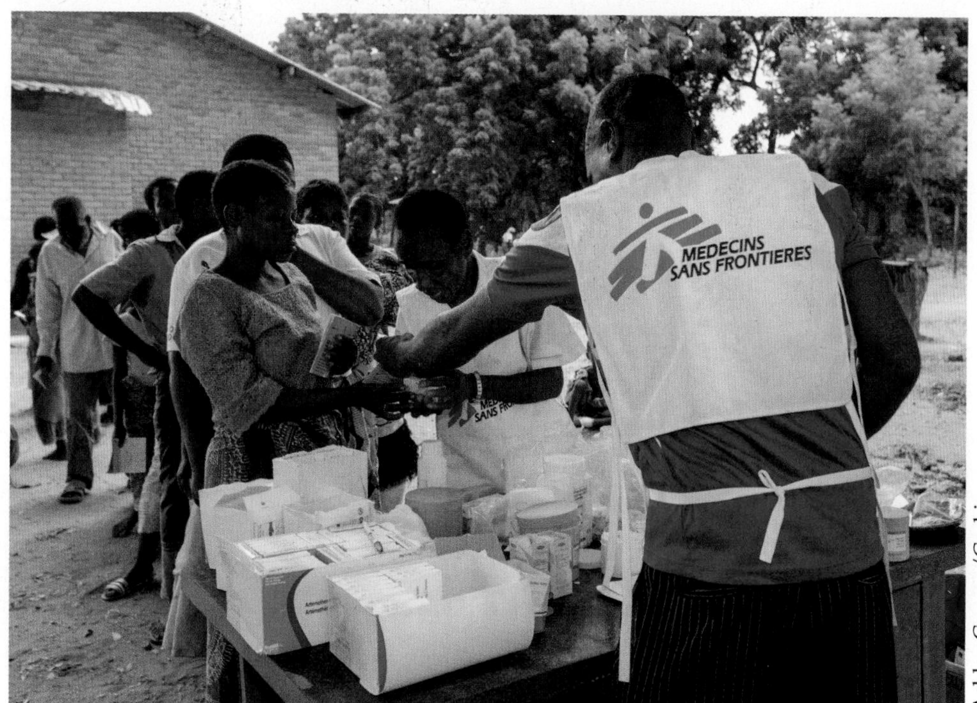

Ashley Cooper/Corbis

A Doctors Without Borders representative distributes malaria drugs to victims of a 2015 flood in Malawi.

was expelled ~~with~~ after criticizing the government's mistreatment ~~for~~ of refugees and the misuse ~~in~~ of relief funds.

(16) ~~On~~ During/In the following decades Doctors Without Borders provided medical services to help victims of wars and disasters ~~around~~ in Sudan, Sierra Leone, Rwanda, and Haiti. (17) ~~With~~ In addition ~~for~~ to medical treatment, nutrition, and clean drinking water, Doctors Without Borders also provides psychological support ~~with~~ for/to victims of war and disaster. (18) In 1999, Doctors Without Borders received the Nobel Peace Prize for its work ~~of~~ on behalf ~~for~~ of victims around the world.

(19) Some members ~~in~~ of Doctors Without Borders formed a separate organization called Doctors of the World, which supported the idea ~~in~~ of using armed intervention to achieve humanitarian goals. (20) Doctors Without Borders, however, insisted ~~for~~ on the group's original mission to operate independently, without ties to national governments.

EXPLORING ONLINE

grammar.ccc.commnet.edu/grammar/quizzes/preposition_quiz1.htm

Graded preposition quiz

a4esl.org/q/f/z/zz36mas.htm

Interactive preposition quiz

CHAPTER 35

Adjectives and Adverbs

A. Defining and Using Adjectives and Adverbs

TEACHING TIP

Ask students to rewrite sentences containing tired adjectives like *nice* or *great* with more exact words; urge them to do this every time they revise.

Adjectives and **adverbs** are two kinds of descriptive words. **Adjectives** describe or modify nouns or pronouns. They explain what kind, which one, or how many.

1. A *black* cat slept on the piano.
2. We felt *cheerful*.
3. *Three* windows in the basement need to be replaced.

- The adjective *black* describes the noun *cat*. It tells what kind of cat, a *black* one.
- The adjective *cheerful* describes the pronoun *we*. It tells what kind of mood we were in, *cheerful*.
- The adjective *three* describes the noun *windows*. It tells how many windows, *three*.

Adverbs describe or modify verbs, adjectives, and other adverbs. They tell how, in what manner, when, where, and to what extent.

4. Joe dances *gracefully*.
5. *Yesterday* Robert left for a weekend of skydiving.
6. Brigit is *extremely* tall.
7. He travels *very* rapidly on that skateboard.

ESL TIP

ESL students may be stymied by the correct order of adjectives in a sentence like "The man in the *long red woolen* scarf turns." For Charles Darling's helpful charts, search online for "Royal Order of Adjectives" or "Royal Order of Adverbs."

- The adverb *gracefully* describes the verb *dances*. It tells how Joe dances: *gracefully*.
- The adverb *yesterday* describes the verb *left*. It tells when Robert left: *yesterday*.
- The adverb *extremely* describes the adjective *tall*. It tells how tall (to what extent): *extremely* tall.
- The adverb *very* describes the adverb *rapidly*, which describes the verb *travels*. It tells how rapidly he travels: *very* rapidly.

Many adjectives can be changed into adverbs by adding an *-ly* ending. For example, *glad* becomes *gladly*, *hopeful* becomes *hopefully*, *awkward* becomes *awkwardly*.

Note the pairs on this list; they are easily confused:

Adjectives	Adverbs
awful	awfully
bad	badly
poor	poorly
quick	quickly
quiet	quietly
real	really
sure	surely

8. The fish tastes *bad*.
9. It was *badly* prepared.

- In sentence 8, the adjective *bad* describes the noun *fish*.
- In sentence 9, the adverb *badly* describes the verb *was prepared*.

10. We drove the *slow, rusting* van.
11. We drove the *slowly rusting* van.

- In sentence 10, the adjectives *slow* and *rusting* describe the noun *van*: it moves slowly and it is rusting.
- In sentence 11, the adverb *slowly* modifies the adjective *rusting* to describe a van that is gradually rusting.

PRACTICE 1

Circle the correct adjective or adverb in parentheses. Remember that adjectives modify nouns or pronouns; adverbs modify verbs, adjectives, or adverbs.

1. Have you ever seen (real, really) emeralds?

2. Try to do your work in the library (quiet, quietly).

3. We will (glad, gladly) take you on a tour of the Crunchier Cracker factory.

4. Lee, a (high, highly) skilled electrician, rewired his entire house last year.

5. She made a (quick, quickly) stop at the scanner.

6. It was (awful, awfully) wet today; the sleet filled our shoes.

7. The fans from Cleveland (enthusiastic, enthusiastically) clapped for the Browns.

8. Are you (sure, surely) this bus stops in Dusty Gulch?

9. He (hasty, hastily) wrote the essay, leaving out several important ideas.

10. It was a funny joke, but the comedian told it (bad, badly).

11. Tina walked (careful, carefully) down the icy road.

12. Sam swims (poor, poorly) even though he spends hours posing on the beach.

13. Sasha the crow is an (unusual, unusually) pet and a (humorous, humorously) companion.

14. The painting is not (actual, actually) a Picasso; in fact, it is a (real, really) bad imitation.

15. It is an (extreme, extremely) hot day, and I (sure, surely) could go for some (real, really) orange juice.

ESL TIP
Refer students to this additional quiz on choosing adjective or adverb word endings: **a4esl.org/q/f/z/zz60fck.htm**.

TEACHING TIP
Encourage students to use correct forms in casual speech. When words like *real* are used incorrectly in conversation (as in *I'm real glad to see you*), the errors are more likely to find their way into writing.

B. The Comparative and the Superlative

The **comparative** of an adjective or adverb compares two persons or things:

1. Ben is *more creative* than Robert.
2. Marcia runs *faster* than the coach.

- In sentence 1, Ben is being compared with Robert.
- In sentence 2, Marcia is being compared with the coach.

The **superlative** of an adjective or adverb compares three or more persons or things:

3. Sancho is the *tallest* of the three brothers.
4. Marion is the *most intelligent* student in the class.

TEACHING TIP
You might combine Part B with a spelling review (e.g., rules about doubling the final consonant or adding *-er* and *-est* to words ending in *-y*).

ESL TIP
Point out that superlative forms of adjectives are preceded by *the*: *the longest yard, the most outrageous costume.*

- In sentence 3, Sancho is being compared with the other two brothers.
- In sentence 4, Marion is being compared with all the other students in the class.

Adjectives and adverbs of one syllable usually form the **comparative** by adding *-er.* They form the **superlative** by adding *-est*.

TEACHING TIP
A trick to help students avoid errors like "more better" is to remember to write just one *-r* in any comparison—either *-er* or *more*, not both.

Adjective	Comparative	Superlative
fast	fast*er*	fast*est*
smart	smart*er*	smart*est*
tall	tall*er*	tall*est*

Adjectives and adverbs of more than one syllable usually form the **comparative** by using *more.* They form the **superlative** by using *most*.

Adjective	Comparative	Superlative
beautiful	*more* beautiful	*most* beautiful
brittle	*more* brittle	*most* brittle
serious	*more* serious	*most* serious

TEACHING TIP
An activity likely to engage students is an analysis of adjectives, comparatives, and superlatives in advertising. Bring in ads or have students do so. Locate and discuss the use of adjectives. Groups might wish to write ads for a product they use—or for one they invent.

Note, however, that adjectives that end in *-y* (like *happy*, *lazy*, and *sunny*) change the *-y* to *-i* and add *-er* and *-est*.

Adjective	Comparative	Superlative
happy	*happier*	*happiest*
lazy	*lazier*	*laziest*
sunny	*sunnier*	*sunniest*

PRACTICE 2

Write the comparative or the superlative of the words in parentheses. Remember: use the comparative to compare two items; use the superlative to compare more than two. Use *-er* or *-est* for one-syllable words; use *more* or *most* for words of more than one syllable.*

1. The ocean is ____colder____ (cold) than we thought it would be.
2. Please read your lines again, ____more slowly____ (slowly) this time.
3. Which of these two roads is the ____shorter____ (short) route?

*If you have questions about spelling, see Chapter 40, "Spelling," Part G.

4. Which of these three highways is the ___shortest___ (short) route?

5. Leola is the ___busiest___ (busy) person I know.

6. That red felt hat with feathers is the ___most unusual___ (unusual) one I've seen.

7. Today is ___warmer___ (warm) than yesterday, but Thursday was the ___warmest___ (warm) day of the month.

8. The down coat you have selected is the ___most expensive___ (expensive) one in the store.

9. Each one of Matt's stories is ___funnier___ (funny) than the last.

10. As a rule, mornings in Los Angeles are ___hazier___ (hazy) than afternoons.

11. Is Paolo ___taller___ (tall) than Louie? Is Paolo the ___tallest___ (tall) player on the team?

12. If you don't do these experiments ___more carefully___ (carefully), you will blow up the chemistry lab.

13. This farmland is much ___rockier___ (rocky) than the farmland in Iowa.

14. Therese says that Physics 201 is the ___most challenging___ (challenging) course she has ever taken.

15. Mr. Wells is the ___wisest___ (wise) and ___most experienced___ (experienced) leader in the community.

PRACTICE 3

Proofread the following paragraph for comparative and superlative errors. Cross out unnecessary words and write your corrections above the lines.

TEACHING TIP

You might wish to lead a discussion or debate about Wikipedia. Can it realize the potential of a free Internet, or does bias and sabotage affect its credibility? The *Exploring Online* task following this exercise is an excellent way to teach students how to evaluate sources.

(1) Wikipedia is a free online encyclopedia that offers information about thousands of topics. (2) Created in 2001, it has become one of the most ~~popularest~~ popular sites on the Internet—and one of the most controversial. (3) Unlike *Britannica* and other encyclopedias of ~~a more early~~ an earlier time, Wikipedia is not an expensive set of books; it exists only online at *www.wikipedia.org.* (4) Its ~~most great~~ greatest innovation is also its ~~most~~ biggest problem: readers can also help write content. (5) The "wiki" software allows anyone who visits the site to add or edit an entry. (6) Supporters believe that thousands of minds produce entries that

are often ~~completer~~ more complete and ~~accurater~~ more accurate than those in traditional encyclopedias. (7) Yet mistakes and sabotage have occurred. (8) A U.S. congressperson changed his Wikipedia profile to make it ~~positiver~~ more positive. (9) The entry on Harriet Tubman, rescuer of southern slaves, gave the wrong birthplace and stated as fact several disproved stories. (10) People have planted lies and jokes in some entries. (11) Wikipedia's 800 volunteer administrators labor to approve each change, making sure that a revised entry is more ~~effectiver~~ effective than the previous one. (12) While correcting such errors is ~~more easier~~ easier and ~~fast~~ faster than in print encyclopedias, some teachers and professors caution students not to cite Wikipedia as an information source.

EXPLORING ONLINE

www.wikipedia.org

Choose a subject that you know something about and evaluate the Wikipedia entry. First, read the Wikipedia article; take notes or print it. Now visit the library and check the facts. Ask the librarian if you need help. Did you find any false information, or is the entry reliable? How would you rate Wikipedia, based on this one entry?

C. A Troublesome Pair: *Good/Well*

TEACHING TIP

The error most commonly made is using *good* in place of *well* (as in *Julian plays ball very good*). Point out that although we might hear this in casual speech, it is a red flag error in writing. Before students complete Practice 4, you might suggest that they name the missing word's part of speech *before* they choose *good* or *well*.

Adjective	**Comparative**	**Superlative**
good	better	best
bad	worse	worst
Adverb	**Comparative**	**Superlative**
well	better	best
badly	worse	worst

Be especially careful not to confuse the adjective **good** with the adverb **well**:

1. Jessie is a *good* writer.
2. She writes *well*.

- *Good* is an **adjective** modifying *writer*.
- *Well* is an **adverb** modifying *writes*.

PRACTICE 4

TEACHING TIP

Have students work in pairs to replace the often overused word *good* (and *well* when appropriate) in Practice 4 with more accurate descriptors.

Fill in either the adjective *good* or the adverb *well* in each blank.

1. Corned beef definitely goes ___well___ with cabbage.
2. How ___well___ do you understand Spanish?
3. He may not take phone messages very ___well___, but he is ___good___ at handling computer problems.
4. Exercise is a ___good___ way to stay in shape; eating ___well___ will help you maintain ___good___ health.
5. Tony looks ___good___ in his new goatee.
6. This is a ___good___ arrangement: I wash, you dry.
7. On rainy nights, Sheila loves to curl up with a ___good___ book.
8. The old Persian carpet and oak desk are a ___good___ match; they go ___well___ together.
9. Both teams played ___well___; it was a ___good___ game.
10. They are ___good___ neighbors and are ___well___ liked in the community.

PRACTICE 5

TEACHING TIP

Students who use *worse* in place of *worst* might not hear the difference in pronunciation between the two words. Have groups create sentences using both words to reinforce their understanding of the difference.

Fill in the correct comparative or superlative of the word in parentheses.

1. Lucinda is a ___better___ (good) chemist than she is a mathematician.
2. Bascomb was the ___worst___ (bad) governor this state has ever had.
3. When it comes to staying in shape, you are ___worse___ (bad) than I.
4. Of the two sisters, Leah is the ___better___ (good) markswoman.
5. You can carry cash when you travel, but using a credit card is ___better___ (good).
6. Our goalie is the ___best___ (good) in the league; yours is the ___worst___ (bad).

7. When it comes to bad taste, movies are ____worse____ (bad) than television.

8. Your sore throat seems ____worse____ (bad) than it was yesterday.

9. Gina likes snorkeling ____better____ (good) than fishing; she loves scuba diving ____best____ (good) of all.

10. A parka is the ____best____ (good) protection against a cold wind; it is certainly ____better____ (good) than a scarf.

PROOFREADING STRATEGY

To help you proofread for *adjective* and *adverb* errors, use two highlighters to code the text. Read slowly, and **mark every adjective purple and every adverb gray** (or colors of your choice), as in the sentences below from one student's paper.

Next check every purple and gray word, one by one. **Ask yourself what word each one describes.** For example, *What word does talented describe?* (*Talented* describes *Jada*, a noun; thus, the adjective *talented* is correct.) *What does the word real describe?* (*Real* describes *talented*, an *adjective*, so *real* is incorrect.) *What word does beautiful describe?* (*Beautiful* describes *plays*, a verb, so the adjective *beautiful* is incorrect.)

> My friend Jada is ~~real~~ really talented. She writes songs and plays the guitar ~~beautiful~~ beautifully. She has the ~~most amazingest~~ amazing voice in our group.

PRACTICE 6 REVIEW

Proofread the following essay for adjective and adverb errors, using the proofreading strategy. Correct the errors by writing above the lines.

JULIA MORGAN, ARCHITECT

(1) Julia Morgan was one of San Francisco's ~~most~~ finest architects, as well as the first woman licensed as an architect in California. (2) In 1902, Morgan became the first woman to ~~successful~~ successfully finish the program in architecture at the School of Fine Arts in Paris.

(3) Returning to San Francisco, she opened her own office and hired and trained a very talented staff that ~~eventual~~ eventually grew to thirty-five full-time architects. (4) Her first major commission was to reconstruct the Fairmont Hotel, one of the

A view of Hearst Castle in San Simeon, California, Julia Morgan's masterpiece

Aresium Art/Shutterstock.com

city's ~~bestest~~ best-known sites, which had been ~~bad~~ badly damaged in the 1906 earthquake. (5) Morgan earned her reputation by designing elegant homes and public buildings out of ~~inexpensively~~ inexpensive and available materials and by treating her clients ~~real good~~ really well. (6) She went on to design more than eight hundred residences, stores, churches, offices, and educational buildings, most of them in California.

(7) Her ~~bestest~~ best customer was William Randolph Hearst, one of the country's ~~most rich~~ richest newspaper publishers. (8) Morgan designed newspaper buildings and more than twenty pleasure palaces for Hearst in California and Mexico. (9) She maintained a private plane and pilot to keep her moving from project to project. (10) The ~~most big~~ biggest and ~~famousest~~ most famous of her undertakings was ~~sure~~ surely Hearst Castle. (11) Morgan worked on it ~~steady~~ steadily for twenty years. (12) She converted a large ranch overlooking the Pacific into a hilltop Mediterranean village composed of three of the ~~beautifullest~~ most beautiful guest houses in the world. (13) The ~~larger~~ largest of the three was designed to look like a cathedral and incorporated Hearst's fabulous art treasures from around the world. (14) The finished masterpiece had 144 rooms and was larger than a football field. (15) Hearst Castle is now one of the most visited tourist attractions in California and seems to grow ~~popularer~~ more popular each year.

EXPLORING ONLINE

a4esl.org/q/f/z/zz60fck.htm

Choose the correct adjective or adverb, and check your answers.

grammar.ccc.commnet.edu/grammar/adjectives.htm

Everything you wanted to know about adjectives

CHAPTER 36

The Apostrophe

A. The Apostrophe for Contractions

TEACHING TIP
Students should understand that the apostrophe has just two main uses: (1) to form a contraction, and (2) to indicate possession. A writer should be able to justify every apostrophe with one of these two rules.

Use the **apostrophe** in a **contraction** to show that letters have been omitted.

1. *I'll* buy that coat if it goes on sale.
2. At nine *o'clock* sharp, the store opens.

- *I'll*, a contraction, is a combination of *I* and *will*. *Wi* is omitted.
- The contraction *o'clock* is the shortened form of *of the clock*.

Be especially careful in writing contractions that contain pronouns:

TEACHING TIP
Your students may be confused about using contractions in academic writing. They should ask for their instructors' views before turning in a written assignment.

Common Contractions

I + am = I'm	it + is or has = it's
I + have = I've	we + are = we're
I + will or shall = I'll	let + us = let's
you + have = you've	you + are = you're
you + will or shall = you'll	they + are = they're
he + will or shall = he'll	they + have = they've
she + is or has = she's	who + is or has = who's

PRACTICE 1

Proofread these sentences and, above the lines, supply any apostrophes missing from the contractions.

1. If you're applying for a job, you'll need a good résumé.
2. In fact, it's important to have several versions of your résumé.
3. Employers are busy, and they've been known to skim a résumé in a few seconds.
4. To be successful, you'll have to create a résumé that's clear and concise.
5. Consider what company you're applying to and what they're looking for.
6. Ask yourself, "Who's going to read this, and what do they need to see?"
7. Today, many people upload their résumés to employer websites, and they're often surprised by the lack of response they get.
8. Computers often scan résumés, and it's not uncommon for the software to be confused by italics, bullet points, and underlining.
9. Applicants aren't the only ones frustrated by this problem; employers worry they're losing valuable talent.
10. Job seekers should upload a plain font version of their résumé so scanning software won't be thrown off by specialized text.

TEACHING TIP
It's/its, they're/their/there, you're/your, and *who's/whose* are some of the most often-confused words in the English language. Take a few moments to cover the differences, and perhaps have the class write sentences to demonstrate their mastery.

TEACHING TIP
You might take a few moments to have students think critically about the effect of contractions in writing. (They create an informal tone often inappropriate for formal academic assignments and workplace documents.)

B. The Apostrophe for Ownership

Use the apostrophe to show ownership: Add an *'s* if a noun or an indefinite pronoun (like *someone, anybody,* and so on) does not already end in *-s*:

1. I cannot find my *friend's* book bag.
2. *Everyone's* right to privacy should be respected.
3. *John and Julio's* apartment has striped wallpaper.
4. The *children's* clothes are covered with mud.

- The *friend* owns the book bag.
- *Everyone* owns the right to privacy.

TEACHING TIP
Many students confuse plurals and possessives—e.g., incorrectly adding an -'s at the end of a noun to form a plural. Take a few minutes to underscore the difference.

- Both John and Julio own one apartment. The apostrophe follows the compound subject *John and Julio*.
- The *children* own the clothes.

Note that apostrophes can distinguish between ownership by one person and ownership by several people:

5. Bill's and Nancy's children are coming this weekend.
6. Bill and Nancy's children are coming this weekend.

- In sentence 5, Bill and Nancy individually have children. He has his children, and she has hers. *Bill* and *Nancy* each has an apostrophe to indicate that they each have children.
- In sentence 6, Bill and Nancy have children together. The single apostrophe follows the subject *Bill and Nancy*.

Add only an apostrophe to show ownership if the word already ends in *-s*:*

7. My *aunts'* houses are filled with antiques.
8. The *knights'* table was round.
9. *Mr. Jonas'* company manufactures sporting goods and uniforms.

- My *aunts* (at least two of them) own the houses.
- The *knights* (at least two) own the table.
- *Aunts* and *knights* already end in *-s*, so only an apostrophe is added.
- *Mr. Jonas* owns the company. *Mr. Jonas* already ends in *-s*, so only an apostrophe is added.

TEACHING TIP
Students often have difficulty distinguishing between *its* and *it's*. Tell students to read sentences out loud and substitute *it is* for *its* or *it's*. If the sentence sounds right (*It is going to snow*), they should include the apostrophe. If not (*The college changed it is policy*), they shouldn't add the apostrophe.

Note that **possessive pronouns never take an apostrophe:** *his, hers, theirs, ours, yours, its*:

10. *His* car gets 20 miles to the gallon, but *hers* gets only ten.
11. That computer is *theirs; ours* is coming soon.

PRACTICE 2

Proofread the following sentences and add apostrophes where necessary to show ownership. In each case, ask yourself if the word already ends in *-s*. Put a *C* after any correct sentences.

1. The college's new parking structure opens next week.
2. Martha and David's house is a log cabin made entirely by hand.

---

*Some writers add an *-'s* to one-syllable proper names that end in *-s*: James's bike.

TEACHING TIP
You might enjoy telling students about the Apostrophe Protection Society, which aims to save this mark from bad writers who misuse it: **www.apostrophe.org.uk.**

3. Somebody's smartphone was left on the sink.
4. During the eighteenth century, ladies' dresses were heavy and uncomfortable.
5. The children brought their bicycles into the gym. C
6. Mr. James' fried chicken and rice dish was crispy and delicious.
7. The class loved reading about Ulysses' travels.
8. The Surgeon General's latest report was just released.
9. Our city's water supply must be protected.
10. He found his ticket, but she cannot find hers. C
11. Every spring, my grandmother's porch is completely covered with old furniture for sale.
12. The faculty's complaints are not being taken seriously.
13. Celia's final, a brilliant study of pest control on tobacco farms, received a high grade.
14. The men's locker room is on the right; the women's is on the left.
15. The program is entering its final year. C

C. Special Uses of the Apostrophe

Use an apostrophe in certain expressions of time:

1. I desperately need a *week's* vacation.

- Although the week does not own a vacation, it is a vacation of a week—*a week's vacation*.

Use an apostrophe to pluralize lowercase letters, words, and numbers that normally do not have plurals:

2. Be careful to cross your *t*'s.
3. Your *8*'s look like *f*'s.
4. Don't use so many *but*'s in your writing.

Use an apostrophe to show omitted numbers:

5. The class of '72 held its annual reunion last week.

PRACTICE 3

Proofread these sentences and add an apostrophe wherever necessary.

1. Can you wear size 7's or 8's?
2. Can you send me more 1040's for my income tax seminar?
3. That could cost me a day's pay.
4. Those 9's look crooked.
5. Speaking in Boston, he reminded everyone about the Spirit of '76.

PROOFREADING STRATEGY

Knowing the two main uses of apostrophes—contractions and possessives—will help you avoid the mistake of sticking apostrophes where they don't belong, such as into plural nouns or possessive pronouns like *hers* or *its*.

Go through your draft and highlight every word that contains an apostrophe. If you are using a computer, use the "Find" feature to locate all apostrophes in your draft.

For every apostrophe, you should be able to answer YES to one of two questions:

Is this apostrophe used to form a contraction?

Is this apostrophe used to indicate possession?

Yes / No—encounters / Yes

Example: Lee's dive trip didn't include any shark encounter's, but he wasn't sorry.

To find missing apostrophes, highlight all words ending in *-s*. If the word is a plural, leave it alone. If the word is a possessive noun, add an apostrophe.

Sandel's / OK—plural / OK—plural / other's

Example: In Professor Sandels course on justice, students debate important ethical issues yet respect each others opinions.

PRACTICE 4 REVIEW

Proofread the following essay for apostrophe errors, using the proofreading strategy. Correct the errors by adding apostrophes above the lines where needed and crossing out those that do not belong.

THE TRUE STORY OF SUPERMAN

(1) Sometimes, things just dont work out right. (2) That's how the creators of Superman felt for a long time.

(3) Supermans first home wasnt the planet Krypton, but Cleveland. (4) There, in 1933, Superman was born. (5) Jerry Siegels story, "Reign of Superman," accompanied by Joe Shuster's illustrations, appeared in the boys own magazine, *Science Fiction*. (6) Later, the teenagers continued to develop their idea. (7) Superman would come to Earth from a distant planet to defend freedom and justice for ordinary people. (8) He would conceal his identity by living as an ordinary person himself. (9) Siegel and Shuster hoped their characters strength and morality would boost peoples spirits' during the Great Depression.

(10) At first, the creators werent able to sell their concept; then, Action Comics' Henry Donnenfield bought it. (11) In June of 1938, the first *Superman* comic hit the stands. (12) Superman's success was immediate and overwhelming. (13) Finally, Americans had a hero who wouldnt let them down! (14) Radio and TV shows, movie serials, feature films, and generations of superheroes' followed.

(15) While others made millions from their idea, Siegel and Shuster didnt profit from it's success. (16) They produced Superman for Action Comics for a mere 15 dollars a page until they were fired a few years later when Joe Shusters eyes began to fail. (17) They sued, but they lost the case. (18) For a long time, both lived in poverty, but they continued to fight. (19) In 1975, Siegel and Shuster finally took their story to the press; the publicity won them lifelong pensions. (20) The two mens long struggle had ended with success.

EXPLORING ONLINE

grammar.ccc.commnet.edu/grammar/quizzes/apostrophe_quiz2.htm
Graded practice: Apostrophe or no apostrophe? This is the question.

journalism.ku.edu/node/276
Apostrophe practice makes perfect.

CHAPTER 37

The Comma

A: Commas for Items in a Series

B: Commas with Introductory Phrases, Transitional Expressions, and Parentheticals

C: Commas for Appositives

D: Commas with Nonrestrictive and Restrictive Clauses

E: Commas for Dates and Addresses

F: Minor Uses of the Comma

A. Commas for Items in a Series

Use commas to separate the items in a series:*

1. You need *bolts*, *nuts*, and *screws*.
2. I will be happy to *read your poem*, *comment on it*, and *return it to you*.
3. *Mary paints pictures*, *Robert plays the trumpet*, but *Sam just sits and dreams*.

TEACHING TIP
Students may have been taught that the final comma preceding the conjunction is optional. Encourage them always to insert that last comma to avoid possible confusion or misreading.

Do not use commas when all three items are joined by *and* or *or*.

4. I enjoy *biking* and *skating* and *swimming*.

*For work on parallelism, see Chapter 21, "Revising for Consistency and Parallelism," Part C.

PRACTICE 1

Punctuate the following sentences.

1. Our sales offices are located in Boston Chicago and San Francisco.
2. We accept cash checks and money orders.
3. The new energy bar contains nuts for proteins whole grains for fiber and raisins for iron.
4. I lost my wallet and had to replace my driver's license credit cards and car registration.
5. The storm damaged the roof flooded the basement and ripped our patio umbrella.
6. Students should review their lecture notes study chapters 1–10 and listen to their instructors' podcasts before taking the final exam.
7. Two senators the British ambassador and four members of Congress attended the trade conference.
8. Jane and Natalie ski in winter swim in summer and work out in the gym year-round.
9. To qualify for this job you must have the following: an associate's degree in business two years' experience in retail sales and two letters of recommendation.
10. We import cheese from Denmark spices from India and sausage from Germany to produce our deluxe pizzas.

B. Commas with Introductory Phrases, Transitional Expressions, and Parentheticals

Use a comma after most introductory phrases of more than two words:*

1. *By four in the afternoon*, everybody wanted to go home.
2. *After the game on Saturday*, we all went dancing.

*For more work on introductory phrases, see Chapter 22, "Revising for Sentence Variety," Part C.

TEACHING TIP

It is common for students to overuse commas. Stress that the secret of correct comma usage is memorizing and practicing the comma rules described in this chapter.

ESL TIP

In some languages, like Spanish, commas are used freely to separate parts of a sentence. Have your ESL students explain comma use in their native language and contrast it with English use.

Use commas to set off transitional expressions:

3. Ferns, *for example*, need less sunlight than flowering plants.
4. Instructors, *on the other hand*, receive a lower salary than assistant professors.

Use commas to set off parenthetical elements:

5. *By the way*, where is the judge's umbrella?
6. Nobody, *it seems*, wants to eat the nut burgers.

- *By the way* and *it seems* are called parenthetical expressions because they appear to be asides, words not really crucial to the meaning of the sentence. They could almost appear in parentheses: *(By the way) where is the judge's umbrella?*

Other common parenthetical expressions are *after all*, *actually*, *as a matter of fact*, and *to tell the truth*.

PRACTICE 2

Punctuate the following sentences.

1. Thoughtlessly he left the keys in the car.
2. None of the guests by the way complained about our service.
3. After every banquet we make a thorough inventory of supplies.
4. Nearing the top of the mountain the hikers paused to rest and regroup.
5. To conclude this discussion may I suggest we take some questions?
6. Unfortunately they won't accept a check.
7. We never promised to hire or even promote anyone this summer.
8. Milwaukee unlike Phoenix has access to ample sources of fresh water.
9. After the film is released we can discuss television rights.
10. Before going on this diet you should talk with your doctor.

C. Commas for Appositives

Use commas to set off appositives:*

1. Yoko, *our new classmate,* is our best fielder.
2. *A humorous and charming man,* he was a great hit with my parents.
3. This is her favorite food, *ketchup sandwiches.*

- Appositive phrases like *our new classmate, a humorous and charming man,* and *ketchup sandwiches* rename or describe nouns and pronouns—*Yoko, he, food.*

4. Entrepreneur Bezos launched the largest online retailer.
5. His company, Amazon, started selling books and CDs in the 1990s.

- A one-word appositive is not set off by commas when it is essential to the meaning of the sentence. Without the appositive *Bezos,* we do not know who launched *the largest online retailer.*
- A one-word appositive is set off by commas when it is not essential to the meaning of the sentence. The name *Amazon* does not affect the sentence's meaning.

PRACTICE 3

Punctuate the following sentences.

1. The Rock, the popular wrestler and actor, starred in movies and made a video with musician Wyclef Jean.
2. Long novels, especially ones with complicated plots, force me to read slowly.
3. Rolando, a resident nurse, hopes to become a pediatrician.
4. I don't trust that tire, the one with the yellow patch on the side.
5. Tanzania, a small African nation, exports cashew nuts.
6. Watch out for Phil, a man ruled by ambition.
7. Ms. Liu, a well-known nutritionist, warns against rapid weight loss diets.
8. An exchange student from Kiev, Maria, will give a lecture about the Ukraine tonight.

---

*For more work on appositives, see Chapter 22, "Revising for Sentence Variety," Part D.

9. We support the Center for Science in the Public Interest, a consumer education and protection group.

10. My husband, Bill, owns two iPads.

D. Commas with Nonrestrictive and Restrictive Clauses

TEACHING TIP
You may want to remind students that nonrestrictive relative clauses, covered in Part D of Chapter 22, are a type of parenthetical expression that requires commas.

A **relative clause** is a clause that begins with *who, which,* or *that* and modifies a noun or pronoun. There are two kinds of relative clauses: **nonrestrictive** and **restrictive.***

A **nonrestrictive relative clause** is not essential to the meaning of the sentence:

1. Raj, *who is a part-time aviator*, loves to tinker with machines of all kinds.

- *Who is a part-time aviator* is a relative clause describing *Raj.* It is a nonrestrictive relative clause because it is not essential to the meaning of the sentence. The point is that *Raj loves to tinker with machines of all kinds.*
- **Commas** set off the nonrestrictive relative clause.

A **restrictive relative clause** is essential to the meaning of the sentence:

2. People *who do their work efficiently* make good students.

- *Who do their work efficiently* is a relative clause describing *people.* It is a restrictive relative clause because it is *essential* to the meaning of the sentence. Without it, sentence 2 would read, *People make good students.* But the point is that certain people make good students—*those who do their work efficiently*.
- Restrictive relative clauses do *not* require commas.

PRACTICE 4

TEACHING TIP
Remind students that *who* refers to persons; *which* and *that* refer to things.

Set off the nonrestrictive relative clauses in the following sentences with commas. Note that *which* usually begins a nonrestrictive relative clause and *that* usually begins a restrictive clause. Remember: restrictive relative clauses are *not* set off by commas. Write a C after each correct sentence.

1. Olive, who always wanted to go into law enforcement, is a detective in the Eighth Precinct.

2. Employees who learn to use the new software may soon qualify for a merit raise. C

*For more work on nonrestrictive and restrictive clauses, see Chapter 22, "Revising for Sentence Variety," Part D.

3. Polo, which is not played much in the United States, is very popular in England.
4. A person who always insists upon telling you the truth is sometimes a pain in the neck. C
5. Statistics 101, which is required for the business curriculum, demands concentration and perseverance.
6. Robin, who is usually shy at large parties, spent the evening dancing with Arsenio, who is everybody's favorite dance partner.
7. This small shop sells furniture that is locally handcrafted. C
8. His uncle, who rarely eats meat, consumes enormous quantities of vegetables, fruits, and grains.
9. People who show up late are going to miss the orientation. C
10. Gettysburg, which is the site of a major Civil War battle, draws many tourists every spring and summer.

E. Commas for Dates and Addresses

TEACHING TIP
Have students recall an important day in their lives and then write one sentence stating what happened and the full date of the event. Ask pairs to share what they wrote, exchanging pages to check each other's skill with commas.

Use commas to separate the elements of an address. Note, however, that no punctuation is required between the state and ZIP code if the ZIP code is included.

1. Please send the books to *300 West Road, Stamford, CT 06860.*
2. We moved from *1015 Allen Circle, Morristown, New Jersey,* to *Vorland Lane, Dubuque, Iowa.*

Use commas to separate the elements of a date:

3. The sociologists arrived in Tibet on *Monday, January 18, 2014,* and planned to stay for two years.
4. John DeLeon arrived *from Baltimore in January* and will be our new shortstop this season.

Do not use a comma with a single-word address or date preceded by a preposition:

5. I expect to have completed my B.A. in physical education by June 2019.

PRACTICE 5

Punctuate the following sentences. Write a *C* after each correct sentence.

1. The unusual names of many American towns reflect our history and sense of humor. C

2. In February 1878, Ed Schieffelin told friends that he was joining the California Gold Rush, and they warned, "The only thing you'll find out there will be your own tombstone." C

3. But Schieffelin found silver in Arizona and named his settlement Tombstone now famous for the shootout at the O.K. Corral on October 26 1881.

4. The residents of another mining town wanted to honor the chicken-like ptarmigan bird but an argument about the word's spelling led them to select Chicken Alaska, instead.

5. It was Christmas Eve December 24 1849 when residents of a small rural community chose to name their town Santa Claus.

6. Every Christmas since the 1920s volunteers have replied to the thousands of children's letters that pour into the town's post office located at 45 N. Kringle Place Santa Claus Indiana 47579.

7. Hell, Michigan, got its name when crusty resident George Reeves was asked his opinion and replied, "I don't care. You can name it Hell if you want to." C

8. At a 10K race there on August 13 2005 runners went home with T-shirts announcing "I Ran Thru Hell."

9. On January 20 2000 the town of Halfway Oregon became the "World's First Dot Com City" when it officially changed its name to Half.com.

10. Choosing the right name can be difficult, as the folks who founded Nameless Tennessee can attest.

F. Minor Uses of the Comma

TEACHING TIP
Commas in direct quotations are covered in Chapter 38.

Use a comma after answering a question with *yes* or *no*:

1. *No*, I'm not sure about that answer.

Use a comma when addressing someone directly and specifically naming the person spoken to:

2. *Alicia*, where did you put my law books?

Use a comma after interjections like *ah*, *oh*, and so on:

3. *Ah*, these coconuts are delicious.

Use a comma to contrast:

4. Harold, *not Roy*, is my scuba-diving partner.*

PRACTICE 6

Punctuate the following sentences.

1. Yes, I do think you will be famous one day.
2. Well, did you call a taxi?
3. The defendant, ladies and gentlemen of the jury, does not even own a red plaid jacket.
4. Cynthia, have you ever camped in the Pacific Northwest?
5. No, I most certainly will not marry you.
6. Oh, I love the way they play everything to a salsa beat!
7. The class feels, Professor Molinor, that your grades are unrealistically low.
8. He said march, not swagger.

*For help using commas with coordinating and subordinating conjunctions—and help avoiding run-ons, comma splices, and fragments—see Chapters 27 and 28.

9. Perhaps ^ but I still don't think that argument makes sense.

10. We all agree ^ Ms. Crawford ^ that you are the best jazz bassist around.

PROOFREADING STRATEGY

Armed with these comma rules, you can proofread effectively for comma errors.

1. **Circle or highlight every comma in your draft.** This forces your eye and brain to focus on each one of them. If you are writing on a computer, use the "Find" feature to locate all your commas.
2. For every comma, ask, *Does one of the eight comma rules explain why this comma needs to be here?* If you aren't sure, review the rules in the chapter. Make any needed corrections, like this:

C (introductory phrase)
For centuries, vampire stories have been told around the world.
X (appositive—add second comma)
Stephenie Meyer, author of the four *Twilight* books ^ weaves vampires into a teenage love triangle.

C (items in a series)
Twilight, *New Moon*, *Eclipse*, and *Breaking Dawn* have sold 100 million
X (not coordination—remove comma)
copies, and have been translated into 37 languages.

PRACTICE 7 REVIEW

Using the proofreading strategy, proofread the following essay for comma errors—either missing commas or commas used incorrectly.

PIXAR PERFECT

TEACHING TIP
To reinforce their knowledge of comma rules, you might want to ask students to identify the applicable rule for each comma they add to Practice 7.

(1) A company called Pixar has transformed animated films. (2) It was started in 1986 by Steve Jobs ^ the co-founder of Apple Computer and creator of the iPod and iPhone. (3) Applying technical imagination to storytelling ^ Pixar has produced some of the most successful and beloved movies ever made. (4) *Toy Story, A Bug's Life* ^ *Finding Nemo*, *Monsters, Inc.*, *Wall-E*, *Inside Out*, and *Finding Dory* appeal to both children and adults by combining engaging stories ^ memorable characters, and cutting-edge computer animation.

Everett Collection, Inc.

Sadness, Anger, Fear, Disgust, and Joy in *Inside Out*

(5) Pixar's action-packed plots carry emotional punch. (6) *Monsters, Inc.* for example explores the theme of facing fears as it follows two monsters attempting to return a wayward toddler to her room. (7) In *Inside Out* an eleven-year-old girl's emotions try to help her adjust to a new school house and city.

(8) Pixar populates these plots with lovable heroes and diabolical villains. (9) Although none of them is technically a human characters like Woody, Buzz Lightyear, Sully and Dory win moviegoers' hearts with their "humanity." (10) Woody is upset when a new toy replaces him as the favorite. (11) Lonely Wall-E longs to win the heart of shiny Eve. (12) The characters seem even more real because stars like Ellen DeGeneres, Tom Hanks, Amy Poehler, and Billy Crystal bring their voices to life.

(14) Finally Pixar animators use the latest computer-animation technology and meticulous detail to create realistic 3-D images. (15) Monster Sully's shaggy blue coat ripples in the wind for example because animators created a separate computer model for each of its 2.3 million individual hairs. (16) To convey strong emotion with almost no words *Wall-E*'s animators studied the movements of machines like NASA's Mars Rover and watched silent films and those with little dialogue such as *2001: A Space Odyssey.*

(17) Pixar's films have impressed critics as well as audiences. (18) In fact its movies have won more than two hundred Academy Awards Golden Globes and other top film prizes.

EXPLORING ONLINE

www.pixar.com/behind_the_scenes

The site "Behind the Scenes" offers a tour of the Pixar process through the experience of the director, artists, and technicians who work on a film and bring it to life.

EXPLORING ONLINE

owl.english.purdue.edu/owl/resource/607/01

Quick rules for commas and review

grammar.ccc.commnet.edu/grammar/quizzes/commas_fillin.htm

Where have all the commas gone?

CHAPTER 38

Mechanics

A: Capitalization

B: Titles

C: Direct Quotations

D: Minor Marks of Punctuation

A. Capitalization

TEACHING TIP
You may wish to begin this lesson by reviewing with students the distinction between proper nouns/adjectives and common nouns/adjectives.

TEACHING TIP
Explain to students that although *African American* and *Caucasian* are capitalized, the words *black* and *white* usually are not.

Always capitalize the following: *names, nationalities, religions, races, languages, countries, cities, months, days of the week, documents, organizations,* and *holidays.*

1. The *Protestant* church on the corner will offer *Spanish* and *English* courses starting *Thursday, June* 3.

Capitalize the following *only* when they are used as part of a proper noun: *streets, buildings, historical events, titles,* and *family relationships.*

2. We saw *Professor Rodriguez* at *Silver Hall,* where he was delivering a talk on the *Spanish Civil War.*

Do not capitalize these same words when they are used as common nouns:

3. We saw the professor at the lecture hall, where he was delivering a talk on a civil war.

ESL TIP
Many ESL students do not understand the importance of capitalization. Native Spanish speakers may need to review the rules regarding nationalities in order to avoid errors like this one: *My chinese neighbor is a chef.*

Capitalize *North, South, East, West* when they refer to a geographical region. Do not capitalize them when they refer to a direction, like *left* or *right*.

4. The tourists went to the *South* for their winter vacation.
5. Go south on this boulevard for three miles.

Capitalize academic subjects only if they refer to a specific named and numbered course:

6. Have you ever studied psychology?
7. Last semester, I took *Psychology* 101.

Capitalize most abbreviations.

8. The *NYPD* is working with the *FBI*.

PROOFREADING STRATEGY

Incorrect capitalization is a red-flag error in college writing. If capitalization is one of your error patterns, try this:

1. Circle or color code every **proper noun** (nouns of specific people, places, and things) and **capitalized word**.
2. Now check one by one to **make sure that you have correctly capitalized**. This student coded her proper nouns yellow:

Lady Gaga
Example: In February, 2012, lady gaga launched her new Born This
Way University
way Foundation at Harvard university. The foundation uses digital
kindness bravery
tools to promote Kindness, Bravery, acceptance, and empowerment.

PRACTICE 1

TEACHING TIP
People are still debating whether to capitalize certain words associated with the Internet. Most dictionaries capitalize *Internet, World Wide Web,* and *Web page,* but the words *e-mail* and *online* are never capitalized.

Capitalize wherever necessary in the following sentences. Put a *C* after each correct sentence.

1. Barbara Kingsolver, a well-known novelist, nonfiction writer, and poet, was
A A M
born on ~~a~~pril 8, 1955, in ~~a~~nnapolis, ~~m~~aryland.

K I
2. She grew up in rural ~~k~~entucky and then went to college in ~~i~~ndiana; after
E
graduating, she worked in ~~e~~urope and since then has lived in and around
T A
~~t~~ucson, ~~a~~rizona.

TEACHING TIP

Urge students to use uppercase and lowercase letters (rather than all capitals) in *all* written work, including e-mail messages. Text written in all caps not only is hard to read but also seems to shout at the reader. Using good writing and well-chosen words is the best way to hold readers' attention.

ESL TIP

Here is an engaging activity that might prompt shy ESL students to share. Ask all students to write a brief autobiography—with people, places, pets, and dates capitalized correctly. Then have volunteers read their work aloud as class members learn about each other and listen for words that should be capitalized.

3. In college, Kingsolver majored first in music and then in biology; she later withdrew from a graduate program in biology and ecology at the ~~u~~University of ~~a~~Arizona to work in its ~~o~~Office of ~~a~~Arid ~~l~~Land ~~s~~Studies.

4. Kingsolver's first novel, *The Bean Trees*, has become a classic; it is taught in ~~e~~English classes and has been translated into more than 65 languages.

5. The main character, named ~~t~~Taylor ~~g~~Greer, is considered one of the most memorable women in modern ~~a~~American literature.

6. In a later novel, *The Poisonwood Bible*, Kingsolver follows the family of a ~~b~~Baptist minister in its move to the ~~c~~Congo.

7. The fanaticism of ~~r~~Reverend ~~p~~Price brings misery to his family and destruction to the villagers he tries to convert to ~~c~~Christianity.

8. Kingsolver's writing always deals with powerful political and social issues, but her novels don't sound preachy because she is a wonderful storyteller. C

9. She has won awards and prizes from the ~~a~~American ~~l~~Library ~~a~~Association and many other organizations; she also has earned special recognition from the ~~u~~United ~~n~~Nations ~~n~~National ~~c~~Council of ~~w~~Women.

10. This gifted writer, who plays drums and piano, performs with a band called ~~r~~Rock ~~b~~Bottom ~~r~~Remainders; other band members are also notable writers—~~s~~Stephen ~~k~~King, ~~a~~Amy ~~t~~Tan, and ~~d~~Dave ~~b~~Barry.

B. Titles

Capitalize words in a title except short prepositions, short conjunctions, and the articles *the*, *an*, and *a*. Always capitalize the first and last words of the title, no matter what they are:

1. I liked *The Invisible Man* but found *The House on the River* slow reading.

Italicize or underline the titles of long works: *books*,* *newspapers and magazines*, *television shows*, *plays*, *record albums*, *operas*, and *films*.

Put quotation marks around shorter works or parts of longer ones: *articles*, *short stories*, *poems*, *songs*, *scenes from plays*, and *chapters from full-length books*.

*The titles and parts of sacred books are not italicized or underlined and are not set off by quotation marks: Job 5:6, Koran 1:14, and so on.

TEACHING TIP
Caution students to use *either* quotation marks *or* italics, not both.

2. Have you read Hemingway's "The Killers" yet?
3. We are assigned "The Money Market" in *Essentials of Economics* for homework in my marketing course.

- "The Killers" is a short story.
- "The Money Market" is a chapter in the full-length book *Essentials of Economics*.

Do not underline or use quotation marks around the titles of your own papers.

PRACTICE 2

Capitalize these titles correctly. Do not underline or use quotation marks in this practice.

1. I W C B
   inside women's college basketball
2. T G F L W
   the genius of frank lloyd wright
3. T M E T
   the middle east today
4. A I G M I
   an insider's guide to the music industry
5. T O T
   the orchid thief
6. A A G T
   an american's guide to tokyo
7. H B W
   how to build a website
8. A H V A M
   a history of violence in american movies
9. H P G F
   harry potter and the goblet of fire
10. C D R
    currents from the dancing river

PRACTICE 3

Wherever necessary, underline (to indicate italics) or place quotation marks around each title in the sentences below so that the reader will know at a glance what type of work the title refers to. Put a *C* after any correct sentence.

EXAMPLE Two of the best short stories in that volume are "Rope" and "The New Dress."

1. African American writer Langston Hughes produced his first novel, Not Without Laughter, when he was a student at Lincoln University in Pennsylvania.

2. By that time, he had already been a farmer, a cook, a waiter, and a doorman at a Paris nightclub; he had also won a prize for his poem "The Weary Blues," which was published in 1925 in the magazine *Opportunity*.

3. In 1926, Hughes wrote his famous essay "The Negro Artist and the Racial Mountain," which appeared in *The Nation* magazine; he wanted young black writers to write without shame or fear about the subject of race.

4. Because he spoke Spanish, Hughes was asked in 1937 by the newspaper the *Baltimore Afro-American* to cover the activities of blacks in the International Brigades in Spain during the Spanish Civil War.

5. For the rest of his life, he wrote articles in newspapers such as the *San Francisco Chronicle*, *The New York Times*, and the *Chicago Defender*.

6. In fact, for more than twenty years he wrote a weekly column for the *Chicago Defender* in which he introduced a character named Simple, who became popular because of his witty observations on life.

7. The stories about Simple were eventually collected and published in five books; two of those books are *Simple Speaks His Mind* and *Simple Takes a Wife*.

8. In 1938, Hughes established the Harlem Suitcase Theater in Manhattan, where his play *Don't You Want to Be Free?* was performed.

9. Because Hughes' poetry was based on the rhythms of African American speech and music, many of his poems have been set to music, including "Love Can Hurt You," "Dorothy's Name Is Mud," and "Five O'Clock Blues."

10. Few modern writers can rival Hughes' enormous output of fine poems, newspaper articles, columns, and novels. C

TEACHING TIP
Remind students that quotation marks are always used in pairs; when proofreading, they should verify that they provided the end quotation mark.

ESL TIP
Direct and indirect quotations challenge ESL students because presenting the words or ideas of others is not as strictly controlled in some languages as it is in English. Further, the shifting of verb tenses in reported speech is problematic, and paraphrasing can lead to wordiness or awkward meaning.

ESL TIP
In languages such as Russian and Spanish, quotation marks are placed differently than in English. Ask students to compare how English quotation marks look versus those in their languages.

C. Direct Quotations

1. He said, "These are the best seats in the house."

- The direct quotation is preceded by a comma or a colon.
- The first letter of the direct quotation is capitalized.
- Periods always go *inside* the quotation marks.

2. He asked, "Where is my laptop?"
3. Stewart yelled, "I don't like beans!"

- Question marks and exclamation points go inside the quotation marks if they are part of the direct words of the speaker.*

4. "That was meant for the company," he said, "but if you wish, you may have it."
5. "The trees look magnificent!" she exclaimed. "It would be fun to climb them all."

- In sentence 4, the quotation is one single sentence interrupted by *he said*. Therefore, a comma is used after *he said*, and *but* is not capitalized.
- In sentence 5, the quotation consists of two different sentences. Thus a period follows *exclaimed*, and the second sentence of the quotation begins with a capital letter.

PROOFREADING STRATEGY

If quotation marks are one of your personal error patterns, try this strategy.

1. **Scan your draft** for sentences in which you give **someone's exact words**.
2. **Check these sentences** for correct use of commas, quotation marks, and capitalization.
3. Make sure that you have provided both **beginning and end quotation marks**.

The police officer asked, "Do you know how fast you were going?"

Mike answered, "I was texting so I couldn't see the speedometer."

*For more work on the distinction between direct quotation and paraphrase, see Chapter 18, "Using Direct and Indirect Quotation (Paraphrase)," Part C.

PRACTICE 4

Insert quotation marks where necessary in each sentence. Use the proofreading strategy to make sure you have capitalized and punctuated correctly.

1. The sign reads don't even think about parking here.
2. The author of the report wrote more students are studying foreign languages than ever before.
3. Well, it takes all kinds she sighed.
4. The mayor exclaimed take shelter during the hurricane!
5. The article said Most American children do poorly in geography.
6. These books on ancient Egypt look interesting he replied but I don't have time to read them now.
7. Although the rain is heavy she said we will continue harvesting the corn.
8. Give up caffeine and get lots of rest the doctor advised.
9. The label warns this product should not be taken by those allergic to aspirin.
10. Red, white, and blue Janice said are my favorite colors.

TEACHING TIP
Explore with students some ways that quotations might improve their writing. Quotations can enliven a narrative, provide expert opinion, or improve an introduction or conclusion.

D. Minor Marks of Punctuation

The Colon

Use a colon following an independent clause to show that a direct quotation will follow or to introduce a list:*

TEACHING TIP
Remind students that colons must follow an independent clause to introduce a list. Many students will mistakenly use colons after a verb (*We need: first aid kits, blankets, and tents*). Remind them to place a colon only where they could put a period (*We need camping supplies: first aid kits, blankets, and tents*).

1. This is the opening line of his essay: "The airplane is humanity's greatest invention."
2. The writing center needs additional supplies: toner cartridges, legal pads, pencils, and two laptops.

Use a colon to separate the chapter and verse in a reference to the Bible or to separate the hour and minute:

3. This quotation comes from Genesis 1:1.
4. It is now exactly 4:15 P.M.

*Avoid using a colon after any form of the verb *to be* or after a preposition.

Parentheses

Use parentheses to enclose a phrase or word that is not essential to the meaning of the sentence:

5. Herpetology (the study of snakes) is a fascinating area of zoology.
6. She left her hometown (Plunkville) to go to the big city (Fairmount) in search of success.

The Dash

Use a dash to emphasize a portion of a sentence or to interrupt the sentence with an added element:

7. This is the right method—the only one—so we are stuck with it.

The colon, parentheses, and the dash should be used sparingly.

PRACTICE 5

Punctuate these sentences with colons, dashes, or parentheses.

1. Calvin asked for the following items two light bulbs, a pack of matches, a lead pencil, and a pound of grapes.
2. They should leave by 11 30 P.M.
3. The designer's newest fashions magnificent leather creations were generally too expensive for the small chain of clothing stores.
4. Harvey the only Missourian in the group remains unconvinced.
5. She replied, "This rock group The Woogies sounds like all the others I've heard this year."
6. If you eat a heavy lunch as you always do remember not to go swimming immediately afterward.
7. By 9:30 P.M., the zoo veterinarian a Dr. Smittens had operated on the elephant.
8. Note these three tips for hammering in a nail hold the hammer at the end of the handle, position the nail carefully, and watch your thumb.

9. Whenever Harold does his birdcalls at parties as he is sure to do everyone begins to yawn.

10. Please purchase these things at the hardware store masking tape, thumbtacks, apple-green paint, and some sandpaper.

PRACTICE 6 REVIEW

Proofread the following essay for errors in capitalization, quotation marks, colons, parentheses, and dashes.

THE PASSION OF JACKSON POLLOCK

(1) Jackson Pollock born Paul Jackson Pollock was a major american abstract artist whose revolutionary style influenced generations of painters. (2) His parents, Stella May née McClure and LeRoy Pollock, were born in iowa and moved to Wyoming. (3) Traveling throughout the west with his father, Jackson Pollock

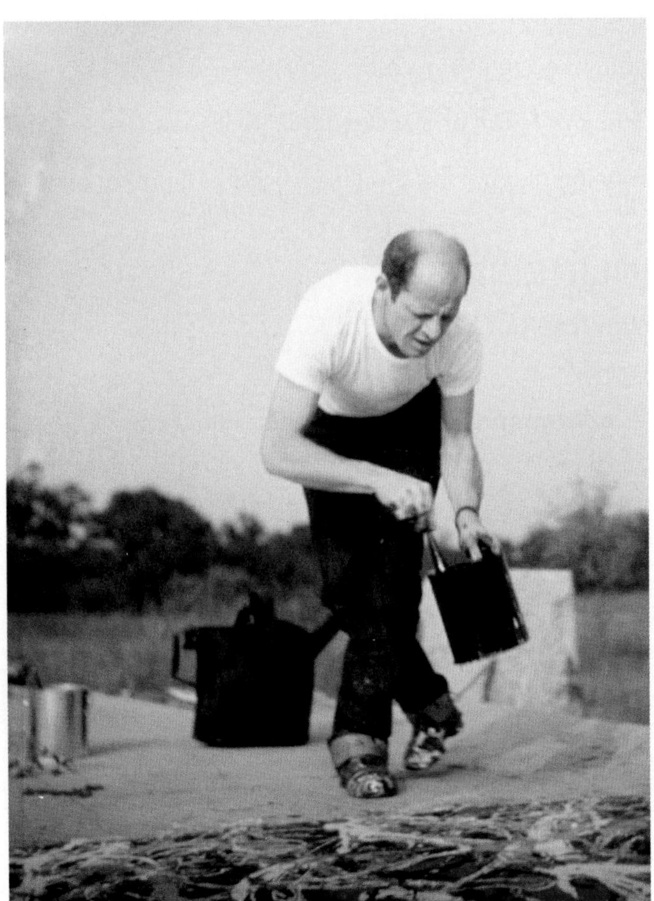

Photo Researchers/Alamy Stock Photo

Jackson Pollock at work

developed an interest in native american culture. (4) While living in California, Pollock attended manual arts high school in Los Angeles but was expelled. (5) During the great depression, Pollock worked for the government as an artist.

(6) Moving to New York, Pollock attracted the attention of Peggy Guggenheim, a wealthy art collector, who commissioned him to paint a Mural in her townhouse. (7) Jackson began to experiment with new methods of applying paint, developing what he called his drip method. (8) Jackson did not use a brush to paint a canvas resting against an easel the method favored by most artists but used a number of unconventional tools hardened brushes, sticks, and basters. (9) His works consisted of swirls, drops, and splashes of colors. (10) In August 1949, *Life* magazine profiled his work in an article titled Jackson Pollock Is he the greatest living painter in the United States?

(11) Pollock battled a series of personal problems depression, alcoholism, and economic insecurity. (12) On August 11, 1956, at 1015 P.M., he was killed in a car crash near his home. (13) His Widow Lee Krasner maintained his estate and continued to promote his art. (14) In 2000, Ed Harris best known for his roles in *The Right Stuff* and *A Beautiful Mind* directed and starred in *Pollock*, an award-winning film tracing the life and work of one of america's most original artists.

EXPLORING ONLINE

esl.fis.edu/grammar/satz/capital1.htm

Graded capitalization practice

grammar.ccc.commnet.edu/grammar/quizzes/punct_fillin.htm

Mixed practice: test your skill with many marks of punctuation.

CHAPTER 39

Putting Your Proofreading Skills to Work

TEACHING TIP
Lead a discussion about the effect that error-filled written work has on the reader, especially in academic and professional settings.

Throughout this unit, you have tried out proofreading strategies for different kinds of errors. This chapter gives you the opportunity to put your proofreading skills to work in even more challenging situations. As you proofread the paragraphs and essays that follow, you must look for any—and every—kind of error, just as you would in the real world of college and work. The first four practices tell you what kinds of errors to look for; if you have trouble, go back to those chapters and review. The other practices, however, contain a random mix of errors with no clues at all.

- Before you start, review your **Personal Error Patterns Chart** that you learned to keep in Chapter 25. Watch out for the errors you tend to make.
- Use the **proofreading strategies** that work best for you, like color highlighting, reading out loud, and reading from the bottom up. Apply your favorite strategies here.
- Refer to the proofreading checklist at the end of this chapter for a quick reminder of what to look for.
- Keep a **dictionary** handy. If you are not sure of the spelling of a word, look it up.

PRACTICE 1 PROOFREADING

TEACHING TIP
Make sure your students have learned their individual *error patterns* and know to proofread carefully for these. Remember: one error repeated ten times looks like ten errors!

Proofread this paragraph, correcting errors above the lines. To review, see these chapters:

Chapter 28	run-ons, comma splices, fragments
Chapter 29	present tense problems, subject-verb agreement
Chapter 31	past participle problems
Chapter 32	noun errors
Chapter 36	apostrophe errors

(1) A *Popular Mechanics* article listed the smartphone as the most important invention, outranking ~~. (2) Outranking~~ the lightbulb, television, and even the computer. (3) In less than a decade, the smartphone has changed ~~change~~ the way people ~~works~~ work, ~~lives~~ live, and ~~socializes~~ socialize. (4) Over ~~With over~~ a billion people worldwide now use ~~used~~ smartphones. (5) Today's ~~Todays~~ smartphones are pocket-sized computers, and their uses are infinite. (6) Workers are freed from their desks, and they can read and send email while shopping or waiting in a dentist's office. (7) It's no wonder why many professionals feel more productive. They ~~they~~ no longer miss critical calls or have to wait for someone to return from lunch to answer a simple question. (8) A doctor can monitor patients while traveling, and patients can be reminded when to take their medication. (9) Almost three million apps have ~~has~~ been developed, letting users personalize smartphones to make their lives easier. (10) Once people had ~~has~~ to use calculators, alarm clocks, and cameras, but now smartphones have these tools. (11) One of the greatest smartphone innovations is ~~are~~ GPS capability, which saves people from getting lost or having to stop to ask for directions. (12) ~~Childrens~~ Children can ~~lets~~ let parents know exactly where they are if they need help or a ride home. (13) The smartphone is ~~are~~ a virtual office for many sales reps, allowing them to contact customers, place orders, and post promotional videos. (14) Companies no longer ~~needs~~ need to maintain costly field offices. Special ~~special~~ apps let them use smartphones to build a network from a single location. (15) Smartphones, however, have ~~has~~ their critics, who argue they have ~~has~~ disrupted personal relationships and eroded our sense of privacy.

PRACTICE 2 PROOFREADING

Proofread this paragraph, correcting errors above the lines. To review, see these chapters:

Chapter 28	run-ons, comma splices, fragments
Chapter 29	present tense problems, subject-verb agreement
Chapter 30	past tense problems
Chapter 31	past participle problems

(1) Mount Everest is the tallest mountain in the world, the ~~. (2) The~~ highest point on Earth, and the dangerous dream of every mountain climber. (3) Everest is set in the Himalaya Mountains of central Asia and rises ~~rise~~ 29,028 feet. (4) The deadliest threat

TEACHING TIP
Consider having students work in groups on the first few practices. They can talk about the errors as they identify them, thus reinforcing learning and boosting their confidence. Or turn one or more of the practices into a game. The first team to find and correct all of the errors wins.

ESL TIP
owl.english.purdue.edu/owl/resource/678/01 and **a4esl.org** are two especially helpful sites for ESL/ELL writers.

to climbers ~~are~~ is not the steep, icy slopes or even the bitter cold and ferocious winds. ~~it~~ It is the lack of air. (5) Air at the top of Everest has only one-third the oxygen of air below, so without preparation, the average person would live less than an hour at the summit. (6) In fact, altitude sickness ~~begin~~ begins at 8,000 feet, with headache, nausea, and confusion. (7) At 12,000 feet, the brain and lungs ~~starts~~ start filling with fluid, which can lead to death. (8) How, then, has anyone ever climbed Everest~~,~~? ~~the~~ The answer is acclimatization. (9) Mountaineers climb slowly, about 2,000 feet a day, and they drink huge amounts of water. (10) They also carry oxygen. (11) Amazingly, in 1980, the first person to climb Everest solo was also the first to climb it without oxygen. (12) That was Reinhold Messner from Italy~~.~~, (13) ~~Who~~ who later wrote in *Climbing* magazine that the lack of air "saps your judgment and strength, even your ability to feel anything at all. I don't know how I made it." (14) Over 219 climbers have died scaling Mount Everest~~,~~; nonetheless, this danger keeps tempting others to try their skills and their luck.

PRACTICE 3 PROOFREADING

Proofread this paragraph, correcting errors above the lines. To review, see these chapters:

Chapter 28	run-ons, comma splices, and fragments
Chapter 30	past tense errors
Chapter 31	past participle problems
Chapter 35	adjective and adverb errors

ESL TIP
A popular ESL proofreading technique is to ask students to check their work *from the end*, starting with the last sentence, proceeding to the next-to-the-last sentence, and so on, to the first sentence. This process requires students to slow down and proof their work carefully.

(1) Martin Scorsese has ~~directs~~ directed some of the most influential motion pictures ~~produce~~ produced in the last 45 years. (2) His 1973 film *Mean Streets* ~~star~~ starred Robert De Niro and Harvey Keitel~~.~~, (3) ~~Actors~~ actors he would work with in many of his later films. (4) His 1980 film *Raging Bull* was ~~great~~ greatly admired by critics. ~~some~~ Some considered it the greatest movie of the year and Scorsese's best achievement.

(5) Over the next several years, Scorsese ~~become~~ became famous directing intense, violent movies about gangsters. (6) *Goodfellas* and *Casino* are ~~consider~~ considered classic films that explored the dark side of the American dream. (7) Scorsese ~~depart~~ departed from the gangster film to make *The Last Temptation of Christ*, a controversial depiction of Jesus starring Willem Dafoe. (8) Scorsese is known for his attention to detail. He ~~careful~~ carefully studied historical records and photographs to recreate nineteenth-century New York~~.~~ (9) ~~For~~ for his film *Gangs of New York*, set in 1863.

AF archive/Alamy Stock Photo

Martin Scorsese directing Leonardo DiCaprio in the 2006 film *The Departed*

(10) He also conducted ~~extensively~~ extensive research about the eccentric millionaire Howard Hughes to make *The Aviator*, starring Leonardo DiCaprio.

(11) Scorsese's films have ~~receive~~ received a total of eighty Academy Award nominations, and twenty of his films have won Oscars. (12) In 1990, Scorsese ~~establish~~ established the Film Foundation, an organization dedicated to film preservation. (13) Today, many critics consider Martin Scorsese the greatest director since Hitchcock.

PRACTICE 4

PROOFREADING

Proofread this paragraph, correcting errors above the lines. To review, see these chapters:

Chapter 21	parallelism errors
Chapter 28	run-ons, comma splices, fragments
Chapter 29	present tense problems, subject-verb agreement
Chapter 32	noun errors
Chapter 35	adjective and adverb errors

TEACHING TIP
Urge students to review the errors they fail to identify in this chapter's practices. Suggest that they either return to relevant chapters or complete additional online exercises such as those in *Exploring Online* at the end of this chapter.

(1) Do you know your learning style? (2) Finding out might help you succeed in college. (3) A learning style is a preferred way of taking in new information. (4) The four major learning styles ~~is~~ are *visual, auditory, reading/writing*, and *hands-on*. (5) Most people use all of these ~~method,~~ methods; however, one method might

work ~~more better~~ better than others. (6) For example, Lupe discovered in college that she has a dominant *visual* learning style. (7) New facts or concepts are ~~most clearest~~ clearest to her if they are presented in diagrams, charts, photographs, or videos. (8) Lupe realized that she can deepen her understanding by drawing pictures to depict the information she hears and reads. (9) Nathan, on the other hand, has a dominant *auditory* ~~style he~~ style; consequently, he needs to hear spoken explanations and also talk about what he is learning. (10) He absorbs course work best by reading aloud, ~~participation~~ participating in class discussions, and tape-recording and then listening to his notes. (11) Terrell has a *reading/writing* style~~.~~ (12) ~~Because~~ because his mind soaks up information best in the form of written words. (13) Terrell enjoys learning through books, handouts, PowerPoint presentations, and notes, and he benefits from writing summaries and journal entries to process what he sees and hears. (14) The fourth learning style—*hands-on*—~~describe~~ describes the preference of Emilio, who learns most ~~efficient~~ efficiently by moving, doing, and using all his ~~sense~~ senses. (15) Whenever possible, he tries to handle objects, participate in performances, conduct hands-on experiments, and use trial and error. (16) An understanding of learning styles ~~give~~ gives each of these students new skills to help master any academic subject.

TEACHING TIP

Remind students that although programs like Microsoft Word can help them identify spelling and some grammatical errors in their papers, computers are far from foolproof. Proofreading is still the job of every writer.

PRACTICE 5 PROOFREADING

This passage contains many of the errors you have learned to avoid in Unit 6. Proofread each sentence carefully, and then correct each error above the line.

(1) How much water are you drinking? (2) Experts ~~disagrees~~ disagree over how much water people ~~needs.~~ need, (3) ~~With~~ with most considering the traditional "eight glasses a day" more than adequate for adults. (4) The amount of water people ~~requires~~ require varies with their age, weight, activity, and weather conditions. (5) The ~~mayo clinic~~ Mayo Clinic ~~remind~~ reminds people that they get roughly 20 percent of the water they need from food. ~~some~~ Some fruits and vegetables are up to 90 percent water by weight. (6) Other beverages, such as juice, coffee, and tea, are mostly water, and they should be ~~count~~ counted toward a person's daily fluid intake.

(7) In addition to the amount of water people should drink, there is the question of what kind of water they should consume. (8) Is bottled water better ~~then~~ than

tap water? (9) In the United States, the ~~e~~ E nvironmental ~~p~~ P rotection ~~a~~ A gency ~~monitor~~ monitors the safety of the nation's public water supply. (10) With some exceptions, tap water is safe to drink, and it contains minerals that may be missing in bottled water. (11) Some environmentalists ~~argues~~ argue that consumers' love of bottled water ~~had lead~~ has led to ~~increase~~ increased pollution, with Americans discarding millions of plastic containers that end up in landfills. (12) Many ~~chooses too~~ choose to save both money and the environment by filtering their tap water and ~~use~~ using reusable bottles.

PRACTICE 6 PROOFREADING

This essay contains many of the errors you have learned to avoid in Unit 6. Proofread each sentence carefully, and then correct each error above the line.

(1) Some of the most ~~popularest~~ popular programs on television today are the *CSI* dramas, which depict crime scene investigators using state-of-the-art equipment and old-fashioned detective work to solve crimes. (2) These shows not only entertain 60 million viewers a week but have also ~~stimulate~~ stimulated great interest in forensics as a ~~career, in~~ career; in fact, demand for training has reached record levels. (3) According to the American ~~a~~ A cademy of ~~f~~ F orensic ~~s~~ S ciences, the many jobs in forensics ~~allows~~ allow people to apply their love of science to the pursuit of justice and public safety.

(4) Forensic scientists are curious, detail-oriented people ~~whom~~ who like to think and ~~puts~~ put puzzles together. (5) They also need to work ~~good~~ well in groups. (6) Unlike *CSI* characters on TV, who perform many varied tasks, real forensic scientists usually specialize ~~on~~ in one area and then pool their expertise to help police nab criminals. (7) For example, crime scene examiners go to the places where crimes have occurred to locate, photograph, collect, and ~~transportation of~~ transport physical evidence like fingerprints and blood samples. (8) On the other hand, crime laboratory analysts stay in the ~~lab.~~ lab, (9) ~~Using~~ using microscopes, DNA tests, firearms tests, and other techniques and ~~equipments~~ equipment to make sense of crime scene evidence.

(10) Each of these jobs ~~require~~ requires a bachelor's degree. (11) Two ~~specialtys~~ specialties requiring a master's degree are forensic ~~anthropology;~~ anthropology, which involves identifying people from skeletal ~~remains. And~~ remains, and psychological ~~profiling.~~ profiling, (12) ~~Using~~ using behavioral

clues to "read" the mind of a killer or other criminal. (13) One specialty, medical examiner, requires a medical degree. (14) Although this is the highest-paid forensics ~~career.~~ career, (15) ~~It~~ it requires someone with a tough personality who is able to perform autopsies on crime victims to determine the exact cause of death. (16) Real-world forensic scientists admit that their jobs are not quite as glamorous as those of their television ~~counterparts~~ counterparts; however, they describe their work as challenging, interesting, and ~~with rewards~~ rewarding.

PRACTICE 7 PROOFREADING

This essay contains many of the errors you learned to avoid in Unit 6. Proofread each sentence carefully, and then correct each error above the line.

IN THE MARKET FOR A USED CAR?

(1) For several year's now, used car sales have exceeded new car sales. (2) Good used cars can be ~~founded~~ found at dealers. (3) ~~And~~ and through newspaper ads. (4) You might also let your friends know ~~your~~ you're in the market for a used car, they might know of someone who wants to sell ~~their~~ his or her car. (5) Wherever you look for a used car keep the following tips in mind.

(6) First shop before you need the car. (7) This way you can decide exactly what type of car ~~suit~~ suits you ~~most~~ best. (8) Do you want a compact. (9) ~~Or~~ or a midsize car? (10) What features are important to you? (11) Should you get an ~~american-made~~ American-made car or a ~~japanese, german~~ Japanese, German, or other import? (12) If you shop when you ~~are'nt~~ aren't desperate, you are more likely to make a good choice and negotiate ~~good~~ well.

(13) Second narrow your choices to three or four cars, and do some research. (14) Start with the ~~*kelley blue book used car price manual*~~ *Kelley Blue Book Used Car Price Manual*, online at www.kbb.com. (15) The ~~blue book~~ Blue Book as its called for short gives the current value by model year and features. (16) Its also a good idea to check ~~*consumer reports*~~ *Consumer Reports* magazine. (17) Every ~~april~~ April issue lists good used car buys and cars to avoid. (18) Based on what you learn go back and test-drive the cars that interest you the ~~mostest~~ most. (19) Drive each for at least an hour, ~~drive~~ Drive ~~in~~ on winding roads, ~~in~~ on hills, and in stop-and-go traffic ~~in~~ on the highway.

(20) When you do decide on a car ask your mechanic to look at it. (21) Be sure to get a written report that ~~include~~ includes an estimate of what repair's will cost. (22) Money

TEACHING TIP

Have students identify the main pattern of organization used in the essays in Practices 7 and 8. They should recognize that "In the Market for a Used Car?" is a process essay, and "Gators and Crocs" is a comparison and contrast essay.

spent at this point is money spent wise, if the seller wont allow an inspection, take your business elsewhere.

(23) When you buy a used car you want dependability and value. (24) Follow these tip's, youll be able to tell a good buy when you see it.

PRACTICE 8 PROOFREADING

This essay contains many of the errors you learned to avoid in Unit 6. Proofread each sentence carefully, and then correct each error above the line.

GATORS AND CROCS

(1) With their scaly bodies slit eyes and long tails, alligators and crocodiles look a lot like dinosaurs. (2) In fact alligators and crocodiles descended from the same family as dinosaurs. (3) While its true that alligators and crocodiles look a lot alike, they differ in three ways.

(4) First alligators and crocodiles are found in different parts of the world. (5) Alligators be found in china, central america, and south america. (6) On the other hand, crocodiles are found in africa (especially around the nile river), australia, southeast asia, india, cuba, and the west indies. (7) Only in the southern united states is both alligators and crocodiles found. (8) In all cases however alligator's and crocodile's live in hot, tropical regions. (9) Reptiles are cold-blooded, so at temperatures below 65 degrees, alligators and crocodiles gets sluggish and cannot hunt.

(10) Alligators and crocodiles also differ in appearance. (11) Alligators has broader flatter snouts that are rounded at the end. (12) Crocodiles has narrower almost triangular snouts. (13) The best way to tell the difference is to view both from the side when they have their mouths closed, you can see only upper teeth on an alligator, but you can also see four lower teeth on a croc. (14) If you get really close you can see that alligators have a space between they're nostrils whereas the nostrils of crocs are very close together.

(15) Finally alligators and crocodiles are temperamentally different. (16) Alligators are not aggressive they are even a bit shy. (17) They will lie in wait along a riverbank for prey when on land, they move slow and uneven. (18) Crocodiles, however, are much more aggressive. (19) They are fast and mean.

they often stalk ~~they're~~ their prey. (20) The ~~a~~A ustralian freshwater crocodile and the ~~n~~N ile crocodile can even run on land, with their front and back legs working together like a dog's. (21) Nile crocodiles kill hundred~~'~~s of people every year.

(22) Alligators and crocodiles have outlived the dinosaurs, but they might not survive hunters who want to turn them into shoes, wallets, briefcases, and belts. (23) In 1967, the ~~u.s.~~ U.S. government declared alligators an endangered species. (24) Fortunately, ~~a~~A merican alligators have repopulated and are now reclassified as threatened. (25) Importing crocodile and alligator skins ~~are~~ is banned worldwide, but some species ~~is~~ are still threatened. (26) These frightening and fascinating ancient creatures need help worldwide if they are to survive.

PROOFREADING STRATEGY

A proofreading checklist like the one below can be an effective tool for remembering what to look for when reviewing your own writing.

Proofreading Checklist

- Check for sentence fragments, comma splices, and run-on sentences.
- Check for verb errors: present tense *-s* endings (verb agreement), past tense *-ed* endings, past participles, and tense consistency.
- Check for incorrect singular and plural nouns, incorrect pronouns, confused adjectives and adverbs, and incorrect prepositions.
- Check all punctuation: commas, apostrophes, semicolons, and quotation marks.
- Check all capitalization.
- Check spelling and look-alikes/sound-alikes.
- Check for omitted words and typos.
- Check layout, format, titles, dates, and spacing.
- Check for all personal error patterns.

EXPLORING ONLINE

writingcenter.unc.edu/handouts/proofreading

How to proofread: a brief audiovisual demonstration

grammar.ccc.commnet.edu/grammar

Interactive grammar and writing help. Explore, learn, review!

owl.english.purdue.edu/owl/resource/561/01

Overview of proofreading, with useful tips

writers' WORKSHOP

Adopt a New Point of View

No matter how excellent the content of an essay, report, or business letter, grammatical errors will diminish its impact. Ironically, errors call attention to themselves. Learning to proofread your writing may not seem terribly exciting, but it is an all-important skill.

When this student received the interesting assignment to *write as if you are someone or something else,* he decided to see what it was like to be a roach. His audience: humans. His tone: wacky. In your group or class, read his essay, aloud if possible. Underline details or sentences that are especially effective or humorous, and **proofread** as you go. If you spot any errors, correct them.

It's Not Easy Being a Roach

(1) It's not easy being a roach. My life ~~consist~~ consists of the constant struggle to survive. We have existed for millions of years, yet we still do not get the respect that we deserve. We have witnessed the dawn of the dinosaur and the building of Rome. We have experienced two world wars, enjoyed the benefits of cable television, and feasted our eyes on many women taking showers. Being small has its advantages, and it doesn't hurt to be quick either. Because we have ~~live~~ lived so long~~.~~, you ~~You~~ would think that respect would be ours, but that is not the case.

(2) We are looked upon as pests rather than ~~pets,~~ pets. We ~~we~~ are quieter than household pets. We don't eat much, and contrary to popular belief, we are very clean. Sure, some of us ~~prefers~~ prefer the wild life of booze, drugs, and unprotected sex with other insects, but that doesn't mean that most of us are not seeking a happy life that includes love and affection from you humans. I think it's high time that you appreciated our value as insects, pets, and potential lifelong companions.

(3) I might have six legs, but that doesn't mean I can handle all the burdens that come with being a roach. My wife is pregnant again, which means 10,000 more mouths to feed. It's bad enough that I have to find a meal fit for ~~thousands~~ thousands; I also live in fear of becoming a Roach McNugget. For some strange reason, rodents consider us food. Do I look scrumptious to you? Does my body ignite wild fantasies of sinful feasting? I think not. Mice and rats refuse to respect us because they see us as midnight munchies.

(4) I don't ask for much—a home, some food, and maybe an occasional pat on the head. If I can't have these simple things, I would prefer somebody simply step on me. A fast, hard crunch would do—

no spraying me with roach spray, no Roach Motel. I may be on the lower end of the species chain, but that doesn't mean I'm not entitled to live out my dreams. I am roach and hear me roar!

(5) When you humans kill each other off with nuclear bombs, we will still be around. With luck on our side, we will grow into big monsters because of exposure to radiation. Then I don't think those of you who ~~remains~~ remain will enjoy being chased around by giant, glowing roaches—all because you humans didn't want to hug a roach when you had the chance.

(6) One more thing: stop trying to kill us with that pine-scented roach spray. It doesn't kill ~~us it~~ us. It just makes us smell bad. If I want to smell like pine trees, I will go and frolic in some wood, naked and free. You people really tick me off.

—Israel Vasquez (student)

1. How effective is Mr. Vasquez's essay?

 ___Y___ Strong thesis statement? ___Y___ Good supporting details?

 ___Y___ Logical organization? ___Y___ Effective conclusion?

2. Discuss your underlinings. What details or lines in the essay did you like the most? Explain as exactly as possible why you like something or why it made you laugh. Answers will vary.
3. Mr. Vasquez's sense of humor comes through to readers. Does he also achieve his goal of presenting a roach's point of view? Answers will vary.
4. Would you suggest any revisions? Is this essay effective or offensive? Why? Does the final paragraph provide a strong and humorous conclusion, or does it seem like an afterthought? Answers will vary.
5. This essay contains several serious grammar errors. Can you find and correct them? What two error patterns does this fine writer need to watch out for? verb agreement and comma splices; one past participle error

GROUP WORK

In writing as in life, it is often easier to spot other people's errors than our own. In your group or class, discuss *your* particular error patterns and how you have learned to catch them. Do you have problems with comma splices, *-ed* verb endings, or prepositional phrases? Discuss any proofreading tricks and techniques you have learned to spot and correct those errors successfully in your own papers. Have someone jot down the best techniques that your group mates have used, and be prepared to share these with the class.

WRITING AND REVISING IDEAS

1. Adopt a new point of view; discuss your life as a bird, animal, insect, or object.
2. Write as a person of another gender, ethnic group, or period in history.

UNIT 7

Strengthening Your Spelling

CHAPTER 40

Spelling

A: Suggestions for Improving Your Spelling

B: Computer Spell Checkers

C: Spotting Vowels and Consonants

D: Doubling the Final Consonant (in Words of One Syllable)

E: Doubling the Final Consonant (in Words of More Than One Syllable)

F: Dropping or Keeping the Final *e*

G: Changing or Keeping the Final *y*

H: Adding *-s* or *-es*

I: Choosing *ie* or *ei*

J: Spelling Lists

A. Suggestions for Improving Your Spelling

Accurate spelling is an important ingredient of good writing. No matter how interesting your ideas are, if your spelling is poor, your writing will not be effective.

ESL TIP

To ESL students in particular, English spelling is difficult and unpredictable. Point out that many other languages have more regular spelling rules than English does.

Some Tips for Improving Your Spelling

- **Look closely at the words on the page**. Use any tricks you can to remember the right spelling. For example, "The *a*'s in *separate* are separated by an *r*," or "*Dessert* has two *s*'s because you want two desserts."
- **Use a dictionary**. Even professional writers frequently check spelling in a dictionary. As you write, underline the words you are not sure of, and look them up when you write your final draft.

- **Use a spell checker**. If you write on a computer, make a habit of using the spell-check software. See Part B for tips and cautions about spell checkers.
- **Keep a list of the words you misspell**. Look over your list whenever you can and keep it handy as you write.
- **Look over corrected papers for misspelled words (often marked *sp.*)**. Add these words to your list. Practice writing each word three or four times.
- **Test yourself**. Use flashcards or have a friend dictate words from your list or from this chapter.

ESL TIP

Encourage nonnative students to invest in an ESL dictionary, which may include a website with spelling, vocabulary, and grammar activities.

- **Review the basic spelling rules explained in this chapter**. Take time to learn the material; don't rush through the entire chapter all at once.
- **Study the spelling list in Part J, and test yourself on these words**.
- **Read through Chapter 41, "Look-Alikes/Sound-Alikes," for commonly confused words (*their, there,* and *they're,* for instance)**. The practices in that chapter will help you eliminate some common spelling errors from your writing.

B. Computer Spell Checkers

TEACHING TIP

Suggest that students who save their papers as electronic files use an online dictionary—like **www.dictionary.com**—to check their spelling during the proofreading phase of the writing process.

Almost all computer programs are equipped with a spell checker. A spell checker picks up spelling errors and gives you alternatives for correcting them. Get in the habit of using this feature as your first and last proofreading task.

What a spell checker cannot do is think. If you've mistyped one word for another—*if* for *it,* for example—the spell checker cannot bring it to your attention. If you've written *then* for *than,* the spell checker cannot help. Proofread your paper *after* using the spell checker. For questions about words that sound the same but are spelled differently, refer to Chapter 41, "Look-Alikes/Sound-Alikes." Run the spell checker again after you've made all your corrections. If you've introduced a new error, the spell checker will let you know.

PRACTICE 1

Read this e-mail, which "passed" spell-check. Can you find and correct all the errors that the spell checker missed?

Attention ~~knew~~ new students:

Once you ~~halve past~~ have passed the ~~finale~~ final entrance exam, you can ~~than~~ then apply ~~four~~ for a ~~lone~~ loan. Applications are ~~excepted~~ accepted online or by ~~male~~ mail. Make ~~shore~~ sure you include information about ~~awl~~ all sources of income. ~~Weather your~~ Whether you're planning to attend full or part time, ~~you're~~ your application ~~well~~ will receive a ~~through~~ thorough review ~~bye are~~ by our staff. Thank ~~ewe~~ you for your attention to this ~~massage~~ message.

ESL TIP
You may need to review the English vowel sounds for ESL learners because differences in pronunciations can lead to misspellings. In some languages, such as Spanish, a long *i* is often pronounced *ee*, so the word *ship* can sound like *sheep*.

ESL TIP
Tell ESL students that one consonant sound in English can also have variable spellings, e.g., *elephant* and *fire*. Have students list spelling-sound variants for *f, c, k, q, j,* and *g*.

C. Spotting Vowels and Consonants

To learn some basic spelling rules, you must know the difference between vowels and consonants.

The **vowels** are *a, e, i, o,* and *u.*
The **consonants** are *b, c, d, f, g, h, j, k, l, m, n, p, q, r, s, t, v, w, x,* and *z.*
The letter *y* can be either a vowel or a consonant, depending on its sound:

daisy	**sky**
yellow	**your**

- In both *daisy* and *sky, y* is a vowel because it has a vowel sound: an *ee* sound in *daisy* and an *i* sound in *sky.*
- In both *yellow* and *your, y* is a consonant because it has the consonant sound of *y.*

PRACTICE 2

Write *v* for vowel and *c* for consonant in the space on top of each word. Be careful of the *y.*

EXAMPLE
c v c v c
h o p e d

1. c v c v
   r e l y
2. c v c c v c c
   p e r h a p s
3. v c c c v v c
   i n s t e a d
4. c v c c
   y a w n
5. c v c c v
   f o r g e
6. c v c c v c c v c
   b y s t a n d e r

TEACHING TIP
Point out that, for some words, failing to double the consonant creates a word with a different sound and meaning (e.g., *hoped/hopped, riper/ripper, staring/starring*). Ask your students to think of other similar pairs.

D. Doubling the Final Consonant (in Words of One Syllable)

When you add a suffix or an ending that begins with a vowel (like *-ed, -ing, -er, -est*) to a word of one syllable, double the final consonant *if* the last three letters of the word are consonant-*v*owel-*c*onsonant or *c-v-c.*

plan + ed = planned	**swim + ing = swimming**
thin + est = thinnest	**light + er = lighter**

- *Plan, swim,* and *thin* all end in *cvc;* therefore, the final consonants are doubled.
- *Light* does not end in *cvc;* therefore, the final consonant is not doubled.

PRACTICE 3

Which of the following words should double the final consonant? Check to see whether the word ends in *cvc*. Then add the suffixes *-ed* and *-ing*.

EXAMPLES

Word	Last Three Letters	*-ed*	*-ing*
drop	*cvc*	*dropped*	*dropping*
boil	*vvc*	*boiled*	*boiling*
1. tan	cvc	tanned	tanning
2. brag	cvc	bragged	bragging
3. mail	vvc	mailed	mailing
4. peel	vvc	peeled	peeling
5. wrap	cvc	wrapped	wrapping

PRACTICE 4

Which of the following words should double the final consonant? Check for *cvc*. Then add the suffixes *-er* or *-est*.

EXAMPLES

Word	Last Three Letters	*-er*	*-est*
wet	*cvc*	*wetter*	*wettest*
cool	*vvc*	*cooler*	*coolest*
1. deep	vvc	deeper	deepest
2. short	vcc	shorter	shortest
3. red	cvc	redder	reddest
4. dim	cvc	dimmer	dimmest
5. bright	ccc	brighter	brightest

E. Doubling the Final Consonant (in Words of More Than One Syllable)

When you add a suffix that begins with a vowel to a word of more than one syllable, double the final consonant *if*:

1. the last three letters of the word are *cvc*, and
2. the accent or stress is on the *last* syllable.

begin + ing = beginning **control + ed = controlled**

TEACHING TIP
Review with students what *suffixes* and *stressed syllables* are.

TEACHING TIP
Have students come up with their own examples in order to reinforce their knowledge of the rule.

- *Begin* and *control* both end in *cvc*.
- In both words, the stress is on the last syllable: *be-gin′*, *con-trol′*. (Pronounce the words aloud and listen for the correct stress.)
- Therefore, *beginning* and *controlled* double the final consonant.

listen + ing = listening **visit + ed = visited**

- *Listen* and *visit* both end in *cvc*.
- However, the stress is *not* on the last syllable: *lis′-ten*, *vis′-it*.
- Therefore, *listening* and *visited* **do not** double the final consonant.

PRACTICE 5

Which of the following words should double the final consonant? First, check for *cvc*; then check final stress. Then add the suffixes *-ed* and *-ing*.

TEACHING TIP
Encourage students to say the words in Practice 5 aloud so they can hear the stressed syllable.

EXAMPLES

Word	Last Three Letters	-ed	-ing
repel	cvc	repelled	repelling
enlist	vcc	enlisted	enlisting
1. happen	cvc	happened	happening
2. admit	cvc	admitted	admitting
3. offer	cvc	offered	offering
4. prefer	cvc	preferred	preferring
5. compel	cvc	compelled	compelling

F. Dropping or Keeping the Final *e*

When you add a suffix that begins with a vowel (like *-able, -ence, -ing*), drop the final *e*.

move + ing = moving **pure + ity = purity**

- *Moving* and *purity* both drop the final *e* because the suffixes *-ing* and *-ity* begin with vowels.

When you add a suffix that begins with a consonant (like *-less, -ment, -ly*), keep the final *e*.

home + less = homeless **advertise + ment = advertisement**

- *Homeless* and *advertisement* keep the final *e* because the suffixes *-less* and *-ment* begin with consonants.

Here are some exceptions to memorize:

argument	courageous	knowledgeable	simply
awful	judgment	manageable	truly

TEACHING TIP
Ask students to explain how each of the exceptions deviates from the rules.

PRACTICE 6

Add the suffix indicated for each word.

EXAMPLES hope + ing = *hoping*
hope + ful = *hopeful*

1. love + able = lovable
2. love + ly = lovely
3. pure + ly = purely
4. pure + er = purer
5. complete + ing = completing
6. complete + ness = completeness
7. enforce + ment = enforcement
8. enforce + ed = enforced
9. arrange + ing = arranging
10. arrange + ment = arrangement

PRACTICE 7

ESL TIP
English spelling can seem confusing, even perverse, to ESL writers—e.g., differences between the pronunciation and spelling of *tough (tuff), through (throo), dough (doe), bought (bawt).* Urge students to memorize rules, keep personal spelling lists, and practice!

Add the suffix indicated for each word.

EXAMPLES come + ing = *coming*
rude + ness = *rudeness*

1. guide + ance = guidance
2. manage + ment = management
3. dense + ity = density
4. polite + ly = politely
5. motive + ation = motivation
6. sincere + ly = sincerely
7. like + able = likable
8. response + ible = responsible
9. judge + ment = judgment
10. fame + ous = famous

G. Changing or Keeping the Final *y*

When you add a suffix to a word that ends in *-y*, change the *y* to *i* if the letter before the *y* is a consonant.

Keep the final *y* if the letter before the *y* is a vowel.

happy + ness = happiness **portray + ed = portrayed**

- The *y* in *happiness* is changed to *i* because the letter before the *y* is a consonant, *p*.
- The *y* in *portrayed* is not changed because the letter before it is a vowel, *a*.

However, when you add *-ing* to words ending in *y*, always keep the *y*:

copy + ing = copying **delay + ing = delaying**

Here are some exceptions to memorize:

day + ly = daily pay + ed = paid
lay + ed = laid say + ed = said

PRACTICE 8

TEACHING TIP
Practicing with flashcards may help students learn to apply the rules more consistently.

Add the suffix indicated to each of the following words.

EXAMPLES marry + ed = *married*
buy + er = *buyer*

1. try + ed = tried
2. vary + able = variable
3. worry + ing = worrying
4. pay + ed = paid
5. enjoy + able = enjoyable
6. wealthy + est = wealthiest
7. day + ly = daily
8. duty + ful = dutiful
9. display + s = displays
10. occupy + ed = occupied

PRACTICE 9

Add the suffix in parentheses to each word.

1. beauty (fy) beautify
(ful) beautiful
(es) beauties
2. lonely (er) lonelier
(est) loneliest
(ness) loneliness
3. betray (ed) betrayed
(ing) betraying
(al) betrayal
4. study (es) studies
(ous) studious
(ing) studying

H. Adding *-s* or *-es*

Nouns usually take an *-s* or an *-es* ending to form the plural. Verbs take an *-s* or *-es* in the third person singular (*he, she,* or *it*).

Add *-es* instead of *-s* if a word ends in *ch, sh, ss, x,* or *z* (the *-es* adds an extra syllable to the word):

box + es = boxes **crutch + es = crutches** **miss + es = misses**

Add *-es* instead of *-s* for most words that end in *o*:

do + es = does	**hero + es = heroes**
echo + es = echoes	**tomato + es = tomatoes**
go + es = goes	**potato + es = potatoes**

Here are some exceptions to memorize:

pianos sopranos radios solos

When you change the final *y* to *i* in a word,* add *-es* instead of *-s*:

fry + es = fries **marry + es = marries** **candy + es = candies**

PRACTICE 10

Add *-s* or *-es* to the following nouns and verbs, changing the final *y* to *i* when necessary.

EXAMPLES sketch *sketches*
echo *echoes*

1. watch watches
2. tomato tomatoes
3. reply replies
4. company companies
5. bicycle bicycles
6. piano pianos
7. donkey donkeys
8. dictionary dictionaries
9. boss bosses
10. hero heroes

I. Choosing *ie* or *ei*

Write *i* before *e*, except after *c* or in an *ay* sound like *neighbor* or *weigh*.

achieve, niece **deceive** **vein**

---

*See Part G of this chapter for more on changing or keeping the final *y*.

TEACHING TIP
Tell students that the "*i* before *e*" rule does not apply to words in which the *i* and *e* are pronounced as two sounds (as in *science*) instead of one (as in *brief*).

- *Achieve* and *niece* are spelled *ie*.
- *Deceive* is spelled *ei* because of the preceding *c*.
- *Vein* is spelled *ei* because of its *ay* sound.

However, words with a *shen* sound are spelled with an *ie* after the *c: ancient, conscience, efficient, sufficient.*

Here are some exceptions to memorize:

either	height	seize	their
foreign	neither	society	weird

PRACTICE 11

Fill in either *ie* or *ei*.

1. bel i e ve
2. e i ght
3. effic i e nt
4. n e i ther
5. cash i e r
6. ch i e f
7. soc i e ty
8. rec e i ve
9. fr i e nd
10. consc i e nce
11. h e i ght
12. ach i e ve
13. v e i n
14. for e i gn
15. perc e i ve

PRACTICE 12 REVIEW

Test your knowledge of the spelling rules in this chapter by adding suffixes to the following words. If you have trouble, the part in which the rule appears is shown in parentheses.

		Part			Part
1. nerve + ous	nervous	(F)	6. occur + ed	occurred	(E)
2. drop + ed	dropped	(D)	7. carry + ing	carrying	(G)
3. hope + ing	hoping	(F)	8. tomato + s/es	tomatoes	(H)
4. busy + ness	business	(G)	9. believe + able	believable	(F)
5. radio + s/es	radios	(H)	10. day + ly	daily	(G)

PRACTICE 13 REVIEW

Circle the correctly spelled word in each pair.

1. writting, writing
2. receive, recieve
3. begining, beginning
4. greif, grief
5. relaid, relayed
6. piece, peice
7. resourceful, resourcful
8. argument, arguement
9. marries, marrys
10. thier, their

TEACHING TIP

Tell students that imprecise pronunciation can translate into spelling errors. Those who habitually say "probly" and "accidently," for example, are less likely to spell those words *probably* and *accidentally*.

J. Spelling Lists

Commonly Misspelled Words

Following is a list of words that are often misspelled. As you can see, they are words that you might use daily in speaking and writing. The trouble spot, the part of each word that is usually spelled incorrectly, is in bold type.

To help yourself learn these words, you might copy each one twice, making sure to underline the trouble spot, or copy the words on flashcards and have someone test you.

Commonly Misspelled Words

1. absen**c**e
2. a**c**quaint**a**nce
3. a**c**ross
4. a**dd**ress
5. **a** lot
6. an**sw**er
7. a**pp**ointment
8. a**pp**roxim**a**te
9. arg**u**ment
10. a**thle**te
11. begi**nn**ing
12. beha**vi**or
13. bu**si**ness
14. cal**e**nd**a**r
15. ca**reer**
16. cons**cie**nce
17. cons**cious**
18. crow**ded**
19. def**ini**te
20. d**es**cribe
21. desp**er**ate
22. di**ffe**rent
23. dis**app**oint
24. disa**pp**rove
25. do**e**sn't
26. ei**ghth**
27. emba**rrass**
28. envir**on**ment
29. espe**cial**ly
30. ex**agge**rate
31. exe**rcise**
32. famil**iar**
33. fina**lly**
34. for**eign**
35. gove**rn**ment
36. gramm**a**r
37. guid**ance**
38. hei**ght**
39. **ill**egal
40. immed**iate**ly
41. import**ant**
42. in**teg**ration
43. in**telli**gent
44. int**ere**st
45. int**er**fere
46. jew**el**ry
47. jud**gm**ent
48. knowle**d**ge
49. labor**a**tory
50. maint**ain**
51. maint**enance**
52. math**e**matics
53. me**a**nt
54. mor**t**gage
55. ne**cessa**ry
56. nerv**ous**
57. notic**ea**ble
58. o**cc**asion
59. occu**rre**nce
60. opin**ion**
61. opt**i**mist
62. partic**u**lar
63. **per**form
64. **per**haps
65. perso**nn**el
66. **phys**i**cally**
67. po**ssess**
68. poss**i**ble
69. practic**al**
70. **pre**fer
71. pre**jud**ice
72. privil**ege**
73. prob**ab**ly
74. **psy**cholo**gy**
75. p**ur**sue
76. reco**gn**ize
77. ref**er**ence
78. r**hy**th**m**
79. ridic**ul**ous
80. **sch**ed**ule**
81. **scie**ntific
82. sep**a**rate
83. sim**ilar**
84. s**in**c**e**
85. sp**ee**ch
86. stren**gth**
87. su**cc**e**ss**
88. **sur**prise
89. **tau**ght
90. temper**a**ture
91. th**orou**gh
92. though**t**
93. thr**ough**
94. tire**d**
95. tr**uly**
96. unti**l**
97. us**ua**lly
98. vac**uu**m
99. w**eight**
100. wri**tt**en

TEACHING TIP

Encourage students to keep a personal spelling list of problem words in their notebooks and to review the correct spellings frequently.

Personal Spelling List

In your notebook, keep a list of words that *you* misspell. Add words to your list from corrected papers and from the exercises in this chapter. First, copy each word as you misspelled it, underlining the trouble spot; then write the word correctly. Study your list often. Use this form:

	As I Wrote It	Correct Spelling
1.	probly	probably
2.		
3.		

PROOFREADING STRATEGY

If poor spelling is one of your personal error patterns, refer to your Personal Spelling List of errors and a dictionary as you write, and try these strategies:

1. Use the **bottom-up proofreading technique**. Read your draft sentence by sentence from the last sentence to the first. This will help you spot possible misspellings and typos more easily.
2. Ask **someone who is a good speller** to read your draft and help you spot any misspellings and typos. Then correct these yourself; this will help you learn correct spellings. Tutors in your college's writing lab or classmates who have a good eye for errors can be excellent sources of help.

PRACTICE 14 REVIEW

Using the bottom-up technique described above, proofread the following essay for spelling errors. (Be careful: There are misspelled words from both the exercises in this chapter and the spelling list.) Correct errors by writing above the lines.

SNIFFING FOR A CURE

(1) In addition to the joy and love they bring to humans, some dogs ~~peform~~ perform ~~practicle~~ practical tasks as well, from guiding the blind to detecting bombs. (2) But a recently proven canine skill may be the most ~~surpriseing~~ surprising and ~~usefull~~ useful of all: dogs can smell cancer. (3) In 1989, a medical journal reported that a woman's dog kept ~~niping~~ nipping at a mole on her leg. (4) The pooch's ~~wierd~~ weird behavior sent her to the doctor, who diagnosed cancer and saved her life. (5) ~~Similer~~ Similar stories of dogs sniffing cancers had been told for years, but this one dropped a small bomb.

(6) It grabbed the ~~intrest~~ interest of Dr. Michael McCullough, a ~~sientist~~ scientist in California. (7) He knew that dogs pick up scents 10,000 times better than humans. (8) McCullough also knew that tumors release ~~diffrent~~ different chemicals from healthy

cells; these chemicals must have odors. (9) He and his team trained five dogs to ~~reconize~~ recognize breath samples from early-stage breast and lung cancer patients. (10) ~~Incredably~~ Incredibly, in 2006, their results showed that the dogs' ~~succes~~ success at sniffing out breast cancer was 88 percent and lung cancer, 99 percent!

(11) Research in Germany confirms that ~~traned~~ trained dogs could save thousands of lives by catching cancer early. (12) The goal is to get a Breathalyzer-like sample from every ~~pateint~~ patient during routine medical exams. (13) Our best friends might be our best disease detectors, too.

EXPLORING ONLINE

esl.fis.edu/grammar/spell/1a.htm

Interactive spelling test

www.esldesk.com/esl-quizzes/misspelled-words/index.htm

Challenge yourself: more than 500 commonly misspelled words in English. Learn new words and quiz yourself.

CHAPTER 41

Look-Alikes/ Sound-Alikes

The pairs or sets of words in this chapter might look alike or sound alike, but they have different meanings. The chapter will teach you how not to make the mistake of confusing *its* and *it's* or *affect* and *effect* in your writing. Review the chart below, carefully reviewing any words that confuse you. Add these to your Personal Error Patterns Chart, and complete the practice exercises in this chapter.

Word	Meaning	Example
a	Used before a word beginning with a consonant or a consonant sound	*a* man; *a* house; *a* union (here *u* sounds like the consonant *y*)
an	Used before a word beginning with a vowel (*a, e, i, o, u*) or silent *h*	*an* igloo; *an* apple; *an* hour (the *h* in *hour* is silent)
and	Joins words or ideas together; shows addition	Emma *and* Daisuke are taking the same biology class.
accept	To consent to receive	I *accepted* his offer of help.
except	Other than; excluding	Everyone *except* Marcelo thinks it's a good idea.
affect	To have an influence on; to change	Her father's career as a chef *affected* her decision to attend culinary school.
effect	(noun) The result of a cause or an influence	Careful proofreading had a positive *effect on* Carl's grades.
	(verb) To cause	The U.S. Senate is attempting to *effect* changes in foreign policy.
been	Past participle form of *to be*; usually used after the helping verb *have, has,* or *had*	She has *been* a poet for ten years.
being	The *–ing* form of *to be*; usually used after the helping verb *is, are, am, was,* or *were*	They are *being* helped by the salesperson.

buy by	To purchase Near; by means of; before	My aunt *buys* antique furniture at garage sales. They walked *by* and didn't say hello.
it's its	Contraction of *it is* or *it has* A possessive that shows ownership	*It's* time to go fishing. Industry must do *its* share to curb pollution.
know knew no new	To have knowledge or understanding Past tense of the verb *know* A negative Recent, fresh, unused	Carlos *knows* he has to finish by 6 P.M. I *knew* it. He is *no* longer dean of academic affairs. I love your *new* hat.
lose loose	To misplace; not to win Too large; not tightly fitting	Be careful not to *lose* your way on those back roads. This shirt is not my size; it's *loose.*
past passed	That which has already occurred; it is over with The past tense of the verb *to pass*	Never let the *past* interfere with your hopes for the future. The wild geese *passed* overhead.
quiet quit quite	Silent, still To give up to stop doing something Very; absolutely	The woods are *quiet* tonight. Last year I *quit* drinking. He was *quite* tired after skateboarding for two hours.
rise raise	To get up by one's own power To lift; to grow or increase	The moon *rises* at 9 P.M. *Raise* your right hand.
sit set	To seat oneself To place or put something down	*Sit* up straight! Don't *set* your workout clothes on the dining room table.
suppose supposed	To assume or guess Ought to or should (it is followed by *to*)	Nhean *supposes* that geology will be interesting. You were *supposed* to wash and wax the car.
their there they're	A possessive that shows ownership Indicates a direction; also a way of introducing a thought A contraction: *they* + *are* = *they're*	They couldn't find *their* wigs. I wouldn't go *there* again. *There* is a fly in my soup. If *they're* coming, count me in.
then than	Afterward; at that time Used in a comparison	First we went to the concert, and *then* we had pizza and champagne. She is a better student *than* I.
through though	In one side and out the other; finished; by means of Although (used with *as, though* means as if)	The rain came *through* the open window. I am *through* with geometry! *Through* practice, I can do anything. *Though* he rarely speaks, he has a huge vocabulary. It was *as though* I had never ridden a bicycle.

to	Toward *To* can also be combined with a verb to form an infinitive	We are going *to* the computer lab. Where do you want *to* go for lunch?
too	Also; very	Eugene is going skydiving, *too.* It is *too* cold to swim.
two	The number 2	There are *two* new nursing courses this term.
use	To make use of	Why do you *use* green ink?
used	In the habit of; accustomed to (it is followed by *to*)	I am not *used* to getting up at 4 A.M.
weather	Refers to atmospheric conditions	In June, the *weather* in Spain is lovely.
whether	Implies a question	*Whether* or not you succeed depends on you.
where	Implies place or location	*Where* have you been all day?
were	The past tense of *are*	We *were* driving south when the hurricane hit.
we're	A contraction: *we + are = we're*	Since *we're* in the city, let's go to the zoo.
whose	Implies ownership and possession	*Whose* Kindle is that?
who's	A contraction of *who is* or *who has*	*Who's* knocking at the window?
your	A possessive that shows ownership	*Your* knowledge astonishes me!
you're	A contraction: *you + are = you're*	*You're* the nicest person I know.

Personal Look-Alikes/Sound-Alikes List

In your Personal Error Patterns Chart or your notebook, keep a list of look-alikes and sound-alikes that you have trouble with. Add words to your list from corrected papers and from the exercises in this chapter; consider such pairs as *adapt/adopt, addition/edition, device/devise, stationery/stationary,* and so forth.

First, write the word you used incorrectly; then write its meaning or use it correctly in a sentence, whichever best helps you remember. Now do the same with the word you meant to use.

	Word	Meaning
1.	*though*	*means although*
	through	*We hiked through the woods.*
2.	________	________
	________	________
3.	________	________
	________	________
4.	________	________
	________	________

PRACTICE 1

Write a paragraph using as many of the look-alikes and sound-alikes as possible. Exchange paragraphs with a classmate and check each other's work.

PRACTICE 2

Read each sentence carefully and then circle the correct word or words. If you aren't sure, refer to the chart.

1. The Trail of Tears has long (been, being) one of the United States' most shameful memorials.
2. This historic trail traces the path traveled by 16,000 Cherokee forced (buy, by) the U.S. government to leave (their, there) homelands.
3. Like their Seminole, Chickasaw, Choctaw, and Creek neighbors (whose, who's) lands the white settlers wanted, the Cherokee marched westward at gunpoint (threw, through) five states.
4. From Tennessee through Arkansas, they walked in snow and bitter winter (weather, whether), many without warm clothing or even shoes.
5. Weakened by starvation, disease, and cold, they pushed (too, to) Indian Territory in what is now eastern Oklahoma.

The Trail of Tears, painted by American artist Robert Lindneux in 1942

The Granger Collection, New York

6. In March 1839, about 12,000 reached (their, they're) final destination, a thousand miles from home.

7. Behind them (where, were) the graves of 4,000 grandparents, parents, (an, and) children who were unable to complete the punishing journey.

8. In the Cherokee language, this relocation is called *Nu na do ul tsun yi,* which means "The Place (Where, Were) They Cried."

9. Today, the Trail of Tears cuts the American landscape like (a, an) scar.

10. (Its, It's) a (quiet, quite) but powerful reminder of (passed, past) mistakes that most Americans hope will not be made again.

PRACTICE 3

The following paragraphs contain 19 look-alike/sound-alike errors. Proofread for these errors, writing the correct word choice above the line.

(1) If ~~your~~ you're fighting a cold, feeling blue, or just wanting to live a long, healthy life, you should ~~no~~ know about a force more potent ~~then~~ than pills: your friends. (2) Researchers are discovering that friendship is ~~quiet~~ quite important to both physical and psychological well-being. (3) People with strong friendships are less likely ~~then~~ than others to get colds, perhaps because ~~there~~ they're less stressed. (4) Friends help us fight serious diseases, ~~to~~ too. (5) A 2006 study of 3,000 nurses with breast cancer found that women with good friends were ~~for~~ four times more likely to live than women with no close friends. (6) Interestingly, ~~there~~ their survival rates were not ~~effected~~ affected by ~~weather~~ whether or not they had husbands. (7) Both sexes live longer if they have close friends, ~~through~~ though.

(8) Friendship even ~~rises~~ raises our confidence level as we face challenges. (9) University of Virginia researchers ~~use~~ used a fascinating model to study this. (10) They took students to the base of a steep hill, put weighted backpacks on them, ~~an~~ and asked them to estimate the steepness of the hill they ~~we're~~ were about to climb. (11) The students who stood next to ~~there~~ their friends gave lower estimates of the hill's steepness than those who stood alone. (10) The longer the friends had known each other, the less steep the hill looked ~~two~~ to them! (11) Our friends not only help us cut ~~lose~~ loose and have fun but also make tough times a bit easier.

PRACTICE 4 CRITICAL THINKING AND WRITING

Review your answers to Practice 3. Did you find and correct all 19 errors? Now reread the description of the experiment conducted by the University of Virginia (paragraph 2). Do you agree that this experiment shows that friends make us more confident in facing challenges? If so, can you think of two reasons why this might be true? If you don't think this research shows that friendship makes us more confident, why not?

PROOFREADING STRATEGY

If you tend to confuse the look-alikes/sound-alikes, **keep your Personal Error Patterns Chart updated** with the specific words you misuse, such as *their* and *there, affect* and *effect,* and *your* and *you're.*

Every time you proofread, **search your draft for every one of the words you confuse**. If you are using a computer, use the "Find" feature to locate them. Then double-check the meaning of the sentence to make sure that you've used and spelled the word correctly.

PRACTICE 5 REVIEW

The following essay contains a number of look-alike/sound-alike errors. Proofread for these errors, paying special attention to the words on your Personal Error Patterns Chart. Write each correct word above the line.

ISABEL ALLENDE

(1) Possibly the best-known female writer of Latin-American literature, Isabel Allende has survived many political and personal tragedies. (2) Most of those events have found ~~there~~ their way into her books. (3) Born in 1942, Allende was ~~raise~~ raised by her mother in Chile after her parents' divorce. (4) When her uncle, President Salvador Allende, was killed during a military coup in 1973, she fled. (5) For the next 17 years, she lived in Venezuela, ~~were~~ where she was unable to find work and felt trapped in ~~a~~ an unhappy marriage.

(6) One day, learning that her grandfather was dying in Chile, Allende began to write him a long letter; that letter grew until it became her first novel. (7) Still her most famous book, *The House of the Spirits* established Allende's style of writing, which combines political realism and autobiography with dreams, spirits, ~~an~~ and magic. (8) The novel, which was banned in Chile, was translated into more ~~then~~ than 25 languages and in 1994 was made into a movie.

(9) ~~Buy~~ By 1988, Allende had divorced, moved to northern California, remarried, and written her fourth novel, *The Infinite Plan*, which is her second husband's story. (10) Her next book traced the profound ~~affect~~ effect on Allende of the death of her daughter, Paula. (11) The book *Paula*, like *The House of the Spirits*, was ~~suppose~~ supposed to be a letter, this time ~~too~~ to her daughter, who lay in a coma in a Madrid hospital.

(12) After *Paula* was published, Allende stopped writing for several years. (13) She started again in 1996, on January 8, the same day of the year that she had begun every one of her books. (14) The result was *Aphrodite*, a nonfiction book about food and sensuality that was ~~quiet~~ quite different from Allende's ~~passed~~ past work. (15) With renewed energy to ~~right~~ write again, Allende spun the tale of an independent woman who leaves her home in Chile to move to San Francisco during the Gold Rush. (16) Two novels, *Daughter of Fortune* and *Portrait in Sepia*, complete her story.

(17) Isabel Allende is famous for ~~been~~ being a passionate storyteller ~~who's~~ whose writing captures both the Latin-American and the universal human experience. (18) As the first Latina to write a major novel in the mystical tradition, she not only created a sensation, but she paved the way for other female Hispanic writers, including Julia Alvarez and Sandra Cisneros.

EXPLORING ONLINE

grammar.ccc.commnet.edu/grammar/notorious2.htm#quizzes
Excellent look-alikes/sound-alikes quizzes

a4esl.org/q/h/homonyms.html
Confused by English words that sound alike? Practice and learn with these quizzes.

writers' WORKSHOP

Discuss a Time When You Felt Blessed

Some writers are naturally good spellers, and others are not. If you belong to the latter group, this unit has given you some techniques and tools for overcoming your spelling problems.

In your group or class, read this student's essay, aloud if possible. Underline the ideas and sentences you find especially effective. If you spot any spelling errors, correct them.

Rain

(1) It is interesting to watch the way people act when rain starts falling. Most run for cover, ~~especialy~~ especially the women who just got ~~there~~ their hair done. The guy with the brand new shoes also ~~trys~~ tries to find a dry spot. Many people think, "~~They're~~ There goes the day." That's what I thought before I went to the big sand box.

(2) It happened last year around March. President Bush decided Iraq was a threat to the United States, and of course being a Marine meant I was one of the first to go. Our first weeks were the hardest because we had to get ~~aclimated~~ acclimated to the ~~whether~~ weather. Iraq has got to be one of the ~~hotest~~ hottest places on Earth, and I swear that you can be motionless and still be soaked with sweat. The glare almost hurts, even in sunglasses. Those days I prayed for rain as I never thought I would.

(3) It ~~finely~~ finally happened in the middle of June; I was outside my tent doing pushups with a fellow Marine. The sky did not darken or cloud up. Instead, the rain came down in one great splash as if the sky had held on for awhile and just could not hold on any longer. We all smiled at the sky and then ~~noded~~ nodded at each other. At that moment, we felt we were ~~been~~ being blessed. Some guys took ~~there~~ their shirts off, and some started jumping around like little kids. Not one of us ran for cover, and those who were inside ~~there~~ their tents came out to join in the celebration. For a few minutes, we all forgot that we were at war.

(4) That rain gave us new energy and hope. We knew from that day on that everything was going to be all right. Even those who disliked each other shook hands in the name of rain. We felt more ~~then~~ than special because God had shown us his blessings.

(5) When I got back home last August, I took my girlfriend to the movies. As we left the theater, it started to rain. Everybody started ~~runing~~ running into the subway station, and most looked

frustrated
~~fustrated~~ because the rain had ruined their night. My girlfriend started pulling my arm, but I slowed my pace. She asked if I was crazy because I was not rushing like everyone else. I smiled at her and told her that I wanted to walk in Central Park. She laughed at me; however, she agreed because, as she said, I had just come back from war, and she wanted to please me. During our walk, I felt the same joy I had felt that day in June. I told her how that moment blessed us in the hell of war, and how special rain can be.

—Gayber E. Guzman, Student

1. How effective is Mr. Guzman's essay?

   __Y__ Strong thesis statement? __Y__ Good supporting details?

   __Y__ Logical organization? __Y__ Effective conclusion?

2. Discuss your underlinings. What details or lines in the essay did you like the most? Explain as exactly as possible why something struck you as interesting or moving.
3. Every narrative should have a clear point. What point does Mr. Guzman make by telling this story? Living through war made him appreciate "small things" like rain.
4. Have you had an experience of sudden appreciation for small things or of knowing clearly what really matters? What prompted this insight?
5. This student's spelling errors are distracting in an otherwise thoughtful and well-written essay. What suggestions would you make to him for improving his spelling? Review Chapter 40 on doubling consonants, final *y*, and commonly misspelled words. Watch out for look-alike/sound-alike errors.
6. Do you see any error patterns (one error made two or more times) that this student needs to watch out for? He misspells *their* three times; spelling in general is a problem.

GROUP WORK

In your group, find and correct the spelling errors in this essay. See if your group can find every error. Hint: There are 15 misspelled or confused words.

WRITING AND REVISING IDEAS

1. Discuss a time when you felt blessed.
2. Discuss something you took for granted and fully appreciated only after it was gone.

UNIT

8

Reading Strategies and Selections

CHAPTER 42

Reading Strategies for Writers

A: Active Reading

B: An Annotated Essay

C: Specific Reading Strategies

D. Connecting Reading and Writing

A. Active Reading

Active reading is a set of strategies that helps you take a close look at a text, especially when you are reading to learn. When you approach a text that is meant to help you gain a better understanding of a topic, you need to slow down and use strategies that help you look more closely.

The first active reading strategy is to **activate your prior knowledge**. Using what you already know about a topic to understand new knowledge helps you make connections and comprehend what you are reading much more effectively. When you are learning a new skill (such as driving), you begin with foundational information. After days, weeks, or months of practice, those foundations have become part of your prior knowledge. Now, when you drive in five o'clock traffic on the highway for the first time, you will be taking in the new information and processing it with your prior knowledge.

Think about the title of this chapter: Reading Strategies for Writers. Readers use strategies to help them find the main idea, locate supporting details, define difficult vocabulary words, and draw conclusions about a text. Active reading will help you read and study more efficiently.

The following guidelines will help you become a more effective reader and writer.

TEACHING TIP

Ask students to use their prior knowledge about different reading strategies. Make a list of the reading strategies.

1. **Note the title.** A title, of course, is your first clue as to what the selection is about. For example, the title "The Addiction Solution We Never Use" lets you know that the selection will discuss a solution for addiction and probably the reasons it isn't used or should be used.

A title may also tell you which method of development the author is using. For instance, a selection entitled "Gaga or Madonna?" might be a comparison/contrast essay, perhaps contrasting the two performers' creativity or lasting impact. A selection entitled "Stages of a Child's Moral Development" might be a process piece explaining how a child learns to make moral choices.

2. **Highlight or underline main ideas**. If you read a long or difficult selection, you may forget some of the important ideas soon after you have finished the essay. However, highlighting these key ideas as you read will later help you review more easily. You may wish to number main ideas to help you follow the development of the author's thesis.

3. **Keep track of your reactions**. Feel free to express your agreement or disagreement with the ideas in a reading by commenting in the margins. This is called **annotating**. For example, you might think about whether or not you agree with the author's point. You might write comments like, "yes," "no," "Important—compare with Jessica Bennett's essay," or "Is he kidding?" You might also highlight, underline, or put brackets around key ideas. Annotating is a highly personal process. Find a method that works for you.

   You will often be asked to write a "reaction paper," or a composition explaining your thoughts about or reaction to the author's ideas. The comments that you have recorded will help you formulate your response.

TEACHING TIP

Show students how to annotate online texts.

4. **Prepare and ask questions**. As you tackle more difficult reading selections, you may come across material that is hard to follow. To increase your understanding, start by rereading the passage; sometimes a second reading will help you pick up on ideas you didn't see before. If you are still having trouble, add a question mark next to the passage. This will remind you to ask a teacher, tutor, or classmate for clarification later on. You may also jot down any specific questions that you have about a reading.

   Do not be embarrassed to ask for explanations in class. Instructors appreciate careful readers who want to be sure that they completely understand what they have read.

5. **Note possible composition topics.** As you read, you may think of topics for compositions related to the ideas in the selection. Write down these topics. These notes may become useful if your instructor asks you to write an essay based on the reading.

6. **Note effective writing.** If you are particularly moved by a portion of the selection—a phrase, a sentence, or an entire paragraph—underline or highlight it. You may wish to quote it later in class or use it in your composition.

7. **Circle unfamiliar words.** As you read, you will occasionally come across unfamiliar words. If you can't guess what the word means from its context—from how it is used in the sentence or in the passage—do not interrupt your reading to look it up. Interruptions can cause you to lose the flow of ideas in the selection. Instead, circle or highlight the word and check it in a dictionary later.

TEACHING TIP

Have students turn to one of the reading selections in Chapter 43 and point out examples of effective writing.

ESL TIP

Urge ESL students to refrain from circling too many words.

8. **Vary your pace.** Some essays can be read quickly and easily. Others may require more time if the material is difficult or unfamiliar. Be careful not to become discouraged, and avoid skimming a particularly difficult section just to get through it. Do not give in to the temptation to check your email, Facebook page, or other social media. Extra effort will pay off.

9. **Reread.** If possible, budget your time so you can read the selection (or particularly difficult sections of the selection) a second or even a third time. One advantage of rereading is that you will be able to discuss or write about the reading with more

understanding. Ideas that were unclear may become obvious; you may even see new ideas that you failed to note the first time around.

Another advantage is that by the second or third reading, your responses may have changed. You may agree with ideas you rejected the first time; you may disagree with ones you originally agreed with. Rereading gives you a whole new perspective!

10. **Do not overdo it.** Marking the selection as you read can help you become a better reader and writer. However, too many comments may defeat your purpose. You may not be able to decipher the mass—or mess—of underlinings or highlights, circles, and notes that you have made. Be selective.

B. An Annotated Essay

The following essay has been marked, or annotated, by a student. Your responses might be different. Use this essay as a model to help you annotate other selections in this book—and reading material for your other courses as well.

MARTIN LINDSTROM

What Your Supermarket Knows About You

1 The global financial crisis of 2008 hit consumers hard. Two years later, and they're still reeling. Spending is down across the board, and even the more affluent are watching their pennies. In this fearful climate, retailers are applying ever more scientific and psychological tactics to lure them back. This was made clear to me on a memorable day in 2010 when I visited the laboratory outside of Chicago of one of the world's largest consumer goods manufacturers.

affluent = wealthy people

Main idea: retailers use special tactics to get us to buy things

2 After driving for nearly two hours, I reached my destination: a huge, imposing warehouse, with no outward signage, and a vast parking lot full of cars. A friendly receptionist checked my identity, had me sign all sorts of paperwork, and directed me through a door labeled Control Room. It was massive, and resembled images I've seen of NASA's operations area—row upon row of people staring intently at hundreds of screens, only they were monitoring shoppers pushing carts around the aisles of a supermarket that had been designed to test their responses to different marketing strategies. "Take a careful look at this lady," said one of the monitors, pointing to a middle-aged woman on the screen. "She's about to enter our latest speed-bump area. It's designed to have her spend 45 seconds longer in this section, which can increase her average spend by as much as 73%. I call it the zone of seduction."

Is this an illustration essay?

Why so secret? I didn't know this kind of research existed

3 This particular section of the market was different from the usual aisle. For a start, it had different floor tiles—a type of parquetry imparting a sense of quality. And instead of the cart

1st example of a tactic: "speed-bump area" with different floor tiles

parquetry = wood laid in a geometric pattern

The grocery store where I shop has a fancy section like this

gliding imperceptibly across nondescript linoleum, it made a clickety-clack sound, causing the shopper to instinctively slow down. The shopper's speed was displayed at the top of the screen, and as soon as she entered the zone, her pace noticeably slowed. She began looking at a tall tower of Campbell's soup, and then plucked a can off the top. Bingo! The sign in front of the display read: "1.95. Maximum three cans per customer." Before the shopper slowly sauntered off, she had carefully selected three cans for her cart.

Sophisticated as we may be, there's no getting away from our more primitive survival technique of hoarding food to see us through lean times. So when we come across a deal that appeals to this ancient instinct, dopamine is released in our brain, giving us an instant rush of pleasure. My guide explained the exercise: "Yesterday we ran exactly the same offer, with two distinct differences. There was a dollar sign in front of the price, and no 'Maximum 3 cans per customer' line. We also gave the shoppers smaller-sized carts and changed the floor tiles." These seemingly small changes translated into big differences. On the first day of the experiment, only 1 in 103 purchased Campbell's soup. Today, however, it seemed that 1 in every 14 succumbed—a sevenfold increase. 4

Is this why some people become shopaholics?

True. I'm more likely to buy when there is a deal on food.

Do smaller carts make people think they've bought more?

succumbed = gave in

Over several months of experimenting with signage, the team noticed that using a dollar sign in front of the price decreases our likelihood of making the purchase. The dollar sign is a symbol of cost, rather than gain. Removing the sign helps the consumer sidestep the harsh reality of outstanding bills and longer-term financial concerns. No doubt the larger cart and the changed floor tiles also played their part, but what was most surprising was our need to hoard. The dictum allowing only three cans per customer sealed the deal. 5

2nd example: no dollar sign

3rd example: size of shopping cart

4th example: limiting the number of items per customer

dictum = order, command

The next time you go grocery shopping, take a look at the signs, the type of floor, and even the carts. Everything has been designed with an eye towards getting you to grab those three cans of something that was not on your list. The more attention you pay to the details, the more aware you'll become of how you're being manipulated. One thing is for certain; whoever made those three cans will be watching you just as closely. 6

I always buy things off my list. Am I being manipulated by store tactics?

Writing ideas–

- *Visit Wal-Mart and identify tactics and their effects.*
- *Think more about how all stores convince us to buy. What other ways do they manipulate customers? Clothing stores–lively music, flattering light, "skinny mirrors"?*
- *Observe shoppers and their behavior in the store.*
- *Ways to be a wiser, savvier consumer*

C. Specific Reading Strategies

Reading strategies help readers of all levels become even better readers, and they will help you throughout college and beyond. Two active reading strategies you can add to your reading toolbox are SQ3R and REAP. These are instructions you can follow to ensure that you are reading texts actively. Try each strategy and decide which works best for you.

SQ3R: Survey, Question, Read, Recite, Review

1. **Survey the text.** Preview the information to gain an overall idea of a text's major topics, organization, parts, and features. When you complete this step, you'll be able to form a mental framework that will allow you to better understand how specific paragraphs, sections, or chapters fit in. Your purpose is not to read the whole text but to get an overview of what to expect.

   For shorter texts, start by reading any introductory materials and headings. Then read the first sentence of each paragraph or section. If there are review summaries or questions at the end, read those to get an idea of the major concepts covered in the selection. Glance over any illustrations or photographs and read their captions. If you are surveying a longer text, like a book, start by reading the title and the table of contents. Flip through a chapter to get a sense of its important features, such as headings, images, or learning objectives.

2. **Formulate questions.** Turn the title and the headings into questions; then, as you read, actively look for the answers to those questions. For example, if the heading is "The Medieval Castle," you could turn it into "What was the medieval castle like?" If the heading is "The War of 1812," you could create the question "What caused the War of 1812?" or "What happened during the War of 1812?"

3. **Read.** Read entire sentences and paragraphs in a section. Read only one section at a time. In a textbook, you'd read from one heading to the next and then stop. As you read, look for the answers to the questions you formed in step two. Mark the text as you go. Highlight or underline those answers and other important information. You may want to take notes on the answers to these questions or other details as you read.

4. **Recite.** After you read a section of material, stop and say aloud the answers to the questions you created in step two. If you can't answer a question, reread the information until you can. Think about actors and actresses. They recite their lines over and over again to learn them instead of simply reading them.

5. **Review.** After you've read the entire selection, go back through it and see if you can still answer all of the questions you formed in step two. Don't reread unless you can't answer a particular question.

REAP: Read, Encode, Annotate, Ponder

1. **Read** the text to understand the author's ideas and the information given.

2. **Encode**, or *translate the text's message into your own words*. One way to practice encoding is to imagine you are writing an e-mail to a friend about an interesting text you read for one of your classes. Your friend is expecting the message to sound like you, not like a college textbook.

3. **Annotate** the text, or *write notes or comments about it* (as you learned in Part A of this chapter, step 3). These notes can take the form of objective summaries or more subjective reactions to the ideas and information. Refer to the essay in Part B for an example. If you need to return to the text later, you can save time and read your annotations instead of the entire text. If you are annotating online, you can share these annotations with your classmates or your instructor.

4. **Ponder**, or *continue reflecting on what you have read and the notes you have written.* In this stage, you also read or discuss other people's responses to the same text in order to more fully explore its content. This sharing can take place in the classroom or outside of it.

   Ask yourself *what if* questions and *why* questions in response to the text you have read. Some students ask and answer the following questions after each reading: So what? Who cares? Now what? When you are writing about the text, these three questions individually or together can help you write effective conclusions.

D. Connecting Reading and Writing

Strong readers are strong writers. **Reading** and **writing** are closely connected activities. In fact, writing about what you've read can help you retain and comprehend information more successfully. Building a strong foundation in reading skills will help you be a better writer in the long run. Here are some strategies that can help you approach reading with a positive attitude:

- Think of your reading assignments as a chance to learn something new.
- Participate in class discussions about what you've read.
- Ask for help if you don't understand something in your reading assignment.
- Remain actively involved in the reading process.
- Summarize what you've read. This activity blends reading and writing and tests your comprehension.

Being aware of the key elements of a piece of writing—ideas, organization, voice, word choice, sentence fluency, and conventions—can help you better comprehend a reading and develop your own written responses to what you've read. The following chart explains these key elements:

Ideas	Every piece of writing expresses ideas, starting with a main idea and using supporting ideas to provide evidence.
Organization	To create meaning, ideas need to be organized. Readers expect to be able to follow a sensible pattern of organization, such as time order, compare and contrast, or cause and effect. As you read, pay attention to how the author organizes his or her thoughts. Are they clear? Do they follow a logical order? When you write, pay attention to how you organize your thoughts on paper.
Voice	A text has voice, or tone, which refers to the way the writer writes for a reader. Voice reflects the writer's attitude about the topic and text. When you write, be aware of how the tone of your writing comes across and how it might affect your readers.
Word Choice	Academic texts contain specific terminology, while personal texts might use more informal language. As you read, look at the quality of the words: are they interesting and clear? When you write, choose words that are specific, clear, and fitting to your assignment.
Sentence Fluency	In a reading selection, sentences carry ideas, and they must flow smoothly from one idea to the next and communicate ideas clearly in order to be effective. When you write, strive for sentence fluency. Try reading your writing out loud to see if your sentences flow smoothly together.
Conventions	Conventions are rules for grammar, usage, and mechanics that produce clear and correct text. As you read an assignment, pay attention to these conventions: to what degree does the author follow these conventions? As you write, follow the rules of grammar, usage, and mechanics. If you need help, see a tutor or your instructor for guidance, or refer to Units 6 and 7 in this book.

WRITING ASSIGNMENT

Choose one of the reading selections from Chapter 43 and use either the SQ3R or REAP strategies from Part C to actively read the text. Then choose one of the options below to respond to it:

1. Write an effective summary of the text, referring to Chapter 18 if needed.
2. Use a style of writing that is similar to what the author uses to write your own essay. Choose your own topic, or write about the same topic as the author but use a different perspective.

CHAPTER 43

Reading Selections*

ELLEN GOODMAN	*Multitasking or Mass ADD?*
RYAN RIGNEY	*How to Make a No. 1 App with $99 and Three Hours of Work*
BRENT STAPLES	*A Brother's Murder*
EVETTE COLLINS	*I Freed Myself When I Embraced My Locks*
DAVE BARRY	*Driving While Stupid*
ANA VECIANA-SUAREZ	*When Greed Gives Way to Giving*
LAURENCE BENHAMOU	*Everything You Need to Know About Generation Z*
ROBERTO A. FERDMAN	*Americans Are Having Dogs Instead of Babies*
ELISSA ENGLUND	*Good Grammar Gets the Girl*
IAN FRAZIER	*On the Rez*
KAREN CASTELLUCCI COX	*Four Types of Courage*
WANG PING	*Book War*
LEONARD PITTS	*A Risk-Free Life*
MICHAEL LEVIN	*The Case for Torture*
MELISSA M. EZARIK	*Mandatory Student Volunteerism Benefits Everyone Involved*
HISHAM ALMIRAAT	*Arab Bloggers: A Blessed Generation?*
ALI S. KHAN	*Preparedness 101: Zombie Apocalypse*
CADE METZ	*Robots Will Steal Our Jobs, but They'll Give Us New Ones*
CHRISTINE HARRINGTON	*Motivation*

*For a list of the readings organized according to theme, see the thematic index.

ELLEN GOODMAN

Multitasking or Mass ADD?[1]

Many busy people believe that multitasking—doing two or more things at once—makes them more efficient and successful. The more e-mails, text messages, phone calls, and Internet downloads they can juggle, the more productive they feel. But recent studies turn this idea upside down. In this article from the Record Searchlight, *Pulitzer Prize–winning columnist Ellen Goodman argues that our misguided passion for multitasking comes at a high price.*

Once I considered myself a champion multitasker. This was in the days when the Olympic event of technological multitasking was unloading the dishwasher while talking on the phone. Fast forward: I am at a computer with a land phone to my left and an iPhone to my right. As I type into my Word program, Google is alerting me to the latest news in the health care debate, e-mails are coming in on two of my three accounts, and I have a text message from my daughter. Even this, however, puts me at the low end of the multitask scale since I am not Facebooking while surfing the Net, downloading iTunes, and driving. 1

The truth is that I am terrible at multitasking. Worse yet, I have believed that my inability to simultaneously YouTube and IM makes me a technological dinosaur. Surely, the younger generation look down at my inability to text and talk the way I look down on someone's inability to walk and chew gum at the same time. More to the point, I have lived with the conviction that the people watching TV while Twittering and surfing the Web have a secret skill, like polyphonies who can sing two notes at the same time. 2

Now I find out from Stanford's Clifford Nass that there is no secret. High multitaskers are not better at anything, even multitasking. They are worse. Nass, who teaches human-computer interactions, led a research team that studied 100 students, high and low multitaskers. The high ones focused poorly, remembered less, and were more easily distracted. They couldn't shift well from one task to another and they couldn't organize well. They couldn't figure out what was important and what wasn't. 3

"We didn't enter this research trying to beat on multitaskers but to find out their talent," says Nass. "And we found out they had none." 4

Nass has yet to study whether they were bad at paying attention to begin with or were driven to distraction. But there's a suspicion, he says, that "we may be breeding a generation of kids whose ability to pay attention may be destroyed." Before I exhale in relief and bond with others waving this research in front of their children's (distracted) faces, a couple of things have to be noted. First of all, as Nass ruefully says, many multitaskers believe they are the efficient exception. They can talk and chew e-mails at the same time. Second and related, simultaneous media immersion[2] has become the new norm. 5

1. ADD: Attention Deficit Disorder: inability to focus one's attention and concentrate on a task
2. immersion: deep involvement

This is what normal looks like. It's the norm in offices where people are often required to keep chat rooms open and respond to e-mail within 30 minutes. It's in sports arenas where fans in mega-buck seats actually watch the game on big-screen TVs and text friends. It's in college classrooms where the professor's lecture competes with the social networking site on a laptop. It's also the new social norm. It's part of a world in which people walk together side by side talking separately on cell phones. Where you hear the click of a friend's keyboard while you're talking on the phone. And where Nass recently watched two students holding a serious conversation while one was surfing the Internet. 6

If the ratcheting up of media multitasking is teaching us not to pay attention, is it also training us not to expect attention? Nass, who is turning his research to everything from airline pilots to fourth-graders, has begun to wonder about students. "I don't know that this generation values focused attention. The notion that attention is at the core of a relationship is declining," he suspects. "Is saying to someone 'I am going to give you my undivided attention' still one of the greatest gifts I can give?" Or has multitasking led us to a kind of attention infidelity? 7

What we are learning is our limits. Not just on the highway where texting-while-driving is as common as it is terrifying, but at the dinner table where kids insist (wrongly) that they can text and talk, at the office where multitasking is multidistracting, and in relationships where face-to-face competes with Facebook. It turns out that we have only so many coins to pay attention. How do we hold their value in a media world? 8

I'll explain just as soon as I answer this e-mail. . . . Now then, where was I? 9

LANGUAGE AWARENESS AND VOCABULARY QUESTIONS

1. In paragraph 2, the author uses a metaphor to describe herself: a technological dinosaur. What does she mean?
2. What does *multidistracting* mean in relation to multitasking, according to the reading?

COMPREHENSION AND ANALYSIS QUESTIONS

1. What is the main idea of paragraph 8?
2. Do you multitask? What tasks do you often perform simultaneously? After reading this article, do you still believe that you are good at shifting your attention among several things at once?
3. What, according to the author, are some negative effects of multitasking? Would you add any other drawbacks to her list? Are we really "breeding a generation of kids whose ability to pay attention may be destroyed" (paragraph 5)? If so, what effects would that have on their lives?

TEACHING TIP

You might wish to discuss student texting in class. Is undivided attention in class a gift to *oneself*—whether one is listening, participating, or writing?

WRITING ASSIGNMENTS

1. For one or two days, conduct an experiment: refuse to multitask. When you talk on the phone, don't surf the Internet or send text messages. When you eat dinner or do homework, do only that. Then write a frank essay about the benefits and drawbacks you experienced when you focused on one thing at a time.
2. Harvard Medical School now sends young doctors to art classes. Apparently, doctors who learn to pay close attention to works of visual art become much better at studying and diagnosing their patients during visits. Why do you think this might be true? Should everyone go to art class? Write an essay explaining your reasoning.

TEACHING TIP

Your students might enjoy this classic video "test" showing that multitasking is harder than we think: **www.youtube.com/watch?v=vJG698U2Mvo.**

RYAN RIGNEY

How to Make a No. 1 App with $99 and Three Hours of Work

"How to Make a No. 1 App with $99 and Three Hours of Work" by Ryan Rigney from *Wired*, March 2014. Used by permission.

Have you ever dreamed of creating an app that was a number one best-seller? According to the author, this dream might not be so difficult to achieve. In this article, Ryan Rigney examines how you can make a top-rated app with as little as $99 and three hours of free time.

You don't need to be a programmer to break into the App Store's top charts. All you need is 100 bucks and a free afternoon. 1

You'll need a halfway decent idea, of course, but once you've got that nailed down, you can easily buy the source code, get an online tutorial on how to use it and within hours have a game ready to play. That explains why 95 of the 300 or so new apps released on Apple's iTunes store one day last week were riffs[1] on *Flappy Bird,* the mega-hit its creator pulled at the height of its popularity. There's *Flappy Wings, Splashy Fish,* even *Crappy Bird.* 2

For some reason, a surprising number of these apps, like *Flying Cyrus, Cyrus Flyer* and *Jumping Miley,* feature the disembodied[2] head of pop star Miley Cyrus. One of the most downloaded of this unlikely sub-genre[3] is *Flappy Miley Wrecking Ball Pro,* created by Gregory Storm. He uploaded the game on February 12, just two days after *Flappy Bird* flew the coop. Never mind that he'd only heard of *Flappy Bird* the week before. "I had no idea what a *Flappy Bird* was," Storm said. "Never played it. Hadn't seen it." 3

So how was he able to create *Flappy Miley* so quickly? Easy: He bought everything he needed. 4

The first step was purchasing the source code to *Flappy Crocodile.* 5

On sites like Chupamobile, billed as "a stock photo agency, but for app development," programmers can sell their app's source code to others. This is hardly a new idea in the videogame business, but just as the democratization[4] 6

1. riffs: variations of an original work
2. disembodied: removed from the body
3. sub-genre: type or category
4. democratization: the process of making something available to everyone

of development has allowed people to create games with small budgets and sell them at low prices, so too has it created a market where middleware[5] mavens[6] can sell source code to would-be developers for next to nothing.

You need an app for your restaurant? Chupamobile has templates for $50 each. Want to create a match-three game like *Bejeweled*? A clone of *Tiny Wings*? The rights to the source code are just a few clicks and a few bucks away. Just $99 gets you an open-ended, royalty-free[7] license to use the *Flappy Crocodile* code to create a single app and sell it in perpetuity.[8] Even if you make a million bucks, you don't owe another cent to the guy who did the heavy lifting. 7

In the case of *Flappy Crocodile,* that guy is Vojtech Svarc, a 26-year-old app developer from the Czech Republic. He's spent the past six years jumping from one online business to another: website scripting, e-books, Google AdSense and practically everything else. Svarc got into the app business about a year ago, but quickly realized that investing large amounts of cash into a single app and hoping it would be discovered among the 1 million or so already on the App Store might not be the best use of his time. Then he thought, what if building an app could be more like building a website? 8

"When building a website, there is no need to start from scratch as there [are] plenty of templates out there to choose from," Svarc said. "Using templates cuts the cost and time down, and it allows you to get your products out there quickly." 9

Svarc watched the App Store and noticed that any time an app made waves, similar apps would be buoyed to the top. Speed, he thought, was key to taking advantage of that. App templates would allow developers to build trendy apps in no time. "When I saw the media attention *Flappy Bird* was getting," Svarc said, "I knew this [was] a ride I need to be on." 10

So far, he says, about 100 developers have paid him $100 each to use *Flappy Crocodile.* Svarc says *Tiny Flying Drizzy,* which was the No. 1 free game on the App Store earlier this week, is based on his engine. 11

Anyone with a C-note and ten seconds can license the source code to a videogame. But what do you do then? Don't you need programming skills to actually modify the code? 12

Nope. You don't need any special skills at all. To prove it, I bought a license to use *Flappy Crocodile.* 13

I've worked on a mobile game before, but I'm a terrible programmer. Still, I could see that my $100 had bought me a complete package: Svarc had included every asset,[9] function and plugin you'd need to publish and sell a *Flappy Bird* clone. It also included a voucher for an online course, led by Svarc and app developer Yohann Taieb, that walks you through the process of creating your first app. It covers everything from registering for an Apple developer license to reskinning the graphics and adding in-game advertising to uploading your finished product. 14

I had a little trouble setting things up properly at first because of how I'd set up the open-source game engine Cocos2d while developing my own apps. With a little adjustment I had *Flappy Crocodile* running smoothly in Xcode, Apple's iOS development software. 15

5. middleware: software that creates a bridge between an operating system and an application
6. mavens: experts on a particular subject
7. royalty-free: without the requirement that one pay the creator for the use of copyrighted material
8. perpetuity: the state of continuing forever
9. asset: a piece of software

With minimal effort and zero coding required, I could now start replacing any of the game's art or sound with my own files. A drag and a drop later, *Flappy Crocodile*'s cheery background song became "Type of Way" by Rich Homie Quan. 16

Then I found the folder containing the files for animating the crocodile. I opened up Photo Booth and snapped a selfie, cut out my head using Photoshop, then replaced the crocodile sprite with my face. I compiled the new code, feeling more than a little surprised when the iPhone simulator launched successfully, allowing me to direct my own head through a gauntlet of pipes. In less than an hour, I'd changed *Flappy Crocodile* into *Flappy Ryan.* 17

Gregory Storm put more spit and polish into his clone than I did. 18

"My wife knew an awesome animator named Reinaldo Rocha," he said, "and he was able to get us preliminary sketches within an hour." Storm swapped in Rocha's drawings of Cyrus, which featured flapping ears and a tongue that is forever sticking out. 19

He made several other tweaks before submitting the game to the App Store, all of them minor: The static[10] background image is different, and all the sound effects have been changed. Otherwise, everything from the menus to the pipes are straight from the source code. Some app templates require users to "re-skin" everything, from the graphics to the music to the sound effects, before they upload the app. *Flappy Crocodile*'s license agreement has no such restrictions. 20

Assembling an app using inexpensive source code and zero knowledge of programming is limited to simple app games today, but it won't be long before you can use the same trick to build more elaborate games. There's already a similar sharing economy where developers use the low-cost game development engine Unity. And anyone can buy complex elements of game design like artificially intelligent enemies. Buy the code, slap it into your game, and you're done. 21

"Things like rendering a silhouette when the player moves behind an obstacle, or handling palette swapping characters, used to be done on a game-by-game basis. Now I can buy a standardized solution for the price of a pizza," game developer Mike Bithell said in a blog post on the Unity website. 22

It takes significantly more effort to create a high-quality game in Unity than it does to whip out a *Flappy Bird* clone, but we're reaching the point where non-coders will be able to make increasingly complex games and throw in snazzy features as easily as ordering an extra large with pepperoni. More and more popular indie[11] and mobile games have begun using Unity in recent years—*République, Plague Inc.* and *Rust,* to name just a few—and this is one of the reasons. 23

The widespread availability of source code and templates is just putting small developers on par with big players in the app market, says Storm. Big Fish Games, he notes, has published more than 100 hidden object games on the App Store. 24

"I highly doubt they build from scratch for every new title," Storm says. "They aren't trying to be original and recreate the wheel. They're trying to maximize their proven formulas and repeat them by re-skinning and using the same source code over and over." 25

10. static: showing little to no change
11. indie: independent

Creating such games, he says, is like appearing on the cooking competition show *Chopped*. "Everybody has the same basket full of odd ingredients and you have a short time to make something tasty with them or you'll lose out," Storm says. "It's my job to take the same source code that everybody else has been given and spice it up." 26

Still, with so much competition it isn't easy for a guy like Storm to make a killing. With all of his costs—buying the art, hiring a freelance[12] programmer to help with updates, etc.—he says he's spent about $2,500 creating *Flappy Miley*. If it sticks around—say, if Miley Cyrus twerks her way back into the news—Storm could rake it in. But in the volatile[13] app marketplace, that's a big "if." 27

"At this point we've just about made our money back," Storm says, "so it looks like a fun night at the Olive Garden is in our future." 28

LANGUAGE AWARENESS AND VOCABULARY QUESTIONS

1. How is creating a game using a template similar to appearing on the television show *Chopped*?
2. What does it mean to re-skin a game?

COMPREHENSION AND ANALYSIS QUESTIONS

1. Summarize the steps you would need to take after purchasing a source code to *Flappy Crocodile* if you were interested in making a revised version of the game.
2. Why does the author think that it is smarter for app developers to purchase a game template instead of creating a game from scratch?
3. Why does the author describe the app marketplace as *volatile*?

WRITING ASSIGNMENTS

1. App developers are making a profit by selling game templates, which leads to multiple apps being produced that are similar to one another. Explain why you find this to be an ethical (or unethical) approach to game development.
2. Many high schools now offer classes on how to develop apps. What are the benefits and drawbacks to classes like these being offered in some high schools?

12. freelance: working on one's own
13. volatile: likely to change rapidly, usually for the worse

BRENT STAPLES

A Brother's Murder

Brent Staples grew up in a rough, industrial city. He left to become a successful journalist, but his younger brother remained. Staples' story of his brother is a reminder of the grim circumstances in which so many young men of the inner city find themselves today.

It has been more than two years since my telephone rang with the news that my younger brother Blake—just twenty-two years old—had been murdered. The young man who killed him was only twenty-four. Wearing a ski mask, he emerged from a car, fired six times at close range with a massive .44 Magnum, then fled. The two had once been inseparable friends. A senseless rivalry—beginning, I think, with an argument over a girlfriend—escalated[1] from posturing,[2] to threats, to violence, to murder. The way the two were living, death could have come to either of them from anywhere. In fact, the assailant had already survived multiple gunshot wounds from an accident much like the one in which my brother lost his life. 1

As I wept for Blake I felt wrenched backward into events and circumstances that had seemed light-years gone. Though a decade apart, we both were raised in Chester, Pennsylvania, an angry, heavily black, heavily poor, industrial city southwest of Philadelphia. There, in the 1960s, I was introduced to mortality, not by the old and failing, but by beautiful young men who lay wrecked after sudden explosions of violence. The first, I remembered from my fourteenth year—Johnny, brash lover of fast cars, stabbed to death two doors from my house in a fight over a pool game. The next year, my teenage cousin, Wesley, whom I loved very much, was shot dead. The summers blur. Milton, an angry young neighbor, shot a crosstown rival, wounding him badly. William, another teenage neighbor, took a shotgun blast to the shoulder in some urban drama and displayed his bandages proudly. His brother, Leonard, severely beaten, lost an eye and donned a black patch. It went on. 2

I recall not long before I left for college, two local Vietnam veterans—one from the Marines, one from the Army—arguing fiercely, nearly at blows about which outfit had done the most in the war. The most killing, they meant. Not much later, I read a magazine article that set that dispute in a context. In the story, a noncommissioned officer—a sergeant, I believe—said he would pass up any number of affluent, suburban-born recruits to get hard-core soldiers from the inner city. They jumped into the rice paddies with "their manhood on their sleeves," I believe he said. These two items—the veterans arguing and the sergeant's words—still characterize for me the circumstances under which black men in their teens and twenties kill one another with such frequency. With a touchy paranoia born of living battered lives, they are desperate to be *real* men. Killing is only machismo taken to the extreme. Incursions[3] to be 3

1. escalated: increased
2. posturing: trying to appear tough
3. incursions: attacks, violations

punished by death were many and minor, and they remain so: they include stepping on the wrong toe, literally; cheating in a drug deal; simply saying "I dare you" to someone holding a gun; crossing territorial lines in a gang dispute. My brother grew up to wear his manhood on his sleeve. And when he died, he was in that group—black, male and in its teens and early twenties—that is far and away the most likely to murder or be murdered.

I left the East Coast after college, spent the mid- and late 1970s in Chicago as a graduate student, taught for a time, then became a journalist. Within ten years of leaving my hometown, I was overeducated and "upwardly mobile," ensconced[4] on a quiet, tree-lined street where voices raised in anger were scarcely ever heard. The telephone, like some grim umbilical, kept me connected to the old world with news of deaths, imprisonings and misfortune. I felt emotionally beaten up. Perhaps to protect myself, I added a psychological dimension to the physical distance I had already achieved. I rarely visited my hometown. I shut it out. 4

As I fled the past, so Blake embraced it. On Christmas of 1983, I traveled from Chicago to a black section of Roanoke, Virginia, where he then lived. The desolate public housing projects, the hopeless, idle young men crashing against one another—these reminded me of the embittered town we'd grown up in. It was a place where once I would have been comfortable, or at least sure of myself. Now, hearing of my brother's forays[5] into crime, his scrapes with police and street thugs, I was scared, unsteady on foreign terrain.[6] 5

I saw that Blake's romance with the street life and the hustler image had flowered dangerously. One evening that late December, standing in some Roanoke dive among drug dealers and grim, hair-trigger losers, I told him I feared for his life. He had affected the image of the tough he wanted to be. But behind the dark glasses and the swagger, I glimpsed the baby-faced toddler I'd once watched over. I nearly wept. I wanted desperately for him to live. The young think themselves immortal, and a dangerous light shone in his eyes as he spoke laughingly of making fools of the policemen who had raided his apartment looking for drugs. He cried out as I took his right hand. A line of stitches lay between the thumb and index finger. Kickback from a shotgun, he explained, nothing serious. Gunplay had become part of his life. 6

I lacked the language simply to say: Thousands have lived this for you and died. I fought the urge to lift him bodily and shake him. This place and the way you are living smells of death to me, I said. Take some time away, I said. Let's go downtown tomorrow and buy a plane ticket anywhere, take a bus trip, anything to get away and cool things off. He took my alarm casually. We arranged to meet the following night—an appointment he would not keep. We embraced as though through glass. I drove away. 7

As I stood in my apartment in Chicago holding the receiver that evening in February 1984, I felt as though part of my soul had been cut away. I questioned myself then, and I still do. Did I not reach back soon enough or earnestly enough for him? For weeks I awoke crying from a recurrent dream in which I chased him, urgently trying to get him to read a document I had, as though reading it would protect him from what had happened in waking life. His eyes shining like black diamonds, he smiled and danced just beyond my grasp. When I reached for him, I caught only the space where he had been. 8

4. ensconced: settled comfortably

5. forays: undertakings, trips

6. terrain: ground

LANGUAGE AWARENESS AND VOCABULARY QUESTIONS

1. What does the phrase "embraced as through glass" (paragraph 7) suggest?
2. In paragraph 4, the author describes himself as "upwardly mobile." What does he mean?

COMPREHENENSION AND ANALYSIS QUESTIONS

1. Staples says that he was "introduced to mortality" in Chester, Pennsylvania, in the 1960s (paragraph 2). What does he mean?
2. What does the author mean when he says his brother grew up to "wear his manhood on his sleeve" (paragraph 3)? Does he imply that there are other ways of expressing masculinity?
3. Staples begins his narrative by describing the moment at which he hears of Blake's death. Why does he *start* with this event, instead of moving toward it?

WRITING ASSIGNMENTS

1. In a short essay, answer the following questions: Do you think Brent Staples could have done more to change his brother? Can we really influence others to change their lives?
2. In a group with three or four classmates, discuss the most significant problem facing young people in the inner city today. Is it crime? Drugs? Lack of educational or employment opportunities? Choose one problem and decide how it can be solved. Your instructor may ask you to share your solution with the class. Then write your own paper, discussing the problem you think is most significant and proposing a solution.

EVETTE COLLINS

I Freed Myself When I Embraced My Locks

What does it mean to reach a place of true self-acceptance? For some, self-acceptance comes quickly. For others, the journey takes a bit longer with many stops along the way. In this article, the author writes about her own personal journey to self-acceptance.

When I was a little girl, every day was a bad hair day. In the morning, my grandmother would wash my hair, then straighten it with a hot pressing comb,[1] yanking my naturally thick, kinky[2] hair, and jerking my head in every 1

1. hot pressing comb: a metal comb that is heated and used to straighten hair
2. kinky: tightly twisted or curled

direction. The heat from the comb was so intense that I would wince[3] before Grandma ran it through my hair. And though she did her best to be careful, the imprint of the comb's teeth was left on my ears, neck and temples. The heavy stench of burnt hair and hair grease filled the kitchen. I hated this ritual so much that I hoped she would forget to do it. And even worse than the physical discomfort that came from straightening my hair was Grandma's commentary: "Lord, your hair is a job to do! Look at this nappy[4] mess! Keep still! Stop moving around!"

And so it began, my lifelong obsession with straight hair. In addition to the daily reminders from Grandma, I had the media to help me along in my self-loathing. The models in fashion magazines all had flowing coiffures that bounced and behaved, not tight, coarse coils like mine. Advertisements targeted at black women promise freedom from the oppression[5] of the hot pressing comb with the use of harsh chemical relaxers.[6] 2

When I first heard about relaxers, I thought my prayers had been answered. I wanted one when I was younger, but the older, wiser women in my family warned me against it. They had experienced hair loss when they had relaxers, and they didn't want that to happen to me. But I was tired of getting my hair pressed only to have it revert back to its natural state after getting wet. I was tired of wearing wigs because my frustration with my hair had gotten to the point that I just chose to cover it up. So naturally, I ignored my elders' advice and got my first relaxer at the age of 19. When I saw my new hair in the mirror, I was in awe. It was sleek and shiny, flowing past my shoulders, down my back, swinging when I turned my head. I finally had the straight hair I had coveted[7] for so long. I felt like the sexiest woman in the world. My confidence increased, and suddenly flirtatious men were coming from every direction. It felt great to be noticed. 3

For a while, the style was easy to maintain—if my hair got wet, it wouldn't revert, and my comb could glide right through it. Unfortunately, the maintenance of my new hairstyle was costly. I couldn't afford to return to the salon to get touch-ups, so once the relaxer was replaced by the new hair that grew underneath it, I was forced to go back to wearing wigs. 4

In 2002, a year after having a steady job, I decided to return to the same salon to get my hair relaxed again, and got my touch-ups every two or three months. Eventually I began to notice that my hair was breaking off. I would comb my hair and big clumps would come right out. In about nine months, my hair that once hung to the middle of my back was stopping slightly above my shoulders. Turns out the elders were right after all. 5

3. wince: frown in pain or distress
4. nappy: tightly curled
5. oppression: being subjected to unjust or harsh treatment or control
6. relaxers: chemicals that, when placed on curly hair, cause the strands to straighten
7. coveted: desired or wished for intensely

My mother noticed my hair loss and persuaded me to stop using chemicals, plunging me back, yet again, into a conundrum[8] that I'd struggled with my entire life: what to do about my thick, kinky, misbehaving hair. Chemicals were out of the question, and I was tired of wearing wigs. Suddenly, a frightening thought occurred to me—"Am I going to have to wear my hair nappy?" The only natural style that I knew about was the Afro, but when I started to research the many possibilities for styling my hair naturally, I was pleasantly surprised to find the Afro is just the beginning. 6

Now that I've worn my hair naturally for two years, I can't imagine putting another relaxer in my hair. Wearing my hair naturally has opened my eyes to my own beauty, and eliminated some major hassles. I don't miss being in the salon from morning till sunset. I don't miss running from rain clouds. Most importantly, I don't miss hair loss. 7

One day, about five months after I started wearing my natural hair, I was out getting lunch when I heard words that sounded almost foreign to me: "Your hair is so thick and pretty!" The woman who complimented me not only put a smile on my face, she confirmed something I had struggled to convince myself of—that my natural hair was beautiful, too. I'm now proud to wear it, to show other black women that our hair is gorgeous just the way it is. It took me years to get to a peaceful place about my hair, but in the end, I got it all straightened out. 8

LANGUAGE AWARENESS AND VOCABULARY QUESTIONS

1. The term *ritual* (paragraph 1) commonly has a religious connotation. Why does the author use it to describe her childhood hair treatments?
2. What makes the author's decision about her hair a *conundrum* (paragraph 6)?

COMPREHENSION AND ANALYSIS QUESTIONS

1. Why is straight hair so important to the author and her grandmother?
2. According to the article, why did the author begin to lose her hair?
3. In the end, what decision does the author make regarding her hair? What are her reasons? How does this decision benefit her? Use specific examples from the reading.

WRITING ASSIGNMENTS

1. The author feels different because her natural hair doesn't look like the hair she sees represented in the media. Describe a time when you or someone you know felt that you didn't fit in with a group. What were the reasons? How did you respond? Compare your reaction with the author's.

8. conundrum: a perplexing or difficult problem

2. Every society has its own idea of what physical characteristics are beautiful. Research cultural standards of beauty in three countries of your choice. For example, you might consider hair styles (as in this article), body types, or body decoration or tattoos. How are these standards of beauty similar? How do they differ?

DAVE BARRY

Driving While Stupid

Humorist Dave Barry loves to poke fun at Miami, his hometown ("Motto: an automatic-fire weapon in every home"). Barry has written over thirty books, none of which, he claims, contains useful information; he won a Pulitzer Prize for his humor columns, which ran in over five hundred newspapers. Barry aspires to "continued immaturity followed by death." In this Miami Herald *column, he takes on bad drivers.*

So I have to tell you what I saw on the interstate the other night. First, though, you must understand that this was not just any old interstate. This was I-95 in downtown Miami, proud home of the worst darned drivers in the world. 1

I realize some of you are saying: "Oh yeah? If you want to see REALLY bad drivers, you should come to MY city!" Listen, I understand that this is a point of civic honor, and I am sure that the drivers in your city are all homicidal[1] morons. But trust me when I tell you that there is no way they can compete with the team that Miami puts on the road. 2

I know what I'm talking about. I have driven in every major U.S. city, including Boston, where the motorists all drive as though there is an open drawbridge just ahead, and they need to gain speed so they can jump across it. 3

I have also driven in Italy, where there is only one traffic law, which is that no driver may ever be behind any other driver, the result being that at all times, all the motorists in the nation, including those in funeral processions, are simultaneously trying to pass. 4

I have ridden in a taxi in the Argentinean city of Mar del Plata (literally, "Cover your eyes"), where (a.) nobody ever drives slower than 65 miles per hour, even inside parking garages, and (b.) at night, many motorists drive with their headlights off, because—a taxi driver told me this, and he was absolutely 5

1. homicidal: murderous; intending to kill someone

INCONSIDERATE, STUPID DRIVERS THIS LANE ONLY
ZUVELA.

Tony Zuvela/CartoonStock Ltd

serious—this extends the life of your bulbs. When he said this, we were in a major traffic jam caused by an accident involving a truck and a horse.

I have also ridden on a bus in China, plowing through humongous[2] traffic snarls involving trucks, cars, bicycles, ox-drawn carts and pedestrians, all aggressively vying[3] for the same space, and where the bus driver would sometimes physically push pedestrians out of the way. I don't mean with his hands. I mean with the BUS. 6

My point is that I have seen plenty of insane driving techniques, and I am telling you for a fact that no place brings so many of these techniques together as Miami, where a stop sign has no more legal significance to most motorists than a mailbox. The police down here have given up on enforcing the traffic laws. If they stop you and find a human corpse in your trunk, they'll let you off with a warning if it's your first one. 7

So I've seen pretty much everything on the roads here. Nevertheless, I was surprised by the driver on the interstate the other night. I heard him before I saw him, because his car had one of those extremely powerful sound systems, in which the bass notes sound like nuclear devices being detonated[4] in rhythm. So I looked in the mirror and saw a large convertible with the top down overtaking me at maybe 600 miles per hour. I would have tried to get out of his path, but there was no way to know what his path was, since he was weaving back and forth across five lanes (out of a possible three). 8

2. humongous: huge, enormous
3. vying: competing
4. detonated: exploded

Fortunately, he missed me, and as he went past, I got a clear view of why he was driving so erratically:[5] He was watching a music video. He was watching it on a video screen that had been installed where the sun visor usually goes, RIGHT IN FRONT OF HIS FACE, blocking his view of the road. I don't want to sound like an old fud,[6] but this seems to me to be just a tad hazardous. I distinctly recall learning in driver's education class that, to operate a car, you need to be able to see where the car is going, in case the need arises (you never know!) to steer. 9

Of course, more and more, drivers do not have time for steering, as they are busy making phone calls, eating, reading, changing CDs, putting on makeup, brushing their teeth, etc. I recently received mail from an alert reader named Kate Chadwick who reports that she drove behind a man who was SHAVING HIS HEAD, with his "visor mirror positioned just so, windows wide open for hair disposal, and for a significant portion of the ride, no hands on the wheel." 10

But at least these drivers are able, from time to time, to glance at the road whereas the guy I saw on I-95 basically could see only his video. I hope you agree with me that this is insane. I also hope you are not reading this in your car. 11

LANGUAGE AWARENESS AND VOCABULARY QUESTIONS

1. What does the author suggest when he states that "the bass notes sound like nuclear devices being detonated" (paragraph 8)?
2. In paragraph 2, the author mentions civic honor. What is civic honor?

COMPREHENSION AND ANALYSIS QUESTIONS

1. Summarize the driver distractions that the author discusses in this reading.
2. Barry's subject is serious, but the essay is funny. Do you think Barry's use of humor makes his point more or less effective?
3. How does Barry develop his persuasive thesis that Miami drivers are the worst in the world? How does he answer the opposition who might claim that other towns have the worst drivers?

WRITING ASSIGNMENTS

1. Review Chapter 16, Part A, and then write a humorous illustration essay about self-defeating ways in which people work, study (or don't), or try to impress others. You might title your essay "Working (Attending College, or Dating) While Stupid."
2. Discuss a time when you engaged in or witnessed dangerous behaviors. What happened? What did you learn from the experience?

5. erratically: without a fixed or regular path
6. fud: a fussy and old-fashioned person

ANA VECIANA-SUAREZ

When Greed Gives Way to Giving

Ana Veciana Suarez, "When Greed Gives Way to Giving," THE RECORD, October 10, 1999, p. L5 (MIAMI HERALD). Used by permission of Tribune Media Services.

If you suddenly made millions of dollars, what would you do with the money? Here Miami Herald *columnist Ana Veciana-Suarez reports one man's surprising response to that situation. Like many newspaper writers, she employs a casual tone and style, but the questions she raises are profound.*

In the flurry of life, you probably missed this story. I almost did, and that would have been too bad. Over in Belleville, Minnesota, a 67-year-old man named Bob Thompson sold his road-building company for $422 million back in July. He did not, as we would expect, buy himself a jet or an island, not even a new home. Instead, Thompson decided to share the wealth. 1

He divided $128 million among his 550 workers. Some checks exceeded annual salaries. And for more than 80 people, the bonus went beyond their wildest expectations: They became millionaires. Thompson even included some retirees and widows in his plan. What's more, he paid the taxes on those proceeds—about $25 million. 2

Employees were so flabbergasted[1] that the wife of an area manager tearfully said: "I think the commas are in the wrong place." The commas were right where they belonged. Thompson had made sure of that, had made sure, too, that not one of the workers would lose his or her job in the buyout. 3

I sat at the breakfast table stunned. I just don't know too many people or companies that would do something like that. Sure, many employers offer profit-sharing and stock-option plans. But outright giving? Nah. Employees rarely share in the bounty when the big payoff comes. In fact, many end up losing their jobs, being demoted,[2] seeking transfers, or taking early retirement. Insecurity—or better yet, the concept of every man for himself—is a verity[3] of work life in America. 4

Yet here is one man defying all of the stereotypes. I search for clues in his life, but find nothing out of the ordinary, nothing that stands out. He started the business in his basement with $3,500, supported by his schoolteacher wife. He has owned the same modest house for 37 years. His wood-paneled office has no Persian rugs or oil paintings, only photos of three children and five grandchildren. He admits to an indulgence or two: a Lincoln and an occasional Broadway show. 5

Yet he possesses something as priceless as it is rare: generosity. And he seems to be sheepishly modest even about that. "It's sharing good times, that's really all it is," he told a reporter. "I don't think you can read more into it. I'm a proud person. I wanted to go out a winner, and I wanted to go out doing 6

1. flabbergasted: astonished; shocked
2. demoted: reduced in status or rank
3. verity: truth or reality

the right thing." We all want to do the right thing, but blessed by a windfall,[4] would we have done as Thompson did? Maybe. I don't know. Honestly, I'm embarrassed to say I'm not sure I would have.

Perhaps, however, the more appropriate question is this: In our own more limited circumstances, do we share with others in the same spirit Thompson showed? Do we give beyond expectations? For most of us, generosity comes with limits. It is, by and large, a sum without sacrifice, a respectable token. 7

Some might say that Thompson's munificence[5] was token-like. After all, the $153 million is less than a third of his $422 million payoff. That kind of reasoning, however, misses the mark. Few of us give away even 10 percent, and if our income increases, the tendency is not to share more but to buy more, to hoard[6] more. Not Thompson. After finishing with his employees, he plans to continue giving away much of what's left of the $422 million. 8

I suspect he is on to something. In a society where success tends to be measured in what we can acquire, this guy instead is preaching and practicing the opposite. Success, he is telling us, is in the giving back. He seems to have mastered what many of us have yet to understand: the difference between need and want, between the basic essentials and our inchoate[7] desires. He has, by golly, defined *enough.* Maybe that's all the wealth he needs. 9

LANGUAGE AWARENESS AND VOCABULARY QUESTIONS

1. What does the author suggest when she states that generosity is "a sum without sacrifice, a respectable token" (paragraph 7)?
2. Based on the reading, how does Bob Thompson define *enough* (paragraph 9)?

COMPREHENSION AND ANALYSIS QUESTIONS

1. What is the main idea of paragraph 6?
2. The author first tells the factual story of Bob Thompson's "windfall" and then discusses its meaning. What does she believe is the point, or importance, of his story?
3. Do you agree with the author that generosity is a rare quality in today's society? If so, why do you think this is true? If you know a truly generous person, describe his or her generosity to the class.

WRITING ASSIGNMENTS

1. Veciana-Suarez discusses two definitions of success: the idea that success is acquiring as much as we can and Bob Thompson's idea that success is "giving back" (paragraph 9). Which of these is closer to the truth for you? Write an essay honestly exploring your personal definition of the word *success.*

4. windfall: sudden, unexpected good fortune or personal gain
5. munificence: great generosity
6. hoard: accumulate in a private supply, usually more than needed
7. inchoate: only partially formed or developed

2. What career path have you chosen to pursue or are considering now? Will that career lead you to your idea of success? Write about the top three rewards of that career for you (for example, salary, mental stimulation, security, fun, the chance to give back, to travel, and so on).

LAURENCE BENHAMOU

Everything You Need to Know About Generation Z

"Everything You Need to Know about Generation Z" by Laurence Benhamou from Agence France-Presse. Used by permission.

Baby Boomers. Generation X. Millennials. You might have heard of these names that refer to different generations: groups of people that are born within certain year brackets and are thought to share similar characteristics. In this article, Laurence Benhamou examines Generation Z—or those born after 1995—who, according to the author, are "independent, stubborn, and always in a rush." Do you agree with the author's description?

Facebook? Of course. Books? Definitely not. Video games? For sure. Sport? No way. Speed? Yes. Patience? Not so much. 1

This, in a nutshell, is the life of the "Generation Z"—independent, stubborn, pragmatic[1] and always in a rush. 2

These youngsters, born after 1995 and unaware of a world without Internet, live a life that seems a million miles removed from the hopes, dreams and morals of previous generations. 3

They are so hooked into the digital world that some academics have nicknamed them the "mutants." 4

Here are a few of the habits of Generation Z: 5

Daily life

They want everything, everywhere and immediately. They surf on two screens simultaneously. They don't mind paying through the nose for the latest smart phone but turn up their nose at paying for a film or a song when you can get that for free online. 6

Aged 13 to 20, they get all the latest trends from social media and find the morals of their elders out-of-date. 7

Their fashions are those found worldwide over the web: they watch American blockbusters like "Hunger Games" or "Divergent," listen to Korean K-pop and, when they dance, they "twerk." 8

When they speak, their vocabulary is peppered with acronyms, incomprehensible[2] to those not in the know. "Swag" is the new "cool." 9

And their new idols are Internet stars, like PewDiePie, who has the world's most subscribed YouTube channel. 10

Their friends

People from Generation Z find it easier to talk online than in person. Their friends on social media are as important to them as their friends in 11

1. pragmatic: practical
2. incomprehensible: impossible to understand

real life but sometimes they do actually meet up in person with these "virtual" pals.

More than eight out of 10 are hooked on social networks and more than half of them think that this is where their real social life takes place. 12

They are on dating websites from the age of 16—sometimes before. 13

What they know

Even as young as they are, they have already seen so many technologies become obsolete.[3] For this reason, they have become the ultimate "self-educators," learning how to use new stuff via self-help videos on YouTube. 14

As for the web, violence, porn, they've already seen it all. 15

What they watch

According to US consultancy Sparks and Honey, the average Generation Z-er spends more than three hours a day in front of a screen. 16

They live in constant "FOMO," fear of missing out. They can't stand the idea of not being in the loop when something new and exciting comes out. 17

Facebook is their main poison, despite its flagging popularity among some Americans. Photos on Instagram, quick messages on Snapchat. Twitter and Tumblr are omnipresent.[4] 18

But it's not all passive: Generation Z are also putting themselves out there on YouTube or "Vlogging" (video blogging), hoping to become the next "Fred" (Lucas Cruikshank), who made his name at the grand old age of 13. 19

Everyone surfs the web while watching the TV and they think that everything is possible with technology. But, they have a short attention span and tend to skim-read rather than read properly, which can lead to difficulty at school. 20

Generation Z at work

This is a generation that wants to create their own company—between 50 percent and 72 percent want to run their own start-up. 21

The idea of "business" brings up negative responses: "complicated," "brutal," "a jungle." 22

They believe success comes from their "network" rather than from qualifications and they prefer a flat organisation to a hierarchy at work. 23

They want to succeed and achieve, with 76 percent aiming to make their hobby their job. 24

The future of Generation Z

These are children of the crisis and it shows in their outlook. Most of them say they are "stressed out" by what they see as a bleak[5] future, especially in terms of economy and environment. 25

Given the same pay, 25 percent of the Generation Z in France would choose the most "fun" company, 22 percent the most innovative and 21 percent the most ethical. 26

3. obsolete: no longer used
4. omnipresent: always present; common
5. bleak: not hopeful

But like any idealistic[6] generation, they want to change the world and love the idea of volunteer work, which a quarter of Americans in their late teens are already doing. 27

LANGUAGE AWARENESS AND VOCABULARY QUESTIONS

1. The author states that some academics have nicknamed Generation Z "the mutants" (paragraph 4). What does this comparison mean?
2. What does *pragmatic* mean in relation to Generation Z (paragraph 2)?

COMPREHENSION AND ANALYSIS QUESTIONS

1. Summarize the habits of Generation Z.
2. Why is having a fun job important to Generation Z?
3. How is Generation Z an idealistic generation?

WRITING ASSIGNMENTS

1. Find an article about Generation X. Write a paragraph that evaluates the similarities and differences between Generation X and Generation Z.
2. Describe four of your parents' or grandparents' values, and explain why Generation Z thinks each of those values is out-of-date.

ROBERTO A. FERDMAN

Americans Are Having Dogs Instead of Babies

"Americans are Having Dogs Instead of Babies" by Roberto A. Ferdman from QZ.com, April 2014. Used by permission.

More and more young people today are delaying getting married and having children, opting instead for companionship in the form of small dogs. In this article, author Roberto A. Ferdman examines this popular trend among young Americans.

The fewer babies Americans give birth to, the more small dogs they seem to buy. 1

Birth rates in the US have fallen from nearly 70 per 1,000 women in 2007, to under 63 last year—a 10% tumble. American women birthed almost 400,000 fewer little humans in 2013 than they did six years before. The drop-off has come exclusively among 15- to 29-year-olds. This chart, taken from a recent report by the US Department of Health, does a pretty decent job of showing how much of the growing disinterest in having babies is due to younger women: 2

6. idealistic: having high hopes for the future

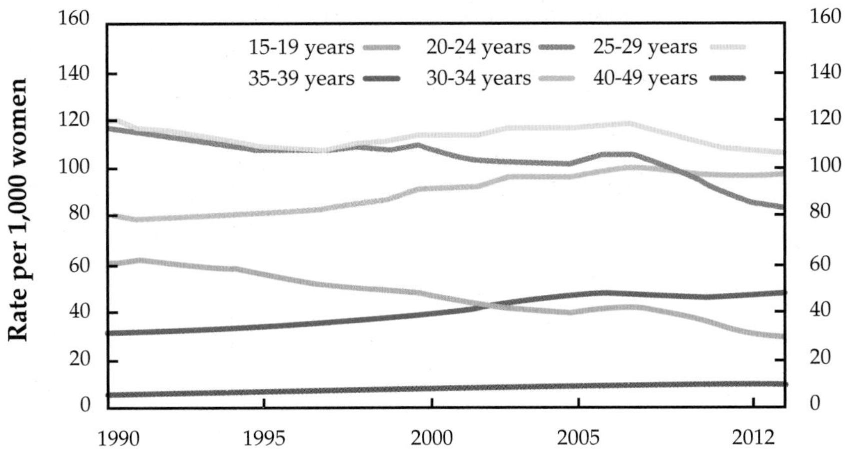

Birth rates, by selected age of mother: United States, 1990–2012

Source: CDC/NCHS, National Vital Statistics System

Meanwhile, the ownership of small dogs—that is, pets weighing no more than 20 pounds (9 kilograms)—is doing just the opposite. Americans have been buying more and more small dogs each year since 1999. The population of little canines more than doubled in the US over that period, and is only projected to continue upwards, according to data from market research firm Euromonitor. 3

"You do not have to go to many pet shows to realize that the numbers of small and tiny dogs are on the increase," a report by Pets International opined in 2010. 4

And rightly so. The number of small dogs has grown so fast that they are now the most popular kind nationwide. 5

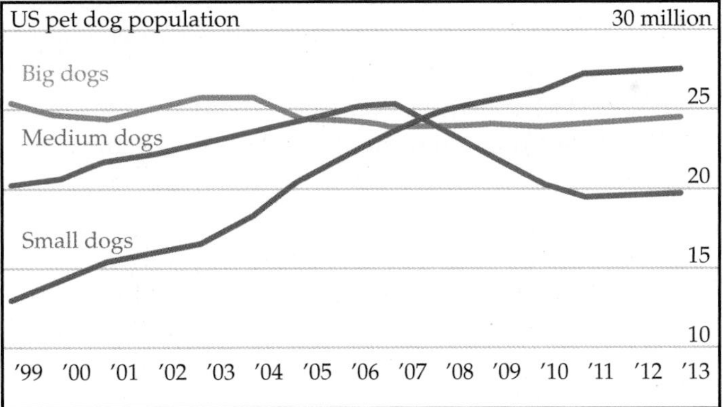

U.S. pet dog population, 1999–2013

Source: Euromonitor

It could just be a coincidence that Americans are birthing fewer babies at the same time as they're buying a lot more little dogs. But there's pretty good reason to believe it isn't, Damian Shore, an analyst at market-research firm Euromonitor, told Quartz. "There's definitely some replacement happening there," he said. 6

One telling sign that the two are not entirely unrelated is that the same age groups that are forgoing[1] motherhood are leading the small dog charge. 7

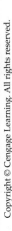

1. forgoing: doing without

"Women are not only having fewer children, but are also getting married later. There are more single and unmarried women in their late 20s and early 30s, which also happens to be the demographic[2] that buys the most small dogs," Shore said.

There's also evidence people are treating their dogs a bit more like little humans these days. Premium dog food, the most expensive kind, has grown by 170% over the past 15 years, and now accounts for 57% of the overall dog food market. 8

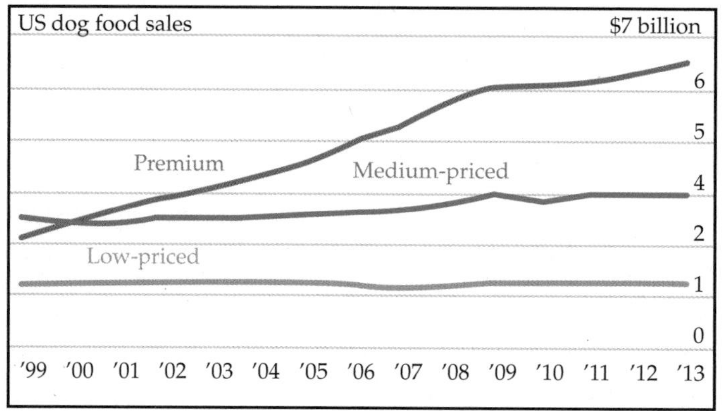

U.S. dog food sales, 1999–2013

Source: Euromonitor

There are now tools to monitor your dog's fitness, ice cream trucks exclusively for canines, and vacations designed exclusively for dog-having people. "The animals in our homes are family. They're like children," David Grimm, the author of the book *Citizen Canine*, told *Wired* this week. 9

Of course, small dog ownership isn't rising just because people want kid substitutes. Fashion trends aside, small dogs are also emblematic[3] of a national migration[4] to cities, where big dogs are harder to keep. Nearly 80% of Americans live in urban areas. "Smaller homes and apartments are also helping drive the growing popularity of smaller dogs," Shore said. 10

But the national trend towards later motherhood is certainly playing its part. And those who treat their pooches and pugs like babies may be on to something. A study last year found that dogs form bonds of dependency[5] with their owners not unlike the ones babies form with their parents. 11

LANGUAGE AWARENESS AND VOCABULARY QUESTIONS

1. The author quotes David Grimm as stating that "the animals in our homes are family" (paragraph 9). What is Grimm suggesting?
2. What does the word *dependency* mean in relation to the main idea of the article?

2. demographic: group of similar people within a population
3. emblematic: representative of
4. migration: movement from one place to another
5. dependency: need for someone

COMPREHENSION AND ANALYSIS QUESTIONS

1. Summarize the findings in the "US pet dog population" chart.
2. Explain why pet owners are buying premium dog food instead of low-priced dog food.
3. The author states that "small dogs are also emblematic of a national migration to cities" (paragraph 10). What does this mean?

WRITING ASSIGNMENTS

1. Write an illustrative paragraph that explains why more women in their late twenties and early thirties today are single and unmarried.
2. Imagine you are booking a vacation with a small dog. Research dog-friendly vacations, including accommodations, and write about your findings.

ELISSA ENGLUND

Good Grammar Gets the Girl

Elissa Englund, "Good Grammar Gets the Girl" from www.statenews.com/index.php/article/2005/09/good_grammar_gets_the_girl. Reprinted by permission of the author and State News.

Can excellent grammar help you find romance? Elissa Englund thinks it can. A senior at Michigan State University in 2005, she had just joined an online dating service and was struck by the importance of grammatical first impressions. She wrote this humorous article, with tips for improving "grammatical hotness," for the college newspaper. Today Ms. Englund works as a copyeditor for Time *magazine in New York City. You can check out her blog and photographs at* **TooManyCommas.com.**

TEACHING TIP

Have fun with your class by reading aloud and correcting some of the errors and bloopers the author records.

In the few weeks that I've been a member of an online dating service, I've had an interesting range of people contact me. Meet Craig (not his real name). He's a 28-year-old Virgo seeking a lady who is "fun to be around." He says he finished college and is employed full-time. All in all, he seems like a pretty together guy—until you read his message. 1

"Hi! I love to have fun weather it at work or hang out with friends," wrote Craig in his introductory conversation, which I've left with the original grammar. "I'm an optimistic because like is to short too be a pessimistic." 2

In our second conversation, he informed me, "I don't like it when people play games and our dishonest. I have been burned to many times." 3

Sorry, Craig. You seem a little "to dumb" to date. 4

I'm sure Craig is actually very smart. I'm sure he's very sweet. But in the online dating world, that just won't cut it, babe. Our society has reverted to the written word as one of the initial means of conversation. Although these love letters generally aren't written on parchment with quill pens, many first impressions are based solely on how you express yourself through the English language. 5

With the explosion of the Internet, many couples have exchanged their first flirting words through instant messages, e-mail, and online dating services. Grammar isn't just a subject taught in seventh grade or a thing you worry about when writing a cover letter any longer. If you can't spell, use grammar, or express yourself through writing, you're going to be in trouble with the ladies. 6

But have no fear! There are options, one of them being a nifty thing called spell check. But spell check, as I'm sure you know, can fail you. Poor Craig, for example, had no misspellings but a slew[1] of incorrect usages. "Our" should have been "are." He mixed up "too" and "to" and "weather" and "whether." And this girl deleted him from her contact list forever. 7

Sure, maybe I'm shallow. But it makes as bad of an impression as a guy wearing a muscle shirt and daisy dukes to a swank[2] club. It makes you seem trashy, not sweet. 8

But I'm not totally heartless, so for all of you who are lacking in grammar hotness, I'm here. Clip out these rules. Tape them to your computer. And most importantly, reread something before sending it on. A lot of times, you'll catch the errors yourself. Be the Internet Romeo we all know you can be. Nobody ever rejected a guy because his grammar was too good. I promise. 9

How to use stellar[3] grammar to get a hot date: 10

1. With plurals, never use an apostrophe.

   Hotter than Zack Morris:[4] "I'm looking for girls who love to laugh."

   Fewer dates than Screech Powers:[5] "All my past girlfriend's dumped me when I cheated."

2. Possessives almost always use an apostrophe.

   Singular:

   Zack: "I always treat my girlfriend's mother with respect."

   Screech: "I still steal my sisters diary and read it."

   Plural:

   Zack: "My friends' favorite thing about me is my sense of humor."

   Screech: "My last three girlfriend's parents hated me."

3. Know the difference between "it's" and "its." "It's" is a contraction of "it is"; "its" is possessive.

   Zack: "It's sexy when a girl is successful and intelligent."

   Zack: "Here's a rose; I had the florist trim its thorns."

   Screech: "I like when its raining because I can see through your shirt."

1. slew: large number
2. swank: elegant and expensive
3. stellar: excellent
4. Zack Morris: handsome character on the 1990s high school sitcom *Saved by the Bell*
5. Screech Powers: nerdy character on *Saved by the Bell*

4. "They're" is a contraction of "they are." "There" refers to direction or location. "Their" is ownership. Likewise, "you're" is a contraction of "you are," and "your" is ownership.

   Zack: "There is something about your personality that is so magnetic."

   Screech: "You're dress looks great, but it would look better on my floor."

5. Have you ever read Tupac Shakur's[6] poetry? Yeah, it's awful. Apparently, it's thug not to capitalize and to nix[7] spelling whole words to abbreviate "you" to "u," "are" to "r," and "for" to "4." But it makes you look like an eighth grader passing notes.

   Zack: "I have a surprise for you when we go out tomorrow."

   Screech: "i can't wait 4 us 2 get 2gethr so u can c my bed."

Being a communication Casanova is really quite simple; it just requires that you take the effort to memorize a few quick rules and reread your writing before hitting "send." Consider it the online dating equivalent of running a comb through your hair and flossing your teeth. The extra effort shows, and the ladies will notice. And if you think you're already a syntax Superman, look me up. I'll be waiting, red pen in hand. 11

LANGUAGE AWARENESS AND VOCABULARY QUESTIONS

1. What does the author mean when she says, "Be the Internet Romeo we all know you can be" (paragraph 9)?
2. The author uses the word *reverted* in paragraph 5. Use context clues to determine the meaning of the word. Use an online dictionary to verify your answer.

COMPREHENSION AND ANALYSIS QUESTIONS

1. What is the main idea of paragraph 5?
2. Englund develops her essay with grammatically correct and incorrect examples. How effective are these examples? Why does she pretend they are written by sitcom characters Zack and Screech? Working with a partner, find and edit all of the errors in the incorrect examples.
3. This essay is humorous, but it aims to persuade. How effective is the writer's argument?

TEACHING TIP
You might have the class work in teams, correcting all of Screech's sentences. Reward the winners with small prizes.

WRITING ASSIGNMENTS

1. Many people have become concerned about the erosion of good writing skills caused by widespread use of texting lingo, with its abbreviations, misspellings, and dropped capitalization and punctuation. Is this concern a

6. Tupac Shakur: widely admired American rap singer who was murdered at age 25
7. nix: to reject or eliminate

valid one? What are other positive and negative consequences of heavy use of texting lingo among young people?

2. If you were writing an article for the college newspaper with the purpose of calling students' attention to the importance of clear and concise writing, how would you do it? Plan a strategy, brainstorm, and write your article. Once you have revised and proofread your article, submit it to the newspaper for publication.

IAN FRAZIER

On the Rez

Do you think a single act of courage or heroism can reverse decades of misunderstanding? In his book* On the Rez*, Ian Frazier tells the true story of SuAnne Marie Big Crow, who faced a taunting crowd and decided to answer its jeers with a surprising gift.

Some people who live in the cities and towns near reservations treat their Indian neighbors decently; some don't. In Denver and Minneapolis and Rapid City police have been known to harass Indian teenagers and rough up Indian drunks and needlessly stop and search Indian cars. Local banks whose deposits include millions in tribal funds sometimes charge Indians higher interest rates than they charge whites. Gift shops near reservations sell junky caricature[1] Indian pictures and dolls, and until not long ago beer coolers had signs on them that said INDIAN POWER. In a big discount store in a reservation-border town a white clerk observes a lot of Indians waiting at the checkout and remarks, "Oh, they're Indians—they're used to standing in line." Some people in South Dakota hate Indians, unapologetically, and will tell you why; in their voices you can hear a particular American meanness that is centuries old. 1

When teams from Pine Ridge play non-Indian teams, the question of race is always there. When Pine Ridge is the visiting team, usually the hosts are courteous and the players and fans have a good time. But Pine Ridge coaches know that occasionally at away games their kids will be insulted, their fans will feel unwelcome, the host gym will be dense with hostility, and the referees will call fouls on Indian players every chance they get. Sometimes in a game between Indian and non-Indian teams the difference in race becomes an important and distracting part of the event. 2

One place where Pine Ridge teams used to get harassed regularly was the high school gymnasium in Lead, South Dakota. Lead is a town of about 3,200 northwest of the reservation, in the Black Hills. It is laid out among the mines that are its main industry, and low, wooded mountains hedge it around. The brick high school building is set into a hillside. The school's only gym in those days was small, with tiers of gray-painted concrete on which the spectator benches descended from just below the steel-beamed roof to the very edge 3

1. caricature: cartoon

of the basketball court—an arrangement that greatly magnified the interior noise.

In the fall of 1988 the Pine Ridge Lady Thorpes[2] went to Lead to play a basketball game. SuAnne was a full member of the team by then. She was a freshman, fourteen years old. Getting ready in the locker room, the Pine Ridge girls could hear the din from the Lead fans. They were yelling fake Indian war cries, a *"woo-woo-woo"* sound. The usual plan for the pre-game warm-up was for the visiting team to run onto the court in a line, take a lap or two around the floor, shoot some baskets, and then go to their bench at courtside. After that the home team would come out and do the same, and then the game would begin. Usually the Thorpes lined up for their entry more or less according to height, which meant that senior Doni De Cory, one of the tallest, went first. As the team waited in the hallway leading from the locker room, the heckling got louder. Some fans were waving food stamps, a reference to the reservation's receiving federal aid. Others yelled, "Where's the cheese?"—the joke being that if Indians were lining up, it must be to get commodity cheese. The Lead high school band had joined in, with fake Indian drumming and a fake Indian tune. Doni De Cory looked out the door and told her teammates, "I can't handle this." SuAnne quickly offered to go first in her place. She was so eager that Doni became suspicious. "Don't embarrass us," Doni told her. SuAnne said, "I won't. I won't embarrass you." Doni gave her the ball, and SuAnne stood first in line. 4

She came running onto the court dribbling the basketball, with her teammates running behind. On the court the noise was deafening. SuAnne went right down the middle and suddenly stopped when she got to center court. Her teammates were taken by surprise, and some bumped into each other. Coach Zimiga, at the rear of the line, did not know why they had stopped. SuAnne turned to Doni De Cory and tossed her the ball. Then she stepped into the jump-ball circle at center court, facing the Lead fans. She unbuttoned her warm-up jacket, took it off, draped it over her shoulders, and began to do the Lakota shawl dance. SuAnne knew all the traditional dances (she had competed in many powwows as a little girl), and the dance she chose is a young woman's dance, graceful and modest and show-offy all at the same time. "I couldn't believe it—she was powwowin', like, 'Get down!'" Doni De Cory recalls. "And then she started to sing." SuAnne began to sing in Lakota, swaying back and forth in the jump-ball circle, doing the shawl dance, using her warm-up jacket for a shawl. The crowd went completely silent. "All that stuff the Lead fans were yelling—it was like she *reversed* it somehow," a teammate says. In the sudden quiet all they could hear was her Lakota song. SuAnne dropped her jacket, took the ball from Doni De Cory, and ran a lap around the court dribbling expertly and fast. The audience began to cheer and applaud. She sprinted to the basket, went up in the air, and laid the ball through the hoop, with the fans cheering loudly now. Of course, Pine Ridge went on to win the game. 5

For the Oglala, what SuAnne did that day almost immediately took on the status of myth. People from Pine Ridge who witnessed it still describe it in terms of awe and disbelief. Amazement swept through the younger kids when they heard. "I was, like, '*What* did she just do?'" recalls her cousin Angie Big 6

2. Lady Thorpes: named for Native American Jim Thorpe, one of the greatest athletes of all time

Crow, an eighth grader at the time. All over the reservation people told and retold the story of SuAnne at Lead. Anytime the subject of SuAnne came up when I was talking to people on Pine Ridge, I would always ask if they had heard about what she did at Lead, and always the answer was a smile and a nod—"Yeah, I was there," or "Yeah, I heard about that." To the unnumbered big and small slights of local racism that the Oglala have known all their lives SuAnne's exploit made an emphatic reply.

Back in the days when Lakota war parties still fought battles against other tribes and the Army, no deed of war was more honored than the act of counting coup. To "count coup" means to touch an armed enemy in full possession of his powers with a special stick called a coup stick, or with the hand. The touch is not a blow, and serves only to indicate how close to the enemy you came. As an act of bravery, counting coup was regarded as greater than killing an enemy in single combat, greater than taking a scalp or horses or any prize. Counting coup was an act of almost abstract courage, of pure playfulness taken to the most daring extreme. Very likely, to do it and survive brought an exhilaration to which nothing else could compare. In an ancient sense that her Oglala kin could recognize, SuAnne counted coup on the fans of Lead. 7

And yet this coup was an act not of war but of peace. SuAnne's coup strike was an offering, an invitation. It gave the hecklers the best interpretation, as if their silly, mocking chants were meant only in good will. It showed that their fake Indian songs were just that—fake—and that the real thing was better, as real things usually are. We Lakota have been dancing like this for centuries, the dance said; we've been doing the shawl dance since long before you came, before you got on the boat in Glasgow or Bremerhaven, before you stole this land, and we're still doing it today. And isn't it pretty, when you see how it's supposed to be done? Because finally, what SuAnne proposed was to invite us—us onlookers in the stands, namely, the non-Lakota rest of this country—to dance too. She was in the Lead gym to play, and she invited us all to play. The symbol she used to include us was the warm-up jacket. Everyone in America has a warm-up jacket. I've got one, probably so do you, so did (no doubt) many of the fans at Lead. By using the warm-up jacket as a shawl in her impromptu shawl dance she made Lakota relatives of us all. 8

"It was funny," Doni De Cory says, "but after that game the relationship between Lead and us was tremendous. When we played Lead again, the games were really good, and we got to know some of the girls on the team. Later, when we went to a tournament and Lead was there, we were hanging out with the Lead girls and eating pizza with them. We got to know some of their parents, too. What SuAnne did made a lasting impression and changed the whole situation with us and Lead. We found out there are some really good people in Lead." 9

America is a leap of the imagination. From its beginning people have had only a persistent idea of what a good country should be. The idea involves freedom, equality, justice, and the pursuit of happiness; nowadays most of us probably could not describe it much more clearly than that. The truth is, it always has been a bit of a guess. No one has ever known for sure whether a country based on such an idea is really possible, but again and again we have leaped toward the idea and hoped. What SuAnne Big Crow demonstrated in 10 the Lead high school gym is that making the leap is the whole point. The idea does not truly live unless it is expressed by an act; the country does not live unless we make the leap from our tribe or focus group or gated community or demographic[3] and land on the shaky platform of that idea of a good country which all kinds of different people share.

LANGUAGE AWARENESS AND VOCABULARY QUESTIONS

1. What does the author suggest when he states that "the host gym will be dense with hostility" (paragraph 2)?
2. What is *commodity cheese* (paragraph 4)?

COMPREHENSION AND ANALYSIS QUESTIONS

1. How was the Pine Ridge girls' basketball team usually treated when they played games at Lead? What larger problem between Indians and non-Indians in South Dakota was reflected in this behavior?
2. SuAnne's performance of the Lakota shawl dance to a silent gymnasium full of people is described in powerful detail. What descriptive details does the author include to make that scene come alive for the reader?
3. What did the students at Lead discover during SuAnne's dance that caused them to change their opinions about Lakota Indians? What made the Pine Ridge players decide that "there are some really good people in Lead" (paragraph 9)?

WRITING ASSIGNMENTS

1. SuAnne Marie Big Crow's actions that day made her a heroine for the people of the Pine Ridge reservation. With a group of classmates, brainstorm the qualities that make someone a hero or heroine. Then select two or three of these qualities and write an essay defining heroism. You may wish to illustrate with an anecdote of your own about someone who performed like a heroine in a difficult situation.
2. How can we promote tolerance in the world? Think of a conflict that you have experienced or heard about—perhaps between two ethnic groups, gangs, families, or individuals. What specific actions would you recommend to help promote understanding and tolerance between the two sides?

3. demographic: group of similar people within a population

KAREN CASTELLUCCI COX

Four Types of Courage

Adapted from "Four Types of Courage" by Karen Castellucci Cox and Susan Fawcett.

"In these times when many students wonder anxiously what the future will bring, courage may be more important than ever," claims Karen Castellucci Cox, a professor of English at City College of San Francisco. In this inspiring essay, she examines four different kinds of courage first set forth by psychologist Rollo May, applying his categories to contemporary challenges.

Most people think they know what courage is. When asked to name a courageous person, many pick a Hollywood hero like Jack Bauer, the impossibly capable action star of television's *24.* Others choose real-life heroes, often those who confront great physical danger like firefighters or soldiers. Indeed, our culture teaches us to view courage as a kind of Rambo-style bravado. Consider these cases, however: Chardee, a battered wife who finally leaves her husband; Luis, who goes against his family's wishes to pursue his dream of becoming an actor; Ann, who cares for a father with Alzheimer's disease, patiently having the same conversations day after day yet infusing their small apartment with good cheer and kindness. Do any of these people exhibit courage? In his classic book *The Courage to Create,* American psychologist Rollo May invites us to examine more deeply the quality he believes is essential to a meaningful life. Courage, he insists, is not just one emotion among others, but the foundation on which all other virtues and values rest. May divides courage into four distinct types—physical, social, moral, and creative. 1

Physical courage is familiar to most people: the ability to confront bodily pain or danger with self-possession, usually for a greater goal or good. For example, when Hurricane Katrina hit the Gulf Coast in August 2005, causing devastating floods in New Orleans, local police raced to curb looting and rescue the stranded. These officers had no experience facing such a catastrophic[1] emergency and little training in search-and-rescue. Yet they risked their lives to save desperate and angry citizens amid surging water, threat of disease, and even sniper fire. The pressure proved too much for some; several dozen deserted. But the truly remarkable fact was that 1,700 men and women continued to report to work each day, exhibiting the brand of physical courage that May believes capable of transforming society. 2

Physical courage has lost much of its usefulness in contemporary life, May cautions. Whereas our society once applauded the self-reliant pioneer, now we egg on the Tony Sopranos,[2] who justify their violence with talk of disrespect or frontier justice. What masquerades as physical courage in television, films, music videos, and games is often little better than the bully's swagger on the playground. A more productive physical courage, like that of the New Orleans officers, puts the body on the line, not to overpower or harm others, but to serve and protect them. 3

1. catastrophic: disastrous
2. Tony Soprano: lead character in *The Sopranos,* a dramatic HBO series about a Mafia family

The second category, social courage, is the type demanded of us in daily life. This is the courage to have meaningful relationships, to dare to reveal who we really are, to tell the truth in public forums despite the risks. The child who faces peer disapproval to befriend an unpopular classmate demonstrates social courage. The 55-year-old woman who goes back for her college degree though she fears she will feel out of place demonstrates social courage. The employee who volunteers to give a business presentation despite a lifelong terror of public speaking demonstrates social courage. Marriage, parenthood, any relationship that calls for an engagement of the heart and mind invites this brand of courage. May writes, "It is easier in our society to be naked physically than to be naked psychologically or spiritually." But when one chooses to open oneself, despite real risks of embarrassment, rejection, or worse, the reward is the chance of making a profound connection in a world of superficial ones. 4

Moral courage may exact an even heavier toll. The one who exhibits moral courage usually recognizes the suffering of others and decides to help despite the consequences. Aung San Suu Kyi is such a figure. The daughter of a diplomat and a general who was assassinated after negotiating Burma's independence from Great Britain in 1947, Suu Kyi was inspired by her parents to spend her life promoting democracy and human rights in Burma. When an oppressive military gained control of the government in 1988, Suu Kyi stepped into a leadership position, helping to found a democratic party and speaking publicly throughout Burma. Her inspiring vision drew huge crowds, and when her popularity became a threat, she was followed, harassed, and arrested. Suu Kyi spent a total of fifteen years under house arrest, a sacrifice that meant living apart from her grown sons and not being able to visit her dying husband in England. Her moral courage was recognized when she won the Nobel Peace Prize in 1991. Beloved by Burmese citizens and admired worldwide as a democratic leader, she was re-arrested and held under house arrest until 2010. 5

John Sciulli/Getty Images

Paul Rusesabagina, the inspiration for the movie *Hotel Rwanda,* speaks at a press conference for the film at the 2004 Toronto International Film Festival.

Moral courage is found as well in ordinary people who take a stand. Between April and July 1994, nearly one million people were killed in a mass genocide[3] in Rwanda; Hutu extremists murdered their Tutsi[4] neighbors while the international community looked the other way. But one man, Paul Rusesabagina, did not look the other way. The son of farmers and a modest hotel manager, Rusesabagina at first wanted to protect only his wife and children. Gradually, however, he began to comprehend the scope of the brutality. He devised a way to hide Tutsi refugees in his hotel until they could be carried to safety. In all, Rusesabagina is responsible for single-handedly saving the lives of 1,268 people. His story, told in the film *Hotel Rwanda,* is a reminder that moral courage can be found wherever a person chooses action over apathy.[5] 6

The final category is creative courage, "discovering new forms, patterns" and solutions that no one has yet imagined and that might even promote a better future. A writer, musician, or inventor shows creative courage when he or she rejects the status quo,[6] seeing beyond what *is* to create something new. President Lincoln called Harriet Beecher Stowe the "little woman who 7

3. genocide: the systematic and planned execution of an entire national, racial, or ethnic group
4. Hutu . . . Tutsi: two of the three ethnic groups that occupy Rwanda and Burundi
5. apathy: lack of interest or concern
6. status quo: existing condition or state of affairs

wrote the book that started this great war." Her 1851 novel *Uncle Tom's Cabin,* while it didn't actually provoke the Civil War, created a groundswell[7] of public outrage against slavery through its detailed and moving descriptions. Another example is *Rent,* one of the longest-running shows on Broadway. *Rent* was the first musical to address the HIV health crisis through life-affirming personal stories aimed at the general public. An uplifting musical form helped the public face difficult issues.

Not just the arts, but all professions, require creative courage. Tim Berners- 8
Lee, for instance, is credited with inventing the World Wide Web, maybe the most important innovation of our time. In 1991, he set up the first website and began networking his computer with others around the country. Concerned that patenting his discovery would make the growing Web too expensive for general use, Berners-Lee chose to keep the technology public. In doing so, he passed up a personal fortune and risked mockery for his "foolish" insistence that the World Wide Web should belong to everyone.

Of course, the four types of courage sometimes overlap. Tobacco executive 9
Jeffrey Wigand was motivated by moral courage when he revealed in the 1990s that Big Tobacco[8] was hiding the truth about nicotine causing cancer. This whistle-blower[9] demonstrated physical courage as well, refusing to be silenced by veiled threats of violence. Wigand's social courage was tested as the case hit the media, the business community shunned[10] him, and his own family deserted him. And when his old life was shattered, this man somehow found the creative courage to build a new one.

"Courage has many faces," writes Katherine Martin, the author of *Women* 10
of Courage. "We lose much when we dismiss it in ourselves, thinking we don't measure up." The classification that May sets forth invites us to find and cultivate courage in our own lives, to ask what blocks our daring, and then to stand and try.

LANGUAGE AWARENESS AND VOCABULARY QUESTIONS

1. What does the phrase "courage has many faces" (paragraph 10) mean?
2. Using context clues, define the word *bravado* (paragraph 1). Use a dictionary to determine if your definition is accurate. How does the word apply to the first paragraph?

COMPREHENSION AND ANALYSIS QUESTIONS

1. What is social courage?
2. How does the author classify courage in this essay? That is, what four categories of courage does she identify? What is the source of these categories?

---

7. groundswell: a sudden gathering of force
8. Big Tobacco: nickname for the three most powerful tobacco companies in the United States
9. whistle-blower: an employee or member of an organization who exposes misconduct or corruption
10. shunned: rejected, ignored

3. In the last sentence, the author invites us to ask ourselves "what blocks our daring." What does she mean? What kinds of obstacles "block our daring"?

WRITING ASSIGNMENTS

1. Discuss a time when you or someone close to you displayed one or more of the four types of courage described in this essay.
2. Write a classification essay about another concept, emotion, or term—such as success, friends, mistakes, or lies—and break it into different types or "faces."

WANG PING

Book War

Have you ever lived in a country whose government tried to control what you read, said, wore, or even believed? Author Wang Ping grew up in China during the violent "Cultural Revolution" of the late 1960s when Communist chairman Mao Zedong closed schools, banned books, and imprisoned or killed thousands of citizens. In this true story, a curious child tries to learn in a place where reading the wrong book could bring a death sentence.

TEACHING TIP
The original *Little Mermaid* by Hans Christian Andersen had a tragic ending, which has been altered in many adaptations of the tale.

I discovered "The Little Mermaid," my first fairy tale, in 1968. That morning, when I opened the door to light my stove, I found my new neighbor, a girl a few years older, sitting under the streetlight, a book in her lap. The red plastic wrap indicated it was Mao's collected work. She must have been there all night long, for her hair and shoulders were covered with frost, and her body shivered violently from cold. Another loyal Maoist, I thought to myself. Then I heard her sobbing. I got curious. What kind of person would weep from reading Mao's words? I walked over and peeked over her shoulders. What I saw made me freeze in fear and excitement. The book in her hands had nothing to do with Mao; it was Hans Christian Andersen's fairy tales, the story of "The Little Mermaid." Since I had heard the story in my kindergarten, I was determined to read it myself someday. Just when I was ready, the Cultural Revolution began. Schools were closed, books, condemned as "poisonous weeds," were burnt on streets, and the rest were confiscated.[1] 1

My clever neighbor had disguised the "poisonous weed" with the scarlet cover of Mao's work. Engrossed[2] in the story, she didn't realize my presence behind her until I started weeping. She jumped up, fairy tales clutched to her budding chest. Her panic-stricken face said she was ready to fight me to death if I dared to report her. We stared at each other for an eternity. Suddenly she 2

1. confiscated: seized
2. engrossed: completely absorbed

started laughing, pointing at my tear-stained face. She knew then that her secret was safe with me.

She gave me twenty-four hours to read the fairy tales, and I loaned her *The Arabian Nights,* which was missing the first fifteen pages and the last story, but no matter. The girl squealed and danced in the dawn light. When we finished each other's books, we decided to start an underground book exchange network. With strict rules and determination, we had books to read almost every day, all "poisonous" classics. 3

Soon I excavated[3] a box of books my mother had buried beneath the chicken coop. I pried it open with a screwdriver, and pulled out one treasure after another: *The Dream of the Red Chamber, The Book of Songs, Grimms' Fairy Tales, Romeo and Juliet, Huckleberry Finn, American Dream,* each wrapped with waxed paper. 4

I devoured them all, in rice paddies[4] and wheat fields, on my way home from school and errands. I tried to be careful. The consequences could have been catastrophic,[5] not only for myself but also for my entire family, had these books fallen into wrong hands. But my "enemy" was my own mother. Once she discovered I had unearthed her treasure box, she set out to destroy these "time bombs," combing every possible place in the house. It was a hopeless battle. My mother knew my habits, my little tricks. I couldn't outsmart her. Whenever she caught me red-handed, she'd order me to tear the pages and place them in the stove, and she'd sit nearby, tears in her eyes, muttering: "This is for your safety, everyone's safety." And my heart, our hearts, turned into ashes. 5

When the last book was gone, I went to sit in the chicken coop. Hens surrounded me, pecking at my closed fists for food. As tears flowed, the stories became alive from inside. They flapped their wings and flew out of my mouth like mourning doves. I started telling them to my siblings, friends, and neighbors; stories I'd read from those forbidden treasures, stories I made up for myself and my audience. We gathered on summer nights, during winter darkness. When I saw stars rising in their dimmed eyes, I knew I had won the war. 6

LANGUAGE AWARENESS AND VOCABULARY QUESTIONS

1. What does the author suggest when she writes that books were considered poisonous weeds (paragraph 1)?
2. In paragraph 5, the author says that she devoured the books. In the context of this reading, what does *devoured* mean?

COMPREHENSION AND ANALYSIS QUESTIONS

1. Explain how the author "won the war."

3. excavated: dug up
4. rice paddies: flooded land used for growing rice
5. catastrophic: disastrous

2. Why does the author's mother destroy her own books once she finds out that her daughter loves them too?

3. Wang Ping uses many similes and metaphors (poetic comparisons, see Chapter 23, Part D) in telling her story. For example, to the mother, the books her daughter is reading are "time bombs" (paragraph 5). Why does she say this? Find another example of poetic language in the text and explain what it means.

WRITING ASSIGNMENTS

1. What activity or right, if any, would you risk your life to fight for if the government suddenly forbade you from engaging in that activity? Explain your answer.

2. Do Americans value literacy? Why or why not?

LEONARD PITTS

A Risk-Free Life

If you could tinker with the genes of your unborn children to protect them from a disease—or even to select their gender or physical traits—would you do it? How far would you go to take control of nature and of chance? Pulitzer Prize–winning columnist Leonard Pitts argues that people who seek this level of control are denying one of life's most basic truths.

I don't have the heart—or, perhaps more accurately, the heartlessness—to beat up on a lady whose only sin was the desire to have a healthy baby. So don't read any of what follows as a criticism of the woman—her name has not been released—who went to a geneticist[1] to have her eggs screened for the gene that causes Alzheimer's.[2] 1

That disease is a clear and present danger in the life of this woman. Her family is reportedly one of about a dozen in the world carrying a genetic flaw that virtually assures them of developing Alzheimer's—and doing so while tragically young. A sister started showing symptoms at the age of 38, a brother at 35. Experts say it's a virtual certainty that this woman, who is 30, will develop the mind-destroying affliction[3] by the time she's 40. 2

Her problem was that she desperately wanted a child. Now, as just reported in the *Journal of the American Medical Association*, she and her husband have one. And another is on the way. It's likely that when the woman's daughter, who was born a year ago, turns 10, her mom will no longer recognize her. Had she been conceived by normal means, the daughter would have faced a 50-50 3

1. geneticist: a scientist who studies genes, which pass traits from parents to children
2. Alzheimer's: an incurable brain disorder characterized by memory loss, confusion, loss of language, and finally death
3. affliction: a state of suffering or pain

chance of suffering a similar fate. Instead, she and her sibling have been freed from what amounts to a family curse.

If I were in this woman's place, I can't tell you that I wouldn't have done 4
the same thing she did. At the same time, I'd be lying if I didn't admit to being troubled by some of the moral and ethical doors that are swinging open here.

It is not, it seems to me, that big a leap from screening for fatal disease to 5
screening for hair color, height, weight or susceptibility[4] to allergies. Given that many cultures value females less than they do males, will we see fewer girls being born? Will self-hating blacks sign up to give their children light skin and so-called "good" hair? Will self-hating Asians want to do away with almond eyes? Will there come a day when the fertility doctor hands you a checklist and you choose characteristics—one from Column A, two from Column B—putting a human being together like you would a meal in a take-out restaurant?

I fear—and believe—the inevitable answer to all of the above is yes. It's in 6
our nature. We seek to remove from the equation that gremlin,[5] chance.

That's an old impulse that you and I have raised to a whole new level. The 7
world has never seen control freaks like us. We make bestsellers out of self-help books that purport[6] to help us put our emotional and financial houses in order. We line up to buy the latest gadget that promises to save time and simplify chores. We put the whole world in an electronic box that sits on a desk. We seek uniformity, predictability, security.

But guess what? Stuff still happens. As they did when the cliché[7] was fresh, 8
the best laid plans of mice and men still manage to go astray. You wonder when or whether human beings will ever concede that their ability to guarantee their own destinies is finite[8] at best. We do what we can, but we can never do enough. So the two children who are now freed from the threat of Alzheimer's still face the risk that they will suffer cancer, heart disease, stroke, or someday step off the curb in front of a city bus. In the words of Gilda Radner,[9] "It's always something."

Indeed. For her, it was ovarian cancer. And I guess it would be easy to 9
look at a thing like that and regard it as an intrusion upon your life. But life IS ovarian cancer. It's Alzheimer's, it's heart attack, it's mental illness, it's uncertainty, and it is suffering. Yet it is also, in the very same instant, laughter that makes your head swim, faith that makes your heart soar. It is triumph, hope, pleasure and, with apologies to Al Green,[10] love and happiness as well.

To live is to be surprised, I think. And shocked. You wake up in the morning 10
to find out what happens next.

I have no condemnation[11] for a mother who only wanted the best for her 11
children. But at the same time, I think there's something foolish and self-defeating in this impulse we have to make life risk-free. That's a contradiction in terms.

4. susceptibility: the state of being easily affected
5. gremlin: a trouble-making elf
6. purport: to claim
7. cliché: overused, worn-out expression
8. finite: having a limited existence
9. Gilda Radner: American comedienne and actress who died from ovarian cancer in 1989
10. Al Green: American soul singer, one of whose hits was "Love and Happiness"
11. condemnation: strong disapproval

LANGUAGE AWARENESS AND VOCABULARY QUESTIONS

1. The author begins paragraph 8 with a cliché: "the best laid plans of mice and men still manage to go astray." What is the meaning of this phrase? Does it make this reading more effective? Why or why not?
2. What does it mean to have a risk-free life?

COMPREHENSION AND ANALYSIS QUESTIONS

1. Summarize the author's argument.
2. Do you agree or disagree with the actions of the woman who had her eggs screened for the gene that causes Alzheimer's disease? Would you have done the same thing?
3. Do you think that the author's fear about a future when we'll probably be "putting a human being together like you would a meal in a take-out restaurant" (paragraph 5) is valid? Why or why not?

WRITING ASSIGNMENTS

1. Narrate a time when you tried to control a situation, but hurt, shock, or the unexpected occurred anyway. What happened? What lessons did you learn from this experience?
2. Contrast someone you know who often takes risks with someone you know who avoids risks. Think of attitudes and behaviors that reveal the differences between them, and select three points of contrast to structure your writing.

MICHAEL LEVIN

The Case for Torture

"The Case for Torture" by Michael E. Levin, NEWSWEEK, June 1982. Reprinted by permission of the author.

Leaders like Martin Luther King, Jr., and Mahatma Gandhi have preached nonviolence no matter what, and many people agree that deliberately injuring another person is wrong. However, philosophy professor Michael Levin argues in this startling essay that torture is sometimes necessary.

It is generally assumed that torture is impermissible,[1] a throwback to a more brutal age. Enlightened societies reject it outright, and regimes suspected of using it risk the wrath of the United States. 1

I believe this attitude is unwise. There are situations in which torture is not merely permissible but morally mandatory. Moreover, these situations are moving from the realm of imagination to fact. 2

1. impermissible: not allowed

Suppose a terrorist has hidden an atomic bomb on Manhattan Island which will detonate at noon on July 4 unless . . . (here follow the usual demands for money and release of his friends from jail). Suppose, further, that he is caught at 10 A.M. of the fateful day, but—preferring death to failure—won't disclose where the bomb is. What do we do? If we follow due process—wait for his lawyer, arraign him—millions of people will die. If the only way to save those lives is to subject the terrorist to the most excruciating possible pain, what grounds can there be for not doing so? I suggest there are none. In any case, I ask you to face the question with an open mind. 3

Torturing the terrorist is unconstitutional? Probably. But millions of lives surely outweigh constitutionality. Torture is barbaric? Mass murder is far more barbaric. Indeed, letting millions of innocents die in deference[2] to one who flaunts his guilt is moral cowardice, an unwillingness to dirty one's hands. If you caught the terrorist, could you sleep nights knowing that millions died because you couldn't bring yourself to apply the electrodes? 4

Once you concede that torture is justified in extreme cases, you have admitted that the decision to use torture is a matter of balancing innocent lives against the means needed to save them. You must now face more realistic cases involving more modest numbers. Someone plants a bomb on a jumbo jet. He alone can disarm it, and his demands cannot be met (or if they can, we refuse to set a precedent[3] by yielding to his threats). Surely we can, we must, do anything to the extortionist[4] to save the passengers. How can we tell 300, or 100, or 10 people who never asked to be put in danger, "I'm sorry, you'll have to die in agony, we just couldn't bring ourselves to . . ." 5

Here are the results of an informal poll about a third, hypothetical,[5] case. Suppose a terrorist group kidnapped a newborn baby from a hospital. I asked four mothers if they would approve of torturing kidnappers if that were necessary to get their own newborns back. All said yes, the most "liberal" adding that she would administer it herself. 6

I am not advocating torture as punishment. Punishment is addressed to deeds irrevocably[6] past. Rather, I am advocating torture as an acceptable measure for preventing future evils. So understood, it is far less objectionable than many extant[7] punishments. Opponents of the death penalty, for example, are forever insisting that executing a murderer will not bring back his victim (as if the purpose of capital punishment were supposed to be resurrection, not deterrence[8] or retribution).[9] But torture, in the cases described, is intended not to bring anyone back but to keep innocents from being dispatched.[10] The most powerful argument against using torture as a punishment or to secure confessions is that such practices disregard the rights of the individual. Well, if 7

2. deference: respectful submission
3. precedent: a possible example in similar situations
4. extortionist: one who gets something by force or threat
5. hypothetical: assumed to be true for the purposes of argument
6. irrevocably: in a manner that is impossible to change
7. extant: existing
8. deterrence: prevention of similar acts
9. retribution: punishment
10. dispatched: killed

the individual is all that important—and he is—it is correspondingly important to protect the rights of individuals threatened by terrorists. If life is so valuable that it must never be taken, the lives of the innocents must be saved even at the price of hurting the one who endangers them.

Better precedents for torture are assassination and preemptive[11] attack. No Allied[12] leader would have flinched at assassinating Hitler[13] had that been possible. (The Allies did assassinate Heydrich.[14]) Americans would be angered to learn that Roosevelt could have had Hitler killed in 1943—thereby shortening the war and saving millions of lives—but refused on moral grounds. Similarly, if nation A learns that nation B is about to launch an unprovoked attack, A has a right to save itself by destroying B's military capability first. In the same way, if the police can by torture save those who would otherwise die at the hands of kidnappers or terrorists, they must. 8

There is an important difference between terrorists and their victims that should mute talk of the terrorists' "rights." The terrorist's victims are at risk unintentionally, not having asked to be endangered. But the terrorist knowingly initiated his actions. Unlike his victims, he volunteered for the risks of his deed. By threatening to kill for profit or idealism, he renounces civilized standards, and he can have no complaint if civilization tries to thwart him by whatever means necessary. 9

Just as torture is justified only to save lives (not extort confessions or recantations),[15] it is justifiably administered only to those *known* to hold innocent lives in their hands. Ah, but how can the authorities ever be sure they have the right malefactor?[16] Isn't there a danger of error and abuse? Won't We turn into Them? 10

Questions like these are disingenuous[17] in a world in which terrorists proclaim themselves and perform for television. The name of their game is public recognition. After all, you can't very well intimidate a government into releasing your freedom fighters unless you announce that it is your group that has seized its embassy. "Clear guilt" is difficult to define, but when 40 million people see a group of masked gunmen seize an airplane on the evening news, there is not much question about who the perpetrators are. There will be hard cases where the situation is murkier. Nonetheless, a line demarcating[18] the legitimate use of torture can be drawn. Torture only the obviously guilty, and only for the sake of saving innocents, and the line between Us and Them will remain clear. 11

There is little danger that the Western democracies will lose their way if they choose to inflict pain as one way of preserving order. Paralysis in the face of evil is the greater danger. Some day soon a terrorist will threaten tens of thousands of lives, and torture will be the only way to save them. We had better start thinking about this. 12

11. preemptive attack: striking first, before the enemy does
12. Allied: in World War II, the Allied powers included the United States, Britain, France, the Soviet Union, and China
13. Hitler: dictator of Nazi Germany who ordered the murder of millions of Jews and others
14. Heydrich: a Nazi organizer of mass executions
15. recantations: denials of previous statements
16. malefactor: evildoer
17. disingenuous: falsely innocent-seeming
18. demarcating: setting boundaries

LANGUAGE AWARENESS AND VOCABULARY QUESTIONS

1. What does Levin mean when he asks "Won't We turn into Them?" (paragraph 10)
2. What does the word *idealism* mean in the context of this reading (paragraph 9)?

COMPREHENSION AND ANALYSIS QUESTIONS

1. According to Levin's article, when should torture be admissible?
2. What arguments *against* torture does the author answer in paragraph 4? Are his answers convincing? His introduction also answers the opposition (paragraphs 1 and 2). Why do you think Levin spends so much time answering the opposition in this essay?
3. Why does Levin argue that torture should never be used as punishment (paragraph 7)?

WRITING ASSIGNMENTS

1. Conduct an informal poll of parents based on a hypothetical kidnapping case, as Levin does in paragraph 6. Ask at least five parents whether they would support torture of the kidnapper and why. Organize your findings and write a paper presenting them.
2. Write a reply to Michael Levin's essay. Develop an argument against torture under any circumstances. For ideas search "Amnesty International, torture test" or "United Nations, torture."

MELISSA M. EZARIK

Mandatory Student Volunteerism Benefits Everyone Involved

Source: From "Good Deeds are Good Indeed" by Melissa M. Ezarik. Published in CAREER WORLD, September 2003. Copyright © 2003 by Weekly Reader Corporation. Reprinted by Permission of Scholastic Inc.

For some students, mandatory volunteerism is just another means to graduation. But for others, volunteering in their community can be life-changing. Many people volunteer not only because it helps others, but also because it helps them feel good. In this article, Melissa M. Ezarik discusses how volunteering benefits students—in high school and beyond.

Many public schools, including all of those in Maryland, require students to perform public service in order to graduate; however, what starts as a forced school requirement can lead to a lifelong passion for the volunteer. Students who volunteer find their own self-esteem rises as they become valuable members of the community. Their service to others often leads them to develop important life skills such as teamwork and leadership. Volunteering can also lead a young person toward a career goal. But the best reward of all is the way in which volunteers help others to lead more enjoyable lives. 1

When Rachel Doyle's grandmother passed away in 1999 in a Nevada nursing home, it was because of loneliness and refusing to eat. The next year, as a junior in high school, Rachel founded a nonprofit organization in hopes of preventing the same thing from happening to other grandmothers. 2

Called GlamourGals, the New York–based organization pairs teens with female residents in nursing homes. After the teens collect donations of facial cleansers, cosmetics, and instant camera film, they meet at the home to perform makeovers on the residents. 3

"The women love it! They smile and tell life stories about when they were our age and their experiences with makeup," says Rachel, now 20, and a junior at Cornell University. "After the makeover, the women smile for the camera—some of them pose like 1930s starlets.[1] They are so cute!" 4

The elderly women feel a renewed sense of their own beauty. But they're not the only ones to benefit. "Many think that volunteering is all about what you give. But what catches you by surprise is how much you receive in return," Rachel says. 5

Everyone Benefits from Mandatory Public Service

Within the past 10 years, more and more teens have stepped up as volunteers, some because their schools require students to perform service work. 6

For example, Maryland requires 75 hours of student service for graduation. But what started as a school assignment for three friends at Montgomery Blair High School in Silver Spring, Maryland, has become their passion. Then-sophomores Matthew Yalowitz, Sarah Thibadeau, and Annie Pierce created the Montgomery Ultimate Story Exchange (MUSE) three years ago. 7

Elementary students are invited to join an after-school club where they're matched up with a high school mentor.[2] Each week, the young students send their creative writing to the mentors via e-mail. The mentors respond with compliments and suggestions on the writing. "That e-mail can make a huge impact on the students," says Matt, now 18. One student from Liberia [in Africa], for example, was a shy, hesitant writer at first. With his mentor's encouragement, he eventually wrote about his family and life in Liberia. From then on, the boy opened up. 8

Everyone benefits. The kids learn that writing and technology can be fun, and the high school students become proud role models. The program now has 40 mentors. Over time, the founders of MUSE have watched their dream become reality. 9

Volunteering Makes One Feel Good

Luke Fritsch also volunteers with youngsters. As a T-ball coach for the past two years, the 18-year-old says he enjoys it when the kids spot him around town. Hearing an enthusiastic "Hi, Coach!" or getting a compliment from a parent, he says, "really makes my day." 10

Samuel Richard Prunty, a freshman at the University of Wisconsin in Madison, has made a difference in the lives of people he's never even met. His parents helped start a fund to raise money for projects in East Africa. "Many of the projects we help fund are for children. I know that I have touched them, 11

1. starlets: young movie actresses
2. mentor: someone who gives advice or help to a less experienced (and often younger) person

by the letters and [by] seeing their happy faces in the pictures we receive," he says. "It makes it worth the time and effort."

Volunteerism Promotes Skill Building

As a bonus, volunteering can help you build skills that are useful in school and 12
in the workplace too. Here are some of the skills participants often develop.

Organizational skills. Rachel learned that founding a program takes lots 13
of planning. Before the first GlamourGals makeover was held, Rachel spent months writing grant applications, soliciting[3] donations, raising money, recruiting volunteers, and learning how nonprofits work. The first event went smoothly because of her careful coordination.

Communication skills. The MUSE founders found themselves speaking in 14
front of the state legislature[4] when it considered dropping the service work requirement for schools. How well did they communicate the reasons it should remain in place? "The bill was defeated," Matt says. In his future career in political science or international relations, that public speaking practice will definitely come in handy.

Luke's coaching taught him how to communicate with kids. "I have learned 15
to make things concise[5] and interesting to hold their attention," he says.

Samuel's volunteer work has taught him to deal with all kinds of people. 16
This has paid off at his job at the local library. "If you're nice and helpful, it makes someone's day a lot better," he says.

Whether starting a program from scratch or taking on a leadership position 17
at an organization, volunteering can mean learning to take charge.

Jim West/Alamy Stock Photo

High school students in Michigan prepare and serve dinner at a shelter for homeless men in Detroit.

3. soliciting: asking for
4. legislature: a group of lawmakers
5. concise: brief, not including unnecessary information

Even one of the first steps toward volunteering—finding a good organization—can boost your ability to communicate clearly. Great Givers, a program that helps teens get into volunteering, suggests asking an organization you're interested in a few questions before you sign up. Some important ones are: What exactly would I be doing as a volunteer? What results has the program achieved? What percentage of donations actually go to the program? 18

Teamwork. Samuel has learned that a volunteering event is most successful when everyone pitches in. He remembers this lesson whenever it's time to buckle down and get a group project completed at school. 19

Rachel says she feels a sense of teamwork, not only among the caring people who work for GlamourGals, but also from her supportive family. "I could not have done it alone," she says. 20

Leadership. Whether starting a program from scratch or taking on a leadership position at an organization, volunteering can mean learning to take charge. Rachel has watched GlamourGals grow from one chapter to 10. She speaks at youth conferences, encouraging other teens to do fundraising and take on leadership roles in organizations. Her work has even been featured in a number of national publications[6] and television shows. "It is almost surreal[7] how much the program has grown, and the success it has achieved," she says. 21

Volunteers Make a Real Difference

Volunteering now can help you get a jump on your career goals. "Knowing that I wanted to become a teacher, I have actively searched for opportunities to interact with kids," says Luke, a freshman at the University of Wisconsin, Eau Claire. "The thrill that you get out of helping younger generations grow and become better people," he adds, is what continues to draw him to the profession. 22

While volunteering didn't influence Samuel's main career choice, he says that learning how rewarding it was to serve others did help him make another choice. In college, he'll be studying to be an electrical engineer, but at the same time, he'll be serving his country as an Air Force R.O.T.C. member. 23

Of course, among the best things about volunteering are the personal rewards. Once, Rachel was giving a makeover to a woman who didn't seem to be enjoying it. "I kept up the energy, smiling and laughing," Rachel says, remembering how disappointed she felt that her efforts didn't seem to be working. 24

A few days later, the nursing home activities director called to explain that the woman had been severely depressed and had not been eating for a while. After the makeover, she had started eating again. That's when Rachel knew for sure that her program was making a real difference. 25

TEACHING TIP

Ask students to research volunteer opportunities available in their community. Make a list on the board or create a wiki for students to share their findings.

LANGUAGE AWARENESS AND VOCABULARY QUESTIONS

1. According to the article, what is mandatory student volunteerism?
2. What does Rachel Doyle mean when she says her GlamourGals experience has been *surreal* (paragraph 21)? What has made the experience surreal?

6. publications: books, magazines, journals, etc.
7. surreal: having the qualities of a dream

COMPREHENSION AND ANALYSIS QUESTIONS

1. Summarize the skills that volunteerism promotes.
2. What are the positive effects of mandatory student volunteerism?
3. How can volunteering help people choose a career?

WRITING ASSIGNMENTS

1. Research an issue in your community, and develop a plan to help those in need. Discuss the plan with your classmates, and write separate e-mails that outline your plan to the following audiences: fellow students, instructors, administrators, and politicians.
2. Think about the classes you are taking this semester, or think about your field of study. Create a list of ways students in your classes or others in your field of study could come together to help others in your community. Choose your top three ideas and write a proposal paragraph for each. Discuss the proposal with your classmates in small groups or as a class.

HISHAM ALMIRAAT

Arab Bloggers: A Blessed Generation?

Source: Hisham Almiraat/Global Voices Advocacy

When you post your viewpoints on the Internet—on social media or a blog—you probably take for granted the freedom of expression that we have in America. Do you ever think about censorship? Have your ideas ever been flagged or censored? In some countries around the world, freedom of expression is far from a given right. What happens when the Internet is used by activists as a voice for political and social change, and governments attempt to silence these voices? In this article, Hisham Almiraat discusses these issues and the challenges faced by activist bloggers in the Middle East.

Your generation is blessed. Everybody has a phone now, internet is accessible everywhere, satellite TV is available in almost every home. What more do you need?" 1

This was thrown at me by a middle-aged Jordanian taxi driver who took me from the Amman airport to the Arab Bloggers Meeting last month. I was trying to share with him my frustration about the situation of freedom of expression in the Arab world. 2

Three years earlier, I may have agreed with the man's comment. Today it seems to encapsulate[1] almost all that is wrong with the way some of us still think about how technology can change things. 3

It's true that communications technology has revolutionized[2] the way we learn about the news or the way we spread ideas—or even the way we relate 4

1. encapsulate: to sum up
2. revolutionized: having changed something thoroughly

to each other. Three years back, it even seemed that it had finally succeeded in cracking the wall of censorship[3] and fear that plagued[4] the Arab region for decades. Social media platforms, blogs and the increasing availability of smart phones allowed a generation of citizen journalists to report and inform, while activists could mobilize and organize at a level not seen in the region for decades.

It seemed that people no longer had to worry about censorship and government control over the media. *We* were the media. 5

A lot of us believed that the mere[5] access to modern means of communications had acted as the catalyst[6] that allowed the sweeping wave of protests to continue, gather pace and arguably succeed. Today, not many of us are ready to make that unblinking assumption. 6

New challenges

The challenges faced by bloggers in the Middle East and North Africa have shifted substantially[7] ever since. 7

(By blogger, I don't only mean a person keeping a blog, but rather anyone using the Internet for political or civic engagement.)[8] 8

Since our last Arab bloggers meeting in Tunis in 2011, at least two major changes have occurred: 9

For one thing, bloggers are no longer expected to be "mere" commentators. From simple observers to active participants, a lot of them had to adapt to a new, more complex political reality where a lot more is demanded of them. 10

This called for a whole set of new skills and resources that those most active, most influential or those who agitated[9] for the revolution didn't necessarily have in store. They are looked at for answers, ideas, actions in so many more areas and ways than they used to be. And in a bitterly polarized region[10] where things are moving so fast and so much is happening every day, the task can seem crushing—almost paralyzing. 11

I know that this has caused many around me to question their role. I also know that it's been cause for frustration about the lack of resources pro-democracy[11] activists generally have access to. Some of us just couldn't cope and gave up trying. Some even stopped being active online. 12

Secondly, the nature of the threats against freedom of expression online has equally shifted: Prior to the revolutions, governments in the region seemed resigned to the idea that Internet filtering was the primary way to stifle free expression on the web. 13

But now they seem to have learned a new lesson: Censorship may be cheap and efficient, but it is relatively easy to expose. Surveillance on the other hand is more subtle and much harder to identify. 14

3. censorship: the act of limiting access to information
4. plagued: having caused continual trouble
5. mere: unimportant or insignificant
6. catalyst: a person or thing that causes a quick change or action
7. substantially: to a great extent
8. political or civic engagement: when individuals or groups identify and address issues of political or public concern
9. agitated: feeling or appearing troubled or nervous
10. polarized region: a geographical area where there is a sharp divide between belief systems
11. pro-democracy: aimed at creating a democratic government

Over the last three years, electronic surveillance and interception 15
technology[12] have very much become the name of the game. A multi-billion dollar market has sprung up and many governments in the region seem happy to cash in. Today, with very few exceptions, many of those governments spend huge sums of money on expensive, state-of-the-art electronic surveillance and interception technology, most of it developed by western private companies.

Take the case of my country, Morocco, for example: 16

In 2012, the country purchased a two million USD program called Project 17
Popcorn, developed by French company Amesys. It is said to be able to intercept and monitor all sorts of communications at a country-wide scale.

The same year, a Moroccan online activist group was visited by "Da Vinci," 18
a sophisticated virus worth half a million US dollars and developed by a Milan-based company, revealingly named Hacking Team. It is said to be able to compromise[13] any operating system, take control of specifically targeted computers and communicate keystroke records[14] and private files to a distant server.

For all we know, this is only the tip of the iceberg. 19

Similar instances were flagged in places like Bahrain, the United Arab 20
Emirates, Syria, Egypt. And the list is growing.

As a result, while censorship remains a major weapon against free speech 21
in the region, electronic surveillance, with its chilling[15] effect on free speech, is becoming a serious threat.

It's no surprise that three years after the start of the Arab revolutions, the 22
situation of online freedom of expression in the region seems almost as bleak[16] as it did before 2011.

Planting the seeds for a better future

How are we coping with the new reality? Are there any new and creative 23
forms of online activism[17] that have succeeded in the last three years and that we can learn from?

How can we ultimately play an effective role in improving the Internet 24
freedom situation in our countries? And to what extent can we rely on technology to protect us online?

These are but some of the questions that participants at the fourth Arab 25
Bloggers Meeting (#AB14) set out to answer.

For four days, the meeting (co-organized by Global Voices Advocacy and 26
the Heinrich Böll Foundation) brought together 70 bloggers, activists, artists, and trainers came from all over the world, including from 16 Arab countries. Participants, like myself, were full of questions and keen to share their stories and skills while also anxious to learn from their peers.

Perhaps the most important lesson I left with is the idea that despite our 27
broader access to modern means of communication in the region today, they

12. interception technology: tools that are used to receive electronic transmissions before they reach the intended party
13. compromise: to expose to danger
14. keystroke records: records of every stroke, or depression, made on a keyboard or mobile device, usually recorded by a malicious software program (called "spyware" or "malware")
15. chilling: horrifying or frightening
16. bleak: without hope
17. activism: the act of using vigorous action or involvement as a means of achieving political or other goals

seem to only work at the periphery[18] and not necessarily as a major factor for change as a lot of us seemed to think three years back.

There's a need to find ways to connect and combine online activity with the "offline" efforts of people who traditionally work to effect change in the real world. And that process seems to work towards change only when technology succeeds in mobilizing[19] and organizing a broader and diverse sector of society. 28

Arab bloggers today are fighting a tough fight—an asymmetrical[20] warfare, where it is no longer a question of access to technology alone, but also a larger, more fundamental[21] question of user rights, of how technology is governed and whether it's free from government interference. 29

The ominous[22] feeling that someone may be looking over our shoulders makes it difficult, even for the most daring among us, to operate freely. 30

But this is not a lost battle. We may not be so blessed of a generation after all, but I feel like AB14, by bringing us together, has succeeded in planting the seeds for a better future. 31

LANGUAGE AWARENESS AND VOCABULARY QUESTIONS

1. What does "freedom of expression" mean? How is the term used in the article? How would you define it?
2. In paragraph 1, the author recounts how a middle-aged taxi driver referred to his generation as "blessed." What does he mean? Does the author agree? Why or why not?

COMPREHENSION AND ANALYSIS QUESTIONS

1. According to the author, how has the role of the blogger changed in the three years between the Arab Bloggers Meeting of 2011 and the meeting in 2014?
2. Almiraat makes the point that "the nature of the threats against freedom of expression online has equally shifted." What is this shift? Give specific examples from the article.
3. The author points out that "Arab bloggers today are fighting a tough fight." What is this "tough fight?" What solutions (if any) are there?

WRITING ASSIGNMENTS

1. Write a response in which you reflect on how bloggers use writing to encourage political and social change. Why do some governments see these actions as threatening?
2. Think about a political or social issue that you care greatly about. Write a "blog post" in which you try to convince readers to side with your point of view. Use specific examples to support your idea.

18. periphery: the outer regions
19. mobilizing: preparing and organizing for action
20. asymmetrical: consisting of parts or pieces that don't fit together
21. fundamental: of absolute importance
22. ominous: threatening

ALI S. KHAN

Preparedness 101: Zombie Apocalypse

From Center for Disease Control and Prevention (http://blogs.cdc.gov/publichealthmatters/2011/05/preparedness-101-zombie-apocalypse/) 05.06.2011

Have you ever thought about what you would do in the event of an emergency? How prepared are you for natural disasters such as earthquakes, floods, or tornadoes? What about zombies? What would you do in the event of the zombie apocalypse? In this article, Dr. Ali S. Khan, Assistant Surgeon General and director of the Centers for Disease Control and Prevention's (CDC) Office of Public Health Preparedness and Response (OPHPR), discusses how you can be prepared.

There are all kinds of emergencies out there that we can prepare for. Take a zombie apocalypse[1] for example. That's right, I said z-o-m-b-i-e a-p-o-c-a-l-y-p-s-e. You may laugh now, but when it happens you'll be happy you read this, and hey, maybe you'll even learn a thing or two about how to prepare for a real emergency. 1

A Brief History of Zombies

We've all seen at least one movie about flesh-eating zombies taking over (my personal favorite is *Resident Evil*), but where do zombies come from and why do they love eating brains so much? The word *zombie* comes from Haitian and New Orleans voodoo[2] origins. Although its meaning has changed slightly over the years, it refers to a human corpse mysteriously reanimated to serve the undead. Through ancient voodoo and folk-lore[3] traditions, shows like *The Walking Dead* were born. 2

In movies, shows, and literature, zombies are often depicted[4] as being created by an infectious virus, which is passed on via bites and contact with bodily fluids. Harvard psychiatrist Steven Schlozman wrote a (fictional) medical paper on the zombies presented in *Night of the Living Dead* and refers to the condition as Ataxic Neurodegenerative Satiety Deficiency Syndrome caused by an infectious agent. The Zombie Survival Guide identifies the cause of zombies as a virus called solanum. Other zombie origins shown in films include radiation from a destroyed NASA Venus probe (as in *Night of the Living Dead*), as well as mutations[5] of existing conditions such as prions, mad-cow disease, measles and rabies. 3

The rise of zombies in pop culture has given credence[6] to the idea that a zombie apocalypse could happen. In such a scenario zombies would take over entire countries, roaming city streets eating anything living that got in their way. The proliferation[7] of this idea has led many people to wonder "How do I prepare for a zombie apocalypse?" 4

1. apocalypse: a disastrous event involving widespread destruction or damage
2. voodoo: a religion of West African origin that is practiced in the Caribbean and the southern United States and is characterized by animism (the belief that natural and inanimate objects possess souls), sorcery (the use of magic), spiritual possession, and other supernatural beliefs
3. folk-lore: the traditional beliefs, customs, and stories of a group of people that are passed down from generation to generation
4. depicted: shown or portrayed
5. mutations: changes in the structure of a gene that result in a new form
6. credence: an acceptance that something is true
7. proliferation: rapid increase; a large number of something

Well, we're here to answer that question for you, and hopefully share a few tips about preparing for real emergencies too! 5

Better Safe than Sorry

So what do you need to do before zombies . . . or hurricanes or pandemics[8] for example, actually happen? First of all, you should have an emergency kit in your house. This includes things like water, food, and other supplies to get you through the first couple of days before you can locate a zombie-free refugee camp (or in the event of a natural disaster, it will buy you some time until you are able to make your way to an evacuation shelter or utility lines are restored). Below are a few items you should include in your kit; for a full list visit the CDC Emergency page. 6

- Water (1 gallon per person per day)
- Food (stock up on non-perishable[9] items that you eat regularly)
- Medications (this includes prescription and non-prescription meds)
- Tools and Supplies (utility knife, duct tape, battery powered radio, etc.)
- Sanitation and Hygiene (household bleach, soap, towels, etc.)
- Clothing and Bedding (a change of clothes for each family member and blankets)

TEACHING TIP

Ask students to discuss whether this ad from the CDC is effective or not.

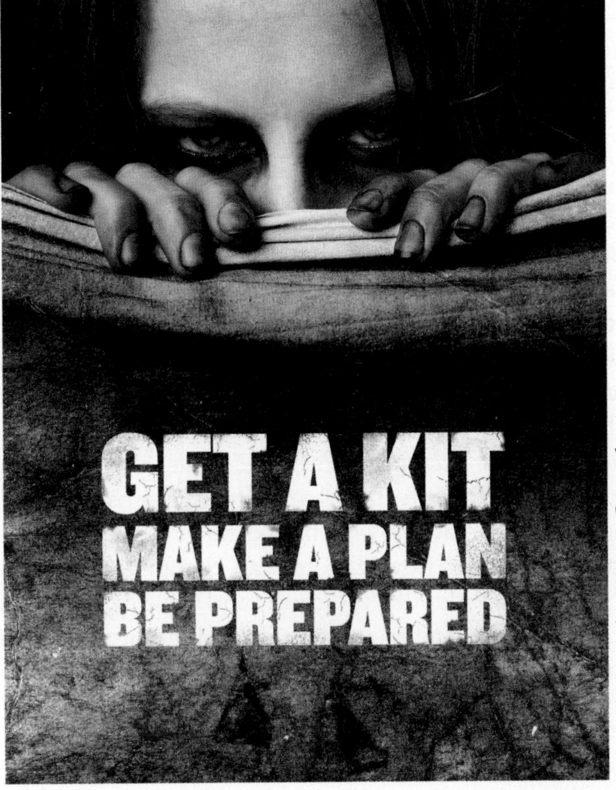

Source: Centers for Disease Control

8. pandemics: outbreaks of a disease over large portions of the country or the world; widespread diseases or illnesses
9. non-perishable: unlikely to go bad quickly

- Important documents (copies of your driver's license, passport, and birth certificate to name a few)
- First Aid supplies (although you're a goner if a zombie bites you, you can use these supplies to treat basic cuts and lacerations that you might get during a tornado or hurricane)

Once you've made your emergency kit, you should sit down with your family and come up with an emergency plan. This includes where you would go and who you would call if zombies started appearing outside your door step. You can also implement this plan if there is a flood, earthquake, or other emergency. 7

1. Identify the types of emergencies that are possible in your area. Besides a zombie apocalypse, this may include floods, tornadoes, or earthquakes. If you are unsure contact your local Red Cross chapter for more information.
2. Pick a meeting place for your family to regroup in case zombies invade your home . . . or your town evacuates because of a hurricane. Pick one place right outside your home for sudden emergencies and one place outside of your neighborhood in case you are unable to return home right away.
3. Identify your emergency contacts. Make a list of local contacts like the police, fire department, and your local zombie response team. Also identify an out-of-state contact that you can call during an emergency to let the rest of your family know you are ok.
4. Plan your evacuation route. When zombies are hungry they won't stop until they get food (i.e., brains), which means you need to get out of town fast! Plan where you would go and multiple routes you would take ahead of time so that the flesh eaters don't have a chance! This is also helpful when natural disasters strike and you have to take shelter fast.

Never Fear—CDC is Ready

If zombies did start roaming the streets, CDC would conduct an investigation much like any other disease outbreak. CDC would provide technical assistance to cities, states, or international partners dealing with a zombie infestation. This assistance might include consultation, lab testing and analysis, patient management and care, tracking of contacts, and infection control (including isolation[10] and quarantine[11]). It's likely that an investigation of this scenario would seek to accomplish several goals: determine the cause of the illness, the source of the infection/virus/toxin, learn how it is transmitted and how readily it is spread, how to break the cycle of transmission and thus prevent further cases, and how patients can best be treated. Not only would scientists be working to identify the cause and cure of the zombie outbreak, but CDC and other federal agencies would send medical teams and first responders[12] to help those in affected areas (I will be volunteering the young nameless disease detectives for the field work). 8

10. isolation: separation of sick people with a contagious disease from people who are not sick
11. quarantine: separation and restriction of the movement of people who have been exposed to a contagious disease to see if they become sick
12. first responders: people trained to respond in an emergency, such as paramedics or firefighters

LANGUAGE AWARENESS AND VOCABULARY QUESTIONS

1. What is the origin of the word *zombie*? How has the definition changed over time? Cite specific examples from the article.
2. What is an *apocalypse*? Define this word in the context of the article.
3. According to the author, "pop culture has given credence to the idea that a zombie apocalypse could happen" (paragraph 4). What is "pop culture"? Define the term and use specific examples from the article to support your definition.

COMPREHENSION AND ANALYSIS QUESTIONS

1. What is the main point of Khan's article?
2. According to the article, what steps would the Centers for Disease Control (CDC) take to conduct an investigation in the event of a zombie apocalypse?
3. Why does the author use the zombie apocalypse as a basis for discussing emergency preparedness? Is this technique effective? Why or why not? Use specific examples from the article to support your point.

WRITING ASSIGNMENTS

1. Think about where you live. What disasters (natural or otherwise) might your area be vulnerable to? Are you prepared? Why or why not? If not, what could you do to make sure you're better prepared?
2. Write a response in which you discuss how you would prepare for a disaster. List the items you would include in an emergency kit, as well as the specific steps of an emergency plan for you and your family.

CADE METZ

Robots Will Steal Our Jobs, but They'll Give Us New Ones

"Robots Will Steal Our Jobs, But They'll Give Us New Ones" by Cade Metz from *Wired*, August 2015. Used by permission.

If a machine could do your job for you, would you want it to? How would you feel about being replaced by a robot? A Jetsons-style reality isn't as far off as you might think, and while the idea of a robot workforce has some people excited, others are unsure. In the following article, Cade Metz explores both sides of this topic.

At the Dusseldorf[1] airport, robotic valet parking is now reality. You step out of your car. You press a button on a touch screen. And then a machine lifts your car off the ground, moving all three tons of it into a kind of aerial[2] parking bay. Built by a German company called Serva Transport, the system saves you 1

1. Dusseldorf: a city in western Germany
2. aerial: in the air

time. It saves garage space, thanks to those carefully arranged parking spots. And it's a sign of so many things to come.

But the one thing it doesn't do, says J.P. Gownder, an analyst with the Boston-based tech research firm Forrester, is steal jobs. In fact, it creates them. Before installing the robotic system, the airport already used automatic ticket machines, so the system didn't replace human cashiers. And now, humans are needed to maintain and repair all those robotic forklifts. "These are not white-collar jobs," Gownder tells *Wired*. "This is the evolution of the repair person. It's harder to fix a robot than it is to fix a vending machine." 2

Gownder uses the Dusseldorf parking garage as a way of showing that the coming revolution[3] in robotics and artificial intelligence may not squeeze the human workforce as much as some pundits[4] have feared. In a widely cited study from 2013, Oxford professors Carl Frey and Michael Osbourne say that machines could replace about 47 percent of our jobs over the next 20 years, but in a new report released today, Gownder takes a more conservative view. Drawing on government employment data and myriad[5] interviews with businesses, academics, and, yes, pundits, Gownder predicts that new automation[6] will cause a net loss of only 9.1 million U.S. jobs by 2025. The horizon of his study is much closer, but his numbers are well under the roughly 70 million jobs that Frey and Osbourne believe to be in danger of vaporization.[7] 3

"While these technologies are both real and important, and some jobs will disappear because of them, the future of jobs overall isn't nearly as gloomy as many prognosticators[8] believe," Gownder writes in the report. "In reality, automation will spur[9] the growth of many new jobs—including some entirely new job categories." 4

AI Versus Humanity

Yes, the revolution is coming. Gownder points to a robot at the ALoft hotel in San Francisco that delivers towels and toothpaste and other stuff. At Vanguard Plastics in Connecticut, a machine called Baxter is manufacturing goods in ways machines never could in the past. The likes of Google and Amazon are pushing even further into this area with everything from warehouse drones to self-driving cars. 5

Perhaps more importantly, the giants of the 'net are rapidly advancing the art of artificial intelligence, teaching online services to recognize images, understand natural language, and even carry on conversations—the kinds of artificial intelligence that will empower robots to tackle ever-more complex tasks. Using the AI that Google and Facebook use to identify photos on the 'net, researchers have already built machines that can, say, teach themselves to screw on a bottle cap. 6

3. revolution: a sudden or complete change
4. pundits: experts in a particular subject or field
5. myriad: a lot of
6. automation: the use of largely automatic equipment in manufacturing or other production processes
7. vaporization: rapid change
8. prognosticators: people who use current evidence to predict future trends or ideas
9. spur: prompt or encourage

"Today's technology is different than what we've seen in the past," says Martin Ford, the author of the recent book *Rise of the Robots: Technology and the Threat of a Jobless Future.* "The technology is taking on cognitive tasks. We now have machines and algorithms[10] that can, at least in a limited sense, think." 7

As this tech evolves, concern is certainly warranted,[11] not only because of how these technologies will affect the workforce but because, some argue, smarter robots could wind up becoming more harmful robots. After seeing the latest artificial intelligence in action, Elon Musk, the founder of electric car company Tesla and the space exploration outfit SpaceX, worries that such AI may turn on humans in more direct ways, so much so that he has donated millions to efforts that seek ways of keeping AI "beneficial to humanity." But Gownder rightly points out that such technology is still in the early stages of development—and that it still requires much help from humans. 8

'Job Transformation, Not Job Replacement'

Humans must build these machines and program them and repair them. But they must also *train* them. This is true of "deep learning" AI, and it's true of robots like Baxter. Baxter must be programmed to perform certain tasks, and that involves physically moving his limbs back and forth. 9

IBM is touting the arrival of Watson, a broad collection of online tools that use artificial intelligence to help diagnose disease, among other things, and so many others are exploring similar work. But whatever the message from IBM, such tools operate alongside humans, not in lieu[12] of them. "Watson is like a robotic colleague," says Gownder. "It's job transformation, not job replacement." 10

Andrew Moore, the dean of the school of computer science at Carnegie Mellon University who previously worked in AI and robotics at Google, agrees. He says that he has seen no evidence that this technology is stealing jobs—and that, as time goes on, it will likely create an enormous number of jobs. 11

"Technology does change the mix of jobs. You're going to see doctors taking more of the role that involves the personal interaction with patients and less of the role of trying to keep huge amounts of evidence in their head. The nurse may become more prestigious[13] than the doctor," Moore says. "But if you look around, there are also new kinds of creative roles being produced across the market. There are so many jobs that didn't exist just a few years ago." 12

This is the larger message of Gownder's report. Robotics and AI will change the way we work, but it won't necessarily take away our work. Today's warnings over the rise of AI, he says, are reminiscent[14] of that handwringing over so many other technological advances in the past—and after all these centuries, the workforce is still there. 13

10. algorithms: processes to be followed by a computer in calculations or other problem-solving operations
11. warranted: justified
12. in lieu of: in place of
13. prestigious: having high status; well-respected
14. reminiscent: suggesting something by resemblance

It should be said, however, that Gownder's study only looks so far down the road. And as Ford says, even Gownder's rather conservative estimate—9.1 million jobs lost—is still rather significant. Robotics and AI will continue to progress—at an unprecedented[15] rate—and though Gownder believes the doomsayers have overblown the threat of widespread automation, he too sees reason for concern—and for continued debate. "The rate of change matters," Gownder says. "We must keep our eyes open." 14

LANGUAGE AWARENESS AND VOCABULARY QUESTIONS

1. "AI" stands for "artificial intelligence." What is AI? According to the article, what are the benefits of AI? What are the drawbacks? Give specific examples from the article to support your point.
2. Who or what is "Baxter"? "Watson"? What is a "drone"? Give specific examples from the article to support your answers.

COMPREHENSION AND ANALYSIS QUESTIONS

1. According to the article, robots have already taken over certain jobs that humans used to do. What are these jobs? Cite one or two examples from the article.
2. One concern related to the rise of robots is that humans in certain sectors of the workforce will lose their jobs. But the author suggests that moving certain tasks to robot workers will actually create new jobs for humans. What are the new jobs that humans will do? Why can't robots do these jobs, too?
3. The author writes, "As this tech evolves, concern is certainly warranted, not only because of how these technologies will affect the workforce but because, some argue, smarter robots could wind up becoming more harmful robots" (paragraph 8). What are the concerns surrounding AI? How might AI be harmful to humanity? Give specific examples from the article to support your point.

WRITING ASSIGNMENTS

1. Think ahead to a future with robotics and AI and how robots or artificial intelligence might impact our society at large. Do you think robots or AI will help or harm society? Is it possible for these technologies to do both? Use specific examples to support your answer.
2. Think of a major issue that impacts the world today. How could robotics or AI be used to solve or improve this problem? Don't be afraid to be creative and "think outside the box" when developing your answer. Possible issues you might explore: climate change, the pollution of the oceans, world hunger.

15. unprecedented: never done or known before

CHRISTINE HARRINGTON

Motivation

"Motivation" by Christine Harrington from *Student Success in College*, 2e, © Cengage Learning, 2016.

Maybe this sounds familiar: you start the semester excited and ready to do well in your classes, but once you realize how much work you have to do, you feel less enthusiastic. In this excerpt, Christine Harrington explains how students can get and stay motivated in order to succeed.

Motivation, the drive that gets us to begin and complete tasks, is strongly related to success. Not surprisingly, there is extensive[1] research showing that motivated students perform better academically (Walker, Greene, & Mansell, 2006; Waschull, 2005). This is in part due to the fact that motivated students exert[2] more effort on tasks (Goodman et al., 2011). Getting and staying motivated increase your effort and ultimately your achievement. 1

Your motivation level will fluctuate[3]—this is normal. It is therefore necessary to find ways to boost your motivation when it starts to drop. Most students typically start a semester very motivated, eager to perform well academically. This process may begin with purchasing all new school supplies and feeling excited about starting a new academic journey. This is often followed by a commitment to make school a priority. New beginnings offer an opportunity for a fresh start, and this can foster high levels of motivation. A few weeks or so later, it is typical for motivation levels to drop. This is when students start to realize how much work they need to do in order to meet with success. Lower motivational levels can lead to lower effort put forth, which then results in lower performance. It is therefore important to continually work on being motivated. Using the following theory-based[4] motivational strategies will help you get back on track when your motivation begins to drop. 2

Reward Yourself: Behavioral Motivators

One of the most commonly used motivational strategies is the reward. Rewards are at the heart of the behavioral approach to motivation. Behaviorism is the belief that consequences guide our actions. More specifically, behaviorists such as Skinner believe that we continue to engage in behaviors that have positive consequences or rewards, and we stop doing behaviors that have negative consequences (Myers, 2014). You can probably think of personal examples where you continued to do something because you wanted the reward that followed. Perhaps you spent a lot of time studying for an exam because you wanted a good grade. Maybe you are attending college because you want the reward of a college degree or a high salary. You may have also been motivated by wanting to avoid a negative consequence. Maybe you put time and effort into an academic task to avoid a bad grade or a negative reaction from your family. Although both positive and negative consequences play a role in motivation, we will focus on positive consequences since we have committed ourselves to a strength-based mindset.[5] 3

1. extensive: large in size, amount, or area
2. exert: to make a physical or mental effort
3. fluctuate: to shift back and forth; to change in level, strength, or value
4. theory-based: relating to the general idea of a subject or area of study rather than its truth or reality
5. mindset: a set of attitudes held by someone

Rewards work for two main reasons. First, they serve as a positive consequence; according to behaviorists, this reinforces our behaviors. In other words, we want to continue receiving rewards, so we continue to engage in the behavior that garners[6] them. 4

The second reason that rewards work is because the positive feeling of getting a reward becomes associated or connected to the task. This results in more positive feelings about the task itself, and we are more likely to engage in tasks that we feel good about doing. 5

Reward Strategies

- Celebrate the positive feeling of accomplishing a task.
- Reward yourself with a fun activity.
- Share your accomplishments with friends and family so they can celebrate with you.
- Be sure the reward is personally meaningful to you.
- Match the reward to the task—small rewards for small tasks and big rewards for big tasks.

Stay Positive and Believe in Yourself: Cognitive Motivators

Although behaviorism probably gets more attention, the cognitive approach to motivation is also extremely powerful. Cognitive theorists such as Beck believe that our thoughts impact our mood and behaviors, and so they aim their interventions on the thinking process (Myers, 2014). According to this approach, it is our interpretation of the events in our lives that leads us to be more or less motivated. This is particularly true when we have a negative experience. Let's look at an example: Jessica and Alex both failed a midterm exam. 6

Jessica: Oh no! I failed the exam. I will probably fail the course, and will eventually fail out of college. I was not meant to go to college. 7

Alex: Oh no! I failed the exam. I am worried about being able to pass the class. It is worth 20% of my final grade, which is a lot, but I did receive an A on the midterm project, which was also worth 20% of the final grade. I will meet with my professor to discuss study techniques so I can pass the course.

Cognitive theorists believe that this experience will be interpreted differently by different students and therefore result in different reactions. Jessica will likely be less motivated than Alex to work hard in this course even though they both had the same experience. 8

According to this cognitive perspective,[7] we can increase motivation by looking at our thought patterns and reducing negative thoughts, particularly ones that are not based on accurate information. Looking at the situation from a positive yet productive viewpoint can significantly increase motivation levels. The great news here is that this entire theory is based on the power of thoughts, and thoughts are changeable! Granted, thoughts often occur automatically and it may seem like you can't control them, but you can. 9

6. garners: gathers or collects

7. perspective: a particular attitude toward something; a point of view

Keeping the situation in perspective is an important part of the process. Failing a test is definitely not good; however, it doesn't have to mean it is the end of the world, either. As you saw in the example, Alex was able to keep this test grade in perspective, citing how much this grade counted and recalling other grades already received. 10

Shifting from negative to positive, productive thinking involves looking for data or evidence to support our thinking. What evidence do you have to support your thought? What evidence do you have that contradicts[8] your thought? Using the exam example, here are some questions you can ask yourself to explore the evidence: 11

- What percentage of my grade is based on this one test?
- Do I have any other grades in this course? If so, how much do these assignments count?
- What is the highest grade I can now earn in the class? Grade calculator applications are great tools for this purpose.
- Have I ever passed a college-level assignment? How did I accomplish this?
- Has anyone ever failed a test but still passed the course?
- Are there college graduates who failed exams or even courses?
- What actions can I take to perform well in the future?

If you don't know the answer to one of the questions, you can ask someone else or investigate it. The main idea of this approach is that you look for data or evidence that either supports or contradicts your thinking. This keeps your thoughts in check, helping to ensure that your thinking is not exaggerated and remains productive in nature. 12

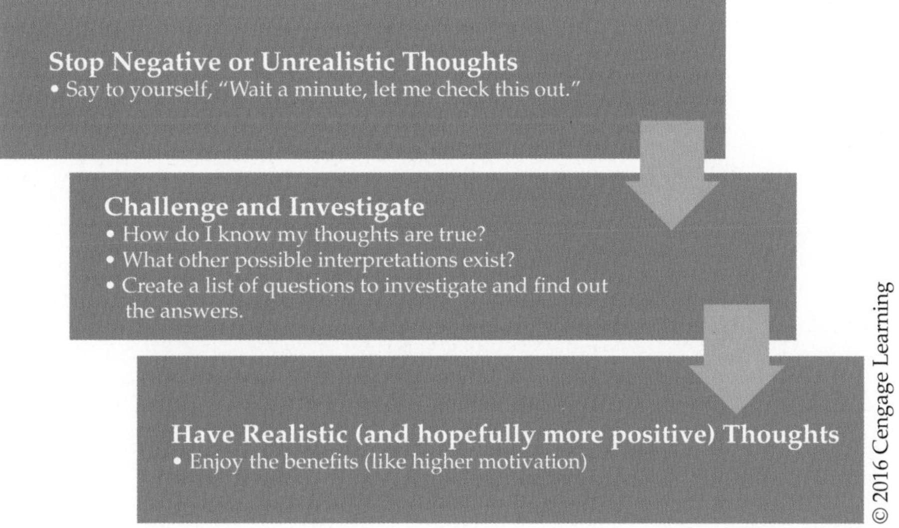
Stop Negative or Unrealistic Thoughts
• Say to yourself, "Wait a minute, let me check this out."
Challenge and Investigate
• How do I know my thoughts are true?
• What other possible interpretations exist?
• Create a list of questions to investigate and find out the answers.
Have Realistic (and hopefully more positive) Thoughts
• Enjoy the benefits (like higher motivation)
© 2016 Cengage Learning

Using the cognitive approach to improve motivation

8. contradicts: opposes the truth of, especially by claiming the opposite

LANGUAGE AWARENESS AND VOCABULARY QUESTIONS

1. The article highlights different types of motivators. What is behaviorism, and how does it work as a motivator? Cite specific examples from the article to support your response.
2. What is cognitive motivation, and how does it work as a motivator? How does it differ from behaviorism? Cite specific examples from the article to support your response.

COMPREHENSION AND ANALYSIS QUESTIONS

1. According to the author, why is it important to get and stay motivated?
2. The author points out that motivation levels fluctuate over time and that this fluctuation is normal. According to the article, what can happen if motivation levels fall too low? What can be done to increase motivation?
3. The author suggests that "productive thinking involves looking for data or evidence to support our thinking." What questions can you ask yourself to explore the evidence? Cite specific examples from the article.

WRITING ASSIGNMENTS

1. The article gives the following example:

   Jessica and Alex both failed a midterm exam.

   Jessica: *Oh no! I failed the exam. I will probably fail the course, and will eventually fail out of college. I was not meant to go to college.*

   Alex: *Oh no! I failed the exam. I am worried about being able to pass the class. It is worth 20% of my final grade, which is a lot, but I did receive an A on the midterm project, which was also worth 20% of the final grade. I will meet with my professor to discuss study techniques so I can pass the course.*

   Write a response in which you reflect on this example. Who do you relate to more: Jessica or Alex? Why?
2. Think about the motivating factors in your own life. Do you practice behaviorism, cognitive motivation, or a combination of both? Why? Give specific examples to support your answer.

APPENDIX

Additional Help and Practice for ESL/ELL Students

Count and Noncount Nouns

Count nouns* refer to people, places, or things that are separate units. You can always count them and often physically point to them. Note that, in English, the following nouns are used as plural count nouns: *police, jeans, pajamas, Middle Ages, scissors, shorts*.

Count Noun	Sample Sentence (Note the underlined words used with count nouns)
television	The marketing department purchased ten large-screen **televisions**.
drive	John had to buy a new flash **drive** to hold the graphics he completed for art class.
assignment	How many **assignments** did you complete last night?
police	The **police** are stationed around the perimeter of the house.

Noncount nouns refer to things that you cannot count separately. Some noncount nouns refer to ideas, feelings, and other things that you cannot see or touch; other noncount nouns refer to food or beverages.

*For more on nouns, see Chapters 32 and 26, Part A.

Noncount Noun	Sample Sentence (Note the underlined words used with noncount nouns)
integrity	A politician's **integrity** is frequently tested.
information	We have been waiting for some **information** about the exam.
homework	How much **homework** do you have to finish tonight?
milk	**Milk** is available with 2 percent fat, 1 percent fat, and no fat.

Three signs can help you identify noncount nouns: (1) nouns that have the same verb form (for example, *help, to help; cash, to cash*), (2) words that occur only in noun form (e.g., *equipment, vocabulary*), and (3) nouns with certain endings.

Following is a list of common endings on noncount nouns. This is not complete but is meant as a guide.

Endings on Many Noncount Nouns

-ance / ence: insurance, patience, persistence
-ness: frankness, nervousness
-age: courage, postage, luggage, leverage
-sure or *-ture:* pressure, furniture
-fare: welfare, warfare
-th: health, warmth, wealth, strength, truth
-ice: advice, juice, practice
-tion: information, inspiration, respiration, transportation
-esty / ity: honesty, continuity, integrity
-ware / wear: software, sportswear, silverware
-ment: development, equipment
-work: homework, metalwork (exception: network)

PRACTICE 1

Choose the correct word in each pair in the following sentences. Be prepared to explain your choice.

1. After moving to the condominium, they decided to buy new (furniture, furnitures).
2. An important key to learning a second language is memorizing (vocabulary, vocabularies).
3. The crew took a lot of video (equipment, equipments) to the film shoot.
4. This class was difficult because of all the (homework, homeworks) we had to complete.

5. This class was difficult because of all the (exercise, exercises) we had to complete.

6. The (scissor, scissors) lay on the color copier.

7. Waldo set up some computer (network, networks) for the company.

8. The patient's (respiration, respirations) seemed normal.

Some nouns have both count and noncount meanings. Usually, the count meaning is concrete while the noncount meaning is abstract. Note that the count and noncount meanings of some nouns (for example, *corn, iron*) differ significantly.

Count Meaning	Noncount Meaning
Almost all of the **lights** in the office went out. Only the exit **light** is still burning.	Technicians can now send messages as pulses of **light** through optic wires.
Some loud **sounds** are coming from the street. The last **sound** was a shout of victory from a sports fan.	The speed of **sound** is slower than the speed of light.
I found a great store with **teas** and **cakes** from different countries. I bought a loose green **tea** and a chocolate **cake** there.	Do you like **tea** with **cake**? Would you prefer green or black **tea**?
Two broken **irons** lay on the washer in the laundry room. One working **iron** sat in the cabinet.	**Iron** is a strong metal used to make heavy machinery.

PRACTICE 2

Circle the correct word in each pair in the following sentences. Be prepared to explain your choice.

1. I always have (coffee, coffees) with dessert. Please give us two Persian (coffee, coffees) and two orders of baklava.

2. You have work (experience, experiences) in this field, I see. Tell me about your various (experience, experiences) at the ABC Company, where you held several positions.

3. Ship builders use a lot of (iron, irons) to build cruise and war ships.

4. Most modern (iron, irons) are made of plastic and steel, so they are light and easy to use.

5. To make Maria's wonderful salsa, you need to grill some fresh (corn, corns).

6. He had several (corn, corns) from years of wearing tight leather shoes.

7. If all cars had both front and side air bags, more (life, lives) would be saved.
8. How (time, times) passes! We have met several (time, times) by chance since we became engineers.

Articles with Count and Noncount Nouns

Indefinite Articles

The words *a* and *an* are **indefinite articles**. They refer to one *nonspecific* (indefinite) thing. For example, "a woman" refers to *any* woman, not a particular woman. The indefinite article *a* or *an* is used before a singular count noun:*

Singular Count Noun	With Indefinite Article
music video	a music video
question	a question
umbrella	an umbrella

The indefinite article *a* or *an* is never used before a noncount noun:

Noncount Noun	Sample Sentence
music	*Correct:* I enjoy music. *Incorrect:* I enjoy a music.
courage	*Correct:* She displayed courage. *Incorrect:* She displayed a courage.

Be careful: An indefinite article *can* be used with a quantifier (a word that specifies the noun's quantity) and a noncount noun:

Noncount Noun	Noncount Noun with Quantifier
information	The hackers were looking for *a piece of information* that was classified.
news	Let me give you *a bit of news*.

PRACTICE 3

Cross out *a* or *an* if it is used incorrectly in the sentences below. Be ready to explain your answers.

1. We need ~~a~~ special luggage for the camping trip.
2. She gave us ~~an~~ advice that helped our project succeed.

---

*For information about when to use *an* instead of *a*, see Chapter 41.

3. She gave us *a* piece of advice that helped our project succeed.
4. They are transferring to *a* university located somewhere in Los Angeles.
5. To drive on California freeways, one needs ~~*a*~~ patience.
6. I am in the mood for ~~*a*~~ fish, perhaps *a* piece of salmon and *a* green vegetable.
7. Mr. Lee will offer ~~*a*~~ help if you give him *a* call.
8. We heard ~~*a*~~ laughter coming from the other room.

Definite Articles

The word *the* is the only **definite article** in English. It usually refers to one or more specific (definite) things. For example, "the doctor" refers not to *any doctor* but to a specific doctor. "The doctors" refers to two or more specific doctors. **The article *the* can be used before any singular or plural count noun:** *the moon, the soccer players, the Chinese ambassador.**

The can be used before a noncount noun *only* if that noun is specifically identified, usually by a prepositional phrase† or relative clause.‡

Noncount Noun	Sample Sentence
food	*Correct: The* food at the party was delicious. (specific food) *Incorrect:* All living things must have *the* food to survive. (nonspecific food)
poetry	*Correct: The* poetry that she writes is richly detailed. (specific poetry) *Incorrect:* He enjoys reading *the* poetry. (nonspecific poetry)

Review of Article Usage

	Count Nouns		Noncount Nouns
	Singular	**Plural**	
Indefinite	Use *a/an.* *A chair would be useful. Let's buy one.* (refers to a nonspecified chair)	No article *Chairs come in many different styles.* (refers to nonspecified chairs)	No article *Furniture comes in many different styles.* (refers to nonspecified furniture)
Definite	Use *the.* *The chair we bought is comfortable.* (refers to a specific chair)	Use *the.* *The chairs we bought are comfortable.* (refers to specific chairs)	Use *the.* *The furniture we bought is comfortable.* (refers to specific furniture)

*In fact, every singular count noun must be preceded by a "determiner": that is, by a definite or indefinite article; by a pronoun such as *his, her, their, our,* and *my;* by *this, that, these, those;* by a word such as *many, most, all, both, every,* or *some;* or by a number.

†For more on prepositional phrases, see Chapter 34.

‡For more on relative clauses, see Chapter 22, Part D.

PRACTICE 4

Write the article *the* where needed in each blank. Write X where no article is needed. Be prepared to explain your answers. (More than one answer is correct in some cases.)

Who said that _X_ life never changes? Recent research has shown that _the_ human body has changed significantly, especially during _the_ past two hundred years. Dr. Robert Fogel at _the_ University of Chicago and other scientists around the world have concluded that a significant change in _X_ people's physical size has taken place. They note that _X_ modern humans are much taller and heavier than _X_ people were only a couple of centuries ago. _The_ same scientists also found that humans today are much healthier than their ancestors. _X_ Chronic diseases occur ten to twenty-five years later than they used to, and older people today experience fewer disabilities. _The_ same trend was also found for _X_ mental health. _The_ average IQ, for example, has increased for decades, and mental illnesses are diagnosed and treated much more effectively today. Because of these changes, we now enjoy _X_ happier, healthier, longer, and more productive lives.

Verbs Followed by a Gerund or an Infinitive

A **gerund** is the *-ing* form of the verb used as a noun.

Watching my weight is harder during the cold months.
They enjoy *hiking* in the Rocky Mountains.

In the first sentence, *watching* is the simple subject of the sentence.* In sentence two, *hiking* is the object of the verb *enjoy*.† Some common English verbs can be followed by a gerund. Example: Joaquin quit *smoking*.

Verbs That Can Be Followed by a Gerund

appreciate	consider	enjoy	mention	quit	risk
avoid	discuss	finish	mind	recommend	suggest
complete	dislike	keep	postpone	remember	understand

*For more on simple subjects, see Chapter 26, Part A.
†For more on objects of verbs, see Chapter 33, Part D.

The verbs in the previous box are never followed by an infinitive (*to* + the simple form of the verb):

Verb	Sample Sentence
dislike	*Correct:* I *dislike* **cooking** on weeknights. *Incorrect:* I *dislike* **to cook** on weeknights.
discuss	*Correct:* Let's *discuss* **taking** a trip to Asia. *Incorrect:* Let's *discuss* **to take** a trip to Asia.

Other English verbs can be followed by an **infinitive** (but never by a gerund). Example: He expects *to graduate* in June.

Verbs That Can Be Followed by an Infinitive

afford	attempt	demand	hope	mean	offer
agree	choose	expect	intend	need	refuse
appear	dare	fail	learn	plan	wish
ask	decide	forget	like	promise	

Some verbs can be followed by a **noun or pronoun and** an **infinitive** (but never by a gerund). Example: She asked *him to dance.*

Verbs That Can Be Followed by Noun or Pronoun + Infinitive

advise	caution	expect	invite	persuade	teach
allow	convince	hire	order	remind	tell
ask	encourage	instruct	permit	require	want

The verbs listed above are never followed by a gerund:

Verb	Sample Sentence
afford	*Correct:* They can *afford* **to buy** the tickets. *Incorrect:* They can *afford* **buying** the tickets.
agree	*Correct:* I *agree* **to lend** you $100 this week. *Incorrect:* I *agree* **lending** you $100 this week.
plan	*Correct:* He *plans* **to move** to Ohio this summer. *Incorrect:* He *plans* **moving** to Ohio this summer.

A few verbs can be followed by ***either*** **a gerund or an infinitive without a change in meaning.** Example: They ***began*** to **write.** They ***began*** **writing.**

Verbs That Can Be Followed by a Gerund or an Infinitive

begin	hate	prefer
continue	like	start
dislike	love	try

Some verbs can be followed by ***either*** **a gerund *or* an infinitive,** but the meaning of the verb changes depending on the form (gerund or infinitive) used:

> He stopped *seeing* her. (**Meaning:** He is not seeing/dating her anymore.)
> He stopped *to see* her. (**Meaning:** He made a stop to see/visit her.)

PRACTICE 5

Circle the correct form (gerund or infinitive) to follow the verb in each sentence.

1. Many Americans enjoy (to watch, watching) television.
2. Because this is the store's busy season, we will postpone (to visit, visiting) our friends until spring.
3. Yuri asked Mia (to repair, repairing) the washing machine.
4. Mae Lee regretted (to miss, missing) the auto show.
5. Barring any unforeseen problems, the family expects me (to complete, completing) my degree by this summer.
6. Bae will persuade Edgar (to join, joining) us at the library.
7. Please keep (to sing, singing). We both want (to hear, hearing) another song.
8. Remember that Bruno's party is a surprise, so please do not mention our (to go, going) to the bakery and (to buy, buying) this huge cake.

PRACTICE 6

Circle the correct verb in each sentence. If you need help, review the verb lists.

1. I (prefer, want) listening to NPR during breakfast.
2. Ichiro (suggests, hopes) to finish his coursework this semester so that he can graduate in May.
3. Given the high cost of housing, he (plans, recommends) sharing an apartment with another serious student.
4. The mayor (hoped, advised) the city council not to pass legislation that would hurt local retailers.
5. Now that she has a good job, she can (afford, consider) to buy a new car.
6. I enjoyed the evening very much. I (appreciate, thank) your inviting me.
7. Several students (decided, kept) working after the chemistry lab closed.
8. He (loves, anticipates) to get up early and go running along the river.

Index

Thematic Index of the Reading Selections

These thematic clusters suggest some ways to group and discuss the reading selections in Unit 8.

Family Roles and Relationships

Heroes and Courage

Examining Popular Culture

Dealing with Loss

Technology: Blessing or Threat?

Success and Failure

Social Rights and Responsibilities

Identity and the Minority Experience

Preventing Violence and Bullying

Money and Consumerism

Rhetorical Index

The following index first classifies the paragraphs and essays in this text according to rhetorical mode and then according to rhetorical mode by chapter. (Those paragraphs with added errors for students to correct are not included.)

Rhetorical Modes

Illustration

Narration

Description

Process

Definition

Comparison and Contrast

Classification

Cause and Effect

Persuasion

Rhetorical Modes by Chapter

2 Prewriting to Generate Ideas

3 The Process of Writing Paragraphs

4 Achieving Coherence

5 Illustration

6 Narration

Narration

7 Description

Description

8 Process

Process

9 Definition

Definition

10 Comparison and Contrast

Comparison and Contrast

11 Classification

Classification

12 Cause and Effect

Cause and Effect

13 Persuasion

Persuasion

14 The Process of Writing an Essay

Illustration

Narration

Process

Comparison and Contrast

Cause and Effect

Persuasion

Mixed Modes

15 The Introduction, the Conclusion, and the Title

Illustration

Comparison and Contrast

Cause and Effect

22 Revising for Sentence Variety

23 Revising for Language Awareness

24 Putting Your Revision Skills to Work

39 Putting Your Proofreading Skills to Work

41 Look-Alikes/Sound-Alikes

Rhetorical Modes in the Reading Selections

Classification

Cause and Effect

Persuasion

Revising and Proofreading Symbols

The following chart lists common writing errors and the symbols that instructors often use to mark them. For some errors, your instructor may wish to use symbols other than the ones shown. You may wish to write these alternate symbols in the blank column.

Standard Symbol	Instructor's Alternate Symbol	Error	For help, see Chapter
adj		Incorrect adjective form	35
adv		Incorrect adverb form	35
agr		Incorrect subject-verb agreement	26; 29
		Incorrect pronoun-antecedent agreement	33, Parts A and B
apos		Missing or incorrect apostrophe	36
awk		Awkward expression	23
cap		Missing or incorrect capital letter	38, Part A
case		Incorrect pronoun case	33, Part D
(,)		Missing or incorrect comma	27, Parts A and B; 36
coh		Lack of coherence	4
(:)		Missing or incorrect colon	38, Part D
con d		Inconsistent discourse	20, Part C
con p		Inconsistent person	21, Part B
con t		Inconsistent verb tense	21, Part A
coord		Incorrect coordination	27, Part A
cs		Comma splice	28, Part A
(-)		Missing or incorrect dash	38, Part D
dev		Incomplete paragraph or essay development	3, Parts C, D, and E; 14, Parts D, E, and F
dm		Dangling or confusing modifier	22, Part E
ed		Missing *-ed,* past tense or past participle	30, Part A; 31, Part A
frag		Sentence fragment	22, Part D; 27, Part B; 28, Part B
¶		Missing indentation for new paragraph	3, Part A
(())		Missing or incorrect parenthesis	38, Part D
||		Faulty parallelism	21, Part C
pl		Missing or incorrect plural form	32
pp		Incorrect past participle form	31
(.)(!)(?)		Missing or incorrect end punctuation	22, Part B
quot		Missing or incorrect quotation marks	38, Part C
rep		Unnecessary repetition	3, Parts D and F
ro		Run-on sentence	28, Part A
(;)		Missing or incorrect semicolon	27, Part C
sub		Incorrect subordination	27, Part B
sp		Spelling error	40
		Look-alike, sound-alike error	41
sup		Inadequate support	3, Part F
title		Title needed	15, Part C
trans		Transition needed	4, Part B; 14, Part E
trite		Trite expression	23, Part C
ts		Poor or missing topic sentence or thesis statement	3, Parts A and B; 14, Part B
u		Lack of paragraph or essay unity	3, Part F; 14, Parts D, E, and F
w		Unnecessary words	24, Part B
⌒		Too much space	39
ℯ		Words or letters to be deleted	39
?		Unclear meaning	23, Part A
^		Omitted words	39
∼		Words or letters in reverse order	39